CRIMINOLO

We work with leading authors to develop the
strongest educational materials in criminology,
bringing cutting-edge thinking and best
learning practice to a global market.

Under a range of well-known imprints, including
Longman, we craft high-quality print and electronic
publications which help readers to understand and
apply their content, whether studying or at work.

To find out more about the complete range of our
publishing, please visit us on the World Wide Web at:
www.pearsoned.co.uk

CRIMINOLOGY

THEORY AND CONTEXT

Third edition

John Tierney

Senior Lecturer in Criminology, School of Applied
Sciences, Durham University

Harlow, England • London • New York • Boston • San Francisco • Toronto
Sydney • Tokyo • Singapore • Hong Kong • Seoul • Taipei • New Delhi
Cape Town • Madrid • Mexico City • Amsterdam • Munich • Paris • Milan

Pearson Education Limited

Edinburgh Gate
Harlow
Essex CM20 2JE
England

and Associated Companies throughout the world

Visit us on the World Wide Web at:
www.pearsoned.co.uk

First published 1996 by Prentice Hall
Second edition published 2006 by Longman
Third edition published 2010

ISBN 978-0-273-72277-9

British Library Cataloguing-in-Publication Data
A catalogue record for this book is available from the British Library

Library of Congress Cataloging-in-Publication Data

Tierney, John.
    Criminology : theory and context / John Tierney. — 3rd ed.
        p. cm.
    Includes bibliographical references and index.
    ISBN-13: 978-0-273-72277-9 (pbk. : alk. paper)
    ISBN-10: 1-4058-2361-5
    1. Criminology—History. 2. Criminology—Great Britain—History. 3. Crime—Sociological aspects. 4. Crime—Sociological aspects—Great Britain. I. Title.
    HV6021.T54 2009
        364—dc22   2009030701

10 9 8 7 6 5 4 3 2
14 13 12 11 10

Typeset in 11.25/13 StonePrint by 75
Printed in Great Britain by Henry Ling Limited., at the Dorset Press, Dorchester, DT1 1HD

For Ben, Dominic and Christian

Tierney has made an enormous contribution by offering a thorough, comprehensive, and accurate review and record of the field . . . the book should be read by all students of criminology looking for an account of the essential themes, key debates and contemporary twists in the theoretical explanation of crime.

Professor Colin Sumner

Criminology is marked by almost all those qualities one might hope to find in an introduction to a burgeoning and often incoherent discipline. It is a near encyclopedic summary of major American and British work that succeeds in being well structured, accessible, clearly written, judicious and historically informed. That is quite a feat.

Professor Paul Rock, LSE

This new edition of John Tierney's 1996 textbook repeats and vindicates the approach of the successful first edition. It looks *outwards*: at the market demands of students for a reliable guide not to disembodied 'problems' or 'issues', but to criminology as 'thinking about crime'. Tierney's guidebook correctly does this by looking *inwards* – a textbook that carefully explains the texts of criminological theory as a living history.

Stan Cohen
Emeritus Professor of Sociology,
London School of Economics

CONTENTS

Preface to the first edition xii
Preface to the second edition xiii
Preface to the third edition xiv

Introduction 1
The organisation of the book 2
Selecting material 3

Part I   Preliminaries and Early History

    1   Criminology, crime and deviance: some preliminaries 7
        Key themes 7
        Introduction 7
        Good old common sense 7
        Setting the scene 9
        Criminology 11
        Crime 13
        Deviance 21
        Other terms and concepts 25
        Selected further reading 25

    2   Measuring crime and criminality 27
        Key themes 27
        Introduction 27
        Official statistics 27
        The 'dark figure' of crime 29
        Public reporting 29
        Changes in the law 30
        The role of the police 31
        Ways of seeing 33
        The implications for criminal statistics 34
        Victim surveys 35
        The usefulness of criminal statistics 43
        Local crime surveys and left realism 46
        Recent crime trends 47
        Selected further reading 49

3   Criminology and criminologists up to World War Two 51
     Key themes 51
     Introduction 51
     Tree of sin, tree of knowledge 51
     The criminological tree of knowledge: separating the tree from the wood ... 53
     Classicism and positivism 54
     Positivist criminology 56
     The turn of the century to the 1930s 59
     Eugenics 62
     Selected further reading 64

Part II   World War Two to the Mid-1960s

4   The discipline of criminology and its context – 1 69
     Key themes 69
     Introduction 69
     The emergence of criminology 70
     Sociological criminology 77
     Sociological criminology in Britain from the 1950s to the mid-1960s 78
     Sociological criminology in the United States 82
     Selected further reading 86

5   Social disorganisation and anomie 87
     Key themes 87
     Introduction 87
     The sociology and criminology of Emile Durkheim (1858–1917) 87
     The Chicago School 95
     Mertonian strain theory 102
     Selected further reading 107

6   Strain, subcultures and delinquency 109
     Key themes 109
     Introduction 109
     A. K. Cohen: developments in strain theory 109
     R. Cloward and L. Ohlin: opportunity knocks 112
     Selected further reading 115

7   Criminological theory in Britain 116
     Key themes 116
     Introduction 116
     American influences 116
     Sociological criminology in Britain 119
     Developing a British perspective 122

Cultural diversity theory 122
Schools and the 'problem of adjustment' 126
Subcultural theory: taking stock 128
Selected further reading 131

Part III The Mid-1960s to the Early 1970s

8   **The discipline of criminology and its context – 2** 135
     Key themes 135
     Introduction 135
     The development of sociological criminology in Britain 135
     The break with orthodoxy: the new deviancy 136
     The New Left 142
     Radicals and the new deviancy: the impact on British criminology 144
     Selected further reading 146

9   **New deviancy theory: the interactionist approach to deviance** 147
     Key themes 147
     Introduction 147
     Labelling theory 148
     Learning to become 'deviant' 149
     Primary and secondary deviation 151
     The amplification of deviance 152
     Conceptualising deviance 153
     Criticisms of the new deviancy 154
     Selected further reading 160

Part IV The 1970s

10   **The discipline of criminology and its context – 3** 165
     Key themes 165
     Introduction 165
     Deviance and politics 165
     The sociology of law: making laws, making deviants 167
     Criminology in the 1970s: other directions 172
     Orthodox criminology 176
     Radical critiques and the growth of the New Right 178
     Selected further reading 183

11   **Post-new deviancy and the new criminology** 184
     Key themes 184
     Introduction 184
     Deviance and power 185

American conflict theory 186

Politicising deviance 189

Critical criminology 190

Marx and Engels on crime 193

Taylor, Walton and Young and the politicisation of deviance 196

Politicising deviance: nuts, sluts, preverts . . . and revolutionaries? 196

Youth subcultures and politics 198

Critical criminology: deviance, crime and power 202

Phenomenology and criminology 209

Ethnomethodology 210

Control theory 211

Feminist perspectives and criminology 216

Selected further reading 219

Part V   The 1980s to the Mid-1990s

12   The discipline of criminology and its context – 4 223

Key themes 223

Introduction 223

The shift to the right in British politics 224

Criminology's external history 226

Social organisation 228

The growth of policy-oriented research 230

The nature and context of research 233

Policy-oriented research and the left 237

British criminology in the late twentieth century 239

Selected further reading 244

13   Criminological theory 245

Key themes 245

Introduction 245

Mainstream criminology 245

Longitudinal research and criminal careers 246

The historical roots 257

Feminism and criminology 258

Gender and crime 271

Administrative criminology 277

Right-wing classicism 283

Neo-positivism and right realism 284

Radical criminology 289

Critical criminology and left realism 292

Final remarks on this period 298

Winning the fight against crime? 300
Selected further reading 301
Postscript 302

Part VI The Mid-1990s into the New Millennium

14 The discipline of criminology and its context – 5 305
Key themes 305
Introduction 305
New Labour, old problems 306
Restorative justice 312
Imprisonment 314
Social policy and New Labour 315
Crime prevention, crime reduction and community safety 316
Crime and criminal justice: the wider context 320
Criminology in the new millennium 326
Selected further reading 332

15 Theorectical perspectives: recent developments 334
Key themes 334
Introduction 334
Postmodernist perspectives 336
Feminist perspectives 341
Perspectives on masculinities 348
Control perspectives 351
Cultural perspectives 355
Critical perspectives 358
Final remarks 376
Selected further reading 377
Postscripts 379

References 383
Name index 419
Subject index 424

PREFACE TO THE FIRST EDITION

This book is written as an introduction to criminology, or, more specifically, sociological criminology. The aim has been to write an accessible and comprehensive text, but one that does not shirk from engaging with what are sometimes complex issues and debates. The approach is based on a good many years' experience teaching criminology and related subjects to a wide range of groups. Now some thanks.

Writing this book has meant a frequently obsessive preoccupation with a century of criminological thought, and lengthy sojourns in, if not quite a garret, at least an attic room where I watched the seasons roll by through a Velux window. My thanks to my wife and sons for putting up with the resultant disruptions to family life, and for continuing to provide much appreciated encouragement. I hope that I can make up for all those games of Subbuteo I should have played with my youngest son, but didn't because I was consorting with various criminal and criminological miscreants. A welcome respite from writing, especially during those periods when my brain seemed to be turning into taramasalata, was provided by the Thursday night folk music sessions at the Colpitts pub in Durham, which offered comradeship and an incentive to work out some new guitar tunings.

My thanks to those colleagues at New College Durham and at the University of Northumbria who provided encouragement. For various reasons my thanks are also due to the following people – some of whom I've never met. To Stan Cohen for *Folk Devils and Moral Panics,* and to the person who a while ago lent me a copy and got me started; to Colin Sumner for helping to keep key conceptual debates alive; to the late Steven Box for writing the best Preface to a criminology book (Box, 1981); to Mike Brogden who has been a friendly face at some dire conferences; to Martin Scorsese for the film *Goodfellas,* which should be part of a criminology starter pack; to the anonymous reviewer of the original book proposal who generously described me as not part of the mainstream; and to Dick Hobbs, Barbara Hudson and Mike Maguire, who offered extremely useful criticisms and comments on an earlier draft of the book. Needless to say, I take responsibility for the final product.

PREFACE TO THE SECOND EDITION

Since writing the first edition of this book the only constant in my life has been the Velux window mentioned in the earlier Preface. Shortly after the book was published I moved from New College Durham to the University of Durham's Department of Sociology and Social Policy (now School of Applied Social Sciences). Although I ended up with a less grand-sounding job title than previously, in terms of teaching and research this proved to be a productive move. It gave me an opportunity to work alongside various criminologists, namely, Bob Roshier, Dick Hobbs, Jim Sheptycki, the late Ian Taylor and Robin Williams (who has evolved into a criminologist). All of them, for countless reasons, contributed to the experience of living in 'interesting times', and deserve thanks. So too does Georgios Antonopoulos for his help in tracking down various pieces of information for this book. Of those referred to in the first Preface, I've yet to meet Martin Scorsese (who tends not to turn up at criminology conferences). Finally, and for all sorts of reasons, thanks to my three sons, Ben, Dominic and Christian, whose qualities and accomplishments never fail to amaze me.

PREFACE TO THE THIRD EDITION

For the benefit of what I suspect is a small minority of readers who actually read prefaces, I am happy to report that the Velux window continues to soldier on. As I do, and with a slightly grander-sounding job title than last time.

This preface to the third edition gives me an opportunity to add a few more thanks to my previous lists. To Stan Cohen, Paul Rock and Colin Sumner for their much appreciated comments about this book. To Tom Morello for permission to use the lyrics to his song 'The Fabled City' as a postscript to this edition. And, of course, to Nigel Mellor and Willy Russell for permission to use their words as postscripts for the first and second editions respectively. Each was chosen because I felt that they articulated sentiments highly relevant to three recent periods in history. To colleagues in Durham University's School of Applied Social Sciences for support and encouragement. And special thanks to my son Ben and Tim Dillon for designing the cover of this third edition. Additional thanks are due to artist Ryan Graeff for permission to use his 'Bandit' image.

INTRODUCTION

Since the late 1960s the area of study broadly described as criminology has expanded enormously in Britain. Nowadays all sorts of writers, researchers and teachers make many and varied contributions to issues of crime and social control, and represent various political and theoretical positions. Within academic criminology contributions come from many different discipline areas: psychology, psychoanalysis, geography, history, economics, political science, jurisprudence, biology, sociology, and so on. Clearly, given the vast army of participants in the 'criminological project', there are competing views regarding the agenda to be followed. In fact, one of the central questions that will accompany the discussion of criminology's history here is what is it *for*? The book is as much about criminology's history as an academic discipline as it is about criminological theory.

Although important ideas and pieces of research from other disciplines will be referred to, the primary focus is unashamedly sociological criminology. The book is also unashamedly concerned with important *theoretical* developments. There is little detailed discussion of specific forms of crime such as ram-raiding, burglary or bank robbery, though there are plenty of references to research based upon these themes. At the risk of disappointing the reader before we have begun, the argument here is that we can only make sense of specific types of contemporary crime by having a grasp of the theoretical ideas and debates that have sprung up over the years. This is why all criminology programmes in British universities devote a significant amount of time to theoretical criminology.

A central dimension to the book is an engagement with conceptual debates over 'what things mean'. Our everyday worlds are filled with references to crime, criminals, punishment, discipline, the law, and so forth, but what do these terms *mean*? How have these meanings and understandings been constructed? What impact does crime have on people's lives? To what extent are meanings and understandings shared by society's members? How have these phenomena been approached within academic criminology? Throughout the book, therefore, the reader will be invited to consider seriously a range of questions and issues that are often taken for granted.

Although I have attempted to present these debates and issues in such a way as to make them accessible, I have also been concerned to avoid simplifying them to the point of distorting the material and patronising the reader. One of the things I've noticed whilst researching this book is that sometimes the ideas and theories of classic, or at least frequently referred to, writers suffer the fate of messages in Chinese whispers: the original message becomes distorted, or caricatured or oversimplified.

This book, therefore, is an invitation to the reader eventually to read those original texts, so that they can judge them for themselves.

This is also a book about social and political history, in so much as the main concerns and general shape of criminology as it has developed over the years cannot be understood without considering the context provided by that history.

THE ORGANISATION OF THE BOOK

The book is structured around two central themes:

1 The historical development of criminology as an academic discipline, primarily within a British context.
2 The main criminological theories that have emerged as the discipline has developed, together with an overview of contemporary criminological theory. This will involve drawing on theoretical work from countries other than Britain, especially the United States.

The material is organised on the basis of six parts, each made up of a number of chapters.

Part I comprises three chapters. Chapter 1 sets the scene by identifying some problems associated with defining terms such as crime and deviance. In particular, the role of criminology in challenging accepted common-sense understandings of these phenomena is discussed. Chapter 2 takes us into a discussion of some of the difficulties faced when measuring the amount and distribution of crime in society; these difficulties are both 'technical' and 'conceptual'. Chapter 3 introduces a historical dimension by examining the history of criminology from the nineteenth century through to World War Two. Unlike the rest of the book, in this chapter the theme of criminology's development as an academic discipline within specific social and political contexts, and the theme of developments in criminological theory, are combined.

In Parts II, III, IV, V and VI, however, as sociological influences begin to appear, these two themes are, for analytical purposes, separated out for each historical period. Each part thus addresses a particular historical period. The first chapter in each part aims to provide an introduction to the social and political changes over that period, and their impact on the nature and social organisation of criminology as a discipline. This not only allows an appreciation of the importance of these external influences but, by focusing on criminology as a discipline, it establishes a framework within which the discussion of theory in subsequent chapters in that part can be situated. By analogy, it is rather like walking the Wembley turf and acclimatising to the stadium before actually playing in a Cup Final. Where there has been 'delayed action' regarding the influence of a particular theory on British criminology, then reference will be made to earlier periods.

SELECTING MATERIAL

There are some interesting problems in writing an introductory text such as this. One specific problem is that over the years the amount of published work in criminology has grown enormously, assuming a kind of wedge shape, with the thin end receding into the past. Why, we might ask, should introductory texts continue to reproduce this work from the past?

One can often pick up a modern author's sensitivity to the recycling of older theories. They almost apologise for reproducing a well-known and well-used quotation, or revisiting some well-trodden ground. There are no apologies here, though: most of the major passages are quoted in an effort to provide a comprehensive introduction. This earlier material is often interesting in its own right, and what is well-trodden ground to the professional criminologist may be entirely new to the reader. Furthermore, this material is important in that it will have influenced subsequent criminologists, and may continue to exercise a powerful influence in some quarters. An understanding of modern criminological theory presupposes familiarity with what has gone before. Although this clearly involved making judgements, I have dwelt on certain theoretical ideas and debates from the past because I feel that they have an important contemporary resonance. Acknowledging that they may not mean much to the reader at this stage, some examples to look out for are: in the nineteenth century, Durkheim on modernity; in the 1920s and 1930s, discussions of disorganisation and the urban criminal area by the Chicago School; and, in the 1960s, the conceptual problems raised by new deviancy theory. In the final analysis, of course, any introduction to criminology would be glaringly incomplete if it did not discuss the earlier work. Having said that, a large portion of the book concerns itself with more recent developments in terms of the discipline, its context, and its theories.

PART I

PRELIMINARIES AND EARLY HISTORY

CRIMINOLOGY, CRIME AND DEVIANCE: SOME PRELIMINARIES

Key themes
- Good old common sense
- Setting the scene
- Criminology
- Crime
- Deviance

INTRODUCTION

This first chapter invites the reader to think critically about terms such as 'crime' and 'deviance' and, indeed, the notion of 'criminology' itself. Challenging taken-for-granted, common-sense understandings is an important dimension to this. The chapter indicates some of the ongoing disputes and debates within criminology regarding its subject matter, conceptual language, research methodologies and purpose. The chapter includes a brief discussion of sources of crime-related data; this is returned to in the next chapter.

GOOD OLD COMMON SENSE

One of the tasks of criminology should be to question taken-for-granted assumptions regarding what crime and deviance are, what criminals are like, and so on. It should, in other words, question common-sense knowledge. However, as Howard Becker has pointed out, the term 'common sense' is used to mean two different things. Sometimes common sense describes an approved quality of mind:

> the common man [*sic*], his head unencumbered by fancy theories and abstract professional notions, can at least see what is right there in front of his nose. Philosophies as disparate as pragmatism and Zen enshrine a respect for the common man's ability to see, with Sancho Panza, that a windmill is really a windmill. [From now on, rather than

clutter up the text with '*sic*', whenever a quoted author uses such genderised language, disapprobation can be taken as given.]

(Becker, 1974: 50)

This meaning of common sense is found in injunctions such as 'Use your common sense', and, expressed like this, is difficult to criticise. In reality, though, it is not always easy to distinguish this common sense from the second type, though we all like to think of ourselves as Sancho Panza. This second, less estimable, way in which the term 'common sense' is used is described by Becker as follows:

> Common sense, in one of its meanings, can delude us. That common sense is the traditional wisdom of the tribe, the *mélange* of 'what everybody knows', that children learn as they grow up, the stereotypes of everyday life.

(Ibid.: 49)

Defined in this way, common sense refers to generally held views about the social world which in some cases can, and should, be contradicted, or at least questioned by the social sciences. As Becker describes it, there is the possibility of delusion, of being misled by common sense. This is congruent with the observation made by the anthropologist Alfred Kroeber: 'That a belief is common is as likely to stamp it as a common superstition as a common truth' (Kroeber, 1952: 27). From this perspective, generally held beliefs about the nature of crime, criminals, deviance and associated themes need to be carefully scrutinised and, if necessary, challenged. This challenge, though, involves more than just setting the record straight by providing 'factual' information. Fundamentally, it is to do with the taken-for-granted meanings of these categories. They are not neutral objects, given in nature, but are social constructions, and as such are the outcome of processes involving relationships of power. As Pat Carlen says: 'the very task of theory is to engage in a struggle over the "meaning of things" (including all material and ideological constructs)' (Carlen, 1992: 62).

Common sense is particularly active in debates about crime and criminals, and participants will, of course, insist that theirs is the 'no nonsense' rather than the 'delusion' variety. Over the years a steady stream of politicians, journalists, researchers and practitioners have, sometimes tentatively, sometimes confidently, explained the 'causes of crime', or announced a treatment/punishment package that they believe will actually work. We have had a bewildering galaxy of causal explanations, taking in bad genes, chromosome deficiencies, deformed personalities, unemployment, deprivation, trendy parents, lone parents, trendy lone parents, simple greed, blocked opportunities, peer group pressure, status frustration, too much money, too little money and artificial colouring in fish fingers. Suggested treatment/punishment regimes have been equally wide ranging, and some of them have been tried out. Thus offenders have been incarcerated in hulks on the River Thames, transported to Australia, hanged, pelted with eggs in village stocks, tortured in dungeons, given short sharp shocks in detention centres, injected with mind-altering drugs, sterilised, made to face their victims, sent on safari to Africa and locked up in prison. Each of these wildly varying causes and treatments may very well represent common sense for some people.

SETTING THE SCENE

This first chapter will indicate some of the basic conceptual debates within criminology. This will entail a preliminary examination of how the academic terrain of criminology may be mapped out, and some of the attendant difficulties involved in defining the core terms 'crime' and 'deviance'. The chapters that follow will examine these issues in greater detail.

One of the tasks of criminology is to unravel, or deconstruct, the concept of crime and in the process challenge common-sense understandings that are taken for granted. It is not uncommon for politicians and journalists, for instance, to ignore the complex structures and processes within which crime and criminality are constituted, and to rely instead on a dangerous rhetoric whereby crime is reduced to a simple causal factor. Critically questioning what is meant by 'crime' opens up a whole range of questions lying at the heart of the criminological enterprise such as:

1 *What type of crime?* It is commonplace for crime to be discussed as if it was more or less one specific type of behaviour, and the emphasis is usually on 'conventional' crime such as burglary and robbery. 'Crime', though, covers a vast number of quite different sorts of activity, including white-collar and corporate crime, domestic violence, ram-raiding, child sexual abuse, and rape.

2 *Explanations of crime?* Clearly, given the wide range of possibilities, it is futile to believe that one explanation can be found which covers all crime. Furthermore, even if one particular type of crime is examined, the problems involved in seeking out an explanation are still enormous. In fact, if we narrowed it down to one particular person who stole a bar of chocolate from a store, trying to explain why they did it raises immensely complex issues.

3 *Who decides what is a crime?* Crime only exists because laws exist; therefore crime is not a fixed, absolute quality of an act. Over the years laws change and vary from one society to another. Furthermore, although all legal jurisdictions are likely to have laws prohibiting, say, murder, there is wide variation in how this offence is defined. If we take as an example a case where someone is assaulted, goes into a coma, and subsequently dies. Whether or not the assailant can be charged with murder varies from one jurisdiction to another, depending upon, among other things, the length of time the victim is in a coma before they die.

4 *When does a crime exist?* This is an intriguing question. Some criminologists, loosely described as 'realists' – and not to be confused with left and right realists discussed later – approach crime statistics as if there exists a real, objective amount of crime 'out there'. The task, then, is to develop suitable methods for accurately measuring these crimes. Others take an 'institutionalist' view and argue that crime *rates* are socially constructed: that is, they are produced by organisational behaviour and various subjective processes on the part of, say, the police. More extreme versions go further and argue from a 'constitutive' position that 'crime' itself does not have an independent existence, but is socially constructed. Thus crime is seen as a social entity created not by an offender, but by control agents who, in specific cases, designate an act as 'criminal'. From this perspective, crime is a product of various processes mediating between an original act and a final judgement regarding its criminal or non-criminal status. Using this reasoning they reject, for example, the view that last night a certain number of cases of 'threatening behaviour' occurred in the town centre, and yet only some were discovered, the remainder forming part of the 'dark figure' of crime. Thus, because this offence is dependent on interpretations by, say, the police, it cannot exist as a 'real' thing detached from these interpretive processes. Crime is therefore not conceptualised in the same way that, for instance, the number of individuals carrying the Aids virus is conceptualised. Some have argued that a crime only exists as a social entity when a court finds a person guilty.

It is important to appreciate that debates regarding the definition of key terms are not merely semantic quarrels, a luxurious digression from the real business of criminology. Because phenomena such as crime and deviance are not theoretically neutral objects waiting 'out there' to be identified and analysed, it is necessary to consider seriously how best to conceptualise these areas of study. How they are conceptualised will have profound implications for the types of theories developed. Unfortunately, for a large part of its history academic criminology has often not suspended what Colin Sumner calls 'a commonsensical acceptance of these categories' (Sumner, 1990: 26). As a result, many analyses have proceeded within a conceptual framework built upon 'what everyone knows', with crime and deviance treated as if they were non-problematical, ahistorical categories of harmful/immoral behaviour. This is not necessarily because criminologists have been, or are, unaware of the conceptual difficulties inherent in these categories. In practice, a criminologist will often put the debate to one side because it is not thought relevant to the particular project in hand. The bracketing off of these fundamental conceptual debates is, perhaps, most vividly apparent when the mass media – say, television – invite a criminologist to comment on a crime-related issue. Due to the structural constraints imposed by the genre itself, with its demands for bite-sized nuggets of sagacity, the criminologist who launches into a detailed critique of the concept of crime is unlikely to be asked back again.

The complexity of these definitional issues makes life difficult for writers of introductory textbooks, and for those delivering introductory lectures in criminology. Usually the problems are resolved, or at least temporarily ameliorated, by offering a brief discussion on why defining criminology is complex, and why basic terms such as 'crime' and 'deviance' are difficult to define and measure. Following an overview, *en passant*, of 'problems with crime statistics', and 'crime as a socially constructed entity', the rest of the chapters or lectures may proceed, sustained by a few working definitions. This partly accounts for the heavy use of inverted commas in such textbooks (or, in the case of a lecture, the frequent use of jiggling fingers as sign language for inverted commas). The vocabulary of criminology is replete with terms requiring this treatment, for example, 'true' or 'real' crime rates, the 'dark figure' of crime, 'deviant', 'mad', 'bad', 'pervert', 'immoral', 'meaningless violence', 'hooligan', 'under-socialised', 'sick', 'maladjusted', 'hyperactive', and so on. Essentially, the message being transmitted, quite correctly, is that these are risky concepts.

CRIMINOLOGY

It would be reasonable for students of criminology to ask at the outset: What is criminology and what do criminologists do? The complexities surrounding this apparently simple enquiry can be indicated by noting that it is not unusual for elderly criminologists still to be debating these questions as they head for their dotage. The term 'criminology' obviously suggests that 'crime' lies at its core, and the *Shorter Oxford Dictionary* stretches the definition to 'the scientific study of crime'. This, however, merely points the student in a general direction. As a definition it is loaded with interesting epistemological problems. From a more academic viewpoint, *A Dictionary of Criminology* defines criminology as:

> The study of crime, of attempts to control it, and attitudes to it. Crime is interpreted in its widest sense, so as to include minor as well as major law-breaking, and also conduct which, but for the special status or role of those involved, would be regarded as law-breaking; e.g. excessive punishment of children by parents, antisocial practices of commercial undertakings.
>
> (Walsh and Poole, 1983: 56)

Moreover, a glance at the four editions of *The Oxford Handbook of Criminology* (Maguire *et al.*, 1994, 1997, 2002, 2007), for instance, indicates the wide range of activities in which criminology takes an interest: the politics of law and order; crime data; violent, white-collar, professional and organised crime; crime prevention; policing; pre-trial processes; sentencing policies; probation and community sanctions; prisons; 'race', gender and mental disorder and crime; victims, and so on.

And what of 'deviance'? If criminology is the study of crime, can criminologists study deviance and still work within recognised academic parameters? During the 1960s a large number of academics, some of whom had previously described themselves as criminologists, began to call themselves sociologists of deviance. This signalled a shift from the study of crime, as such, to the study of a broader range of rule-breaking activities, some illegal, some not. Today there are those who continue the sociology of deviance tradition, but academics have on the whole reverted back to the label of 'criminologist', though they may well engage in the study of what they see as non-criminal forms of deviance (having said that, quite a few working in this field, however, use the term as a flag of convenience).

Although there are clearly basic parameters whereby criminology has an identity and recognisable shape, it is by no means a totally integrated, theoretically homogeneous discipline. Internal divisions and disputes can be outlined as follows.

A range of disciplines

Over the years, those describing themselves as criminologists have based their work on many different academic disciplines, first one, then another, becoming dominant. As Stan Cohen puts it: 'Somewhat like a parasite, criminology attaches itself to its host subjects (notably, law, psychology, psychiatry, and sociology) and drew from them methods, theories and credibility' (Cohen, 1988: 4). At the same time, representatives of the various disciplines have given temporary attention to issues of crime and criminality, without, as it were, leaving their original discipline and emigrating to criminology. Frances Heidensohn (1989: 3) paints a suitable image:

> crime has sometimes featured as a social science tourist attraction, a Taj Mahal or Tower of Pisa, which everyone visits – once. Hence major theorists such as Durkheim, Parsons or Merton have made key but brief appearances on the crime scene.

Competing focuses

Criminologists continue to debate whether the proper focus of criminological study should be the offender, the offence, reactions to offending, the victim, or various combinations.

Competing agenda

There are extensive debates within criminology regarding what the discipline should really be aiming to achieve. Should it, for example, concern itself in the main with investigating the causes of crime, or with providing data and ideas useful in terms of penal or policing policy? Or should it be part of a struggle for civil liberties, or reform of the criminal justice system, or the transformation of society? The range of possibilities is immense.

Rival theories

Reflecting broader debates within the social sciences, criminologists have over the years subscribed to rival theoretical schools such as functionalism, Marxism, interactionism and phenomenology, to take sociological criminology as an example.

Varieties of methodology

Again reflecting more general debates and developments within the social sciences, criminologists have argued the case for a range of different research methods: quantitative and qualitative; positivist and phenomenological; dispassionate and politically committed, and so on.

Political orientations

Although not always explicitly stated, criminology, like any social science, is an academic terrain containing various competing political orientations. Disputes are not always restricted to traditional political antagonists: sometimes the most vitriolic exchanges are found among those ostensibly sharing the same political sympathies.

CRIME

Standard definitions of crime equate it with behaviour that breaks the criminal law. The term is also used to denote a single event, for example 'a crime was committed last night', or such events collectively, as in 'crime today is a major problem'. Dictionary definitions will generally add an evaluative dimension such as 'evil act'. Although at first glance these statements may appear uncontroversial, they are in need of some discussion. Indeed, there are significant conceptual issues at stake here, though as I have said, they are not always addressed, even within criminology. In this context we can endorse what Colin Sumner (1990: 26) has written:

> The first step of any intellectually rigorous enquiry into matters of crime and deviance must be to suspend a commonsensical acceptance of these categories and to investigate the social relationships, ideologies and contexts which combine to form them and give specific historical meaning.

Writers sympathetic to this view will endeavour to challenge generally accepted assumptions regarding what crime and deviance are, what criminals are like, and so on. This does not mean that all criminologists are agreed on how best to conceptualise these phenomena. In an analysis of criminology and the state, Robert Reiner (1988: 138) raises one of these conceptual debates. He begins by giving a standard legal textbook definition of crime as: 'an illegal act, omission or event . . . the principle consequence of which is that the offender, if he is detected and it is decided to prosecute, is prosecuted by or in the name of the State'. Following this he quotes an often cited and, from the perspective of jurisprudence, definitive statement by Lord Atkin in a 1931 case:

> The domain of criminal jurisprudence can only be ascertained by examining what acts at any particular period are declared by the State to be crimes, and the only common nature they will be found to possess is that they are prohibited by the State.
>
> (Ibid.: 138)

Reiner uses these statements as a vehicle for making the point that lawyers have for a long time accepted that no human activity is, in an absolute sense, criminal. On the same theme, he also notes a famous observation made by the labelling theorist Howard Becker, which caused a stir among criminologists in the 1960s: 'deviance is not a quality of the act the person commits, but rather a consequence of the application by others of rules and sanctions' (ibid.: 138). This, says Reiner, 'may have been news to criminology, but it was platitudinous to criminal lawyers'.

There are a number of important conceptual issues lying just below the surface here, which take us beyond the point that Reiner is making. The observant will have noticed, for instance, that though Reiner is referring to crime, in the quotation Becker uses the term 'deviance'. This raises the question, to what extent can these two terms be used interchangeably? However, the specific point being made by Reiner can be commented on. It is true that the judge, Lord Atkin, and the sociologist, Becker, are both stressing that crime and deviance respectively are relative concepts. In other words, that no act possesses an inherent quality of 'crime' or 'deviance'. A close scrutiny of what Atkin and Becker are saying, though, shows that they are approaching this idea from different directions, so that it means different things. Atkin is saying that what is defined as criminal depends upon the nature of the criminal law in that society. And, by inference, within a particular society the law changes over time, and also varies between one society and another at the same moment in time. So, although law may be necessary, at least as far as the eye can see into the future, the nature of that law – what is in a legal sense banned – is always contingent on the nature of that society. The law, therefore, does not express absolute moral strictures. As it happens, this idea (in the context of deviance) is discussed by Becker (1963: 9) a few pages on from the quotation given by Reiner above: 'deviance is created by society . . . social groups create deviance by making the rules whose infraction constitutes deviance'. In the passage quoted by Reiner, Becker is looking at the relative nature of deviance from a different point of view to this. In the earlier passage the focus is on *specific* acts which are labelled as 'deviant', not because they are inherently deviant, but because of a process of interaction between the 'deviant' and those in a position to apply the label. Unlike Atkin, Becker is going further than simply referring to the defining framework created by an already existing set of rules at a general level. He is referring to particular cases and the processes at work whereby deviance is socially constructed. This is to shift the emphasis away from the factors that 'cause' the behaviour in the first place, to the dynamics involved in the definition of *some* of these behaviours as 'deviant'.

This discussion of Becker directs attention to the actual processes of criminalisation and deviantisation: that is, to how the law or norms operates in practice. This was not what Lord Atkin was referring to. Although the law may appear to be a tightly formulated and impersonal set of codified legal rules, it is often ambiguous and less clear-cut. Furthermore, in practice the criminal law is locked into a whole series of organisational demands and processes, as well as being subject to individual interpretations. All of this will have enormous implications for the way in which crime is constructed within a particular society. The policing of the 1984–85 miners' strike in Britain, for instance, illustrates well how legal statutes and common law powers can, via police discretion, provide an extremely flexible resource. The highly discretionary dimension continued into the courts:

> The role of judges and the courts during the strike have been equally questionable. With regard to the criminal law, most controversial of all has been the systematic use by magistrates of restrictive bail conditions to prevent miners from effectively picketing or participating in the strike. Magistrates have forged close relationships with the police, have declared their hostility to striking miners and have accepted the wide discretion used by the police in defining offences.
>
> (Fine and Millar, 1985: 14)

From the point of view of critical criminologists, the creation of the law and its enforcement, as well as decisions *not* to legally ban certain acts, are not neutral processes guided by the common good. Rather, they reflect the interests of the powerful in society. On the other hand, some writers take the view that the criminal law, and hence what is defined as crime, reflects a society-wide consensus regarding wrongful behaviour (this issue is returned to below when discussing 'deviance'). It is difficult to disagree with the argument that in contemporary Britain there is general agreement among the public regarding the wrongfulness of, for instance, murder, rape and burglary. The problem, though, is that 'crime' embraces an enormous range of acts and omissions, and it would be equally difficult to argue with any certainty that all of these acts and omissions are disapproved of at the level of a consensus, in other words, that the criminal law in its entirety reflects the 'will of the people'.

Some criminologists argue that there is a consensus in society regarding basic moral standards, but this is not always reflected in criminal law. Therefore, they say, criminology should focus on those acts that violate codes of conduct based upon these shared moral standards, rather than on crime *per se*. Sellin (1938), for example, argued that the subject matter of criminology should be those acts that violate what he called universal 'conduct norms', whether or not the acts are technically criminal. The problem here, though, is one of actually identifying such norms, a problem that Sellin failed to resolve. This kind of approach, whereby what is studied by criminology is detached from legal definitions of crime, does mean that the criminologist would no longer be restricted to studying only those activities that happen to be defined as illegal within a particular jurisdiction, at a particular moment in time – a huge advantage in the eyes of some criminologists. Schwendinger and Schwendinger (1975), for instance, attempted to develop a radical version of such an approach. They argued that criminologists should define 'crime' (and therefore their subject matter) in terms of universal codes of conduct relating to fundamental human rights: 'individuals who deny these rights to others are criminal . . . imperialism, racism, sexism and poverty can be called crimes according to the logic of our argument' (*ibid.*: 148).

Measuring crime

Finally, as part of this preliminary look at the notion of crime, it will be useful to examine briefly attempts to measure the amount, nature and distribution of crime in society. At this stage questions of reliability and usefulness need not concern us (these will be part of the more detailed discussion of criminal statistics in the next chapter). The main aim is to indicate the sources of information available and to relate these to conceptualisations of crime.

Official crime statistics
Criminal statistics for England and Wales are published annually by the Home Office (in the publication *Criminal Statistics*), though quarterly updates are also published (similar statistics covering Scotland and Northern Ireland are published by, respectively, the Scottish Office and the Northern Ireland Office). These are the crime figures that are reproduced in the mass media (nowadays in tandem with figures from the *British Crime Survey* – see below) accompanied by, if the figures show a decrease on the previous year, a sigh of relief – or, if they show an increase, by a sigh of anxiety. For a government, a decrease will signal an opportunity for self-congratulation that its criminal justice policies are working; an increase is obviously more of a problem, and can stimulate wonderous verbal sorcery from government sources in an effort to vindicate their policies.

The figures themselves are based on what are called 'notifiable offences' recorded by the police forces of England and Wales, and the more serious offences are meant to be in this category. However, although offences such as homicide and rape are included, some of the offences so classified will be seen by many people as not particularly serious. Supposedly less serious 'summary offences' (made up largely of motoring offences), which are dealt with by the magistrates' courts, are not recorded in the crime statistics. There are, however, figures available for 'persons proceeded against', and these add up to about three times the number of persons convicted or cautioned for notifiable offences. The latest Home Office figures show that in England and Wales, in the 12 months up to the end of September 2008, 4,836,900 offences were recorded by the police.

Victim surveys

These have become increasingly popular over the last few years in Britain and in the United States. They can be incorporated into a conservative or a radical criminological tradition, and they reflect a growth in that field of criminology called victimology (Walklate, 1989, 2007; Hoyle and Zedner, 2007). Victim surveys are based on asking people if they have been the victim of a crime, usually over a twelve-month period, and whether they reported this to the police. Various supplementary questions may then be asked. In this country the largest victim surveys are the *British Crime Surveys* carried out under the auspices of the Home Office in 1982, 1984, 1988, 1992, 1994, 1996, 1998, 2000 and, since 2001, on an annual basis. As well as these national surveys, a number of smaller-scale, localised surveys have been carried out, and these purport to provide more detailed in-depth data on victim experiences.

One of the aims of a victim survey is to gather supplementary or alternative information to that provided by official statistics and, in particular, to obtain some idea of the number of offences that are not reported to the police by the public, and therefore not recorded. In this context it should be noted that in some cases crimes are reported, but are then not considered to be crimes by the police. Inevitably, and using common-sense language, all victim surveys show that there is more crime committed than appears in official statistics. The concept used here is the 'dark figure' of crime.

It is frequently pointed out that the *British Crime Surveys* indicate that, because of a lack of reporting by the public, only around one in four crimes committed are recorded in official statistics. This is an average figure derived from a widely varying propensity to report, depending on the nature of the offence as perceived by the victim. Criminal damage (vandalism), for instance, is much less likely to be reported than the theft of a car. The one-in-four ratio, though, has to be treated with caution, in that some categories of offence used in the *British Crime Surveys* are different to those used by the police, and there are certain offences which, by definition, will not be picked up by such surveys, for example shoplifting and fraud. In fact, Sparks *et al.* (1977) suggest that about eleven times more crime is committed than is recorded in official statistics; this gives an enormous 'dark figure' of crime.

Self-report studies

These are questionnaires asking people if they have committed any of the offences listed (for example, over the last twelve months). Clearly it is asking a lot of someone to admit to breaking the law, and so self-report studies strive to minimise potential problems by stressing anonymity, and by using back-up data from official records and even polygraphs (lie detectors). Depending on the sample used, researchers will attempt to correlate amounts and types of offending behaviour with variables such as class and age.

Carried out for, and published by, the Home Office, the annual *Offending, Crime and Justice Survey* provides detailed information based upon self-reported offending in England and Wales. Whilst the age of respondents in the first survey in 2003 ranged from 10 to 65 years, subsequent surveys have focused on a younger age group of 10 to 25-year-olds. To a large extent the surveys are longitudinal, in that each year they seek to question the same sample of individuals; however, as some of these drop out, new people are added in order to maintain an overall sample of around 5,000. The most recent survey (Roe and Ashe, 2008) found that 22 per cent of respondents said they had committed one of the survey's twenty core offences during the previous twelve months; however, the bulk of this offending was occasional and relatively trivial. Ten per cent said they had committed one of the serious offences and, according to the survey, groups of serious offenders tended to overlap with groups of frequent offenders.

Since their inception self-report studies have consistently discovered significantly more widespread offending among the general public than official information would suggest. Again, though, it has to be stressed that this kind of blanket statement is in need of qualification. The seriousness of offence and frequency of offending have to be considered, along with the actual methods of research used, before reaching too many conclusions.

Police and court records
These provide another, official, source of information for criminologists. Unlike the sources above, here we are dealing directly with individuals who have been defined and processed by the criminal justice system, this procedure culminating in a conviction or a caution. Maguire (1994: 271) mentions an eye-catching piece of information derived from these sources:

> not many more than one in ten offences recorded by the police result in a caution or a conviction: in other words, in the vast majority of cases, nothing is officially known about those responsible. Indeed, it has been further calculated . . . that only about one in fifty of the comparable crimes identified by the British Crime Survey result in a conviction – a figure which drops as low as one in 200 where 'vandalism' (criminal damage) is concerned.

Other sources
In recent years we have seen huge increases in the amount and type of criminal justice-related data available for analysis; this has been facilitated by the expansion in

computer-based data storage systems. It has also been encouraged by the managerialist emphasis now placed on auditing and performance indicators by central government. Crime and Disorder Reduction Partnerships in each borough, district and unitary authority in England and Wales, for instance, were, following the 1998 Crime and Disorder Act, obliged to conduct three-yearly local audits of crime and disorder. More recently, the 2006 Police and Justice Act placed a statutory duty on local partnerships to conduct these audits on an annual basis (they were also given the new title of 'strategic assessments'). While these tend to rely largely on police data, they are expected to collect data from a wide range of other sources, for example the health service, social services and probation, and they often commission their own local research (increasingly, information of this sort is being stored in regional data warehouses). Thus vast amounts of data relating to such things as crime mapping, the whereabouts of certain types of offenders, and victims and the fear of crime are now available (though access to 'sensitive' data is constrained by certain protocols – see Tierney and Hobbs, 2003). These data are collected by, or for, a whole range of agencies and organisations, including the Home Office, the police, universities, local authorities and private research companies.

Varieties of crime

With the above as a backdrop, we can return to a discussion of the concept of crime. It should be apparent that the word 'crime' can crop up in various contexts, and refer to a variety of phenomena. This can be illustrated further by listing some of the chief ways in which 'crime' is used, though in each case it is describing different phenomena:

1 Crimes deemed to be such by a court finding a defendant guilty.
2 Crimes recorded by the police as notifiable offences.
3 Crimes reported to the police by the public.
4 Crimes reported to, or discovered by, the police, but not recorded by them.
5 The dark figure of crime.
6 Crimes actually committed.
7 There is a seventh, rather different category that could be added, and has already been referred to briefly. This is where the term 'crime' is used to describe activities that are not at present against the law, but from the perspectives of some observers are wrong or immoral. Thus someone might say, 'It's a crime the way he treats his wife', meaning that although not illegal, the husband's behaviour is 'wrong', and perhaps should be made illegal. On a more complex level, this principle has been applied to such things as racism, sexism and imperialism (see Schwendinger and Schwendinger, 1975).

When discussing the measurement of crime in society, some criminologists have used the iceberg analogy, in which recorded crime is seen as merely the tip of the iceberg.

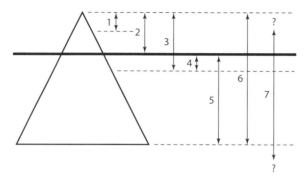

Figure 1.1   *Profile of the seven conceptions of crime*

Whatever the ultimate value of this analogy, it can be used as a basis for illustrating graphically the seven ways of conceptualising crime noted above (see Figure 1.1). Proportions are based upon artistic licence rather than reality.

This discussion can be extended to include the notion of a 'crime rise' and the notion of a 'criminal', to point to similar conceptual problems when using these terms.

Varieties of crime rise

As Jason Ditton (1979) has shown, the notion of a 'crime rise' can mean a number of things:

1 As a result of new laws, acts that were previously non-criminal now become criminal.
2 More criminal acts are discovered.
3 Methods of classification change so that acts previously defined as non-criminal are now criminal.
4 There is more mass media coverage of crime.
5 More criminal acts are committed.

Varieties of criminal

As with 'crime' and 'crime rises', the term 'criminal' can also be used to mean different things. An interesting question (with an answer that is less obvious than might be thought) is, what is a criminal? Here are a number of possible answers:

1 Someone who really committed the offence and is found guilty by a court.
2 Someone who is found guilty but did not commit the offence.

3   Someone who committed the offence, and the offence is recorded, but has not been caught.

4   Someone who committed the offence, but no one is aware of it, except the offender.

Thus, for all three terms – crime, crime rise and criminal – there are various definitional possibilities. The fact that these possibilities exist reminds us that criminologists need to have a clear understanding of what they mean when they use these terms. Finally, we turn to the concept of deviance.

DEVIANCE

Sociological definitions of deviance generally contain two elements: non-conforming behaviour with respect to accepted norms, and strong disapproval of such behaviour. Deviance can therefore be criminal or non-criminal. This view of deviance is illustrated by the following examples: 'Deviance may be defined as non-conformity to a given norm, or set of norms, which are accepted by a significant number of people in a community or society' (Giddens, 1993: 116); 'behaviour which somehow departs from what a group expects to be done or what it considers the desirable way of doing things' (Cohen, 1971: 9); 'the violation of the accepted norms or social rules of a group or society . . . the reaction to them is invariably one of disapproval, fear, suspicion, hostility or outrage' (Bilton *et al.*, 1981: 563).

A crucially important point to make is that because a criminologist describes some act they are studying as 'deviant' does not mean that they personally consider the act to be 'bad', 'immoral' etc. They are merely recognising, or assuming, that within society, or some section of society, the act is strongly disapproved of, because it is judged to have violated certain norms and values. Likewise, when a criminologist refers to deviance in a generalised sense, outside specific examples, there is no implication that they are, in effect, referring to a set of 'bad', 'immoral' etc. types of behaviour on a collective level. In general conversation and within the mass media, though, the word 'deviance' is very often used as shorthand for types of behaviour that supposedly possess these negative qualities. In view of this, it is possible for a student new to the subject to enrol on a university course entitled, say, 'The Sociology of Deviance' under the mistaken impression that, in some absolute sense, the course is 'really' a course devoted to the sociological study of bad, immoral, perverted and unnatural behaviour. This is one reason why some critical criminologists argue that in order to shift the emphasis away from an assumption of inherently 'bad' behaviour, criminological studies should focus on the rules themselves and their application, that is, on deviantisation processes, and not on those labelled 'deviant'.

The advent of a sceptical – and, on one level, radical – 'new deviancy theory' in the 1960s marked the beginning of an attempt seriously to interrogate the concept of 'deviance', though by then the concept had had a relatively short lifespan. Although they were not necessarily answered, this led to a number of critical questions being placed on the agenda:

- Whose rules are being broken?
- In whose interests do these rules operate?
- Why are the rules there in the first place?
- Who is doing the disapproving?

The last question, asking *who* is doing the disapproving, is a good starting point for a discussion of the concept of deviance. One of the central sociological problems in this context concerns the issue of a consensus; that is, a general agreement or majority view over what is considered acceptable behaviour. Traditional criminologists have tended to assume that there is a consensus, which is then translated into phrases such as 'public opinion'. Functionalist approaches to deviance, for example, have built their work around the assumption of a consensus as the product of socialisation processes. Those outside the posited consensus are then viewed as either deviant themselves, or marginal groups whose opinions are perverse and therefore unimportant.

For radical criminologists, or radical sociologists of deviance, especially Marxists, the notion of consensus proved to be particularly awkward. This was because a capitalist society such as Britain or the United States was seen as being composed of different classes and groups, giving a plurality of cultural formations with different understandings of 'accepted behaviour'. Developing an interactionist perspective, new deviancy theorists such as Edwin Lemert (1967), for instance, saw deviant behaviour as being more or less evenly distributed throughout society. The search for the initial causes of deviance was seen as futile, because causes will vary enormously from one individual or group to another. The emphasis was therefore on reactions to some of the behaviour, reactions which lead to the application of the label 'deviant'. From this perspective, only some of the rule breakers are discovered and labelled. Sociologically, then, these are 'deviants', and it is their behaviour and reactions to it that should be the proper concern of sociology. Consequently, notions of consensus are spirited away, and attention is turned to the labelling process and the unfortunates who are unlucky enough to be selected by those possessing the power to label.

However, the arbitrariness inherent in this model suggests that in theory literally anyone could be selected for doing anything. In practice, though, behaviours earmarked as deviant are not randomly selected. Therefore, consideration should be given to the nature and distribution of the power to accomplish labelling, and the structural settings within which specific labelling processes operate. And there is still the thorny issue of consensus. If a plurality of cultures and subcultures exists in society, each with their own quite different feelings about acceptable and unacceptable behaviour, how is the public labelling of individuals and groups to be made palatable? Outside a totalitarian society, presumably there has to be a degree of public disapproval, some congruence of opinion among the various groups regarding the labelled behaviour. The issue then becomes one of determining the nature and source of this disapproval, by examining, for example, the role of ideology.

Radical criminologists wishing to develop a Marxist approach to understanding deviance also had to grapple with the idea of consensus. This was apparent in the 'new criminology' of Ian Taylor, Paul Walton and Jock Young (1973), where they presented a radical Marxist alternative to new deviancy theory. They rejected the view that a consensus existed, but met problems when actually defining what 'deviance' was. In fact, in this study no definition was forthcoming. They attempted to solve the problem of a consensus by arguing that although there was none, people thought there was, because of the influence of the mass media and education. This suggested that individuals did not really disapprove of certain behaviours that are labelled 'deviant', but at the same time believed that most people did.

In the mid-1970s the Marxist Colin Sumner (1976) developed a different approach. He argued that deviance was best conceived of as a social censure – an adverse judgement – existing at the level of ideology. This is to depart from conceptualising deviance in terms of actual behaviour. To complicate matters further, at about the same time another Marxist writer, Paul Hirst (1975a), rejected out of hand the project of developing a 'Marxist perspective' on deviance. For him, deviance was a pre-given bourgeois concept, not a Marxist theoretical object, and therefore was not a proper area for study, except in the form of revisionism. So, by the mid-1970s the debates were beginning to intensify.

More recently, so-called left realist criminology has accepted the existence of a consensus with respect to certain sorts of 'conventional' crime. Put simply, this position states that it is absurd to believe that large numbers of people, and especially those who are victims, do not strongly disapprove of crimes such as rape, burglary and robbery. To many people, though, this will appear to be a pretty unremarkable statement. In fact, presented in this way such statements mask complex theoretical issues pertaining to the deviantisation of certain defined criminal acts.

The left realist position takes us back to the notion of 'strong public disapproval' whereby deviance is defined, but can deviance be conceived of in crude numerical terms? Furthermore, how do we know that people in general strongly disapprove of a particular type of behaviour or person? Obviously, it is reasonable to make this assumption with respect to some behaviour. However, can we say the same about all examples of so-called deviance as defined in the literature of criminology? Certainly, research does point to a significant consensus among the public with regard to the core areas of the criminal law as generalised categories (cf. Braithwaite, 1989). And West (1982) found that even known offenders disapproved of their children's delinquent behaviour. On the basis of localised crime surveys left realists have argued that 'the major crimes *as presently defined in criminal law,* are agreed upon by the mass of the population' (Young, 1987: 355, original emphasis).

However, even if we accept this proposition uncritically, the range of behaviours constituting the academic study of deviance over the years is much broader than this. A quick glance at the books in the criminology section of a university or college library, where the author has designated the activities as 'deviant', will indicate the possibilities: the blind, Mods and Rockers, Hell's Angels, those with learning difficulties, 'Paki'-bashers, gays and lesbians, naturists, 'obese' people, school truants, marijuana users and 'topless' barmaids. If a consensus is the lynchpin of a definition of deviance, how is that consensus to be measured? The danger is that a researcher may simply feel, using common sense, that a consensus exists; indeed, they might create a stigmatised group as a result of doing the research. How could feelings of disapproval over a vast range of potential behaviours be ascertained anyway? No national survey, for instance, has been instituted asking people what they feel about all these behaviours; and it would be of only limited value. How do we discover what people 'really' feel, and what does that mean? An individual may nominally be against some behaviour, and yet do it themselves. On the other hand, they may feel that they should pretend to be against something because they believe that everyone else is.

The difficulties surrounding this issue can be summed up with this, albeit crude, scenario. Imagine a sociologist of deviance decides to do research on a specific type of deviant behaviour. How is he or she to know that this *is* an example of deviance? Are they to be debarred from doing this research because deviant status cannot somehow be objectively assessed? Does it matter? Given these sorts of problems we can perhaps understand how tempting it is to dispense with the definitional niceties, and just get on with studying an activity because it can be reasonably assumed that someone, somewhere, will disapprove of it. Unfortunately, as well as ignoring the central conceptual problem, this criterion probably applies to any activity. The question remains: how is deviance to be recognised?

Debates about how deviance and crime should be conceptualised bubbled to the surface with the radicalism of new deviancy theory, post-new deviancy theory, and left criminology, which became influential during the 1960s and 1970s. Many of the writers involved dispensed with the concept of crime because it was so problematic. As Heidensohn (1989: 8) says:

> Since the concept (of crime) is so flexible and the records so unreliable, and so far outside of the control of researchers, there has been a tendency to avoid confrontation, to argue against any engagement with the concept or especially with official records.

And as she points out, for some the solution was to focus on deviance – though the problems are still there in abundance. From the mid-1970s, however, the focus in the main shifted back to 'crime', and conceptual debates about 'deviance' have tended to be shelved. Sumner (1990: 15) makes this telling observation: 'Students still ask "Whatever happened to the theoretical debate about deviance in the early

1970s?"' He goes on to say that within radical criminology there has been a failure to 'reconceptualize "deviant behaviour"'. Certainly, more recent work has been concerned with reconceptualising crime rather than deviance, but the 'failure' does not only apply to so-called radical criminology.

OTHER TERMS AND CONCEPTS

The following is a brief discussion of some associated terms and concepts that students of criminology will come across in their reading.

The **criminal law**, against which crime is defined, arises from: **common law** (or law made by judges), referred to as legal precedents; **Acts of Parliament**, which create legislation or statutory law; **delegated legislation**, which is legislation derived from persons or bodies other than Parliament; and directives from the **European Union**. **Crime** and **offence** technically mean the same thing, though in the literature 'crime' is often used to describe more serious offences. **Arrestable offences** are more serious offences, or offences with a fixed penalty, meaning that a police officer is legally entitled to take the alleged offender into custody. **Non-arrestable offences** are those where a police officer issues a summons to an alleged offender to appear in court at some future date, or issues an on-the-spot fine. However, failing to give a credible name and address (Mickey Mouse, Disneyland would be in this category) will result in an arrest. There is no consensus regarding the precise meaning of **delinquency**, though it usually refers to the offending behaviour of young people, and the behaviour can stretch from serious criminal offences to relatively minor non-criminal activities. **Doli incapax** means that in England and Wales a child under 10 years (8 years in Scotland) cannot be guilty of a criminal offence. Prior to 1998 it was 14 years. However, in the case of children aged 10–13, the prosecution is obliged to prove that at the time of the offence the child was aware that their actions were wrong. **Adult offenders** are those aged 18 years and over; **young offenders** are those aged 14–17 years inclusive; **child offenders** are those aged 10–13 years inclusive.

Selected further reading

(All texts discussed under 'further reading' at the end of each chapter are not listed in order of precedence.)

There are a number of excellent general textbooks available to students. Four editions of the encyclopaedic *Oxford Handbook* have now been published, and all four are worth reading:

Maguire, M., Morgan, R. and Reiner, R. (eds) (1994, 1997, 2002, 2007) *The Oxford Handbook of Criminology,* 1st, 2nd, 3rd and 4th edns, Oxford: Oxford University Press.

For an overview of criminological theory and the context of its development in the United States, see: **Lilly, J. R., Cullen, F. T. and Ball, R. A. (2007)** *Criminological Theory: Context and consequences*, **4th edn, London: Sage**.

Now in its fifth edition, **Downes, D. and Rock, P. (2007)** *Understanding Deviance*, **5th edn, Oxford: Oxford University Press**, is a classic British text written by two major figures in British criminology.

Sumner, C. (ed.) (2004) *The Blackwell Companion to Criminology*, **Oxford: Blackwell Publishing**, provides a collection of critical discussions of a range of key themes and issues, many of which have emerged recently within criminology; at the time of writing it is only available in hardback.

Two well-written and accessible introductory textbooks that discuss criminological theory and processes of criminal justice are: **Hale, C., Hayward, K., Wahidin, A. and Wincup, E. (eds) (2009)** *Criminology*, **2nd edn, Oxford: Oxford University Press**; and **Newburn, T. (2008)** *Criminology*, **Cullompton: Willan**.

Now in its seventh edition, **Clarke, E. J. (2007)** *Deviant Behavior*, **7th edn, Basingstoke: Palgrave Macmillan** is a highly regarded theoretical discussion of deviance.

Walters, R. (2003) *Deviant Knowledge: Criminology, politics and policy*, **Cullompton: Willan** is a critical discussion of the political and ideological contexts within which criminological research is conducted.

Two interesting theoretical models of crime are the 'pyramid of crime' and the 'prism of crime' introduced and discussed, respectively, by: **Hagan, J. (1977)** *The Disreputable Pleasures*, **Toronto: McGraw-Hill Ryerson**; and **Henry, S. and Lanier, M. M. (1998)** 'The prism of crime: arguments for an integrated definition of crime', *Justice Quarterly*, 15(4), pp. 609–27.

For an accessible overview of legal terms and legal processes, see: **Williams, K. S. (2009)** *Textbook on Criminology*, **6th edn, Oxford: Oxford University Press**.

CHAPTER 2

MEASURING CRIME AND CRIMINALITY

Key themes

- Official statistics
- The 'dark figure' of crime
- Public reporting
- Changes in the law
- The role of the police
- Ways of seeing
- The implications for criminal statistics
- Victim surveys
- The usefulness of criminal statistics
- Local crime surveys and left realism
- Recent crime trends

INTRODUCTION

Here we discuss in more detail the various sources of information relating to crime and criminals. The reader is introduced to the key processes at work in the social construction of crime and criminals; for example, the role played by the police, who act as 'gatekeepers' to the criminal justice system. The chapter includes an up-to-date overview of statistical data on amounts and types of crime, a commentary on their usefulness or otherwise, and a review of historical trends.

OFFICIAL STATISTICS

How much crime?
How many criminals?
How many victims?

It is impossible to give any accurate or straightforward answers to the questions posed
. . . Not only does everything depend on what is meant by 'crime', 'criminals' and
'victims', but even if there were to be broad agreement on the definition and scope of

these basic terms, it is very apparent that most of the extant methods of measuring the nature and amounts of crime, criminality and victimization would be inadequate to the task.

(Bottomley and Pease, 1986: 1)

Give or take a few qualifications, all criminologists would probably go along with this sobering assessment, which appears on the first page of an important analysis of crime data. Criminologists can answer questions (or find the information) regarding such things as the number of people residing in HM prisons in England and Wales at a given moment, or the number of offences of criminal damage recorded by the police in a given year. The questions posed by Bottomley and Pease, though, refer to qualitatively different phenomena. In fact, the quotation indicates two issues at stake here. One concerns the accuracy of data, and the other concerns the conceptual meaning of the phenomena that the data purport to represent. Put another way, it is not just a question of how close official statistics are to 'real' amounts of crime; it is also a question of what processes are involved in the construction of such figures and, ultimately, what is meant by crime anyway.

This does not mean that all statistical information pertaining to crime, either official or not, is useless and unworthy of serious attention by criminologists. It does mean, though, that such information has to be treated with extreme caution. Of course, a judicious amount of caution is not always exercised by those who comment on, and use, these statistics, for example in support of a political programme. Furthermore, as Jack Douglas (1971b) has pointed out, criminological knowledge produced by academics can be put to all sorts of nefarious uses by those representing particular ideological interests; to this extent, criminological knowledge can be 'dangerous knowledge'.

There is, however, one question that at the level of common sense may be viewed as one to which criminologists should be able to provide an answer: is there more crime now than there was in the past? This question can form the basis of a more extended discussion.

Echoing Bottomley and Pease, the immediate response has to be that no simple answer can be given, for any engagement with the question necessarily triggers layers of statistical and conceptual problems. To begin with, what is meant by 'the past'? Pre-World War Two? A hundred years ago, or beyond? A crude reading of the official criminal statistics for the last century – at least up until the 1990s – would leave no option but an affirmative answer to the original question. Apart from a few fluctuations – notably a dip at the end of the 1940s, and between 1950 and 1955 – total amounts of crime, and crime rates based upon offences per 100,000 of the population, continued to rise steadily.

From the turn of the twentieth century up to World War One, under 100,000 offences were recorded by the police of England and Wales for each year. Currently, the figure is 4,836,900 (for the twelve months up to the end of September 2008). The categories of theft/handling stolen goods and burglary add up to about 35 per cent of all offences recorded, a much smaller proportion of total recorded crime than in the mid twentieth century. In the case of violence against the person and criminal damage, the opposite is true, with each representing about 20 per cent of recorded offences. Theft of or from a vehicle currently stands at around 700,000 per year, a figure which in itself is seven times the total number of offences recorded annually in the first part of this century. Needless to say, all information of this nature needs careful scrutiny, and especially so if we extend the picture to include international comparisons, for then such factors as different jurisdictions and offence classification systems have to be incorporated into tortuously complicated analyses (for a more detailed up-to-date review of official crime statistics see Maguire, 2007).

Not surprisingly, many viewed the gradual increases in recorded crime during the twentieth century in Britain, and in many other industrialised nations, with some dismay, seeing them as confirmation that there was less crime committed in the past. Indeed, a majority of the public thought this even when recorded crime began to decrease from the mid 1990s. However, even if crimes are simply viewed as objective events waiting 'out there' to be discovered and recorded, there are still huge problems involved in interpreting criminal statistics and making comparisons across time. If conceptual problems relating to the meaning of crime are considered alongside these 'technical' problems, then analyses become more complicated. For the moment, though, it will be useful to concentrate on criminal statistics at a technical level; that is, to examine those factors that will determine their shape and 'accuracy' (there are good, extended discussions in Wiles, 1976a; Jupp, 1989; Maguire, 2007).

THE 'DARK FIGURE' OF CRIME

The concept of a dark figure of crime has been mentioned earlier, when the iceberg analogy was introduced. It refers to those 'hidden' crimes that are not recorded by the police, and are therefore absent from official statistics. Data from victim surveys are used to estimate the magnitude of this dark figure – Sparks *et al.* (1977) suggest that it is eleven times the official figure, though this latter statistic is an overall average which hides enormous variation between one offence and another.

Whether or not the 'dark figure' is an appropriate way in which to think about crime is an issue that can be left to one side for now. What has to be stressed is that it cannot be assumed that amounts of unrecorded crime have stayed constant throughout history, as the following discussion of some of the main variables determining amounts of recorded crime will illustrate.

PUBLIC REPORTING

Given that about 80 per cent of crime known to the police comes to their attention as a result of information from the public, the willingness of the public to report crime is a crucial factor. Obviously, statistical comparisons across time will need to take this into consideration. As a result of motor insurance being legally compulsory, we can expect very high levels of public reporting and police recording of vehicle theft. Likewise, the spread of household contents insurance, and the requirement to notify the police of loss of property before a claim can be made, will increase the reporting of burglary. With other types of offence – for example, sexual offences, domestic violence and child abuse – the evidence from victim surveys suggests substantial under-reporting. Finkelhor's (1979) study of American students, for instance, found that 19.2 per cent of women and 8.6 per cent of men had experienced sexual molestation as children, though only rarely had they disclosed this to another person.

In more recent years there have been increases in amounts of these offences recorded by the police. A plausible argument is that this results as much from such things as greater publicity and improvements in police procedures as from increases in the incidence of such offending.

Other factors to note in the context of public reporting are the spread of telephones, making contact with the police easier, and neighbourhood watch schemes, whose *raison d'être* is to encourage public reporting. There is also the degree of public tolerance of certain sorts of behaviour. If a more sensitised public exists, with a lowered tolerance threshold, then we can expect reporting to increase. Thus the official crime rate can go up as members of a society become more demanding in terms of notions of civility and propriety.

CHANGES IN THE LAW

This factor in itself illustrates the massive problems involved in determining whether or not there is 'really' more crime today than in the past. Over the years new laws are introduced, and others repealed, which means that legal rules are in a constant state of flux. Compared to the early part of this century, the net of criminalised behaviour has widened considerably – for example, with respect to the use of drugs, the treatment of children and commercial fraud. In general terms, then, the further back one goes in history, the more difficult it is to make judgements about the moral health of a society on the basis of criminal statistics. On the other hand, providing there have been no significant recent legislative changes, comparisons between the present and the recent past are more valid. Since New Labour came to power in 1997, though, the introduction of new laws has led to the creation of around 3,000 new offences.

Changes in the law also involve changes in the counting rules and the classification of offences as imposed upon the police by the Home Office. A most striking, and consequently often referred to, example of this characteristic concerns the offence of criminal damage (vandalism). According to official statistics, in 1976 there were 93,000 offences of criminal damage in England and Wales, whilst in the following year this had increased to 297,400. One explanation might be that during this twelve-month period there was a huge upsurge in criminal damage, an anarchic festival of paint spraying and property destruction. Needless to say, this was not the case. The real reason for the increase was that the 1976 figure excluded criminal damage valued at £20 and under, whilst in 1977 the police had been instructed by the Home Office to record instances of criminal damage valued at this figure and under as well. Of course, relying on monetary value, for any class of offence, will mean that all subsequent figures are influenced by inflation.

The implications of changes in the law (and the power to make these changes) can be illustrated further by a recent case tried in an Italian court. At the conclusion of the trial in early 2009, Englishman David Mills, who is the estranged husband of British Labour minister Tessa Jowell, was found guilty of accepting a bribe of £400,000 as a reward for giving 'distorted evidence' at two previous trials where the Prime Minister of Italy, Silvio Berlusconi, was a defendant. Mills, a legal adviser to Berlusconi on off-shore dealings, was sentenced to four and a half years in jail, and fined heavily. He is to appeal against the sentence. Although Berlusconi was indicted to appear with Mills, in 2008 the Prime Minister's government passed a law giving him, along with other senior officials, immunity from prosecution. This immunity is currently under consideration by the country's constitutional court, however:

> The Italian government recently secured Berlusconi's position further with a clause inserted in a bill to reform the judiciary. If approved by parliament, it will mean that, even if such immunity were lifted, the judge residing over the case that ended yesterday would not be able to apply its outcome automatically to Berlusconi. She would be obliged to begin proceedings all over again.
>
> (Hooper and Stratton, 2009)

THE ROLE OF THE POLICE

In view of the fact that criminal statistics are derived from information supplied by the various police forces, the 'gatekeeping' role of the police is of central importance. The nature of this role will vary over time, as well as between one force (and even one officer) and another. This introduces yet more variables into the process of constructing crime statistics.

The importance of the police can be outlined by distinguishing between a reactive and a proactive dimension. Reactive policing refers to responses to specific incidents by the organisation or individual officers. The incident may come to light because of information from the public, or through direct experience. The proactive dimension to the police role is usually associated with general policing policies based upon a mix of Home Office directives, discussions within the police at a national level (for example, via the Association of Chief Police Officers, ACPO), and policies emanating from a particular force. A proactive dimension, however, can exist at the level of the individual too, such as when an officer develops local contacts, or keeps an eye on certain establishments.

All of these various aspects of the police role need to be situated within an organisational as well as broader social structural context. In terms of the organisation, note would have to be taken of, for instance, management styles and resources available to a particular police force. The broader social structural context will include the social composition and policing problems pertaining to that force's area, political pressures from government, legal powers and constraints, modes of accountability, and so on.

Thus we can see that a whole range of factors will be at work shaping the manner in which offences and offenders are dealt with by the police. Obviously, it is absurd to assume that these have been constant through history. All of these factors will, in various ways and in varying degrees, affect the actual decision-making process with respect to amounts and types of offences that are eventually included in the national criminal statistics. This can be illustrated by taking a few key examples.

Fundamentally, the police have to decide if an indictable crime has taken place, and, if so, within which particular category of offence it should be included (remembering that the counting rules are subject to periodic change by the Home Office). For instance, in those cases where no suspect is apprehended it is by no means always unambiguously clear what type of offence is being dealt with. In an assault case, how severe are the victim's injuries? Did the shopper really have a wallet containing £1,000 picked from their pocket? How serious has the criminal damage to be before it is recorded? Furthermore, as we shall see, police officers are part of a complex interactional and interpretive process whereby particular understandings of reality are negotiated (e.g. Bittner, 1967; Cicourel, 1968; Manning, 1977; Tierney, 1987).

At a national and local level police forces will set priorities regarding the targeting of particular types of offence. These law enforcement priorities will be derived from various sources: the Home Office and central government, perceived public anxieties, local policing plans, and problems flagged-up by local crime and disorder audits. At specific moments, the result of this may be a sudden statistical increase in the incidence of a targeted offence, or what appear to be startlingly high levels of illicit drug use and child sexual abuse, or appalling standards of driving in certain police force areas. Hence the necessity of seeing such information as the artefacts of police organisation and practice, rather than as a statistical photograph of objective reality. In this context we can note Maguire's (1994: 249) comment that:

> Prior to 1968, there was little consistency between police forces on how many offences were to be recorded when events of these kinds came to their notice. Following the recommendations of the Perks Committee in 1967, clearer 'counting rules' were established . . . which tidied up some of the discrepancies between forces, but at the same time they appear fairly arbitrary and, undoubtedly, understate the relative frequency of some offences.

Other factors associated with the police which could increase or decrease amounts of crime that are recorded, irrespective of 'actual' amounts taking place, can be listed briefly, as follows:

- The number of police officers – this has risen from about 110,000 in 1980 to over 140,000 today, the highest number on record (Bullock and Mulchandani, 2009). In addition there are around 30,000 full-time equivalent police community support officers and special constables.
- The use of increasingly sophisticated technology, such as computers.
- More efficient systems of administration.
- More expenditure on policing – in England and Wales, 1992–93, total spending on the police was £5.42bn, an 87 per cent rise in real terms since 1979. Today it is over £12bn, a 77 per cent increase since 1997 when the Labour government was elected to office. In 2006–07, £26bn was spent on criminal justice in England and Wales, almost 40 per cent more in real terms than was spent in 1997–98 (HM Treasury, 2008). Annual per capita expenditure on the criminal justice system in England and Wales is higher than that of any other EU country (and the United States).

WAYS OF SEEING

Having established a broad analytical framework within which policing operates, we can now examine in more detail what is often referred to as 'cop culture' and the bearing that this has on the production of criminal statistics:

> An understanding of how police officers see the social world and their role in it – 'cop culture' – is crucial to an analysis of what they do, and their broad political function. It is a commonplace of the now voluminous sociological literature on police operations and discretion that the rank-and-file officer is the primary determinant of policing where it really counts – on the street.
>
> (Reiner, 1992: 107)

As a result of the nature of the occupation and the structural pressures to which it is subject, police officers construct shorthand characterisations pertaining to types of public, location and event. In particular, the public become 'dramatis personae': persons of the drama. This process is predicated on the necessity of gathering together the elements of what could be a chaotic and confusing world in order to make sense of it, as well as control it – and sometimes this involves crude stereotyping. In different ways, of course, we are all caught up in this kind of process. However, with respect to the police it is a fundamental occupational requirement, and has important implications for the rest of us. It is well summed up by Cicourel (1968: 67), who says that the police develop:

> theories about individuals and groups, morality and immorality, good and bad people, institutions, practices and typifications of community settings, and such theories or conceptions are employed in routine ways . . . the officer's preconstituted typifications and stock of knowledge at hand lead him to prejudge much of what he encounters . . . particular ecological settings, populated by persons with 'known' styles of dress and physical appearance, provide the officer with quick inferences about 'what is going on'.

In this way chaos is transformed into order. There may be rioting in progress at the time, but police typifications allow all events to be understood, meaningfully interpreted, and thus at least mentally ordered:

> People are expected to fill categorical niches and fall into line with the commonsense police theory about human nature. The observed facts are assembled under the umbrella of a commonsense theory. The facts are not taken as a means to disconfirm the police theory of human nature.
>
> (Manning, 1977: 237)

Broadly speaking, members of the public tend to get assigned to one of two categories: 'respectable' or 'non-respectable'. According to the Policy Studies Institute (PSI) report on the Metropolitan Police: 'In this scale the "respectable" working class and the suburban middle class stand highest, while the "underclass" of the poor and the rootless, together with groups regarded as deviant, such as homosexuals or hippies, stand lowest' (Smith and Grey, 1985: 435). Phil Scraton discusses how these understandings become part of police practices: 'The regular, institutionalized use of these images leads to their incorporation into the general ideology of police operations and practices. They . . . form a central part of the political management of communities' (Scraton, 1985: 105). So what, from a police point of view, does the ideal citizen look like? This question is perhaps answered most succinctly by the PSI report. Referring to police culture, the report says: 'It is a milieu in which people who do not speak with a London or other regional accent and men who do not dress like football managers are definitely made to feel out of place' (Smith and Grey, 1985: 435).

THE IMPLICATIONS FOR CRIMINAL STATISTICS

Taken together, the cirumstances outlined above constitute a complex mix of factors shaping police policies and practices across the board. The nature and impact of these factors, for example political and public pressure, organisational and managerial demands, and police ideologies and culture, will not, of course, remain constant in terms of their contribution to the construction of recorded crime. If changes in the law, methods of classifying offences and the propensity of the public to report crime to the police are also taken into account, then the hazards inherent in using official criminal statistics from different moments in history as a measure of the moral health of a society become apparent.

Although the primary focus of this section is on amounts of crime as represented by these statistics, we might note that the issues raised in our discussion of policing will have important ramifications for other aspects of crime and criminality as socially constructed phenomena. The types of offences that end up in the statistics and act as one representation of the 'crime problem' – for example, conventional property crime rather than corporate fraud – will be partly a function of the activities of the police. So too will be the types of offenders who are officially labelled and processed by the criminal justice system. We will return to these issues at a later stage. For the moment what our discussion illustrates is that the criminal statistics are the product of dynamic and complex processes involving the law, the police, offenders, victims and witnesses.

VICTIM SURVEYS

Essentially, the analysis so far of criminal statistics has taken place within a more or less common-sensical framework, employing an accepted and familiar definition of crime. This has meant questioning the accuracy of those statistics, though there have been some hints of other, conceptual, agendas. The analysis, therefore, has been situated within the more conventional parameters associated with criminological positivism. Biderman and Reiss (1967) describe this approach as 'realism' (not to be confused with left realism). From the point of view of realism, the problems with criminal statistics are – to use the term I introduced earlier – basically technical. That is, there is an assumption that a 'real', objective amount of crime exists in society, but only some of it is actually recorded. Therefore, there is a 'dark figure' of crime. Looked at from this perspective, the task of criminology is to improve the tools of research in order to determine as accurately as possible the posited 'real' amount of crime. Institutional processes involving interpretation and negotiation, whereby criminal statistics and the 'crime problem' are constructed, are thus neglected in these analyses.

On occasion, some researchers have taken this way of considering crime a step further and have treated recorded crime as if it is a slice of a large homogeneous cake, a representative sample of the whole. The same sort of logic has been applied to convicted offenders, leading to the conclusion that if the prisons are mainly populated by poorer people, then poorer people must be more involved in crime than the better-off. The problem is neatly summed up by Steven Box (1981: 181):

> It is as though some researchers would have approached the question of how many colours there are in Joseph's coat by placing one fragment under a microscope and

35

declaring, after studying the fragment intensely, that the coat's multi-colouredness was a myth for only one colour had been revealed after the most elaborate scientific investigation.

In recent years victim surveys have become increasingly popular, as, indeed, has that field of study called victimology, now accepted as one of the normal concerns of criminology: 'Victims, once on the margins of criminological research, are now a central focus of academic research' (Zedner, 2002: 429).

For realists there are obvious attractions in victim surveys in that they seem to offer a technique for discovering and measuring more accurately amounts of crime. At the same time, victim surveys have attracted the attention of some less conventional, more radical criminologists. One of the attractions for those with a more sceptical mind than realists, is that victim surveys appear to bypass the institutional processes and allow the researcher to get to the heart of the matter directly. Furthermore, victim surveys have been latched on to by criminologists on the right and on the left, with right-wing versions tending to mobilise findings around a 'get tough' law and order stance, whilst left-wing versions have used them to argue for general improvements in the lives of oppressed sections of society. (An awkward issue is that sometimes victims are also offenders.)

While there are many important debates and issues surrounding the uses and abuses of victim surveys, in this section the focus is (again) essentially on their value as ways of measuring amounts of crime in a society; that is, we are still operating within a more or less 'realist' framework.

Victimology

Victimology, through the use of victim surveys, is centrally concerned with gathering information on the experiences of victims of crime. Broadly speaking, two different traditions can be discerned. At its inception in the United States during the 1940s (with the work of Von Hentig, 1948, and Wertham, 1949) the emphasis was on the psychological characteristics and social circumstances – for example, 'lifestyles' – of those most likely to find themselves victims of crime. Whilst this tradition continues today, during the 1960s, and again in the United States, a second tradition focusing on measuring the extent of hidden crime developed.

Victim precipitation is perhaps the term most closely identified with the first of these traditions. This was introduced into the vocabulary of criminology by Wolfgang (1958), and arose from his analysis of homicides. For Wolfgang, victim precipitation had a very precise meaning, namely, that in a significant number of cases which he looked at, the homicide victim was the first to use force. Other writers, however, began to use the term more loosely, so that it came to refer to instances where victims actually provoked or hastened their own victimisation, for example by the way they dressed or the places they visited. The classic study based upon this sort of reasoning – and for obvious reasons much criticised by feminists – is Amir's (1971) investigation of rape, where he argues that in the cases he examined, almost one-fifth of victims precipitated the assault (for example, gave out the 'wrong signals').

More recent work (e.g. Sparks et al., 1977; Mayhew, 2000) has tried to develop more sophisticated models of victimisation. Here, a range of factors such as age-linked vulnerability, lifestyle management, a lack of power to complain and types of neighbourhood are analysed. This kind of research shifts the focus of attention away from the perceived culpability, or even stupidity, of the victim towards other socially structured factors over which the victim may have little control.

The second tradition began during the 1960s in the United States with large-scale national surveys of victims' experiences. Their primary aim was to shed some light on the dark figure of crime, and such surveys are therefore particularly relevant to the theme of this section.

Surveying victims

The first British example of a victim survey at a national level is, in a modest way, found in the *General Household Survey* of 1972, which included a question about being the victim of a burglary. The first specialised mass survey, though only carried out in London, was by Sparks et al. (1977). In 1982 the first of a series of large-scale national surveys – the *British Crime Survey* – specifically designed to cover a wide range of offences and bring to light hidden crime, was carried out under the auspices of the Home Office (Mayhew and Hough, 1983). Since then a large number of *British Crime Surveys* have been completed (Hough and Mayhew, 1985; Mayhew et al., 1989; Mayhew and Maung, 1993; Mirrlees-Black et al., 1996; Mirrlees-Black et al., 1998; Kershaw et al., 2000; Kershaw et al., 2001; Simmons et al., 2002; Simmons and Dodd, 2003; Dodd et al., 2004; Nicholas et al., 2005; Walker et al., 2006; Nicholas et al., 2007; Kershaw et al., 2008).

Information is gathered by asking household members aged over 15 years a set of standardised questions. In the latest *British Crime Survey* there were over 40,000 respondents. Up to the 1992 survey, the households used were chosen randomly from electoral registers; however, from 1992 onwards the Postcode Address File was used (for technical discussions of the *British Crime Survey* methodology, see Bolling et al., 2003 and Grant et al., 2006). This change was made because of earlier criticisms that a significant minority of people are in fact absent from electoral registers. The main questions in these surveys are concerned with people's experiences as victims of crime, though other, supplementary questions are included; for instance, questions relating to the fear of crime or decisions not to report an offence to the police. The survey is now conducted on a 'rolling' basis and, since 2001, the results are published annually alongside police data on recorded crime (there are separate surveys for England and Wales, Northern Ireland and Scotland).

Supporters of these surveys have argued that as well as providing a more accurate picture of criminal victimisation in general, they also bring to light the experiences of particularly vulnerable groups whose victimisation rates were hitherto grossly under-estimated by official data (for example, victims of racially motivated violence). Because victim surveys inevitably discover relatively large amounts of previously 'hidden' crime, they can generate increased public fear of crime. This perhaps accounts for the general tone of *British Crime Surveys,* which has been one of balanced reassurance. Thus, in the style of the presenters of TV's *Crimewatch* at the end of each programme, efforts are made to point out that as individuals the chances of being a victim of a serious crime are not especially high; for example, in the words of the 1989 survey, the 'statistically average' adult will have their home burgled only once in every 37 years.

Obviously, such statistics, being averages, mask the inequalities in victimisation rates between one neighbourhood and another, one type of housing and another, and one group of people and another; council house tenants, for example, are more likely to be victims of burglary than owner-occupiers. It was this sort of critique that helped to stimulate an interest in more detailed, localised victim surveys in Britain during the 1980s. By focusing on specific neighbourhoods, and using research methods that were thought to be more sensitive in nature, the aim was to gain more valuable, detailed knowledge of patterns of victimisation. In the main, these localised studies were carried out by criminologists sympathetic to the so-called left realist perspective, and sponsored by local Labour Party-controlled councils. As such, this research has been incorporated into a left realist call to 'take crime seriously'. This links data generated by victim surveys to what left realists see as a progressive reform programme in areas such as policing and crime prevention policies.

Findings

It is true that by their nature victim surveys show higher levels of crime than do official statistics, and so send out a message that there is even more crime being committed than we thought. However, once a number of similar surveys have been conducted, and it is possible to draw out trends over a suitable period of time, then a different picture may emerge. A good example of this is discussed by Bottomley and Pease (1986).

Between 1971 and 1981 the number of domestic burglaries in the official statistics rose from 204,560 to 349,692, confirming widespread fears that burglary was growing significantly in frequency. As Bottomley and Pease say, this could mean that the proportion of burglaries reported to, and recorded by, the police remained constant, and the increase actually happened. Or, it could mean that there was no increase, but more burglaries were reported and recorded. In this context the data from the 1972, 1973, 1979 and 1980 *General Household Surveys* make interesting reading. As mentioned earlier, these surveys asked if households had been the victims of a burglary during the past twelve months. Surprisingly, these surveys found no increase in the incidence of burglary in private households over the period from 1971. The first *British Crime Survey* was conducted in 1982 and asked for recollections from 1981. The figure for household burglaries from this survey was within 1.3 per cent of the figure from the 1980 *General Household Survey* (when people were interviewed in 1979, and asked to recall the previous twelve months). This suggests that there was no massive and sudden increase in burglary missed by the *General Household Survey* of 1980. In conclusion, Bottomley and Pease (1986: 23) state: 'This surely clinches the view that the increase in burglary during the 1970s was almost completely illusory'.

Although the *British Crime Survey* (BCS) brings to light a large number of crime incidents that are not present in police recorded crime figures, it should be noted that this only applies to particular offence categories, rather than crime in general. Furthermore, comparing BCS figures with recorded crime figures for each of these categories shows wide variation in the number of offences picked up. Thus, as Maguire (2002: 352) says: 'The BCS . . . provides *an alternative, rather than directly comparable, overall picture of crime to that offered by police statistics*' (emphasis in original).

It is often said that the BCS brings to light four times as much crime as shown in recorded crime figures. This results from a misleading interpretation of an analysis of the first survey. This (averaged) ratio only applies to those offences directly comparable with those compiled by the police; one-third of BCS offence groups are in fact not directly comparable. As a result, the survey does not purport to offer a more accurate picture of victimisation rates for *all* offences. The latest survey estimates that there were 10.5 million crimes against adults in 2007–08, compared with 4.8 million crimes recorded by the police, the latter including victims of all ages, not just those aged 16 and over.

Local victim surveys

Although sympathetic to the basic principle of focusing on victims of crime, some criminologists argue that because of the large sweeps involved, mass surveys are unable to draw out deeper, more detailed information on the nature and distribution of crime:

> Inevitably, therefore, national crime surveys obscure the way in which victimization is concentrated in different communities and among particular groups within those communities . . . By drawing samples from small neighbourhoods, these (local crime) surveys have described much more accurately the experiences of different sections of the population.
>
> (Anderson *et al.*, 1991: 5)

As a consequence, since the mid-1980s there has been a parallel growth in localised crime surveys (Kinsey, 1984 (Merseyside); Jones *et al.*, 1986 (Islington, London); Crawford *et al.*, 1990 (Islington); Anderson *et al.*, 1990 (Edinburgh); Anderson *et al.*, 1991 (Edinburgh); Hartless *et al.*, 1995 (Glasgow)). However, following the introduction of the 1998 Crime and Disorder Act which, as mentioned previously, obliged local Crime and Disorder Reduction Partnerships to conduct three-yearly audits of crime and disorder (now annual strategic assessments), we have seen a huge increase in local victim surveys, though the quality of these surveys does vary enormously. One of the earlier surveys will be examined in order to illustrate the sort of information these local surveys generate.

The first Islington survey
According to Jones *et al.* (1986: 5) *The Islington Crime Survey* is much more focused than the national surveys and 'embraces a much greater part of the whole process of criminalization':

> the pattern of victimization, the impact of crime, the actual police response to both victim and offender, the public's requirements as to an ideal police response and the public's notions of appropriate penalties for various offences.

The survey certainly provides a great deal of detailed information on victimisation patterns in Islington. It found, for instance, that victims of burglary were more likely to be young rather than old, men rather than women, and black rather than white. With theft or robbery it was the other way round, apart from black people, who were more at risk than white people. As far as assault was concerned, the survey says: 'Black people on average are almost twice as likely as other people to be victims of assault and women half as likely again as men to be assaulted' (ibid.: 65).

This contrasts sharply with the BCS, 1982, which reported that young men were more likely to be the victims of assault than any other group, though this survey did pinpoint young men who regularly went out drinking a few nights per week; they were also the most likely assailants. The reason women were at greater risk of assault than men in the Islington survey is that the researchers uncovered relatively large amounts of domestic violence against women. The Islington survey also discovered a much higher incidence of sexual assault than the *British Crime Surveys*. In fact, only one case of unreported attempted rape came to light in the first two *British Crime Surveys*, and 17 and 18 cases of sexual assault in each year of the sweep, whilst the Islington survey estimated that there were 1,200 sexual assaults in the area covered by the study. According to the authors, this discrepancy arises from the greater sensitivity of the researchers, as well as the way in which questions were phrased. The underreporting by women of rape, attempted rape and other forms of sexual assault has been highlighted by a large number of victim surveys. According to Hall (1985), for instance, only 8 per cent of rape victims informed the police.

The greater assault rate in Islington for black people when compared with white people was congruent with the national findings of the 1992 BCS. However, interestingly, the second Islington survey found very little difference in assault rate between white people and people of Afro-Caribbean background. Zedner (1994: 1215) gives some possible explanations for this disparity:

> It may be that Afro-Caribbeans in Islington are so exposed to violence that they tend to underreport assaults against them. Alternatively, it may be that the high concentration of ethnic minority populations in this inner London borough levels out disparities in the victimization of whites and blacks.

It should be appreciated that local crime surveys carried out by 'left realists' – such as the Islington survey – are not simply attempts to gather better knowledge about crimes and victims. They constitute the basis of a much broader criminological project involving the development of crime control policies, and theoretical models seeking to explain criminal behaviour. Thus left realism attempts to engage in a direct, practical way with issues of law and order. At root this means entering a terrain traditionally colonised by the political right, and in the process developing a critique of other radical left positions characterised by the left realists as 'left idealism'. This project has coalesced around the slogan 'take crime seriously', an injunction based upon the left realist view that:

1 Not only do poorer people have to cope with all the usual problems associated with social and economic deprivation, they also have to cope with being more at risk from crime; and
2 following on from this, the fear of crime is not an irrational moral panic generated by the mass media, but a realistic assessment of the situation.

According to the left realists, data from local crime surveys can then be used as a basis for developing crime control policies at a local level.

Victim surveys: limitations and problems

A whole range of criminal offences are not picked up by victim surveys (victims aged under 16 years are not part of the *British Crime Surveys*, for instance). In addition, these tend to be underrecorded in official statistics, the combined effect of which is to give a misleading picture of the 'crime problem'. By questioning people as individual members of households there are certain offences that, although often creating victims, cannot be identified. The following examples will illustrate this.

Corporate crime and organised crime

> The amount of illegal profit made from multinational and national corporation crimes, as well as the illicit gains from 'organised crime' (or crimes of the 'mafia' or 'cosa nostra'

or some other official mystifying synonym), is enormous, and, beside it, the value of goods stolen or otherwise illegally acquired by 'conventional, ordinary' criminals drops into insignificance.

(Box, 1981: 235)

Clearly, the responses of households in victim surveys will give no inkling of the magnitude of corporate and organised crime. Leaving aside, for now, a more detailed discussion of these aspects, it can be noted that there is a large and important literature of 'exposé' criminology which analyses the illegal activities of big business (e.g. Pearce, 1976; Chambliss, 1978; Henry, 1978; Levi, 1987; Yeager, 1991) and organised and professional crime (e.g. Taylor, 1984; Hobbs, 1988; Block, 1991).

Occupational crime

This can involve persons of high or low status within an organisation. White-collar occupational crime can be carried out *against* the company (for example, fiddling expenses), or *for* the company, when it enters the realms of corporate crime (the classic study is Sutherland, 1983, originally published 1949; for a recent overview of this area, see Nelken, 2002). Ditton's (1977) study of fiddling among bread salesmen provides an example of the criminal activities of those further down the hierarchy.

Other examples of offences hidden from victim surveys are:

- *Theft from businesses.* This will involve such things as shoplifting and insurance fraud.
- *Criminal damage.* Vandalising public or non-household property will not, of course, be registered in victim surveys.
- *'Crimes without victims'.* This term is used to describe offences such as illicit drug use, certain illegal sexual activities, or offences connected with the Obscene Publications Act.
- *Taxation and social security fraud.* Clearly, victim surveys cannot measure offending rates in these areas.
- *Non-household crime.* Homeless people, and those living in a hostel or institutional setting are not surveyed.

In addition, there are likely to be instances where respondents in victim surveys have been victims of crime but, because of circumstances, or the design or conduct of the interview, their victimisation will not come to light; for example:

- Where respondents are too frightened, embarrassed or ashamed to admit that they are victims (e.g. having property stolen whilst visiting a prostitute, or experiencing a sexual assault).
- Where they are simply unaware that they are victims (e.g. believing that a purse has been lost when it has been stolen).

Walklate (1989) offers a perceptive discussion of the need for research to be sensitive to the individual's understanding of his or her own victimisation, and that ready-made categories used by the police or researchers may not be appropriate. In this context she quotes Kelly who, with reference to sexual violence against women, argues that the victims' experiences should be seen as forming a continuum:

> Using the concept of a continuum highlights the fact that all women experience sexual violence at some point in their lives. It enables the linking of more common, everyday abuses women experience with the less common experiences labelled as crimes. It is through this connection that women are able to locate their own particular experiences as being examples of sexual violence.
>
> (Ibid.: 33)

This dimension is important, too, in a general sense, for different people will have different understandings and thresholds regarding the seriousness and harmfulness of what has happened to them. The victim's own perception of events will have implications for how he or she responds to questions in victim surveys. Furthermore, how elaborated a victim's account is will be linked to their articulacy when answering questions.

Finally, the information from victim surveys is, of course, dependent on people being honest and accurately remembering what has happened to them.

Thus, although victim surveys, national and local, do provide valuable alternative sources of information about the extent of crime and patterns of victimisation, their limitations have to be acknowledged.

THE USEFULNESS OF CRIMINAL STATISTICS

The discussion so far of statistics, especially official statistics, has been quite critical. Many criminologists, though, whilst generally accepting these criticisms, would argue that this does not mean that they are therefore of no value. One example of this is associated with the *class conflict* approach to statistics. From this perspective, the fact that criminal statistics, as well as statistical information relating to the operation of the criminal justice system in general, reflect the activities of the various organisations and individuals involved, is precisely why they can be usefully employed. As the label applied to this perspective suggests, the main emphasis is on exploitative class relations in a capitalist society:

> Only by understanding that statistics are produced as part of the administration and control of a society organised around exploitative class relations can we grasp their full meaning; and only with the aid of this understanding can we determine their uses, and usefulness, in critical social research.
>
> (Miles and Irvine, 1981: 127)

Thus in a sense criminal statistics are 'rehabilitated', but only if they are read as products of conflictual class relations. The statistics may not, in terms of common sense, reflect the reality of crime, but for class conflict theorists they do provide an insight into the class-based nature of the criminal justice system. From this point of view, crime-related statistics, though manipulated to suit the interests of the powerful, do none the less provide useful indicators of the inequalities and biases inherent in the system itself, and indeed in capitalist society in general. The overrepresentation of working-class, as opposed to bourgeois, crime in the statistics, and the over-representation of black and poorer people in the prison populations of capitalist societies, are not seen as simply the result of their greater criminality. In an unequal society, it is argued, only the naive believe that a fair and equal system of justice can be delivered. Thus, crime-related statistics can be used as the basis for developing critical explanations of these inequalities.

From a different perspective, Bottomley and Pease (1986: 159) recognise that 'criminal statistics provide few, if any, significant answers to many of the important traditional questions of evaluation' (such as, is crime under control?), but add: 'On the other hand, criminal justice statistics are informative in a variety of ways, and should not be discarded as meaningless, as has sometimes been their fate'. Indeed, they call for an increase in routine statistical information pertaining to the workings of the criminal justice system, and see such descriptive material as forming the basis for more informed discussion. As an example, they point out how this kind of information can act as an antidote to the often lurid and misleading stereotypes of crime and criminals found in the mass media and pub conversations:

> Simple descriptive studies can sometimes have a powerful influence that their lack of technical or theoretical complexity may at first belie – consider, for instance, the important effect upon public attitudes towards capital punishment of basic information about the 'typical' murderer as someone caught up in a stressful domestic situation to which no other solution is seen but a tragic murder–suicide attempt, or the important message from research that most house burglaries involve only quite modest financial losses and no violence by the burglar, and happen during the day.
>
> (Ibid.: 169)

Some of the other areas identified by the authors where statistical information will be useful are as follows:

- The crime mix of particular neighbourhoods.
- Mechanisms at work whereby crimes come to the attention of the police.
- The ways in which different branches of the police service are used.
- The rates of cautioning between one force and another.

- Links between criminal activity, police clear-up rates and various community-based initiatives.
- Disparities in sentencing between one part of the country and another.

Today the police in this country are expected to base their work on targeted problem solving, which necessarily requires the support of statistical data. A 1994 report by the National Board for Crime Prevention argued in favour of the police prioritising their work in this way. The report pointed out that 44 per cent of all reported crime is suffered by just 4 per cent of victims of crime, and that large increases in recorded crime during the 1980s was mainly due to these victims being victimised more often. The report concluded that the police should therefore concentrate on those making up the 4 per cent. Obviously data of this kind require careful scrutiny, although in the context of this discussion it is the nature of the recommendations that is of relevance.

Statistical information from other areas of the criminal justice system may also be drawn on. Among its European neighbours, only Spain and Luxembourg have higher rates of imprisonment than England and Wales. Based on the number of prisoners per 100,000 in the population, the following gives imprisonment rates for these and a sample of other European countries (by way of comparison, the figure for the United States is 756):

Spain – 160
Luxembourg – 155
England and Wales – 152
Scotland – 145
Greece – 109
Portugal – 103
Netherlands – 100
France – 96
Italy – 92
Germany – 89
Northern Ireland – 78
Sweden – 74
Norway – 69
Finland – 64

At the time of writing, the prison population in England and Wales stands at 82,240, which is about 8,000 more than the official capacity; in 1991 it was 42,000. Most are male (94.7 per cent) and from unemployed/working-class backgrounds, and over 20 per cent are members of minority ethnic groups. The imprisonment rate for black people is around eight times that for white people (if white people were imprisoned at the same rate the prison population would increase to approximately half a million).

The average annual cost of keeping a prisoner inside is now £41,000. A recent report by the charity Barnardo's (2008), based upon government data, found that there are more children (10–14 years) in custody in England and Wales than in any other neighbouring European country. According to the report, between 1996 and 2006 the use of custody for this age group rose by 550 per cent (to a total of 572 in 2006). This increase has resulted from various legal changes that have made it much easier for children to be sentenced to custody for relatively minor offences, such as summary offences and breach of community orders. A further example worth noting is that each year in England and Wales, about 30 parents are imprisoned because their children have truanted from school.

Clearly, this kind of statistical information provides a useful backdrop to debates about the value of imprisonment. Likewise, the relative costs and merits of cautioning, non-custodial sentences and imprisonment can only be seriously considered in the light of relevant statistical information.

LOCAL CRIME SURVEYS AND LEFT REALISM

Local crime surveys carried out by left realists, such as the Islington surveys, have two central aims. They seek to show, first, that those people living in the area being studied see crime as a significant problem and, second, that this is a rational assessment on their part; that is, that crime really is a problem, and the fear of crime is therefore understandable. The corollary of this is that current official definitions of crime provide suitable anchor points, especially as they are seen to reflect a consensus, at least as far as 'conventional' crime (burglary, street robbery, for example) is concerned. This approach is at variance with a radical tradition in criminology that questions the requirement to be constrained by a particular state's definition of crime at a particular moment in history. It is also at variance with those critical criminologists, characterised by left realists as left idealists, who are purported to play down the harmfulness of conventional crime, to see the fear of crime as a moral panic generated by the mass media, and to emphasise corporate and white-collar crime as the real problem.

Those carrying out local surveys are aware that official/police categories are not able to accommodate the myriad experiences that various victims have. Sometimes these experiences do not at face value involve a criminal offence, but are, none the less, harmful or frightening. However, although left realist crime surveys may sometimes spread the net beyond what are nominally criminal offences, and include other activities, these still tend to be referenced against official definitions of crime. Anderson *et al*. (1991: 37), for example, do this:

> In terms of the law, the incidents so far described are all criminal offences. In terms of young people's lives, however, there are many other examples of general harassment, abuse and frightening and stressful events which may fall outside the law, but which contribute to general levels of anxiety and fear of crime.

Relevant activities are therefore those that either, as above, contribute to 'anxiety and fear of crime', or represent a sort of mild version of a criminal offence, for example various threats. Apart from anything else, this does raise the issue of what it is that criminologists should study: where is the line to be drawn? There are other activities that are also harmful, distressing and frightening, and yet, nominally, no law breaking is involved. On the other hand, there will be criminal offences committed that do not have harmful repercussions. Furthermore, there will be many criminal activities that are harmful, and yet victims will be unaware that they are victims of that activity, for instance the adulteration of foodstuffs. Victim surveys are always dependent upon people having knowledge of their victimisation.

This indicates one of the central difficulties with the local surveys of left realism. While much useful information may be forthcoming, they do tend to be rooted in a concrete, 'essentialist' framework, with positivist overtones. By concentrating on the experiences of a specific neighbourhood at a specific moment in time, and relying on a taken-for-granted set of crime-related concepts, such studies inevitably foreclose the project of developing a non-parochial theoretical criminology. In this hard-headed, 'non-idealist' world of realism there is no requirement for esoteric debates about what the criminologist should properly study: whether the capitalist state's current definition of crime is too narrow or too wide, or whether 'problematic situations' rather than crime should be the intellectual currency. Thus the Islington surveys are content to take official definitions as working categories, and to accept as satisfactory the victim's interpretation of events as 'criminal'. If the victim's account appears to match official discourse, then the reality of the crime is assumed. In this way, 'real' fears and 'real' crimes are brought blinking into the light.

This is not to say, of course, that left realism is wrong; clearly, victims of crime are damaged by their experiences, and they need protecting. Rather it is that a criminological project based on questionnaires about criminal victimisation is partial – the data produced are elements of a wider jigsaw.

RECENT CRIME TRENDS

Annual recorded crime figures and the result of the *British Crime Survey* are now published at the same time. Following yearly increases during the 1980s and early 1990s, from 1993 to 1997 there was a sustained fall in total amounts of recorded crime in England and Wales (from 5,526,000 to 4,545,000). Since then, give or take some slight fluctuations, amounts of recorded crime gradually increased to a figure of 5,934,000 for 2003–04, followed by a gradual decrease to 4,836,900 for the twelve-month period up to September 2008. However, according to the Home Office, when the figures are adjusted to take changes to the 'counting rules' into account, the trend has been downwards since 1993. Changes introduced in 1998 mainly affected violent crime, and led to some previously less serious, non-notifiable assaults being categorised as notifiable. In 2002 a national crime recording standard was introduced for all police forces. This meant that since then the police have to take a victim's account at face value, until proven otherwise. Clearly, this will inflate the number of offences recorded, and is a further illustration of the socially constructed nature of criminal statistics. A further dimension to this is that changes in recording practices are designed to provide a more comprehensive and realistic picture of crime by being victim-led. This means that, for instance, if a number of cars are vandalised at the same time in a street, each is recorded as a separate offence. More recent changes have made the business of untangling trends in recorded crime (to put it mildly) even more complicated, as illustrated by this piece of information:

> With the introduction of Public Service Agreement (PSA) Delivery Agreement 23, grievous bodily harm (GBH) without intent has been moved into the 'most serious violence against the person' offence category (annual counting comparisons are not yet available). There was a clarification in the counting rules (around circumstances that may indicate intent) covering offences of GBH with intent and thus when it is appropriate to record a crime as attempted GBH with intent. This had the effect of increasing figures in some forces, GBH with intent being a major component of 'most serious violence'.
>
> (Home Office, 2009: 3)

The police themselves are not immune to confusion over the counting rules. In October 2008, for instance, recorded crime figures showed an apparent 22 per cent increase in the most violent crime category over the previous twelve months. According to Home Office officials, this was because up to seventeen police forces had 'misinterpreted' the counting rules (Travis, 2008).

The 10.5 million crimes against adults living in private households estimated by the latest *British Crime Survey,* represents a decrease of 1 per cent over the previous year (which is not statistically significant). Data from the survey show that crime overall has more or less halved since it peaked in 1995, and the risk of being a victim of crime has fallen from 40 per cent to 23 per cent, the lowest figure since the first survey. Violent crime is estimated to have nearly halved since 1995, a figure at variance with that based upon recorded violent crime figures, which indicate a significant increase. From the point of view of the Home Office, this has resulted from changes in the counting rules (as discussed above) and other 'extraneous factors', and does not reflect a real increase. However, as Maguire (2007: 273–4) says:

> This may well be the case with relatively minor incidents, but it is perhaps less plausible with the most *serious* offences of violence (principally serious woundings), which were relatively unaffected by the changes in counting rules and continued to increase each year even before the introduction of the NCRS (National Crime Recording Standard).

The latest (at the time of writing) quarterly recorded crime figures covering July–September 2008 show a 4 per cent increase in domestic burglary and an 18 per cent increase in street robberies committed at knifepoint, over the same period in 2007, causing concerns among Home Office ministers that the impact of the recession may reverse the longer-term historical trend.

A final point to make here is that regardless of the accuracy of the above figures, *British Crime Surveys* continue to show that, on the whole, the public (and especially tabloid readers) believe that crime is on the increase.

Selected further reading

Although published some time ago, **Bottomley, A. K. and Pease, K. (1986)** *Crime and Punishment: Interpreting the data*, **Milton Keynes: Open University Press** provides a useful theoretical perspective on crime statistics.

For an example of a local victim survey, see **Jones, T., Maclean, B. and Young, J. (1986)** *The Islington Crime Survey*, **Aldershot: Gower**. Overviews of victims and the field of victimology are provided by **Walklate, S. (ed) (2007)** *Handbook of Victims and Victimology*, **Cullompton: Willan**. One of the best discussions of the 'fear of crime' is **Lee, M. (2007)** *Inventing Fear of Crime: Criminology and the politics of anxiety*, **Cullompton: Willan**.

In their edited collection, **Jupp, V., Davies, P. and Francis, P. (eds) (2000)** *Doing Criminological Research*, **London: Sage**, address various dimensions to the research process, as does **Westmarland, L. (2009)** *Researching Crime and Justice,* **Cullompton: Willan**.

A well-informed insight into quantitative research will be found in **Hirschfield, A. and Bowers, K. (eds) (2001)** *Mapping and Analysing Crime Data: Lessons from research and practice*, **London: Taylor & Francis**.

For an interesting discussion of the notion of 'crime waves', see **Sacco, V. F. (2005)** *When Crime Waves*, **London: Sage**, and on the theme of discretion and interpretation on the part of key players in the criminal justice system: **Gelsthorpe, L. and Padfield, N. (eds) (2003)** *Exercising Discretion: Decision-making in the criminal justice system and beyond*, **Cullompton:Willan**.

Christie, N. (2004) *A Suitable Amount of Crime*, **Abingdon: Routledge** examines the social construction of crime, as 'unwanted acts', in various countries.

An excellent discussion of crime statistics, their sources and meaning is provided by **Maguire, M. (2007)** 'Crime data and statistics', in M. Maguire, R. Morgan and R. Reiner (eds) *The Oxford Handbook of Criminology*, **4th edn, Oxford: Oxford University Press**.

Up-to-date information on official crime statistics is provided by **Kershaw, C., Nicholas, S. and Walker, A. (eds) (2008)** *Crime in England and Wales 2007–2008: Findings from* *the British Crime Survey and police recorded crime*, Home Office Statistical Bulletin 7/08, London: Home Office. A full range of official data on crime and the criminal justice system is available from: http://www.homeoffice.gov.uk/rds/pubsintro1.html.

An enlightening historical discussion of the uses and abuses of criminal records is provided by Thomas, T. (2007) *Criminal Records: A database for the criminal justice system and beyond*, Basingstoke: Palgrave Macmillan.

CHAPTER 3

CRIMINOLOGY AND CRIMINOLOGISTS
UP TO WORLD WAR TWO

> ## Key themes
>
> - Tree of sin, tree of knowledge
> - The criminological tree of knowledge
> - Classicism and positivism
> - Positivist criminology
> - The turn of the century to the 1930s
> - Eugenics

INTRODUCTION

The historical development of criminology as an academic discipline has been less neat and tidy than some accounts would suggest. It certainly did not achieve its present form as a result of a straightforward, linear progression, involving the careful assembly of an agreed body of knowledge and understanding. Indeed, even how we might recognise the 'first' criminology, or a 'real' criminologist, remain contested issues.

An interesting question is: when did the first 'real' criminology emerge? Some point to eighteenth-century classicism, others to nineteenth-century positivism. This chapter outlines the development of criminology in Britain from the late nineteenth century up to World War Two. It was during this period that criminology attempted to establish credibility as an academic discipline. According to the British criminologist David Garland, *modern* criminology emerged during this period, and was the product of a convergence between classicism and positivism.

TREE OF SIN, TREE OF KNOWLEDGE

In volume 1 of Marx's (1969) *Theories of Surplus Value,* there is a frequently quoted section, only two pages in length, on the theme of crime – or rather it was frequently quoted when criminologists were, for whatever reason, less bashful about drawing on Marx. With few direct references in Marx's work to crime *per se,* it is not surprising that this section should be seized upon as a 'criminological' discussion. Unfortunately, the section – entitled 'Apologist conception of the productivity of all professions' – was often read out of context and consequently misunderstood. It was written primarily as an attack on those economists who would ascribe the quality of 'productive' to an almost infinite range of human activities. Thus it cannot be understood if it is taken out of the context of his criticisms of conceptualisations of productive labour then found in the field of political economy.

For Marx, it was not a question of whether or not some activity was 'useful' or even whether the activity created physical objects. Productive labour is labour that produces surplus value for capitalism. The veracity or usefulness of Marx's model is not at issue here, but it is necessary to make the general point. What is worth noting is that in the process of criticising what to him were specious and imprecise notions of productive labour, Marx (1969: 387–8) does provide the reader with a rapid sequence of observations of interest when examining the place of crime and criminology in society:

> The criminal produces not only crimes but criminal law, and with this also the professor who gives lectures on criminal law and in addition to this the inevitable compendium in which this same professor throws his lectures onto the general market as 'commodities'. This brings with it augmentation of national wealth . . . The criminal moreover produces the whole of the police and of criminal justice, constables, judges, hangmen, juries etc.; and all these different lines of business, which form equally many categories of the social division of labour, develop different capacities of the human spirit, create new needs and new ways of satisfying them. Torture alone has given rise to the most ingenious mechanical inventions, and employed many honourable craftsmen in the production of its instruments . . . The criminal produces . . . also art, belles-lettres, novels . . . The effects of the criminal on the development of productive power can be shown in detail. Would locks have reached their present state of excellence had there been no thieves? . . . Doesn't practical chemistry owe just as much to adulteration of commodities and the efforts to show it up as to the honest zeal for production?

Crude readings have seen in this passage a version of functionalism, where crime is conceived of as being functionally useful for society, and hence necessary and inevitable. In a similar vein some writers have concentrated on references further on in the text to the criminal 'arousing the moral and aesthetic feelings of the public', and breaking the 'monotony . . . of bourgeois life', thereby keeping it from 'stagnation'. Such attempts to draw out an early 'functions of crime' argument misconstrue what Marx was saying, though we might note that some of his observations do represent a remarkable precurser to what Durkheim was famously to debate a few years later. Having said this, it is equally misleading to dismiss the functionalist overtones in favour of the view that this section is nothing more than an amusing digression, an excuse for some tongue-in-cheek mockery of 'bourgeois apologists'. Marx is making some important points regarding the connections between criminals and their crimes, and the economic, social and cultural development of capitalism. He happens to do this by employing the device of irony.

This use of irony by Marx has been stressed by some writers, notably Taylor *et al.* (1973) and Hirst (1975a), though the irony goes beyond the situation where, in Hirst's words, 'The most upright citizens depend for their livelihood on the criminal classes' (ibid.: 212). In fact the irony operates on two levels. First, it is used in a Socratic sense, that is, with a pretence of ignorance. Here Marx takes on the part of a bourgeois apologist and, in the manner of a devil's advocate, argues that the activities of the despised low-life criminal are somehow 'productive'. In this way he hoped to hold up for ridicule understandings of productive labour current in bourgeois political economy. Second, he uses irony in the sense of a perverse conjunction between the desirable and the undesirable: specifically, between crime and such things as job opportunities, increased national wealth, inventions, novels and, significantly, knowledge. This is succinctly summed up by Marx (1969: 388): 'And hasn't the Tree of Sin been at the same time the Tree of Knowledge ever since the time of Adam?' Thus for the entire history of the world, criminals and their crimes have stimulated the production of knowledge on a number of fronts, including more recently a criminological one. And in the contemporary world what is called the 'fight against crime' is very big business indeed. Across the globe, governments and private organisations spend vast amounts of money on efforts to prevent crime, to apprehend and deal with criminals, and so on. Furthermore, and in tandem with this, a global media devotes much of its time to fictional and factual accounts of crime and the culprits involved.

THE CRIMINOLOGICAL TREE OF KNOWLEDGE: SEPARATING THE TREE FROM THE WOOD

At the time Marx was making the above observations, no distinct discipline called criminology existed, and no one described themselves as criminologists. In fact, we had to wait until the last decade of the nineteenth century before the term criminology came into general use. Of course, the fact that no discipline was around with the name 'criminology', and no individuals were identified as criminologists, does not necessarily mean that criminology in some form or other did not exist. Obviously, what is recognised today as criminology did not appear overnight as a fully grown 'tree of knowledge'. The problem that historians have had is in identifying a recognisable early criminology and then tracing its subsequent development. For hundreds of years various thinkers and writers have spent a great deal of time discussing phenomena of interest to criminologists. After all, issues of defined 'bad' behaviour, immorality, social control, punishment and order have been central to religious, political and social thought down through the ages. What, though, makes such a discussion specifically *criminological*? A contemporary criminologist who has tried to answer this question is David Garland. He proceeds by establishing initially a basic definition of modern criminology: 'Modern criminology, like other academic specialisms, consists of a body of accredited and systematically transmitted forms of knowledge, approved procedures and techniques of investigation, and a cluster of questions which make up the subject's recognized agendas' (Garland, 1994: 25).

Accepting this definition of modern criminology, we might ask if there was something in the past that, although lacking some or even all of these attributes, could none the less be classified as criminology, albeit 'old' or 'pre-modern', or whatever. Garland's answer to this is a qualified 'yes', and he offers a convincing argument to support the view that:

> Discourse about crime and punishment has existed, in one form or another, since ancient times, but it is only during the last 120 years that there has been a distinctive 'science of criminology', and only in the last fifty or sixty years has there been in Britain an established, independent discipline organized around that intellectual endeavour.
>
> (Ibid.: 27)

Others have been less restrained in discovering a 'real' criminology deep in past history. Drapkin (1983), for instance, has trawled the writings of ancient scholars, latching on to any references to crime and punishment. As Garland says, though, not only do these historians operate with a notion of 'criminology' stretched beyond reasonable boundaries, they also fail to see these early discourses within their contemporary contexts, that is, situate them within particular institutional structures, involving particular assumptions and agendas.

CLASSICISM AND POSITIVISM

Over the past thirty years or so a more or less consensual reading of criminology's history grew up among British writers (e.g. Taylor *et al.*, 1973; Roshier, 1989). In these accounts the beginning of criminology lies in the classical criminology of the eighteenth century. However, it was not until the latter part of the nineteenth century that attempts were made to develop an explicit, recognisable 'science' of criminology. This is normally given the general label of positivist criminology.

Positivism represented a quite different agenda to that of the earlier classical school. Although it would be wrong to give the impression that classicism incorporated a unified body of knowledge, with internal unanimity regarding philosophical assumptions and ideas, it did have one, fundamentally important thread running through it. Classical criminology was centrally concerned with the establishment of a reformed, equitable and efficient system of justice (the two most influential writers were Beccaria and Bentham). Classical writers concerned themselves with the creation of, they believed, a fairer, better regulated social order. Drawing on utilitarian philosophy, and in particular the pleasure–pain principle, the aim was to create a system where punishment proportional to the crime would act to deter would-be offenders. This would take place within a rational, codified legal order. The focus was therefore on the criminal act, rather than the criminal actor. Indeed, no differentiation in terms of special attributes was made between the criminal and the non-criminal.

Garland's main argument is that modern criminology grew out of a convergence between the 'governmental project' of classicism, covering a period from the late eighteenth century to the last quarter of the nineteenth century, and the 'Lombrosian project' associated with late nineteenth-century positivism. The term governmental project is used because classicism was oriented towards criminal justice administration. In contrast, the Lombrosian project of positivism is so called because of the influence of Cesare Lombroso, a criminological positivist *par excellence*. It was he who popularised the notion of genetically determined, distinct criminal types. Via a crude physiognomy, he argued that criminals were atavistic beings, that is, throwbacks to an earlier stage of human evolution, who were physically different from non-criminals. This is a fascinating, though totally discredited, idea.

The late nineteenth century saw the publication of a number of works purporting to represent 'scientific' criminology. The repercussions were felt across Europe, and the touchstone for this criminology was the positivist criminology of key writers such as Lombroso (1876), Ferri (1895) and Garofalo (1914) – the Italian school. Lombrosian anthropology, however, was less influential in Britain than in other parts of Europe. Likewise, the positivism of the French sociologist Auguste Comte did not find particularly fertile ground among British criminologists. However, as Garland (1994: 79) says: 'the project of positivism (in a more modest version), and its corresponding methods, formed the broad intellectual basis for the criminological programme'.

With the strongest influence coming from psychiatric medicine, and research locked into penal imperatives, this was the beginning of scientific criminology in Britain.

Using the prisons as ready-made laboratories, criminals were classified into psychological types, with the promise of finding both the causes of crime and the most efficacious ways of dealing with them. Above all, the project was to be *scientific*; research would proceed by empirical investigation and according to scientific principles, principles borrowed from earlier studies of animals and the material world. It was believed that only through science could truth be found. Thus was born a causal–corrective tradition in British criminology that was to continue largely unchallenged until the 1960s. This was the ultimate promise held out by criminology: to establish the causes of crime and then suggest ways in which society could correct the problem.

Not surprisingly, from the late nineteenth century until the 1960s a consensus was sustained which viewed the earlier classical criminology as not 'real' criminology at all. Vold (1958), for example, saw classical criminology as mere pre-scientific 'Administrative and Legal Criminology'.

By the late 1960s there had been another fundamental shift in criminological thinking, and with it a reassessment of classical criminology. Now it came to be rehabilitated as the first 'real' criminology. This reflected a move away from an increasingly derided positivist criminology, with its deterministic views on criminal behaviour. Now there was to be an emphasis on 'voluntarism', on people creating their own social worlds, and this was seen as being in accord with the 'free will' model of classical criminology.

POSITIVIST CRIMINOLOGY

There is always a danger of oversimplification when trying to paint in some historical background, of ending up with such broad brushstrokes that the past becomes a caricature of itself, smoothed out and shed of all those irksome details that confound an apparent coherence and elegant simplicity. Part of the problem concerns the selection of supposedly representative and influential writers in order to draw out some posited 'mainstream' or 'dominant' ideas. Do we, for instance, study only those ideas that received official recognition and became incorporated into policy? Or do we judge the importance of a text according to the manner in which it was received by contemporary academic peers?

Obviously there was no precise date, no magic moment, when modern criminology suddenly appeared. The development of criminology into a distinct academic discipline was a gradual process, and this process was linked in various ways (depending on one's reading of history) to 200 years or more of crime-related intellectual discourse. It was also linked to sweeping economic, social and political transformations that took place, as British society moved from feudalism to agrarian capitalism to mature capitalism. More recently, in the post-war period, the progress of criminology has been connected to such things as an increasingly interventionist central state, the growth of the welfare state, and the expansion of higher education. Certainly, by the beginning of the 1960s criminology was established as a modern academic discipline, with all that that meant: full-time specialists working in university departments or in specialised institutions; an agenda of research questions and approved methodologies; its own learned journals; postgraduate programmes; and various forums for the exchange of ideas.

When discussing the history of criminological thought, it is not controversial to point to the late nineteenth century as the time when 'scientific' criminology first appeared on the scene. Nor is it controversial to describe this as positivist criminology. What is controversial, at least nowadays, is then to go on to label indiscriminately as 'positivist' the bulk of British criminology that developed since the late nineteenth century up to the 1960s, though the application of this label has not always been seen as problematic.

From the late 1960s, there grew within sociology a sustained critique of positivism among those influenced by the ideas of interpretive sociology. Specifically, this critique was aimed at functionalism, and, because functionalism was, not unreasonably, viewed as a conservative social theory, the critique was also embraced by more radical, left-oriented sociologists. The success of this onslaught in terms of the subsequent development of sociology is well known. The critique was generally successful among students too, even early on in their criminological studies. This is well illustrated by my own experiences as an A-level sociology examiner during the late 1970s and early 1980s. Most of the candidates were 'anti-positivism' and 'pro-phenomenology', even those who clearly had no idea what phenomenology was. Indeed, it was not uncommon to read quite malignant, no holds barred, tirades against alleged functionalist miscreants such as Talcott Parsons.

The critique of positivism within sociology in general was paralleled with a critique of positivist criminology, for by the beginning of the 1970s sociology had become the dominant discipline within academic criminology. Garland (1994) has argued that it is misleading to characterise the period from the late nineteenth century to the 1960s as a period of positivist hegemony, with the new deviancy of the 1960s arriving on the scene to rescue the discipline from its clutches. This overgeneralised and demonising view of history has had two important results:

1 As Jock Young (1988: 168) puts it, 'the long lineage of radical positivism in Britain was forgotten'.
2 There was a failure to appreciate the various strands of criminological thought developing from the turn of the century, and that some of the most influential work, especially in the first two decades of the twentieth century, did not easily fall into the category of positivism.

In order to assess these debates it is necessary to be reminded of what is meant by sociological positivism. Cuff and Payne (1979: 159) offer the following standard definition based upon two propositions:

1 The kinds of explanation sociology should produce about the social world should be the same as those produced in the natural sciences, i.e. law-like statements which have the form, 'A causes B' . . .
2 Sociology should as far as possible make use of the same sorts of method as are used in the natural sciences for constructing and testing their explanations. An essential implication is that sociologists need to model their approach on the logic of that exemplary tool of the natural sciences – the experimental method.

What are the implications of this for a specifically criminological positivism? Three central questions are associated with this type of criminology, if and when such a creature can be identified: Why do some individuals break the law? How can criminals be reformed? What can be done to prevent them wanting to break the law in the first place? According to Jeffery (1960) and Matza (1964), attempts to answer these questions proceed within a characteristic framework derived from three fundamental assumptions: determinism, differentiation and pathology.

Determinism means that factors outside of the individual's control – be they biological, psychological, sociological, or some combination – push that individual into criminal behaviour. From this perspective, crime does not result from choice, or rational decision making, but rather from force of circumstance. This model of crime contrasts sharply with that associated with classical criminology, which emphasises the ability of members of society to make rational choices about whether or not to commit crime, similar to a cost–benefit analysis. In this formulation, the 'cost' of crime equates with punishment proportional to the crime, and ideally this acts as a deterrent. As we shall see, different sorts of causal theories developed within criminology through the twentieth century, each stressing different, more or less deterministic, factors.

There is an intriguing contradiction between positivist conceptions and conceptions built into the legal system. The courts, of course, are willing to take such things as age and mental state into consideration when judging a person's guilt. The determinism of positivism, however, removes personal culpability, by making the wrongdoer into a victim of behaviour-determining factors. This certainly does not square with notions of justice based upon just deserts or retribution, and indicates why positivism leads naturally to a 'treatment' model; that is, to attempting to 'cure' the offender. In practice, this uneasy tension has been managed by what is usually referred to as the neoclassical principle of mitigation; for example, by allowing the psychologist or social worker into the court to plead for the defendant. It is an important issue that continues to generate much debate within criminology, namely, to what extent, and in what ways, is the offender to blame?

The second assumption made by positivist criminology, according to Jeffery and Matza, is *differentiation*. What this means is that criminals are differentiated in kind from non-criminals. Depending on the type of criminology involved, criminals have been viewed as different because of their biological constitutions, because they possess certain abnormal or negative psychological traits, or, from a sociological direction, because they have learned attitudes and values which lend themselves to law breaking.

The third assumption, *pathology*, follows on from differentiation, in that criminals are seen as being different to non-criminals because of something going 'wrong' at a biological, psychological or sociological level.

Before turning to developments in the first part of the twentieth century, it will be useful to note two important issues that are usually seen as featuring prominently in positivist criminology: the problematic nature of the concept of crime, and the tension between heredity and environment.

The *raison d'être* of positivism has been its promise to enlist the services of science. Discarding the deadweight of pre-scientific knowledge as mere prejudice and dilettantism, positivist criminology would apply the methods and principles of scientific thought. However, such a criminology had to resolve a crucial problem concerning the concept of crime itself. Because it was appreciated that what was defined as crime changed over time, and from one society to another, it was clear that this central concept, as legally defined, did not offer a fixed, objective, scientific anchor point. To fall back on definitions of crime current in a particular society at a particular moment in history would seem to subvert the positivist project of producing general theories. Consequently, attempts were made to arrive at some objective concept of 'natural' or 'real' crime. The magnitude of this endeavour can be readily appreciated, and positivism met serious problems on two levels. First, in practice, abstracted conceptions simply reflected a writer's personal moral feelings. Moreover, if the solution was to tap into perceived 'public sentiments', and emphasise deviance rather than crime, the problem of relativism remained unsolved, in that supposedly consensual attitudes and values in a society (if they can be identified) are themselves shaped by particular cultures. Second, positivist criminologists eventually tended to surrender to legally defined categories anyway, and even early on in the twentieth century they used prison inmates as subjects for research: that is, they used individuals whose criminal status was obviously derived from legal definitions. We might also add that one of the main criticisms of positivism made by the 'new deviancy' theorists of the 1960s and 1970s was that they accepted uncritically official crime statistics.

The second issue featuring prominently in positivist criminology is that of heredity versus the environment. Some positivists concentrated on what they saw as genetically determined predispositions to criminality, whilst others focused on environmental factors, and the effect of these on the individual. Hereditarians usually acknowledged, though, that the social circumstances of the individual were of *some* importance. Stressing the 'environment' can, of course, still mean subscribing to a deterministic explanation of criminality.

THE TURN OF THE CENTURY TO THE 1930s

It is a complex business unravelling the varieties of positivism, quasi-positivism or non-positivism prevalent in British criminology during the first three decades of the twentieth century. From the available evidence, at the end of the nineteenth century there was strong support for the notion of biological determinism, though this support tended not to follow the Lombrosian idea of linking criminality to external physical features. In Britain the main stress was on genetically determined psychological traits such as 'feeble-mindedness' and 'moral degeneracy' and their links with criminality. After this early, crude attempt at 'scientific' criminology, which continued up to World War One, mapping developments during the 1920s and 1930s becomes rather more hazardous. In particular we have to be wary of making sweeping statements to the effect that British criminology simply continued along a positivist pathway. Some writers, influential during the interwar years, clearly represented the positivist tradition, but others did not. Of course, a problem here, as mentioned earlier, is deciding on which writers best represent this period.

Research carried out under the banner of 'criminology' continued to be dominated by medical practitioners employed within the prison service; usually they had received training in psychiatric medicine. The result was that much of this research was locked into the institutional requirements of the courts and prisons. Taking the individual's mental state as the starting point, criminological investigations were designed to facilitate the more effective organisation of prison regimes and treatment programmes. Thus psychiatry, defined as psychological medicine, and then psychology, were the main influences in this period. Any influence from sociology was conspicuously lacking (for example, the work done by the Chicago School during the interwar years). This is not surprising given that research was largely driven by the needs of the system, and was carried out by those with a vested interest in that system. They were also concerned with legitimising criminology as an academic discipline. This did not mean that social factors were ignored. Such things as 'inadequate' family life, poverty, single parenthood and illegitimacy were often on the agenda. However, these were invoked within a psychological frame of reference. For hereditarians, negative social factors were seen as the outcome of inborn, abnormal mental states – for example, 'inadequate' people created 'inadequate' families – whilst environmentalists saw such things as poverty leading to abnormal mental states.

By the beginning of the 1920s, mainstream criminology in Britain had moved away from seeing the criminal as a distinct type of human being, towards a model based upon a spectrum of mental traits and conditions. Fundamentally, these attributes were judged in terms of diagnosed pathological conditions labelled 'low intelligence', 'feeble-mindedness', and so on.

We can explore this situation further by looking at a number of influential writers around in the 1920s and 1930s. This will show that a plurality of views existed within criminology, and that the appellation 'positivism' may not always apply. Garland suggests that mainstream criminology in the 1920s and 1930s was best represented by the work of W. Norwood East, a writer who, although sharing with positivism a desire to develop objective, empirically based research, did not support a deterministic approach. Neither did he take the view that all criminals were suffering from some psychological disorder. Other writers, however, such as Hamblin Smith and Grace Pailthorpe, did argue that the 'abormal' mental state of the individual led to criminal behaviour.

Those linking heredity to criminal dispositions took into account what they saw as genetically inherited mental traits. This is well illustrated by the work of Charles Goring, a medical officer in the prison service. Between 1902 and 1908 he carried out a psychiatrically based study of over 1,500 prisoners. In his report, published in 1913, he concluded that 'there is no such thing as a physical criminal type'. Although this is a clear refutation of the Lombrosian view, Goring was not seeking to suggest that criminals were 'made' rather than 'born'. In 1919, following his death, an abridged version of the report was published, and this contains an introduction by a collabora-tor in the research, Karl Pearson, who points out that Goring was 'much surprised' to find that there was 'relatively little influence of environment' in criminality. Goring (1919: 211–12) himself wrote:

> Relatively to its origin in the constitution of the malefactor, and especially in his men-tally defective constitution, crime in this country is only to a trifling extent (if to any) the product of social inequality, of adverse environment, or of other manifestations of what may be comprehensively termed 'the force of circumstances'.

One of the most influential studies from the 1920s, carried out on delinquent youth by Cyril Burt (1925: 29), also argued the case for hereditary factors (Burt's reputation has suffered since the revelation in the 1970s that he doctored the figures in various pieces of research): 'if our inquiry is to begin at the very beginning, it must go back to influences that were operative long before the child himself was born. We must review not only his birth and early life, but his ancestry also'.

By the late 1930s, mainstream criminology was linking criminal behaviour to a range of psychological and social factors, against the backdrop of a continuing debate about the relative importance of genetic endowment. This is a tradition that has car-ried on into the work of modern psychologists. As Roshier (1989: 26) says:

> The quest for identifiable crime-prone personality types has included learning theorists as well as heredity theorists, psychoanalysts ('anti-social' or 'affectionless' personality theories), and studies not concerning themselves with the question of how such types come about.

By the time we reach World War Two psychology was clearly in pole position within criminological discourses, with different emphases given to 'heredity' (inborn psy-chological dispositions to crime, or an inborn lack of mental defences against 'proper' attitude formation), and 'environment' ('bad' social conditions detrimen-tally affecting psychological growth).

Interestingly, the same kind of policy-influencing framework was reflected in debates about future secondary education taking place in the late 1930s and during the war. A belief in the genetic basis of intellectual ability, derived in large part from the now discredited research of Cyril Burt, was built into the 1938 Spens Report and 1943 Norwood Report, and then enshrined in the tripartite system ushered in by the 1944 Education Act. The reform of education was, of course, only part of a massive transformation in British social policy following World War Two, and we have to appreciate the strong feelings building up during the war around a welfare theme. Here were reflected Fabian ideas pertaining to the intervention of the central and local state into the social and economic life of the country in order to improve that life. The same rationale was apparent in discussions and policy formulations relating to offenders, especially young offenders, during and after the war. Thus there was an increasing presence of social work, psychotherapy and treatment, and reformative strategies. The movement towards welfarism was, in effect, one way of resolving the tension between 'heredity' and 'environment'. Improvements in health and housing, and an end to poverty, and so on, in a sense made the debate redundant. Put crudely, whatever the importance of genetic endowment might be, society is lumbered with it. At least the social environments of ordinary people can be improved, which, it was reasoned, would minimise the unwanted effects of 'bad' environments, for example crime. Geoff Pearson refers to a 1946 Conservative Party report, called *Youth Astray*, which from a contemporary vantage point makes startling reading: 'The behaviour of boys and girls is mainly the outcome of conditions, social, economic, and to some extent hereditary, for which they themselves cannot be blamed. The blame – for blame there is – rests largely upon society' (Pearson, 1983: 14).

EUGENICS

There was during the interwar years, however, an alternative response to welfarism among some of those convinced of the importance of genetics. The frequent identification of criminality with low intelligence, feeble-mindedness, moral degeneracy and the like led some down a eugenics road and the sad attractions of, among other things, sterilisation. The eugenics movement achieved a significant following in Britain, as well as on the continent and in the United States. Essentially it was concerned with improving the perceived genetic stock, which meant devising ways of preventing those defined as degenerate, of low intelligence, or otherwise deviant, from producing offspring. The word 'eugenics' was coined by Francis Galton in the 1860s by placing the Greek word for 'well' next to the Greek word for 'born'. This mission to purify the genetic pool of what was bizarrely referred to by some as the 'British race', or 'Nordic race', was rather sullied by Nazi Germany taking the arguments to their logical conclusion in the gas chambers of Auschwitz.

These various strands within criminology between World War One and World War Two are brought together in a significant book by Claude Mullins (1945). The book is significant not because it had any particular impact on policy, or because of its academic excellence, but rather because of its nature. The title, to begin with, says it all: *Why Crime? Some causes and remedies from the psychological standpoint*. In addition, because the author was a self-taught psychologist and a magistrate, he acts as a kind of melting pot for academic, lay and judicial opinion. Interestingly, he begins by referring to the lack of popular support for genetic explanations of criminality:

> The popular view among those interested in the subject is that criminals are what they are because society has made them so. This view accords with modern political tendencies and is based upon the assumption that if society had provided for all a satisfactory

social and economic environment, there would be few criminals. Those holding this view find that it generates soothing feelings of anger against the scheme of things . . . they believe that the delinquent, rather than his victims or society, is really the aggrieved party.

(Ibid.: 2)

As the book proceeds, and his own personal opinions emerge, it is clear that Mullins was sceptical of these 'political tendencies', tendencies associated with the welfarism discussed above. While pointing out that 'No one would maintain that the inheritance, whether biological or psychological, can be directly a cause of crime' (ibid.: 9), he went on to observe that 'Delinquency is closely associated with the low-grade and the mentally deficient' (ibid.: 48). His conclusion was to thoroughly commend the findings of the 1934 government Departmental Committee on Sterilization, which stated that they were:

impressed by the dead weight of social inefficiency and individual misery which is entailed by the existence in our midst of over a quarter of a million mental defectives and of a far larger number of persons who, without being certifiably defective, are mentally subnormal.

(Cited by Mullins, ibid.: 49)

This Committee said that all witnesses before them 'recognized heredity as an important factor in the causation of these conditions'.

Mullins (1945: 49) continues:

The Sterilization Committee expressed the opinion that many low-grade parents 'would be glad to be relieved of the dread of repeated pregnancies and to escape the recurring burden of parenthood, for which they are so manifestly unfitted' . . . There must be few of those who have had close contacts with such people who would disagree with this statement . . . The only practical way of preventing people of low-grade intelligence from being overwhelmed with unwanted children, to the immense detriment of such children, is by the sterilization of the fathers.

It is not worth dwelling overlong on Mullins' text, but there is a section in a chapter on 'Illegitimate Children' which manages to combine prejudice towards such children with surreal psychology and anti-trade unionism:

adoption (of illegitimate children) frequently brings severe psychological dangers . . . many medical psychologists will say that a trauma will also remain in the child's unconscious which at any time may result in a crisis. Such a trauma may produce throughout life a hostility towards some one or society generally. An excellent illustration of this was . . . a well-known miners' leader in the decades between the wars. His uncompromising nature . . . its explanation probably lay in the fact that he was a foundling, adopted into the home of a miner and his wife . . . But all his life his pugnacity and his dogged reluctance to meet the other side in any way were in all probability the legacy from his birth, and though his foster-parents' love and care doubtless had their beneficial effect, they could not eradicate what birth and the earliest reception into the world had produced.

(Ibid.: 102)

The eugenics movement was founded on pseudo-science and racism, and was particularly successful in the United States during the first sixty years of the twentieth century (for an excellent discussion, see Black, 2003; and for a discussion of eugenics within the context of DNA profiling and cloning, in particular the re-emergence of the issue of race in present day genetics and medicine, see Duster, 2003). Viewed by the authorities as having 'bad blood lines', showing signs of 'feeble-mindedness', belonging to the wrong 'race', being 'deviant', etc., hundreds of thousands of Americans were prevented from having children. At least 60,000 were coercively sterilised; thousands more were erroneously placed in mental institutions, not permitted to marry, and in some cases 'un-married' by state officials. It was not until the evidence of Nazi extermination camps emerged that the eugenics movement began to lose influence, and when the war ended, what were formerly known as eugenics institutions were renamed genetics institutions. In spite of attempts during the 1920s and 1930s to persuade British governments of the benefits of the forced sterilisation of the 'feeble-minded' and 'degenerate', the necessary legislation was never introduced. However, in some American states, laws allowing sterilisation remain on the statute books. Between 1972 and 1976, 3,406 Native American women and 142 men were sterilised as a result of an Indian Health (*sic*) Service programme (Black, 2003).

The views of people such as Mullins were, at the time, out of step with 'modern political tendencies', tendencies that led to the creation of the modern welfare state – but these views did not disappear. As we shall see when discussing the 1980s and 1990s, reports of the demise of the above type of criminology turned out to be greatly exaggerated.

Selected further reading

Roshier, B. (1989) *Controlling Crime*, Milton Keynes: Open University Press, offers a well-informed, accessible discussion of the classical perspective in criminology and its enduring influence. An edited collection of the writings of Beccaria – one of the major figures in classical criminology – is: Bellamy, R. (ed) (1995) *Beccaria: On crimes and punishments and other writings*, Cambridge: Cambridge University Press.

Beirne, P. (1993) *Inventing Criminology: Essays on the rise of* 'homo criminalis', Albany, NY: State University of New York Press, is a sophisticated analysis of classicism and positivism in early criminology.

Mannheim, H. (1940) *Social Aspects of Crime in England Between the Wars*, London: **Allen & Unwin**, was written by someone who was there at the time.

For a succinct, though comprehensive, overview, see **Garland, D. (2002)** 'Of crimes and criminals: The development of criminology in Britain', in M. Maguire, R. Morgan and R. Reiner (eds) *The Oxford Handbook of Criminology*, 2nd edn, Oxford: Oxford University Press.

An important book on the history of the eugenics movement is **Black, E. (2003)** *War Against the Weak: Eugenics and America's campaign to create a master race*, New York: Four Walls Eight Windows.

PART II

WORLD WAR TWO TO THE MID-1960S

CHAPTER 4

THE DISCIPLINE OF CRIMINOLOGY
AND ITS CONTEXT – I

Key themes

- The emergence of criminology
- Sociological criminology
- Sociological criminology in Britain from the 1950s to the mid-1960s
- Sociological criminology in the United States

INTRODUCTION

From now on, the focus is largely on sociological criminology, tracing its emergence in the United States in the early part of the twentieth century, and in Britain in the 1950s, and its development up to the present day. The chapters that follow are structured around major historical periods. Thus for each historical period there is a chapter outlining the broader social and political context within which the development of criminology as an academic discipline can be situated. This, in turn, is followed by a companion chapter(s) that discusses in detail the theoretical ideas and agendas associated with the various criminological perspectives that have emerged over the years. This begins here in Chapter 4 with a discussion of the social and political contexts within which early versions of British and American sociological criminology emerged.

The emergence of a recognised academic discipline called 'criminology' was not pre-ordained or inevitable; it was not an ology waiting to happen. Similarly, no master plan was guiding the discipline towards some 'true' state. Debates regarding what criminology is, or should be, continue unabated. Indeed, they have increased in intensity as time has gone on.

The academic terrain of criminology has been, and still is, colonised by theories and research projects that have their intellectual bases in a range of pre-existing academic disciplines. As we have seen in the last chapter, in Britain during the first part of the twentieth century that discipline was psychological medicine/psychology. Crime and criminality, though, have been studied from the perspective of biology, anthropology, economics, sociology, and so on. Criminologists, therefore, have either opted for a strategy of broadly based eclecticism, where they synthesise, or at least draw on, a number of disciplines, or for an approach rooted in their own academic specialism.

The choice of an eclectic approach was to a large extent a feature of the criminology that developed during the period under review in this chapter. This raises the interesting issue of whether there is an extant body of theoretical knowledge with uniquely criminological characteristics. What is the distinction, say, between the sociology or psychology of crime and criminology? After all, the specialist area of, for instance, the sociology of the family did not lead to a separate academic discipline called 'familyology'.

In the ebbs and flows of subject dominance and changing research agendas, 'criminology' became a flag of convenience, under which a motley crew could sail. Its status as a separate academic discipline derived from the institutional trappings accumulated over the years: specialist research centres and departments, parking spaces on library shelves, academic journals, professorships, conferences and the like. This allowed for a concentration of scholarship and the potential for cross-fertilisation of ideas; but the work produced has always remained rooted in earlier disciplines, either as a primary focus, or some sort of synthesis.

THE EMERGENCE OF CRIMINOLOGY

By the end of the 1950s criminology had, in many circles, achieved the status of a recognised academic discipline. Indeed, as one measure of this, according to Radzinowicz's (1961) review of this period, Britain was second only to the United States in terms of government funding for criminological research during the 1950s.

In the last chapter mention was made of Garland's distinction between two different criminological projects, first one then the other becoming dominant as the discipline developed in history. On the one hand, there is the 'governmental project', where criminology's *raison d'être* was its practical usefulness for administrators, and on the other, the 'Lombrosian project', where criminology was oriented towards the production of scientific knowledge. According to Garland, by the end of the 1950s there had been a convergence between these two projects: criminology laid claim to proper academic/scientific status, and at the same time offered useful knowledge for those involved in the administration of the criminal justice system.

This raises important and complex philosophical issues relating to the role of the social sciences in general, and, as we shall see, these become particularly pertinent within the context of versions of critical criminology. For the moment, one point to make is that irrespective of whether or not one believes that criminology should be 'useful', it is necessary to consider the basic framework within which criminological research is carried out. There is a distinction between research carried out within the constraints and demands imposed by a funding body, according to an agenda they set, and research carried out because it is interesting and will further academic knowledge and understanding. Those involved in each type of research might even agree that criminology should, for instance, help in the 'fight against crime', but there is a huge difference between research that is locked into some administrative require-ments and research that is not (though nowadays such freedom is increasingly diffi-cult to come by). This tension also has implications for the development of theory. Hope (2006: 245) attributes this observation to the American criminologist Travis Hirschi: 'There are two kinds of theory – theory, and grant-theory.'

In Garland's view, then, research carried out during the 1940s and 1950s satisfied both administrative and academic demands due to a happy coincidence of the two projects. On a general level this was undoubtedly the case, though a more detailed analysis shows that there were differences of opinion within criminology. Without this administrative and academic convergence, it is probably true to say that crimi-nology's evolution into a legitimate and recognised academic discipline would have been more drawn out. Whatever the personal preferences of the criminologists involved might have been, the promise of a 'scientific' understanding of crime and its treatment was a seductive one for governments in the post-war period – a period of optimism founded on notions of social planning and social engineering.

Before we examine the implications of this for criminology, it will be useful to step back a little and consider the social and political climate in British society at that time. The Fabian-influenced social reform movement, referred to in the earlier discussion of the 1930s, gathered momentum as World War Two ran its course. The idea of social reform in the shape of better housing, healthcare and education, and freedom from abject poverty, captured the imagination of large numbers of the population, espe-cially the working class. During the war, cinema audiences got used to seeing govern-ment information films giving glimpses of a post-war future when the quality of life would be greatly improved for everyone. Magazines such as *Picture Post* began to carry similar messages, with photographs of model council housing estates, where kids had plenty of green spaces to play in, and a trip to the lavatory was not an expedition through the elements to the outer reaches of a backyard. Many people lived in grossly inadequate housing, and dreaded the onset of illness because of the costs involved. Memories of the 1930s and the high levels of unemployment were still fresh in the minds of those once unemployed men and women now fighting for Britain. The sacri-fices that people at the front and at home were being asked to make demanded a prom-ise of something better than the pre-war world that had gone before. The idea that winning the war would be rewarded merely by a return to the old days of glaring class inequality and privilege would not have been much of an incentive. Driven by welfarist principles, Britain after the war was to be a land fit for heroes.

In spite of this, many people were surprised when Churchill's wartime charisma failed to ensure a Conservative general election victory in 1945. As it turned out, the Labour Party won by a significant majority, and their manifesto committed them to a radical programme of social and economic reform. Not only was the welfare state to be established, but key sectors of the economy were to be nationalised. Clearly, the Labour Party's victory reflected the fact that a large number of voters were in accord with their plans for post-war reconstruction. An interesting explanation of their victory is attributed to my ex-father-in-law, John Tracy. In his view it was because the men and women fighting overseas were rarely able to read the mainly Conservative-supporting newspapers.

This, then, was the social landscape in which studies of crime and delinquency continued to develop in the 1940s and 1950s, and the nature of these studies became part of the *zeitgeist* of post-war Britain. Criminology was thus infused with the ideas of social reform within a political philosophy of social democracy.

Institutional roots

One measure of criminology's growing importance during the two decades of the 1940s and 1950s is provided by looking at the institutional roots laid down by the discipline. The specialised criminology course which began at the London School of Economics in 1935 continued to develop under the leadership of Mannheim. A Department of Criminal Science was set up at the University of Cambridge in 1941, though this was concerned with research and publishing rather then teaching. Eventually the Home Office-funded Institute of Criminology grew out of this department. The government funding of criminological research, originally sanctioned by the 1948 Criminal Justice Act, indicates the congruence between governmental social policy and the directions taken by British criminology at that time. In 1950, the Institute for the Scientific Treatment of Delinquency (ISTD), established in 1932, published the *British Journal of Delinquency*, Britain's first specialist criminological journal. A shift in emphasis from delinquency to the broader concept of crime is reflected in the decision to alter the title of this journal to the *British Journal of Criminology* in 1960.

As criminology was trying to find its feet and establish itself as a legitimate academic discipline, debates about the types of behaviour or social problems criminology should study were joined by debates about how and why these should be studied: for example, whether research should be tailored to meet the needs of the Home Office, and whether the research should be driven by perspectives derived from psychology, psychoanalysis or sociology. One outcome of these debates was the setting up of the British Society of Criminology by a breakaway group dissatisfied with the lack of interest in theoretical analysis within the Scientific Group for the Discussion of Delinquency Problems, an organisation founded in 1953 by the ISTD, and strongly influenced by psychoanalysis and a 'social problems' approach. Finally, in 1957 the Home Office Research Unit was established, and the Home Office continues to be an important centre for criminological research in this country (today there are a number of Home Office Research Units).

Main characteristics

In his review of developments in British criminology during the post-war period, Stan Cohen (1981) argued that the institutions discussed above, within which criminology took root, exhibited four main characteristics: pragmatism, the interdisciplinary conception, correctionalism and positivism. In general terms, these describe the characteristics of criminology in this country up to the 1960s, though as Cohen concedes, there were a few individuals and pieces of research that deviated from the mainstream. However, it was not until the second half of the 1960s that significant breaks occurred, leading eventually to a new orthodoxy. Cohen's four characteristics can be examined in turn.

Pragmatism essentially refers to an approach based on empiricism and a strong orientation towards research with direct, practical consequences. In other words, a commitment to the provision of what is perceived to be useful knowledge, rather than to the construction of social scientific theory. As has been commented on earlier, promulgating the view that criminology was 'useful' was important in these early days from the point of view of gaining official acceptance and legitimation. The idea also fitted in neatly with the social reformism associated with the post-war period. This emphasis on pragmatism is, according to Cohen, well represented in the views of Radzinowicz, one of the leading criminologists at the time. Radzinowicz celebrated what he himself described as the 'pragmatic position', a position that precludes attempts to build an all-embracing theory, or theoretical schools of thought. In consequence, existing data and ideas, from whatever source, constituted an intellectual smorgasbord from which the criminologist might select as required. This again raises the question of what it is that identifies criminology as a distinct academic discipline. Can the approach recommended by Radzinowicz create something peculiarly 'criminological'? Can it fashion a legitimate, though hybrid, discipline, based as it is on dipping into the handiwork of already established academic disciplines?

Explaining why criminology was characterised by this stress on pragmatism, Cohen (1981: 222–3) points to:

> the fact that the whole idea of 'schools' of criminal law and criminology in the Continental sense is quite alien to the British legal tradition . . . The strong American socio-legal tradition was virtually absent in Britain. There was, thus, little opportunity for either a legally or sociologically based theoretical criminology to emerge.

He also refers to the argument, originally put forward by Anderson (1968), that on a different level, pragmatism has been a traditional feature of Britain's national culture. With reference to sociology, Anderson highlights a general distrust of theory and a failure to build any classical traditions at the time when European counterparts were doing just that. In Britain, sociology is historically associated with charity, social work and Fabian institutions. As Cohen (1981: 223) puts it:

> In a much wider sense, the pragmatic tradition could be seen as part of the national culture; the amateur, muddling-along ethos of British life, combined with the Fabian type

of pragmatism in which disciplines with obvious practical implication like criminology are located. Behind many enterprises in such fields, the attitude is: find out the right facts, then let the well-meaning chaps (for example, in the Home Office) make the obvious inferences and do the rest. Contrast, for example, the highly professional and research-based collection of information for policy-making in an American official commission with the typical Royal Commission – with its motley collection of peers, bishops, judges, very part-time experts and 'informed laymen', and its unbelievably slow rate of productivity.

The second characteristic of post-war British criminology identified by Cohen is *interdisciplinary conception*. By this he means that the empiricism and pragmatism which permeated criminology lent itself to the utilisation of a broadly based mix of disciplines. This suggests that the eclectic approach was pursued not only because it apparently produced 'useful', practical knowledge, but also because it corresponded with the dominant view that it was in the nature of criminology to be an eclectic discipline. The work carried out by the big institutions of criminological research during the 1940s and 1950s, and which, as a totality, constituted 'British criminology', was based on a range of perspectives such as psychology, psychiatry, psychoanalysis, forensic science, medicine and sociology. However, an examination of these institutions individually does show that there were differences in the emphasis given to these various disciplines. While the dominant view seems to have been that no one discipline had cornered (or should corner) the market as a 'master discipline', research in specific institutions did tend to be skewed towards one or other of them. In fact, psychology and psychiatry were the most prominent. The minor role played by sociology is worthy of special note, and is returned to below.

Garland (1994) has identified three primary strands in the criminology that had emerged in the 1950s: administrative, psychoanalytical and sociological. The first of these was originally labelled 'administrative criminology' by George Vold (1958), in an effort to disparage a type of criminology lacking commitment to the development of a scientific, theoretically oriented model. This critique was mainly aimed at the Cambridge Institute of Criminology, then under the tutelage of Radzinowicz, and the Research Unit at the Home Office. Drawing on an eclectic mix of academic disciplines, administrative criminology describes a criminology that is fundamentally geared towards doing research which will be of direct practical use to government agencies concerned with criminal justice matters, for example the prisons and the courts.

The psychoanalytical strand exemplified the clinical approach to criminology. Studies set within a psychological and psychiatric framework attempted to fathom the causes of crime, to classify different types of offender, and, in the process, to develop theoretical models. Again, although these studies had scientific aspirations, they were ultimately locked into some notion of 'useful' knowledge – useful, that is, to the policy process. This kind of criminology was associated with the ISTD, the Maudsley Hospital, the Tavistock Institute, the British Society of Criminology and the *British Journal of Criminology*. According to Cohen (1981: 224), these institutions 'heavily weighted the field towards psychology and psychiatry', and 'This weighting remained despite the later contributions by sociologists'.

The sociological strand was largely associated with a growing number of sociological criminologists working under Mannheim at the London School of Economics in the 1950s. Mannheim, who came from a legal background, favoured a multidisciplinary approach, but did gradually come to develop a sociological perspective on crime and delinquency (Mannheim, 1965). Overall, however, British criminology contained relatively little written from a specifically sociological direction.

Cohen's third characteristic of post-war criminology – *correctionalism* – he describes as correction, reform and the problem of values. Although there were some exceptions, with writers such as Walker (1965) arguing for scientific detachment and a commitment to theoretical knowledge, on the whole, says Cohen, British criminology was strongly tied to government-led demands for a more efficient, albeit humanely reformed, correctional system (though there is no logical necessity for these two ambitions to coincide in practice). There was, therefore, a great stress on the treatment of offenders, and modes of intervention in the lives of predicted offenders. In essence, Cohen's reasonable complaint is that criminology had developed a largely unreflexive posture, whereby key assumptions, that should have been critically interrogated, were more or less taken for granted as 'givens'.

The fourth, and final, characteristic for Cohen (1981: 229) is what he calls the *positivist trap*, and he attributes this to the dominance of clinical interests: 'the search for clinical or statistical proof of causation, the commitment to scientific determinism, the denial of authenticity and meaning to deviance'.

This mobilisation of 'scientific' criminology in the battle against recidivism and the prevention of delinquency among those 'at risk' was more of a promise than a reality. As David Downes (1978: 490) puts it: 'no clear idea had emerged of what might be inflicted on "pre-delinquents", should an adequate predictive instrument be devised, a seemingly remote possibility in any case'.

The lack of impact made by these correctionalist ideas, due to their inherent inadequacies, partly explains, says Downes, why no sustained criticisms, or indeed worries, developed during the 1950s. Put another way, the clinical alchemy feeding the correctionalist's dreams of scientific intervention into the lives of supposed 'pre-delinquents' was so underdeveloped and hazy that it was not looked upon as a real threat. However, says Downes, by the early 1960s and the advent of people such as the psychologist Hans Eysenck, these interventions on the basis of, say, aversion therapy concentrated the minds of more liberally inclined criminologists wonderfully. Thus began a shift towards a more critical criminology impatient with the (dangerous) correctionalist principles lying at the heart of mainstream criminology.

An 'everything' of crime

Criminologists working in the post-war period obviously felt that they were engaged on a project that was distinctively 'criminological'. Using an interdisciplinary approach that entailed dipping into and borrowing from various already established relevant areas of study was precisely why criminology was seen as a distinct academic discipline. Somehow, the process of extracting the various factors – psychological, psychoanalytical, biological or sociological, etc. in nature – viewed as acting in combination on offenders, or potential offenders, constituted the business of doing criminology. An approach anchored in a single discipline – for example, a psychology or sociology of crime – would have negated efforts to construct a separate, qualitatively different, way of studying crime and criminality. Thus, criminology became, potentially, an 'everything' of crime. Interestingly, this view was officially endorsed in 2007 when 'benchmark statements' for criminology as an academic discipline were produced by the government's Quality Assurance Agency (benchmark statements provide content guidance for degree programmes in this country).

In this context Cyril Burt's (1925) pre-war study, *The Young Delinquent*, is a good example. Using a sample of 400 children, Burt sought to identify those factors in a child's life that produce individual psychological variations. In particular, he was interested in those factors which in combination are associated with delinquency and, hence, can be used as predictors of future delinquency. Burt's work reflected his background in psychology and his professional role of educational psychologist in so far as he linked the various factors to psychological differences. However, the process of selecting the key factors was broadly based, relying as he did on all sorts of indices and measurement techniques: for example, psychoanalysis, IQ tests and the investigation of social and material circumstances. It was this commitment to a multifactorial approach that endeared him to post-war criminologists. So too did his focus on the *individual* delinquent and, as a corollary, on the need to devise individually tailored treatment programmes. One other feature of Burt's work, which was to dominate much of the British criminology that followed, was its pathological frame of reference: some parents had 'defective' relationships with their children, some children had 'bad' temperaments, and so on.

Burt's study stands as a direct precursor of much of the criminology produced in the 1940s and 1950s. It concentrated on young offenders, and attempted to predict in a 'scientific' manner which children would be most likely to end up as delinquent. This endeavour to predict delinquency has been described by Stan Cohen as an 'obsession in British criminology'. Certainly, as we shall see, British criminology has been seduced by notions of 'prediction' and dominated by studies of youthful delinquency. In the immediate post-war period this was partly connected to the fact that official statistics continued to show apparent increases in amounts of juvenile crime. And, predictably, the research pathway relating to the treatment of young offenders marked out by Burt was also followed, with research explicitly linked to the penal requirements of the Borstal system.

SOCIOLOGICAL CRIMINOLOGY

As criminology began to emerge as a separate discipline during the 1940s and 1950s, where was sociology? The short answer is that sociological criminology did exist and some studies were carried out within a loosely defined sociological framework. However, as a contributing discipline it played a minor role over that period in Britain, and continued to do so until the middle of the 1960s. From then on things changed and the influence of sociology increased dramatically.

In order to understand why this was so we have to take account of the central features of both the emerging criminology and sociology itself during the period under review. As we have seen, mainstream criminology made a virtue out of an interdisciplinary multifactorial approach. This, by definition, precluded embracing a specifically sociological analysis, though it did not preclude the incorporation of ideas and theories from sociology, at least in principle. However, in comparison with, notably, psychologically grounded criminology, sociological criminology was thin on the ground. Furthermore, according to Cohen (1981: 227), British criminology was operating within a fairly crude conceptual framework: 'Curious notions about sociology being concerned with "area" or "environmental" factors appear, sociology is identified with statistics, and concepts such as anomie, sub-culture or deprivation are distorted'.

It was also, as far as influences from other countries were concerned, something of a closed shop. This is particularly striking with respect to potential influences from the United States where, by World War Two, a large and important body of sociological criminology had developed.

The way in which mainstream criminology coalesced around a commitment to pragmatism is also important. The desire to produce knowledge useful to criminal justice administrators, and especially to those working within the penal system, enabled criminology to achieve recognition as a legitimate discipline. Unfortunately, sociology failed to convince the pragmatists that it was able to offer much of value. The promise held out by criminology of being of practical use was predicated on a primary concern with the individual delinquent or pre-delinquent, and this clearly lent itself to a strong influence from psychiatry and psychology. In that context, even a more mature and sophisticated sociology would, because analyses are pitched at the level of the 'social', have had difficulty in gaining mainstream acceptance. The 'social problems' orientation of mainstream criminology finds a parallel with social work, with its emphasis on casework. Here, too, with knowledge evaluated on the basis of such things as 'relevance', 'practical application' and a promise to make problems 'manageable', sociology has traditionally assumed a secondary status to psychology.

This illustrates the continuing importance of the 'governmental project' (Garland, 1994) in the post-war years. Under these conditions, for sociology to become influential – and thereby earn centrally administered funds, respectable status, and a seat at the top table – it needed to prove its worth by producing what was seen as useful knowledge, which equates to knowledge that will help in the 'fight against crime'. Eventually, some sociology was able to do this, as exemplified by the research carried out at the Home Office. However, a coextensive process was at work from the late 1960s onwards which offered an alternative to this administrative route to discipline status. Some strands of sociological criminology opted out of the government project in favour of an academic – rather than 'Lombrosian' – project. Sociology was able to disengage itself from the government project to a significant degree because its discourse gathered together a large internal audience, irrespective of any claims to 'usefulness'. From the late 1960s there was a massive expansion in university, and then polytechnic, courses in sociology, and a concomitant growth in the publication of sociological texts. One outcome was increasing interest in sociological studies of crime, though at that period these were likely to be described as the sociology of deviance.

While the themes of much of this work would have shocked many of the criminologists from the 1940s and 1950s, it was just as much a product of that time in history as theirs was a product of the immediate post-war period. By the beginning of the 1970s there had been a spectacular expansion of this sociological area of study, characterised by a kaleidoscopic outpouring of bold, brash, unsettling and sometimes wild virtuosity. As a consequence, sociological criminology (or whatever it was labelled) could to a large extent be sustained by its own internal resources, with a growing audience for the books and papers that were produced among undergraduates, postgraduates, researchers and teachers. In this way market forces began to play a part, as publishing houses became aware of the trend. Furthermore, the work produced could be as theoretical as the author wanted: it did not have to gain acceptance on the basis of some perceived usefulness to the Borstal system. Indeed, that sort of administrative criminology became the focus of criticism: disengagement from the Establishment was celebrated. Of course, one result of this disparaging attitude towards the pragmatic approach was a corresponding lack of direct political influence, a point that raises an interesting debate that surfaced more recently within the context of the growth in influence of 'left realism'. This is discussed later on.

SOCIOLOGICAL CRIMINOLOGY IN BRITAIN FROM THE 1950s TO THE MID-1960s

Winning the World Cup made 1966 an auspicious year for English soccer: it was also an auspicious year for sociological criminology. In his short, though now classic, account of criminology over this period, Stan Cohen (1981: 227) tells us: 'there was virtually nothing before the post-1965 wave following Downes's book *The Delinquent Solution*'. Apart from being the most theoretically sophisticated British sociological study of youth crime then available, Downes's research on delinquency in the East End of London arrived at a time when sociological criminology was poised to develop very significantly in Britain. The study is also important in that it was part of a lineage that over a decade or so had started (albeit spasmodically) to draw on American sources. It is ironic, though, that soon after Downes's book appeared, British criminology, under the influence of other, fresh ideas from the United States, shifted direction towards the so-called new deviancy. In a short period of time an alternative to mainstream criminology was developed by a number of young, and soon to be very influential, British criminologists.

Looking back from the vantage point of today to the time when Downes's book was published, the lack of sociological research on crime seems remarkable. Downes (1966: 100) described the situation as follows:

> What aspects of American Theorisation are substantiated by post-war findings on juvenile delinquency in England? Any attempt to answer this question involves a revelation of the paucity of English work on the sociology of crime . . . Concentration on penology, the psychology of crime, and legal and statistical studies of delinquency . . . has involved the almost complete neglect of the very questions with which American sociologists pre-occupy themselves.

Soberingly, he suggested that sociological work, when it did begin to take off in this country in the 1950s, did so from a position established by the Victorian researcher Henry Mayhew. It was as if British painting had lain dormant since the time of the Pre-Raphaelites: 'Despite the almost single-handed efforts of Mannheim, the sociological study of crime and delinquency slowly revived only during the 1950s, almost a century after the publication in 1862 of Mayhew's massive documentation of the London "underworld" and slums' (ibid.: 100–1).

Given that there was only a handful of British sociologically based studies of crime in existence by 1966, it is quite easy to list the key examples: H. D. Willcock (1949); T. Ferguson (1952); T. Ferguson and J. Cunnison (1951, 1956); J. B. Mays (1954, 1959); M. P. Carter and P. Jephcott (1954); T. Morris (1957); H. Jones (1958); D. Lowson (1960); T. R. Fyvel (1961); J. L. Spencer *et al.* (1961). In addition to these, there were also studies essentially concerned with the statistical distribution of young offending: J. H. Bagot (1941); A. M. Carr-Saunders *et al.* (1942); W. R. Little and V. R. Ntsekhe (1959); J. W. B. Douglas (1964). Studies by P. Sainsbury (1955) and P. Scott (1956), although often referred to in this context (the former, for example, being reproduced in a set of readings on the sociology of crime by Carson and Wiles, 1971), were carried out by psychiatrists.

This meagre list, then, more or less constituted the sociology of crime and delinquency in Britain up to the mid-1960s, thus reinforcing the point made earlier: that criminology during this period was not much interested in sociology, preferring instead the pragmatic, interdisciplinary approach, with strong leanings towards clinical positivism. Clearly, sociological criminology was marginal to the concerns of the mainstream. One result was that until picked up by some of the writers listed above, the large amount of sociological criminology produced in the United States since the early 1920s was virtually ignored in this country. Cohen suggests that this was not always because of mere ignorance, or a perception of it as irrelevant. Even Mannheim, who did most in the late 1930s and the 1940s to introduce sociological perspectives into criminology, is accused by Cohen (1981: 227) of a 'certain parochialism . . . with his apparent policy of selecting for his textbook American work only when British or European work could not be found'. This situation was slowly remedied during the 1950s as two of the most influential early sociological studies of crime (Mays, 1954; Morris, 1957) introduced American ideas and research.

Although British criminology was not much interested in sociology, the reverse is also true: British sociology was not much interested in criminology. Yet in the light of what has already been said about the nature of criminology this detachment can perhaps be easily forgiven. Criminology as it was constituted provided few attractions for the dedicated sociologist. However, a failure to appreciate the continuities between the general concerns of sociology (for example, social order) and the concerns of criminology is less easily explained. According to Cohen, some of the reasons for this resistance to criminology derived from features internal to the discipline of sociology itself in Britain, such as a view that studying criminals or deviants was peripheral to core sociological projects. Other reasons, he says, derived from the 'other side', from the traditional framework within which crime was studied. This framework was guaranteed to put sociologists off: 'the moralistic, non-abstract ways in which deviance was studied and the early identification of this field with social work, reformative or correctional concerns' (1981: 231). On a more personal level, Cohen has painted an unflattering picture of sociology departments during most of the 1960s, with antagonism towards issues of crime and deviance being encountered among all political and theoretical persuasions.

The sociological studies of crime developing in the 1950s represented a move away from an interdisciplinary, clinically based mainstream criminology. Instead of juggling with a multiplicity of biological, psychological and social factors which, in one way or another, were seen as creating individual criminals, sociology explicitly focused on the social context of crime. This social context was the neighbourhood, thus sociological criminology developed within the strong British tradition of area–community studies, a tradition that has endured (e.g. Willmott (1966); Parker (1974); Baldwin and Bottoms (1976); Gill (1977); Bottoms *et al.* (1987); Evans *et al.* (1992)).

The 'social' dimension had been acknowledged in pre-war criminology, even though it had tended to be lost due to the preoccupation with clinical psychology. Mainstream criminological research at that time was littered with concepts such as 'inadequacy', 'maladjustment' and 'low intelligence', and these 'conditions' were often associated with poverty and the slum neighbourhood. On a political level, as we have seen, one important feature of post-war Britain was an increasingly interventionist state, and this included an expanding social welfare programme. Thus an emphasis was placed on the social bases of various defined social problems, among which was crime. This was clearly congruent with the concerns of a Fabian-influenced sociological criminology.

One striking characteristic of the sociological studies of crime carried out during the 1950s and first half of the 1960s, and listed above, is that they all concentrated on young people and their delinquencies. This is not surprising, perhaps, given growing panics about juvenile crime, and the message from official statistics that the peak age of offending was 14. This was also the period that saw the emergence of distinctive youth subcultures, beginning in 1953 with the Teddy Boys, as well as the social category of 'teenager'. These developments helped to accentuate the well-documented tendency to associate adolescence with unruly or troublesome behaviour (Pearson, 1983; Muncie, 1984).

During the decade preceding the publication of Downes's book, then, a sociological alternative to mainstream criminology began to emerge in Britain. As we shall see when this work is examined in more detail, British criminologists were at last acknowledging, and drawing on, American research, and shifting the spotlight away from individualism towards the socio-cultural context of delinquency, towards the neighbourhoods in which delinquent youth lived. However, this type of research started much later in Britain than in the United States, and this, combined with the facts that few sociologists were interested in the field and that there was much less money available to fund research, meant that by the mid-1960s, relatively few studies aimed at testing the explanatory models had been carried out.

While the late 1960s saw a rapid growth in the number of sociologists in Britain who did have an interest in crime and deviance, this interest was by then being sustained in the main by the promise held out by a different kind of sociological criminology. The emphasis now was on the sociology of deviance, and the emerging paradigm was referred to as new deviancy theory. Inevitably, this shift had occurred originally in the United States and the work produced there provided a fecund source of ideas for British criminologists. Very quickly, and in spite of being only relatively short-lived, the earlier sociological criminology was itself labelled, disparagingly, as 'mainstream', or 'orthodox', and became the target for intense criticism. Obviously, these criticisms can only be fully appreciated after we have examined the respective models. However, the discussion so far, aimed at plotting briefly the direction taken by sociological studies of crime, does perhaps give a hint of the nature of some of these criticisms.

Fundamentally, the earlier work had made no attempt to grapple with the definitional issues surrounding the use of terms such as 'crime' and 'delinquency'; state definitions were taken as given. On a less abstract level, these studies were content to rely on official statistics regarding the distribution of crime, and this helped to concentrate research not just on youthful delinquency, but also specifically on lower-working-class males; middle-class deviance was more or less ignored, as was corporate crime. This situation links up with an assumption of a consensus over norms and values: although some studies pointed to delinquency being normal in certain areas, these areas tended to be conceived of as enclaves of criminality within a larger society founded upon a monolithic law-abiding citizenry. There was too, in these studies from the 1950s, a strong social work ethos, and a positivist orientation towards seeking out the causes of delinquency, or identifying 'at risk', 'pre-delinquent' children, with a view to devising appropriate treatment regimes. Above all else, though, earlier sociological criminology was accused of ignoring the part played by the various control agencies in the actual construction of deviance.

Before turning to these developments in British criminology from the late 1960s, it will be useful to cross the Atlantic and have a look at sociological criminology in the United States from the early part of the century up to the impact of new deviancy theory.

SOCIOLOGICAL CRIMINOLOGY IN THE UNITED STATES

When sociological perspectives on crime started to appear, the discipline of criminology in the United States and in Britain was dominated by analyses pitched at the level of the individual. In extreme examples, attempts were made to trace the source of criminal behaviour directly to biological or psychological factors within the individual. The assumption was that something was wrong with the individual, rather than with society. The sociological challenge to this type of theorising developed much earlier in the United States than it did in this country. Although biologically and psychologically based versions of positivism by no means disappeared, a shift towards seeing crime as the outcome of social circumstances began as early as the turn of the twentieth century in the United States.

It was during the 1920s and 1930s, though, that two particularly important and influential traditions in the sociology of crime and delinquency emerged, one based on the work of the Chicago ecologists, the other on Robert Merton's 'strain theory'. Until the 1950s, however, this work was 'wilfully excluded' (Cohen, 1981) by criminologists in Britain. The situation began to change when Mays (1954) acknowledged the contribution made by some of this American research, but Morris (1957) was the first British criminologist to seriously tap into, and give a voice to, American sociological criminology. From then on American research became increasingly influential, and by the late 1960s the floodgates had opened.

The Chicago School

Some of the reasons sociology began to influence criminological thought in the United States much earlier than it did in Britain can be briefly noted. To begin with, as an academic discipline, sociology had established an institutional foothold by the end of the nineteenth century. The first university sociology department was set up in

1892 at, significantly, the University of Chicago. As a consequence, by the beginning of the twentieth century sociology had already achieved a degree of legitimacy, and a power base, including resources for research, from which to develop. For those academics connected with the sociology department in Chicago, the city itself stood before them like a vast social laboratory. Even by American standards the city had grown rapidly. Only 4,100 people lived there in 1833 when the city incorporated; by the late 1890s the number had risen to 1 million. This spectacular growth continued into this century, so that by 1910 the population had doubled to 2 million. As well as indigenous Americans, such as black people moving up from the southern states, the population was swelled by immigrants from all over the world. Chicago was therefore characterised by a hugely diverse range of social groups, and for many of these the move to the city was a move into urban deprivation. Small wonder that criminologists were fascinated by the social life of the city in which they lived. Working within an urban sociology tradition, the Chicago School sought to illuminate the socio-cultural dynamics of crime and delinquency in Chicago's mean streets.

Drawing on the familiar imagery of the 'urban jungle', and equating city life with crime and other social problems, many Americans viewed the rapidly expanding cities with some apprehension. The city became an 'issue'. In this context we might note the growth of the 'progressive movement' during the first part of the century. This movement, based on liberal principles, concerned itself with the human costs of capitalist growth in America: the city slums, poor working conditions, the lack of healthcare provision, and so on. By the 1920s the movement had gathered a great deal of support, not just among the urban poor, but also among more powerful groups in society, who saw in its reformism an acceptable alternative to more radical groups, such as the American Communist Party. A general climate of opinion was therefore developing that was sympathetic to the work of the Chicago School: in other words, to research that stressed the social contexts of crime. In many ways this is similar to the influence exerted by Fabianism in Britain in the post-war period. At each respective time in history, reformist ideas helped to create conditions conducive to the emergence of a criminology curious about the social contexts of crime. In America the framework within which this criminology was nurtured was urban sociology; in Britain it was community studies. In each case there was a promise of gathering data and constructing explanations that would prove useful for social policy makers.

As we shall see, much of the research carried out by the Chicago School (also known as the Chicago ecologists) concerned itself with juvenile delinquency, just like the sociological criminology in Britain in the 1950s and 1960s. In general terms this meant relating delinquency (the distribution of which was derived from official statistics) to the nature of the social processes associated with the areas in which it occurred. For the Chicago ecologists, social disorganisation was identified as the key explanatory concept (Shaw and McKay, 1942). They were also interested in talking to people, and in this vein carried out a great deal of pioneering work based on in-depth interviews (referred to as the 'life history' approach (Shaw, 1930)). Often there was a social policy dimension to this research. Shaw and McKay, for example, two of the most famous researchers from this period, were attached to a child guidance clinic, although they had close connections with the University of Chicago sociology department, and as such were committed to discovering ways of preventing delinquency. Indeed, Shaw established the 'Chicago Area Project' in the early 1930s, which was a community-based set of initiatives aimed at, for instance, creating better-organised neighbourhoods and providing facilities that would divert youngsters away from delinquent activities. In an assessment of the Project fifty years on, Schlossman *et al.* (1984) credit it with achieving some success in reducing amounts of recorded delinquency in the areas concerned.

One important figure who did depart from this typical concentration on juveniles was Sutherland, who was a professor in the sociology department at Chicago from 1930 to 1935. In the 1940s Sutherland (1940, 1949) turned the spotlight on to white-collar crime (a term he coined), that is, crime committed by persons of high status. This was well in advance of any criminological research on this theme in Britain.

Early 'strain theory'

An alternative approach to explaining crime was put forward by Robert Merton (1993) in 1938. Although Merton was not a criminologist, but a notable figure in sociology, and though his original formulation covered only a few pages, his basic ideas have endured in criminological thought. Unlike the Chicago ecologists, who located the source of criminal behaviour in the socio-cultural characteristics of the neighbourhoods in which they lived, Merton located the source within the social structure of American society itself. For him, crime did not result from the deviant values of the slum neighbourhoods, but rather from mainstream, conventional values into which all Americans were socialised. He argued that the core values stressed material success, but that the problem was that not everyone was equally placed to achieve this success. Hence the existence of 'strain' in some people's lives. In essence, then, property crime resulted from a lack of equality of opportunity, and was therefore a product of social structure. The – to many – startling conclusion was that American society was criminogenic.

Given that crime, for Merton, was a function of relative deprivation, the obvious way to ease the crime problem was to create more opportunities for the poor, so that they had better chances of legitimately achieving material success. As it happens, Merton was himself brought up in a slum neighbourhood, and was well aware of the routine disadvantages experienced by those around him.

Merton's introduction of strain theory into criminology was to have a long-term and profound influence on the shape of sociological studies of crime and delinquency. In the United States, the general principles were picked up and elaborated by, for example, Cohen (1955) and Cloward and Ohlin (1960).

Strain theory and crime policy

The beginning of the 1960s saw a change in the political climate of the United States. The ideas of the strain theorists found fertile ground in a Kennedy administration that had openly embraced a policy of equal opportunities. While the country had achieved massive economic growth in the post-war period, the ideology of the American Dream was subverted by the persistence of poverty, the endemic racial discrimination and disadvantage faced by black and Hispanic people, and rising levels of recorded crime. In terms of social policy, the emphasis shifted from purely community-based schemes that attempted to divert youngsters away from crime, to broader, federally funded initiatives directed at increasing the opportunities available to the disadvantaged. There were direct links here with Merton's version of strain theory. If crime resulted from a lack of legitimate opportunities to achieve the goal of material success, then increasing those opportunities should lead to less crime.

The need to establish equality of opportunity within the education system was centre stage; improving the educational qualifications of the disadvantaged would improve their chances in the job market. Consequently, with the opening up of legitimate avenues to success, there would be less pressure to opt for the illegitimate avenues provided by crime. The aim, of course, was not the creation of a classless society; somehow, equality of opportunity was to be fashioned out of a society where the class structure remained intact. It was a profoundly liberal philosophy that aimed to create a capitalist system with a human face. Criminologists who belonged to the strain theory camp had found some powerful political allies. Of course, the notion of the American Dream still resonates strongly throughout that society. In his first speech as president elect in November 2008, Barack Obama (2008) said:

> If there is anyone out there who still doubts that America is a place where all things are possible, who still wonders if the dream of our founders is alive in our time, who still questions the power of our democracy, tonight is your answer.

There was another dimension to Merton's work that helped it to become influential at this time. By using the concept of relative deprivation, he stressed that it was not deprivation *per se* that was important, but rather the ways in which individuals subjectively experienced deprivation. Specifically, the impact of blocked opportunities was dependent upon the aspirations that people had; from this perspective, problems arise when available opportunities cannot meet these aspirations. Merton, therefore, seemed to offer a plausible explanation of why during periods of affluence recorded crime rates, puzzlingly, continued to rise.

The state-sponsored 'war against poverty' intensified when Kennedy's successor, Lyndon Johnson, took office. Under the direction of the Office of Economic Opportunity – a title that summed up the prevailing ethos – large sums were spent on 'Operation Head Start' and other big initiatives, and these continued into the 1970s. While analyses vary in their explanations, the consensus appears to be that in spite of billions of dollars being expended, the programmes were not significantly successful. As far as recorded crime rates are concerned, these climbed inexorably throughout the 1960s and 1970s.

The link between theory and practice was even more explicit, and finely tuned to delinquent youth, in the case of two other strain theorists, Cloward and Ohlin. As Lilly *et al.* (2007: 74) describe it:

> their opportunity theory 'resonated well with the liberal domestic politics of John F. Kennedy,' and particularly with the president's call for equal opportunity. Indeed, the fit between strain theory and the prevailing political context was so close that Lloyd Ohlin was invited to Washington, D.C. to assume a Health, Education and Welfare post and to assist in formulating delinquency policy.

One outcome of this was the 'Mobilization for Youth' (MFY) delinquency prevention programme; Cloward was appointed director of research. MFY eventually became more radical in its demands than many powerful groups could tolerate: 'MFY promoted boycotts against schools, protests against welfare policies, rent strikes against "slum landlords", lawsuits to ensure poor people's rights, and voter registration' (ibid., 75). And there were claims 'by the *New York Daily News* that the staff was infested with "Commies and Commie Sympathizers"' (ibid., 75). In the end this sort of radicalism led to such programmes being allowed to die. There is a parallel here with the Community Development Projects set up in the 1970s in Britain: once they strayed from fairly narrow parameters – say, helping establish playgroups – complaints of 'going too far' started to appear.

Selected further reading

Radzinowicz, L. (1961) *In Search of Criminology,* London: Heinemann, is a review of this period written by one of its leading figures.

A retrospective account is provided by a later leading figure in British criminology: Cohen, S. (1981) 'Footprints in the sand: A further report on criminology and the sociology of deviance in Britain', in M. Fitzgerald, G. McLennan and J. Pawson (eds) *Crime and Society: Readings in history and theory,* London: Routledge & Kegan Paul/Open University Press.

CHAPTER 5

SOCIAL DISORGANISATION AND ANOMIE

Key themes

- The sociology and criminology of Emile Durkheim (1858–1917)
- The Chicago School
- Mertonian strain theory

INTRODUCTION

In this chapter we examine the important and highly influential early American sociological criminology associated with, first, the Chicago School and, second, Robert K. Merton. The Chicago School was concerned to develop understandings and explanations of crime and the city, while Merton achieved lasting importance within criminology for his version of what came to be known as 'strain theory'. However, because of his enormous influence on the theories of both the Chicago School and Merton (as well as other criminologists), the chapter begins with a discussion of the work of the French sociologist Emile Durkheim, paying particular attention to concepts of social disorganisation and anomie.

THE SOCIOLOGY AND CRIMINOLOGY OF EMILE DURKHEIM (1858–1917)

It is platitudinous to say that Durkheim's influence on sociology, including sociological criminology, has been immense. Unlike Marx and Weber, the other two giants of sociological theory, Durkheim devoted a significant amount of space to the phenomena of crime and deviance. The main links between Durkheim and subsequent developments in the field of criminology can be summarised as follows:

- His work was influential in shifting analyses of criminality away from sources rooted in the individual towards sources that were socio-cultural in nature.
- He was a proponent of the positivist school of thought, especially with reference to methodology: that is, he attempted to develop an objective, scientific understanding of society.

- He characterised societies as 'healthy' or 'unhealthy'/'pathological', assessed in terms of degrees of organisation or disorganisation, and by employing the concept of 'anomie'. These ideas were to have a considerable influence on the Chicago School and R. K. Merton in the period up to World War Two.
- His evolutionary view of social development and the application of social Darwinian principles also influenced the Chicago ecologists, who conceived of the social life of the city in terms of dynamic social processes involving interactions between the inhabitants and their environments.
- He influenced functionalist writers through his discussion of the importance of a consensus regarding norms and values, and the socialisation processes through which this was achieved.
- Later writers were to utilise his argument that crime was both normal and functionally useful.
- His work also represents an interesting early precursor of labelling theory. He argued that the quality of 'crime' or 'deviance' is 'not the intrinsic quality of a given act but that definition which the collective conscience lends them' (Durkheim, 1982: 101).
- Finally, his analysis of the social bonds that secure a cohesive, integrated society, pointed the way to the emergence of control theory much later on in the twentieth century.

Durkheim's sociology

There is not the space to present a detailed discussion of the sociology of Durkheim, and in any case such discussions are widely available (e.g. Lukes, 1973; Giddens, 1978; Fenton, 1984). The intention here is to examine those aspects of his work that are particularly pertinent to issues of crime and deviance, and influenced the ideas of subsequent writers.

A key contributor to functionalist sociology, and strongly committed to positivist principles based on scientific method, Durkheim sought to study human beings and their societies from a fundamentally sociological perspective. By so doing he wished to repudiate those who reduced human behaviour to individual psychological or biological impulses. This is not to say that he rejected the psychological dimension, but rather that he saw psychological states of mind as deriving from the nature of society itself. Indeed, he was centrally concerned with the effects that social forces had on the individual member of society, though sometimes the distinction between the two dimensions is not always clear-cut.

His desire to show the importance of the social dimension is exemplified in his famous study of suicide (Durkheim, 1970). Taking what appears to be one of the most personal, individualised actions, and hence ostensibly more amenable to psychological than sociological modes of analysis, Durkheim in fact located the sources of suicide not in the psyche of the individual, but in a social reality external to the individual. In this way he wished to illustrate how a society was not just a collection of individuals; that it was something more than the sum of its parts. On the basis of a comparative study of different countries, Durkheim noticed that suicide rates had, over time, assumed a definite pattern. They remained fixed at a certain level within the same society, the variation between one society and another also remained fixed, as did the suicide rates pertaining to different groups within the same society (for example, Jews and Catholics). In view of the fact that over these time periods the actual individuals living in the various societies obviously changed, he concluded that the primary source of differential suicide rates lay in an external social realm; there were, in other words, suicidogenic forces at work that were external to the individual. We will return to this below.

Achieving social order

Durkheim was fundamentally concerned with the 'problem of order' and, indeed, this is often referred to as the central 'problem' of sociology. This concern with order and regulation led him to consider issues of crime, deviance and difference. At the time Durkheim was writing, European society was attempting to come to terms with modernity. Industrialisation and urbanisation had profoundly altered the nature of European societies. Rapid, and sometimes abrupt social upheavals had occurred, especially in his own country, France. Not surprisingly, many social thinkers directed their energies at trying to make sense of these changes and their impact on social life. They often looked back to an earlier, pre-industrial golden age of 'community' and, in the process, making unfavourable comparisons with modern life, for example Tonnies (originally 1887, see Loomis, 1957). Others, for example Simmel (1903), directed their worries specifically at the city, which was seen to exemplify modernity and all its ills. Durkheim also counterposed the past – in the shape of traditional, 'primitive' societies – with the present, though he took the view that whilst there was a real danger of sliding into irretrievable disorganisation, those with power could actively intervene to prevent this happening. Sociology, he believed, would provide the knowledge base for such interventions, and in fact he eventually worked with the French government on the design of the state education system.

Mechanical and organic solidarity

In common with other eminent sociological theorists such as Comte and Spencer, Durkheim viewed social change from an evolutionary perspective and, applying Darwinian logic, saw societies as analogous to biological organisms. Just as animals and plants adapt to suit changing circumstances over periods of time, so human societies, as they evolve, have the potential to adapt by developing appropriate social institutions. Societies that did adapt in this way to social change would, from this perspective, be 'healthy'; those that did not, 'pathological'. However, his belief in the need for governmental intervention, guided by scientific knowledge, suggests a departure from the notion of natural selection in the social sphere, and also raises questions about the relative importance of human agency in managing social change.

Durkheim argued that in pre-industrial, traditional societies, social order was based upon a certain kind of social solidarity that he called 'mechanical solidarity'. These societies lacked the complex web of mutually dependent institutions characterising modern societies. Instead they were composed of fragmented, small, tribal or clan-based segments. Solidarity was achieved through an all-encompassing set of norms and values referred to as the 'collective conscience'. Although this constraining moral force was external to the individual – in the form of 'social facts' – through a process of socialisation it became internalised by society's members:

A social fact is every way of acting, fixed or not, capable of exercising on the individual an influence, or an external constraint; or again, every way of acting which is general throughout a given society, while at the same time existing in its own right independent of its individual manifestations.

(Durkheim, 1982: 59)

In this type of society social order was fundamentally rooted in moral regulation. Unlike the situation in modern societies, there was no place for individualism: the individual was, in effect, subsumed or 'lost' within the tribe or clan. Reactions to nonconformity would be harsh and retributive in character.

On the other hand, and according to Durkheim, a central feature of modern societies was individuation. Here individual members are freed from the tyranny of 'sameness', and this illustrates how Durkheim rejected a commonplace late-nineteenth-century sentiment that bemoaned the loss of 'real community'. He did recognise, however, that freeing the individual from the constraints of mechanical solidarity brought with it its own dangers in terms of social order. In his view human nature was composed of two selves: the social self (socialised and integrated), and the egoistic self (unsocialised and unintegrated). The egoistic self, freed from constraining social forces and left to its own devices, naturally possessed desires that knew no bounds. If modern societies were to stress individualism – that is, to have as a central value the right of individuals to realise their own potential – then, Durkheim argued, some restraining mechanism had to operate, otherwise disorder would reign – for example in the form of crime and deviance. For Durkheim, order in modern societies was predicated on the social integration deriving from functionally interdependent institutions, and the division of labour was to play a central role. Modern industrial society is based upon a diverse range of work tasks, tasks that continue to become increasingly specialised. He saw a 'natural' division of labour – that is, one where the individual's work task matched their talents and abilities – as the source of functional interdependency. Although treated as individuals, and perceiving of themselves as individuals, society's members would appreciate the necessity of working together for their mutual benefit. The division of labour is 'the sole process which enables the necessities of social cohesion to be reconciled with the principle of individuation' (Durkheim in Lukes, 1973: 147).

He called this type of solidarity 'organic solidarity', though his discussion of a 'forced' division of labour indicates that Durkheim was aware that modern European societies had some way to go before this happy state of social integration could be said to have arrived. In essence, a forced division of labour is one where people's jobs do not match their abilities, hence his argument that selection processes based upon equality of opportunity were a necessary pre-condition.

The increasing modernisation of society, then, represented a move away from social order based upon mechanical solidarity to one based upon organic solidarity. This entailed a process of individuation, whereby the all-consuming moral regulation of the collective conscience associated with traditional societies, and encompassing all aspects of human behaviour, receded, and social integration deriving from functional interdependency emerged. This did not mean, however, that Durkheim saw no need for moral regulation via a collective conscience; quite the contrary. He believed that a lack of moral force, and with it adherence to a normative system, was an ever-present danger, and *in extremis* would produce a condition of 'anomie'. In an anomic society there are no moral constraints on the individual's limitless desires. Even a society with a division of labour based upon equal opportunities still needed a consensual moral force. The difference would be that in modern societies the collective conscience, whilst having a central moral core, would be flexible enough to allow a high degree of individualism. For Durkheim a modern collective conscience should be constituted by a cluster of values regarding individual dignity, equal opportunities, the work ethic and social justice. Legal rules and rules based on custom would still be required if organic solidarity was to be maintained. With the decline in influence of religious beliefs, Durkheim saw it as imperative that governments intervened in economic and social life in order to establish suitable institutional arrangements and processes of socialisation conducive to the creation of social cohesion. As Sumner (1994: 12) has pointed out in an illuminating discussion of the relevance of Durkheim's thought to contemporary Britain:

> By arguing that the urgent duty and task of the state was to bring the anomic condition
> of society to an end, Durkheim's position is rounded off and he can clearly be seen as an
> early theorist of what we would now call social democracy.

The two concepts egoism and anomie (together with 'altruism' and 'fatalism') also crop up in Durkheim's study of suicide mentioned earlier. Taking a specific example of 'deviant' behaviour, he links certain types of 'pathological' society, as external entities, to the state of mind of individuals living in those societies. His conclusion was that: 'Suicide varies with the degree of integration of the social group of which the individual forms a part' (Durkheim, 1970: 209).

Four different types of suicide were said to result: egoistic, altruistic, anomic and fatalistic (the last type, in fact, is only treated as a footnote, since Durkheim felt that it could be ignored because of its rarity in modern societies). *Egoistic* suicide was the product of 'excessive individualism', whereby individuals are cast adrift from other members of society and are isolated from the shared norms and expectations. At times of trouble such individuals lack the 'mutual moral support' of work, family or community networks. There is a strong link between these ideas and a later development in criminological theory known as control theory. *Altruistic* suicide, on the other hand, occurs when the individual is overintegrated into the group, so that they cease to have a separate, personal identity, thereby denigrating their own worth. This type of suicide includes, for instance, those who take their own lives out of a sense of duty. *Anomic* suicide results from times of upheaval, when the force of moral regulation is weakened – for example, during times of economic slumps or booms – and normative constraints on behaviour cease to be effective. This is sometimes referred to as a state of 'normlessness'. In this situation there is an absence of a moral force in society through which the individual is able to accept their place in the world and the rewards they receive. Lacking this moral restraint an insatiable, though futile, desire for 'more' is released. As Box (1981: 98) puts it:

> Durkheim viewed human aspirations as naturally boundless, and, as he saw it, the trick of social control was not to give people what they want – that would be impossible – but to persuade them that what they have is about all they morally deserve.

Crime as inevitable and necessary

Durkheim is also associated with the argument that crime is both inevitable and necessary. For him crime is a social fact, just as a stable suicide rate is a social fact. If such things are found in an 'average' society, then they are normal; hence crime is normal. In order to appreciate the reasoning behind this, it is important to consider what has already been said regarding Durkheim's views on modernity and individualism. While he endorsed the high moral premium placed on individualism in modern societies, he also recognised that the existence of a flexible, less draconian collective conscience, which provided the breathing space for the individual, would inevitably lead to degrees of nonconformity, and some of this nonconformity would be criminalised. Even in a society composed entirely of saints, he hypothesised, there would still be crime. Extraordinarily high moral standards would be enshrined in the collective conscience, giving an extremely low tolerance threshold, so that what to us are negligible examples of rule breaking become for the saintly brethren terrible acts. This suggests that in the real world it is futile to attempt to eradicate crime by introducing more repression. By closing down areas of freedom through increasingly repressive legislation, previously trivial acts of nonconformity become serious transgressions. In response, the net of legal sanctions is spread even wider, forever criminalising more and more acts.

In order for no crime to exist there would, from Durkheim's perspective, have to be total agreement regarding norms and values among all members of society, but for him 'a uniformity so universal and absolute is utterly impossible' (Durkheim, 1982: 100). An opposite situation arises when there is a weak collective conscience, bringing with it a state of anomie. Here the limitless desires of the individual would be subject to no moral constraint. However, as Bob Roshier (1977) has pointed out, following Durkheimian logic a crime-free society is theoretically possible not only where the collective conscience is all-consuming (albeit in reality an impossible situation for Durkheim), but also where the collective conscience ceased to exist – a society of devils. In this situation there would be no basis for defining any act as criminal, and although such a society is not one that most people would consider emigrating to, it would none the less be crime-free.

An important dimension to this discussion of the inevitability of crime has been highlighted by Sumner. The framework that Durkheim developed opened up a theoretical space for the concept of 'deviance', and therefore a specialism called the sociology of deviance. By illustrating how modernity, by definition, frees the individual from the conformity of a traditional society, bringing with it an inevitable diversity of behaviour, Durkheim acknowledged that some of this diversity will, again inevitably, be socially sanctioned (or censured) as crime or deviance, or in some cases left alone as mere difference. This raises the question of how these various categories are arrived at in practice.

Of course many people would agree with Durkheim that crime is inevitable; the view that it is also necessary, though, has struck some people as very odd. Roshier has pointed out that accidents at work are inevitable, but that does not mean that they are necessary. According to Durkheim, apparently, crime is necessary because it is functionally useful: it helps to maintain a healthy society. Crime does this, he believed, by fulfilling an 'adaptive' function and a 'boundary maintenance' function.

The *adaptive* function of crime is to introduce new ideas into society, thereby preventing that society from stagnating. The criminals concerned are, therefore, innovators who help society to adapt to changing circumstances – unfortunately for the criminals their ideas are ahead of their time. From this viewpoint too much conformity – that is, too little crime – would put the brakes on a society's development. Durkheim gives as an example Socrates, who although condemned in his own time as a criminal, eventually had a beneficent and progressive influence on society through his (criminal) ideas.

In the second case, the *boundary maintenance* function, crime is seen as operating rather like a medieval morality play. Through such things as public hangings, media reporting and conversations between people, the criminal event is inserted into people's lives and functions to reaffirm the boundary between 'good' and 'bad' behaviour. The collective nature of these responses, according to Durkheim, promotes social solidarity. In common with most supporters of the functions-of-crime argument, Kai Erikson (1966) draws on the boundary maintenance function discussed by Durkheim rather than the adaptive function. Using a dispute among members of an early Puritan group in the United States as a case study, Erikson argues that the public trial and then banishment of the dissident minority who refused to follow the elders was functionally necessary in terms of the social solidarity of the whole group. The response of the majority is seen as drawing the new moral boundaries in that society.

An important critique of what he calls the functions-of-crime myth is provided by Roshier (1977). As far as the adaptive function of crime is concerned, Roshier accepts that this is what Durkheim argued, but maintains that he was wrong. In the case of the boundary maintenance function, on the other hand, he argues that this in fact was not what Durkheim was saying, and that Erikson, therefore, has misinterpreted his original source. With respect to Durkheim's view that crime involves innovation and allows society to adapt and progress, Roshier says that to illustrate the validity of this proposition we would have to take specific examples of activities that were previously criminal and show how they eventually contributed to a healthy society, as well as demonstrate that the fact that they were originally criminal was a necessary characteristic of these activities. Roshier concludes that it is the functional value of the *ideas* associated with such activities that is important, not their criminal status. Thus, in the case of Socrates, criminalising his ideas was not required in order to make them subsequently useful. Roshier also points out that while certain activities such as pornography or prostitution might be functionally useful for society, it is not their status as crimes (if they were criminalised) that endows them with this usefulness. In his view society could simply allow a diversity of behaviour, and this would throw up innovative ideas. Durkheim, of course, would argue that this is precisely what modern, individualistic societies do, with the inevitable consequence that some of this diversity is criminalised. His position seems to be that given the likelihood that those behaviours and ideas seen as most threatening to society will be criminalised, then, with the passage of time, there will be an inevitable tendency for diversity of a criminal nature to fulfil this adaptive function. However, this still leaves the question: Does the behaviour by necessity have to be criminal? Durkheim appears to be arguing that crime will fulfil this adaptive function *inevitably* rather than *necessarily*.

Turning to the boundary maintenance function of crime, Roshier argues that Durkheim's views have been misinterpreted by Erikson and others, and offers this as a key passage:

> If then, when (a crime) is committed, the consciences which it offends do not unite themselves to give mutual evidence of their communion, and recognize that the case is anomolous, they would be permanently unsettled. They must re-enforce themselves

by mutual assurances that they are always agreed. The only means for this is action in common. In short it is the common conscience which is attacked, it must be that which resists, and accordingly the resistance must be collective.

(Durkheim quoted in Roshier, 1977: 5)

According to Roshier, Durkheim is not saying that crime, as such, maintains the moral boundaries between right and wrong in a particular society, but that a collective response to crime – that is, social control – fulfils this function. If there is no crime or deviance, then by definition social solidarity exists, because there is complete consensus over norms and values. For Durkheim, though, this situation is not only impossible to achieve, but the very idea is not congruent with the values placed on individualism in a modern society. Thus, again, Durkheim is saying that the existence of crime is inevitable, and as Roshier points out, responses to it must be collective. In the specific case discussed by Erikson, it could be argued that the deviance of the dissenting group was not a necessary pre-condition for the acceptance of the new moral boundaries. If no split had occurred, then arguably the moral boundaries would have been universally agreed upon anyway.

THE CHICAGO SCHOOL

Durkheim once commented that the platform of the railway station in Paris on to which France's rural workers alighted, and made their first contact with a new life in the city, seemed to possess magical qualities. As soon as their feet touched the platform, all religious beliefs disappeared.

Throughout the nineteenth century social thinkers in Europe had been variously appalled, excited or fascinated by the consequences of urbanisation, and one of the main consequences was judged to be an increase in crime. As the nineteenth century developed, studies of urban life and criminality were increasingly influenced by the ideas of positivism, though explanations of crime tended to emphasise social rather than individual factors. A positivist commitment to scientific method is well represented in the statistical work of the Belgium mathematician Quetelet, and the French lawyer Guerry. Referring to their endeavours as 'social physics' and 'moral statistics' respectively, they analysed official records relating to the amount and distribution of crime in the city. The published statistical results were seen as scientific measures of the moral life of the city. This sort of social scientific research eventually began to influence research in Britain. Motivated by a strong sense of a philanthropic, reforming mission, figures such as Fletcher, Mayhew and Booth amassed a wealth of highly detailed information on the dark side of city life. By the late nineteenth century, however, and especially because of the influence of Lombroso, attempts to locate the social bases of crime began to be superseded by positivistic studies oriented towards the individual.

The early social researchers produced graphic descriptions of life among the urban poor, and in the process introduced the notion of the criminal area. Cities were associated with crime, but it was in certain parts of the city that crime and deviance were seen to be concentrated. Then, and now, there are potent images of dark and 'dangerous places'. Nineteenth-century accounts made reference to the undeserving poor, debauchery, disorder and insanity; nowadays it is the underclass, the inner city and deprived council estates, social disorganisation and 'yob culture'. From Mayhew's writings on the rookeries of Victorian London to contemporary accounts of life in the deprived inner cities and outer council estates of Britain, there stretches a deep seam of criminological research.

Whilst the late-nineteenth-century shift to positivist explanations that sought to locate the sources of criminality within the individual set in motion a continuing tradition of this type of criminology, the stress on the social aspect was to re-emerge powerfully soon afterwards in the United States in the shape of the Chicago School. Some of the organisational features of the department of sociology at the University of Chicago have already been discussed. So too has the way in which the city of Chicago provided a social laboratory for these sociologists during the 1920s and 1930s; Chicago seemed to encapsulate all of the salient characteristics of the modern city.

The members of the Chicago School were clearly acquainted with, and influenced by, the work of Durkheim. This manifested itself on a number of fronts:

- Crime and crime rates were viewed as social phenomena, and were not to be explained in terms of the individual's biology or psychology.
- Crime was linked to social disorganisation, whereby family and community-based bonds were weakened. Low levels of social integration were associated with high levels of crime.
- It was the social life of certain neighbourhoods that was seen as 'pathological', and not the people living in them. Criminal behaviour was regarded as a normal response to an abnormal situation; in a spirit of optimism it was viewed as a temporary phenomenon arising out of periods of rapid social change.
- Drawing on social Darwinism, crime was seen as part of an evolutionary process of adaptation.
- A certain amount of crime in society was accepted as inevitable and of no threat to that society.
- There should be government intervention to improve the sources of social organisation in the criminal areas of the city.

The key figure behind the work of the Chicago School was Robert Park, an ex-journalist who had studied sociology in Germany, and who had apparently dabbled in delinquency himself in his younger days. Park established the basic framework for research by arguing that the city was best viewed as an ecological system, comparable to the ecological systems associated with plants and animals. He also argued that in order to carry out proper research, researchers should go into the city and discover at first hand what was going on. This led to a large number of ethnographic studies being conducted by sociology department members, and indicates an attempt to integrate two research methodologies: a quantitative one oriented towards positivism and a qualitative one oriented towards interpretive sociology.

As the name suggests, a social ecological perspective sees the city in terms of a web of interdependent relationships created by people as they adapt to a changing environment. According to this perspective, these adaptations follow an evolutionary pattern and are comparable to the modes of adaptation found among species of plants and animals as they adjust to changes in their environments. Thus cities such as Chicago had not developed on a random basis, but rather this development was patterned according to 'natural' social processes. The outcome is that cities evolve their own particular types of neighbourhood, each with their own type of social life. Some of these are stable, well-organised neighbourhoods, but others are more socially disorganised, and it is here that social problems, including crime, are concentrated. Proponents of a social ecological model argued that neighbourhoods have periodically to cope with an influx of outsiders (e.g., new immigrants or business organisations), leading to conflict and a 'struggle over space'. Eventually, equilibrium is restored, but not without winners and losers according to the Darwinian principle of the survival of the fittest. From this perspective the city is in a state of flux, as market forces and evolutionary processes lead to the the migration of people from one neighbourhood to another; those who leave then conform to the values and norms of their new neighbourhood. In the most deprived areas, characterised by transient populations who are unable to put down roots, will be found those values and norms most conducive to criminal behaviour. Thus the Chicago ecologists rejected explanations of criminality that focused on particular individuals. For them, the fact that neighbourhoods with high crime rates continued to have high crime rates even when the original inhabitants had moved out, showed that it was not the people but rather the social characteristics of the neighbourhood that led to crime – some areas were criminogenic.

In a book published in 1925 one of Park's colleagues, Ernest Burgess, attempted to map out the results of these processes in Chicago. His 'social map' of the city consisted of five zones forming concentric circles. In the middle stood the Central Business District, where banks, insurance companies and the like had their offices. Four residential zones then radiated out from this central area, with each zone containing various subsections. Of particular importance was the Zone of Transition, which skirted the Central Business District. It was here that most of Chicago's poorest citizens lived: new immigrants and various groups lacking access to urban survival kits. Housing was of low quality and largely comprised cheap lodging houses nestling in the shadows of decaying factories. According to Burgess, this was the zone in which crime was likely to be concentrated. The next zone contained the houses of the more respectable working class and was the escape route from the ghetto. The assumption seemed to be that in general, and given time, most people would be successful in their escape attempts.

Clifford Shaw and Henry McKay (1942), two researchers from a local child guidance clinic with close ties with the sociology department at Chicago, attempted to test Burgess's model by looking at the distribution of juvenile delinquency in the city. Their findings supported the ecological thesis that even when individuals living in a particular neighbourhood moved on to greener pastures, crime rates remained the same in the neighbourhood they had left behind.

The high rates of juvenile crime found in the Zone of Transition were said to be linked to the social disorganisation in those areas. In the absence of strong normative controls from the family and the community, juveniles were likely to engage in delinquent activities. This was an idea that was eventually to influence the development of control theory. Although Shaw and McKay had, through their analysis of crime statistics, satisfied themselves that criminal areas existed and could be identified, they agreed with Park that in order to establish precisely what processes were at work, it was necessary to talk to and observe at first hand those involved. Thus were born two important research methods associated with the Chicago School: first, the construction of 'life histories' via in-depth interviews, and second, the use of participant observation as the basis for what Matza (1969) calls the 'appreciative' study of delinquency. This indicates the acknowledged debt that the Chicago School owed to writers in the symbolic interactionist tradition, such as Thomas, Cooley and Mead. A research strategy that sought to present the social world from the point of view of those being studied, and to 'tell it like it is', lay at the core of symbolic interactionist methodology. The result was that the Chicago School generated a large number of detailed, appreciative studies during the 1920s and 1930s, some of which have now achieved the status of classics. Some of the more notable examples are: *The Hobo*, Anderson (1975), first published in 1923; *The Gang*, Thrasher (1963), first published in 1927; *The Jack-Roller: A delinquent boy's own story*, Shaw (1930); *The Natural History of a Delinquent Career*, Shaw and Moore (1931); *The Professional Thief: By a professional thief*, Sutherland (1937); *Brothers in Crime*, Shaw, McKay and MacDonald (1938); and in a similar vein, though set in Boston, *Street Corner Society*, Whyte (1955), written in 1930, and first published in 1943.

In their studies of juvenile offenders, Shaw and McKay extended the explanations offered by ecological theory by introducing the concept of cultural transmission. Delinquent values, they argued, became established in criminal areas, and were then passed on to a new generation of youngsters. It is, therefore, an explanation of delinquency deriving from learning theory. Criminal areas, where those sorts of values predominated, were counterposed against a mainstream, consensual culture into which law-abiding juveniles were socialised.

Shaw and McKay's ideas were picked up by Edwin Sutherland, who spent the first half of the 1930s at the University of Chicago. Sutherland's work, though, marked an important theoretical change of direction which was to permeate the Chicago School as the 1930s progressed. There had always been an inherent tension at the heart of social disorganisation theory. The use of appreciative research methods had presented the social world of the delinquent as coherent and meaningful to the participants. However, by relying on the notion of social disorganisation as a way of explaining that delinquency – and with it the assumption that there existed a conformist, consensual mainstream society that was by definition socially organised – the social world of the delinquent was pathologised. Sutherland's (1939) important contribution was to depathologise the criminal area. He did this by developing a model of criminality based upon assumptions of cultural plurality. Instead of social disorganisation, he spoke of differential social organisation, and questioned the ready acceptance of the existence of consensus. Neighbourhoods, in his view, were not disorganised, but rather organised in different ways, one outcome being differential crime rates. And with his concept of 'differential association' Sutherland analysed criminality in terms of a person's exposure to particular cultural influences, seeing this as the mechanism whereby some became criminals and others did not: 'a person becomes delinquent because of an excess of definitions favourable to violation of law over definitions unfavourable to violation of law' (Sutherland quoted in Taylor *et al.*, 1973: 126).

In this formulation Sutherland is arguing that delinquency is learned in the same way that any other types of behaviour are learned. Through differential association the individual not only learns how to commit crime – for example, how to break into a car – but also the moral outlook and motivations conducive to criminal behaviour. Through his refinement of the concept of differential association Sutherland had, by the 1940s, made a significant break with dominant explanations of criminality. For Sutherland these were too narrowly focused on deprived youth, and made an unwarranted assumption that crime was basically a product of poverty. His 1937 study of a professional thief signalled this change of emphasis, but it was his classic study of white-collar crime, first published in the late 1940s, that finally left the slum behind. Crime, he argued, was widespread among those with high status in America. Unfortunately, most of this crime remained invisible, so that official crime statistics gave a misleading impression of the nature of criminal behaviour. Sutherland believed that differential association was able to explain white-collar and corporate crime as well as the crime committed by the youth living in the Zone of Transition.

The Chicago School: an assessment

There is no doubt that the ideas generated by the Chicago School had a significant influence on subsequent sociological criminology. In particular, as we have seen, those associated with the sociology department at Chicago locked into a nineteenth-century tradition of providing accounts of life among the urban poor. By developing more sophisticated theoretical explanations and research methodologies, they were then instrumental in influencing an important modern tradition of areal studies in

Britain and the United States. The use of participant observation and a 'life histories' approach has continued to influence many rich ethnographic studies. In addition, elements of what became known as control theory, and the foundations for the growth of subcultural approaches should be noted.

Looking back over the two decades of the 1920s and 1930s at the huge amount of work produced by the Chicago School, however, it is clear that it does not stand as a single, agreed body of knowledge. As Heidensohn (1989: 18–19) puts it:

> There is no single definitive view in their work; indeed, as was inevitable in such a productive group, ideas diverged between different writers and even within the work of one man . . . their work was not systematised and did not generate a 'finished system of sociology'.

In many ways those involved were finding their feet. They were caught up in a variety of theoretical influences and cross-currents. Individuals changed their mind, and sometimes contradictory ideas coexisted for a while. With reference to their use of life histories, Matza (1969) speaks approvingly of their commitment to 'appreciative' sociology, to a sociology concerned with letting people tell their own stories. And yet researchers such as Shaw and McKay were also strongly committed to pinning down the causes of crime, and to social policy-based interventions that would lead to a reduction in criminal behaviour. This is an approach that Matza disparages for being 'causal-corrective'. Likewise, although many were influenced by the ideas of symbolic interactionism, which sees individuals as actively constructing their social worlds through interactions with others, the Chicago School is frequently criticised for its positivism – for example, the deterministic view that environments determine people's behaviour. In fact, as we have seen, Sutherland's contributions during the 1930s moved the Chicago School away from seeing society as a consensus, and some localities as enclaves of disorganisation and criminal values, towards a position of cultural pluralism. Again, though, this was a tension that was never fully resolved, and returns us to one of the central issues in Durkheim's work: how can social order be achieved in a modern society that places a high premium on individualism, and with it the cultural space for pluralism and diversity?

Although Sutherland went on to address the issue of white-collar crime in the 1940s, one particularly striking feature of the work of the Chicago School during the 1920s and 1930s is that with one exception (Landesco, 1968) it ignored organised crime, as well as the crimes of the powerful and the 'respectable'. This, remember, was a period in Chicago's (and America's) history that saw Prohibition, large-scale crime syndicates, gangland luminaries such as Al Capone, and significant levels of corruption among city officials and politicians. Hollywood did not miss the opportunities, but it is therefore ironic that the Chicago sociologists did. Sumner (1994: 31–2) provides one of the few discussions of the Chicago School that includes some details relating to these wider criminal activities: 'Two billion dollars' worth of business shifted from the old established brewers and the bar-owners to the bootleggers and the "hoods"; money which they continually reinvested in gambling, prostitution, labour unions, regular business and extortion'. In an interesting, and telling, footnote, he adds: 'As Harold Finestone, a doctoral student there in the 1930s, once told me in conversation, in response to my query about the lack of studies on the mob itself: the mob was the government at that time, and you don't do fieldwork on the government, do you?' (ibid.: 51).

Finally, we can conclude this section by briefly outlining some of the main criticisms that have been levelled at the Chicago School:

- There was a reliance on, and faith in, official crime statistics.
- Writers such as Shaw referred to 'delinquent areas'. What was unclear, though, was the distinction between an area in which delinquents lived, and areas in which delinquency took place.
- The earlier work has often been accused of being tautological. Crime is seen as a product of social disorganisation, and yet crime is an example of social disorganisation.
- The ecological models of the city, with their descriptions of the 'natural area', missed out of the equation class conflict and an unequal distribution of power – for example, the actions of slum landlords.
- On the same ecological theme, there tends to be a picture of criminals as determined creatures, moulded by their environments.
- To what extent was an ecological system used merely as a metaphor, as opposed to an actual description of social life in the city?
- By concentrating on poor areas, the Chicago School overpredicted the crimes of the poor; clearly, not all poor people engaged in criminal behaviour. Thus it has been said that their work served to perpetuate dominant stereotypes.
- With reference to the later theory based upon cultural transmission, the origins of the delinquent culture being transmitted were never clearly explained.
- The notion of differential association developed by Sutherland has been criticised for not being amenable to empirical verification, because of the enormous range of experiences that individuals have.
- It has been argued that close analysis of the data shows that crime rates in particular localities were in fact not stable over periods of time.
- There are the usual criticisms of a life histories approach – for example, the truthfulness of those being interviewed.
- In common with most criminological research at that time, the victims of crime were ignored, along with the reactions of control agents and their role in the construction of deviance.

MERTONIAN STRAIN THEORY

Robert K. Merton was a key figure in the functionalist school of thought that dominated American sociology during the 1940s and 1950s. Although not a criminological specialist, functionalism's primary interest in the nature of social order inevitably led him to consider issues of crime and deviance. The classic, and much discussed, article in which Merton (1993) first presented his ideas was originally published in 1938 (and subsequently revised) in his book *Social Theory and Social Structure*. The title of this article, 'Social structure and anomie', indicates a connection with Durkheim, and it stands as the seminal work within a criminological tradition known as 'strain theory'.

In simple terms strain theory, as the name suggests, is an attempt to answer the question that common sense perhaps impresses upon us: what sorts of 'faulty' social conditions make some people act in deviant ways? (We should note in passing the presupposition in the question that deviance must be a result of something going wrong.) At the time that Merton was writing, and in spite of the contributions of the Chicago School, answers to the question 'What went wrong?' tended to focus on the individual. Merton, on the other hand, was committed to a sociological level of analysis, where the sources of deviance are traced to the nature of the social structure. Rejecting efforts to individualise, or 'atomise' the causes of deviance, he argued that deviance arose in certain groups, 'not because the human beings comprising them are compounded of distinctive biological tendencies but because they are responding normally to the social situation in which they find themselves' (Merton, 1993: 250). It is worth pausing here to consider in more detail the concept of 'strain' as used by Merton.

When being interviewed in 1987 (see Cullen and Messner, 2007), that is half a century after *Social Theory and Social Structure* was first published, he argued against the by then commonplace view that his theory should be described as strain theory. However, it is clear that he had a very specific social-psychological version of strain theory in mind, and it is this that he was keen to distance himself from. With this version, the focus is on the individual, and their deviant behaviour is seen as a psychological response to 'strains' in their life (for more recent examples of this version of strain theory, see Kornhauser, 1978 and Agnew, 1987). Merton, on the other hand, focused on rates of deviance in society as a whole, on an aggregate level, seeing these as the result of anomie inherent in the social structure of American society (and for more recent examples of this version of strain theory, see Bernard, 1987 and Messner and Rosenfeld, 2001). This thoroughly sociological approach, an approach reflecting the fundamental concerns of structural functionalism (at that time the dominant paradigm within American sociology), therefore, operates on the same conceptual level as Durkheim's study of suicide, in that the sources of 'strain' are located in society, rather than the individual. Baumer (2007) has recently sought to develop a 'multi-level' theoretical analysis that attempts to combine each of these versions of strain theory into a single theory.

For Merton the 'social situation' referred to in the above quote is the product of a disjunction between, on the one hand, culture, and on the other, social structure. Individuals living in American society, as participants in the American Dream, are, he says, socialised into desiring certain cultural *goals*; chief among these is the goal of material success. At the same time, the social structure provides various legitimate *means* through which material success can be achieved – passing examinations, working hard in business, and so on. However, when there is a lack of fit between the goals and the means – that is, when opportunities are blocked for individuals because of their social class position, even though the message is that everyone can succeed if they have the ability – then problems of 'strain' arise: there is a 'contradiction between the cultural emphasis on pecuniary ambition and the social bars to full opportunity' (ibid.: 260). Merton describes this type of society – where there is a lack of equality of opportunity, coupled with a strong emphasis on material success – as 'anomic'. Deviant behaviour is seen as resulting from reactions to situations of anomie.

According to Merton, this tendency towards deviance is not simply a result of limited opportunities for some people. As he notes, there are societies where very few opportunities for social advancement exist, and the gap between rich and poor is enormous, and yet relatively little deviant behaviour occurs. The crucial factor for Merton is where socialisation processes strongly emphasise the achievement of material success. He saw the United States as just such a society. A disjunction between this cultural goal and the opportunities, or legitimate means, within the social structure for achieving it, creates strains which, says Merton, individuals will adapt to in different ways. On the basis of this reasoning, he suggested the following 'ideal type' set of 'modes of adaptation', where (+) signifies 'acceptance', (−) signifies 'rejection', and (±) signifies 'rejection of prevailing values and substitution of new values' (see Table 5.1).

Apart from 'conformity', where individuals accept both cultural goals and the institutionalised means, irrespective of how they are actually performing, the categories represent various sorts of deviant adaptation. 'Innovation' describes a situation

Table 5.1   *A typology of modes of individual adaptation*

	Modes of adaptation	Cultural goals	Institutionalised means
I	Conformity	+	+
II	Innovation	+	−
III	Ritualism	−	+
IV	Retreatism	−	−
V	Rebellion	±	±

where the individual has been socialised normally into accepting the goal of material success, but, faced with a lack of legitimate means for achieving the goal, resorts to deviance. In this formulation, this constitutes the source of property crime. With 'ritualism', the individual has given up on the goals and merely goes through the motions: 'The original purposes are forgotten and close adherence to institutionally prescribed conduct becomes a matter of ritual' (ibid.: 251). Although this adaptation involves conformity to the means, it is, for Merton, deviant in so far as the individual has jettisoned the goal of material success. 'Retreatism' occurs when the individual gives up on both the goals and the means, and in effect drops out of normal society. Here Merton had in mind hobos and drug addicts. Finally, 'rebellion' applies to those individuals who reject the dominant cultural goals, together with the legitimate means for achieving them, in favour of alternative goals and means; political revolutionaries would occupy this category.

Invoking as it does notions of winning and losing, and playing or not playing according to the rules, Merton's version of strain theory has often induced commentators to search for analogies with games. In fact Merton himself mentions football, wrestling, athletics and poker. Usually, though, a game analogy crops up within the context of a sentence such as 'in Merton's theory it is as if society was like a . . .' The best-known British example is probably a 'fruit machine', introduced by Laurie Taylor (1971). Taylor goes on to explain how the machine is rigged (a lack of opportunities), leading different players to respond in different ways according to Merton's typology. Heidensohn (1989) prefers to use an analogy with a bowling alley. One imagines criminology lecturers worldwide bringing out their own particular favourites (mine is poker) when they discuss Merton (readers can choose their own).

Merton's anomie

Although Merton uses the Durkheimian concept of anomie, and develops a theoretical explanation of deviance as illustrated above, the meaning that he gives to anomie is not consistent. For much of the article he in fact follows Durkheim and uses the concept to describe a society where there is a lack of moral regulation:

> contemporary American culture continues to be characterized by a heavy emphasis on wealth as a basic symbol of success, without a corresponding emphasis upon the legitimate avenues on which to march towards this goal.
>
> (Merton, 1993: 255)

A lack of moral regulation has unleashed an unrestrained desire for material success; individuals want everything, but are no longer willing to play according to the rules. Clearly, under these circumstances an increase in property crime is likely. However, as some commentators have pointed out, Merton moves away from this Durkheimian definition of anomie and gives it a rather different meaning: 'Durkheim's conception of anomie raised problems for Merton because the logical and empirical implications of it ran counter to his beliefs about the social distribution of deviant behaviour' (Box, 1981: 98–9).

If American society was anomic in the sense that Durkheim used the term, then deviant behaviour would be distributed among all social classes. Although mentioning problems with official statistics, and referring to white-collar crime, Merton (1993: 259) did none the less conclude that deviance was in general linked to poverty:

> Of those located in the lower reaches of the social structure, the culture makes incompatible demands. On the one hand, they are asked to orient their conduct toward the prospect of large wealth . . . and on the other, they are largely denied effective opportunities to do so institutionally.

Thus in order to remain true to his belief that deviance was concentrated among the deprived, Merton had to move away from Durkheim's definition of anomie, for that would apply to the whole of American society. In terms of his understanding of the distribution of deviant behaviour, he logically saw anomie as the product of a lack of equality of opportunity within a society that, on the one hand, celebrated supposed opportunities for all and, on the other, placed enormous emphasis on the desirability of material success. From this perspective, the end result was relative deprivation, that is, a situation where people feel 'cheated', in that their (to them) realistic expectations regarding material success have not been met. As discussed earlier, the ideas of strain theory, including Merton's version, were to influence those political administrations that saw the creation of equality of opportunity via poverty programmes as the way to solve the problem of crime.

Criticisms

While Merton's work has been, and continues to be, highly influential within criminology, it has over the years been subject to a barrage of criticism. Some of the main criticisms can be summarised as follows:

- There is too much reliance on official statistics.
- As a theory it predicts too much lower-class crime.
- The various modes of individual adaptation are difficult to classify in reality. Thus value judgements are likely to be used when assigning individuals to specific categories.
- Although the source of deviance lies in the social structure, responses of a deviant nature are conceptualised in individual terms. This ignores the importance of collective responses.

- It is unclear why particular individuals opt for one type of adaptation rather than another.
- The theory does not explain non-utilitarian deviance: that is, deviance such as rape or criminal damage that is not oriented towards material success.
- The theory cannot accommodate the wide variety of deviant motivations and types of deviant behaviour (e.g. domestic violence, rape and murder).
- How and why does addiction, associated with 'retreatism', result from anomie? Could addiction not lead to anomie?
- There is an assumption of a monolithic culture oriented towards material success, and this ignores the plurality of cultural values. It may be that lower-class individuals typically set their sights on extremely modest goals in the full knowledge that to do otherwise would be unrealistic.
- Social control as a factor shaping deviant behaviour is ignored.
- The theory fails to address those situations where means exceed goals: that is, where individuals have 'too much', leading them into deviant behaviour.
- Has Merton exhausted the possibilities with respect to modes of adaptation? In other words, is it logically possible to continue his table using permutations based upon (±) and (+)/(−)? In an interesting recent discussion, Murphy and Robinson (2008) suggest adding 'Maximizer' to Merton's original typology: 'someone who simultaneously uses and incorporates legitimate and illegitimate means of opportunity in the pursuit of profit and/or monetary gain (the American Dream)' (ibid.: 502).
- He ignores those situations where deviant behaviour occurs prior to a lack of success in achieving cultural goals.
- He fails to appreciate that deviant motivations may be oriented towards emotional or sensual pleasure (Katz, 1988; Young, 2003b).

Since they were first introduced to the world, Merton's ideas have inspired a large volume of research on anomie, crime and deviance. Some criminologists have, for instance, drawn on Merton's theory and applied it to analyses of white-collar and corporate crime (Menard, 1995; Passas and Agnew, 1997), whilst Paranaby and Sacco (2004) have focused on celebrity and deviance. It should be noted, though, that whilst Merton believed that the strains in American society would have a greater impact on poorer, rather than richer people, leading to more deviance among the former, he did acknowledge that deviance was in evidence among all sections of society – see Merton (1957) for a discussion of deviance within the scientific community. From a social-psychological perspective, Agnew (1992) has examined the strains arising from the 'removal of positively valued stimuli' (for example, due to bereavement) and the 'presentation of negative stimuli' (for example, the trauma associated with being a victim of crime) and subsequent deviant behaviour. Following Merton, Messner and Rosenfeld (2001) agree that the excessive stress placed upon material success in the United States perpetuates a condition of anomie, and with it a high level of crime.

However, they disagree with Merton that creating greater equality of opportunity will necessarily lead to a reduction in anomie and attendant criminal behaviour. This, they argue, is because the cultural goal of material success is so deeply embedded within non-economic institutions, such as schools and families, that it is never seriously challenged. Messner and Rosenfeld describe their approach as 'institutional-anomie theory'.

Selected further reading

The following two books were written by the leading lights of the Chicago School during the 1930s: **Shaw, C. R. (1930)** *The Jack-Roller*, **Chicago, IL: University of Chicago Press**; **Shaw, C. R. and McKay, H. D. (1942)** *Juvenile Delinquency in Urban Areas*, **Chicago, IL: University of Chicago Press**. A special issue of the journal *Theoretical Criminology*, **11(4), November 2007**, is made up of a series of contemporary articles on Shaw's *The Jack-Roller*.

A classic ethnographic study from the Chicago School is: **Thrasher, F. M. (1963; first pub. 1927)** *The Gang*, **Chicago, IL: University of Chicago Press**.

A large number of classic texts from the Chicago School are reproduced in **Beirne, P. (ed) (2005)** *The Chicago School of Criminology, 1914–1945*, **Abingdon: Routledge**.

For a general discussion of Durkheim's work, see **Lukes, S. (1973)** *Emile Durkheim, His Life and Work: Historical and critical study*, **Harmondsworth: Penguin** and **Fenton, S. (ed) (1984)** *Durkheim and Modern Sociology*, **Cambridge: Cambridge University Press**.

Merton's use of strain theory and the concept of anomie can be found in **Merton, R. K. (1993; first pub. 1938) 'Social structure and anomie', in C. Lemert (ed)** *Social Theory: The multicultural readings*, **Boulder, CO: Westview Press**. The journal *Theoretical Criminology*, **11(1), February 2007** is devoted largely to a number of articles on Merton, anomie and relative deprivation.

All the general textbooks referred to at the end of Chapter 1 discuss criminological theory during this period.

CHAPTER 6

STRAIN, SUBCULTURES AND DELINQUENCY

> **Key themes**
> - A. K. Cohen: developments in strain theory
> - R. Cloward and L. Ohlin: opportunity knocks

INTRODUCTION

In the United States, the 1950s and 1960s saw the emergence of versions of strain theory linked to the dynamics of adolescent delinquent subcultures. This chapter discusses the work of A. K. Cohen, and R. Cloward and L. Ohlin, the major figures associated with subcultural strain theory.

A. K. COHEN: DEVELOPMENTS IN STRAIN THEORY

In *Delinquent Boys*, published in 1955, Albert Cohen offers his own version of strain theory. As with Merton before him, Cohen attempts to explore sociologically those features of American society that create strains for some people, leading eventually to delinquent behaviour. His conclusion is similar to Merton's in that he sees criminogenic pressures as being inherent in the society itself:

> those values which are at the core of the 'American way of life', which help to motivate the behavior which we most esteem as 'typically American', are among the major determinants of that which we stigmatize as 'pathological' . . . the problems of adjustment to which the delinquent subculture is a response are determined, in part, by those very values which respectable society holds most sacred.
>
> (Cohen, 1955: 137)

He also follows Merton by assuming that the bulk of delinquency is found within the lower working class, though unlike Merton, Cohen concentrates specifically on adolescence: 'The delinquent subculture is mostly found in the working class' (ibid.: 73). Having said that, Cohen's work is riddled with caveats through which he is at pains to point out, for instance, that not all lower-working-class boys become delinquent, and that delinquency also exists among middle-class boys. He also departs from Merton by drawing on psychology and includes the notion of 'psychogenic factors'. Here again there are various caveats. He accepts that there may be different types of delinquency, each resulting from different causal processes, but he is particularly interested in what he sees as those processes causally linked to most delinquent activity: 'in the majority of cases psychogenic and subcultural factors blend in a single causal process, as pollen and a particular bodily constitution work together to produce hay fever' (ibid.: 17). From this we can clearly see that Cohen believed that some individuals, whatever their social circumstances, were predisposed to delinquency; he was interested in what triggered it. As a result of these various caveats, Cohen was left with a core of what he described as 'typical' adolescent delinquency, and he therefore focused on young, lower-class males committed to the delinquent values of the subculture.

There are also links between Cohen's work and Sutherland's theory of differential association, and this indicates another departure from Merton's version of strain theory. Whereas Merton conceived of deviant adaptations in individual terms, Cohen followed Sutherland and saw delinquency as a collective response; in other words, he highlights delinquent subcultures. Furthermore, although, like Merton, he invokes the idea of the American Dream, its saliency derives from differential access to status rather than to material success.

Cohen's basic argument is that American society is dominated by what he calls middle-class, mainstream norms and values, and through the mass media and the education system these permeate the whole of society. It is against these that individuals are judged. Unfortunately, lower-class boys, referred to by Cohen as 'corner boys' (a term he borrowed from William Foote Whyte (1955)), are ill-equipped, because of their socialisation, to compete with middle-class boys in the status stakes. The corner boy is pictured as organising his life around working-class values, finding satisfaction in the close-knit companionship of his mates. It is, however, a milieu that inhibits vertical mobility. The outcome is that in early adolescence such boys are faced with a 'problem of adjustment', as they are denied the status more readily given to their middle-class counterparts:

> In the status game, then, the working-class child starts out with a handicap and, to the extent that he cares what middle-class persons think of him or has internalized the dominant middle-class attitudes toward social class position, he may be expected to feel some 'shame'.
>
> (Cohen, 1955: 110)

Cohen outlines three 'ideal type' responses open to the corner boy, and again he draws on Whyte's terminology: the 'stable corner boy', the 'college boy', and the 'delinquent boy'. The stable corner boy response involves an ambivalent acceptance of one's lot in life, with individuals accommodating themselves to their situation as best they can, and this may include some mild acts of delinquency. The college boy response, as the name suggests, applies to those lower-working-class boys who, having to a significant extent internalised middle-class cultural norms, aspire to improve themselves through educational success, and hence compete with the middle class on their own terms. The delinquent boy response is the one that Cohen is particularly interested in. Using the Freudian concept of 'reaction formation', he argues that some boys, faced with a lack of status by the carriers of middle-class culture who are able to judge them, join together with others in the same situation and develop a delinquent subculture. While acknowledging that Merton's version of strain theory can explain criminal activities carried out for monetary gain, in Cohen's view it cannot explain day-to-day, working-class delinquency which, he argues, is mainly non-utilitarian and negativistic (e.g., fighting and vandalism).

The psychological concept of reaction formation describes a situation where the individual who is denied something they desire, reacts by disparaging it to excess. In the context of Cohen's study the denial of status leads some to seek out others who share the same 'problem of adjustment'; the resultant subculture develops an exaggerated hostility towards middle-class values. In effect, it is a contra-culture within which middle-class norms and values are inverted; now an activity is 'right' because mainstream culture says it is 'wrong'. This raises an important issue.

For Cohen, a crucial aspect of this process of delinquency creation is that the corner boys care about their lack of status:

> most children are sensitive *to some degree* about the attitudes of *any persons* with whom they are thrown into more than the most superficial kind of contact. The contempt or indifference of others, particularly of those like schoolmates and teachers, with whom we are constrained to associate for long hours every day, is difficult, we suggest, to shrug off.
>
> (Ibid.: 123, original emphasis)

The candidate for delinquency cares, according to Cohen, because:

> To the degree to which he values middle-class status, either because he values the good opinion of middle-class persons or because he has to some degree internalized middle-class standards himself, he faces a problem of adjustment and is in the market for a 'solution'.
>
> (Ibid.: 119)

However, as Box (1981) has shown, this suggests that the delinquent boy can feel either resentment or shame/guilt, or both. The working-class boy may resent the low status that he is given, simply because it is difficult to be indifferent, but this does not mean that he sees his own culture as inferior and desires middle-class status. A feeling of resentment might lead to delinquency, but it might also lead to an angry resignation. The important element in Cohen's theory, though, is reaction formation, and this requires more than resentment. Reaction formation requires the shame/guilt and the rejection of something previously desired, in this case middle-class status. Thus Cohen's theory of delinquency is based upon the assumption that the typical working-class delinquent to some degree internalises middle-class norms and values prior to the creation of the subculture. Put another way, the assumption is that middle-class culture is widely dispersed and accepted throughout all social classes. This has been picked up by some of Cohen's critics, in particular those who have developed an explanation of delinquency based upon cultural diversity. Proponents of this approach have questioned the view that middle-class norms and values are internalised by lower-working-class boys early on in their lives. There has also been much criticism of the characterisation of delinquent working-class boys as vehemently anti-middle-class culture (e.g. Short and Strodtbeck, 1965; Downes, 1966). In fact, Cohen saw the values associated with the delinquent subculture as taking on a life of their own, rather as the Chicago School had done, which would put even greater pressure on some boys to become delinquent. If this is true, we might query why working-class boys need to have internalised middle-class values in the first place in order for them to become delinquent. Other critics have made the familiar claim that such studies rely too much on official statistics regarding the social class distribution of delinquency, and in so doing underestimate the extent of middle-class delinquency (e.g., Kitsuse and Dietrick, 1959).

Finally, a note about the policy implications of Cohen's work. As with Merton, the message is that crime results from strains inherent in the structure of American society, and these are basically to do with a lack of equality of opportunity. According to the logic of this formulation the way to tackle crime is to create equality of opportunity, in other words, to make the reality of life in America correspond to the ideology of opportunities for all, irrespective of social class origins. There is, though, a fundamental contradiction at the core of this type of reasoning. Although the goal of equality of opportunity may be desirable, the notion of equality of opportunity to succeed implies equality of opportunity to fail; they are two sides of the same coin. In the work that we have looked at so far from strain theorists, there is no suggestion that class society should be eradicated. On the contrary, each writer is committed to an unequal class society, but people should have an equal chance to win or lose in that society. Indeed, the concept of equality of opportunity presupposes the existence of social class inequality. However, if such a divided society exists, then how are people able to line up equally? Poverty programmes, for example, may be introduced so that the chances of those at the 'bottom' are improved, but the model is predicated on the continuing existence of a 'bottom' and a 'top'.

R. CLOWARD AND L. OHLIN: OPPORTUNITY KNOCKS

When discussing the development of criminology during the post-war period it was pointed out that the explanations of delinquency associated with strain theory fitted

well with the ideas of the Kennedy administration of the early 1960s. This was particularly apparent with respect to the contribution made by Richard Cloward and Lloyd
Ohlin in their study *Delinquency and Opportunity,* published in 1960. Again, the central themes of strain theory are in evidence. There is a basic assumption that delinquent behaviour results from something going 'wrong' and, as a corollary: 'under
normal circumstances, that is the absence of strains and tensions, individuals will not
be motivated to break the law' (Box, 1981: 103).

Furthermore, and as with Cohen, although individual psychological factors may be
implicated in triggering specific types of response, the source of 'strain' lies in the
nature of society itself. This, of course, does not amount to a critique of American
capitalist society as such. It is, rather, a critique of the way that society is actually
working. Fundamentally, strain theory lends itself to social policies oriented towards
managing the opportunity structure so that the disadvantaged have a better chance
to succeed, whilst at the same time ensuring that disincentives to succeed because of
reduced income and status differentials do not intrude. It is a tall order. Indeed, as we
have seen, by the 1970s the perceived failure of programmes such as Operation Head
Start was shifting the emphasis away from 'equal opportunities' towards a rudimentary policy of control and containment.

Cloward and Ohlin had the explicit intention of forging together the ideas of Merton ('strain') and Sutherland ('differential association'), but their work also illustrates
the continuing influence of Durkheim on American criminological theory. Essentially
Delinquency and Opportunity addresses two issues: first, how the opportunity structures of mainstream American society lead some people to fail and become involved
in delinquency and, second, how the opportunity structures within criminal subcultures create, in turn, their own failures.

When analysing the causal factors associated with delinquency Cloward and
Ohlin's (1960: 32) basic research question is: 'Under which conditions will persons
experience strains and tensions that lead to delinquent solutions?' Clearly, it is the
impact of these conditions on the individual, conceived of in terms of strains and tensions, and leading to delinquent motivations, that they are interested in. In Mertonian fashion they begin by arguing that in modern societies such as the United States,
people are socialised into believing that those with ability will 'get on'. Through qualifications gained in the education system people will be matched to the job that suits
them. The actual achievement of this kind of society – a meritocracy – would create a
system of functional interdependence, as envisaged by Durkheim. However, in the
real world, say Cloward and Ohlin, some fail to achieve a social position commensurate with their ability; unfortunately, there are not enough higher-status jobs to go
round. Faced with queues of equally able applicants, employers fall back on criteria
other than ability, such as class, religion or style of dress. For Cloward and Ohlin the
lower-working-class victims of these processes, who feel that they have been treated
unjustly, are those most likely to become delinquent. This introduces a moral dimension and, again, makes links with Durkheim. There are no strains for those who fail

and yet subjectively believe that their failure is the result of a lack of ability, for they will resign themselves to their fate. The angry failures, on the other hand, do not, and they are in a situation where they are likely to withdraw their support for conventional, legitimate norms. Although Cloward and Ohlin follow Cohen and argue that most delinquent youth will come from lower-working-class backgrounds, they point to a different source within that social class. For them delinquency is most likely to occur among those who have earlier on committed themselves to middle-class norms, given some evidence of their ability, and have therefore been encouraged in their quest for higher status. In short, it is the 'college boy' who is most at risk: 'all available data support the contention that the basic endowments of delinquents, such as intelligence, physical strength and agility, are equal to, or greater than, those of their non-delinquent peers' (ibid.: 42).

Cloward and Ohlin's theory represents an application of the Durkheimian logic that social order requires the existence of a hierarchical system where each person feels that what they have achieved is all that they are morally entitled to. This raises a number of issues. For instance, they seem to assume that those working-class youth who fail to achieve success, but see themselves as being of low ability, will passively accept their failure. The possibility that they might turn to delinquency is ignored, as is the possibility of them adopting non-compliant, non-delinquent political strategies. In addition, equality of opportunity is conceived of as a system for separating the wheat from the chaff. The assumption is that the 'chaff' really exist – 'ability' is regarded as a natural, fixed level of intelligence, rather than a product of educational experiences – and what is required is a suitable system for identifying those with low ability. Importantly, though, such a system must at least appear fair to the failures; they must be convinced that their failure is morally deserved.

The main concern of Cloward and Ohlin, however, is with those working-class boys who supposedly possess high ability, but who none the less still fail. In the absence of a sufficient number of higher-status jobs to satisfy the demand represented by the pool of ability among all social classes, it is difficult to see how improving opportunities would in itself lead to a decrease in the number of angry failures. Without a corresponding expansion in actual job opportunities, social peace could only be achieved through other strategies, such as a more powerful ideology that convinced people of their morally deserved failure, or, some might say, more powerful modes of social control. There is one problematic aspect of their work that is shared with other strain theorists. This is their argument that lower-working-class delinquent boys have at a prior stage accepted middle-class norms and values.

Opportunity structures in the world of delinquency

Cloward and Ohlin argue that the social world of the delinquent contains the same sort of inequalities as the social world of the non-criminal – though we might question this neat dichotomy between 'goodies' and 'baddies'. Drawing on Sutherland's theme of differential association, they discuss the various opportunities available for learning the techniques and absorbing the motivations necessary for criminal behaviour. On this basis they suggest three different types of criminal subculture:

1 *Criminal.* This is a subculture oriented towards property crime, and will tend to be found in more socially organised lower-class neighbourhoods. Here informal social control networks centred on experienced adult criminals ensure that delinquent youth confine themselves to well-planned, utilitarian activities rather than such things as vandalism and gang warfare.
2 *Violent.* These are also referred to as conflict subcultures, and are associated with the more socially disorganised neighbourhoods which approximate to the Zone of Transition identified by the Chicago School. Delinquent activity is much less restrained than in the criminal subculture, and tends towards violent, gang-oriented behaviour.
3 *Retreatist.* This subculture is primarily associated with illegal drug use, and arises among those boys who have failed in both criminal and violent subcultures. In effect they represent the lumpen proletariat of the delinquent world.

Selected further reading

The seminal works on subcultural strain theory are: **Cohen, A. K. (1955)** *Delinquent Boys,* **London: Free Press**, and **Cloward, R. and Ohlin, L. (1960)** *Delinquency and Opportunity,* **London: Collier Macmillan**.

CHAPTER 7

CRIMINOLOGICAL THEORY IN BRITAIN

> ## Key themes
>
> - American influences
> - Sociological criminology in Britain
> - Developing a British perspective
> - Cultural diversity theory
> - Schools and the 'problem of adjustment'
> - Subcultural theory: taking stock

INTRODUCTION

The development of sociological criminology in Britain lagged behind its development in the United States. This chapter looks at the influence of the Chicago School and American subcultural theory on British criminologists in the 1950s and 1960s. In general, it was the Chicago School and the notion of the 'criminal area', rather than subcultural strain theory, that had the greatest influence. However, important studies based upon subcultures did emerge in Britain, though from the perspective of cultural diversity theory. The chapter concludes with a critique of the concept of delinquent subcultures by Matza and Sykes.

AMERICAN INFLUENCES

We have seen that there are important differences between the Chicago School and the subcultural strain theorists, such as Cohen, and Cloward and Ohlin, in their analyses of the processes that lead to criminal behaviour. They also differ in the way in which they conceptualise those areas of the city in which crime is believed to be concentrated. As we shall see, the respective positions raised an issue that influenced the early British sociologies of crime in the 1950s, and has resonated within criminology up to the present day.

On the basis of a social ecological model, the Chicago School saw the city in terms of 'natural areas'. These had their own ecological systems, and were differentiated according to the types of people living there and the relationship between their lifestyles and the physical environment. Some of these were identified as 'criminal areas'. These areas were characterised by run-down housing, transient populations and high levels of immigration and poverty. Crime in these areas was initially linked to social disorganisation, though later on, partly because of the influence of Sutherland, there was a move towards the idea of differential social organisation. This acknowledged the existence of a plurality of norms and values in the city. Although the subcultural strain theorists developed different understandings of the origins of delinquency, they agreed with the Chicago School that delinquent subcultures existed in certain lower-working-class areas. However, a central dispute concerned the relationship between such areas and the rest of the city, and indeed the rest of society.

For the Chicago School, the criminal area consisted of a delinquent culture, and inhabitants absorb the corresponding norms and values, and these are at variance with those of a supposed conformist, mainstream society. Youngsters became delinquent out of a 'natural' process of cultural transmission. Cohen, and Cloward and Ohlin, on the other hand, stress the ways in which the inhabitants are connected to, and influenced by, the wider mainstream culture, described as 'middle class'. Lower-class boys, specifically, are seen as to some extent internalising the norms and values of middle-class society:

> all their lives, through the major media of mass indoctrination – the schools, the movies, the radio, the newspapers and the magazines – the middle-class powers-that-be that manipulate these media have been trying the 'sell' them middle-class values and the middle-class standard of living.
>
> (Cohen, 1955: 124–5)

The 'reaction formation' suggested by Cohen, and the 'alienation' of Cloward and Ohlin's 'college boys' presuppose that this internalisation of middle-class values has occurred. Lower-working-class youth could not be insulated from mainstream middle-class culture, for the internalisation of this culture, at least to some extent, is necessary for a delinquent reaction to take place. The dispute between cultural transmission theorists and strain theorists essentially boils down to the issue of whether those living in a so-called criminal area become delinquent because they conform to the norms and values of the area, or because they have been rejected by a middle-class value system which, to a significant degree, they have internalised. The question is: do lower-working-class lads typically desire, then are denied, middle-class status?

It is an issue that was to figure in the early British sociologies of crime, and for some time afterwards. However, before exploring that debate, there is another dimension to the work of the Chicago School and the subcultural strain theorists that needs commenting on. In these and subsequent accounts, there is a danger of constructing distorted stereotypes of what life is like among the urban poor. Certainly, this is especially apparent in highly moralistic contributions from the mass media, and their references to lone parents, absent husbands, children who are 'out of control', 'no go' areas, and 'yob culture'. Drawing on the idea of an 'underclass', it is as if some urban neighbourhoods have been cut adrift from decent, law-abiding society. In an effort to emphasise the positive, rather than the negative, aspects of coping with the grim reality of unemployment and social deprivation in modern Britain, one commentator has written:

> I am sick and tired of the moral high ground being divided up between the haves and the have-nots. If this is the high ground give me the low ground any day. I am at home in the low ground – it is where I grew up and where I see women on their own struggling to bring up their children as best they can with little money and support. It is in the moral foothills that I see people look after their dying relatives day in and day out. Amongst this misery I also see more ingenuity than in a thousand sermons.
>
> (Moore, 1995: 5)

A problem with the Chicago School's description of the working-class criminal area is that it automatically equates non-delinquent values with some posited 'mainstream' middle-class society. Concomitantly, delinquent values, and thus such things as immorality and selfishness, are equated with lower-working-class culture. It is as if this culture is intrinsically delinquent: that is, the opposite of respectable, hard-working, mainstream America, and possessing no non- or anti-delinquent resources. The move from delinquency to non-delinquency, therefore, has to be accomplished through factors on the 'outside'.

In the case of the subcultural strain theorists, it is true that they do see the lower working class as not being cut adrift from the wider society, and in varying degrees subscribing to values associated with respect for other people's property, courtesy and non-violence. However, these are only absorbed by the lower working class because they have a moral conduit into the wider, mainstream culture. In fact, these values are presented as middle-class values. Thus again the image is one of the less well off having no intrinsic source of 'decent', non-delinquent values. The implication is that left to their own devices, and without the benefit of middle-class morality via schools and the mass media, these working-class neighbourhoods would become irredeemably delinquent. As a description of American society, Cohen's work in particular offers a highly idealised, one-sided picture of what he calls middle-class culture. Obviously, working-class children in 1950s America were, through the education system and the mass media, exposed to a range of norms and values from outside their family and neighbourhood. With the growth in mass communications, this is even more the case today. It would, though, be misleading to see all of these influences as being, by definition, 'middle-class', 'decent' and non-delinquent. In Britain the readers of some tabloid newspapers, for instance, are likely, in varying degrees, to be exposed to sexism, racism, ethnocentricity and homophobia. It would perhaps be reckless to judge these as necessarily benign, civilising influences on the lower working class.

SOCIOLOGICAL CRIMINOLOGY IN BRITAIN

It was not until the 1950s that the sociological criminology produced in the United States since as far back as the 1920s began to influence criminology in Britain. This delay was related to the fact that up to the 1960s criminology was not much interested in sociology and, conversely, sociology was not much interested in criminology. Although there were some internal disputes, the early British sociologies of crime did share certain features: they were strongly empirical, and owed more to the Chicago School than to the strain theorists; they concentrated on young offenders; they favoured an areal or community studies approach; they assumed that delinquency was in the main carried out by lower-working-class males; and they were oriented towards Fabian-influenced correctionalist principles. Importantly, though, they did represent a move away from focusing on the individual offender, via the strong influence of psychology, towards a consideration of the socio-cultural context of delinquency. The strength of individualised approaches at this time is indicated by the amount of criticism received by one major writer, Mays, for failing to carry out psychological tests to measure 'maladjustment'. This work created a framework for the subsequent development of sociological criminology in Britain.

It also provided an opportunity to assess the extent to which American ideas and explanations, based upon criminal areas and delinquent subcultures, could be transposed to a British context. Unlike conflict or labelling theory, for instance, these 'middle-range' theories are, of course, potentially more culture-bound (in Britain, for example, there was an important municipal housing market, and there seemed to be an absence of American-style adolescent gangs). It is worth noting that in the early British work the same issues discussed above regarding the nature of lower-working-class culture, and its relationship to the rest of society, bubbled to the surface.

The general tendency was to follow the Chicago School, rather than the strain theories of Cohen, and Cloward and Ohlin. Thus although 'criminal areas' were identified, where children were socialised into delinquent values, the delinquent subcultures were not seen as resulting from reactions to a denial of desired middle-class status. Conceptualisations of class structure and class dynamics were, however, fairly crude, and in this respect were similar to the American analyses. Non-delinquent, and by implication 'decent', values were often equated with some perceived 'middle-class' culture, as if these values were somehow intrinsic to the culture of an area where the head of the household had a job nominally corresponding to the Registrar-General's understanding of social class. Even in those cases where the writer acknowledged the existence of non-delinquent values among sections of the lower working class (e.g., Carter and Jephcott, 1954) the values were still essentially middle class; some people were poor, but middle class in lifestyle and outlook. As with the American work, it was as if lower-working-class culture was in its natural state delinquent; it only became non-delinquent when it borrowed ideas from the middle class.

The two figures in British criminology who were largely responsible for introducing American ideas into this country were John Barron Mays and Terrence Morris. Mays's (1954) *Growing Up in the City: A study of juvenile delinquency in an urban neighbourhood* was centred on an inner-city slum area in Liverpool. Mays drew on the ideas of the Chicago School, but toned down the concept of social ecology. He did, though, subscribe to the idea of the criminal area in which delinquency was concentrated, and used extensive interviewing as a basis for his research. Mays's central argument was that delinquency was widespread, and involved virtually all of the adolescents living in the area. The source of this delinquency, said Mays, was not strains or tensions in the boys' lives, as Cohen had argued, but, rather, it developed 'naturally' out of normal socialisation. He did, though, utilise the concept of subculture: 'This to the best of my knowledge is the first reference, in British literature at least, in which the notion of subculture is invoked to account for juvenile crime', and he argued that the bulk of delinquency was 'not so much a symptom of maladjustment as of adjustment to a subculture in conflict with the culture of the city as a whole' (Mays, 1975: 63). In spite of using the word 'conflict', he was not arguing that delinquency was a conscious rebellion against middle-class society. He found no 'reaction formation' due to a prior internalisation of middle-class values, as Cohen had done. However, he did concur with Cohen to the extent that the boys in Liverpool, not surprisingly, resented being treated as inferior. Although there was a small minority who involved themselves in serious delinquency, on the whole Mays paints a picture of socially and economically deprived young people trying to make the best of a bad job. In general, their delinquent behaviour represented an attempt to inject some fun into their lives. Given the overwhelming power of the delinquent subculture found in accounts such as Mays's, a question that is often asked is: why do all of the boys not become delinquent? The mordant answer from Mays is that they all do, but only some are unlucky enough to get caught. After leaving school, however, the boys' involvement in delinquency begins to decline and eventually, apart from a small core, ends by adulthood. He therefore repudiated the commonly held view that today's youthful delinquents are tomorrow's adult criminals.

In their study of Radby, a mining town in the Midlands, Carter and Jephcott (1954) argued that whilst working-class neighbourhoods might appear homogeneous, they were in fact socially differentiated. 'Respectable', non-delinquent families gravitated towards each other, and lived in the same streets, referred to as 'white' streets; 'rough', delinquent families lived together in the 'black' streets (fifty years on their choice of colours seems strikingly unfortunate). This division into 'respectables' and 'roughs' could not, they found, be traced back to the particular jobs that people had. The general pattern, they argued, was for delinquent youth to be brought up in delinquent families; delinquency was thus culturally transmitted, both in the family and on the street. For Carter and Jephcott, these values, then, persisted into adulthood, to be passed on to children. They, in fact, criticised Mays for failing to recognise this continuity between the values of adults and the values of children. Inevitably, the 'respectables' are seen as working-class people who have actually adopted supposedly middle-class values. So, once again, these values – respect for property and people, for instance – are not conceived of as *just* values, but they are specifically identified with the 'middle class', as if they were one of the key defining features of middle class-ness, but not working classness.

Although he was a psychologist, Sainsbury's (1955) study of suicide in London also drew on the work of the Chicago School. In particular he refers to the 'ecology of London', and identifies what he also calls 'natural areas'. On the other hand, Sains-bury rejected the view that poverty equals social disorganisation equals delinquency. He discovered that the greatest amounts of poverty did not correspond with the most socially disorganised areas. Delinquency, he argued, did correlate with poverty, but not with social disorganisation, though suicide, the main focus of the study, did.

The title of Morris's (1957) book, *The Criminal Area: A study in social ecology,* indi-cates the direct link with the Chicago School, though as we have said, in common with British writers at this time, the full ramifications of the ecological model were not accepted. He did, however, approve of the concept of the criminal area, and used this as the framework for his areal study of delinquency in the London suburb of Croydon. For Morris, though, a deteriorating physical environment coupled with the existence of poverty did not in themselves explain why some youngsters came to be involved in delinquent behaviour. Neither did he consider areas associated with high levels of delinquency to be socially disorganised. Morris, therefore, reconceptualised the notion of a delinquent area, by seeing it as the product of two crucial variables: the housing policies of the local authority, and social class. As a result of decisions made by housing departments, and in particular decisions based upon a policy of placing 'problem' families together on the same estates, certain neighbourhoods had the 'potential' for the development of delinquent behaviour. This was an idea that stimulated a large amount of research in Britain on the theme of housing classes, and the struggle for housing space (see, for example, the well-known study by Rex and Moore (1967) of Sparkbrook in Birmingham).

Morris's explanation of delinquency owes much to Sutherland's theory of differen-tial association. The boys living together on 'problem estates' form delinquent sub-cultures because of their socialisation into the norms and values of the area, norms and values carried by the people living there. Unlike the argument from the Chicago School, this suggests that if such people were relocated they would take their culture with them, along with their possessions in the removal van – which approximates to a 'pollution' explanation of delinquency. In fact, in an attempt to explain why all chil-dren do not become delinquent, and arguing against Mays, Morris uses as an analogy the spread of diseases such as cholera in the nineteenth century. Some people, he says, were more resistant than others to the disease. Using the same logic, the resistance to delinquency in Croydon was explained in terms of the 'adjustment' to socio-economic factors made by the family. This contagion view of delinquency found in the theory of differential association has often been criticised, essentially because it presents a mechanistic model of becoming delinquent. The individual is pictured as in a sense soaking up the various 'bad' (or 'good') influences that they happen to come into contact with, rather like Pavlov's dogs.

DEVELOPING A BRITISH PERSPECTIVE

If British sociological criminology could never hope to match the sheer volume of research carried out by its counterparts in the United States, at least by the 1950s British researchers had begun to recognise and draw on this research. Furthermore, by the time the 1960s arrived, a more distinctly British approach to adolescent delinquency was building up.

One difficulty was that adolescent gangs – in the sense of identifiable, distinct groups of adolescents, whose *raison d'être* was to engage in specifically delinquent activities – proved hard to find in Britain. Research increasingly centred on the notion of youth culture, and the delinquency with which it was sometimes associated. Even in the United States the existence and nature of so-called gangs continued to generate debate within criminology. Short and Strodtbeck (1965) in their study in Chicago, for instance, were sceptical that specialised gangs existed. One's position on this matter, of course, depends upon one's definition of a 'gang'. As far back as 1927, Thrasher (1963) in *The Gang* provided a sociological definition, though too often the term has been used very loosely, more or less simply to describe an 'unruly' group of individuals who spend a certain amount of time together. In order to achieve conceptual integrity, though, a sociological definition has to do better than this. Following Thrasher, therefore, a delinquent gang should more properly be seen as a collectivity possessing a number of key features such as permanence, face-to-face contact, a sense of identity among members, territoriality, usually a name, and a central concern with acts of delinquency. Unfortunately, in many studies the concept of subculture is used as if it were synonymous with gang.

CULTURAL DIVERSITY THEORY

As the discussion of the work of Mays and Morris has indicated, British sociological criminology in the main favoured an approach to delinquent behaviour that had more in common with the Chicago School than with the strain theorists, although there were moments of tension. This pedigree continued into the 1960s and came to be referred to as cultural diversity theory (it also had other names: differential association theory, cultural transmission theory and affiliation theory). Essentially, cultural diversity argues that society is composed of a number of different cultures, these usually being linked to social class and neighbourhood. Generally there is an assumption that a dominant 'mainstream', conformist, culture exists, with other alternative delinquent cultures described as subcultures. Delinquency, from this perspective, results from normal socialisation, through which individuals conform to the norms and values of these delinquent subcultures. People learn to be delinquent in exactly the same way that they learn to be non-delinquent; no pathological motivations need explaining. Unlike the subcultures described by Cohen, though, delinquent subcultures are not seen as reactive and anti the dominant mainstream culture, although they are, by definition, in conflict in a normative sense with that culture (should it exist).

In his study of delinquent youth in England, the American anthropologist Walter Miller (1958) outlined the central elements of cultural diversity theory. Focusing on lower-working-class culture as the prime source of delinquency, Miller argued that the adolescents involved were conformists rather than nonconformists or rebels. Their delinquency reflected their conformity to what he termed the 'focal concerns' of the working-class neighbourhood: trouble, toughness, smartness, excitement, fate and autonomy. He also noted that many of the boys in his study lived in lone parent families, with that parent being a mother rather than a father. This led him to suggest that the machismo associated with delinquency functioned to express and register the boy's escape from his mother's apron strings.

Peter Willmott's (1966) study of adolescent boys living in Bethnal Green in the East End of London contains a section on the theme of delinquency. The book illustrates some of the uncertainties around at the time. Willmott is sympathetic to Cohen's status frustration theory, as well as to the cultural diversity theory of Miller. Thus he is able to write: 'Some . . . argue that the motive is above all "status frustration" – that is, the boys behave as they do to hit back at the society that has rejected them and to show their contempt for its values' (Willmott, 1966: 161). But he then goes on to say:

> there is no widespread and continuing sense of resentment, revolt or frustration among the local boys. Many boys are 'delinquent', in the sense that they sometimes break the law, and particularly steal. But, since most boys do not feel rejected or frustrated, the theory does not explain their transgressions. It can help to explain only the delinquency of the minority.
>
> (Ibid.: 161)

One of the difficulties was that Willmott came across only a small minority of boys who were seriously involved in delinquency. He refers to the typology introduced by Whyte – 'corner boys' and 'college boys' – though his preferred terms are 'working class' and 'middle-class' (the latter, strangely, meaning working-class boys who want to be middle class). Each represents a particular type of adjustment to a perceived lack of success in monetary and status terms. The 'working-class' boy accepts his status and financial situation; the 'middle-class' boy wishes to surmount his working-class status by trying to move into a non-manual occupation. There is also a third group identified by Willmott and he refers to members of this group as 'rebels', adding that it is 'probably from boys like this that the seriously delinquent are drawn . . . though it cannot be proved from our figures' (ibid.: 168). In fact, the 'rebel', described as actively deviating from both working-class and middle-class standards, was in a small minority. In his sample of 246 boys, only 'a tenth or less' could be described as 'rebels', and he acknowledges that not all of these were necessarily delinquent. There is in Willmott's study one particularly interesting type of rebel, and it is a type of working-class adolescent rarely commented on, or even recognised, in sociological studies of youth. This is the bohemian or politicised working-class youth. Given the stereotyping of working-class culture in much of the literature, it is perhaps understandable that any serious engagement with, say, avant-garde poetry, music or painting, or with political struggle, will be overlooked in studies of this culture. In the example given by Willmott, the 'rebel' is into jazz, the novels of Kerouac and Mailer, and smokes marijuana. In short, he is nearer to what at that time was a beatnik than a delinquent tearaway or middle-class-style conformist.

Willmott's general conclusion is that serious delinquency is rare in Bethnal Green, though he estimates that one in three of the boys that he interviewed will probably end up in court before they are 21. Most of the boys in his study had no desire for middle-class status and they used their intermittent acts of delinquency as vehicles for a bit of fun and an expression of group solidarity. To this extent he sees them as belonging to a delinquent subculture.

Published in the same year, David Downes's (1966) *The Delinquent Solution* had the distinction of being the most theoretically sophisticated British sociological study of delinquency. Not only did he provide a graphic account of working-class life in Poplar and Stepney in the East End of London, and evaluate the relevance and validity of current influential theories, but he also developed a theoretical understanding of delinquent subcultures that addressed their deeper social and cultural roots. The study did, however, appear just as criminology in Britain was about to be transformed because of the impact of the new deviancy, and it therefore soon found itself assigned to a pre-new deviancy category.

In line with cultural diversity theory, Downes argues that delinquency is fundamentally conformist, in the sense that those involved in the delinquency are conforming to the values of the lower-working-class neighbourhood in which they live; he found no evidence that these delinquent subcultures resulted from antagonisms towards a perceived mainstream culture. This is similar to Miller's formulation, though Miller uses the notion of 'focal concerns' rather than values. According to Downes, there was no discontent with working-class status. In general the boys wanted to be working class, and certainly had no 'problems of adjustment' of the sort discussed by Cohen. Their speech, dress and demeanour were in many ways a celebration of their working classness. This is not to suggest that they felt no dissatisfactions. They saw school as basically a waste of time, and left at the earliest opportunity with few or no academic qualifications. When they entered the world of work there was no expectation, and rarely any realisation, of 'job satisfaction'. However, they did not want to cease being working class and become middle class, though like most people they would have welcomed more money.

Downes describes working-class areas where men have often been in trouble with the law, where there is drug dealing and prostitution and where fights continue into middle age. For the boys their social space is the street, and given the normative expectations to which they conform, it is difficult for them *not* to come into conflict with the law or the norms of 'respectable' working-class and middle-class society. This was not rebellion though: the delinquent subcultures were not contra-cultures. Furthermore, Downes found no evidence of delinquent *gangs*.

As the title of the book suggests, Downes argues that delinquency provides a solution, for some boys, to the central problems they experience. The delinquent subculture provides a way of coming to terms with the profound dissatisfaction experienced in schools and work. What they have achieved:

> is an opting-out of the joint middle- and skilled working-class value-system whereby work is extolled as a central life-issue, and whereby the male adolescent of semi- or unskilled origin is enjoined to either 'better himself' or 'accept his station in life'. To insulate themselves against the harsh implications of this creed, the adolescent in a 'dead-end' job, in a 'dead' neighbourhood, extricates himself from the belief in work as of any importance beyond the simple provision of income.
>
> (Downes, 1966: 236–7)

With neither of these middle-class/skilled-working-class options striking them as particularly attractive, the non-aspirant and non-compliant adolescent 'dissociates' himself from the two spheres of school and work, so that they have no importance or credibility. With no educational aspirations or commitment to seeking out a 'good' job, let alone a career, the adolescent 'deflects what aspirations he has into areas of what has been termed "non-work"' (ibid.: 237), that is, they put their energies into the leisure sphere. If education and work cannot provide the basis for a meaningful life, then it is down to the opportunities provided by the enticing space represented by leisure. The way in which leisure is used, though, has to be seen against the backdrop of the value system in which the boys have been brought up. It is a value system that stresses adventure, daring, toughness and excitement. If these values cannot be lived out in schools or factories, or some substitute attachments found, then they have to be lived out in leisure. Indeed, as Downes puts it, there is an 'edge of desperation' about the boys' reliance on leisure. Unfortunately, because of their class position and outlook, they have neither the money nor the inclination to engage in certain leisure pursuits that could potentially realise their aspirations. In other words, they face blocked opportunities in the world of leisure, opportunities that are available to their better-off, middle-class counterparts. What *is* readily available, though, for the lower-working-class adolescent is delinquency:

> 'Law-breaking is the only area of excitement to which he has absolutely untrammelled access.'
>
> (Ibid.: 249)

An important dimension to Downes's work is his partial incorporation of the ideas of the American criminologists Matza and Sykes (1961) (their work is looked at in more detail later on). Matza and Sykes argue that so-called delinquent values are not at all peculiar to the lower working class, but are present as leisure values throughout society. They are critical of much criminology for, in their view, erroneously polarising the value systems, so that a posited middle-class value system is presented as the normal, non-delinquent value system to which members of society in general conform. Delinquency, they argued, was more or less evenly distributed among all social classes; members of the lower working class just happened to get caught more often. While agreeing with the general tenor of this argument, and accepting as a 'criminological truism' the view that non-delinquency is extremely rare, Downes (1966: 247) disagrees that middle-class adolescents are as frequently and as seriously involved in delinquency as are lower-working-class adolescents: 'Most evidence supports the view that group delinquency is more frequent, persistent, diversified and less amenable to control among male, working class, urban adolescents than in any other sector'.

In Downes's view it is necessary to employ the notion of differential access to leisure goals in order to make Matza and Sykes's argument plausible. Leaving school at the earliest opportunity, working-class adolescents are, he says, more likely to find themselves with 'free time', as they are not involved in studying for examinations, or pursuing apprenticeships or a career. However, because of their dissociation from school and work, they in fact require *more* from leisure – but here they meet blocked opportunities. There is no educational preparation for, and a lack of interest in, 'constructive' hobbies, and the local youth clubs and dance halls usually fail to compensate for what is missing in education and work. In this situation delinquency offers an accessible and attractive way of achieving leisure goals.

SCHOOLS AND THE 'PROBLEM OF ADJUSTMENT'

The role of the school in the lives of working-class boys was explored in more detail by David Hargreaves (1967) in *Social Relations in a Secondary School*. The school in question was a secondary modern school in the north of England taking mainly working-class 11-plus failures. Hargreaves is strongly influenced by the work of Albert Cohen, drawing on the concepts of status frustration and the problem of adjustment, as well as identifying an oppositional contra-culture.

By the fourth and final year, two subcultures – one 'academic', the other 'delinquescent' – had developed in the school, with the latter concentrated in the bottom D stream. While the values of the academic subculture were 'oriented to those of the school and teachers', the values of the delinquescent subculture, though not necessarily delinquent, were in opposition to those of the school. In the familiar terminology of this period, the boys in the top stream were described as conforming to middle-class values, and in Hargreaves's estimation they tended to come from homes that although working class, were themselves oriented to middle-class values. Once again it is as if those working-class families that respect people and property are honorary members of the middle class, and to that extent are actually deviant. Conversely, the delinquescent ones are merely conforming to something that is presumed to be intrinsically working class. It is as if only those working-class professional footballers who have internalised 'middle-class' values are capable of behaving themselves on and off the pitch.

In Hargreaves's account the bottom-stream boys lost status because they had failed on two counts: by not passing the 11-plus examination, and by ending up in the D stream. On top of that they were 'negatively valuated' by teachers, making them feel inferior; they lacked the privileges enjoyed by the A-stream boys; and when leaving school had only a limited range of jobs open to them. The result of all this, not surprisingly, was that the bottom-stream boys felt resentment because of status deprivation. Thus, as Hargreaves puts it, this created a problem of adjustment, leading to a collective, subcultural response, with the subculture adopting an oppositional stance towards the norms and values of the school. Within the subculture, anti-school and anti-teacher behaviour became a source of status for the boys, though in practice the opposition was limited because of the power held by teachers; much of the time the boys fell back on 'sullen compliance'.

The similarities with Cohen's work are obvious, but there is one important difference between the two studies. Unlike Cohen, Hargreaves does not argue that the oppositional subculture was composed of boys who had previously internalised middle-class values, and were then denied status. He does not see the boys' delinquescent behaviour and antagonism towards the school as an example of 'reaction formation'; feeling resentment at a perceived lack of status was sufficient. This detail raises the question of timing in studies such as these. Cohen, presumably, would argue that we would need to know if the boys concerned had at some previous stage internalised, or at least partly internalised, middle-class values. Hargreaves assumes that they have not. The top-stream boys, though, according to Hargreaves, had internalised middle-class values, but for Cohen these were unlikely candidates for delinquency because they had, in 'college boy' style, achieved a degree of academic success and satisfied their aspirations. Alternatively, Cloward and Ohlin would see these college boys as the prime source of delinquency, because of the blocked opportunities they would eventually face. Even if we accept the argument that lower-working-class delinquent boys typically desire, but are then denied, middle-class status, the above discussion illustrates the lack of clarity and consensus in these sorts of studies regarding precisely when status frustration, leading to delinquency, will surface. Indeed, by 1958 Cohen had moved away from the idea of reaction formation as the crucial basis of delinquency (Cohen and Short, 1958).

SUBCULTURAL THEORY: TAKING STOCK

Subculture has proved to be a seductive concept within criminology, whether used in the context of delinquent behaviour, or as a way of understanding youth subcultural formations (see the later discussion of the work of the Birmingham Centre for Contemporary Cultural Studies, for example). At this juncture we can take stock of the subcultural theory that grew up in the 1950s and 1960s. Frances Heidensohn (1989) has usefully summarised the limits of subcultural theory on the basis of five headings: determinism, selectivity, gender, conformity and anomie.

Determinism indicates the strong tendency in subcultural theory, especially under the influence of functionalism, to present an 'over-socialised' view of the delinquent. Adolescents are seen as passive products of the cultural forces around them, responding rather like robots programmed by 'bad' influences. Qualities of reflection, choice and rationality are thus neglected. Under such determining conditions – for example, due to living on a 'criminal' housing estate – it is difficult to explain why *all* of the inhabitants do not become delinquent. This overprediction of delinquency arises because of what Matza (1964) calls an 'embarrassment of riches'; in a sense the theory over-explains delinquency.

Selectivity refers to the types of subculture earmarked for attention. These are the more flashy, exciting examples that in fact involve only a tiny minority of young people. Through such selectivity the mundanity, ordinariness and conformity of large sections of British and American youth are neglected. Furthermore, the much more serious crimes carried out by adults tend to be ignored.

Gender was not seriously addressed within criminology until the late 1960s: 'gender was a sociological issue which ticked away, like a time bomb in the cellars, for generations' (Heidensohn, 1989: 54). Although issues of masculinity and machismo were on the agenda, and sometimes a few pages were even reserved for a discussion of females, the (male) subcultural theorists lacked the conceptual resources to deal adequately with gender. This is not simply to do with the exclusion of girls from their delinquency studies, though. It is to do with the social construction of notions of masculinity and femininity, and the ways in which these are incorporated into the lives of adolescents, as well as the adults with whom they come into contact.

Linked to selectivity, the notion of *conformity* directs us to question critically the inability of subcultural theory to explore the reasons so many young people do not, to any significant degree, engage in delinquency. An understanding of conformity, for example among 'college boys', may very well be an important dimension to an understanding of delinquency.

Finally, we come to the problematic concept of *anomie*. Many subcultural theorists have described the delinquent's world in terms of anomie, or a lack of moral regulation. However, this world is often presented as if it was a self-contained, more or less independent social entity. As Heidensohn says: 'Presumably all these children have homes, parents, siblings, elderly neighbours, churches and clubs. If they don't, then such information needs to be built into the picture, since it is likely to be significant' (ibid.: 57).

Matza and Sykes: dissenting voices

The work of the American criminologists David Matza and Gresham Sykes has already been briefly referred to. As far as a critical reading of subcultural theory is concerned, two of their early papers are particularly important. In the first (Sykes and Matza, 1957) they introduce the concept of 'techniques neutralisation', and in the second (Matza and Sykes, 1961) the concept of 'subterranean values'.

In these two papers Matza and Sykes raised awkward and provocative questions for conventional criminology, including subcultural theory. Essentially they set out to challenge the dominant view in criminology that delinquents were fundamentally different from non-delinquents: that they each inhabited separate moral universes. This formed the basis for Matza's later work in which he developed a critique of the sociological determinism with which much criminological theory was infused (Matza, 1964, 1969). Needless to say, Matza was a major influence on the new deviancy of the late 1960s and early 1970s.

Many of the writers we have looked at have stressed that for some adolescents, because they live in certain neighbourhoods, delinquency was normal. Due to their social circumstances they simply conformed (or because of strains ended up conforming) to a set of delinquent norms and values at variance with those of a supposed mainstream culture. From this perspective, society is composed of a non-delinquent majority subscribing to non-delinquent values, and a delinquent minority subscribing to delinquent values. It was this sharp differentiation between the two that Matza and Sykes rejected. The 'delinquent', they argued, had been falsely characterised as a special kind of person, inhabiting a special deviant world. Although this is a view that satisfies common-sense understandings, and is not uncommon within criminology, it is highly misleading. It depicts the delinquent as being totally and consummately committed to a delinquent way of life. It is as if they brush their teeth and make love in a delinquent way, invariably refuse to help anyone in trouble, and harm people and property at every available opportunity. Within this framework every activity appears to be undertaken without reference to any of the values supposedly associated with law-abiding, mainstream society. For Matza and Sykes this is nonsense. They argue that delinquents are routinely involved in the non-delinquent world, and only occasionally engage in delinquency. Furthermore, those who do engage in delinquency are not just aware of non-delinquent values but, to the extent that anyone else does, they actively believe in them.

Matza and Sykes's attempt to connect the delinquent to law-abiding, non-delinquent society, and thereby stress the similarities rather than dissimilarities, can be illustrated by their concept of 'techniques of neutralisation'. Basically, their argument is that just about everyone breaks the law. However, in order to go ahead with the law breaking, individuals need to convince themselves that what they are doing is not actually wrong. This is different to the excuses that someone might make after they have committed an offence. It is a process through which the individual neutralises the 'badness' or 'immorality' of their actions prior to carrying them out (though the distinction between using techniques of neutralisation before or after some transgressive behaviour is not always made clear by the authors). It thus operates as an important feature of the motivation to commit delinquent acts, or, as Matza puts it, to 'drift' into delinquency. This was part of Matza's project to show how the delinquent is not a determined creature, but exercises, at least to some extent, free will. Techniques of neutralisation indicate how individuals actively make decisions to break rules. However, according to Matza and Sykes, the fact that people have recourse to these techniques beforehand shows that they are aware of, and subscribe to, non-delinquent values. Some hypothetical examples will illustrate the sort of situations they are referring to. Although they are against theft, someone fiddles their expenses at work 'because everybody does it, and it is a perk of the job'. Someone is against violence, and yet hits a man at the bar in the face because 'he said something to my wife'. Someone is in favour of a 30 mph speed limit in a built-up area, and yet travels at 40 mph in their car because 'I was in a hurry'. And so on.

This attempt to illuminate the continuities, rather than discontinuities, between the world of the delinquent and that of the non-delinquent is also apparent in their paper on 'subterranean values'. Here they are strongly critical of studies of delinquency that feel obliged to construct a definitive standard in the shape of 'middle-class' values, against which delinquent values can be measured. For Matza and Sykes, society contains a subculture of delinquency, rather than a number of delinquent subcultures. In other words, delinquent values exist throughout society, among all social classes, and should not be specifically linked to the lower working class. Values stressing such things as hedonism, conspicuous consumption, machismo, excitement and daring are, they say, to be encountered everywhere and are so prevalent that to call them 'deviant' is absurd. However, the middle and upper classes are in a better position than the working class to live out these values in appropriate settings, or in ways that do not invite the attention of control agencies. The working-class delinquent often suffers from 'bad timing'. The notion of subterranean values at least acts as an antidote to those theories that see 'middle-class' culture as exemplifying an unqualified commitment to such things as hard work, keeping to the rules, politeness, and so forth, and its opposite designated as 'working-class' culture. As Downes says: 'far from standing as an alien in the body of society, the delinquent may represent instead a dangerous reflection or caricature' (Downes, 1966: 246).

Selected further reading

British studies by **Mays, J. B. (1954)** *Growing Up in the City,* **Liverpool: Liverpool University Press**; and **Morris, T. P. (1957)** *The Criminal Area: A study in social ecology,* **London: Routledge & Kegan Paul** both drew on the work of the Chicago ecologists and represent early versions of cultural diversity, rather than strain, theory.

Another early example of an approach based upon cultural diversity is **Miller, W. B. (1958) 'Lower class culture as a generating milieu of gang delinquency',** *Journal of Social Issues,* 14(3).

A landmark study of adolescent delinquency and cultural diversity is **Downes, D. (1966)** *The Delinquent Solution,* **London: Routledge & Kegan Paul.**

From the point of view of subcultural theory, it is worth reading two articles by the American criminologists David Matza and Gresham Sykes, where they emphasise the continuities, rather than discontinuities, between so-called 'deviant' and 'non-deviant' worlds: **Sykes, G. and Matza, D. (1957) 'Techniques of neutralization: A theory of delinquency',** *American Sociological Review,* 22; and **Matza, D. and Sykes, G. (1961) 'Juvenile delinquency and subterranean values',** *American Sociological Review,* 26.

Cohen, S. (2001) *States of Denial: Knowing about atrocities and suffering,* **Cambridge: Cambridge University Press** examines techniques of neutralization used by states as a way of denying guilt in relation to violations of human rights.

For accessible and comprehensive overviews of studies of youth and delinquency, see: **Muncie, J. (2009)** *Youth and Crime: A critical introduction,* **3rd edn, London: Sage**; and **Brown, S. (1998)** *Understanding Youth and Crime: Listening to youth?* **Buckingham: Open University Press.**

PART III

THE MID-1960S TO THE EARLY 1970S

CHAPTER 8

THE DISCIPLINE OF CRIMINOLOGY
AND ITS CONTEXT – 2

Key themes

- The development of sociological criminology in Britain
- The break with orthodoxy: the new deviancy
- The New Left
- Radicals and the new deviancy: the impact on British criminology

---

INTRODUCTION

This chapter explores the social and political context within which a massive expansion in sociological criminology (or the sociology of deviance) occurred in Britain from the mid-1960s to the early 1970s. The driving force for this expansion was a new approach to the study of crime and deviance. Developed initially in the United States, it was given the name new deviancy theory. As we shall see, the growth of the New Left, along with a so-called counter-culture in Britain, were important factors accounting for the popularity of new deviancy theory among young academics at that time.

THE DEVELOPMENT OF SOCIOLOGICAL CRIMINOLOGY IN BRITAIN

The relatively small contribution made by sociological perspectives to criminology in Britain up to the mid-1960s effectively ensured the suppression of any significant influence from sociological criminology in the United States. During the second half of the 1960s, however, this situation changed dramatically, as British criminology began to draw increasingly on American sources for ideas and inspiration. From then on, as Downes (1988: 46) puts it: 'For two decades Britain became an off-shore laboratory for the distillation of ideas fermented in the U.S.A'.

This coincided with the expansion of sociology in British universities and polytechnics, and with it a rapid increase in the number of young sociologists interested in the field of crime and deviance. The result was that by the beginning of the 1970s the sociology of crime had shed its marginalised status, though by now the preferred term was the sociology of deviance.

The pillaging of American sources by British sociologists of deviance was not simply because there was so much of it; the innovations associated with new deviancy theory were what proved to be overwhelmingly attractive. Indeed, the apparently sudden interest in this field on the part of British academics was stimulated by new deviancy theory, though in some cases the work had actually been produced some years previously.

THE BREAK WITH ORTHODOXY: THE NEW DEVIANCY

The rush to embrace the ideas of new deviancy theory was the result of factors operating at both the level of criminology/the sociology of deviance, and at a wider societal level.

The new deviancy developing at that time – and variously called labelling theory, social reaction theory, transactionalism and interactionism – was subversive, though what was subverted was not so much the wider society as academic criminology. It did not provide a critique of Western capitalist societies, and generally would not have wanted to, though it did raise questions that subsequent writers utilised in the construction of a much more radical sociology of deviance/criminology. It did, however, mark an important break with earlier criminology, a criminology that was by then being called 'orthodox'.

Within orthodox criminology, debates over the conceptual language of the discipline were conspicuously lacking. Crime was by definition 'bad' because it was against the law; deviance was 'bad' because it was against the norms. Debates about the meaning of such terms became central to the new deviancy. Likewise, the sociological criminology that had grown up since the war was criticised for its causal–corrective concerns and positivist methodologies: track down the causes of crime, then decide on the most appropriate ways of dealing with the criminal. There was frustration with the constraints placed on criminology by social policy and penal and legal practices. Authoritarian versions of orthodox criminology stressed the individual's personal responsibility and the need for punitive action by the agencies of social control. More liberal versions emphasised more or less deterministic 'social factors', or individual/family 'problems' of a psychological nature; problems that could be cured, or solved, or adjusted to, providing that help was given by those with the professional expertise. When 'deviance' was mentioned in these accounts, it was assumed that it represented a pathological state, and the important questions were: What caused it? How can we stamp it out? This was the legacy of British criminology that the new deviancy theorists sought to break away from.

This critical stance was part of a much wider revolt in the social sciences against the set of assumptions underlying the, until then, dominant positivist paradigm.

David Hargreaves *et al*. (1976: 1) very broadly define the debate as being between positivism and phenomenology:

> In an oversimplified form the debate can be characterised as a battle between the more traditional social scientists of this century, who are grouped together under the general label of 'positivists', and the growing supporters of the alternative paradigm, who are grouped together under the general label of 'phenomenologists' . . . Nowhere has this debate been more sharply felt than in that area of social science . . . which is traditionally referred to as deviance.

In fact, the impact of phenomenological sociology on the area of deviance petered out fairly quickly, but Hargreaves *et al*.'s observation is correct if 'phenomenology' is used in the loosest sense. For new deviancy theorists this basically entailed taking account of the subjective world of the actor, seen as the product of meanings constructed through social interaction.

Stan Cohen described the new deviancy theorists as 'sceptical theorists', and for him the new deviancy was part of a revolution:

> This reorientation is part of what might be called the sceptical revolution in criminology and the sociology of deviance. The older tradition was *canonical* in the sense that it saw the concepts it worked with as authoritative, standard, accepted, given and unquestionable.

> (Cohen, 1973: 12)

Many writers viewed what was happening to criminology as cataclysmic: 'The 1960s saw a Renaissance in sociological criminology in Britain' (Wiles, 1976b: 14).

In an attempt to gather together the various cultural threads which contributed to these changes in the sociology of deviance, Geoff Pearson (1975: 51) described the new perspectives gathering momentum in the 1960s as follows:

> This area of scholarship is an odd theoretical cocktail, constructed out of sociology, psychiatry, criminology, social administration, media studies, law, social work, political science, cultural criticism, social psychology, and even some strands of popular culture and music. This interdisciplinary misfit finds its focus in the study of deviants . . . the sociology of labelling is only one of its elements. Within the same domain one finds what passes for 'phenomenology', and also a sort of 'Marxism'. Anti-psychiatry has left its mark . . . a theoretical jigsaw which has earned the reputation of being 'radical' . . . I call this space which opened out in social thought in the 1960s, *misfit sociology*. (Original emphasis)

This gives a whiff of the hotchpotch of sometimes frenetic ideas that grew out of the wild possibilities of the new deviancy. Given the lack of interest in, or even antagonism towards, the sociology of crime/deviance within the discipline of sociology in

Britain, we can understand why criminologists, or sociologists, who considered themselves as radicals, received the new deviancy as it arrived from across the Atlantic with unrestrained enthusiasm. It was a breath of fresh air, bringing with it an invigorating sense of new possibilities. There was a promise of a radical alternative to the moribund perspectives of traditional criminology. The alternative to positivist criminology offered by the new deviancy encouraged a critical frame of mind, and allowed a broader spectrum of sociological theory and method to enter the arena. Also, by focusing on 'deviance' rather than 'crime', it opened out the range of activities encompassed by research. No longer obsessed with juvenile delinquency, the new sociologists of deviance turned their attention to all sorts of groups supposedly having deviant status: nudists, the blind, the mentally ill, the mentally handicapped, poolroom hustlers, Hell's Angels, drifters, dropouts, illegal drug users, blackmailers, and so on. By the early 1970s though, some new deviancy writers were becoming worried that this shift of emphasis was actually contributing to the deviantisation of such groups. One example of this view is provided by Alexander Liazos (1972), who famously used the phrase 'nuts, sluts and preverts'. ('Preverts', incidentally, is the correct spelling, although when used by British writers it is inevitably spelt 'pervert'. The phrase originally appeared in the 1960s film *Doctor Strangelove or: How I Learned to Stop Worrying and Love the Bomb*. It was used by one of the redneck characters.)

After the initial burst of new deviancy activity at the end of the 1960s, the dust began to settle and more careful assessments of the impact could be made. Certainly, new deviancy theory represented a move towards a more sophisticated approach to theory, with deviant motivations and official reactions to deviant behaviour at the core. In the post-new deviancy period from the early 1970s, a number of strands in varying degrees critical of what had gone before began to develop, and these are examined below. What we can note is that since the late 1960s the area of crime and deviance has provided an arena for a discussion of the most fundamental theoretical concerns of sociology.

In this context the issue of the relationship between the 'deviant' and the sociologist is of particular interest. The 1960s saw a move away from a situation where the criminologist in effect lined up with the rule enforcers, to one where the stance adopted was either ambivalent or even explicitly on the side of the deviant. Becker, for instance, one of the most influential American criminologists at the time, argued that the researcher should take sides. This idea had important implications for the way in which new deviancy theory was received in Britain, though there were significant differences between the more liberal sociologists and those on the left, especially what was called the 'New Left'. For the liberal there was, somewhere within new deviancy, the promise of a more humane welfare state, where the 'outsider' was treated with dignity – dignity commensurate with a fuller appreciation of the authenticity of his or her actions. This stance was what 'law and order' letter writers to the press would characterise, derogatorily, as 'soft'. For those on the left, the promise led in a different direction, and brought to the surface what may be described as latent moral ambiguities regarding deviants and their actions. In a review of new deviancy, Jock Young (1975: 63) has written: 'Attacking a theoretical position to which one is opposed often tends towards the erection of an alternative position which is merely an inversion of one's opponent's'. The inversion of traditional criminology created an interesting situation. If crime was previously pathological, it was now 'normal'. If criminologists had previously sided with official versions of reality, they now sided with the deviant's. If previous research was aimed at correction, it was now aimed at 'appreciation'. And – wherein lies the crux of the problem – if crime was previously 'wrong', was it now 'right'? Was there something in crime/deviance that the left could positively appreciate, that is, explicitly approve of?

Various new deviancy luminaries such as Becker (1963), Erikson (1962) and Kitsuse (1962), had replaced the 'absolutism' of earlier criminology with a new 'relativism'. No behaviour, it was argued, was inherently deviant or inherently 'bad'; deviant status depended upon the power to label. This idea was to take some criminologists on the left down some interesting highways.

During the 1960s the orthodox left, as opposed to the emerging New Left, in one sense occupied a similar position to that of the conservative criminologist. Although moral ambivalence on a personal level may have existed, publicly crime was judged to be 'wrong', though of course the respective explanations and solutions would have been different. For the New Left, however, the ideas introduced by new deviancy theory led to a fundamental questioning of common-sense distinctions between crime and non-crime and deviance and non-deviance ('deconstructionism' of this sort is now a staple of postmodernist perspectives). If nothing was inherently immoral or evil, why should official, or ruling-class definitions be accepted? Perhaps some acts labelled deviant are in fact acts that can, from a socialist point of view, be approved of. This is to move beyond the argument that some legal activities, such as arms deals, are more harmful than some illegal activities, to one where certain deviant acts are to be welcomed because they are beneficial in socialist terms. Eventually, this was to lead some radical writers to argue that crime and deviance were forms of political action.

The commitment of new deviancy theory to 'siding with the deviant' was interpreted in different ways. For some it meant organising research and theory around the deviant's version of reality. For others it meant actually *supporting* the actions of at least some defined deviants, and it is here that the moral ambivalence enters, leading to statements such as 'the mass of delinquents are literally involved in the practice of redistributing private property' (Taylor *et al.*, 1973). It can also lead to a full-blooded romanticism, where all so-called deviants are viewed as courageous nonconformists fighting an evil system. If, say, members of the working class are thought to be frustratingly docile, or at best wrapped up in strategies based on economism, then it is perhaps tempting for radical criminologists to see in deviance an example of struggle against the state apparatus of capitalism. It is this that raises the important question of whether a left-wing criminologist or sociologist of deviance should, as it were, align themselves with judges, magistrates, prison governors and police officers, all of whom are in the business of maintaining the status quo, rather than with the deviant who is threatening it. This niggling problem has haunted various types of radical criminology since the 1960s, though it has not always been given explicit attention.

Wider societal factors: the counter-culture

When explaining the friendly reception given to American new deviancy theory by young British sociologists and criminologists during the second half of the 1960s, we also need to consider the broader cultural and political developments that took place. On a cultural level the 1960s saw the growth of the so-called counter-culture, and on a political level, an increasingly influential challenge to the old, orthodox Left from what came to be known as the 'New Left'. Sociologists and criminologists in this country were not immune to the effects of these two movements. Thus, from the mid-1960s a climate of opinion was being generated that was to prove highly conducive to the ideas of the new deviancy.

In essence the counter-culture represented a disengagement with the values of mainstream, conformist culture, and an attempt to create a non-materialistic, more expressive and meaningful alternative. With a subjectivist and hedonistic frame of reference, the emphasis was on personal liberation from the constraints imposed by what was seen as a dehumanised consumer society, where *things* had become more important than people. Hence the resistance to dominant ideas regarding such things as sexuality, drug use and appropriate style of dress.

The primary source of the 'great refusal' (as Marcuse put it) represented by the counter-culture of the 1960s was affluent middle-class youth, and the greatest wrath was reserved for the stultifying middle-class lifestyle associated with affluent subur-bia, the land of 'little boxes' in the song sung by Pete Seeger. In fact, the little boxes from which many of them had come:

> For here were people protesting not against material hardship, but against the emo-tional containment of affluence, a feeling that affluence was not all that there was to life and that public success in the affluent world might be personally meaningless.
>
> (Pearson, 1975: 83)

The rejection of consumerism and conventional mores, and a corresponding commit-ment to cultural diversity, harmonised with the sympathetic, even celebratory, approach to deviance taken by the new deviancy theorists. This is not to say, of course, that British sociologists who latched on to the ideas of the new deviancy were dropouts, who, high on drugs, wrote their books and papers in between listening to Donovan and Jimi Hendrix in a convention-shunning hippy commune. What was important was the way in which elements of the counter-culture permeated into the lives of a whole range of people, though their commitment stopped short of, say, dropping out of society. At the time, in fact, many of the sociologists concerned were undergraduate or postgraduate students, or in some cases young lecturers, and the desire to acquire qualifications and teaching posts, and to write books, indicates a degree of commitment to staying in the system. However, being a student did provide rather more opportunities than did paid employment for experimenting with ideas and lifestyles associated with the counter-culture.

The influence of the counter-culture on a younger generation in Britain was swift and pervasive. Ironically, the commercial interests sustaining a consumer society so vehemently rejected by the counter-culture were responsible for the dissemination of many of these ideas. Within a short space of time commercial interests were eagerly seizing and marketing in a vulgarised form anything that would sell. It is a familiar process which, in this case, was to find its nadir when, in the early 1970s, Marks & Spencer finally brought Woodstock to the High Street when they started selling pale blue trouser suits with a printed pattern of fake stitched patches. In the summer of 1967, with Scott McKenzie's *San Franciso (Be Sure to Wear Some Flowers in Your Hair)* filling the air, holiday-makers in Blackpool and Southend would have seen Indian love beads, cardboard headbands and plastic daffodils by the score. In a classic review of post-war cultural movements, Jeff Nuttall (1970: 200) paints this picture:

> Nine months after the first gatherings in Haight-Ashbury girls and office workers were wandering down the Brighton and Blackpool seafronts, jangling their souvenir prayer-belts, trailing their Paisley bedspreads, brandishing daffodils and trying to look tripped out. The Beatles had gone 'flower power' and it was up to the kids to do their best to follow.

Many commentators saw members of the counter-culture as harbingers of new, personally fulfilling strategies for coping with a future based on leisure. The American sociologist Fred Davis (1967: 12), for instance, in a paper with the attention-grabbing title 'Why all of us may be hippies someday', celebrated the prophetic nature of the counter-culture, suggesting that hippies were 'rehearsing *in vivo* possible cultural solutions to central life problems posed by the emerging society of the future'.

In spite of these commendations, though, various contradictions within the counter-culture began to appear, and critics on the left started to question its radical credentials. Because of its nature, however, the counter-culture was hardly going to deliver a coherent political programme, let alone a socialist one. In reality, when they did participate in the activities of the counter-culture, it was the left at play rather than the left at (class) war; the barricades in Paris in 1968 were built by politicos rather than hippies.

Ultimately, the counter-culture represented a critique of, and reaction to, not so much capitalism as modern, consumer-oriented society abstracted from its economic and political structures. The dissatisfaction shown by those on the political left was eventually paralleled by a dissatisfaction with new deviancy theory among radical sociologists, and with it a corresponding shift to a much 'harder' political stance. The dawning of the Age of Aquarius signalled a romantic celebration of youth. They would lead people back to the Garden of Eden, though they could take some of the artefacts of modern technological society with them, but only some of them. Because they were identified with middle-class suburbia, such things as vacuum cleaners and food processors were frowned upon, whilst electric guitars, stereo systems and synthesisers, also products of an affluent capitalist technology, were acceptable. Youth would change society, but somehow capitalism would still exist.

THE NEW LEFT

For the New Left too, modern life was characterised by a soul-destroying consumerism, though here the target was a specifically capitalist society. Day-to-day social order, the argument ran, was maintained not by overt measures of social control, but by concentrating people's minds on an overriding concern with consumer goods. Important social and political questions were relegated to second place behind questions about the best deodorant or washing machine to use. In the words of Marcuse, capitalist societies were 'one dimensional'. Of course the left in Europe had for a long time equated capitalism with self-centred consumerism, but from the perspective of the New Left, older groups, such as the Communist Party, had become ossified: their formulations and strategies had ceased to provide a meaningful alternative vision.

The New Left also shared with the counter-culture a preoccupation with subjectivism and the need for a personal liberation of thought, out of which will grow a basis for revolutionary change. In the case of the New Left, though, this was explicitly linked to the removal of capitalism. While the New Left did confront capitalism as a system, it was in a manner that many older European socialists found strange. Essentially this was because of the importance attached to the relationship between the personal and the political. Again we see how the influence of a more broadly based intellectual framework was important for the subsequent reception given to the ideas of new deviancy theory by radical sociologists.

The intellectual roots of the New Left lay in what is called the Frankfurt or 'critical' School, whose ideas were developed in pre-war Germany, and during the war when its members were in exile in the United States. Undoubtedly, this school held a formidable array of intellectual talent: Adorno, Horkheimer, Fromm, Benjamin, Lowenthal and Marcuse. The Frankfurt School believed that the view of humankind's relationship to nature that grew out of the Enlightenment, although it discarded the naive animism of an earlier period, was not fulfilling the promise of real social progress. As human beings had manipulated nature, so those with power used technology to manipulate the less powerful. This manipulation, however, did not occur simply at a physical level, for their consciousness and senses were also manipulated, and the Frankfurt School argued that what was needed was a 'sense' liberation. Marcuse, one of the most prominent proponents of these ideas in the 1960s, saw in the sometimes serious, yet at other times silly and childish, behaviour of the counter-culture the possible basis for liberation. A later member of the Frankfurt School, Habermas, commented on the political content of the counter-culture:

> I consider the politicisation of private conflicts a singular result of the protest movement . . . Today, difficulties that a mere 2 or 3 years ago would have been passed for private matters . . . now claim political significance and ask to be justified in political concepts. Psychology seems to turn into politics – perhaps a reaction to the reality that politics, in so far as it relates to the masses, has long been translated into psychology.
>
> (Habermas quoted in Pearson, 1975)

Thus in the 1960s there were points of fusion between the counter-culture and the New Left, and these produced definitions of 'political' notable for their extreme fluidity and flexibility – a theme that was to be picked up by sociologists of deviance in the post-new deviancy period. In a range of publications almost anything was likely to be prefixed by the term 'the politics of': the politics of ecstasy, of madness, of sexuality, of shoplifting, and so on. Those involved in making everything 'political' did so from a number of perspectives, and with varying degrees of sophistication. Poets, journalists, novelists, psychiatrists, cultural pundits, as well as sociologists of deviance, carried forward this break with traditionalism. Many of them also began to use the term 'radical' to underline opposition to traditional ways of thinking, and thus there appeared movements such as radical social work, radical education and radical philosophy.

There was an ironic subtext to all of this that has already been alluded to in the discussion of the counter-culture. This is that the 'radical', 'revolutionary', 'transforming' ideas of the New Left came to be disseminated and popularised by the very capitalist institutions against which the radicalism was aimed. A striking example of this is provided by a book published in 1968 and written by a French student prominent in the uprisings in Paris in that year. The author, Daniel Cohn-Bendit, cannot resist pointing out the contradiction:

> the publishers now come chasing after me, begging me to write about anything I choose, good or bad, exciting or dull; all they want is something they can sell – a revolutionary gadget with marketable qualities . . . publishers are falling over themselves to cash in on the May events. In our commercial world, individual capitalists are perfectly willing to pave the way for their own destruction, to broadcast revolutionary ideas, provided only that these help to fill their pockets . . . They do not even seem to be bothered by the fact that their cash will be used for the next round of Molotov cocktails.
>
> (Cohn-Bendit and Cohn-Bendit, 1968: 11)

RADICALS AND THE NEW DEVIANCY:
THE IMPACT ON BRITISH CRIMINOLOGY

Against a backdrop of counter-cultural and New Left influences, new deviancy theory was absorbed with relish by a generation of British sociologists. Soon, as with Cohn-Bendit, publishers were seeking out work from these radical sociologists. This was important in that, coupled with a growth in sociology in general, and the sociology of deviance in particular, it contributed to a situation where radical criminology broke free of any significant dependence on funding from institutions such as the Home Office, the police and the prisons. Criminological work that was tied to these institutional demands, and often referred to as mainstream 'administrative' criminology, did, it should be noted, continue throughout this period under review – and still continues.

David Garland (1985b) has strongly argued that since its inception criminology has always been linked to 'external' political and ideological demands. In other words, the discipline has been tied to the administrative and ideological constraints imposed upon it by its political paymasters; and we have seen something of this when looking at the nature of criminology up to the 1960s. To this extent, and in spite of pretensions to scientific status, criminological research has conformed with the requirements of the state. However, notwithstanding the validity of Garland's argument, the sociology of deviance/criminology did, at that moment in the late 1960s, provide, at least for radical practitioners, a space in which to work that was relatively free from these constraints. As Jock Young (1988: 164) has said:

> The fall-out from the new deviancy explosion has been considerable. Radical criminology has its powerbase in those areas of what one might call unsubsidised criminology. That is criminology as it is taught in the schools and polytechnics, the universities and the colleges of education. It has not held sway over those parts of criminology which are paid for directly out of central government funds.

Furthermore, many of the ideas derived from radical criminology have also had an impact in areas outside these teaching institutions and 'have entered into the general social perspective of educated sections of the population as they have influenced the thinking of establishment criminology itself' (ibid.).

An important institutional development for the new deviancy in Britain was the creation in 1968 of the National Deviancy Conference (NDC), which acted as a forum for radical criminologists. Continuing well into the 1970s, the conferences organised by the NDC quickly attracted large audiences, and played a key role in augmenting and developing alternatives to mainstream criminology. As Downes (1988: 177) says:

> The great appeal of the NDC was not only to sociologists of crime in search of a congenial forum, but also to younger sociologists who saw in deviance an escape route from the positivist methods and functionalist orthodoxy of much British sociology.

That many of the main figures in British criminology today were closely involved in the NDC is a further indication of its significant contribution to the field of criminology. Achieving senior positions in universities and research centres, the influence of these criminologists on the shape of the discipline in this country has been far-reaching. In fact, the success of the assault on mainstream criminology mounted by these figures was such that their ideas were to become the new mainstream, at least as far as the teaching of criminology was concerned. Now in their fifties and sixties, they did not have to withstand a comparable onslaught from the next generation of radical criminologists, though they may have themselves modified their views. The extraordinary fecundity, in terms of quantity and quality, that characterised the late 1960s and early 1970s was not to be repeated by the new generation – but this was not because of a decline in ability. By the late 1970s cut-backs in the funding of university and polytechnic postgraduate programmes reduced the pool of rising criminologists, and teaching posts in sociology departments had become thin on the ground in the 1980s. This is an important factor when explaining the lack of any substantial paradigmatic challenge from radical criminologists on the scale of that mounted against the mainstream during the 1960s.

The 'unsubsidised criminology' associated with the new deviancy period established a particular intellectual framework, deriving from agreement – at least in the short term – regarding how criminology was to be studied, what was to be studied and why it was to be studied. At the core of new deviancy theory lay the theoretical insights of interactionism, sometimes with bits of Marxism or phenomenology added. The areas studied reflected a move away from an earlier concentration on juvenile delinquency towards a broader concept of 'deviance'. Some of the more important studies from the period illustrate this: soft drug use (Young, 1971); industrial sabotage (Taylor and Walton, 1971); suicide (Atkinson, 1971); white-collar crime (Carson, 1970); surviving long-term imprisonment (Cohen and Taylor, 1972); ideological violence (Cohen, 1969); Teddy Boys (Jefferson, 1973). The 'why' element coalesced around the notion of 'appreciation', and the need to give the deviant an authentic voice. This was a clear departure from the corrective concerns of the criminology that had gone before.

Divisions and disputes

By 1973 various divisions involving the 'how', 'what' and 'why' of criminology had begun to surface among members of the NDC. Disputes over how criminology was to be studied reflected growing criticism of interactionism and the labelling theory associated with it. Some wished to develop a more radical, explicitly Marxist criminology; others opted for the promises offered by phenomenology; some attempted to incorporate the insights offered by another theoretical development originating in the United States, control theory, with interactionism; whilst others wished to refine interactionist criminology.

Disputes over what to study were directed not so much at areas of study *per se* (e.g., skinheads versus hippies), as at the wider moral and political implications of the choices made. Ethnographic research, for instance, was accused by some of aiding the imposition of deviant statuses on marginalised groups, exploiting them in the furtherance of an academic career and providing data useful to those in power. Similar sentiments had been expressed in a famous (or infamous, depending on one's viewpoint) address to the American Sociological Association in 1968 by a young sociologist called Martin Nicolaus. At one point he scandalised his audience by telling them:

> the professional eyes of the sociologist are on the down people, and the professional palm of the sociologist is stretched toward the up people . . . he is an Uncle Tom not only for this government and ruling class but for any.
>
> (Nicolaus quoted in Gouldner, 1971: 10)

This was to a largely conservative audience. To apply a similar critique to the new deviancy theorists, as some radicals were doing, was particularly mordant.

Although these divisions began to become very public in 1973, they had been a latent feature of the new deviancy from the start; by 1973 the divisions had reached critical mass. Within a short space of time the field began to fragment, with different strands flying off in different directions. In conformity with an already established pattern, these divisions appeared first in the United States, and were then picked up shortly afterwards by British counterparts. One of the central unstable elements in new deviancy was the concept of deviance itself: how much mileage was left in it?

In the next chapter the new deviancy is discussed in detail, and in particular one of its chief components, labelling theory (though supporters came to prefer the term labelling *perspective*). This will include an examination of a critical assault on labelling theory, building up between 1968 and 1973, and pursued on two fronts: first, for treating the deviant as a passive 'underdog', and second, for concentrating on 'nuts, sluts and preverts' (I'll retain the original spelling).

Selected further reading

The cultural transformations associated with the 1960s are reviewed in **Nuttall, J. (1970)** *Bomb Culture*, St Albans: Paladin.

A collection of chapters addressing some of this period is **Wiles, P. N. P. (ed) (1976)** *The Sociology of Crime and Delinquency in Britain*, Vol. 2, *The New Criminology*, Oxford: Martin Robertson. See also: **Rock, P. (ed) (1988)** *A History of British Criminology*, Oxford: Oxford University Press.

CHAPTER 9

NEW DEVIANCY THEORY: THE INTERACTIONIST
APPROACH TO DEVIANCE

> **Key themes**
> - Labelling theory
> - Learning to become 'deviant'
> - Primary and secondary deviation
> - The amplification of deviance
> - Conceptualising deviance
> - Criticisms of the new deviancy

INTRODUCTION

This chapter provides a detailed discussion of new deviancy theory – an interactionist approach to the analysis of crime and deviance. Key concepts, such as labelling and moral panic, are explained, together with the work of major British and American theorists. However, the arguments put forward by new deviancy theorists did attract various criticisms, and these are also discussed in this chapter.

As we have seen in the last chapter, new deviancy theory and the interactionist ideas on which it was based began to have a strong impact on criminology, or the sociology of deviance as it became known, in Britain and the United States during the middle to late 1960s. With a shift away from crime towards the broader concept of deviance, interactionism continued to influence criminological thought through the 1970s and, indeed, up to the present day.

Interactionism marked an important break with the causal–corrective approach of traditional criminology, where crime was investigated and explained within the context of social policy and legal and penal processes. In the orthodox criminology looked at earlier, crime and deviance tended to be conceptualised in terms of pathology, according to some assumed yardstick of acceptable behaviour, and the search for causes (of a more or less positivistic nature) was linked to the eradication of the criminal or deviant behaviour. Many of these orthodox studies, especially where they had forgotten the lessons to be learnt from the early ethnographic work of the Chicago School, denied authenticity to the deviant's account of what they did, and thus rendered invalid subjective motivations and purposes. Importantly, this break with a causal–corrective

147

orientation, signalled by the arrival of new deviancy theory, brought with it a reconceptualisation of what criminology, or rather the sociology of deviance, should be about. The development of a sceptical approach meant a disengagement from the commonsense agenda obsessed with answering the question, 'Why did they do it?' in favour of analyses of reactions to perceived deviance, and the subsequent implications for those so labelled. The new deviancy was in fact often referred to as social reaction theory.

The interactionist approach to deviance had its roots in the earlier work of George Herbert Mead (1934) and the symbolic interactionist school, though it did come in a number of guises. Following the symbolic interactionists, attention was on the individual social actor and the ways in which he or she develops perceptions of self and others through social interaction. And it was this subjectivism that allowed for the assimilation (albeit sometimes crudely) of certain ideas from phenomenology. Matza's work with Sykes was clearly relevant to this reorientation in criminology, as was the 'naturalism' of his phenomenological perspective developed later on. Matza's concept of 'appreciation' was particularly influential. Appreciation meant that the sociologist should aim for truthfulness and accuracy in their descriptions of social phenomena, rather than impose their own understandings on them. Thus, instead of carrying out one's study on the basis of presuppositions regarding the (immoral) nature of deviant behaviour, with the hope of eradicating it, the sociologist should attempt to present the behaviour in its own terms. As Matza (1969: 17) puts it: 'These appreciative sentiments are easily summarized: We do not for a moment wish that we could rid ourselves of deviant phenomena. We are intrigued by them. They are an intrinsic, ineradicable, and vital part of human society'.

LABELLING THEORY

Above all, interactionism is associated with labelling theory, though many have questioned its status as a theory and prefer to call it a perspective. As one of the influential members of this school put it, writing retrospectively in the 1970s: 'I have never thought that the original statements by myself and others warranted being called theories, at least not theories of the fully articulated kind that they are now criticized for not being' (Becker, 1974: 41–2). With this qualification, we will refer to it here as a theory.

Labelling theorists focused on the interactions between individuals or groups and those who label or define them as deviant. Out of these interactional encounters – say, between police and 'delinquents' – the participants will construct meanings: namely, images and understandings of both themselves and the others involved. The relationship between definers and defined is conceived of as processual; that is, individuals are involved in a process whereby they subjectively construct a symbolic world. Under certain circumstances these interactions lead to the application of a 'deviant' label. This, in turn, has psychological implications in that those so labelled may come to see themselves in terms of the label. It also has social implications in that such labelling is likely to have an impact on the way in which individuals labelled as deviant are treated by others in the future. This link between labelling and future behaviour was partly derived from Merton's idea of a 'self-fulfilling prophesy'.

From the perspective of labelling theory the quality of 'deviance' does not reside in the behaviour itself, but is, rather, the outcome of responses to that behaviour by various social audiences. Behaviour that is potentially deviant is said to occur all the time, among all sections of society (though, in effect, *all* behaviour is potentially deviant). Which behaviour actually gets labelled deviant depends upon how and where it is carried out, and on the nature of the interactional responses:

- In some instances the individual simply does not get caught. They perhaps possess the resources to cover their tracks.
- Sometimes the audience lacks the power to apply the deviant label. Clearly, relationships of power are central to labelling processes.
- Sometimes the general circumstances allow the behaviour to be normalised. In another context the behaviour may easily be defined as deviant, but contingent factors, such as being on holiday or inebriated, may allow the behaviour, although it might be odd or frightening or whatever, to be kept within the frame of normality.
- Sometimes the individual is able to resist the impact of labelling, perhaps because of others who can protect their non-deviant identity.

Out of these complex interactional processes the participants interpret and negotiate their understandings of what is going on. In short, they construct social reality. The process of becoming deviant reaches a key stage when the recipient of the label begins to accept the label and sees him or herself as deviant.

From this brief outline we can see that interactionism's focus on reactions to perceived deviance marked a radical departure from traditional criminology's concentration on the causal factors leading to deviance in the first place. This is not to say, however, that this dimension to the study of deviance had been entirely ignored in the past. The American criminologist Tannenbaum (1938) provided the first serious discussion of the effects on the young delinquent of negative judgements by the community. One of labelling theory's pivotal concepts, 'primary deviation', was originally introduced by Edwin Lemert in 1951, and Howard Becker's article 'Becoming a marijuana user', one of the most influential and widely quoted texts, was first published in 1953. It was not until 1963, though, that his *Outsiders: Studies in the sociology of deviance*, a collection of essays on marijuana use and reactions to it, first appeared.

LEARNING TO BECOME 'DEVIANT'

Becker's *Outsiders* found an enthusiastic audience among more radical British and American sociologists in the late 1960s. Here was a fundamental critique of a criminological orthodoxy that conceptualised the social world in terms of the normal on one side of the moral line, and deviance/crime on the other. Becker had attempted to bring to light the continuities, rather than discontinuities, between deviant and non-deviant worlds. Significantly, instead of the concept of crime, with its connotations of moral absolutism, he used the concept of deviance, and he shifted attention away from the supposed intrinsic qualities of the rule breaker towards the reactions of the social audience, and the interactional processes leading to the application of the deviant label.

Becker traced the processes through which an individual learns to become a marijuana user. The behaviour is not seen as resulting from deviant motivations; these come later because of the reactions of control agents and their efforts to deviantise those involved. Put another way, prior to any deviant label being applied, the individual chooses not to be deviant, but to use a drug that happens to be strongly frowned upon, and indeed, illegal. Becker aimed to show how deviant identities and understandings depended upon the labelling process. In this way he sought to infuse the user's original behaviour with authenticity – to show how choices are made. This was a challenge to traditional formulations that viewed deviant motivations as resulting from deterministic forces operating prior to any labelling. As Matza (1969: 110) says in a commentary on Becker's analysis: 'it becomes apparent that *anyone* can become a marijuana user and that *no one* has to' (original emphasis).

Two important elements of labelling theory are present in Becker's account: first, an anti-deterministic stance, allowing people to make choices and exercise their wills, and second, following successful labelling by control agents, the notion of a deviant 'career'. For labelling theorists, the original causes of the behaviour, as traditionally understood, are not on the agenda. Modern societies, they say, are composed of different groups with different norms and values, and deviant behaviour – or more accurately, behaviour that could be labelled as deviant – is widespread. However, only some of it becomes officially designated as deviant. More people are doing their own thing than traditional criminology had seemed to realise. And, as Edwin Lemert, another eminent writer in the labelling tradition, argued, trying to establish the original 'causes' is pointless. In his view, all that deviants have in common is that they have been labelled deviant.

As the central canon of labelling theory is that deviance is 'caused' by the reactions of a social audience, then, logically, analyses have to concern themselves with the creation of deviance at that point. The position is well summed up by Becker (1963: 9) in this widely quoted passage:

> Social groups create deviance by making the rules whose infraction constitutes deviance, and by applying those rules to particular people and labeling them as outsiders. From this point of view, deviance is *not* a quality of the act the person commits, but rather a consequence of the application by others of rules and sanctions to an 'offender'. The deviant is one to whom that label has been successfully applied; deviant behavior is behavior that people so label.

The same relativistic view of deviance had also been put forward by two other labelling theorists:

> Forms of behavior *per se* do not differentiate deviants from non-deviants; it is the responses of the conventional and conforming members of society which identify and interpret behavior as deviant which sociologically transforms persons into deviants.
>
> (Kitsuse (1962) quoted in Taylor *et al.*, 1973: 144)

> Deviance is not a property inherent in certain forms of behaviour; it is a property conferred upon these forms by the audiences which directly or indirectly witness them.
>
> (Erikson (1962) quoted in Taylor *et al.*, 1973: 144)

We can see from these quotations that the primary focus of labelling theory is on the application of already existing rules to particular people. From this perspective who gets selected, and why they get selected, become crucial, given the argument that it is not the distinctive quality of the behaviour itself that is the determining factor; no behaviour is in itself deviant. Thus rule breaking, as such, does not designate a person as deviant; a response to that rule breaking is required. According to Becker, particular individuals and groups are labelled deviant because of what he calls 'career contingencies'. These are extraneous factors, external to the actual behaviour itself, and include such things as the dress and demeanour of the participants, the neighbourhood in which they live, and police resources and policies.

PRIMARY AND SECONDARY DEVIATION

The impact of labelling on the deviant's future behaviour was explored by Lemert (1967), who introduced the concepts of primary and secondary deviation. In his view, traditional criminology had put the cart before the horse by assuming that deviant behaviour came first, and then triggered social control responses. At the time this seemed to many a startling proposition:

> This is a large turn away from older sociology which tended to rest heavily upon the idea that deviance leads to social control. I have come to believe that the reverse idea, i.e., social control leads to deviance, is equally tenable and the potentially richer premise for studying deviance in modern society.
>
> (Ibid.: v)

He illustrated this link between reaction and deviance through his research into stuttering in a number of native American tribes in British Columbia. In some of these tribes he found that the language contained concepts relating to stuttering, and that some members of the tribe did stutter. Among neighbouring tribes, however, no such concepts existed, and stuttering seemed to be absent. Clearly, there was no physiological reason why this should be so, and it could not be connected with the contacts that the tribes had had with white people. Lemert found that in the tribes where stuttering existed, great emphasis was placed on oratory and storytelling. Children were socialised into a set of norms and values that placed great stress on not stuttering, and failure to put on a 'good performance' was ridiculed. Lemert concluded that the enormous pressure placed on people to speak 'properly', and the institutionalisation of the social reaction to those that didn't (to the 'deviants'), actually led to the development of stuttering: that is, the social reaction created the deviance. In tribes where these cultural expectations did not exist, there was, of course, no negative reaction, and hence no deviance of this type.

Lemert emphasised the ubiquitous nature of 'deviance'. Most of the time, he argued, individuals 'get away' with such behaviour, meaning that it remains unlabelled, and they are therefore able to maintain a non-deviant self-image, and are not treated as deviant by those around them. He describes this as primary deviation, and as such it is of little interest to interactionists. However, under certain circumstances, again not dependent upon the nature of the behaviour, there is a social reaction and the individuals concerned are labelled as deviant. This is described as secondary deviation, which is seen as: 'deviant behavior, or social roles based upon it, which becomes a means of defense, attack or adaptation to the overt and covert problems created by the societal reaction to primary deviation' (ibid.: 17).

An acceptance of the label, and the carrying out of further deviant acts, may therefore be mechanisms used by those labelled to cope with the problems posed by the labelling. Obviously, the imposition of the label 'deviant' involves, at its core, judgements about a person's moral worth. The label can easily become the new 'master status', superseding a range of other statuses such as mother, teacher and footballer. The early symbolic interactionists, from whom many of these ideas had been drawn, had shown that how an individual is treated by significant others has profound implications for how an individual sees him or herself; the process was encapsulated in Cooley's (1902) concept, introduced at the beginning of the twentieth century, of the 'looking glass self'. Being treated as a 'thief', 'sexual pervert', 'alcoholic', 'mad person', and so on, makes it extremely difficult for those involved to take part in the routines of normal life, and, as Becker said, they 'of necessity develop illegitimate routines'. In this situation the individual is likely to seek out others who have been similarly labelled, which then forms the basis for mutually supporting subcultural groups.

THE AMPLIFICATION OF DEVIANCE

Leslie T. Wilkins (1964) introduced the concept of 'deviancy amplification' as a way of explaining the process outlined above. It describes those paradoxical situations where the social reaction on the part of control agents, which is aimed at stamping out or controlling the deviance, in fact leads to an increase in amounts and frequency. Amplification in this context does not simply mean that publicity given to some deviant behaviour by the mass media leads to 'copycat' behaviour on the part of others. Rather it seeks to identify a process arising from secondary deviation, where those labelled as deviant incorporate the label within their self-image. This has a knock-on effect of producing more reactions from control agents, thereby further consolidating the deviant self-image. In time, this creates a deviancy amplification spiral, as others attracted by the deviant status also become involved. Stan Cohen's (1980) classic study of the Mods and Rockers phenomenon in the 1960s set out to illustrate how deviancy amplification operated with respect to these specific youth subcultures. The title of his book, *Folk Devils and Moral Panics,* contains two further concepts popular with interactionists. Cohen argued that the very actions by police, magistrates and mass media, designed to eradicate the delinquent activities of Mods and Rockers, were in reality counterproductive in that they ultimately created and sustained a much larger 'problem'.

Although interactionists agreed that none of the processes discussed above was inevitable, there was less clear-cut agreement about the nature of the relationship between the changes in self-image resulting from labelling and changes in subsequent behaviour. If secondary deviation involves a change in both thinking and acting, then it would have important implications for traditional studies that attempt to discover the causes of deviance. In such studies, samples of offenders are usually drawn from among those officially processed by the criminal justice system, namely, secondary deviants. However, this research aims at discovering why people offend in the first place: it is seeking out the causes of primary deviance. Thus it is using secondary deviants as a basis for explaining primary deviance, and is therefore somewhat flawed. If the mass of primary deviants escape apprehension, then such research may simply tell us what kind of offenders are likely to get caught and labelled.

CONCEPTUALISING DEVIANCE

As the discussion so far has indicated, interactionism made an important contribution to the sociology of deviance by attempting to develop what is sometimes called a 'constitutive' model. From this perspective, 'deviance' does not have an independent existence, but is socially constructed through processes of interaction. This approach represented a commitment to a thoroughly sociological understanding of deviance, and marked a break with the absolutism characterising common-sense understandings. According to the logic of this argument, no deviance can exist unless it has been labelled as such. Unfortunately, labelling theorists themselves did not always consistently adhere to the conceptual implications of this, which led to many criticisms – some of which will be examined below – and to some spirited defences (e.g. Becker, 1974; Gove, 1975; Plummer, 1979).

In Chapter 1 there was a brief discussion of Reiner's (1988) reference to Becker's statement that 'deviance is not a quality of the act'. Reiner's comment that this was merely a platitude – that lawyers had known all along that in order for crime/deviance to exist there must be rules – is highly misleading. Clearly, as Durkheim had pointed out in the nineteenth century, no behaviour is in itself intrinsically criminal or deviant, just as no painting is intrinsically beautiful. What is defined as 'bad' or 'immoral' in a society changes over time, and varies from society to society. Left like this, Becker's message is, of course, not at all novel; but it was necessary for labelling theorists to reaffirm the point that when analysing deviance we are not dealing with moral absolutes – deviance is a relative concept. However, Becker was saying more than this, as the rest of the sentence quoted by Reiner indicates: '. . . but rather a consequence of the application by others of rules and sanctions'. If he had simply said that deviance exists because rules exist, then it would have suggested that deviant behaviour can exist without a social reaction and the *application* of the rule, a proposition that labelling theorists rejected, at least when they remained faithful to their theory. The crucial argument from labelling theory was that deviance does not exist merely because a rule is broken: deviance results from the labelling of specific cases. Although consistency regarding this theoretical formulation was not always maintained (see, for example, Becker's notion of a 'secret deviant' below) it was, none the less, an insight of central importance. It alerted sociologists to the need to consider carefully the ways in which they conceptualised crime and deviance, and thus pushed them towards complex epistemological questions pertaining to the subject-matter of the sociology of deviance/criminology. These questions still stand, though contemporary criminology does not always engage with them (the issues they raise are many miles away from, say, research on how to 'design out' ram-raiding).

CRITICISMS OF THE NEW DEVIANCY

Given the break with orthodoxy represented by the advent of new deviancy theory, and the nature of the questions it thrust on to the agenda of the sociology of deviance, it was inevitable that it generated much criticism.

A quality of the act?

At what point can a deviant act be said to exist? Obviously, labelling theory was correct to draw attention to the implications for self-image and future behaviour of being labelled, but is it correct to say that a rule-breaking act cannot be deviant (or criminal) until labelling has occurred, or in other words, that deviance is not a quality of the act? The 'constitutive' approach argues that 'deviance' is a social label conferred upon rule breaking. This can be illustrated with a simple example. In 1986 Diego

Maradona pushed the ball into the goal with his 'hand of God' during a World Cup football match between England and Argentina. Clearly (for we can see the video evidence) Maradona broke a rule, but the referee did not see what happened and he let the goal stand; that is, the *crucial* social audience did not label the act as a foul (though England supporters might label Maradona a 'cheat'). The interesting question to ask is, was a foul 'really' committed? Can the quality of foul be given to the act in the absence of labelling? There is one further dimension to this that can be commented on. Labelling involves both a 'deviant' act and a 'deviant' person, though the distinction is not always made explicit. Thus, in the case of Maradona, we have to consider the creation of a 'foul' as well as a 'fouler'. According to the official records no foul occurred, and Maradona was not a fouler. Is it possible that rule breaking can constitute a deviant act (a foul), but the absence of a reaction, of labelling, means that the social category of a deviant (a fouler) is not created? And what are the implications of this for perceptions of self?

Criticism of labelling theory's claim that deviance is not a quality of the act is built up along two broad fronts: first, a critique of what was seen as a logical inconsistency on the part of some writers, and second, a critique of the idea itself. As far as the first of these was concerned, the main criticisms were aimed at Lemert and Becker. In the case of Lemert, it was the concept of 'primary deviation' that was at issue. If, as labelling theory contends, deviance results from labelling, then how can primary deviation, that is, unlabelled deviance, be possible (see Gibbs, 1966)? The same criticism has also been levelled at Becker, and arises from his categorisation of different types of deviance deriving from two variables: actual behaviour, and perceptions of that behaviour by a social audience. Becker (1963: 20) thus offered the following typology:

	Obedient behaviour	Rule-breaking behaviour
Perceived as deviant	Falsely accused	Pure deviant
Not perceived as deviant	Conforming	Secret deviant

As Gibbs (1966), for example, has pointed out, according to the logic of the labelling perspective a 'secret deviant' cannot exist. Although a rule has been broken, the individual concerned has avoided being labelled, so how can it be deviance? (There is a parallel here with the example of Maradona, whose 'deviance' was not seen by the referee.) Becker, says Gibbs, is here confusing two different conceptual models: one sees deviance as rule breaking, the other views it as the result of social reaction. The same critical point is discussed by Taylor *et al.* (1973). From an ethnomethodological perspective Pollner (1974) sees Becker's concept of secret deviant as arising from a confusion between what he calls a mundane/common-sense model of deviance and a constitutive model. Although we can see what Becker meant by secret deviant, for Pollner he had retreated from a proper, constitutive model. In the same vein, Pollner says that the concept of 'falsely accused' is illogical too, for if deviance results from interactional labelling processes, then irrespective of whether or not someone 'really' did it, if they have been labelled deviant, they *are* deviant. From Pollner's standpoint Becker wanted to have his cake and eat it. However, we should note that Becker (1974) did review his original position and say that instead of secret deviant he should have used the concept of 'potential deviant'.

While Pollner criticises Becker's concepts, he approves of the logic of labelling theory which sees deviance as socially constructed. Others, however, have disputed the contention that labelling need occur in order for deviance to exist. In other words, they have insisted that deviance is a quality of the act of breaking strongly sanctioned rules. From this standpoint Maradona did commit a foul. The case for this line of reasoning has been forcefully put by Taylor *et al.* (1973). They agree with Becker, Erikson and Kitsuse that deviance is not an absolute quality intrinsic to an activity, and give as an example the taking of human life: in wartime it can earn a medal, in peacetime a life sentence. Their dispute with writers such as Becker concerns the view that deviance requires a social reaction and labelling in specific cases. For Taylor *et al.* it is quite possible for a secret deviant to exist. To illustrate this they distinguish between 'behaviour' and 'action'. Following Weber, behaviour is simply some physical activity, such as accidentally falling off a ladder, whilst action is of sociological significance because it is behaviour to which meaning has been attached. Therefore, even a secret deviant is generally aware that what they are doing is disapproved of, which is why they remain secret. Taylor *et al.* (1973) thus argue that if the individual (secret) deviant attaches this sort of meaning to their action – meanings shared with the rest of society – then at that moment in time deviance is, objectively, a quality of the act, and no specific reaction is required.

This concern with the meanings lying behind deviance had, by the late 1960s, become part of a major critical assault whereby labelling theory was accused of treating the deviant as a passive 'underdog'. At the same time, a second critical front opened up which homed in on labelling theory's concentration on 'nuts, sluts and preverts'. Each will be examined in turn.

Underdogs

In a classic paper, Alvin Gouldner (1968) argued that labelling theorists had conjured up an image of the deviant as the innocent victim of the application of labels by control agents such as the police: 'man-on-his-back', rather than 'man-fighting-back'. This, he said, made deviance entirely contingent on the whims of authority. For Gouldner, the labelling theory view of marginalised groups was in fact an expression of the liberal, welfare-oriented ideology of the American establishment, whereby all deviants were victims. They were, however, not seen as victims of the system, so much as victims of petty-minded and illiberal agencies and individuals within it.

This 'fighting back' view of the deviant was also in evidence in a paper published in the following year by Horowitz and Leibowitz (1969). Here they argued that a false dichotomy was made by sociologists (including labelling theorists), law makers, social workers, and so forth. Some forms of 'socially' deviant behaviour, they said, should more properly be viewed as 'politically' deviant. They developed this by arguing that traditional definitions of 'political' were too narrow and inflexible. Thus the views of Horowitz and Leibowitz, as well as Gouldner, were clearly in tune with some of the ideas emanating from the New Left/counter-culture configuration at that time. After a decade of riot and protest in the United States, for Horowitz and Leibowitz (1969: 280) an important convergence had occurred in which deviant groups were increasingly using political tactics to further their cause, whilst political groups were increasingly using deviant tactics: 'the result of this trend is estimated to be an increase in the use of violence as a political tactic, and the development of a revolutionary potential among the expanding ranks of deviant sub-groups'.

This attempt to politicise deviance was particularly important as far as the development of the sociology of deviance/crime was concerned over the next few years. Criticising Becker, Taylor *et al.* (1973: 142), for instance, drew directly on Gouldner's (1968) paper when they wrote:

> Becker's confusion stems from his desire to preserve the category deviant for those people who are labelled deviant, but, to do this, is to imply at the outset that rule-breakers, and rule-breakers who are labelled (i.e. deviants), are fundamentally different from each other in their self-perceptions . . . this leads to an over-concentration by Becker and other social reaction theorists on the importance of the application of a label in creating self-conscious commitment to deviant acts.

One of Taylor *et al.*'s primary goals was to present deviance not only as meaningful from the point of view of the participants, but also as a form of *political* action. It is not surprising, therefore, that they attack Becker's proposition that people do not choose to engage in deviance, but rather choose to carry out certain acts of rule breaking which may subsequently be labelled deviant. Because of their general theoretical position, it was necessary for Taylor *et al.* to argue that the deviant makes a conscious choice to be deviant, for this was seen as a political action against bourgeois rules.

Eventually, a growing number of writers were criticising labelling theory for seeing the deviant as a passive victim of the agents of social control, and arguing that as a theory it was just as deterministic as the theories they railed against (e.g. Schervish, 1973; Broadhead, 1974). It was seen as deterministic because it suggested that the reaction caused the deviance. However, sometimes this line of criticism was prone to distort the original claims made by labelling theory. As Plummer (1979: 104) says: 'no labelling theorist seems to espouse the "label creates behaviour" view'. An observation by Akers (1967: 46), for instance, will be familiar to most of those who have studied A-level sociology (it certainly cropped up with monotonous regularity in the examination papers that I used to mark): 'One sometimes gets the impression from reading this literature that people go about minding their own business, and then – "wham" – bad society comes along and slaps them with a stigmatized label'. Labelling theorists, however, did not say that rule breakers were blissfully unaware that they were breaking rules, and suddenly realised that they were when they were labelled. Becker's marijuana users, for example, knew full well that what they did was disapproved of, and indeed illegal, and took pains to conceal their activities. The relevance of the label is that it is a public recognition and stigmatisation of a 'deviant' and has implications for self-perceptions and subsequent treatment by others in society.

The criticism had, perhaps, more substance when it was directed at labelling theory's tendency to examine forms of deviance where sympathy for the deviant, as a victim of labelling, was relatively easily invoked. In particular, this involved 'crimes without victims' for example, soft drug users, dropouts, stutterers and prostitutes. Studies of serial killers, racist murderers, rapists and the like were conspicuously lacking. By doing this, the sociologists concerned gave the impression of approaching deviance in general in, as Gouldner put it, 'a spirit of sentimental romanticism'. As a theory, or perspective, it did most strikingly lend itself to a focus on those who seemed to be treated oppressively by control agents.

The moral ambiguity surrounding much of the research by interactionists reached its apotheosis in Becker's (1967) article 'Whose side are we on?' Here he rejected traditional criminology's condemnatory approach to the study of deviance, and argued instead for an 'appreciation' of the deviant as victim. In some cases this might be appropriate, but, as many commentators have pointed out (e.g. Heidensohn, 1989), it ignores those who are often the deviant's victims.

'Nuts, sluts and preverts'

A second important critical front developed around Liazos's (1972) theme of 'nuts, sluts and preverts' (the misspelling has already been explained). By focusing on marginalised groups with unconventional lifestyles, it was argued that labelling theorists were themselves helping to create deviant labels, and mystifying the reality of deviance and crime; for example:

> The term 'social deviants' . . . does not make sufficiently explicit – as the terms 'scapegoat' or 'victim' do – that majorities usually categorize persons or groups as 'deviant' in order to set them apart as inferior beings and to justify their social control, oppression, persecution, or even complete destruction.
>
> (Szasz, 1973: xxv–xxvi)

Thus, the argument ran, even if one accepted the view from labelling theory that deviant status was ascribed by control agents, and that when in full swing the labelling process led to an acceptance of that status and a commitment to a deviant lifestyle by the individual, they none the less ended up *as* deviant. No matter how they got there, we can all recognise who they are. It was this seeming compliance with the ideologies of dominant groups in society that was now being criticised.

Labelling theory had ignored the deviant activities of the powerful in American society; in fact, in the absence of labelling (by the powerful) these activities were, according to labelling theory, not deviant. Critics argued that many of the activities of the powerful and 'respectable' were more socially harmful than were the activities of those labelled 'deviant'. They pointed to the massive amounts of corporate crime committed in the United States, to the violence of the Vietnam War and other imperialistic excursions, and to the corruption of political administrations. In a study of business crime, Conklin (1977: 4), for example, concluded:

> The direct cost of business crime surpasses the cost of such conventional crimes as larceny, burglary, and auto theft. In 1965, the estimated loss from these four crimes was about $600 million; with inflation and rising crime rates, a better estimate as of 1977 would be about $3 to $4 billion a year. This figure pales in significance when compared with an estimated annual loss of $40 billion from various white collar crimes. Half that amount results from consumer fraud, illegal competition and deceptive practices.

Critical voices questioned the double standards that permeated the culture of American society whereby, for instance, President Nixon could say that abortion was a violation of 'the sanctity of human life', whilst at the same time giving approval to the actions of Lieutenant Calley at My Lai (a Vietnamese village where the civilians were massacred).

Liazos's paper on 'nuts, sluts and preverts' was an important example of this type of critique. He drew attention to the harm done to people as a result of racial disadvantage and discrimination, and to the poverty, ill health, and so on, associated with a capitalist society. In the following year, Thio (1973) produced a similar argument, and castigated the sociology of deviance for failing to disengage itself from the ideological requirements of powerful elites.

More recently, the British criminologist Colin Sumner (1994: 262) has suggested that the 'nuts, sluts and preverts' critique presented by these two papers in 1972 and 1973 could have had a momentous impact on the sociology of deviance in the United States and in Britain, leading to the demise of the concept of deviance itself:

> These two essays took American sociology of deviance to the brink of a dissolution of the field of study, but held back from the crucial theoretical steps of *superseding* the concept of deviance and abandoning the search for a *general* theory of deviance. (Original emphasis)

From this perspective the key to understanding deviance lies not in the behaviour itself, but, rather, in the ideologies that define and shape what is thought to be 'deviant'. According to Sumner, though, the sociology of deviance pulled back from the brink because of the ideas set in motion by the 'underdog' critique: Gouldner's 'man-fighting-back' imagery gave the concept of deviance a new lease of life as the 1970s unfolded, and deviance came to be seen as a form of political resistance (these developments will be looked at in Chapter 11):

> This was hardly a time for sociologists to declare that deviance was a dead concept. Far from it, it was all too tempting to take the concept and give it a new behavioural mean- ing as a political rejection of the established social order. *In this sense, the late sixties gave the concept of deviance a whole new lease of life, a second wind.*
>
> (Ibid.: 258, original emphasis)

Two further criticisms of labelling theory should also be noted. First, it was argued that it had shown a wilful lack of interest in the original causes of deviance – primary deviation, as Lemert had called it. Although writers such as Schur (1971) had argued that, by definition, this was not the intention of labelling theory, critics saw this neg- lect of causes, and a concentration on reaction, as one-sided (Bordua, 1970; Mankoff, 1971; Taylor *et al.*, 1973). For them, deviant motivations and a commitment to a deviant lifestyle should not be linked exclusively to social reactions. These, they argued, can result from causal factors that pre-date any reaction by a social audience. In Mankoff's (1971: 211) words: 'one might attribute career deviance and its conse- quences not to societal reaction but to the continued effects of social structural strains, psychological stress, or disease states which produce initial rule-breaking'.

Second, the interactionist approach was criticised for failing to locate the rules them- selves, the causes of rule breaking, and reactions to perceived deviance within the wider structures of power in society. Although labelling theory had pointed to the central importance of the power to apply the label, analyses had tended to be confined to the actions of relatively low-level agents of social control, such as police officers, teachers, social workers and psychiatrists. This was a critique that, as we shall see, eventually helped to stimulate the development of the 'new' critical criminology of the 1970s, which attempted to establish a political economy of crime/deviance and control.

Selected further reading

There is no substitute for reading the now classic, original American texts: **Becker, H. S. (1963)** *Outsiders: Studies in the sociology of deviance,* London: Macmillan; **Lemert, E. M. (1967)** *Human Deviance, Social Problems and Social Control,* Englewood Cliffs, NJ: Prentice-Hall; **Wilkins, L. (1964)** *Social Deviance: Social policy, action and research,* London: Tavistock; **Matza, D. (1964)** *Delinquency and Drift,* New York: Wiley; **Matza, D. (1969)** *Becoming Deviant,* Englewood Cliffs, NJ: Prentice-Hall, and his 'appreciative' approach, were hugely influential. A British classic is **Cohen, S. (1980)** *Folk Devils and Moral Panics,* 2nd edn, Oxford: Martin Robertson.

For a collection of chapters covering this period, see: **Rock, P. and M. McIntosh (eds) (1974)** *Deviance and Social Control*, London: Tavistock.

A critical American voice was **Gouldner, A. W. (1968)** 'The Sociologist as Partisan: Sociology and the welfare state', *American Sociologist*, May.

The concept of moral panics has been revisited recently in this collection of readings: **Krinsky, C. (ed) (2008)** *Moral Panics Over Contemporary Children and Youth*, Abingdon: Ashgate.

PART IV

THE 1970S

CHAPTER 10

THE DISCIPLINE OF CRIMINOLOGY
AND ITS CONTEXT – 3

Key themes

- Deviance and politics
- The sociology of law: making laws, making deviants
- Criminology in the 1970s: other directions
- Orthodox criminology
- Radical critiques and the growth of the New Right

INTRODUCTION

This chapter looks at various criticisms of new deviancy theory that were already, even among sympathetic writers, building up by the end of the 1960s. It thus sets the scene for a discussion in the next chapter of the different theoretical perspectives that gained influence in the early 1970s. Notably, more radical ideas derived from Marxism were emerging and being absorbed by a growing number of academics working in the field of crime and deviance. At the end of the 1970s, though, there was a decisive shift to the right in British (and not long after, in American) politics with the election of the Thatcher government. This chapter concludes by discussing some of the ways in which the radical left, ironically and unwittingly, helped prepare the ground for this political transformation.

DEVIANCE AND POLITICS

As in the United States, various criticisms of labelling theory began to appear among radical sociologists of deviance, and in the first instance it was the 'underdog' critique that stimulated most work.

In an underdeveloped form, labelling theory had introduced the notion of politics into the field of deviance research. By stressing that the power to impress the deviant label was concentrated in the hands of the relatively powerful few, the deviant process was, to this extent, political. Radical sociologists, however, criticised labelling theory for failing to make connections between processes of interaction and the structures of power in which they were rooted.

As we have seen, some writers in the United States began to extend the ideas of labelling theory. In particular, Horowitz and Leibowitz (1969) argued that some deviant groups were engaging in political action. However, in their enthusiasm to politicise deviance, some British sociologists were quick to read into these formulations rather more than the authors originally intended. Horowitz and Leibowitz's position was that whereas in the past deviant minorities had carried out their deviances more or less privately, they were now entering the public realm, and taking up political modes of protest. It was this *new* activity that was seen as political, not the original deviance. Engaging in homosexual acts, for example, was not regarded as political, but the activities of the Gay Liberation Movement were. Geoff Pearson (1975: 96), for instance, seems to have read more into their paper than was actually there:

> But what emerges in the literature of misfit sociology from the analysis provided by Horowitz and Leibowitz is the imperative that one should understand not only the *labelling process* as a politically derived judgement, but also that *deviant behaviour* itself should be accorded political status. Or, more specifically, that deviance should be grasped as a primitive crypto-political action.

From hesitant beginnings, the project of politicising deviance was to become an important strand of British sociological criminology. Similar developments occurred in other disciplines too: for instance, R. D. Laing's (1967, 1968) 'anti-psychiatry', and efforts to show how the definition and treatment of mental illness were political processes. An early response to Horowitz and Leibowitz came in an article from Stan Cohen (1969), with a fuller version being published in 1973, and from Stuart Hall (1974). Although each of these essentially reiterated the original arguments, they did relate them to events in this country, and also had the merit of recognising, and endorsing, the limited extension of labelling theory offered by Horowitz and Leibowitz. Such restraint, however, was short-lived, as some radical sociologists moved to a position of arguing that some, or even all, crime/deviance was itself a political act – in simple terms, because it was resistance to bourgeois rules. This entailed delving into earlier precursors of this type of work: for example, Goldman (1959) on school vandalism and truancy. It also involved widening the academic net by trawling among the work of radical historians who had produced accounts of revolts from 'below' in Britain's past. Hobsbawm's (1959) concept of 'primitive rebellion' soon became common currency within this genre.

Ian Taylor (1971) identified soccer hooliganism as a form of political protest and, together with Paul Walton and Jock Young, incorporated the politics of deviance into an ambitious attempt to develop a Marxist theory of deviance in a book entitled (in contradistinction to the new deviancy) *The New Criminology* (Taylor *et al.*, 1973). Here, instead of picking out specific types of (usually working-class) deviance as candidates for the appellation 'political', they suggested that 'much deviance is in itself political'. Unfortunately, the authors failed to define either 'deviance' or 'political'. This was, though, an important and influential, if much criticised, text. However, by

1975, with the publication of a follow-up collection of readings (Taylor *et al.*, 1975), Jock Young was already starting to review his position. Whatever the merits of *The New Criminology*, it stands as a supreme example of criminological work nurtured by the twin influences of the New Left and the counter-culture: the New Left in its effort to introduce humanistic Marxism into the field, and the counter-culture because of its commitment to social diversity, to a celebration of 'difference'. As result of this, a serious criticism of the text was that it owed more to anarchism than it did to Marxism.

Geoff Pearson (1976, 1978) continued to plough the crime-as-politics furrow, in particular in a study of so-called Paki-bashing, where he argued that those involved were engaging in 'crypto-political' action. As early as 1973, though, other National Deviancy Conference members were pointing to the dangers of romanticism which they saw as characterising the counter-culture. Paul Rock (1973: 103), for instance, criticised the 'romanticism which views all criminals as primitive innocents who are engaged in inarticulate political conflict with institutional authority'.

The mid-1970s saw the growth in influence of the Birmingham Centre for Contemporary Cultural Studies, and in much of the work we can detect attempts to politicise crime/deviance. Under the direction of Stuart Hall, the Birmingham Centre drew on the work of the Italian Marxist Gramsci, and introduced key concepts, such as hegemony and ideology into the criminological discourse. The Centre is particularly associated with radical youth subcultural theory (see Hall and Jefferson, 1976). The main emphasis was on youth subcultural 'styles', and the ways in which these operate as modes of cultural resistance, and therefore, to that extent, represent forms of political action (Clarke and Jefferson, 1973a, 1973b; Jefferson, 1973; Clarke, 1976). The Centre laid down the foundations for future work that examined, and attempted to refine, concepts such as 'style' and 'cultural symbolisation' (e.g., Hebdige, 1979).

By the end of the 1970s the crime/deviance-as-politics argument had more or less fizzled out within radical criminology, but then, like a firework that had not quite gone out, in the early 1980s it burst into life again. Instead of *working-class* crime, though, it was specifically *black* crime that was characterised as political. It was no coincidence that American versions of this argument had come in the wake of major riots; likewise, the British versions emerged following large-scale urban disorder and resistance in 1980 and 1981 in this country (for a critique, see Tierney, 1988).

So we see that into the 1970s, in spite of the conceptual challenge raised by labelling theory, among radical sociologists the concept of deviance was, albeit in a politicised form, firmly back on the agenda as a quality of the act. Some things really were deviant, and not only that, they were also political.

THE SOCIOLOGY OF LAW: MAKING LAWS, MAKING DEVIANTS

As the above discussion shows, the politicisation of deviance in the late 1960s gave the concept of deviance, as Sumner puts it, a 'second wind', and set in motion a research agenda that placed the actions of the deviant centre stage. Inevitably, the deviants placed under this spotlight were marginalised, relatively powerless groups. At the end of the 1960s, however, another strand of sociological criminology emerged, again partly contingent on labelling theory and the theoretical problems it raised. This second strand developed along a broad pedigree line that included Liazos's 'nuts, sluts and preverts' critique, as well as Gouldner's 'underdog' critique, and was essentially based upon two propositions. First, that definitions of crime and deviance (and, thus, ultimately, the nature of law itself) were linked to the interests of powerful elites or classes; and second, that governments, corporations and 'respectable' members of society were often involved in, and got away with, criminal activities that were much more harmful than so-called deviant activities. In short, rather than concentrate on the nature of officially defined deviant behaviour (as hedonistic, crypto political, prophetic or whatever), this strand of criminological thought turned its attention to the powerful in society, either as self-interested rule makers, or as cynical rule breakers, or as both. Indeed, in *Critical Criminology*, Jock Young (1975: 89) attacked the ruling class in terms of both rule making and rule breaking: 'Radical criminological strategy . . . is to show up the law, in its true colours, as the instrument of the ruling class . . . and that the rule-makers are also the greatest rule-breakers'.

In combination with the earlier *The New Criminology* (Taylor *et al.*, 1973) we can see in fact three central elements of what became known generically as critical criminology: a view of deviants as political rebels; an 'instrumentalist' view of law; and a desire to emphasise ruling-class, as opposed to working-class, crime.

Inevitably, *The New Criminology* generated a great deal of debate and criticism when it was published, and criticism was only marginally assuaged following the publication of *Critical Criminology* (Taylor *et al.*, 1975). The most fundamental question raised was whether a specifically Marxist theory of deviance was, from the point of view of Marxism itself, possible. Fellow Marxist Paul Hirst (1975a: 204), one of the contributors to the second text, argued that Marxists should have nothing to do with deviance: 'there is no "Marxist theory of deviance" either in existence, or which can be developed within orthodox Marxism. Crime and deviance vanish into the general theoretical concerns and the specific scientific object of Marxism'. Hirst's objection essentially revolved around the concept of deviance. For him, the theoretical objects of analysis are, in Marxism, laid down and structured by the concepts that Marx himself devised:

> The objects of Marxist theory are specified by their own concepts: the mode of production, the class struggle, the state, ideology, etc. Any attempt to apply Marxism to this pre-given field of sociology is therefore a more or less 'revisionist' activity in respect of Marxism; it must modify and distort Marxian concepts to suit its own pre-Marxist purposes.
>
> (Ibid.: 204)

Put into simpler language, from this standpoint, using the concept of deviance is a bit like, for instance, using the concept of 'bad art'. Why should Marxists acquiesce to (bourgeois) definitions and treat some art as if it really was 'bad'?

Shortly after this exchange between Hirst and Taylor *et al.*, the Marxist criminologist Colin Sumner (1976) attempted to provide a solution to the problem posed by Hirst. Sumner argued that deviance should be seen as a type of ideology – as a social censure – rather than as behaviour. As we shall see, this was to become an important theoretical issue for radical criminology.

In his critique, Hirst also attacked Taylor *et al.* for romanticising crime – the criminal as revolutionary – and for their 'oppositional' stance regarding law: that is, for seeing all law as acting in the interests of the ruling class ('instrumentalism').

We can now look briefly at developments in radical criminology based upon the two propositions mentioned earlier.

Self-interested rule makers

Attempts to develop a political economy of crime – that is, to develop a theoretical criminology based upon analyses of the creation and functions of the law within a political and economic context – encompassed a range of writers from the late 1960s onwards. Some of these were Marxist theorists, some non-Marxist conflict theorists, with the former tending to be products of a European tradition, the latter of an American one. What united them all was a rejection of the conservative view that the law was a neutral and universally beneficial entity. In various ways, and with varying degrees of sophistication, the political economy of crime perspective attempted to show how the law, both in terms of its substance and its administration, acted to protect the interests of those with power.

In this context, some criminologists during the 1970s began to look afresh at the work of social historians such as E. P. Thompson (1975) and Stedman-Jones (1971), who had documented how the law had been used in the past to control the labouring poor. This acknowledgement of the contribution that historians could make to the study of crime, law and the state was something of a breakthrough in British criminology. As Pat Carlen (1980: 13) says:

> The peculiar isolationism of 'criminology' meant that sociologists of crime could plead for more historical studies of crime without acknowledging that histories of labour and political movements have repeatedly been histories of lawbreaking and criminalization.

Other criminologists decided to explore similar themes by excavating the past themselves: for example, Chambliss (1976), with his study of the vagrancy laws of medieval England, and Kolko (1976) with his study of the meat-packing industry in the United States at the beginning of this century. Graham (1976) provided a contemporary example of such research with his study of drugs legislation in the United States. Graham argued that because of their power, pharmaceutical companies were able to have federal laws aimed at controlling amphetamine production and use significantly weakened. Their action, he maintained, was due to the stake that these companies had in the manufacture of this class of drug.

In a way this kind of criminology takes to its logical conclusion the argument derived from labelling theory that deviance (or crime) is not a quality of the act, but rather results from the application of rules by the relatively powerful. However, unlike labelling theory, radical criminologists began to trace the creation and application of the law to the structural arrangements of a specifically capitalist society. This was one way out of the problem of surrendering to the capitalist state's definition of crime and in effect only being allowed to study what the state allowed: that is, legally proscribed behaviour. As a consequence, during the second half of the 1970s there was a shift away from the 'criminal' or 'deviant' towards issues of law, state and social control, and to a large extent criminology became the sociology of law. Theoretical developments were also becoming more sophisticated, and there was in particular a rejection of a simplistic, instrumental model of the law as a tool of the ruling class. This entailed a number of Marxist writers reassessing the work of Marxist theoreticians from the early twentieth century such as Renner and Pashukanis. One text, especially, stands as a culmination of this project: *Capitalism and the Rule of Law*, edited by Bob Fine (1979) for the National Deviancy Conference and Conference of Socialist Economists. The subtitle, *From deviancy theory to Marxism*, aptly summed up the journey taken by radical criminology over that decade.

It was during the second half of the 1970s that the work of the French writer Michel Foucault began to influence British criminologists. Foucault's (1977, 1979) writings are complex and difficult to classify, but his work played a key role in the development of 'post-Marxist' criminology during the 1980s (Reiner, 1988). Foucault's book, *Discipline and Punish*, published in 1977, in which he analyses the phenomenon of punishment in a historical context, was particularly influential, as it seemed to offer, for some criminologists, a more satisfying alternative to the mechanistic models of the state and systems of discipline. For Foucault, discipline was literally everywhere, and was not the exclusive province of coercive formal state institutions.

In a paper originally published in 1970, and then given a wider audience when it was reproduced in Taylor *et al.*'s (1975) *Critical Criminology*, the American criminologists H. and J. Schwendinger attempted to redraw the map of criminality in a way that seemed to free the radical criminologist from the parameters set by the capitalist state. They proposed a 'human rights' definition of crime: criminal activities, they argued, should be defined in terms of certain universal codes of conduct, rather than the legal codes of a particular society:

> The abrogation of these rights certainly limits the individual's chance to fulfil himself in many spheres of life. It can be stated that individuals who deny these rights to others are

criminal . . . imperialism, racism, sexism and poverty can be called crimes according to the logic of our argument.

(Schwendinger and Schwendinger, 1975: 148)

Another landmark publication in the 1970s that should be noted, and which was also located within this tradition of focusing on the rule makers, was Stuart Hall *et al.*'s (1978) *Policing the Crisis*, a study produced by members of the Birmingham Centre for Contemporary Cultural Studies. Drawing on neo-Marxism and labelling theory, Hall and his colleagues argued that in order to divert attention away from the deep structural economic and social problems afflicting Britain, the state constructed a moral panic during the 1970s regarding so called 'muggings'. According to the authors these crimes of violence were, with the help of the media, linked specifically to supposedly 'black muggers'.

Cynical rule breakers

We can now turn to the other proposition associated with this strand of radical criminology as it developed through the 1970s: that governments, corporations and 'respectable' members of society were often involved in, and got away with, criminal activities that were much more harmful than so-called deviant activities. These are sometimes called 'crimes in the suites' rather than 'crimes in the streets'.

This is the radical end of a criminological tradition that has concerned itself with white-collar crime, a term originally used by the American criminologist Edwin Sutherland (1940). However, as David Nelken (1994) argues, although the term has entered into general usage, and people feel that they know what it means, its use as a descriptive term within criminology is highly problematic. In practice, it functions as a catch-all term encompassing a vast array of criminal activities, involving offenders of high as well as relatively low status:

> If Sutherland merited a Nobel Prize, as Mannheim thought, for pioneering this field of study, he did not deserve it for the clarity or serviceableness of his definition. What, if anything, is there in common between the marketing of unsafe pharmaceuticals, the practice of insider trading, long-firm fraud, computer crime, bank embezzlement and fiddling at work?

(Ibid.: 361)

From the point of view of radical criminology, of course, the crimes of the powerful (Pearce, 1976) – in the form of corporate crime – are of most interest. Sometimes referred to as exposé criminology, research in this field is attractive to radical criminologists because, as well as providing satisfying ammunition to use against the 'real' criminals in society, on a theoretical level it provides evidence that the capitalist system is in itself criminogenic (Box, 1983). A classic American study in this vein from the 1970s was carried out in Seattle by W. J. Chambliss (1978), where a criminal network involving many of the great and the good was uncovered. According to Chambliss, significant sections of the business community, together with politicians and police officers, constituted a large crime syndicate in the city.

CRIMINOLOGY IN THE 1970s: OTHER DIRECTIONS

Whilst radical criminology attempted, along the lines discussed above, to construct a political economy of crime and deviance during the 1970s – and, in Britain, tending to draw on a European Marxist tradition rather than American-style conflict theory – this decade also saw British criminology developing along other pathways. Although some of this work complemented the radical project, overall it reflected the increasingly wide variety of research themes, methodologies, theoretical orientations and political leanings opening up within the discipline of criminology. These alternative pathways will be examined briefly, although not in any particular order of precedence.

Feminism and criminology

The 1970s finally saw the beginning of serious research in Britain on issues of gender, crime and criminal justice from the perspective of feminism. This reflected the growth of feminism in a general sense, in the United States during the 1960s, and in Britain during the 1970s. Carol Smart's (1976) book, *Women, Crime and Criminology*, is identified by most commentators as the first British example of a criminological text written from the standpoint of feminism. Since then, a large and influential literature oriented towards feminist concerns has sprung up. However, just as there is no one feminism, so there is no one 'feminist criminology': different schools of thought have developed out of different political and theoretical traditions. The central common element, though, has been a commitment to ending sex-based discrimination in society towards women. Nevertheless, as we shall see in a more detailed discussion later on, debates over the implications of this for criminology, and even whether a specifically feminist criminology (or criminologies) is possible, continue to flourish.

As with other areas of criminological research, the early feminist work in this country drew heavily on American sources (e.g., Klein, 1973; Chesney-Lind, 1973). As the 1970s came to an end four main themes had emerged in Britain. First, the 'invisibility' of women in existing criminological theories. Up to the mid-1970s criminological theory had to a startling degree ignored female offenders. The assumption seemed to be that *if* women were to be considered, then the particular criminological theory involved could somehow accommodate them without too much bother, or, if a theory linked criminality to 'machismo', then the question of female criminality could be simply dispensed with. In fact, some early feminists sought to incorporate their ideas into existing theoretical frameworks as a progressive step (e.g., Shacklady Smith, 1978), though subsequent writers have been more sceptical. The second theme focused on the relatively few examples of criminological work – written by men – that *had* addressed the issue of female criminality. This work was accused of 'distortion', of offering explanations based on crude, sexist stereotypes (Smart, 1976). The third theme concerned itself with the workings of the criminal justice system, in so far as that system was seen to be profoundly sexist (R. Pearson, 1976; Cashburn, 1979). Finally, the fourth theme was that of female victimisation, especially sexual assault and violence taking place within the domestic sphere (Hanmer, 1978).

That the bulk of criminological theorising concerned itself with men rather than women was a corollary of the much higher rates of offending among men. In Britain and in the United States, statistics have consistently shown that around 80 per cent of those found guilty of, or cautioned for, indictable offences are men (self-report studies of offending behaviour, though, put the sex-crime ratio at around two to one). This was reflected in prison populations in Britain during the 1970s: out of a total of around 50,000 prisoners, about 1,500 are women. Thus, it would appear that the best single predictor of future criminality among, say, a group of schoolchildren is the sex of the child, rather than, for example, the child's social class background. This observation, said feminist writers, should logically have placed issues of gender firmly at the centre of the criminological stage: what is it about masculinity that leads to such relatively high levels of crime, especially with respect to violent crime?

Interactionism, phenomenology and ethnomethodology

As we have seen, American-led interactionist approaches to the study of deviance, and in particular the emphasis on labelling, had an enormous impact on British criminology in the late 1960s. The message from labelling theory was that deviance was created by society, which at first glance seems a less than earth shattering revelation. After all, it was commonplace to link deviant, or criminal, behaviour to social factors such as poverty, rough neighbourhoods, urban life, and so forth. However, for the labelling theorists, 'created by society' meant something rather different. In fact, it had two meanings, though the distinction is not always recognised: first, that society creates the rules against which behaviour is judged, and second, that in specific circumstances certain groups are selected and labelled as deviant by those in a position to do so, for example the police or the mass media. It was the first of these meanings that stimulated radical work which focused on the law makers later on in the 1970s. The second meaning was picked up during the late 1960s and early 1970s by a number of sociologists of deviance (by now the preferred term) and applied to a British context, with the addition of the congruent concept of deviancy amplification, devised originally by Leslie Wilkins (1964). Two notable examples of such research are Jock Young's (1971) study of soft drugs use in Notting Hill, London, and Stan Cohen's (1980) study of the Mods and Rockers phenomenon, the latter introducing the term 'moral panic' into the lexicon of 'informed debate' on law and order.

By the early 1970s, though, various critiques of labelling theory, and indeed new deviancy as a whole, were beginning to stack up, first in the United States, and then in Britain. Although this eventually led to more radical criminologists breaking with labelling theory in favour of a harder, Marxist-informed political economy of crime, a number of the early members of the National Deviancy Conference, together with later adherents, continued to work within an interactionist framework. Thus through the 1970s various writers developed and refined the earlier forms of interactionist theory: Steven Box (1981, first published 1971), for instance, attempted to incorporate labelling theory into yet another American import, control theory.

One result of this was the growth in ethnographic studies of groups defined as deviant. Drawing on the earlier symbolic interactionism of G. H. Mead (1934), labelling theory had argued that it was important to take account of the ways in which those labelled as deviant respond, at both a behavioural level (what they do) and at a mental level (how they think). Under certain circumstances, the argument ran, labelling processes lead to the successful application of the label 'deviant' to a group, and this has fundamental implications for the deviant's self-image. In other words, under appropriate circumstances, labelled groups come to accept the label and see themselves as deviant. Criticisms that this viewed the deviant as mere passive victim (Gouldner, 1968), and was highly deterministic (Akers, 1967), led interactionists to develop more refined theoretical formulations as the 1970s progressed, with a stress on labelling as a 'sensitising' perspective, rather than a heavy-duty theoretical school (Plummer, 1979).

Proponents of interactionism argued that research should be sensitive to the subjective worlds constructed by those labelled as deviant, and indeed, to the subjective worlds of any group being studied. In other words, one of the tasks of the sociologist is to engage in research that will seek to understand the social world from the point of view of the individuals and groups concerned. This was part of a critique of positivism which, it was said, merely imposed the researcher's understandings on to the deviant under the cover of a spurious claim to be 'scientific'. Thus, whilst being sensitive to the subtle changes in meanings that occurred via interactions with control agents, the anti-positivists underlined the importance of providing authentic accounts that the deviant groups would themselves recognise. In this context, ethnography offered the only viable research method. Originally developed by anthropologists, ethnographic research basically involved the researcher joining a group, either covertly or overtly, and, by spending time with the members, gradually building up an in-depth understanding. The 1970s produced a number of important studies of this type, for example, delinquent youth in Liverpool (Parker, 1974); the construction of homosexual identities (Plummer, 1975); and pilferage at work (Ditton, 1977).

These ethnographic studies also reflected the British interest in the phenomenological criminology associated with David Matza. Writing in the 1960s, Matza, whose work came to be known as 'American naturalism', was a strong influence on British new deviancy theorists. His famous injunction to 'tell it like it is' indicates the phenomenologist's commitment to present accounts of human events in their own terms; to adopt an 'appreciative' stance and to see the deviant's world as they see it (Matza, 1969).

Other research during the 1970s also continued to develop some of the elements of interactionist theory, although it did not opt for an ethnographic methodology. Inevitably, where deviant groups were being studied, this involved a rejection of 'correctionalism', that is, a refusal to align criminological research with the practical goal of stamping out the deviance. In the 'sceptical' spirit of new deviancy theory such research was imbued with a strong sense of relativism rather than absolutism (see Taylor and Walton, 1971). Other research, also expressing some of the central ideas of interactionism, turned the spotlight away from defined deviant groups and towards other players in the criminal justice process, such as police officers (Cain, 1973; Holdaway, 1979) and magistrates (Carlen, 1976).

An interest in the subjective worlds of those labelled as deviant, as well as all other participants in interactive processes of meaning construction, is associated with two other theoretical developments in the late 1960s and 1970s, each of which turned their attention to crime and deviance: phenomenology and ethnomethodology. Within the context of this overview of developments in academic criminology, it is not necessary to embark on a detailed exposition of the respective theoretical positions here; that can be left until we return to an examination of criminological theory. However, some markers can be put down.

From the point of view of phenomenology, no objective social reality exists 'out there' waiting to be discovered. What we perceive to be reality is, from this perspective, merely a version of reality (phenomenal reality), constituted by the subjective meanings that the world has for us. Within this theoretical framework a number of forays were made into the criminological terrain by phenomenologists, for example Cicourel (1968) on juvenile justice in the United States; Coulter (1973) on insanity; and Atkinson (1971) on definitions of suicide in coroners' courts. On a general level, Phillipson (1971) produced a phenomenological critique of the sociology of deviance that questioned the entire stock of theoretical knowledge making up that field. As Bob Roshier (1989: 68) has noted: 'Phenomenological sociology, with its micro-level focus on human meaning construction, has mostly ruled out any specific interest in substantive areas of human action such as crime'. Therefore, because phenomenology is ultimately concerned with shared meanings and the nature of knowledge in the most fundamental sense, and adopts a totally relativistic position, as a perspective it drifted away from the specific concerns of criminology or the sociology of deviance.

Ethnomethodology drew on many of the insights of phenomenology, and directs attention to day-to-day, taken-for-granted methods used by individuals to create a meaningful, ordered social world. The relevance of this to criminology manifests itself in detailed examination of the assumptions used to make sense of what appear to be the 'facts' of crime and deviance. As an example, from an ethnomethodological standpoint, the notion of 'law making' has a quite different meaning to the one that it normally has. Law making is not addressed in terms of the formulation of the law of the land at some point in time, by, say, Parliament. Rather, law making is seen as a process that is acted out each day within the courtroom, as each of the participants comes to understand what 'really happened': 'In contrast to the "finished" conception of criminal law . . . ethnomethodology favours a view of criminal law as a continually contingent production of the *in situ* practices of participants in legal proceedings and settings' (Hester and Eglin, 1992: 75).

ORTHODOX CRIMINOLOGY

Whilst criminology was shooting off in all these various directions during the 1970s, with ideas and debates tumbling forth at a breathless rate, orthodox criminology continued to stalk quietly alongside. Furthermore, much of orthodox criminology was still possessed by new deviancy theory's very own folk devil: positivism. It may not have grabbed the headlines, or excited the brain cells of students (except, perhaps, when they were disparaging it), but in terms of volume of work and influence on policy, positivist criminology remained a powerful force, both in Britain and in the United States. Writing in the mid-1980s, Gottfredson and Hirschi (1987: 18) felt able to report: 'In the light of the pervasive distaste for positivism expressed by many modern criminologists, it is surprising to discover that positivistic criminology may today be healthier than ever'. They saw this situation as resulting from positivist criminology's ability to respond to the earlier criticisms and to create 'what is perhaps a healthier and more self-assured positivistic criminology than has heretofore existed' (ibid.). However, as we shall see when discussing criminological theory in detail, and as sometimes happens with medical diagnoses, this confident pronouncement probably coincided with positivist criminology taking a turn for the worse, at least in Britain.

During the 1970s, though, positivist-oriented orthodox criminological research continued unabated in Britain. To a large extent this was due to its powerbase in key research institutions, and in particular, the Home Office. At the same time there was an increase in the amount of in-house research carried out by criminal justice agencies, such as the police, the Prison Department and the probation service. Government-funded social science research within universities, on the other hand, began to be cut back. Although the grandiose promises of the nineteenth century had by then been scaled down to more modest dimensions, criminological research carried out within the positivist tradition continued to appeal to policy makers more than other approaches did, because it still promised to be useful. As always, positivism was committed to discovering the causes of crime (or at least determining correlational factors) and devising ways of treating offenders so that they cease to be offenders. The dominant conceptual framework within which this proceeded was not seen as problematic – clearly much less irksome to a government than the critical stances adopted by other criminologies at the time. A classic example of this type of orthodox criminological research is the massive longitudinal study conducted by West and Farrington (1973, 1977), where they attempted to link delinquency to a range of salient social factors. In spite of all the developments associated with new deviancy and radical criminology, orthodox criminology – the 'criminological establishment' – still maintained a tenacious hold on powerful institutions. This is a point made by Stan Cohen (1988: 82) in his review of British criminology at the start of the 1980s:

> There are more corners and cavities than ten years ago, but for the most part the institutional foundations of British criminology remain intact and unaltered . . . the establishment saw the new theories as simply a fashion that would eventually pass or as a few interesting ideas that could be swallowed up without changing the existing paradigms at all.

Although the 'institutional foundations of British criminology' may have remained intact, the influence of the various strands that grew out of the new deviancy, and, in particular, the impact made by a specifically sociological criminology, should not be underestimated, at least within the context of academic criminology. Many of the concepts from new deviancy theory had, by the end of the 1970s, permeated through the education system, so that most O-level sociology students, let alone undergraduates, would have been introduced to, for instance, moral panics and the amplification of deviance. Theoretical developments over the preceding decade had resulted in a substantial remapping of the terrain of sociological criminology. Questions concerning why people broke the law, and how criminals should be treated, which at one time were taken for granted within criminology, had been replaced by different questions: Why are certain types of behaviour designated illegal? In whose interests do the laws operate? Why are only some people selected as deviant or criminal? And so on. Whatever else we might say about this change of emphasis, for students of criminology the more radical strands did seem to offer something far more interesting than the preoccupations of an earlier orthodox criminology.

Having said this, although interactionism and the various strands of radical criminology had become very influential within the academic world during the 1970s, the limits of this influence have to be recognised. Echoing Stan Cohen's sentiments, Jock Young (1988: 170) has pointed out:

> But what radical criminology did not do to any significant degree is challenge the criminological establishment. For the policy centres in British society were, and remain, remarkably unaffected, both in the Home Office itself and the university institutions which it helps to finance.

Young is specifically referring to positivist criminology in all of its guises (sociological, psychological, biological), and it is important to appreciate that throughout the intellectual turmoil of the 1960s and 1970s, orthodox criminology, with its positivist credentials, lived on, and, significantly, continued to attract official research funding. Its position had, however, been weakened, and, in the next decade, positivism had to contend with a more powerful challenge, though this time from a less obvious source.

At the level of policy, radical criminology had made little impact. Young does refer to its influence on Labour Party thinking, but this occurred just as the Labour Party lost office to a Conservative government, a government still in power in the mid-1990s. However, radical criminology did influence the Labour Party at local government level in some parts of the country. As far as national criminal justice policies were concerned, though, by the end of the 1970s the influence of radical criminology had, not surprisingly, been minimal.

Unlike positivism, which, since its inception, had taken an uncritical stance *vis-à-vis* the concepts of deviance and crime, and offered the promise of discovering the causes and cures of crime, radical criminology had celebrated its disengagement from the requirement to be 'useful' in this sense. Clearly, radical socialist criminology's commitment to the dismantling of capitalism – and, in Taylor, Walton and Young's version, a revolutionary call for 'socialist diversity' – was unlikely to endear it to the main political parties or to the custodians of the criminal justice system. Although feminism was interested in an agenda that confronted official responses to female criminality, women as victims, and the treatment of offenders, its contribution to criminology was still at an underdeveloped stage by the late 1970s.

When attempting to assess the impact of radical criminology on the criminal justice system the tendency, of course, is to expect this impact to be progressive in nature. This has meant that analyses of the period up to the 1980s have usually ignored the possibility that left–liberal thought, inside and outside criminology, may have unwittingly played a part in paving the way for the growth of criminal justice policies with a quite different character.

RADICAL CRITIQUES AND THE GROWTH OF THE NEW RIGHT

The election of a Conservative government in 1979 signalled a decisive shift to the right in British politics and with it the establishment of Thatcherism. A similar political realignment occurred in other European countries and, with the election of a Reagan administration, in the United States too. Soon afterwards, state socialism began to be dismantled across former eastern Europe and the Soviet Union, and 'the market' took centre stage, both as an economic mechanism and as an ideological symbol.

From 1979 onwards, those on the liberal–left spectrum in Britain found themselves having to fight a rearguard action, as they tried to unravel the precise meaning and impact of what has been variously described as new rightism, right-wing authoritarianism and authoritarian populism. Obviously, a range of social, political and economic factors would have to be taken into consideration when accounting for the rise of the New Right, factors beyond the scope of this book. However, one ironic dimension to this will be considered: that over the previous decade left-of-centre (described loosely as 'radical') thought unwittingly helped to prepare the ground for the New Right. This can be illustrated by focusing on two central characteristics of radical thought as it developed from the late 1960s, on a general level as well as specifically within the context of criminology:

1 There was much criticism of institutions and processes in capitalist Britain, especially by socialists, though this criticism tended to remain truncated; constructive and convincing alternatives to contemporary arrangements were in short supply.
2 Radical thought came to be riven by internal divisions. Ideological in-fighting created various schisms, with the Labour Party in particular having to cope with a number of disparate factions; one important outcome was the split resulting from the formation of the Social Democrat Party.

Radical criticism on a general level

Clearly, criticism of aspects of life in capitalist Britain is an expected and appropriate response on the part of radicals; what was perhaps not expected was that this criticism would play a part in helping pave the way for the advent of the New Right. The irony of the situation is encapsulated in a letter that appeared in the journal *New Statesman and Society* in 1988. The writer castigated the journal for allowing the phrase 'chattering classes' to be used in its columns, pointing out that the phrase was used by Prime Minister Thatcher as a term of abuse, as a way of ridiculing liberal-minded, middle-class academics and intellectuals. The phrase is, of course, synonymous with '*Guardian* reader', with the sort of person who joins CND and Amnesty International, uses 'chair' rather than 'chairman', and until recently reprimanded supermarket managers for stocking South African oranges. If such people are to be treated as a joke, are the causes they support worthy of ridicule too?

The irony is that during the 1970s those so labelled joined in the fun themselves, or laughed at comedians who did the job for them. Some of these comedians would fill theatres with members of the 'chattering classes', who would then be treated to being the butt of the comedian's jokes, with inevitable references to vegetarianism, muesli, stripped-pine furniture and polytechnic angst. Some novels followed the same path, Malcolm Bradbury's *The History Man* (about a 'trendy', a.k.a. useless, university sociology lecturer) being a classic of the genre. This was made into a television series. If that was what sociologists were like, if that was how they behaved, why should taxpayers support them with their hard-earned money? The fact that the book was meant to be humorous helped to protect it. Any criticism by a sociologist was likely to be written off as sour grapes and confirmation that sociologists did indeed lack a sense of humour. Thus in the 1970s people began to get accustomed to apparently right-on comedians and writers having a go at liberal to left-minded groups and the causes they supported. Who were these chattering, 'middle-class' victims? In the main they were not particularly well-paid public employees. They did not run private corporations or sell arms to right-wing military dictatorships, but they were fair game for radical humour. It is likely that in subtle ways this process contributed to the creation of a climate in which the value of these groups, their work and the causes they subscribed to, came to be questioned.

If this 'softening up' process was going on at a cultural level, using humour as a vehicle, the connections between much more systematic radical social and political criticism and subsequent developments associated with the New Right are even more remarkable. A wide range of critical analyses of key sectors of British society had begun to appear by the late 1960s. The validity of this work is not at issue here; what is at issue is the way in which these critical analyses failed to develop constructive alternatives, beyond, for instance, vague socialist phrases. The result was an opening up of a political space that was readily colonised by the New Right in the 1980s. The right, then, homed in on the same sectors previously criticised by radicals and were able to put forward concrete solutions (or what purported to be solutions). A cursory glance at the key sectors of British society around which radical critical thought flourished, and which subsequently became locations for Conservative policies, quickly exposes, as Matza would put it, an 'embarrassment of riches'. Here are some examples:

- Nationalised industries were seen as over-bureaucratised examples of pseudo-socialism. As far as the workers were concerned, they operated much as private industries did and, in fact, were necessary for capitalism as they could be used by the state to fine-tune the economy. They were privatised by the Conservative government.
- Manual work, for instance in manufacturing industry and mining, was alienating, physically damaging and demeaning. Huge portions of manufacturing were to disappear and most of the coal mines closed.
- The National Health Service was over-bureaucratised and to a large extent run for the benefit of overpaid professionals. The National Health Service was to be increasingly under-funded and organised around strict notions of cost efficiency and effectiveness, together with an increasing privatisation of services.
- Mental hospitals, we were told, did more harm than good for the patients; decarceration was the clarion call. Under the guise of 'community care', patients were decanted from these hospitals out on to the streets.
- Council estates were bleak, standardised and soulless. Large numbers of council houses were privatised, heralding in a new Georgian front door era.

- When it was not corrupt because of a junket-loving, entrenched political mafia, local government was overstaffed and inefficient. The power of local government was dramatically reduced.
- By dealing with the system's casualties, social workers were in effect propping up the capitalist society. Social work had to cope with financial stringency and a changed orientation towards the whole welfare process.
- Aid programmes to the 'Third World' were seen as both counterproductive because they postponed a socialist revolution among recipient nations, and futile because the real problem lay in a system of world trade dominated by the developed nations. As a proportion of GNP, British aid went on to be significantly reduced.
- Comprehensive schools were great failures because they were simply secondary modern schools and grammar schools under one roof. The opting out system that was introduced gradually recreated a two-tier system.
- The arts were elitist, benefiting only a tiny minority of the population. Here too funding was to be significantly reduced.

Radical criticism within criminology

There were similar developments within criminology. While a huge amount of work appeared during the 1970s that was intensely critical of orthodox, establishment approaches to crime, crime control techniques and indeed to the whole criminal justice system, concrete suggestions regarding how things might be improved were relatively thin on the ground. The New Right, however, did at least appear to have strong, confident ideas regarding a supposed better future. A range of ideas, policies and practices relating to crime and criminal justice were, from the late 1960s, routinely criticised by radical criminologists. Again, whatever the validity of these criticisms, the targets were often the same ones subsequently selected by the New Right. Furthermore, and to inject more irony into this, those features of the criminal justice system being criticised by radicals were arguably more liberal, more humane and less draconian than what were to follow in the 1980s and 1990s. The radical criticism that developed within criminology from the late 1960s coalesced around three main themes:

1 The reality and fear of crime.
2 The causes of crime.
3 Prescriptive policies aimed at controlling crime and dealing with the criminal.

The reality and fear of crime
Following labelling theory, it was commonplace during the 1970s for radical criminologists to argue that crime rises were a function of labelling by control agents, with the police simply recording more offences. Reassuring comparisons were sometimes drawn between contemporary life and life in Britain's cities 100 years earlier. The fear

of crime tended to be equated with moral panics and, looked at objectively, people had to contend with worse things than crime. One outcome of this type of reasoning was that links between crime rises and capitalist development could not be made. If there were no crime rises, then there was nothing beyond 'reaction' to explain. The right, on the other hand, did offer explanations, unpalatable as these were to left–liberal thought, and appeared to be sympathetic to the worries of the public, who did feel that crime was on the increase. However, if necessary, the right could appropriate radical reasoning and argue that official crime rises reflected the greater willingness of the public to report crime to the police, which in turn reflected the government's policies in this area.

The causes of crime

Attempts to fathom the causes of crime were attacked by many radical criminologists as deterministic positivism, and futile anyway. Thus, for instance, theories linking crime to poverty, unemployment and deprivation were criticised for being deterministic, especially by those oriented towards an interactionist paradigm. Ironically, as we shall see, with the rise of the New Right there was a significant shift away from trying to identify the causes of crime. The growth of what has been called administrative criminology in the 1980s led to a greater emphasis being placed on control. From the point of view of the right, if poverty was irrelevant, why waste money on such things as urban aid programmes, which, it was argued, had so obviously failed in the United States anyway?

Prescriptive policies

Among left criminologists and liberal ones within the interactionist tradition, it was not thought proper for criminologists to help the capitalist system, or the forces of law and order, by joining in the fight against crime. There was no desire to line up with the repressive apparatus of the state. The New Right, however, was able to present itself as a force in society that was bothered about crime. Within the context of criminal justice policies, the 'softening up' process was most obviously seen in radical critiques of welfare-oriented treatment models of juvenile justice. Again ironically, those on the right agreed. They attacked what they saw as 'soft', 'kid-gloved' approaches, and argued that people should take full responsibility for their actions and be punished accordingly. Many on the left argued that juveniles should be dealt with on the basis of a 'due process' model of justice, linked to the idea of 'just deserts', rather than the welfare model supposedly enshrined in the 1969 Children and Young Persons Act (e.g., Taylor, Lacey and Bracken, 1980). Interestingly, a similar convergence between left and right occurred in the United States, where rehabilitation through treatment was also criticised: 'The subsequent turn against rehabilitation cannot be explained primarily as a conservative reaction to rising crime rates. It was made possible only by a discrediting of rehabilitation from the Left' (Plattner, quoted by Cullen and Wozniak, 1982: 24).

Divisions within radical thought

The ideological in-fighting within radical thought in general was paralleled by increasing disunity within radical criminology during the 1970s. The major divisions that opened up encompassed labelling theory, critical criminology and recent debates between 'left realism' and 'left idealism'. No concerted challenge to New Right thinking on crime arose; rather, what we saw was a great deal of sometimes vitriolic disputes within radical criminology.

Selected further reading

The flavour of these theoretical developments is well captured by **Pearson, G. (1975)** *The Deviant Imagination,* London: Macmillan.

The shift from new deviancy theory to a Marxist informed criminology is explored in **Fine, B. (ed) (1979)** *Capitalism and the Rule of Law: From deviancy theory to Marxism,* London: Hutchinson.

For a recent and clearly written introduction to Foucault's work, see: **Han-Pile, B. (2008)** *Foucault,* Abingdon: Routledge.

CHAPTER II

POST-NEW DEVIANCY AND THE NEW CRIMINOLOGY

Key themes

- Deviance and power
- American conflict theory
- Politicising deviance
- Critical criminology
- Marx and Engels on crime
- Taylor, Walton and Young and the politicisation of deviance
- Politicising deviance: nuts, sluts, preverts . . . and revolutionaries?
- Youth subcultures and politics
- Critical criminology: deviance, crime and power
- Phenomenology and criminology
- Ethnomethodology
- Control theory
- Feminist perspectives and criminology

INTRODUCTION

This chapter examines attempts to develop a Marxist approach to the study of crime and deviance – the 'new', or critical, criminology – and includes a discussion of Marx and Engels's writings on crime. For critical criminologists, crime and responses to it should be studied within the context of a specifically capitalist society. In such a society, it was argued, the law and law enforcement protect the interests of the ruling class. Some writers argued that criminal or deviant behaviour represented a form of political action, in that it was a way of resisting those with power in society. This period also saw the emergence of radical studies of youth subcultures. The 1970s witnessed other important theoretical developments within criminology, notably, feminist perspectives on crime and criminal justice, control theory and work influenced by phenomenology and ethnomethodology; these too are examined in this chapter.

Interactionism had the rare distinction of having to cope with criticisms from all political directions. Looking back on these criticisms, Becker (1974: 53) commented:

> Moral problems arise in all sociological research but are especially provocatively posed by interactionist theories of deviance. Moral criticism has come from the political centre and beyond, from the political Left, and from the left field. Interactionist theories have been accused of giving aid and comfort to the enemy, be the enemy those who would upset the stability of the existing order or the Establishment. They have been accused of openly espousing unconventional norms, of refusing to support anti-Establishment positions, and (the left field position) of appearing to support anti-Establishment causes while subtly favouring the status quo.

Irrespective of interactionism's 'true' nature, it did play an important role in generating key criminological debates during the 1970s. The strongest criticisms of interactionism, and in particular of labelling theory, probably came from the left. By the beginning of the 1970s labelling theory was already being attacked for its lack of politically radical credentials; the British left came to see it as another version of American liberalism. In response, there emerged a much more radical and politically committed criminology based upon varieties of conflict theory. In the United States this was conflict theory of a pluralistic, non-Marxist type – though later on some of it did become infused with Marxist concepts – whilst in Britain there was a more explicit commitment to neo-Marxist formulations in the shape of critical criminology. The enduring influence of labelling theory, though, should not be overlooked. Conflict theorists picked up on the argument from writers such as Becker and Lemert that deviance had to be seen in relative terms, and that the designation of certain acts as deviant was a function of the distribution of power in society. Furthermore, Lemert had stressed that powerful elites were able to influence how deviant behaviour would be dealt with: whether to 'control or de-control'. However, labelling theory had fallen short of an analysis of the deeper sources of the power to label, and conflict theorists, through their attempts to construct a political economy of crime, were concerned to analyse the structural bases of rule creation and rule enforcement.

Two important theoretical themes emerged in the immediate post-new deviancy period and helped pave the way for conflict theory, and each developed out of a critique of labelling theory: one focused on deviance and power, the other on the politicisation of deviance.

DEVIANCE AND POWER

This theme is associated with those writers who were critical of labelling theory for concentrating on the least powerful, marginalised groups in society, groups conventionally defined as deviant (Gouldner, 1968; Liazos, 1972; Thio, 1973). They also criticised labelling theory for confining their analyses of the power to label to low-level agents of social control. Liazos argued that the sociology of deviance had only a partial view of deviance. It had, he said, neglected the violence perpetrated by the United States government in Vietnam, and the violent, corrupt and fraudulent activities of large corporations. Thio took a similar line, but also argued that powerful elites protected their interests by defining certain forms of behaviour as deviant and, by maintaining an unequal society, sustained the social and economic conditions that caused deviant behaviour among the powerless.

These were issues taken up by conflict theory in the United States as it developed from the late 1960s and through the 1970s. The theme of powerful elites or classes as self-interested rule makers is particularly apparent in the early work of the conflict theorists. Later on, they turned their attention to the powerful as law breakers, via 'exposé' criminology and a focus on the 'crimes of the powerful' and, under the influence of Marxism, to the criminogenic features of capitalism itself.

AMERICAN CONFLICT THEORY

Three criminologists in particular are associated with the early development of conflict theory in the United States: Austin Turk, William Chambliss and Richard Quinney. Although many of their ideas overlapped, summarising their work is complicated by the fact that their ideas (especially in the case of Quinney) underwent some modification during the 1970s, this reflecting the theoretical ferment within radical criminology at that time.

Coincidently, each of these writers introduced their ideas in books published in the same year, 1969. In general terms, all three followed labelling theory by orienting their analyses towards the criminalisation of behaviour, rather than towards the criminal and the sources of criminal behaviour. Thus they adopted a relativistic stance, and rejected the view that deviance/crime was a quality of the act. However, unlike labelling theory, they attempted to explain processes of criminalisation from the point of view of the deeper structures of power in American society. Powerful interest groups were seen as imposing their own definitions of crime on to society. Fundamentally, the law was seen as a coercive instrument used selectively by these sectional interests to preserve their power.

Turk (1969) developed a particular form of conflict theory, largely derived from Ralph Dahrendorf (1959, 1968), in which he emphasised the conflict arising from the unequal distribution of authority, rather than from class relationships rooted in the economic system. The model of authority used owed much to Weber's model of power, where authority is equated with legitimised power. For Turk, relationships based upon authority and subordination would always exist – in socialist as well as capitalist societies – though the sources of authority may alter. At a given moment, therefore, there will always be a dominant group able to impose their own normative system on to society in general. Rather than class, Turk saw subordinate status as deriving from sex, 'race'/ethnicity and age. Those occupying subordinate positions were more likely to find their behaviour criminalised, not because it was inherently criminal or 'bad', but because their normative systems were in conflict with the normative system of the dominant group. As a corollary of this, those most likely to experience criminalisation in American society were male, black and young.

Chambliss carried out his own empirical research in order to substantiate the theoretical claim that the law operated in favour of the powerful in society. His first study (1964) was of the English vagrancy laws initially introduced in the fourteenth century, where he showed how they directly operated in the interests of the ruling class. He argued that feudal landowners used these laws as a mechanism to compel people to work on their land. From the point of view of the landowners the laws were necessary because of the shortages of labour brought about by the Black Death. The vagrancy laws made it illegal for people to give food or shelter to those defined as vagrants. In addition, vagrants were threatened with imprisonment if they refused work offered by a landowner. As Chambliss (1964: 69) concluded:

> There is little question that these statutes were designed for one express purpose: to force laborers . . . to accept employment at a low wage in order to insure the landowner an adequate supply of labor at a price he could afford to pay.

Later on Chambliss did a study of the introduction of a Poll Tax law by British colonisers in their East African colonies. Again, he made the point that the law was used to further the interests of the class in power. The introduction of the Poll Tax law meant that African migrant workers were forced to work on the colonisers' plantations so as to earn enough money to pay the tax. The establishment of a low-wage economy ensured that the workers stayed on the plantation until the season ended, and prevented them from earning sufficient to pay their taxes mid-season.

By the middle of the 1970s Chambliss had moved towards a more overtly Marxist position, drawing now on key concepts such as ruling class (rather than elite) and class conflict. In his article 'Towards a political economy of crime' (Chambliss, 1975), he was arguing that as capitalism develops, so the gaps between proletariat and bourgeoisie will widen, bringing with it increased social conflict. Under these circumstances he saw it as inevitable that the ruling class would gradually impose a more coercive penal law on the working class in the hope of maintaining social order through their submission. As a consequence, he argued, modern capitalist societies are characterised by increasingly oppressive criminal justice systems as social conditions deteriorate, and the corresponding deprivation suffered by large sections of the working class contributes to rising levels of crime. Thus by the middle of the 1970s Chambliss was giving attention to explanations of criminality, rather than concentrating on processes of criminalisation. This engagement with causal questions was also found in the work of another American conflict theorist, David Gordon, at the beginning of the 1970s. Gordon (1971) argued (as Chambliss was to do) that given the selfishness, individualism and competitiveness of a capitalist system, crime represents a perfectly rational response.

Chambliss also took up another theme in his research, a theme that was to be developed further by radical criminologists: namely, the powerful as rule breakers (Chambliss, 1978). For many years he carried out a study of crime and the legal system in Seattle in the United States. His conclusion was that all classes were involved in criminal activities, with the major crime syndicate consisting of both professional criminals and 'respectable', powerful members of the community. In addition, he identified what he called a 'symbiotic' relationship, based upon mutual interdependency, between organised crime and the bureaucratic legal system. Rather than cope with the organisational disequilibrium that would result from bringing those involved in organised crime to justice, powerful players in the legal system preferred to devote most of their resources to the apprehension and punishment of the least powerful criminals, such as drug users and prostitutes. In effect, the criminal justice system and organised crime in the city oiled each other's wheels.

Like Chambliss, Quinney gradually moved towards an explicitly Marxist position, though his own intellectual journey was especially remarkable in that, earlier on, it encompassed some ideas from phenomenology and, later on, theological considerations. The latter stage of this journey found Quinney editing a collection of readings entitled *Criminology as Peacemaking* (Pepinsky and Quinney, 1991). His own contribution to this volume is an eclectic mix of radical social science, humanism and a wide range of religious sources. As the title suggests, the book was aimed at mobilising criminologists not for the traditional 'war against crime', but for a process of reconciliation and healing. Macho cynics are likely to scoff at this enterprise, though there is no evidence that declarations of war on crime in Europe and the United States have been particularly successful.

In his first important contribution, Quinney's (1969) arguments were similar to those found in Turk and Chambliss, in that they stressed the powerful as instrumental law makers. In two books published the following year, though, he introduced a phenomenological dimension (Quinney 1970a, 1970b). Here he addressed the social reality of crime: the ways in which those with power were able to construct subjective understandings of crime and criminality that suited their own interests. On this basis he argued that the perception of crime – that is, the subjectively understood 'reality' of crime (and, indeed, anything else) – was a 'state of mind'; nothing that constituted 'social reality' existed as an objective entity. Thus the 'problem of crime' is shaped by powerful interests in society. However, by 1974 Quinney was criticising the perspective of phenomenology, and had embraced an explicitly Marxist position (Quinney, 1974).

This work was strongly influenced by the Frankfurt School, with its emphasis on the manipulation of consciousness by bourgeois ideological formations, such as the mass media. Quinney (1977) described his Marxian criminology as 'critical criminology', and argued that because of its inherent contradictions, the capitalist system created large numbers of unemployed people – surplus populations. The capitalist state, he said, attempts to manage these surplus populations by welfare and criminal justice policies, in an effort to stave off social disruption. In Quinney's view, these attempts were doomed to failure, being unable to prevent increases in crime. The crime associated with surplus populations is described by him as 'survival crime'; it is crime that arises from living in or at the edges of poverty. However, it was also seen as a form of immature political action – the poor fighting back. In Quinney's work, then, we can see a move away from an earlier, purely instrumental view of the law and legal system, with the suggestion of ruling-class conspiracies, towards a more structuralist position, where law and the criminal justice system are locked into the structural imperatives of capitalism as a whole.

The conceptualisation of crime as the means by which the poor and marginalised fought back that Quinney subscribed to later on in the 1970s, leads directly to the second theme that emerged in the late 1960s within an embryonic radical criminology: the politicisation of deviance.

POLITICISING DEVIANCE

This theme is associated with the 'man-fighting-back' image of the deviant introduced by Gouldner (1968) as a critique of what he saw as labelling theory's defeated, 'man-on-his-back' image, and also with the work of Horowitz and Leibowitz (1969). These writers pointed the way towards theoretical models that placed the actions of the deviant centre stage. Rather than a pathetic victim of labelling by control agents, the individual was now seen as choosing a specifically deviant path as an expression of resistance. Deviance here became linked to political action.

Horowitz and Leibowitz's influential article considerably extended the argument put forward by labelling theorists. Not only was the labelling of certain acts as deviant a political process, they argued, but also some 'socially' deviant acts should more properly be viewed as 'politically' deviant acts. Their charge that traditional definitions of 'political' were too narrow and inflexible was obviously in tune with some of the ideas emanating from the New Left/counter-cultural configuration in America and Europe at that time. The labels 'social' and 'political' deviance were, they said, becoming increasingly redundant in modern America. Developments in the 1960s – and in particular, protest based upon the experience of the ghetto – had produced a convergence between the deviant and the political. Thus political minorities were increasingly stepping outside the repertoire of acceptable tactics to further their causes, and adopting methods and lifestyles normally associated with deviant groups. On the other side, in an effort to make their voices heard, deviant groups were increasingly adopting tactics that were normally thought of as political tactics. In Horowitz and Leibowitz's view, this convergence had occurred because the 'right to dissent', traditionally enjoyed by powerful minorities, had come to be questioned by the elites as these minorities had begun to use deviant tactics. From the other direction, deviant minorities had become less willing to confine their problems to the private sphere, and were using modes of protest traditionally thought of as political. However, powerful interests tended to deny political status to their protests, since they had, so to speak, already been written off as 'social problems'. If, therefore, the actions of political minorities are defined in ways traditionally reserved for deviants, so they will be responded to in similar ways. A classic example of this would be the Stalinist ploy of labelling political dissension in the former Soviet Union as mental illness.

In Britain this theme was taken up by Cohen (1969, 1974) and by Hall (1974). Following Horowitz and Leibowitz, they discussed the tendency of those with power to assign certain kinds of political activity to the 'deviant' category, thereby negating any social criticism informing that activity. It is important to recognise (as Cohen and Hall did) precisely what Horowitz and Leibowitz were saying about *deviance* and politics. They did not argue that deviant acts are, by definition, political, but rather that some deviant groups – the Gay Liberation Movement, for example – were now adopting political modes of protest to further their cause. The original deviance was never seen as political in itself. Unfortunately, on this side of the Atlantic some sociologists (e.g., G. Pearson, 1976) saw in Horowitz and Leibowitz's article an argument that deviance in general was political.

CRITICAL CRIMINOLOGY

I have already described the eagerness with which a generation of young, radical British criminologists seized upon the ideas of new deviancy theory in the late 1960s. This was the beginning of an intensely fertile period, when the foundations for the subsequent development of criminology in Britain were laid.

While interactionism had emerged out of a strongly liberal tradition in the United States, in Britain it attracted the attention of academics with more radical aspirations, reflecting the influence of a European Marxist tradition. From the very beginning there was a tension between interactionism, pulled by a 'do your own thing' counter-culture, and neo-Marxism, whose sympathisers kept one eye on the barricades and the possibility of socialist revolution. In the early British interactionism-inspired research, though, this political radicalism was still underdeveloped, and only hinted at by the use of phrases such as ruling class or bourgeoisie instead of elites, class conflict instead of culture conflict, and capitalism instead of industrial society. By the beginning of the 1970s the tensions and inevitable splits were surfacing within the National Deviancy Conference, new deviancy's forum in Britain.

Eventually this led to attempts to develop an explicitly Marxist criminology, given the title of critical criminology. Although much criticised – in time by the authors themselves – Taylor, Walton and Young's (1973) *The New Criminology* announced this shift in Britain towards a Marxist-informed political economy of crime and deviance. From the title we can see that the sociology of deviance had been eclipsed by a return to criminology, though the book was subtitled *For a social theory of deviance* and was largely devoted to the phenomenon of deviance, which indicated a lingering ambivalence. Their follow-up book, *Critical Criminology* (Taylor *et al.*, 1975), which they edited, drew on a range of contributors, and tried to answer some of the criticism met by the first book.

These early versions of critical criminology were to a large extent based upon a mixture of radical labelling theory and neo-Marxism, a potent brew that ended up with more than a whiff of anarchism. The two themes (discussed above) of deviance and power, and the politicisation of deviance, that emerged in the immediate post-new deviancy period in the United States, and was to some extent incorporated into the work of American conflict theorists (especially Quinney), strongly influenced Taylor, Walton and Young's ideas. The two elements contained in the deviance and power theme were clearly in evidence: 'radical criminological strategy . . . is to show up the law, in its true colours, as the instrument of the ruling class . . . and that the rule-makers are also the greatest rule-breakers' (Taylor *et al.*, 1975: 89). The second theme, the politicisation of deviance, was also a key component of their work. Seeing deviants as political rebels, 'much deviance', they said, 'is in itself political' (ibid.: 221).

Although a few writers in Britain and the United States had produced work on crime and deviance that was influenced by Marxism, until the advent of *The New Criminology* attempts to construct a Marxist theory of crime and deviance had been rare. In response to Paul Hirst, one of their critics, Taylor *et al.* (1975: 283) wrote:

> We can think of no theorist of crime and deviancy in this country, and only two in the USA (John Horton and Tony Platt) who could be accused of the 'Marxism' in deviancy theory he (Hirst) sees to be prevalent. None of the other 'conflict' theorists of crime . . . borrow in any significant fashion from Marxism.

Indeed, the dearth of Marxist criminology was such that until the early 1970s the pre-war work of the Dutch Marxist criminologist Willem Bonger was seen by many as definitive (and was much criticised by Taylor, Walton and Young).

Taylor, Walton and Young's ambitious aim was to help construct a Marxist-informed theoretical understanding of both the processes of criminalisation/ deviantisation, and the aetiology of criminal/deviant activities, by opening up 'the criminological debate by pointing to certain *formal* and *substantive* requirements of a fully social theory of deviance, a theory that can explain the forms assumed by social control and deviant action in "developed" (capitalist) societies' (Taylor *et al.*, 1973: 269, original emphasis). The main features of their work can be summarised as follows:

1 There was a commitment to a 'normative' criminology. By this they meant a socialist criminology that insisted on the need to eradicate social and economic

inequalities inherent in capitalist society. This would be congruent with Marx's view that 'man's true nature could only be realised in a classless society based upon a spirit of community'.

2 The creation of a socialist society would usher in a celebration of 'diversity', though without the need for any activities to be criminalised. Thus they envisaged a future 'crime free' society.

3 They attempted to find a route to understanding human action that avoided the determinism found in positivism, as well as the relativism found in phenomeno-logical accounts of deviance. This was reflected in their endorsement of Gouldner's 'man-fighting-back' image of the deviant, and they advanced the view that deviance had to be seen as the way in which individuals 'actively made' the external world. From this perspective deviance is chosen, and 'much' of it is in fact political. In this context they were critical of Bonger, and of the more recent work of the American conflict theorists for holding on to a deterministic and pathologised view of deviance.

4 Although they stressed voluntarism and choice, they did none the less recognise the structural contexts in which people made decisions, ultimately class society. However, following Marx, they saw the development of class consciousness as the basis for eventual liberation.

5 They spent much time discussing the role of the powerful, via the state and its agencies, in the creation of rules and their enforcement, thereby leaning towards an instrumentalist view of the law. This included those professionals and institu-tions in advanced capitalist societies concerned with the control of, as they saw it, increasing numbers of people.

Critical responses

Inevitably, *The New Criminology* generated a great deal of criticism and debate – including criticism from other Marxists. The most fundamental issue thrown up by these debates was whether, whilst still retaining Marxist credentials, a Marxist theory of deviance was possible at all. Taylor, Walton and Young's strongest Marxist critic at the time was Paul Hirst (whose critique appeared in *Critical Criminology*). Hirst (1975b) argued that Marxists should have no truck with bourgeois concepts such as crime and deviance; to do so would lead only to revisionism. For Hirst, crime and deviance were not 'real' objects of study; Marxist social theory was already specified by its own conceptual language. Using a concept such as deviance was to assume that deviant behaviour was special, and essentially different to non-deviant behaviour. How, then, can deviance be separated out for study? Unfortunately, in *The New Crimi-nology* the authors did not provide a precise definition of deviance. They seemed to be saying that deviance *is* different to conformity in so much as it is purposive infrac-tion of (ideological) rules. Deviants were thus seen as being committed to modes of behaviour that they know are frowned upon by the wider society. The difficulty here is the implication that there is a consensus in society, a notion that they had thoroughly disapproved of when criticising orthodox criminology.

In fact, as the 1970s progressed, the focus switched to crime and law, and the concept of deviance was used less often. Colin Sumner (1976) was one Marxist who felt that it could be retained, providing that it was reconceptualised so as to make it compatible with Marxism. He suggested that deviance was best seen as an ideological 'social censure', or adverse judgement. From this standpoint, 'deviance' does not exist because people decide to break rules, or because they have a deviant label impressed upon them. It exists as an objective phenomenon located within the ideological superstructure of capitalism, irrespective of actual behaviour, or the extent of a consensus. In a later discussion, Sumner (1990: 27) pointed out that social censures 'mark off the deviant, the pathological, the dangerous and the criminal from the normal and the good. They say "stop", and are tied to a desire to control, prevent or punish'. From this perspective, the sociology of deviance should become the sociology of social censures. The focus would therefore be on 'the negative categories of moral ideology', the social censures, rather than on the 'offenders' that they produce.

During the rest of the 1970s a large amount of theoretical work was produced in Britain in varying degrees informed by Marxist ideas. Before we examine that work, it will be useful to return to original sources and see what Marx himself, and his collaborator Engels, had to say about crime.

MARX AND ENGELS ON CRIME

Marxists who return to source to look for detailed analyses of the phenomenon of crime are likely to be disappointed. Marx had little more than a passing interest in crime, and when he did address the subject it was usually treated as part of a wider concern with the political economy of law and right (especially in *The German Ideology* (Marx and Engels, 1965)). Engels spent rather more time specifically on the subject of crime, especially in *The Condition of the Working Class in England* (Engels, 1969).

By modern standards, Marx's writings on crime as such are, arguably, less than adequate. His faith in criminal statistics, his lack of interest in criminal motivations, and his identification of crime with the lumpenproletariat are good examples of this.

Taylor *et al.* (1973: 221) argued that criminology should recognise 'in deviance the acts of men in the process of actively making, rather than passively taking, the external world'. This formulation, although it was intended to be 'Marxist', did appear to be at variance with Marx's own writings on crime. In general, he seemed to view the criminal as 'passively taking', rather than 'actively making', the world. They attempted to resolve this problem by arguing that Marx's work on crime was misleading, and that we should utilise his general body of theory rather than rely on those instances where he specifically takes up empirical challenges.

One of the main difficulties to be overcome by Taylor *et al.*, and indeed by all Marxists, was that Marx saw crime as being concentrated in the lumpenproletariat, and this provided Hirst with one of his main criticisms of 'Marxist' criminology. From Hirst's point of view, Marxists should follow Marx and treat the lumpenproletariat with the contempt they deserve. Lying outside the relations of production – that is, as 'non-productive' labour – and living a parasitic mode of life, they were of no interest as far as revolutionary socialist struggle was concerned. Marx and Engels (1970a: 44) said of the lumpenproletariat:

> The 'dangerous class', the social scum, that passively rotting mass thrown off by the lowest layers of old society, may here and there be swept into the movement by the proletarian revolution, its conditions of life, however, prepare it far more for the part of a bribed tool of reactionary intrigue.

This was not a reflection of some grumpy Victorian morality; it was based upon a view of this stratum as being more likely to inhibit than further a revolutionary cause. It was in the context of a discussion of 'productive' and 'unproductive' labour that Marx referred ironically to the 'productivity' of crime (see Chapter 3, p. 52).

Engels's (1969) *The Condition of the Working Class in England* stands as a denunciation of the life conditions that the working class was subject to at that time (1844–45), and a denunciation of the capitalist mode of production which he saw as producing and sustaining those conditions. He discussed crime within the context of a brutal wage labour system. Out of this system arose economic deprivation and the demoralisation of increasing numbers of the working class. Engels contended that crime was an inevitable response, as summed up in this rather deterministic passage:

> If the influences demoralizing to the working man act more powerfully, more concentratedly than usual, he becomes an offender as certainly as water abandons the fluid for the vaporous state at 80 degrees, Reaumur. Under the brutal and brutalizing treatment of the bourgeoisie, the working man becomes precisely as much a thing without volition as water, and is subject to the laws of Nature with precisely the same necessity; at a certain point all freedom ceases.
>
> (Ibid.: 159)

There are, however, more 'voluntaristic' elements to be found in Engels's discussion. Faced with economic deprivation, he argued, the worker either 'merely strives to make life endurable while abandoning the effort to break the yoke' (ibid.: 145), or he in some way revolts. Using this reasoning, Engels goes on to outline a number of possible, criminal, responses. These 'conflictual' crimes may sometimes be committed by the working class against the working class, and are seen as representing a carica-ture of capitalism itself: 'This war of all against all . . . it is only the logical sequel of the principle involved in free competition' (ibid.: 162). In some cases, though, crime was directed at the rich:

> The working man lived in poverty and want, and saw that others were better off than he. It was not clear to his mind why he, who did more for society than the rich idler, should be the one to suffer under these conditions. Want conquered his inherited respect for the sacredness of property, and he stole.
>
> (Ibid.: 240)

Engels stresses the inevitability of this conflict, and its potential for development into a more mature, class-based economic, then political, struggle against the bourgeoisie: 'The revolt of the workers began soon after the first industrial development, and has passed through several phases . . . The earliest, crudest and least fruitful form of this rebellion was that of crime' (ibid.: 240).

Engels associated different types of criminal activity with different types of con-sciousness. However, *class* consciousness is not present in any of the three types described above: crime determined by conditions of brutality, crime reflecting capi-talist values, and crime based on taking from the rich. *Class* consciousness involves participants having collective class interests: 'As a class, they first manifest opposi-tion to the bourgeoisie when they resisted the introduction of machinery at the very beginning of the industrial period . . . factories were demolished and machinery destroyed' (ibid.: 241).

The fifth possibility for Engels was when the working class used crime in the struggle for socialism.

Marx too saw crime as an inevitable response to the conditions of life created by capitalism. Crime arose as a symptom of the contradictions within capitalism, and as capitalism progressed he believed that the total amount of crime would increase. He did not, however, see crime *per se* as revolutionary. Crime was: 'the struggle of the iso-lated individual against the prevailing conditions' (Marx and Engels, 1965: 367). He was aware that crime covered a spectrum of behaviours, though in each case his over-riding concern was with the efficacy of the behaviour in terms of the workers' struggle for socialism. Thus the fact that crime is 'against' the capitalist's law was irrelevant. However, certain types of crime, such as machine smashing, have a special signifi-cance for Marx and Engels: they represented forms of criminal activity which pre-saged a more mature political struggle. This is an important point when we come to consider attempts by more recent Marxists to politicise criminal behaviour. Whilst Marx was aware of the ways in which law functioned in the interests of capital, he was never led into the position of romanticising crime. Engels, too, in no way romanti-cised crime. Even crime that involved stealing from the 'rich idler' was described as the 'crudest, least fruitful form of rebellion'.

TAYLOR, WALTON AND YOUNG AND THE POLITICISATION OF DEVIANCE

A central thread running through *The New Criminology,* and latched on to by a number of critical criminologists in the 1970s, was that the deviant was actively committed to breaking bourgeois rules, hence 'much' deviance was in itself political. 'Deviance' and 'political' were therefore seen as qualities of the act. Hirst (1975a: 218) was not alone in his retort that:

> The romanticisation of crime, the recognition in the criminal of a rebel 'alienated' from society, is, for Marxism, a dangerous political ideology. It leads inevitably . . . to the estimation of the lumpenproletariat as a revolutionary force.

Obviously, if we adhere to a strict Marx-derived line, and equate criminality with the lumpenproletariat, this does follow. However, this is to assume that all crime has essentially the same qualities, based upon lumpen-type consciousness, which would contradict Hirst's argument that we should not accept bourgeois categories. And, in fact, he referred to crimes such as mob agitation, machine smashing and industrial sabotage as 'having a more obviously "political" quality' (ibid.: 219). The question remains, though, on what basis do we separate political from non-political crime? Marx's view of the lumpenproletariat as the source of most crime, a view that Hirst endorsed, is problematic in that it ignores the vast amount of law breaking carried out by other sections of society, and Hirst's critique of Taylor, Walton and Young to some extent rests on this understanding of the lumpenproletariat, or some supposed modern-day equivalent.

POLITICISING DEVIANCE: NUTS, SLUTS, PREVERTS . . . AND REVOLUTIONARIES?

During the 1970s a number of left, critical criminologists focused on what they saw as the political content of deviant/criminal activities. Some saw virtually all such activities, if carried out by the working class, as forms of political action; others concentrated on specific instances. In his review of Marxist criminology during that period, Ronald Hinch (1983: 69) has written:

> The exact meaning given to crime as a political act, of course, varied. For some . . . the act itself constituted a political statement, while for others . . . the act had to be accompanied by a conscious intent to rebel. In most instances the result was a blurring of the relation between the act, the intent of the act, and the class struggle. Indeed, it appeared that for some . . . the class struggle and crime were inseparable.

Basically, the argument was that some (or all) so-called conventional crime, as well as more obvious forms of working-class resistance, such as urban protest, represented a threat to capitalist society, a society whose structural arrangements had shaped the criminality in the first place. Deviance/crime was characterised as proto-revolutionary activity. One of the strongest advocates of this view, Geoff Pearson (1975: 96–7) argued that since the late 1960s various sociologists had attempted to show how deviant behaviour was in itself political: 'Or, more specifically, that deviance should be grasped as a primitive crypto-political action, in the same way that social bandits in peasant societies, or the machine smashing of the Luddites, represented a primitive political force'.

These two terms 'crypto-political' and 'primitive rebellion', derived from Habermas and Hobsbawm respectively, were widely used at this time. Pearson supported his argument by giving examples of research that had broken with traditional approaches and looked at rule breaking in political terms: Goldman (1959) on school vandalism and truancy (an early precursor of this type of work), I. Taylor (1971) on soccer hooliganism, and his own study of 'Paki-bashing' (Pearson, 1976). Often those engaging in these deviant activities were cast in the role of Robin Hood figures striking out against an unjust society. Thus some vandals, truants, soccer hooligans and Paki-bashers were lumped together within the same analytical scheme as representatives of crypto-political action and, sometimes, as 'folk heroes'.

The problems associated with this kind of reasoning are exemplified by Pearson's Paki-bashing study set in a north-east Lancashire cotton town (for a detailed critique of this study see Tierney, 1980). Although carried out in the mid-1970s, the research was based on incidents that occurred in the summer of 1964, when, according to Pearson, a 'flood' of Paki-bashing hit the town. It was, he argued, 'a primitive form of political and economic struggle . . . a rudimentary form of political action' (Pearson, 1976: 69). He also made the unsubstantiated claim that those involved were viewed as 'folk heroes': 'the misdirected heroism of the Paki-basher' (ibid.: 80). This, in effect, got uncomfortably near to accusing the town's residents of racist complicity. Pearson compared the actions of the Paki-bashers to the political actions of the machine-smashing handloom weavers from an earlier period in Lancashire's history. It is a complex study which is, unfortunately, consistently misunderstood:

> so that a myth has grown up that he was suggesting that high unemployment during the period referred to in the study led to racist attacks on Pakistanis. Given that unemployment in the town was at that time less than 1%, his argument has to be more sophisticated than that.
>
> (Tierney, 1988: 145)

On the basis of Pearson's own sources, the so-called Paki-bashing that occurred hardly constituted a 'flood', and on the evidence available it would be stretching credulity to characterise those involved as latter-day Luddites, folk heroes, or crypto-political revolutionaries. Most of those involved seem to have been motivated by the very unromantic desire for revenge.

YOUTH SUBCULTURES AND POLITICS

As we have seen, most orthodox studies of adolescent delinquency had reflected the message given by official statistics and assumed that in the main delinquency was a feature of working-class life. On the other hand, orthodox studies of youth culture had minimised or ignored the importance of class, seeing youth culture as a largely classless phenomenon, simply structured around the fact of belonging to a certain age group. By the 1970s, studies of youth were concerned to rectify this.

On a different level, we might question the extent to which orthodox studies of youth culture were able to *understand* those they were studying. Consider this curious example from Cyril Smith's (1970: 28) book on adolescence republished (with corrections) in 1970, and conjuring up an image of Cliff Richard being 'discovered' in the *Two I's* coffee bar, circa 1958: 'Teenage culture in Britain was generated, and is still largely sustained by male entertainers performing in coffee bars in city centres'. And, in a rush of elitism:

> The conformity of the young in Britain is in line with the conformity of the adult population . . . for they are the successful products of a stable family life. They have, most of them, belonged to youth organisations managed by adults permeated with the values of the Establishment and breeding respect in them for the churches, monarchy, and their aristocracy . . . They have accepted without protest the weight on their young shoulders of tradition in the public schools and grammar schools, and they become charmed by their privileges.
>
> (Ibid.: 95)

By the 1970s, work explicitly linking youth subcultural formations to class was emerging. Partly because researchers were unable to find structured delinquent gangs in Britain of the sort discovered by American researchers, subcultural theory in this country tended to concern itself with youth subcultures and leisure more than delinquency as such. Of particular importance in this respect was the work produced by the Birmingham Centre for Contemporary Cultural Studies. John Muncie (1984: 97) points to the central elements of this research:

> On the one hand the meaning of subcultural style was examined through various ethnogaphic and semiological analyses: on the other, the political implications of deviancy were explored through investigations of the structural and class position of various subcultures.

This work, then, provided a further example of that strand of radical thought that sought to politicise deviant activities.

The Birmingham Centre research put class and class conflict at centre stage, whilst examining the impact of social and economic change in the post-war period on working-class youth. This involved research on a range of subcultural styles, for example, Teddy Boys, Mods and skinheads. To some extent the researchers agreed with Downes (1966) and saw these styles as products of a parent working-class culture, though they represented an 'intense articulation' of that culture. Clarke *et al.* (1976) argued that ruling-class culture is the dominant culture in society, and is therefore a dominant ideology. This class will endeavour to shape other, subordinate cultures, so that they conform with the dominant ideology. Working-class youth subcultures, they argued, arose as threats to this ideology, because they developed alternative ideas about what a 'teenager' should be like, what leisure should be used for, what is an appropriate dress style, and so on. Clarke and his colleagues at the Birmingham Centre thus put forward the view that youth subcultures were, at a symbolic level, oppositional.

Phil Cohen's (1972) article on the theme of youth subcultures as solutions to stresses and contradictions existing within working-class communities in the East End of London was being described as 'seminal' by the middle of the 1970s. Redevelopment and rationalisation in the East End of London during the post-war period had destroyed traditional neighbourhoods, led to a decline in local job opportunities, and created increasingly privatised families. These changes produced disruptions and dislocations in working-class culture, and Cohen saw the various youth subcultures as providing not 'real' solutions to these problems, but, rather, what he called 'magical' solutions. Young people, he argued, used their subculture as an expression of an 'imaginary relation' (a term he borrowed from the French Marxist Althusser), that is, a relation expressed in terms of symbols (styles of dress, haircuts, etc.) and feelings. Paul Willis (1978) made a similar point in his study of the 'cultural politics' of bike boys and hippies. The view of youth subcultures as attempts to recapture some of the socially cohesive elements of working-class culture destroyed by post-war social change provided an important backdrop to much of the work at the Birmingham Centre.

It is worth pausing to examine the place of consciousness in Cohen's analysis: how did the Teddy Boys, skinheads, and others, understand their actions? This is an important consideration when assessing all attempts to make 'deviant' activities into something political. Cohen's statement that 'The latent function of subculture is . . . to express and resolve . . . contradictions' (1972: 23), implies that those involved did not have as a conscious aim the resolution of contradictions, but rather that their actions fulfilled this function. This use of a form of functionalism seemed to get round the problem of consciousness, yet at the same time created its own problems. Clearly, skinheads, for instance, did not consciously devise a programme aimed at recapturing lost working-class community, but the *sort* of consciousness involved is important. As a subcultural theorist, Cohen took consequences and worked backwards. Thus skinheads presented an already existing representation of an 'imaginary solution', which focused the analysis on subcultural consequences, but ignored the subjective intent as an element in the original formation of the subculture.

Also at the Birmingham Centre, John Clarke and Tony Jefferson (1976) drew up a typology of forms of consciousness among working-class youth. This 'ideal type' classificatory scheme was designed to indicate a range of possible conscious responses to their social worlds. In two of the categories a political dimension was suggested: 'traditional delinquency', where opposition to established authority is limited to illegal activities, and 'deviant youth culture', which was seen as expressing a moment of originality, a creative assertion of deviant consciousness: 'These styles offer a symbolic critique of the established order and, in so doing, represent a latent form of "non-ideological" politics' (ibid.: 148). For the authors, this was the nearest that working-class youth got to opposing a dominant ideology, for in their analysis they dispensed entirely with a more mature political consciousness situated in what they classified as the 'oppositional category'. Now, while working-class adolescents tend not to get involved in large numbers with political movements on the left, they do join and actively participate in such movements, and to an extent that does not justify writing them off completely. The methods of research employed in these kinds of studies will, in fact, generally lead to such examples being excluded from consideration, simply because they begin with a 'deviant' subculture and work backwards.

The title of Corrigan and Frith's (1976: 237) article, 'The politics of youth culture', promised to confront head on the question of just how political youth cultures are: 'We are thinking, for example, of the ways in which kids can use the symbols of pop culture as a source of collective power in their struggle with schools or police'. It was working-class culture at its moment of creation that was seen as representing the most potent mode of resistance: youth cultures were described as the 'crystallisation' of rebellion at the symbolic level. From this vantage point, they are a manifestation of working-class power to redefine and rework meaning systems. Around this general framework Corrigan and Frith attempted to map out the guidelines for a political reading of working-class youth cultures, but the analysis fizzled out with the comment that 'at present we just don't have the sort of knowledge on which clear answers to these questions can be based' (ibid.: 236). I am not sure that that knowledge was ever forthcoming. Again, a basic problem with the material that came from the Birmingham Centre was a failure to come to terms with a clear understanding of 'political', and it is this in particular that dogged subsequent attempts to construct a convincing theoretical framework in this area. The political content of youth subcultures was predicated on their existence as 'struggles' against alternative, dominant, meaning systems, but of interest here are the types of meaning involved, the extent to which the diffusion of youth subcultures weakens this resistance, and the relationship between resistance at a symbolic level and resistance at a concrete material level.

During the 1970s, research continued to be carried out on the theme of youth subcultures and 'style' and 'cultural symbolisation' (e.g., Hebdige, 1979; and see Muncie, 1984, for a review). These studies emphasised that the construction of style was an act of creation and a form of resistance. In particular, attention was focused on the ways in which youth subcultures took over and reshaped or redefined the original cultural meaning attached to an object. Items of clothing, signs such as the swastika, safety pins, hairstyle, and so on, are infused with new symbolic meanings. To this extent, it was argued, some young people are involved in cultural resistance. The task for sociologists was to 'read' the signs, to decode the new meanings (see Hall and Jefferson, 1976). Clarke introduced the concept of 'bricolage' (which he borrowed from Lévi-Strauss) to describe the process of transforming the symbolic meaning of objects.

One of the difficulties with the 'reading the signs' approach to subcultural theory, as Stan Cohen (1980) has pointed out, is that it often seems to distance the perceived meanings of cultural symbols from the subjective intent of the participants. The wearing of a swastika might be decoded as a subversive shock tactic directed at mainstream society, and in the same symbolic universe, therefore, as an unconventional hairstyle. It might, though, simply mean that the wearer is a supporter of fascist movements.

A further point also needs to be made. Given that, according to the Birmingham Centre, youth subcultures do not offer 'real' solutions to contradictions or problems, an important question to ask is: to what extent do they provide even an 'imaginary' solution? The political dimension to subcultures was seen as being located in the sub-culture's control of meaning. The problem with the concept of 'imaginary solution' was that it implied that from the individual's point of view, life actually did become (via his or her 'imaginary relations') exciting, interesting, full of action, or whatever. Thus, although the real problems of life were not altered, it appeared to the partici-pants that, in a sense, they were. Subcultures became a sort of sociological Valium. However, as with Valium, the effects are only temporary, and 'real relations' can break through even in leisure time. The bleaker realities of life are not swept away totally in leisure time, even at the 'imaginary level' and, indeed, are likely to have a strong determining influence on what leisure can offer. To imply that working-class youth subcultures provide a total symbolically constituted resolution of problems is to endow those concerned with unrealistic amounts of power.

Efforts to politicise deviance or the subcultural affiliations of working-class youth did not, at the time, escape criticism. Commenting on his influential study of work-ing-class youth in 'Roundhouse', a neighbourhood of tenements in Liverpool, pub-lished in 1974, Howard Parker put a different slant on 'oppositional' subcultures:

> parents, kids and adolescents basically share so many of the basic structural constraints and social inequalities forced upon them that their world views are consistent and in harmony much more than they are in opposition . . . [this] can be seen to be to a large extent an accommodation to a particular structural situation rather than a perpetuating rejection of dominant values and life styles.
>
> (Parker, 1976: 47)

There was, too, an important theoretical debate between Geoff Pearson and Paul Rock. For Rock (1973: 103), the political status of an activity derived from the meaning that it had for the participants, in other words the type of consciousness involved was crucial: 'Politicized deviancy may be defined as that activity which is regarded as expressly political by its participants'.

Pearson, though, objected to this formulation because, as he put it, 'it reduces politics to a "meaning"'. This criticism of Rock implied a rejection of schools of thought which stressed the primacy of subjective intent or 'meaning'. In Rock's view, deviance only becomes political when those classed as deviants actively worked to change the attitudes and responses of the social audience by redrawing the boundaries between 'moral' and 'immoral'. Thus consciousness and action were inextricably linked, and he refused to make all deviants into political figures, a position he saw as misplaced romanticism. Rock's dourly anti-romantic stance clearly did not accord with Pearson's approach which made the 1964 Paki-bashers into political activists. In effect, Rock's solution to the problem of deciding what was meant by political deviance was to bracket off what are relatively more obvious forms of political deviance – the protests of the poor in the ghetto, Black Power, and so on – and to this extent he dealt with the same groups as Horowitz and Leibowitz, Hall and Stan Cohen. However, both Pearson and Rock ultimately met the same problem: where does the boundary between political and non-political deviance come?

CRITICAL CRIMINOLOGY: DEVIANCE, CRIME AND POWER

The second theme emerging out of the post-new deviancy period – deviance and power – was also in evidence in *The New Criminology*, along with the theme of politicising deviance, as discussed above. The theme of deviance and power encompassed two elements: the powerful as instrumental rule makers, and the powerful as cynical rule breakers. It was the first of these that assumed particular importance among a growing number of critical/radical criminologists in the 1970s, with the concept of 'crime' being preferred to that of 'deviance'.

With the qualification that this describes the discipline-based, intellectual momentum leading to these developments, rather than the sources of the theoretical concepts, Galliher (1978: 253–4) has summed up radical criminology's journey from the 1960s as follows:

> the popularity of the labeling perspective with its emphasis on societal reaction and created deviance seems to have provided the conditions in the discipline for the swift re-emergence of the conflict orientation once it was triggered by the political milieu . . . The conflict perspective stressing powerful interest groups' control of the law, police, and courts, in turn created the intellectual basis for the emergence of Marxism in criminology in the 1970's.

In passing it can be noted that plotting the developments in critical/radical criminology from the middle of the 1970s is accompanied by certain difficulties.

Theoretical discussions were often complicated, sometimes obscure, and occasionally turgid and, in addition, given that this was still a time of intellectual ferment, some writers were adding to the confusion by vacating theoretical positions with which they had been closely associated in favour of different schools of thought.

During the first part of the 1970s, conflict theory and early versions of Marxist criminology had taken an instrumentalist approach to analyses of rule making. However, by the middle of the decade critical academic work was increasingly concerned with developing a more sophisticated understanding of the nature of law, one that transcended the fairly crude instrumentalist approaches. This indicates another important feature of these developments in critical criminology, namely, that attention switched from the actions of the criminal to the legal order and reactions to the criminal, bringing with it an emphasis on the sociology of law.

The powerful as law makers

In the ensuing debate among Marxist writers, a number of key questions emerged:

- In what ways, and to what extent, does law protect the interests of the ruling class?
- Is law, by definition, 'bad' because it is a product of, or is present in, a capitalist society?
- Is it possible to achieve progressive, socialist-oriented, reform of law within the context of capitalism?
- Is law necessary in a socialist society, or can regulation and order be accomplished without a legal order and the criminalisation of some behaviour?

Broadly speaking, critical criminologists saw law as bourgeois law, and therefore the legal order in a capitalist society existed to further the interests of capital by creating appropriate conditions for the pursuit of profit. This required:

- The creation and enforcement of laws, and hence definitions of 'crime', aimed at regulating the workforce and surplus populations.
- The creation of laws pertaining to notions of private property, thereby underpinning the capitalist's right to own the means of production.
- The use of law as an educative device whereby relations between labour and capital are ideologically sanctioned and justified.
- The use of law and penal sanctions against the least powerful who constitute a threat to the system.

However, it was recognised that such formulations raised complex and difficult issues when trying to construct theoretical explanations. The precise nature of the relationship between the state, the ruling class and the legal order was, in particular, an issue that stimulated intense and highly complex debates. Other important issues had to be addressed, and incorporated into theoretical formulations. Some laws, such as those relating to welfare, consumer protection, unfair dismissal and health and safety at work, seemed to act primarily in the interests of the working, rather than ruling, class. Similarly, legislation relating to, for instance, homosexuality and abortion seemed not to be acting directly in the interests of capitalists (see Greenberg, 1976).

An instrumental Marxist approach to law owed much to a well-known statement by Marx and Engels (1970b: 37) in the *Manifesto of the Communist Party*, where, referring to political leadership, they wrote: 'The executive of the modern state is but a committee for managing the common affairs of the whole bourgeoisie'. It was an approach based upon an instrumentalist school of thought in political theory which argued that powerful members of the state apparatus were either themselves capitalists, or they strongly identified, at a subjective level, with the goals and interests of the capitalist class (Miliband, 1969; Domhoff, 1970). The study of law, therefore, was based on the premise that law reflects the interests of the ruling class. This was a similar position to that taken by American conflict theorists, except that conflict theorists tended to use the concept of elites, rather than ruling class, and to reduce the relationship between these elites and the legal order to a sort of conspiracy theory. From this perspective, those with economic power are able to exert direct influence on the state and the legal system. At the same time, they will use whatever ideological means are available in order to present an image of law as neutral and even-handed – both 'in the book' and 'in action' – and in the process construct notions such as the 'rule of law'. From a radical instrumentalist standpoint this merely masks the partiality of law. As Bankowski and Mungham (1975: 29) grimly put it, law is a 'means of domination, oppression and desolation'. For other examples, see Takagi (1974); Quinney (1975); Michalowski and Bohlander (1976); Hepburn (1977).

Structural Marxist approaches

By the second half of the 1970s a number of Marxist-influenced writers were criticising instrumentalist accounts of the legal order. These came to be seen as altogether too neat and tidy and, in the style of conspiracy theory, suggesting that somehow the state and the ruling class form a monolithic whole, working together harmoniously for their own benefit. Thus when dealing with, for instance, the issue of some law appearing to be disadvantageous to the ruling class, instrumentalists argued that it must in some way be advantageous, otherwise it would not have been created (see Thompson, 1975, for a defence of the concept of 'rule of law', and the argument that law is not always oppressive, and is sometimes the result of working-class struggle). Instrumentalist critiques entailed searching for the 'real', nefarious motives lying behind even apparently benign law. Wolfe (1971: 19), for example, has said: 'there are times when sections of the ruling class become sponsors of reform in order to rationalize the system and make it work better'. And, on disputes within the class holding power: 'Superficially, groups within the dominant class may differ on some issues. But they share many interests, and they can entirely exclude members of the other classes from the political process' (Quinney, 1975: 288). This is a view that has permeated into some radical analyses of policing, and is sardonically summed up by Young (1986: 19):

> It is a strange world, bourgeois economists may argue about the logic of capital – as do Marxist economists – but seemingly a local police chief has no problem in understanding what capital requires of him nor does the lone school teacher facing a disruptive class.

Structuralism detaches the workings of the state, the economy and the legal order from the actual individuals concerned. The nature of law, therefore, does not result from the imposition of the will of the powerful as a conscious act, but rather develops as part of the functioning of a total system having reality at a structural level. Put simply, whichever party is in government, capitalism is always in power (Althusser, 1971; Poulantzas, 1973). Furthermore, structuralism sees the institutions of the state as having 'relative autonomy' (Althusser, 1971), although in the final analysis the economy is the determining force. On the basis of this formulation, it logically follows that the state will sometimes introduce laws that do not represent the interests of the ruling class, or that disadvantage certain sections of the ruling class, because of the structural requirement for an ordered, compliant society overall. This is necessary because capitalism is always in a state of tension due to its internal contradictions. It is the capitalist system as a total social formation that is ultimately at stake (Werkentin *et al.*, 1974; Beirne, 1979). For a critique of analyses that reduced the nature of law to the demands of the economy see Cain and Hunt, 1979.

By the end of the 1970s a large body of work, with contributions from a wide range of academic disciplines – though usually built around the sociology of law – had been produced. The intention of this work was to develop a theoretical, Marxist-informed explanation of law, and a better understanding of its practical significance. In this context Fine's (1979) *Capitalism and the Rule of Law* was particularly significant. This was a collection of articles by scholars explicitly committed to a multidisciplinary project of constructing a Marxist theoretical framework for the study of the legal order. Drawing on the work of Gramsci, Althusser, Foucault and the Bolshevik jurist Pashukanis, whose work appeared in the 1920s, the book was seen as marking the triumph of structuralism over instrumentalism. Pashukanis's 'commodity-exchange' theory of law was a major influence, in particular his ideas on the bourgeois *form* of law in capitalist society. Thus he accepted the need for social regulation and order based upon 'rules', but developed a critique of the legal rules specific to capitalism;

for these, he argued, functioned to produce bourgeois social order. In a socialist society, he said, the form of law would disappear, so that regulation was no longer based on state-sponsored legal rules, but on informally generated codes of conduct derived from working-class 'social defence', in line with the needs of socialist construction. This had echoes of Taylor, Walton and Young's arguments for 'socialist diversity' in a crime-free society, which adds a touch of irony, for one of the contributors to this book was Jock Young, who by then was distancing himself from many of the ideas contained in *The New Criminology*, ideas he was labelling as 'left idealism'.

Pat Carlen and Mike Collison's (1980) *Radical Issues in Criminology*, also a collection of articles, directed itself towards a Marxist-informed engagement with practical issues of regulation within capitalist societies, with a view to providing a 'counterbalance to recent libertarian, anarchistic and utopian trends in criminology'. Although the contributors did not share the same 'radical political space', this too reflected the growing criticism of the type of criminology associated with *The New Criminology*, and indicates the direction taken by radical criminology in the 1980s, when a serious debate opened up between so-called left-realists and so-called left-idealists. Laurie Taylor's (1980) article in *Radical Issues in Criminology* was, he said, not a defence of 'legalism' – that is, blind faith in the rule of law – but a defence of 'civil liberties' and the use of law to bring power to heel. This was a common thread running through the book: that socialist theory and practice can be applied to bourgeois law in progressive ways. Clearly, this is an issue that is central to socialist action (or inaction) on the part of criminologists. The book supports the idea of intervening and challenging law, as a springboard to, as the authors saw it, greater things, though there was a clear tension between this and 'mere reformism'.

On a general level the book was 'critical' in the sense of attempting to emphasise problems and contradictions in bourgeois law, criminalisation and penal practices, and problems within current socialist criminology. The critique of the latter centred on those who seemingly did not wish to sully their hands with intervention aimed at changing 'unjust' laws, or ensuring that law makers and law enforcers themselves kept within the law. Paul Hirst's article in *Radical Issues in Criminology* (Hirst, 1980) stands as a critique of those who would, in his terms, look anarchically towards a crime-free and law-free socialist future. He was, therefore, critical of writers such as Pashukanis and his old adversaries Taylor, Walton and Young.

Policing the crisis

Drawing on the language of warfare, Colin Sumner (1981) has described the onslaught by Marxist theoreticians on the ideas associated with *The New Criminology* during the 1970s. Hirst's various critiques had worked like a 'defoliant' on the concepts of crime and deviance; 'Parisian B-52s' in the shape of Althusserian structuralism had 'devastated the terrain'. According to Sumner (1981: 277–8), though, by the end of the 1970s there was a silver lining for Marxist studies of crime indicated by:

1 the return to reading Marx;
2 the epistemological dilution of structuralist Marxism through its confrontation with the nasty business of empirical reality in the booming area of cultural studies;
3 the stimulation of 'quality' Marxist studies of crime and law from outside the sociology of deviance; and
4 the deconstruction of the welfare state and an increased significance of criminal law in a period of heightening social tension.

All of these factors, in Sumner's view, were expressed in Hall *et al.*'s (1978) *Policing the Crisis*. Subtitled *Mugging, the state and law and order*, the book addressed what were seen as moral panics over so-called mugging in the early part of the 1970s, and drew on the cultural studies work of the Birmingham Centre for Contemporary Cultural Studies (where Hall was the director), and Gramsci's writings on hegemony and ideology. The argument was that exaggerated claims were made by control agencies and the mass media regarding an outbreak of mugging. Not only was the amount of mugging inflated, but street robbery was itself incorrectly linked directly to young black males. In a sophisticated analysis the authors argue that the British state was having to cope with considerable social and economic problems, thus creating a 'crisis in hegemony': in other words, the authority of the state was under threat. The response by the state was to deflect attention away from the 'real' bases of the crisis by generating a moral panic over mugging. Although Hall *et al.* never suggested that *no* muggings occurred, what they did argue was that the state overreacted to what was actually going on: special police anti-mugging squads were set up, much space was devoted to 'black muggers' by the mass media, and stiff prison sentences were handed out by the courts. Arguing that the key to support for the established order lies in the creation of 'consent' rather than coercion, Hall *et al.* saw the state tapping into already existing popular stereotypes regarding black youth, and popular explanations of criminality based upon 'permissiveness' and a 'soft' criminal justice system. The 'black mugger' was, therefore, created as a scapegoat for the social anxieties arising from social and economic dislocations.

Powerful law breakers

This is the second strand arising out of the theme of power and deviance, and, as well as featuring in *The New Criminology*, it proved attractive to other writers on the left in the 1970s especially in the United States. This theme is part of a tradition of 'exposé' criminology that can be traced back to Sutherland during the 1940s; the conflict theorist Chambliss, and his study of law breaking among powerful elites in Seattle, has already been examined.

Studies of white-collar and corporate crime were important in that they directed attention away from the powerless and marginalised, and towards other more powerful groups in society, thereby illustrating how conceptualisations of crime derived from official sources lead to a mystification of reality. In an important study of criminal activities among American business corporations, Frank Pearce (1976) showed that the estimated amount of money involved was far in excess of the monetary value of conventional crime. In spite of this, culprits were rarely brought before the courts. On the basis of a number of case studies, Pearce concluded that the main examples of *organised* crime were to be found among the large business corporations in the United States. Pearce developed his argument by attempting to explain why there were so few prosecutions. In his view, prosecutions were rare because to do otherwise would subvert the ideology that the bulk of crime is carried out by the poor, which would create a crisis of legitimacy for the capitalist system. He also included an analysis of the links between big business and organised (as normally understood) crime, in which he paints a picture of a history of collusion, graft and complicity: for example, Ford and General Motors' use of gangsters in the 1930s to threaten and intimidate striking workers.

There is not the space here to examine these points in detail, but a number of writers focused their attention on specific, and sometimes spectacular, examples (for excellent reviews, see Nelken, 1994, 2002). Dowie (1988) brought to light the now well-known case of the Pinto car made by the Ford Motor Company in the 1970s. According to Dowie, Ford went ahead with the manufacture and sale of the Pinto when they knew that, because of a crucial design fault, it was dangerous. He estimated that by so doing, Ford were responsible for between 500 and 900 unnecessary deaths on American highways. Caudill (1977) documented the case of the Scotia Coal Company in Kentucky, which failed to conform with safety requirements, in spite of a record of hundreds of previous violations of safety requirements, and in whose pit twenty-six miners died in an accident. A study of what he saw as lax attitudes towards safety in the North Sea oil industry by Carson (1982) offered a sobering backdrop to the subsequent destruction of the *Piper Alpha* oil rig in 1988, and with it the loss of 168 lives. The nuclear reactor meltdown at Chernobyl, and the chemical explosion at Bhopal, provide further examples where question marks over safety had arisen.

Although this takes us into the 1980s, it is appropriate to dwell on this theme a little longer at this point. Steven Box (1987) provided one of the few analyses of links between economic recession and not just conventional crime, but corporate crime. He referred to an American study by Clinard and Yeager (1981) which did address this dimension. In their estimation: 'financial performance was found to be associated with illegal behavior . . . firms in depressed industries as well as relatively poorly performing firms in all industries tend to violate the law to greater degrees' (quoted in Box, 1987: 99).

Box then went on to examine data from various sources in this country concluding that corporate and white-collar crime did seem to correlate with economic recession.

Figures from the Health and Safety Executive for the period 1980–84 showed a drop in the number of visits to establishments by inspectors coupled with an increase in enforcement notices (by 16 per cent from 30.9 to 35.9 per 1,000 visits). If local authority enforcement notices are added, then between 1975 and 1982 Box found an increase of over 110 per cent. Looking at the incidence of fatal accidents and serious injuries at work as an indicator of 'corporate violations of regulation', Box wrote:

> what has changed markedly during the 1980s is the total number of such incidents. Thus from 1981 when there were 67.9 per 100,000 employees, to 1984 when the figure was 87.0 per 100,000 there was an increase of 28% . . . this is a remarkable increase and it indicates clearly just how far health and safety conditions at work have deteriorated under the impact of recession.
>
> (Ibid.: 101)

A similar story emerged when figures relating to bankruptcy and underpayment of the Wages Council legal minimum wage were examined.

Three other theoretical strands had become influential among some criminologists by the 1970s – phenomenology, control theory and feminism – and these will be examined here.

PHENOMENOLOGY AND CRIMINOLOGY

The fundamental message from phenomenology is that those things and activities that make up the social world do not possess absolute, essential meaning. Out of practical necessity, members of society construct shared perceptions of these things and activities, and thus endow them with meaning. Phenomenal reality, therefore, is reality as we perceive it – as it appears to be for us. Social order requires that to a significant extent these meanings are shared. Those aspects of philosophical phenomenology taken up by sociologists were concerned with the production and nature of this practical knowledge shared by members of society. Clearly, these are deep waters. Question marks are placed against all notions of knowledge, for what is 'knowable' is not an essential 'real' social world, but the social world as it is perceived: a taken-for-granted, common-sensically understood world. This is why phenomenological research is oriented towards providing accounts of the social world from the point of view of participants. Conventional social science is criticised for imposing its own, ready-made conceptual reality on to those being studied (what Schutz, 1972, calls 'constructs of the second degree').

Because phenomenology is concerned with the most fundamental processes involved in the production of meaning, it detaches itself from the study of specific substantive areas as such. Thus although a number of writers in the 1960s and early 1970s utilised the ideas of phenomenology when looking at issues of crime and deviance (e.g. Sudnow, 1965; Bittner, 1967; Douglas, 1967, 1971a; Cicourel, 1968; Matza, 1969; Phillipson, 1971), by the middle of the 1970s phenomenological studies specifically oriented towards crime and deviance had largely petered out.

However, whilst phenomenology did attract a good deal of criticism from within criminology, especially from structuralists who were unhappy with what they saw as its utter subjectivism, it did have some important influences. This was particularly apparent with respect to official statistics relating to the amount and distribution of crime, and the social categories routinely used by criminal justice agencies, and criminologists, such as 'thief', 'alcoholic', 'victim', and so forth. Jack Douglas's (1967) study of the interpretive processes involved in the construction of suicide rates, for instance, provided a strong challenge to positivist approaches that followed the lead taken by Durkheim in his study of suicide. As Douglas argued, suicide was not a 'real' thing existing 'out there' as an objective event; actual suicide rates were produced by organisations and the individuals working in them according to shared meaning systems (see, also, Atkinson, 1979).

ETHNOMETHODOLOGY

Ethnomethodology grew out of sociological phenomenology during the 1960s, and has shown more durability in terms of a continuing contribution specifically to the sociology of crime and deviance. As a perspective it rests on three assumptions (Jones, 1993: 97):

1 Social life is inherently precarious. Anything could happen in social interaction. However:
2 actors never realise this, because
3 they unwittingly possess the practical abilities necessary to make the world appear an ordered place.

Literally defined as 'people's methods', ethnomethodology concerns itself with the empirical exploration of the tacitly understood, everyday methods used by society's members to create order through their interactions (Garfinkel, 1967). As Downes and Rock (1988: 199) said:

> But a number of phenomenologists have become empirical of late. Variously referring to themselves as ethnomethodologists, existential sociologists, and sociologists of everyday life, they rely less obviously upon a search within. They have undertaken meticulous examinations of the conduct of conversation, believing that talk makes a social world.

In a more recent discussion Hester and Eglin (1992) illustrate how ethnomethodologists see crime/deviance not as an objective, independent entity, but, rather, as a product of subjective interpretation. Ethnomethodologists, therefore, use a 'constitu-tive' model, rather than a 'mundane' (Pollner, 1974) or common-sense model; crime/deviance is constituted by an audience's perception of it *as* crime/deviance. An example of mundane reasoning given by Hester and Eglin (1992: 129) concerns the remarks made by a police chief following the trial of some strikers. He was unhappy because the judge had 'thrown out' the charges against them, though in the police chief's view they had acted 'unlawfully':

> from the police chief's point of view, for something to be 'unlawful' it is not crucial that a judge finds it so; rather its unlawfulness exists independently of judicial response . . . Judges, in this view, do not constitute crime in their judicial work, rather they merely respond to its already existing criminal character. This is mundane reasoning par excel-lence: it presumes some independent factual domain of criminality against which human perceptions can either correctly or incorrectly correspond.

For ethnomethodologists, then, Becker's concept of the 'secret deviant', referred to in the earlier discussion of labelling theory, is nonsensical; unlabelled deviance cannot exist. Likewise, in my example of Maradona handling the ball, no foul was commit-ted. These insights from ethnomethodology are important in alerting criminologists to the deeply textured interactional processes at work in the characterisation of cer-tain activities as 'crime' or 'deviance', and raise the issue of just what is meant by 'real-ity'. However, there are people out there shooting cashiers during bank hold-ups, or 'secretly' snorting cocaine, or knowingly inflating their expenses claims. In ethno-methodology's terms none of these is a crime, because that social category has not been assigned to them. But, *something* is going on that makes such activities interest-ing to (some) criminologists. Focusing on the processes that create crime out of such events, whatever its ultimate value, does leave the question of why people do it in the first place, and why there are laws prohibiting such acts, off the agenda.

CONTROL THEORY

Control theory in its modern form (versions of it can be traced back to Aristotle, see Downes and Rock, 2007) is primarily associated with the American criminologist Travis Hirschi and his book *Causes of Delinquency* (1969). To some extent control the-ory's thunder was, at the time, stolen by labelling theory, though more recently it has gained in influence (see Chapter 15). Downes and Rock (2003) identify what they see as possible explanations for control theory's lack of impact:

- It was ignored by many sociologists because its explanation of criminality was seen as too obvious, merely serving to confirm common-sense opinion.
- It gave the appearance of supporting 'law and order'-style calls for more discipline and punishment, which liberal–radical sociologists found unacceptable.

- In a modified form Hirschi recycled a number of variables linked to delinquency originally introduced by Eleanor and Sheldon Glueck, whose work was heavily criticised for its individualised and pathological approach to criminality.

Unlike traditional criminology, control theory does not seek to discover the impulses that cause people to break the law. Instead of asking, 'Why do we break the law?' the theory asks, 'Why do we *not* break the law?' Following the classical school of criminology to some extent, control theory sees human beings as rational decision makers. However, whereas the classical school assumed that these decisions were based upon free will, control theory makes no such assumption; the free will versus determinism debate is left open-ended. Consequently, the question of what causal factors 'make' people into law breakers is not posed by the theory. Therefore, as criminal motivations are not relevant to the theory, the ultimate source of those motivations ceases to be an issue.

By asking the question, 'Why do we not break the law?' control theory is suggesting that something special happens to prevent people acting out whatever impulses they may possess. In other words, conformity is explained in terms of certain controls, which in varying degrees make people *unfree* to break rules. Without these controls, and left to our own devices, we would do whatever was required, as we saw it, to look after our own interests. Again, this draws on classical criminology's view of the individual as essentially self-seeking. Control theory thus paints a picture in which all members of society are potentially free to behave in ways that will sometimes entail breaking the law. The task, then, becomes one of identifying those controls that operate to prevent people taking up the option. Hirschi argued that these controls are located in the social and material bonds that tie individuals to society and to law-abiding behaviour. As rational beings, people make decisions according to the costs and benefits of conformity or nonconformity, and conformity is achieved to the extent that nonconformity is perceived of as a social or material cost. This is not seen as fixed for each individual; circumstances and perceptions can change over time. In a 'post-classical' analysis Bob Roshier (1989: 47) summarised the bonds that Hirschi said tie people to the conventional order:

> He proposes four bonds: attachment (the extent to which individuals have close emotional ties to other people); commitment (the extent to which they see conventional behaviour, for example at school, as offering immediate or long-term rewards); involvement (the extent to which their time is taken up with conventional activities); belief (the extent to which their beliefs about what is permissible or not coincide with conventional ones).

Hirschi's book largely consisted of empirical research, based on a self-report study of over 4,000 12- to 17-year-olds, aimed at testing the theory, and this triggered a number of similar research projects throughout the 1970s. Most of the work on 'attachment' had concentrated on family relationships. According to the theory, those families where emotional ties between children and parents are weak, so that children are relatively unconcerned about their parents' feelings towards delinquency, are more likely to contain delinquent children than are families where the reverse is true. Research has tended to support this idea (e.g. Johnson, 1979; Poole and Regoli, 1979; and Hirschi himself in the United States; and Wilson and Herbert, 1978; and Wilson, 1980 in this country). Wilson, for instance, in a study of families living in a deprived inner-city neighbourhood, found that non-delinquent children tended to live in families where moral upbringing was strict, and where parents had a protective attitude towards their children in what they defined as a non-threatening environment. 'Attachment' in this context derives from the children's concern that delinquency would be frowned upon by parents; it was not simply the result of living in a 'happy' family.

'Commitment' directed attention to the individual's ability to make rational decisions regarding the costs of law breaking. The degree to which we are committed to conforming behaviour is seen to reflect the degree to which we have a stake in society. Those who subjectively feel that their jobs, reputations and standards of living would be placed at an unacceptable risk if they engaged in delinquency, are less free than others who take up this option when tempted. At first glance this reasoning would appear to suggest that delinquency is more likely to occur among the working class than the middle class, simply because they seem to have less at stake materially. However, Hirschi found that the distribution of delinquency did not follow this pattern: there were no class differentials. Hirschi explained this by arguing that 'commitment' has to be seen from a subjective standpoint. What is important is how the individual perceives the nature of their stake in society. In a development of the ideas of control theory, Steven Box (1981, though originally published in 1971) incorporated some of the insights of labelling theory in order to explain why official statistics show delinquency to be largely a working-class activity, whilst self-report studies, such as Hirschi's, show a more even distribution along class lines. Box argued that official statistics deal with 'secondary deviation' (to use Lemert's term), whilst self-report studies uncover 'primary deviation'. In Box's view, it is the nature of the societal reaction which gives the misleading impression that middle-class youngsters are less delinquent.

A good deal of research has been carried out on the relationship between commitment to education and consequent 'involvement' in the conformist behaviour necessary for academic success. Research indicates a strong correlation between underachievement at school and delinquency (e.g. Hargreaves, 1967; Thomas *et al.*, 1977).

The fourth 'bond' discussed by Hirschi, 'belief', referred to the extent to which young people have a commitment to the moral values of conventional society. Again, the evidence from research is that rejection correlates with delinquency (e.g. Cernkovich, 1978). Hirschi found that religious beliefs had little effect on delinquency.

Extending the model

As Box pointed out, this approach to delinquency only addresses the circumstances that make delinquency possible; it does not explain why some actually commit delinquent acts, whilst others under similar circumstances do not. Box developed this further by taking the analysis beyond the situation where an individual is *free* to engage in deviant behaviour, to situations where they are, first, *able* to deviate, and second, *wanting* to deviate.

Whether or not an individual is able to deviate depends, said Box, on the following issues:

- *Secrecy* Although free to deviate, individuals may feel that they cannot conceal what they do. This introduces 'deterrence theory' into the equation, which was central to the classical school of criminology, though it was not part of Hirschi's original formulation. However, as Box points out, proponents of deterrence theory, such as Gibbs (1975), tend to focus on what they see as objective deterrents, when, in his view, it is the individual's subjective understanding of these deterrents that is crucial.
- *Skills* This refers to the need for individuals to possess the necessary abilities for the various deviant possibilities.
- *Supply* Here Box is thinking of the need for individuals to possess the necessary equipment, for example a supply of drugs, or a weapon.
- *Social support* This directs attention to the social groups of which the individual is a member, which may or may not provide encouragement for deviant behaviour. Again, Box stresses the subjective dimension, by arguing that the importance of the group lies in the meaning attributed to it by the individual. He is critical (as Hirschi was) of 'bad company' explanations of delinquency.
- *Symbolic support* This has been examined by a number of writers sympathetic to control theory (e.g. Hindelang, 1974; Austin, 1977; Cernkovich, 1978), and recognises the importance of the group *vis-à-vis* the provision of a framework of moral justification for deviance: for example, 'the victim deserved it'.

Box (1981: 144) continued:

> The analysis cannot stop at this point . . . Why would an adolescent who perceived a delinquent act to be one without many costs (in terms of attachments, commitments, beliefs, sanctions and supports) none the less want to do it?

His answer to this question was derived from Matza and Sykes (1961) and Matza (1964). They outlined four possibilities that might explain what makes delinquency attractive:

1 Individuals get a thrill out of taking risks, perhaps because an activity is banned, and there may, of course, be pleasure in the act itself.

2 Delinquency may provide a means for confirming and acting out gender roles.
3 Sometimes there is material gain.
4 Matza argued that delinquency offered some possibility of acting creatively, of taking control of one's life, albeit in ways that often hurt others.

As we have seen in the earlier discussion of their work, Matza and Sykes did not equate these values with a specifically working-class culture. In their view, they are 'subterranean values' found throughout society.

Control theory in the 1970s

During the 1970s control theory became increasingly influential, especially among more right-wing criminologists (e.g., Wilson, 1975; van den Haag, 1975; Ehrlich, 1975; Hagan, 1977; Nettler, 1978; and, specifically on the theme of gender and criminality, Hagan *et al.*, 1979). As it turned out, this work was to constitute the first phase of an upsurge in right-wing criminology in the 1980s, a criminology drawn in varying degrees to notions of control, deterrence and retribution.

Control theory has also been subjected to critical scrutiny. Control theory contends that it is only designed to make modest claims. Instead of seeking out the answers to 'big' causal questions, it simply focuses on circumstances that 'make delinquency possible'. However, as Downes and Rock (2003: 253–4) say: 'there is a tendency to overdraw the differences between what are presented as the empirically sound but modest claims of control theory and the empirically unsound but more pretentious alternatives'. These modest claims are seen by control theorists as having the virtue of being supported by empirical evidence, though Downes and Rock indicate a number of problems here. In Hirschi's self-report study, for instance, the definition of 'serious delinquency' is described as 'weak in the extreme'. In addition, and speaking from an interactionist, anti-positivist position, control theory, they say, neglects the different motivations lying behind deviant choices: 'Shorn of any meaning, for control theory deprives it of such, deviance is presumably pursued for the sheer gratification of appetites' (ibid.: 238).

Downes and Rock are also critical of control theory for assuming that the acceptance of norms and values is totally dependent upon 'attachments'. There are many different and complex sources of norms and values, and many complex reasons, untouched by control theory, why they are, or are not, subscribed to. Many have criticised control theory for ignoring big structural issues such as class, the nature of law and the role of the law makers and law enforcers. 'Commitment' to school, for instance, may be important, but this needs linking to broader social structural issues relating to the organisation of schooling in general. Finally, as control theorists admit, the theory can only explain relatively trivial primary forms of deviance. Therefore, it is not relevant to analyses of professional crime, or the crimes of the powerful (recent developments in control theory are discussed in Chapter 15).

FEMINIST PERSPECTIVES AND CRIMINOLOGY

Although the material in this book has been presented, broadly speaking, within a chronological framework of decades, obviously this is not meant to suggest that paradigm shifts or key developments in criminological thinking conveniently coincide with particular decades. The difficulties involved in this approach are acknowledged, but some organising principle is necessary. These difficulties are plainly demonstrated in the case of feminism and criminology: obviously there was no sea change in this field as Big Ben heralded in the New Year in 1980, and again in 1990. However, during the 1970s, feminist contributions to criminology were in the early stages of development, and the amount and theoretical sophistication of this work was to increase significantly in the 1980s. Although some American work had preceded it, Carol Smart's *Women, Crime and Criminology*, published in 1976, is generally seen as the first example of British 'feminist criminology', and in common with the rest of the early work, was exploratory, and was subjected to extensive review and reorientation later on. This early work tended to focus on females as offenders, or as victims (of crime or of the criminal justice system).

Critical analyses during the 1970s addressed four themes: invisibility, distortion, the criminal justice system and victimisation.

Invisibility

The discussion so far of the predominant schools of thought in criminology testifies to the neglect of female offenders in the literature. They were not, though, totally absent in criminological theory making – otherwise 'invisibility' would be a misnomer, and the second theme of 'distortion' would be irrelevant. A comparatively small amount of work did attempt to explain female criminality. From a feminist standpoint this was over-influential and wholly unacceptable.

Writers such as Heidensohn (1968, 1985) and Leonard (1982) argued that principal theories such as anomie, differential association and labelling, were aimed at an explanation of male, not female, crime/deviance. This prompted some feminists to pull criminology into the twentieth century by reworking past theories so that they took account of females (e.g., Shacklady Smith, 1978). Others preferred to carry out their own studies on female offenders (e.g., McRobbie and Garber, 1976). The chief contribution of feminism, however, did not derive from a simple desire to achieve some 'balance' by, say, studying more women and fewer men. Fundamentally, feminism made gender, as a social construction, a central issue within criminology, and that obviously involves men as much as women, or, more accurately, 'masculinity' as much as 'femininity'. It is, at the same time, committed to challenging the gender-based discrimination and disadvantage that is characteristic of patriarchal societies.

Various explanations of why females were neglected in criminological research were forthcoming. Heidensohn (1985) pointed to the fact that the discipline had been dominated by men, which affected such things as access to male gangs, cultural assumptions about masculinity and femininity, and a fascination with the macho, working-class deviant. She also noted that their relatively low crime rates made female offenders more difficult to find. In a sense, though, the gender dimension has always featured in criminological studies. It has been inherent in notions of masculinity and the socio-cultural contexts in which (usually working-class) delinquency-prone masculinity is shaped. These have generally proceeded along fairly stereotypical paths, which not only meant that females were excluded, but also that different understandings of masculinity were ignored.

The lower criminality rates for females, as indicated by official statistics, self-report studies and victim studies, clearly led some criminologists in the past, guided as they were by the imperative to find the 'causes' of crime, to concentrate on those largely responsible for crime – males. Apart from pushing to one side those cases where females *do* break the law (see, for example, Campbell's (1981) study of girl delinquent gang members), this failed to appreciate that an understanding of criminality involves coming to terms with the question of why some people do not break the law. What was missing was a theoretical engagement with the observation that females, as well as males, experienced things such as unemployment, poverty, inner-city life, the mass media, unsatisfactory schooling and life as a teenager. Thus one of the most glaring omissions was an analysis of the different ways in which factors such as these impact on females and males. A feminist agenda, according to Smart (1976: 89), had to 'situate the discussion of sex roles within a structural explanation of the social origins of those roles'.

Differences in crime rates for males and females have for many years remained fairly constant at around five or six to one in Britain; other European countries and the United States have similar ratios. Nevertheless, there has been much debate over the accuracy of these figures, hence the use of self-report studies, which purport to give us a better picture of criminality (there is a review of this research in Box, 1983). These studies tend to put the ratio nearer to two to one. As Box observed, though, large amounts of unrecorded crime will be in the categories of corporate crime, domestic violence and sexual assault, and these are either impossible or difficult to pick up in self-report studies. In certain offence categories, of course, women will be overrepresented: for example, prostitution and illegal abortion. Apart from the well-rehearsed problems with self-report studies (sampling, honesty, memory, and so on) some of them fail adequately to differentiate between 'serious' and 'less serious' offences, or to state the frequency with which offences are committed. We will return to this point later.

Distortion

On the theme of 'distortion', the feminist critique was summed up by Smart (1976: xiii) when she argued that the then current stock of criminological explanations of female criminality 'shares an entirely uncritical attitude towards sexual stereotyping of women and girls'. Essentially, the feminist critique emphasised a line of thinking, still around in modern criminology, that stretched back to the genetic theories of Lombroso and Ferrero in the nineteenth century, and in which the assumption was that the normal human being was male, and that the female was therefore an aberration. Combine this with the more specific cultural ideas about women carried around in the heads of these male criminologists and, said feminists, the distorted images of women pervading their work should come as no surprise: 'the majority of these studies refer to women in terms of their biological impulses and hormonal balance or in terms of their domesticity, maternal instinct and passivity' (ibid.: xiv).

Even in the post-war period, studies of female offenders tended to have been cut adrift from the main body of criminological theorising, which had moved away from the crude biological determinism of Lombrosian criminology. Pollak (1950), for instance, thought that women possess two characteristics that not only determined the sorts of offences they committed, but also helped them to cover their tracks more effectively than men: they are naturally deceitful (incredibly, Pollak saw the faking of orgasm as evidence for this), and played social roles based upon privacy (evidence for this was seemingly provided by the concealment of menstruation). It will come as no surprise to learn that feminist writers have reserved particular wrath for Pollak. Later on, Cowie, Cowie and Slater (1968) continued to confuse sex with gender. According to them, because of biologically determined factors boys are less able than girls to cope with stressful situations, hence they are more criminal than girls. However, some girls, they argued, are born with 'masculine traits', which explained their criminal behaviour.

Criminal justice

The 'criminal justice' and 'victimisation' themes were, in this early period, less in evidence within feminist work than the two themes discussed above. This situation was to change significantly in the 1980s though. Research on the theme of criminal justice looked at the ways in which women were dealt with by the various criminal justice agencies such as the police, the courts and the prisons, though the earlier work tended to concern itself with women's imprisonment (Ward and Kassebaum, 1966; Giallombardo, 1966; Heidensohn, 1969). This research drew attention to the disadvantages experienced by female prisoners compared with male prisoners, due to entering a system that was essentially designed for men (for example, women had fewer educational and recreational facilities).

Some writers explored the widely accepted view that women were treated more leniently by the criminal justice system, because it was largely administered by men, who adopted a chivalrous attitude towards them. This was an idea that had been around for some time in criminology (for example, Mannheim, 1940), and according to some criminologists explained the lower official crime rates for women and, if women were brought before the courts, the supposedly more lenient sentences handed out. Anderson (1976), in a review of this debate, pointed the way to subsequent feminist repudiations of the argument that 'chivalry' had a significant and beneficent impact on the treatment of women by the criminal justice system. In an early study of the British courts, Dell (1971) concluded that while a greater proportion of men than women were sent to prison (though women were only rarely involved in violent crime), women were more likely to be held on remand prior to trial or sentencing. Other research carried out in the 1970s found that the treatment of female juvenile offenders was influenced by considerations of 'moral protection', in addition to the actual offence. With males, the tendency was only to see the offence as relevant. This, it was argued, increased the likelihood of juvenile female offenders being sent to an institution (Chesney-Lind, 1973, 1978; Jay and Rose, 1977).

Feminist writers also argued that because of the stereotypical understandings of gender carried by men, women offenders are seen to have offended twice: once from the point of view of the offence itself, and twice because they have transgressed cultural understandings of 'feminine' behaviour. An important component of this characterisation is that women are judged according to particular notions of 'motherly' or 'wifely' roles.

Victimisation

Finally, the theme of victimisation. Research on this theme grew slowly in the 1970s, then mushroomed rapidly through the 1980s, in line with a growing interest in what is known as victimology. The earlier feminist work on women as victims concentrated on sexual crime (Brownmiller, 1975) and domestic violence (Dobash and Dobash, 1979). Studies of rape, child sexual abuse and violence in the home highlighted the low levels of reporting, and signalled an end to the complacency surrounding these areas. Gradually this type of research had an influence at the level of practice – for example, the growth in Women's Aid Refuges (Pizzey, 1973) – and, eventually, in police responses to victims of rape.

Selected further reading

Two key texts oriented towards a political economy of crime and deviance from this period are: **Taylor, I., Walton, P. and Young, J. (1973)** *The New Criminology: For a social theory of deviance,* London: Routledge & Kegan Paul; and **Taylor, I., Walton, P. and Young, J. (eds) (1975)** *Critical Criminology,* London: Routledge & Kegan Paul.

A major study from the Birmingham Centre for Contemporary Cultural Studies was **Hall, S., Critcher, C., Jefferson, T., Clarke, J. and Roberts, B. (1978)** *Policing the Crisis: Mugging, the state and law and order,* London: Macmillan.

Smart, C. (1976) *Women, Crime and Criminology: A feminist critique*, London: Routledge & Kegan Paul is generally seen as the first British analysis from a feminist perspective.

Mungham, G. and Pearson, G. (eds) (1976) *Working Class Youth Culture*, London: Routledge & Kegan Paul provides an edited collection of radical work from this period.

The seminal work on control theory is Hirschi, T. (1969) *Causes of Delinquency*, Berkeley, CA: University of California Press.

Phillipson, M. (1971) *Sociological Aspects of Crime and Delinquency*, London: Routledge & Kegan Paul is an example of a phenomenological analysis.

From the perspective of ethnomethodology, see: Hester, S. and Eglin, P. (1992) *A Sociology of Crime*, London: Routledge, and for a more recent discussion of this subsequently neglected approach to doing criminology: Hester, S. (2007) *Descriptions of Deviance*, Abingdon: Routledge.

A sophisticated study of youth subcultures in the 1970s is Willis, P. (1978) *Profane Culture*, London: Routledge & Kegan Paul, and on the theme of 'style': Hebdige, D. (1979) *Subculture: The meaning of style*, London: Methuen.

Theoretical developments occurring during the period under review in this chapter are examined by Box, S. (1981) *Deviance, Reality and Society*, 2nd edn, Eastbourne: Holt, Rinehart & Winston.

PART V

THE 1980S TO THE MID-1990S

CHAPTER 12

THE DISCIPLINE OF CRIMINOLOGY
AND ITS CONTEXT – 4

Key themes

- The shift to the right in British politics
- Criminology's external history
- Social organisation
- The growth of policy-oriented research
- The nature and context of research
- Policy-oriented research and the left
- British criminology in the late twentieth century

INTRODUCTION

This chapter examines the social and political context of developments within criminology through the 1980s and into the mid-1990s. Of particular importance was a shift to the right in Britain and the United States, and the election of, respectively, Thatcher and Reagan administrations. The 1980s saw the growing influence of conservative ideas within academic criminology. At the same time, there was an increase in policy-oriented research. As far as critical criminology was concerned, by the middle of the 1980s a significant divide between 'left realism' and 'left idealism' had opened up. On a more general level, academic criminology was starting to become increasingly fragmented.

Being brutally honest, one has to say that the task of plotting the various twists and turns, whilst sketching in some social and political background, now becomes more taxing. Relatively clear-cut theoretical shifts gave way to a high degree of fragmentation. In addition, there was a large increase in the amount of academic work subsumed under the title of criminology. By the end of the 1970s developments in non-mainstream criminology, and especially within a specifically radical tradition, were already becoming less obvious. For students of criminology, the discipline's development since the reorientations of the 1960s had, for a while, helpfully gone through relatively easily understood chronological stages: new deviancy theory had challenged an earlier positivism; conflict theory had radicalised the liberalism of labelling theory; and critical criminology had attempted to develop a neo-Marxist political economy of crime. There had also been the beginnings of a feminist tradition and the first murmurings of a victimology. In spite of their internal complexities, these could at least be put into reasonably neat theoretical packages, and to a large extent be identified with conventional political affiliations. At the risk of being scandalously vulgar, students could for a while think in terms of theoretical 'camps'. The embracing of a sociology of law, and with it an intense theoretical interrogation by radical scholars of the political economy of rule making during the second half of the 1970s, made the situation less clear-cut. This did not immediately appear to represent an obvious, challenging theoretical 'camp'. Not only was the work highly complex, but it did not seem to conform to the earlier pattern of a chronological series of paradigms – and why should it? Furthermore, 'criminals' had disappeared from the scene, together with the concept of 'deviance', though the former were to reappear shortly afterwards.

Colin Sumner (1990: 15) observed:

> Students still ask 'Whatever happened to the theoretical debates about deviance in the early 1970s?' . . . Perhaps the revulsion for theory and theoretical wrangling, the return of empirical research, the new popularity of historical work and the general air of hard-nosed realism in the late 1970s and early 1980s, have all contributed to the demise of theoretical dynamics in this field.

This pessimistic reading of developments in sociological criminology became necrological in 1994, when Sumner published a book on the sociology of deviance with the subtitle *An obituary*. What had led to this situation? Early theoretical debate seemed to have disappeared. Challenging paradigms no longer followed one after the other. Theorising seemed to have been supplanted by empirical research. And, on a number of fronts, there was a rush to embrace 'realism'.

THE SHIFT TO THE RIGHT IN BRITISH POLITICS

1979: a political turning point

'Law and order' was a central element of the Conservative Party's election campaign in 1979, though it involved more than a narrowly conceived focus on crime as such. The rhetoric was resplendent with images of militant trade unionists on the rampage; of the dead being unburied and dustbins unemptied; of British culture being 'swamped' by black immigrants; of classrooms in the grip of anarchy; and of a dependency culture, where large sections of the population had grown lazy and undisciplined on the back of a too generous welfare state. At the same time, we were told, the pendulum had swung too far towards the rights of criminals; police officers needed more powers to secure convictions, and the courts were too 'soft'. In the home, an increasing number of parents had abrogated their responsibilities regarding bringing their children up properly. The incoming government was committed to 'getting tough' on law and order.

For the left in Britain, what followed was a drift into an authoritarian law and order society (Hall, 1980, 1988) though as Norrie and Adelman (1989) have pointed out, the sentiments expressed by the Conservatives were in accord with the views of large sections of the working class. Put another way, certain significant common-sense understandings, widespread throughout British society, had found a political voice. However, as various commentators have suggested, the drift in this direction had, in fact, been gathering momentum during the 1970s (see, for example, Pitts, 1988; Norrie and Adelman, 1989). This view acts as a necessary antidote to those who paint a misleading picture of British society in the pre-Thatcher era, as if, for over a decade, the population had enjoyed an age of universal libertinism, where continual saturnalia enveloped everyone in an orgy of decency-sapping permissiveness.

The area of juvenile justice provides a particularly good example. John Pitts shows how a Fabian-influenced Labour Party went some way towards liberalising the system in the 1960s. However, the 1970s saw a move away from a treatment–welfare model of juvenile justice towards the more punitively oriented justice model. The increasing use of custody – in spite of the intentions of the 1969 Children and Young Persons Act – illustrates this. Thus the 'psychologically impaired' children of the 1960s were gradually transformed into the wicked and irresponsible children of the 1970s: undisciplined products of a welfare state that had supposedly made them take too much for granted. In Pitts's view, this trend was to find its culmination in the Thatcher era of the 1980s.

It is impossible to understand the directions taken by criminology during the 1980s and 1990s without taking into consideration the cultural changes in that period, as well as the impact of the social and economic policies of an entrenched Conservative government:

> In practical terms, the government of Margaret Thatcher introduced new legislation to curb the power of sectional interests (including the legal profession as well as the unions); competitive market mechanisms to start to break state monopolies (for example, extending prison privatization); more powers, pay and resources for the police; a major prison rebuilding programme; a 'short, sharp, shock' for recalcitrant, ill-disciplined juveniles; and various measures to make families and communities more self-reliant.
>
> (Jefferson and Shapland, 1994: 266–7)

A number of other developments during the 1980s and 1990s should also be noted: rising levels of unemployment; the decline in manufacturing industry and the impact of this on communities; the 1984–85 miners' strike; rising levels of recorded crime; serious outbreaks of urban rioting; widening differentials in the distribution of wealth and income; and pressure on the government to curb public expenditure.

Good old common sense – again

The election of a Thatcher government marked the endorsement of common-sense amateurism. In a way this was a reversion to an earlier, traditionally British approach to social administration – an approach based upon the pragmatic all-rounder – of cabinets, committees and civil servants, eschewing the 'expert' and the 'intellectual' in favour of the generalist, who, above all, laid claim to common sense. However, whereas in the past this process had been founded on an explicit elitism, where our 'betters' by definition knew best, the 1980s version celebrated the concordance between the common sense of the political elites and the common sense of 'the people'. In the realm of criminal justice policy, the 1980s offered an opportunity for the views of all right-thinking men and women, who 'knew in their hearts' what was wrong, to be put into practice. Well rehearsed during the preceding decade over both lunchtime gin and tonics at the country pub and pints of beer at the working men's club, and underscored daily by the tabloid press, it seemed that the end of the liberal, the do-gooding expert and the intellectual was at hand – the same do-gooding liberals (social workers, teachers, psychologists, and so forth) who, as pointed out earlier, were criticised by radical thought in the 1960s and 1970s. Reviewing Brewer and Lait's *Can Social Work Survive?* a book exemplifying the New Right's thinking, Geoff Pearson writes:

> Mrs Lait concluded that the whole business of childcare should be taken away from permissive educationalists and do-good social workers, and placed instead 'in the hands of ordinary people who have rejected pretentious, self indulgent and unscientific theorising in favour of their own good sense'.
>
> (Quoted in Pitts, 1988: 445)

Just as law enforcement ideologies have presented the police officer as merely a citizen in uniform, so the ideologue of the New Right was merely a citizen in academic dress.

This takes us back to the discussion of common sense in the first chapter, and Becker's distinction between common sense as potentially deluding, tribal gut-feelings, and common sense as practical no-nonsense truth. As always, of course, proponents of the ideas of the New Right saw their common sense as representing the latter.

CRIMINOLOGY'S EXTERNAL HISTORY

In an illuminating analysis of criminology's historical development, David Garland (1985a) refers to the distinction between an academic discipline's 'external' and 'internal' history, an idea originally put forward from the perspective of the philosophy of science by Imre Lakotos. Briefly, the argument is that all scientific disciplines are established within the context of appropriate external social, political and cultural conditions. Eventually, a discipline becomes internally self-sufficient and continues to develop because of its own resources. One outcome of this is that it is no longer tied to catering for the needs of powerful social and political interests: 'In other words, to the extent that this internal logic asserts itself, the social origins of the science will tend to fade into its pre-history' (Garland, 1985a: 2). In Garland's view criminology in Britain had been unable to cast off its dependence upon these external demands, so that it continued to exist as an ideological, rather than scientific project: 'Precisely because criminology's object is a social problem – defined by policies, ideologies and state practices – its "external" origins will always be internal to it' (ibid.: 3). This is an important argument that should at least sensitise us to the ongoing connections between the nature of criminology as an academic discipline and the broader social, political and cultural circumstances. The same point was made by Jock Young (1994: 71) when he said:

> the interior dialogue is propelled by the exterior world. The dominant ideas of a period, whether establishment or radical; the social problems of a particular society; the government in power and the political possibilities existing in a society – all shape the interior discourse of the academic.

If the shift to the right at an external level nurtured the development of a much more self-confident and influential right-wing criminology, both in Britain and in the United States, it posed fundamental problems for radical and liberal criminology. The two characteristics of radical thought referred to earlier – negative criticism and internal divisions – that during the 1970s in a sense helped to prepare the ground for the New Right, went through remarkable transformations during the course of the 1980s, though not in all quarters.

First, radical thought pulled back from criticising such things as publicly owned industries, the teaching profession, social welfare programmes, council housing, the Labour Party, and so on. In the climate of Thatcherism, previous arrangements suddenly looked more attractive than they had at the time. For liberal and left thought, the 1980s and 1990s opened up a period of reclamation and self-appraisal. Within criminology, left realism emerged as the main representative of this trend, especially with its close links with the Labour Party (left realism is discussed later). Outside of a critical strand, radical criminology tended to gravitate towards a liberal democratic baseline, heralding a more explicit commitment to empirical research and even a discussion of policy. Left realism in particular represented a move from pitching analyses at the level of the political economy of capitalism with a stress on the need for radical transformation, to a more modest engagement with concrete reforms. Left realists argued that this was necessary in order to challenge the right's domination of issues of crime and punishment. Importantly, though, it illustrated how many on the liberal–left spectrum did attempt to develop constructive ideas regarding how things might be improved in the short term.

Second, the existence of an external enemy in the shape of Thatcherism worked wonders in healing many of the previous divisions among radical factions. Although critical criminologists continued to develop a neo-Marxist agenda, greater account was taken of the realities of street crime, the victimisation of women and black people, and the dangers of romanticising working-class crime. Across a range of liberal–left thought previous bellicosity gradually disappeared. The overriding truculent debate that continued through the 1980s and into the 1990s was between critical criminology (described by their antagonists as left idealism) and self-styled left realists. This was particularly apparent in the area of black criminality, where some critical theorists, recycling an earlier 'working-class crime as politics' theme, argued that black crime was political. As I have said elsewhere: 'If there was a Richter Scale in the social sciences it would have registered maximum points during these vitriolic exchanges' (Tierney, 1988: 133).

As the 1980s progressed, and the New Right celebrated the idea of common sense, among many radicals there was a corresponding rush to 'realism'. Pared down to its basics, the notion of being realistic seemed to bear a strong resemblance to using common sense. The same process was at work within the Labour Party, which, after a series of election defeats, increasingly assessed its policies in terms of realism – the culmination was 'New' Labour (see Chapter 14). Realism came to suggest a set of qualities based upon 'practical views and policy'. This meant, for example, addressing the here and now rather than a utopian future, taking account of what the public says and feels, taking the reality of crime seriously, and being practical rather than hopelessly theoretical or wildly abstract. Clearly, this raises important issues regarding the nature and role of criminology, issues that have always lain awkwardly at the core of the criminological project.

SOCIAL ORGANISATION

Paul Rock's (1994) survey of 'all identifiable British criminologists' provided the most up-to-date information on what he called the social organisation of criminology in this country: demographic patterns, institutional arrangements and social relations. His findings give us a useful starting point for a discussion of the development of criminological thought since the end of the 1970s.

The survey underlined the fact that academic criminology in Britain was then dominated by a group of criminologists, in their forties and fifties, who were products of an expanding higher education system during the late 1960s and early 1970s – the 'fortunate generation'. Predictably, the bulk of them are men rather than women. The beginning of their academic careers also coincided with the advent of the new deviancy and the break with positivism, and, indeed, many played pivotal roles in developing the sociology of deviance in that period. As well as forming the largest group – 68 per cent of criminologists were aged over 40 – they continued to have a powerful presence in terms of professorial posts and published work. Of course, from this base their influence on academic criminology was widespread: for instance, speaking at conferences, being involved in the recruitment of staff, acting as external examiners, helping to establish and validate new courses, and reviewing proposals for books and articles for journals. In short, the influence of the 'fortunate generation' on the shape of British criminology was, and continues to be, considerable.

Although there has been a growth in the proportion of younger criminologists since the late 1980s, when Rock carried out a similar survey, the overall picture reflected the mixed fortunes of higher education in general, and the social sciences in particular:

> In effect, two demographic waves have moved through post-war British criminology: the greater in the 1970s and the lesser in the latter half of the 1980s; and it was the greater that gave definition to the discipline. Criminologists educated and appointed in the late 1960s and early 1970s form a distinct and self-conscious intellectual generation.
>
> (Rock, 1994: 132)

On a note of pessimism, Rock pointed out that although an expansion may be imminent within departments of law, at the moment the lack of sustained recruitment over the years meant that 'Sociological criminology in particular looks somewhat emaciated' (ibid.: 132). As I have said previously, one result of this has been the absence of decisive theoretical challenges coming from a younger generation, a generation that had to struggle for hard-earned research funding during the 1980s, under strong pressure to pursue empirical research.

The largest proportion of criminologists were now to be found in departments of law – and they had a variety of subject backgrounds – followed by departments of sociology. This reflected more recent increases in undergraduate demand for places on law degrees. Law departments had the highest proportion of female criminologists. The greatest concentration of criminologists, however, was to be found in the Home Office Research and Planning Unit, an institution that continued to influence profoundly the type of research carried out under the banner of criminology in Britain. Not surprisingly, the majority of this research was policy-oriented. Research initiatives coming from another important funding source, the Economic and Social Research Council, took similar directions.

Interestingly, though, Rock's survey illustrated the enduring influence of sociological criminology when it comes to theoretical allegiances, with interactionists forming the largest proportion. This was strongly reflected in the way that criminology was taught within universities:

> Theoretical criminology may no longer seethe and flow but it is what British criminologists continue to teach. Variously called criminology and the sociology of deviance, it looms over all else. Over half the courses offered were so labelled and, in the main, they survey the accomplishments of the past.
>
> (Ibid.: 146)

THE GROWTH OF POLICY-ORIENTED RESEARCH

Mapping the terrain

Having briefly discussed the wider political, social and cultural context, and, following Rock, looked at the social organisation of criminology, we can now examine how the discipline developed through the 1980s and into the 1990s. In view of the large amount of work emerging during this period, and the inevitable disputes over the significance of more recent developments, analyses become a little more hazardous.

Drawing out what appear to be the more important and significant examples of criminological work is bound to be an invidious project. Necessarily, the selection is to some extent arbitrary, and cannot but reflect my own interpretation of events. However, the intention is to give an indication of the main contours of developments in British criminology, whilst paying attention to external and internal pressures on the discipline. The selection of material to illustrate these developments has a qualitative and quantitative dimension to it. By definition, making qualitative judgements involves subjective interpretations with regard to notions of 'importance', 'influence', 'academic virtuousity', and so on. Accusations of bias are less likely to follow when choices rest simply on the sheer volume of work of a certain type that is produced. However, the fact that a particular topic or theme forms the basis for a large amount of research over a given period does not guarantee, of course, that the work is fundamentally important, of high quality, will have long-term effects, or is even interesting from the audience's point of view. We have to acknowledge that fashions and trends come and go within criminology as much as they do within other disciplines and, indeed, within social life in general. What perhaps seemed desperately fascinating and impressive at one time, can seem banal, silly or irrelevant at some future date. Some of us need only look at old photographs of how we used to dress to appreciate this.

Some of the insights of the labelling perspective can be applied to the social production of criminological work. Whether or not a research proposal is funded, or a book or article gains an audience by being published, is the outcome of a range of social processes. It is not simply a question of the work being 'good' or 'bad'. Publishers are well aware of market trends in criminology, and the harsh reality is that some books will not be published if they are thought to be out of tune with these trends. Furthermore, the status of the author will play a part; like all areas of publishing, criminology has its luminaries. These criminologists will also wield influence over what is published via their role as reviewers of proposals for books and articles. Likewise, the kind of research that is successful in the tendering stakes, and attracts funding, will be linked to the demands set by research councils and agencies.

Research topics

Unlike the situation in the 1960s, no one could complain that criminology in the 1980s and 1990s was 'obsessed' with juvenile offenders. Such research had not been abandoned, but it constituted only a relatively small proportion of the total (e.g., West, 1982; Farrington, 1992b; Fergusson *et al.*, 1992; Robins and Rutter, 1990; Agnew, 1991; Nagin and Farrington, 1992; Riley and Shaw, 1985).

Criticism of this 'obsession' is associated with the new deviancy theorists of the late 1960s who, under the banner of the sociology of deviance, turned their attention to various groups defined as deviant, and the labelling processes involved in the construction of deviant identities. This interest in defined deviant groups continued into the 1970s. From the late 1970s onwards, however, the concept of deviance tended to fall into disuse, and with it there was a corresponding decline in studies of specific groups labelled as deviant. With the evaporation of the sociology of deviance, criminal, rather than deviant, activities moved centre stage. Thus during the 1980s and 1990s there was little interest in, for example, youth subcultures, New Age travellers, or the 'nuts, sluts and preverts' of the 1960s. In fact, as the 1980s wore on, and although there were exceptions, the general trend was to address issues of social control and the victims of crime, rather than criminal (let alone deviant) motivations, lifestyles and experiences.

In spite of this, David Downes (1988) argued that by the 1980s three key ideas deriving from new deviancy theory had fundamentally changed 'the nature of "taken for granted" criminological inquiry'. First, that the criminal's (or deviant's) subjective understanding of the world should be considered. Second, that the nature and extent of crime (or deviance) are to some degree a result of social control responses, rather than products of quite separate factors. And third, that crime (or deviance) is ubiquitous, especially if we consider corporate, occupational and domestic crime. However, Downes did point out that while these ideas informed a great deal of research in the 1960s and 1970s, and may have been generally accepted within academic criminology, their influence on actual research in the 1980s had diminished. Ethnographic research that would attempt to tap into the subjectivities of criminal groups began to dry up. The growth of administrative criminology and versions of control theory (see below) set the clock back by separating processes of social control – seen in terms of labelling – from criminal behaviour. And, while domestic violence had figured strongly in feminist contributions to criminology, other kinds of 'normalised' crime – that is, widespread and more or less tolerated crime and, in particular, white-collar crime – had remained relatively underdeveloped areas of research. (There were, however, notable examples of such research: e.g., Carson, 1982; Box, 1983; Levi, 1987; Clarke, 1990; Croal, 1992; Nelken, 1994.)

Observations made by a number of contributors to the first edition of the *The Oxford Handbook of Criminology* (Maguire *et al.*, 1994) indicated the lack of recent research in a variety of areas. Nigel South (1994) opened his chapter on illicit drug use by quoting from Downes's (1988) review mentioned above: 'With a few exceptions . . . sociologists were not engaged by the drugs issue'. And, although more work in this field did come on stream during the 1980s and early 1990s (e.g., Dorn and South, 1987; Pearson, 1987; MacGregor, 1989; Dorn *et al.*, 1992; Strang and Gossop, 1993), South himself concluded by saying: 'However, at present, British criminology and broader policy and practice are ill served by the limited (albeit generally excellent) research upon which we can draw' (South, 1994: 425).

In Michael Levi's (1994: 344) chapter on violent crime we learned: 'By contrast with this focus on "the victim", the causes of violence have received comparatively little criminological attention'. Even in the area of youth crime, which had received much media and legislative attention in the recent past, Geoff Pearson (1994: 1195) made the point: 'We simply do not have the evidence – in the form of government-sponsored statistics, social surveys, reliable self-report studies, etc. – to state with any confidence the actually existing relationships between "youth" and "crime" '.

Criminological research in some areas, then, grew more slowly than might have been expected. But, while emphases changed and research topics were reshuffled, the overall volume of research in Britain continued to grow during the 1980s and 1990s. In terms of amount of research, a number of previously neglected topics came to dominate the field.

One notable example was research on policing. It is interesting that at the end of the 1970s, when a number of polytechnics and colleges were exploring the possibility of mounting degrees in police studies, or criminal justice studies, the Council for National Academic Awards (the now defunct body that in those days validated non-university-sector degree courses) seriously questioned whether there existed a sufficient academic literature on policing in Britain to sustain degree programmes. A decade later, the huge growth in police-related research had dramatically reversed the situation. This trend continued unabated into the 1990s.

The 1980 and 1981 urban riots, and the 1984–85 miners' strike, stimulated research on the topic of public order, and inevitably this frequently overlapped with research on policing. As did an upsurge in research on the themes of 'race', racism and protest, and 'race' and criminality.

Echoing the shift in much of this work away from the offender as such, and towards responses to crime and disorder on the part of criminal justice agencies, the 1980s and 1990s also saw an increase in research on the theme of 'penality', that is, in the widest sense, prisons, probation and community sanctions, and all situated within a socio-cultural context. In some cases this was allied to particular pieces of legislation: for instance, the 1984 Police and Criminal Evidence Act and the 1991 Criminal Justice Act.

Research on victims of crime is a particularly good example of a previously neglected topic that came to the fore in this period. Originally associated with a conservative tradition, this type of research began to attract some of the more radical criminologists in Britain, notably those belonging to the left realist school. Since the beginning of the 1980s studies of victims of crime have grown rapidly in number, and developed along a variety of fronts. An important aspect of this research were the connections between the nature, extent and distribution of victimisation and issues of class, gender, age and 'race'. Raw material relating to the experiences of victims was generated by the periodic large-scale *British Crime Surveys,* carried out by the Home Office, and the more focused local crime surveys.

Empirical and theoretical research carried out within a feminist framework, and taking in such topics as gender and criminality, women as victims (for example, domestic violence and sexual abuse), and women and their treatment by the criminal justice system, continued to thrive. We might note, though, that according to Tony Jefferson and Joanna Shapland (1994: 282), in spite of feminism being 'by one reckoning . . . *the* growth area in criminology during the 1980s . . . the experience of women remained marginal to the *criminological enterprise*' (original emphasis). They also pointed to the marginalisation of research on Northern Ireland and the crimes of the powerful over this period.

With a pedigree that goes back to the Chicago ecologists, research based on the neighbourhood, and on the social and physical environment, continued to be carried out during the 1980s and 1990s. Although studies concentrating specifically on the inner city were fewer in number than might have been expected, the urban rioting at the beginning of the 1990s did trigger research on the experiences of people living in the more deprived areas of the city. Analyses had to recognise, however, that in many cases these areas were not in fact inner-city areas, but rather council estates situated on the outskirts of the city – municipal suburbia. One offshoot of areal studies was policy-oriented research built around some notion of 'community', and concerning itself with initiatives that would encourage residents to take some responsibility for crime control. This was particularly associated with the Home Office, and involved developments such as neighbourhood watch schemes.

The Home Office in particular was also instrumental in carrying out and commissioning research projects organised around the theme of situational crime control. This encompassed a multiplicity of ideas ranging from better street lighting, to more effective house security, to the then Home Secretary's invitation to 'walk with a purpose'. On a general level this kind of research reflected the emergence of what is usually referred to as administrative criminology, itself linked to a rekindling of interest in control theory.

THE NATURE AND CONTEXT OF RESEARCH

As it stands, of course, the above description is of little more than a list of research topics that became popular during that period. With this as a backdrop, the next task is to examine the nature of British criminology as it developed as an academic discipline over the same period. This will entail a consideration of competing criminological discourses and assumptions, around which research was built, together with the broader context in which research was conducted. Later on we will return to this period for a more detailed analysis of criminological theory.

An expanding academic base

As far as the teaching of undergraduate courses in criminological theory was concerned, Rock (1994) had shown that sociological criminology continued to play a dominant role. On the other hand, the contraction in teaching, postgraduate and research opportunities that befell sociology during the 1980s, albeit to some extent offset by a 'second wave' surge at the end of the 1980s, did have an impact on research activities and the production of theory. This partly explains why, since the early 1980s, criminological research in this country was carried out from a widening academic base. Increasingly, contributions were made by criminologists whose roots lay in disciplines other than sociology; for example, political science, law, social history, psychology and economics. Other developments also played a part. A variety of research projects opened up opportunities for the employment of the specialist knowledge offered by these other disciplines. As an example, a central theme of police-related research in the early 1980s was accountability, and given that this raised complex legal and political issues turning on the constitutional position of the police, it was not surprising that lawyers and political scientists quickly became involved. Following the pattern set in the United States, the establishment of degree courses in criminal justice studies in a number of higher education institutions during the 1980s (Tierney, 1989) provided criminology-related teaching and research opportunities for a range of social scientists. Finally, there was an increase in the amount of 'in-house' research carried out by practitioners within criminal justice agencies, as well as by various pressure groups such as Liberty (formerly the National Council for Civil Liberties) and NACRO (the National Association for the Care and Resettlement of Offenders). All of these developments encouraged a broadening of the academic base of criminology.

The research focus

According to Tony Jefferson and Joanna Shapland (1994: 267), criminological research during the 1980s was characterised by 'a gradual contraction of the research focus'. They saw this process as having two dimensions to it. First, the field of vision was narrowed so that research concentrated on elements of the criminal justice system and the practicalities of crime control: the police, prisons, courts, probation and community sanctions, situational crime control, and complementary community-based initiatives such as neighbourhood watch and police–public consultation. Second, analyses tended to lose sight of the broader picture by treating those elements in relative isolation. This contraction in focus was in evidence among radical as well as mainstream criminologists.

Policy and pragmatism

A number of commentators, including Jefferson and Shapland, have pointed to another characteristic of much criminological research in the 1980s and 1990s: a shift away from theory towards a pragmatic, policy-oriented approach. Indeed, this factor and the narrowing of the research focus noted above can be seen as mutually reinforcing processes and, again, they caught the attention of radical as well as mainstream criminologists. This was in evidence at different levels of theoretical research.

On one level, there was a relative decline in macro research that endeavoured to develop a theoretical understanding of issues of crime and crime control within contemporary political, social and economic contexts. This macro research refused to isolate 'law and order' from such things as economic change, government policy and changing ideologies of control. In spite of a decline, however, this type of theoretical research continued to appear (e.g., Hall (1988) and Scraton (1987) on the nature of the authoritarian state; Dahrendorf (1985) on law and order from a position he describes as 'institutional liberalism'; Box (1987) on crime and economic recession; Sumner (1994) linking this agenda to the rise and fall of the sociology of deviance; and Reiner and Cross (1991)).

On another level, the 1980s also saw less research concerned with theoretical analyses of particular areas of criminal justice-related activity in contemporary Britain. However, again, critical work of this sort did appear, and, by the late 1980s and early 1990s, seems to have been on the increase. Some notable examples are: Cohen (1985), Hudson (1987), Lacey (1988), Walker (1991), Garland (1990), von Hirsch (1993), and Hay et al. (1994) on the themes of sentencing, punishment and social control; Brogden (1982) and Reiner (1992, 1994) on the police; Pitts (1988) on the politics of juvenile crime; and Harris (1992) on probation. Important theoretical work that addressed historical developments was also in evidence, notably: Garland (1985a) on punishment and social regulation; Harris and Webb (1987) on the treatment of juveniles; and Sim (1990) on the prison medical service.

Some factors influencing the course of research

The narrowing of the research focus, coupled with a shift towards policy-oriented research, can be linked to a number of key factors at work during the 1980s. The government's commitment to financial stringency had a marked impact on the funding of teaching and research in the social sciences. Increasingly the stress was on 'value for money', which inevitably meant that research had to be seen to be useful in terms of policy. Not only did this lead to an expansion in the research carried out by criminologists at the Research and Planning Unit at the Home Office, it also helped to set the parameters of research initiatives funded by the Economic and Social Research Council – the primary source of funds for university social science departments. The stress on 'value for money', though, was essentially directed at criminal justice agencies, and increasingly the task of criminological research was to evaluate the extent to which these agencies were measuring up to the demand to be efficient and effective. Hence the tendency of research to deal with elements of the system in an isolated fashion, measuring their performance against some posited criteria.

Another factor was the growth in research carried out by the criminal justice agencies themselves (who sometimes funded university research) and by various pressure groups. Obviously, such research conformed to agendas set by the agencies or pressure groups, who in general would hardly finance highly abstract, theoretical work. However, even at the policy level there were in-built limitations. As Roger Hood (1987) has pointed out, setting the research agendas themselves, agendas already circumscribed by central government policy, forecloses on the possibility of radical alternatives. Stan Cohen's (1988: 236) observation made at the beginning of the 1980s now seemed prophetic: 'the content of this type of criminology has switched (and is likely to switch even more) in the direction of "criminal justice"; that is to say, an exclusive concern with the operation of the system'.

The introduction of privatisation within the criminal justice system was also relevant in this context. After a slow start in the 1980s, the momentum of privatisation speeded up in the 1990s, especially with respect to prisons, and although the overall impact in terms of contracts had been small, the principles driving privatisation should not be underestimated:

> The real legacy of the privatization debate has not so far been in actual contracts, but in changing expectations. In 1980 the criminal justice system was thought of as a series of state-run agencies which attempted to contain, punish, or sometimes rehabilitate offenders. Today these agencies are to be managed, offenders to be processed, throughput to be controlled, the system to be modelled. The language of industrial production has been adopted.
>
> (Jefferson and Shapland, 1994: 279)

Also worth noting was the build-up of pressure on academics and their departments to carry out and publish research: the 'publish or perish' syndrome. In the 1990s, university departments found themselves subject to periodic review by external inspectors. On the basis of certain indicators – one of which is research output – they were given a rating (this process has continued into the new millennium). While public accountability is no bad thing, of course, there was a danger that the pressures placed on staff to publish created an edge of desperation, and the possibility of being tempted to avoid time-consuming, innovative theorisation, especially as funding and/or sabbatical leave for such research was in short supply. As Downes (1988: 49) says: 'work from the late 1970s to the present day, has been conducted with a lower level of theoretical intensity but a greater attentiveness to method and project management'.

A number of commentators suggested that internal theoretical squabbles had largely disappeared, with the bulk of criminologists hovering around a consensus, which might also partly explain this diminution in 'theoretical intensity'. It was acknowledged, though, that these placid waters were still disturbed by a handful of 'combative' radicals:

> The second generation of the 1980s consists chiefly of a smaller and younger group of professional scholars. It is a group that missed the period of major recruitment to teaching posts, having to turn instead to research contracts in applied criminology. Their work has necessarily been empirical and policy-oriented . . . there is apparent agreement that many of the earlier problems of theoretical definition and identity have grown stale or have been resolved for most practical purposes.
>
> (Rock, 1988: 63)

Or, alternatively, perhaps these theoretical disputes were swept under the carpet.

These, then, were some of the key factors influencing the shape of criminological research during the 1980s and first half of the 1990s. All of them, of course, have to be seen within the context of economic recession, consistently high levels of unemployment, growing gaps between rich and poor, pressure on the government to cut public expenditure, rising levels of recorded crime, decreasing police clear-up rates and their seeming lack of impact, beyond a certain point, to control criminal behaviour, overcrowding and rioting in the prison system, major examples of urban disorder, and increasing fears about crime.

POLICY-ORIENTED RESEARCH AND THE LEFT

The interest in questions of policy that characterised mainstream criminology over this period was also apparent within areas of radical criminology. As indicated earlier, criminologists on the left had to come to terms with the impact of Thatcherism/Majorism, especially in relation to criminal justice policies. Research associated with the left realist school in particular concerned itself with practical policies pertaining to 'law and order'. Here political sights were lowered. Relatively modest, 'realistic' aspirations based upon an explicitly reformative programme replaced a more radical commitment to major social transformations, though the reforms were seen as progressive and aimed in the direction of an (unexplicated) socialist future.

Embracing the idea of reform manifested itself in developing close links with the Labour Party, especially at local government level, and (traditionally anathema to the left) cooperating with the police in order to develop strategies for reducing levels of crime. And why not? Because, said 'critical' opponents, criminology should not surrender to a conceptual framework and research agenda determined by outside interests, and especially those of the capitalist state.

Although the left realists had advocated the development of a broadly based criminology that will encompass all relevant micro and macro dimensions, according to Jefferson and Shapland (1994: 269) their work had in the main been narrowly focused, because of the central role given to victims' accounts: 'victims' experiences . . . have come to define the new (left) realist project (coupled with, almost by way of a postscript, demands for a more democratically accountable police force . . .) – a more narrow approach'.

Jefferson and Shapland argued that this tendency partly resulted from the 'crisis of Marxism' during the 1980s, and the influence of the French writer Foucault. While one important strand of Foucault's work – based on analyses of the totality and ubiquity of discipline – had inspired radical research pitched at a societal level, and often of a historical nature, a second strand of Foucauldian thought examined the day-to-day manner in which specific institutions exercised power. It is this strand, they argued, that has influenced the left realists. The desire to link criminological research to the administration of justice carried echoes of what Garland called the 'governmental project' of classical criminology.

Although rejecting this move towards narrowly focused, policy-oriented research, critical criminology did, none the less, address concrete issues relating to the operation of the criminal justice system. This was not new, but the impact of Thatcherism/Majorism stimulated an increase in research of this type. Arguing that the 1980s and 1990s had witnessed the growth of an increasingly coercive, authoritarian state, and a narrowing down of areas of freedom, critical criminology emphasised what were seen as the harmful effects of government policy and the injustices permeating the criminal justice system. This type of research was, in fact, a continuation of two traditions already well-established within radical criminology (and discussed earlier): one based on the theme of 'self-interested rule makers', the other on the theme of 'cynical rule breakers'. During the 1980s, critical criminology picked up on the first of these by scrutinising the effects on civil liberties and justice that the implementation of government policy was having. The second theme was originally associated with white-collar crime, but during the 1980s the spotlight was turned on such things as miscarriages of justice, corruption and abuses of power. Research by critical criminologists into substantive criminal justice issues was seen by them as part of a wider critique of a capitalist society characterised by profound inequalities based on class, gender and 'race'. For left realists, the critical criminologists' insistence that criminal *justice* can only be achieved via a radical transformation of society – which leads them to be sceptical of the value of research aimed at devising practical measures for reducing crime – meant that they were unable to offer a realistic and constructive alternative to the 'law and order' policies of the right.

However, by concentrating simply on the question of *why* research should be carried out, there is a danger of reducing the debate between these two schools of radical criminology to a dispute between 'reform' and 'revolution'. As we shall see when examining criminological theory in more detail, the debate between left realism and critical criminology encompassed a range of theoretical issues concerning the production, meaning and uses of knowledge. In short, the debate raised core questions regarding the nature of academic criminology.

BRITISH CRIMINOLOGY IN THE LATE TWENTIETH CENTURY

This examination of the historical development of criminology began with Marx's observation that 'hasn't the Tree of Sin been at the same time the Tree of Knowledge ever since the time of Adam?' The imagery was meant to capture the ironic fact that the livelihoods and reputations of both 'goodies' and 'baddies' (though the distinction is not always clear) were owed to the existence of crime. In the same context Marx refers to 'the inevitable compendium in which this same professor throws his lectures onto the general market', and it is certainly true that the Tree of Knowledge that constitutes British criminology grew enormously during the twentieth century.

One of the obvious difficulties when plotting criminology's historical development is in identifying those movements and ideas that have been particularly significant and influential. The French historian Pierre Vilar (1985: 47) has written: 'The history business has one thing in common with selling soap powder: mere novelty in both can easily pass as innovation'. The same can be said of the 'criminology business'. However, looking at the past has one advantage over looking at the present: with the passage of time, and an opportunity to reflect and take stock, certain key patterns do begin to emerge.

The backdrop

As was argued earlier, criminology has both an 'internal' and an 'external' history. Over the period under review we have seen how changes in the nature of criminology – its discourses, institutional settings and projects – have been shaped by intellectual processes at work within the discipline as well as by wider social, political, economic and cultural factors. The development of criminology during the 1980s and 1990s, therefore, has to be seen against the backdrop of a panoply of 'external' events and movements.

The growing influence of the New Right, and the policies of an (at the time) entrenched Conservative administration, are particularly important. Continuing economic recession, high levels of unemployment and deprivation, and changes in the taxation system, had all helped to sharpen social divisions within British society. The 1995 United Nations international audit of children's rights in Britain provided one illustration. The report accused the British government of violating the UN convention on the rights of children, to which it was a signatory four years previously. A number of areas were pointed to, including what were defined as inadequate benefit allowances, which the report linked to teenage pregnancies and a high divorce rate, and the large number of children living in poverty. According to the Child Poverty Action Group around one-third of Britain's children were living in poverty; twenty years earlier the figure was one in ten. For gypsies and black and Asian people there had been the added burden of racism in its various forms, including an upsurge in racially motivated violence. In addition, the 1980s and 1990s saw spectacular outbreaks of urban disorder, such as occurred in Brixton in 1981 and on Tyneside in 1991. It did not escape the notice of some commentators that serious rioting had taken place during the 1930s and 1880s; these were also periods of severe economic recession. The 1980s and 1990s had also seen large-scale protest relating to specific pieces of legislation, such as the Poll Tax and the 1994 Criminal Justice and Public Order Act. The 1984–85 miners' strike brought a range of issues to the surface concerning the role of the state, and in particular the way in which the strike was policed. Finally, give or take a few year-on-year fluctuations, levels of recorded crime had continued to rise inexorably. One response to this was the greater use of imprisonment; as a proportion of the population, Britain imprisoned more people than most other Council of Europe members (Morgan, 1994; Muncie and Sparks, 1991; Vagg, 1994). One consequence of this policy, in spite of a recent large prison-building programme, was severe overcrowding. Furthermore, over the same period there were serious outbreaks of rioting in prisons.

Some of the main features of British criminology in the late twentieth century

Not surprisingly, these developments have had a profound impact on criminology in this country, irrespective of the political affiliations of the various participants. Left realism represented an attempt to construct a radical criminology that was prepared to address both the causes of crime and practical policies aimed at reducing the victimisation of vulnerable sections of society. The intention was to put forward a radical alternative to the rhetoric of the right. While rejecting this as mere reformism, critical criminologists still felt the need to engage with substantive criminal justice issues in the face of what was seen as a closing down of areas of freedom by the capitalist state. It can also be noted that critical criminology had provided fertile ground for the ideas associated with the abolitionist school of thought (e.g., Bianchi and van Swaaningen, 1986). Originating in its modern form during the 1960s in some of the Scandinavian countries, abolitionism essentially argued that prisons and other punitive elements of the criminal justice system do more harm than good, and that they should therefore be replaced by more humane and effective systems of conflict settlement. Liberal democratic thought had also to come to terms with the increased influence of the New Right, and the implementation of what were seen as illiberal criminal justice policies, though unlike critical criminology, solutions were pitched at a more modest, reforming level. For 'establishment' criminology, and especially that associated with the Home Office, rising levels of recorded crime, and the seeming inability of various forms of penality to either deter or rehabilitate offenders, had led to a disenchantment with positivism's promise to (scientifically) discover the causes and cures of crime. Thus we saw a growth in administrative criminology. This approach incorporated a rational choice model of human behaviour and elements of control theory, and the emphasis was switched to such things as situational crime prevention, the mobilisation of the community, and efforts to improve the efficiency and effectiveness of policing (Heal and Laycock, 1986).

The growing influence of New Right criminology was particularly significant. This had occurred in both Britain and the United States (though a discussion of developments in American criminology will be reserved until later) and has to be seen as not one, homogeneous school of thought, so much as a number of strands clustered around certain key themes.

Traditional conservatives attacked what they saw as the catastrophic failure of liberal welfare-oriented criminal justice policies, and in so doing laid claim to the practical no-nonsense common sense of 'ordinary' people (Brewer and Lait, 1980; Brewer *et al.*, 1981). They were all Sancho Panzas. The ideas of the traditional conservatives were based upon supposed fundamental traditional values. Another strand of New Right criminology was composed of economists whose view of the world derived from the free market principles of nineteenth-century liberalism (Veljanovski, 1990). Drawing to some extent on classicial criminology, crime from this perspective is much the same as any other business activity; criminals make rational choices to break the law, and therefore the aim of criminal justice policies should be to make such 'business' decisions irrational. Some new (or right) realists rejected the traditional punitive law and order policies of the right, though they also rejected the liberal explanations of criminality offered by sociological positivism (Coleman, 1988). Biological positivism, however, was introduced, and linked to the notion of a 'culture of poverty'. Finally, there were those who described themselves as right-wing libertarians. Here there was strong support for decentralisation and an unregulated free market, together with an ideological commitment to the privatisation of public agencies such as the police and the prisons. The libertarians argued that 'victimless' crimes, for example illegal drug use, should be decriminalised. The source of social order, they said, should be moral education and the exercise of self-discipline (Elliot, 1990).

An interesting, and sometimes confusing, aspect of developments in academic criminology during this period was that the various schools of thought did not always represent neat and tidy expressions of expected theoretical or political positions. Thus, for instance, criminologists sympathetic to interactionism were conjoined with those on the right who stressed voluntarism rather than determinism when explaining criminal motivations; the treatment model of juvenile justice, linked derogatorily by the right to the 'excuse making industry', had also been criticised by many on the left; an interest in the victims of crime had been embraced by representatives of the left and the right; and arguments in favour of the legalisation of drugs united some on the left with the libertarian right.

While radical and liberal criminology had to consider how best to respond to the movement to the right in Britain, and in the process cope with pressure to conduct research according to the demands of the funding agencies, feminist work relating to crime and criminal justice had tended to enjoy more independence. This had been double-edged in that although funding for research into specifically feminist concerns had not been in generous supply, and thus perhaps illustrated the marginalisation of feminism in terms of the criminological enterprise, it did allow alternative research agendas to be set and, importantly, allowed space for theoretical development. Clearly, as far as the world of academic criminology was concerned, feminism had been very influential, which helped it to build up its own resources and power bases.

There were two other features of contemporary British criminology that are worth noting, and each concerns the status of theory. First, in tandem with a strong emphasis on narrowly focused, policy-oriented research carried out by highly competent, professional researchers, criminological work, as Downes (1988: 49) put it, 'has been conducted at a lower level of theoretical intensity'. This is not to say that criminology in Britain at the time ignored theoretical analysis, but rather that theoretical analysis tended to have a contracted research focus, concerning itself with specific crime or crime control issues. Thus compared to the late 1960s and 1970s, there were relatively few texts that addressed wider, more fundamental debates. Although some criminologists undoubtedly felt that these debates had already been settled, or that they were irrelevant, the chief explanation for this was probably related to the pressures involved in seeking out research funds, and working to agendas set by the funding agencies. As a consequence, 'major keynote articles and books have become perhaps a rarer, and more endangered species' (Jefferson and Shapland, 1994: 284). The point was well made by Sumner (1990: xi):

> criminology cannot be limited to policy-oriented studies and must retain its integrity as an area of independent, critical enquiry of interest to scholars from a variety of disciplinary backgrounds. A criminology that wants to remain dynamic and worthy of its complex subject matter must therefore constantly renew theoretical debate, explore current issues, and develop new methods of research. To allow itself to be limited by the often narrowly political interests of government departments or the funding agencies' need for parochial 'relevance', especially in an age when 'realism' is so often defined by short-run philosophies, is to promote its own destruction as an intellectual enterprise.

There are, though, examples of work that attempted to develop a wider theoretical discourse, especially within the field of radical criminology (e.g., Cohen, 1988; Sumner, 1990, 1994; Garland, 1992; Scraton and Chadwick, 1991; Newburn, 1992) and, notably, on the part of feminist writers (e.g., Gelsthorpe and Morris, 1990; Smart, 1989; Cain, 1990; Young, 1990; Carlen, 1992; Campbell, 1992).

The second feature had been a significant trend towards an eclectic, 'pick and mix' approach to the use of theory, in the sense that criminologists had, where they felt it was appropriate, drawn on a variety of models and insights from the past, thereby eschewing a commitment to a single school of thought. This is often associated with postmodernism. The postmodern world, it was argued, is one that rejects the 'grand narrative', that is, an all-encompassing, all-explaining intellectual source and world outlook. However it is described, it did appear that within criminology the certainties that nourished the bravado and panache of earlier theoretical work had evaporated somewhat.

Plus ça change

One final observation regarding criminology's historical development is prompted by the growth of the New Right in the 1980s. New Right thinking had one thing in common with much of the British and American criminology that had emerged since World War Two: it concentrated on the crimes of the 'powerless' as opposed to the crimes of the 'powerful'. In so doing, New Right criminology invoked concepts such as the 'underclass' and the 'culture of poverty', and, along the way, had constructed various folk devils such as the 'yob', the 'single mother' and the 'trendy' social worker. In many ways it was reminiscent of a school of thought that was around during the 1930s and 1940s, and was well represented by Claude Mullins's (1945) book, *Why Crime?* discussed earlier. This alone should make us wary of a 'march of progress' view of history.

Like the New Right, Mullins concentrated on the criminality of the less well-off, singling out what he called the 'low grade' and the 'mentally deficient'. His discussion of remedies laid before us in stark terms the dichotomy between, on the one hand, welfare/treatment, and on the other, social control/punishment. Lamenting the general drift towards welfarism, Mullins in effect labelled those who emphasised the social bases of crime (and especially deprivation) as 'excuse makers'. The parallels with New Right criminology are obvious. Like Mullins, the New Right came down on the side of social control. In 1945 it was a pre-emptive strike against an imminent social welfare programme; by the 1980s it was an attack on the supposed failure of that programme. As we have seen, Mullins's preferred instrument of social control was sterilisation; those sections of society prone to commit crime should be prevented from producing a new generation of criminals.

Selected further reading

Rock, P. (ed) (1994) *The History of Criminology*, Dartmouth: Aldershot is a collection of essays on the historical development of criminology up until the mid-1990s.

A review of criminology that includes most of the 1980s is provided by **Downes, D. (1988)** 'The sociology of crime and social control in Britain, 1960–1987', *British Journal of Criminology*, 29(4); and into the 1990s: **Jefferson, T. and Shapland, J. (1994)** 'Criminal justice and the production of order and control', *British Journal of Criminology*, 34(3); **Rock, P. (1994)** 'The social organization of British criminology', in M. Maguire, R. Morgan and R. Reiner (eds) *The Oxford Handbook of Criminology*, 1st edn, Oxford: Clarendon Press.

For a less than optimistic reading of the fortunes of the sociology of deviance, see **Sumner, C. (1994)** *The Sociology of Deviance: An obituary*, Buckingham: Open University Press.

For a review of feminist contributions, see **Gelsthorpe, L. and Morris, A. (1988)** 'Feminism and criminology in Britain', *British Journal of Criminology*, 28(2).

CHAPTER 13

CRIMINOLOGICAL THEORY

Key themes

- Mainstream criminology
- Longitudinal research and criminal careers
- The historical roots
- Feminism and criminology
- Gender and crime
- Administrative criminology
- Right-wing classicism
- Neo-positivism and right realism
- Radical criminology
- Critical criminology and left realism

INTRODUCTION

With Chapter 12 as a backdrop, this chapter discusses the major strands of academic criminology through the decade of the 1980s and into the mid-1990s. This includes an examination of 'mainstream' criminology and so-called administrative criminology. With a primary interest in situational crime prevention (rather than, for instance, the causes of crime), administrative criminology became particularly prominent within establishment criminology during this period. In the context of critical criminology, the respective positions taken by left realism and left idealism – along with right realism – are discussed in detail. So too are contributions from feminist criminologists, whose work placed particular emphasis on issues of gender and inequality.

MAINSTREAM CRIMINOLOGY

The name 'mainstream' is not used to suggest that it played a prominent role within criminological theory, but rather that it continued the empirically grounded, positivist tradition associated with pre-new deviancy criminology. However, it should not be confused with the New Right versions of positivism discussed later. The principle features of mainstream criminology were well summarised by Barbara Hudson (1993: 3):

> Mainstream criminology may itself now be on the theoretical margins, but it continues. It can be identified primarily by an absence of concern with the role of the state in producing crime, an absence of concern with the part played by social reactions in producing criminal identities, and absence of any appreciation of crime and criminal justice as contingent outcomes of socio-political configurations. In mainstream criminology there is no deconstruction of definitions of crime and no fundamental challenge to state punishment strategies or practices: its concern is to assist state correctional policies by providing information about criminals which will facilitate fine-tuning of penal practices.

This summary of the characteristics of mainstream criminology points to its unreconstructed nature, in the sense that it tended to remain true to a particular understanding of what criminology should essentially be seeking to achieve. Although theoretical developments from the new deviancy period onwards were acknowledged, and sometimes incorporated into research, mainstream criminologists have, in general terms, been committed to a core orthodoxy as indicated above. This entailed, first, a concentration on the amount and distribution of so-called conventional crime, such as burglary, theft, criminal damage and certain sorts of violence, in other words, offences that make up the bulk of recorded crime; they are also the types of offences that members of the general public are most likely to worry about. Second, there was a continuing interest in young offenders, reflecting the message from official statistics and self-report studies that this age group is disproportionately involved in crime. Third, there was a strong positivist orientation, expressed in attempts to identify the factors that cause or predict crime.

Although the concerns of mainstream criminology, in particular the search for causal factors, were out of favour with government funding agencies at that time, these concerns did coalesce around questions that continued to dominate public debate, notably: who commits crime and why do they do it? In view of this it will be useful to extend this discussion of mainstream criminology via an examination of the concept of 'criminal career'.

LONGITUDINAL RESEARCH AND CRIMINAL CAREERS

Criminal career research involves plotting the amounts and types of offending of a sample of individuals as they go through life; because of the relatively large time periods covered they are referred to as longitudinal studies. The variables that appear to be associated with the offending are then noted. Proponents point out that longitudinal studies are superior to cross-sectional studies (which provide a 'snapshot' of a number of individuals at a given moment) because changes in behaviour can be linked to changes in relevant variables. As Farrington (1994: 539) said in a comprehensive review of criminal careers:

> Cross-sectional studies make it impossible to distinguish between indicators and causes, since they can merely demonstrate correlations between high levels of one factor (e.g. unemployment) and high levels of another (e.g. offending). However, longitudinal studies can show that offending is greater (within individuals) during some periods (e.g. of unemployment) than during other periods (e.g. of employment).

However, as Farrington acknowledged, longitudinal studies still have to cope with the problem of disentangling dependent from independent variables, that is, causes from symptoms.

Criminal career research does not, in itself, produce criminological theories; rather it is empirical research which aims to provide resources for the testing or development of criminological theories. Historically, such research has concerned itself with conventional, rather than white-collar, crime and has often relied on information from official statistics, although self-report studies are used. The following is a brief discussion of the kind of data generated by criminal career research.

Age and criminality

Research in Britain and other European countries, and in the United States, had shown that by the time they reach their thirties a large proportion of males have been convicted of a criminal offence (see Home Office, 1985; Farrington and West, 1990; and Piquero, 2007, in Britain; Stattin *et al.*, 1989, in Sweden; Wolfgang *et al.* 1987 in the United States). Farrington and West, for instance, found that over one-third of males in London aged up to 32 years had been convicted of at least one criminal offence serious enough to be recorded in the Criminal Records Office. This study is part of an ongoing longitudinal research project called the Cambridge Study in Delinquent Development. Using a sample of 400 males born between 1951 and 1954, the project was set up at the beginning of the 1960s by D. J. West; D. P. Farrington has been the major collaborator. When self-report studies were used, over 90 per cent of adult males admitted to having committed at least one criminal offence (Farrington, 1989). Obviously raw data such as these need to be carefully scrutinised so that such things as frequency and seriousness are taken into account. The comparable figures for females, it should be noted, were much lower (gender and crime is discussed later). The build-up of offences as an individual moves through adolescence and adulthood is referred to as the 'cumulative prevalence' of offending.

According to official statistics and self-report data, there was (and is) a much greater prevalence of offending among teenagers than among other age groups – the peak age for offending, based on cautions and convictions, was 18 years. The Home Affairs Committee (1993) reported that of the indictable offences committed by juveniles, and for which they were cautioned or convicted in 1990, 60 per cent involved theft or handling stolen goods, 17 per cent burglary, 10 per cent violence and 4 per cent criminal damage. Evidence from research, though, indicated that offenders were not specialised: known offenders tended to be involved in different types of offence (Farrington *et al.*, 1988). There was some evidence that specialisation increased with age; sex offenders being the most specialised (ibid.). A significant finding was that a very large proportion of teenagers committed offences, but in the main these are relatively trivial and rarely resulted in a caution or court appearance (most avoided getting caught). Of those arrested and prosecuted, most ceased or significantly reduced their offending by the time they were into their twenties (Belson, 1975; West, 1982). Studies from various countries showed that offending usually began at age 13–15 years, and shoplifting and criminal damage seemed to be the typical offences committed in the early teenage years. Farrington (1992a) found that the 'take off' age for an acceleration in offending was 14 years, and for a decrease, 23 years. His self-report study (Farrington, 1989) discovered that certain types of offences, basically theft, burglary and criminal damage, declined as individuals went through their teens into their twenties, though the decrease was much less for theft from work, assault, drug use and fraud.

It was also discovered that first convictions occurred on average at 17.5 years of age, with those convicted during an earlier pre-adolescence stage most likely to persist in offending (Farrington, 1992a). Many studies pointed to the link between late onset of offending and early desistance (e.g., Home Office, 1987). Whether the link between early onset and later persistence is a result of the behaviour in itself encouraging further offending, the labelling process, or the unfolding of a 'criminal potential', is unclear. A Home Office (1987) study suggested that if burglary or theft were the onset offences, then persistent offending could be predicted. Desistance from offending seems to be associated with the development of a close relationship with a partner (unless the partner was also an offender), job satisfaction, worries about getting caught and a sense of 'maturity' (Shover, 1985).

Socio-economic status and criminality

The link between low socio-economic or low social class status and criminal behaviour has been the subject of much research activity within criminology. As we have seen, many criminological models take this as given. Although this link is reflected in official statistics, data from self-report studies are less conclusive (see Box, 1981, 1987; Rutter and Giller, 1983; Farrington, 1995, for reviews). Certainly in the case of more trivial offences, self-report studies indicate that offending is widespread among all social classes, although in Britain low social classes are still overrepresented (less so in the United States). With respect to more serious offences, studies have tended to point to a correlation between rates of offending and low socio-economic status (Rutter and Giller, 1983). However, some writers (e.g. Box, 1981, and Hindelang *et al.*, 1981) have disputed this.

As measures of criminal activity, there are a number of difficulties with self-report studies, in addition to the obvious ones such as getting respondents to tell the truth. First, they are usually carried out on youths, and therefore exclude many serious offences in the white-collar and corporate crime categories. Second, as Roshier (1989) says, because such studies are generally conducted in school, the serious and frequent offenders are more likely to be absent because of truanting. Third, and again follow-ing Roshier, when more detailed indicators than, for instance, being a manual worker are used, then links between social and economic disadvantage and criminality become more apparent. Fourth, the crudity of questionnaires means that they often fail to distinguish between fairly and very frequent offending (Wilson and Herrn-stein, 1985).

The Cambridge Study was one attempt to deal with detailed indicators. The study found that juvenile and adult offending – official and self-reported – could be pre-dicted on the basis of low family income, poor housing and large family size (Farring-ton, 1992a, 1992b). One of the benefits of criminal career research is that the same individual can be followed through life. Thus the Cambridge Study found that an unstable (unskilled) work record on the part of a boy's father was a predictor of offending by the boy when aged 18 years, and an unstable (unskilled) work record at 18 years predicted offending between 21 and 25 years. In this study conviction rates were found to increase when individuals were unemployed (Farrington, 1986).

Anti-social tendencies

Criminal career research has very often tried to identify various 'anti-social' tenden-cies in early life that are associated with offending later on, or, as West and Farrington (1977) argued, form a totality of which delinquency was one element. Clearly, a term such as anti-social will mean different things to different people, and within criminal career research the term has encompassed a very wide range of activities: for example, smoking, bullying, sexual intercourse, lying, poor concentration and tru-anting. Often the focus has been on the escalation of anti-social/offending behaviour as an individual develops. A large body of research has pointed to links between vari-ous clusters of anti-social behaviour and offending:

> In the Cambridge Study, delinquents tended to be troublesome and dishonest in their primary schools, tended to be aggressive and frequent liars at age 12–14, and tended to be bullies at age 14. By age 18, delinquents tended to be anti-social in a wide variety of respects, including heavy drinking, heavy smoking, using prohibited drugs, and heavy

gambling. In addition, they tended to be sexually promiscuous, often beginning sexual intercourse under age 15, having several sexual partners by age 18, and usually having unprotected intercourse.

(Farrington, 1992b)

I sense some readers of this book shuffling uncomfortably in their seats. Some have traced so-called anti-social tendencies to an even earlier age. In an American study of 3- and 4-year-olds in kindergarten, Spivack, Marcus and Swift (1986) argued that misbehaviour at that age predicted trouble with the police in later life. An even more startling revelation comes from a piece of research by Bates *et al.* (1991) which purported to show that six-month-old baby boys whose mothers judged them to be 'difficult' in terms of temperament, were likely to exhibit anti-social tendencies at age 8. Some studies, for example Eron and Huesmann (1990) and Farrington (1993), found that aggression during boyhood was associated with assaults on spouses and bullying in adulthood, and such men were very likely to have sons who themselves carried out these behaviours when they are adults. However, longitudinal studies do show that around a half of the children defined as anti-social are not so defined by the time that they reach adulthood.

Family context

Longitudinal studies have paid particular attention to family factors, with a view to discovering those factors that predict offending during adolescence. Typically, this research points to the following as predictive factors: irregular and harsh discipline, lax supervision, large family size, lack of parental interest in, and involvement with, the child, parents who exhibit anti-social tendencies, and conflict between parents (West and Farrington, 1973; McCord, 1979; Wilson, 1980; Loeber and Stouthamer-Loeber, 1986).

According to McCord (1979), rejection or lack of interest on the part of the mother predicted the child's later involvement in property crime, whilst violent crime was linked to having been brought up in a family where parental conflict and aggression were in evidence.

The Cambridge Study found that a relatively small number of families were responsible for a very large proportion of criminal behaviour. Indeed, having a convicted parent or sibling was an important predictor of later offending by a child (West and Farrington, 1973, 1977). Having a convicted parent, however, was a predictor of persistence in offending in later life, rather than a predictor of early onset of offending.

In the early 1990s, lone-parent families came under the spotlight in debates about juvenile crime (see, for example, the remarkable convergence between Conservative ministers and self-styled 'ethical socialism' in Dennis, 1993). On a general level, longitudinal studies did tend to show that children brought up in homes broken by divorce or separation (but not death) were more likely to become juvenile and adult offenders than were children brought up in two-parent families (Wadsworth, 1979; Farrington, 1992b), though this was not the case if parental divorce or separation occurred before the child was 5 years old. However, these research findings did not show that family structure, and in particular the lone-parent family, was *per se* criminogenic. Longitudinal researchers acknowledge that abstracting 'lone parent' as a single causal factor is far too simplistic, and ignores factors such as economic and social deprivation and the nature of relationships between spouses and between parents and children. McCord (1982) took a sample of families where the children's natural father had (because of death, divorce or separation) left the home and, for comparison, a sample of unbroken families. She reported that the prevalence of serious offending on the part of the children was as follows:

Lone-parent families:
    62 per cent where the mother failed to give the child affection
    22 per cent where the mother was affectionate

Two-parent families:
    52 per cent where parental conflict existed
    26 per cent where there was little parental conflict

A Home Office study by Riley and Shaw (1985: 45) in the mid-1980s concluded: 'The notion that one-parent families are . . . "criminogenic" receives no support from the results of the present survey'. For a brief, but useful, overview see Rodger (1995).

Moral panics?

In the light of the issues raised during the above discussion of mainstream criminology, and before examining criminological theory, we can complete this section by discussing briefly some high octane debates on the specific theme of juvenile offending and criminal justice policies that emerged.

A striking feature of the juvenile justice legislation introduced between the beginning of the 1980s and the middle of the 1990s is its lack of consistency. To what extent, one might ask, was this a reflection of political expediency or knee-jerk reactions, as opposed to a careful consideration of what might actually 'work'? Importantly, government policy has to be seen against the backdrop of a desire to present a tough law and order stance, and pressure to cut costs via 'value for money' (at the time over £7 billion per year was spent on the criminal justice system).

At the beginning of the 1990s Home Office ministers were congratulating themselves on the apparent success of their juvenile justice policies. Official statistics showed that between 1985 and 1991 the number of offenders aged 17 or under convicted or cautioned had more than halved – 264,000 in 1985 compared with 149,000 in 1991. In 1992 the figure decreased further to 99,000. This contrasted with an increase of 150 per cent in the number of male juvenile offenders convicted or cautioned in the period 1959–77. The decrease from the mid-1980s was only partly explained by a reduction in the juvenile population. There was, too, during the 1980s a significant decrease in the number of juveniles being given custodial sentences. In 1979 the number was 7,900, and in 1984 it was 6,700, falling to 1,500 in 1990, and then rising to 2,000 in 1991.

An optimistic reading would conclude that over the period in question there really was a fall in the number of juveniles who offended. On the other hand, more juveniles may have escaped apprehension; or (which is highly likely) police may have preferred to issue informal cautions rather than formal cautions or setting in motion prosecution procedures. During the 1980s amounts of recorded crime in general continued to increase and, given the disproportionate involvement of juveniles in offending, the apparent decreases seem anomalous. A serious difficulty with all this, of course, is that we cannot know the ages of those committing the majority of recorded offences. As Maguire (1994: 271) points out:

> not many more than one in ten offences recorded by the police result in a caution or conviction . . . only about one in fifty of the comparable crimes identified by the BCS (British Crime Survey) result in a conviction – a figure which drops to as low as one in 200 where 'vandalism' (criminal damage) is concerned.
>
> This being the case, it can obviously not simply be assumed that the characteristics of 'offenders' as a whole can be inferred from those of adjudicated offenders.

In spite of the optimistic glow induced in some quarters by the juvenile crime figures, the early 1990s witnessed a significant upsurge of interest in the 'youth crime problem'. The *Daily Star* in November 1992 pulled no punches, arguing that:

> hardcore child super-crooks are bringing fear to Britain's streets . . . they are our number one crime problem, tearaways just out of primary school who have learned their lessons in motor theft and housebreaking so well they account for *90 per cent* of offences.
> (Quoted in Hagel and Newburn, 1994: 97; emphasis in original)

The mass media provided a rich diet of young thugs 'laughing at the law', 'rat boys', 'criminal tots' in balaclavas who terrorised certain neighbourhoods, and rampaging rioters. The James Bulger case provided a particularly potent image. For many media commentators this was not merely an isolated, idiosyncratic and tragic event (which was how the Mary Bell case in the 1960s, which contained similar features, seemed to be interpreted). Rather, it tended to be presented as a symbol of something having gone profoundly wrong with Britain's children. As public and political debate focused increasingly on youngsters as a generalised threat, a parallel concern was growing which stressed the role of children as victims. In her ongoing study of 11- to 16-year-olds in Cleveland, Browne (1994), for instance, found that for many children the world was a frightening and dangerous place. It was not uncommon for weapons to be carried for self-defence, bullying in schools was endemic and a large number of girls spoke of sexual harassment from male teachers (see also Anderson *et al.*, 1991; Hartless *et al.*, 1995). At the same time various child sex abuse scandals appeared in the media, and there were numerous references to parents being increasingly worried about their younger children playing outdoors and walking home from school alone.

Meanwhile, the judiciary and the police argued that the official statistics were misleading, and that the 1980s had seen not a decrease, but an increase in juvenile crime. This was the dominant view within the mass media, and it was not contradicted by the evidence from academic research. In July 1995, under the headline 'Thatcher's children turn to crime', *The Observer* carried a front page story by Hugill that drew on the findings from three recent pieces of research. In particular that by James who, linking crime to Thatcherism, argued that there had been 'an unprecedented increase in violent crime by and against young people. He reports a 41 per cent increase since 1987 . . . [He] has found that since 1987 juvenile crime figures have risen at a rate of 12,000 crimes a year, three times faster than the average of 4,000 for 1979–86' (Hugill, 1995: 1).

The government, on the other hand, believed that their policies were bearing fruit and amounts of juvenile crime were decreasing. One of their policies had been to divert juveniles from custody, hence the huge decreases in custodial sentences. Subsequently, however, the use of custody increased (for all ages), and the 1994 Criminal Justice and Public Order Act introduced, among other things, secure training centres for 12- to 14-year-olds convicted of serious offences. This was a significant turnaround from the philosophy underpinning the 1991 Criminal Justice Act, and signalled a reversal to a more punitive 'law and order' stance that might satisfy those who believed that the criminal justice system was 'soft' on criminals. It did, however, appear to contradict government celebrations of earlier decreases in recorded offending. The way out of this quandary was for the Home Office to join with judiciary and police and argue that the real problem lay with a hard core of persistent young offenders, and these were now to be targeted. Kenneth Clarke, the Home Secretary who framed the Act, spoke of 'really persistent, nasty little juvenile offenders', and the Prime Minister urged that 'we should understand less and condemn more'. The size of this group of 'persistent' offenders had been the subject of much controversy during the 1990s. The Home Office identified boys in their mid-teens who had been given many informal warnings by the police and who were responsible for the lion's share of juvenile crime. Persistent juvenile offending was one of the issues looked at by the Home Affairs Committee (1993) of the House of Commons. Agencies giving evidence to the Committee, such as the Association of Chief Police Officers (ACPO), the National Association of Probation Officers (NAPO) and Chief Officers of Probation, all agreed that a small group of persistent offenders did exist, and each offered an estimate of the numbers involved (NAPO, for example, thought that there might be 12 to 20 in Newcastle upon Tyne; ACPO suggested around 600 for England and Wales). ACPO also argued that during the decade of the 1980s, and contrary to what official statistics said, juvenile offending had actually increased by 54 per cent. As they saw it, the decrease in the statistics was misleading, and reflected a decline in the proportion of juveniles in the population coupled with a lower police detection rate. Therefore, if these two factors had remained constant, during the 1980s there would have been an increase of 54 per cent in juvenile crime.

Persistent offenders

Clearly, given the nature of the debate, there was plenty of scope for statistical manipulation and astonishing conjecture. In the case of a so-called hard core of persistent offenders, efforts to define and quantify them are fraught with a range of difficulties. For instance, offenders 'known' to the police may subsequently experience greater police scrutiny (for example, when searching for stolen property), leading to them being continually sucked into the system. Although multiple offending may come to light among these groups, such offending among others will go unrecorded. This is particularly important if research is extended into an examination of socio-cultural and other factors associated with offending behaviour, for it cannot be assumed that known offenders constitute a representative sample of all offenders.

An important British study of so-called persistent young offenders was that carried out by Hagel and Newburn (1994) and commissioned by the Home Office Research and Planning Unit. This research took a sample of 531 10- to 16-year-olds in two geographical areas – London and the Midlands – who were selected on the basis of having been arrested at least three times during 1992. The authors acknowledged the view that because self-report studies show that offending by young people is widespread, it is fruitless to search for individual and family characteristics. However, most of this is trivial and infrequent; thus Hagel and Newburn (1994: 78) argued: 'The issue of reoffending refocuses attention on such work, however, for although *most* young people may engage in criminal acts at one time or another, persistent offenders by any definition are a small minority'. They preferred to label their overall sample 'reoffenders', rather than persistent offenders.

Offending profiles
In line with other studies referred to earlier, the research found that reoffenders who specialised in one type of crime were in a minority; only one-fifth were, on the basis of known offending, in this category. However, those who had committed the widest

range of offences were also those who had committed the most offences. Lone offenders were in a minority: over three-quarters of offences were committed in the company of others, and the indications were that many of the offenders knew each other. A majority of reoffenders – 60 per cent – had committed their offences whilst on police or court bail, a finding that provides ammunition for those who have complained about 'bail bandits'. The researchers, though, found that there was often a long gap between offence and final sentence, and the bulk of offenders had spent most of the year on bail.

Violent offences were more common among the sample than among juvenile offenders in general: one-third had committed a violent crime. More serious violence, in the form of grievous bodily harm, was rare, and no offences of rape, manslaughter or murder were recorded. The majority of offences involved property, with the largest proportion covering the range £10–£100 in value.

Not surprisingly, the self-report element of the study showed greater amounts of offending than did police records. Illicit drug use, in particular, was underrecorded: 'drug use among the group was very frequent' (ibid.: 70).

Offender profiles
Hagel and Newburn's study included interviews with 74 of the sample, and although this was a relatively small response rate, as the authors said: 'the survey still provides a unique source of illustrative information about a group that is very hard to interview' (ibid.: 78). Of the reoffenders, thirty-two of those interviewed lived with their mothers only, and five with their fathers, while twenty-two lived with both parents. Most said that they got on well or fairly well with their mothers. Where there was a father figure, expressions of loyalty were only slightly weaker, though relationships with fathers appeared to become less close with the passage of time. Eleven per cent of the interviewed sample were girls, compared with 14 per cent for the total sample of reoffenders.

Closer examination of family circumstances pointed to some inconsistencies; for example, half of those interviewed said that they had run away from home at least once. A further source of information was social services departments. Although gathering together the relevant evidence was quite difficult, the researchers said that the data suggested that a high proportion had experienced social services care in the past, with the vast majority first entering the system because of welfare problems, rather than because of offending behaviour. Half of those interviewed had at one time been referred for counselling or psychological help.

Two out of three of the group were no longer at school, and many had left before they officially should have done. Over half had been permanently excluded. Views on school were generally negative, and truanting was commonplace.

Few of those interviewed had jobs, and lack of money was clearly an important factor in their lives, especially as they were ineligible for state benefits. When asked why they committed crime, money was often mentioned, as were boredom and the excitement experienced from crime, being influenced by others, and wanting to act tough.

Half of the group were living in households where the head of the household was either unemployed or not working. Only a tiny minority lived in a household where the head was in a non-manual job.

Who are persistent offenders?
Obviously, in any given year there will be enormous variation in frequency of offending within the juvenile population – from never to a great deal. There will also be enormous variation in the seriousness of this offending: some will commit a lot of very trivial offences, whilst others will commit relatively few, yet extremely serious, offences. The central theme of Hagel and Newburn's research was how the notion of 'persistent offender' might be defined and the extent to which those so defined possessed certain common characteristics. Of particular importance was an assessment of the number of offenders in their sample who would be classified as persistent offenders eligible for what at the time of the research was a proposed secure training order. This, together with plans to build secure training centres, became part of the 1994 Criminal Justice and Public Order Act. The secure training order was one of three criteria used as a basis for defining 'persistent'. The main conclusions can be summarised as follows:

- Although Hagel and Newburn's (1994) sample represented, as they put it, the 'heavy end' of juvenile offending, it was difficult to identify a distinct group of very frequent offenders. Frequent reoffending coupled with offending over lengthy periods of time was rare. Applying the three different criteria produced three groups of 'persistent offenders'. However, in terms of the individuals comprising these groups, little overlap was found. Put another way, the different measures of 'persistent' did not lead to the identification of one distinct group: 'Only three children out of the full sample of 193 Midlands reoffenders aged 12–14 were defined as "persistent" by all three sets of criteria, whereas a total of 36 were persistent according to one definition or another' (ibid.: 131).
- There were 'no striking differences' (from the point of view of, for example, seriousness of offence) between those identified as persistent by any of the sets of criteria and the rest of the overall sample, apart from the former having committed three or more offences that year.

As Hagel and Newburn (1994: 123) said:

> not only is the process of attempting to define persistence deeply problematic, but because there is a degree of arbitrariness in the way some offenders rather than others become defined as persistent, creating a custodial sentence for that group raises issues both about equality and about efficient resource use.

THE HISTORICAL ROOTS

In the words of Lilly, Cullen and Ball (1989: 194): 'Rather than being a period of new theories cut from the whole cloth, the 1980s were primarily a time that witnessed the revitalization of old theories'. With the exception of feminism, each of the theoretical perspectives or paradigms looked at in this chapter has a direct link with either eighteenth-century classicial criminology, nineteenth-century positivism, or interactionism/neo-Marxism from the 1960s and early 1970s. Classical criminology emphasised 'free will', conceiving of human beings as rational creatures able to weigh up the costs and benefits of crime. Described by Vold (1958) as 'administrative criminology', classicism was primarily concerned with establishing effective and efficient deterrents that would control crime by making the pain of punishment outweigh the pleasure of the offence. Having said that, a rereading of early classical texts by Beirne (1993) suggested that although unrecognised in historical accounts, classicism also contained strong elements of psychological determinism. Positivism concentrated on the offender rather than the offence, and was committed to the application of scientific method. The aim was to discover the causes of criminality – in the earlier period located in the individual's genetic/biological make-up, but later on traced to psychological or social factors. Unlike classical criminology, positivism drew a sharp distinction between criminals and non-criminals. Interactionism shifted attention away from the deterministic search for the causes of crime, and focused instead on the nature of social reactions to behaviour perceived as deviant. Through labelling processes, deviance/crime was thus socially constructed, and was not seen as an inherent quality of the act. Neo-Marxist approaches attempted to develop a political economy of crime through analyses of law making and control within the context of a capitalist mode of production. The links between these approaches and criminological developments in the 1980s and early 1990s can be briefly indicated as follows:

- *Administrative criminology* A direct descendant of the classical tradition, with a primary interest in deterring crime and a lack of interest in the causes of criminality. There were elements of control theory.
- *Right-wing classicism* This too explored ways of deterring people from breaking the law, laying stress on 'rational choice' and the individual's personal responsibility for their actions. With an explicit commitment to the politics of the New Right, there was an acceptance of punishment as retribution. There were libertarian and conservative versions of right-wing classicism.
- *Neo-positivism and right realism* Neo-positivism was a continuation of a long-standing commitment among positivists to develop scientific analyses of crime and criminal. Some versions of neo-positivism, though, were strongly associated with the political concerns of the New Right, and these versions, in combination with elements of control theory, gave rise to what became known as right realism.

- *Radical criminology* Broadly speaking, radical criminology contained two strands. On the one hand, critical criminologists who saw themselves as the true carriers of the radical tradition, and on the other, self-styled left realists committed to 'taking crime seriously'. Critical criminology's roots lie in interactionism and neo-Marxism, whilst left realism has a more eclectic base, drawing, for instance, on subcultural theory and anomie. From the perspective of critical criminology, left realism was essentially reformist liberalism dressed up as radicalism, and had been seduced by the belief that criminal *justice* can be achieved in a fundamentally unjust society. From the other direction, left realism attacked critical criminology for being woefully utopian and ignoring the real concerns of working-class people.
- *Feminist perspectives* These were less obviously linked to the main criminological traditions, as feminist perspectives on crime and social control arose out of broadly based feminist concerns. It is feminism and criminology that will be discussed first.

FEMINISM AND CRIMINOLOGY

Although 'feminism and criminology' is, I think, a reasonable signifier of the theoretical field under review, choosing a title for this part of the chapter was less straightforward than it might appear. The early contributions from feminist writers in the 1970s stimulated a wave of intense theoretical work as the 1980s and 1990s unfolded. Given the increasing complexity of the debates, and the different theoretical and political directions from which writers were coming, it was inevitable that a number of different strands began to emerge. In the context of these debates, not only is the definition of 'feminism' problematic, but so too is the definition of 'criminology'. Although on a general level feminists may have had a common commitment to 'the elimination of gender inequalities' (Dominelli, 1992: 85), it was probably more correct to speak of feminisms rather than feminism. Adamson *et al.* (1988) identified liberal, radical, socialist and black feminisms; Gregory (1986) referred to radical, socialist and bourgeois versions. Different theoretical and political orientations had also developed within the field of criminology. Thus the question of whether or not a feminist criminology existed, was desirable, or was possible, remained unsettled. In their review of feminism and criminology in Britain up to the late 1980s, Gelsthorpe and Morris (1988) mentioned a range of opinion on this. Greenwood (1981) and Brown (1986) supported the idea of an extant feminist criminology, whilst Smart (1981) was sceptical in view of the divisions existing at the level of theory and practice. According to Gelsthorpe and Morris (1988: 97): 'just as we had to talk of "feminisms", we have to talk of feminist criminologies, or, better still, feminist perspectives within criminology'.

They did add, however, that feminist perspectives shared 'certain core elements': they were anti-positivist, critical of stereotypes, place women centre stage and were concerned to develop methodologies which were 'sympathetic to these concerns'. Different, and often competing, strands, though, existed within this broad framework and there had been complex debates about precisely what a feminist analysis of crime and social control would look like. Some writers, such as Cousins (1980), Cain (1989, 1990) and Smart (1990) rejected the idea of linking feminism to the discipline of criminology itself. Using the notion of deconstruction associated with postmodernism, they argued that by attaching themselves to 'criminology', as a given, feminists unwittingly fell into a conceptual trap. This was because criminology is crime-inology – that is, the study of what is assumed to be special behaviour, qualitatively different to non-criminal behaviour, when in fact it has no meaning beyond ideological and institutional contexts. It is rather like feminists studying seventeenth-century 'witches', but defining them in exactly the way that a male witchfinder from that century defined them. Put another way, why should feminists surrender to an already existing 'essentialist' conceptualisation of 'crime', as if the concept itself was not problematic? This is an aspect of doing criminology that has been alluded to in earlier discussions, and does raise important and complex issues. These issues, though, have not been ignored by radical writers, feminist or otherwise (see Sumner, 1990, 1994; Hester and Eglin, 1992). As Pat Carlen (1992: 62) has pointed out:

> fear of the ideological and already institutionalized meanings of the empirical referent is not new among social scientists or political theorists attempting radical critique. Yet the very task of theory is to engage in a struggle for power over the 'meaning of things' (including all material and ideological constructs). The purpose is to produce new meanings that will empower.

Smart (1990) was also critical of efforts by feminists to develop a 'feminist criminology' committed to 'useful', policy-oriented research that was ostensibly aimed at, say, improving the treatment of women by the criminal justice system. Again, this is a familiar theme within radical thought, often turning on the 'reformism' versus 'revolution' debate (see the later discussion of left realism), and was certainly not a view shared by all radical feminists. Moulds (1980) argued that feminist research should be directed towards the creation of a criminal justice system that treated men and women equally, whilst Heidensohn (1986) pointed to cultural differences between male and female offenders that necessitate different types of dispositions by the courts. And Carlen (1990) argued for the abolition of imprisonment for all but a small minority of female offenders.

Heidensohn (1994: 1029) stated: 'something of an epistemological crisis has affected social science and feminism, and studies of crime are implicated'. Put simply, there were still important questions to be answered regarding *what* was to be studied and *how* it was to be studied. Should the focus be on female offenders, or on the concept of gender and its explanatory power with respect to female and male offending? To what extent should studies of social control and jurisprudence be a part of this?

Should the main business of feminism be to illuminate the continuing injustices experienced by females in the criminal justice system? Or should it concentrate on the various ways in which women are victimised? And, from the point of view of methodology, can only women study women (see Harding, 1991 and the concept of 'standpointism' – which suggested that only researchers who share the feelings and experiences of the subject can carry out meaningful research)? Which returns us to the central question: what makes a piece of research distinctively 'feminist'?

In a useful review of some of these debates, Carlen defended the view that feminists should study 'women and crime', but at the same time did not accept that 'a "feminist criminology" was either desirable or possible' (Carlen, 1992: 53). It was not *desirable,* she said, because it suggested that a universal theory that reduces female (and by implication, male) criminality to distinctive biologies can be constructed. The biological fact of being female, and the social context of patriarchy, have, therefore, to be seen in conjunction with a host of other possibilities when explaining criminality, such as poverty, affluence, unemployment, racism, upbringing, education, and so on. A feminist criminology was not *possible,* said Carlen, because:

1 Apart from patriarchy, criminological knowledge has not developed distinctly 'feminist' explanatory concepts.
2 Those things that interest feminists merge into issues of class, racism and imperialism.
3 No single theory can explain:
   (a) why women's crimes are in the main crimes of the powerless;
   (b) why there is a disproportionate number of ethnic minority women in prison; and
   (c) why most women in prison are poor.

Making females visible

As we have seen, early feminist writers complained that traditional criminology had to a large extent made females invisible. Stanley and Wise (1983) argued that in addition to using non-sexist methodologies, and a commitment to the production of practical knowledge, feminist research in criminology should 'make women visible'. Feminist explanations of 'invisibility' highlighted the male domination of the discipline. However, the fact that males appeared to commit most crime (and certain sorts of males at that) cannot be overlooked as a factor shaping the focus of research. After all, the crimes of aristocratic men were also made invisible:

> It so happens that criminological theory has been crime-led, and that the subjects around whom theorizing has been formed have been predominantly white, urban, lower-class, and usually adolescent males in advanced industrial capitalist societies.
>
> (Downes and Rock, 1988: 289)

Since the 1970s there had been a growth in research that had attempted to measure the gaps between male and female crime rates. This was largely triggered by the argument in some quarters (e.g. Adler, 1975; Simon, 1975) that as women became more 'liberated', we could expect their crime rates to move nearer to those of men. Relying on official data is, of course, fraught with a range of well-known problems; for example, the extent to which they reflect organisational practices, rather than criminal activities as such and, in the case of females, how small increases can appear in an exaggerated form because of the small numbers comprising the original base. Box and Hale (1983) found a proportionate increase in conventional property crime for females during the 1970s, but not with respect to burglary or robbery; also, there were no increases for violent offences. According to Home Office figures for England and Wales, the proportion of violent offences attributable to females rose from 9.0 per cent to 11.2 per cent between 1979 and 1989. For other indictable offences proportions varied widely. Self-report studies, as mentioned earlier, tended to put males and females closer together, but seriousness of offence and frequency of offending are not always carefully controlled for. A self-report and victim study of school-age children in Edinburgh (Anderson et al., 1991) attempted to be sensitive to one of these aspects by asking the children themselves to rank various offences in terms of perceived seriousness. The self-report data showed that three to four times as many boys as girls have committed serious offences based on dishonesty and violence, whilst in the case of drug-related offences, the proportion was only slightly higher for boys. When it came to offences ranked as 'less serious', the ratio again varied according to type of offence, as follows:

Offence	Ratio of boys to girls
Rowdy/rude	1.06 to 1
Fighting	1.96 to 1
Shoplifting	1.33 to 1
Broken into car	2.50 to 1
Vandal car	3.00 to 1
Vandal property	1.36 to 1

Source: Based on Anderson et al., 1991: 107.

This still leaves, though, the problem of distinguishing between different *types* of vandalism, shoplifting, and so forth.

In her pioneering book, Smart (1976) referred to the possible danger of a moral panic accompanying feminist efforts to make female crime visible, and the attempt by some writers to equate increased offending with women's liberation would seem to bear this out (this is returned to in Chapter 15). Much feminist work has been devoted to counteracting this kind of reasoning. Smart (1979), for example, argued that what increases there were in female crime rates in fact pre-dated the impact of the women's liberation movement. Carlen (1990) put forward the view that any increases in property crime among women were more likely to be explained by economic recession and deprivation.

There was a double edge to the project of making female crime 'visible'. Those feminists who were unhappy at traditional characterisations of women as passive, and resigned to their fate, whilst men 'rebel' through crime (as 'proto-revolutionary' 'Paki-bashers' or football hooligans, say), may have been tempted to present female crime in a positive light. On the other hand, those who wished to underline masculinity as the primary basis for criminality, could find this approach subverted if large amounts of female crime suddenly materialised. Quite a few important studies were carried out, from a feminist standpoint, which concentrated specifically on female criminals; for example, Campbell (1984) on girl members of delinquent gangs in New York; Campbell (1986), a self-report study of girls and violence; Browne (1987) on female murderers (of their husbands); McLeod (1982) and Miller (1986) on prostitutes; Carlen (1985) on a small group of 'criminal women'; Parton (1992) on the role of mothers in family child sex-abuse cases; MacDonald (1991) on women terrorists; Player (1989) on female burglars.

Challenging 'distortion'

When feminist work on female criminality began to emerge in the 1960s, one of the main arguments was that when women and girls had been made 'visible' within criminology, explanations of their criminality were usually based on versions of biological determinism or psychological reductionism, and their offences tended to be 'sexualised' and presented as 'irrational'. This approach, it was argued, created a climate where responses to female offenders tended to be based on assumptions of 'sickness' or mental illness (Carlen, 1983).

Some feminist writers, such as Leonard (1982), pressed for the modification of important sociologically oriented criminological theories, where women were neglected, so that they took account of gender. Others, such as Smart (1990), argued against the idea that feminists should simply 'insert' women into already existing theoretical frameworks. Clearly, this is a complex issue, which turns on the question of whether existing theories contained the potential both to explain female crime, and draw out the gender dimension to criminal behaviour and reactions to it in general. In a vigorous defence of what some might call 'pre- feminist' criminology, and criticising the 'stark terms' in which gender had been presented by some feminists, Downes and Rock (1988) argued that there was plenty of mileage in the work of major theorists and concepts such as drift, labelling and stigma. They also pointed to subcultural theories and control theories as explicitly providing explanations of the lower crime rates for females:

> Subcultural theories have assumed that females pursue less criminogenic and more attainable goals than men, namely marriage and family life, and are therefore insulated from the social sources of delinquency, the main exception being the strain to sexual deviance. Control theories specify with some precision the far more intensive informal controls that are brought to bear on girls rather than boys, which constitute powerful inhibitors against criminality.
>
> (Ibid.: 283)

If we look at some of the directions taken by feminist research on female criminality in this period, certain tensions become apparent, indicating that it was more appropriate to speak of feminist criminolog*ies*:

1 Some theorists sought to accentuate the gender-based differences between males and females, and the implications of these differences for criminality. Gilligan (1982), for instance, argued that women possess a different personality to that of men.
2 Some theorists pointed out that female offenders have more characteristics in common with male offenders than was traditionally thought. Campbell (1986) argued that gangs composed of boys *and* girls do exist, and although less collective in nature, the girls were involved in more fighting than is commonly assumed. Another example of this was Naffine's (1987) critique of control theories for making females too passive.
3 Some theorists, though, had emphasised that the behaviour of both males and females has to be seen as mediated by other factors such as class or 'race'. Carlen (1988), in her ethnographic study of female offenders, discussed how the women were constrained in their choices by both gender and class. Likewise, Miller (1986), in a study of prostitutes, drew attention to the interrelationship between class and gender.

Heidensohn (1994) indicated three themes around which feminist research had been conducted during the 1980s and 1990s: patriarchy, economic and social marginalisation, and control.

The concept of *patriarchy* – defined basically as male power – is particularly associated with radical feminism, and has tended to be employed when examining the treatment of women by the criminal justice system and the issue of victimisation, rather than female criminality.

Explanations of crime based upon *economic marginalisation*, and the resultant poverty and deprivation, have, as Heidensohn points out, been around in critical Marxist criminology for some time, although for much of that time issues of gender were ignored. Chapman (1980) linked increases in recorded female property crime to economic recession and poverty, which she saw as having a greater impact on women than men. In particular, she pointed to the growth in the number of single mothers, who as a group were especially vulnerable to economic deprivation. *Social marginalisation* arises because of women's 'child care role and their dependency on men or the state for welfare' (Heidensohn, 1994: 1027). This dimension was used to explain the types of offences available to women. Heidensohn was critical of the explanatory power of these approaches, seeing them as essentially positivist, and providing only a partial explanation of female criminality. Not all poor people, for instance, break the law. 'Marginalisation' explanations, though, have been popular with some feminists because they offer a way of challenging the argument that women's liberation leads to more crime (Adler, 1975; Simon, 1975).

Explanations based on *control* theory became increasingly influential among feminists. One reason was that by asking why people don't break the law, rather than why they do, a theoretical space was opened up into which the concept of gender could be inserted. Thus, as far as female criminality is concerned, the fundamental research question becomes: what social controls are at work that can explain the lower crime rates for females (e.g., Hagan *et al.*, 1979; Stanko, 1993)?

Research of this sort pointed to the significance of informal modes of control experienced by women, especially in terms of family and community sanctions and commitments. As a result, men are 'allowed' more freedom to explore deviant routes. According to Hagan *et al.* (1979), even 'career' women are locked into traditional roles *vis-à-vis* the family. Feminist critics of the view that women's liberation leads to more crime, in addition to stressing the links between poverty and crime, had also questioned the extent to which women in Britain are 'liberated'. However, if the lower crime rates for females are seen as a function of greater control, and if those controls were to be lessened, then, according to the logic of control theory, females would have more freedom to engage in crime. The opportunity to commit crime is an important element of this. In a Home Office self-report study of teenage girls, Riley (1986: 38) concluded that: 'given equal opportunities, sex differences in crime participation by young people – as offenders or victims – are minimal'.

Feminists had quite rightly argued that a fully social explanation of crime has to include a consideration of gender issues. This meant addressing the range of social processes at work whereby male and female understandings of 'masculinity' and 'femininity' are constructed, and the ways in which these are linked to specific forms of law breaking. These understandings, however, should also be situated within a broader structural context linking gender to such things as class, 'race' and generation.

The criminal justice system

From the standpoint of radical feminism, women's experiences of the criminal justice system have to be seen within the context of patriarchy. For socialist feminists, the criminal justice system has to be seen as part of a capitalist mode of production. As Gelsthorpe and Morris (1988) argue, though, whatever the merits of these analyses, there is a need to explore in more detail precisely how the various elements of the system operate, and to appreciate that a whole range of mediating factors have to be taken into consideration: 'neither men nor the capitalist mode of production can be singled out as chief conspirators in a plot against women. However ideas about women have been shaped, there is no one unified motivational force underlying that shaping' (ibid.: 99).

As we have seen, one central issue for feminists had been the debate about whether females were treated more leniently by the criminal justice system than men were. Proponents of the view that they were usually pointed to what they saw as the 'chivalry' of the male administrators of the system. Again, this is a difficult area, where evidence either way is inconclusive. However, a large and growing body of feminist work has sought to challenge the leniency argument through detailed empirical studies (e.g. Worrall, 1981; Eaton, 1983, 1985, 1986; Carlen, 1983; Edwards, 1984). Research from the 1970s on this theme has already been discussed.

The police

According to Gregory (1986: 55): 'There is some evidence of leniency towards women both in the different cautioning rates for male and female offenders and in the different incarceration rates of those found guilty'. She then argued that 'paternalism', rather than chivalry, was a more appropriate term; but paternalism, as a form of sexism, could obviously still operate in one's favour. Put another way, it was possible that the police treated women more favourably than men, though for the worst reasons. In fact, Morris (1987) argued that it is at this point in the criminal justice process that chivalry was most likely to be in evidence.

It is important to recognise that the nature of street-level interactions between police and public, and the sorts of decisions that result, involve many other factors than gender, and it is not always easy to assess the relative importance of these various factors. As far as the decision to make an arrest is concerned, research in Britain and the United States shows that the prime factor is seriousness of offence. In line with other research, Harris (1992) found that an offender's demeanour was important (for example, showing respect and being apologetic), as was the offender's previous record. Females, however, were more likely to be cautioned than males. In his review of what is mainly American research, Box (1983) concluded that among those who have committed serious offences, older women, especially if they are white, were treated less aggressively than their male counterparts by the police. In her North American research, Player (1989) found that black women experienced significantly worse treatment than did white women.

Measuring the extent to which sexist attitudes existed among police officers was not easy, though what evidence there was did suggest that a combination of social background and occupational culture did tend to produce sexist stereotyping. The Policy Studies Institute report on the Metropolitan Police (Smith and Grey, 1985) found that policemen would often joke and boast about their sexual activities, sometimes in the presence of female officers, and they enjoyed apocryphal tales involving sexist fantasies. The word 'plonk' was used as a term of abuse to refer to female officers. However, none of this is peculiar to policing as an occupation, and it is important to understand how attitudes reflected in locker-room banter get translated into actual street-level behaviour (see also Young, 1993).

Clearly, it is difficult to make generalisations about the nature of (male) police–female (or male) relationships. There is, for instance, a distinction between women as victims and women as offenders, though Jones (1987) argued that negative attitudes towards women, based upon their supposed inferiority, found among officers influenced their treatment of both victims and offenders. In the case of domestic violence, a large amount of feminist research had been critical of the reluctance of the police to make an arrest (Edwards, 1989), and for defining 'domestics' as not real policework (Faragher, 1981). (See Dunhill, 1989, for a detailed examination of this subject.) Prostitutes in particular complained of unfair treatment by the police, though British research indicated a degree of ambivalence on the part of the police: 'Harassment and entrapment were reported, but also a degree of accommodation. Evidence given by police representatives themselves to a parliamentary committee showed disparaging views of women who prostitute themselves' (Heidensohn, 1994: 1008).

Sentencing

Evidence regarding the lenient, or otherwise, treatment of females by the courts was, according to Smith (1988), in a detailed analysis of available research, inconclusive. On a general level, a number of research findings can be noted. Home Office figures showed that throughout the 1980s there was a gradual decrease in the use of fines for women offenders, and compared to men, a faster growth in the use of imprisonment. Home Office statistics show that about 5 per cent of females convicted of an indictable offence were given a custodial sentence, whilst the figure for males was 20 per cent. Convicted female offenders were more likely than males to be put on probation, though they were less likely to be given a community service order. On the other hand, and echoing earlier research in the 1970s, as well as showing the complexities involved in interpreting the evidence, British research continued to point to the higher proportion of women than men held in custody, either awaiting trial or sentencing (Greenwood, 1983). In a significant number of cases, sentencing delays for women arose because the court required a medical report. Edwards (1984) found that females were much more likely than males to be subject to 'medicalised' interventions by the criminal justice system. In the case of young girls especially, decisions by the courts were strongly influenced by considerations of sexual morality and being 'at risk' (Chesney-Lind, 1986). One outcome was that a higher proportion of girls than boys were taken into care (Eaton, 1986). In an extensive investigation of 'chivalry' within the context of sentencing, Farrington and Morris (1983) came to the conclusion that the apparently more lenient sentences handed out to female offenders were explained by their having fewer previous convictions, and committing less serious offences. On the other hand, Allen (1987) found that women were treated more sympathetically than men when they had committed more serious violent offences.

A number of studies had indicated the particular stereotypes involving non-deviant lifestyles and culturally prescribed family roles that influenced sentencing decisions. Eaton (1986) argued that both men and women who appeared to conform to conventional standards of 'normality' were more likely to benefit from a lighter sentence. Research by Daly (1989) in the United States supported this, pointing in particular to the benefits of having children and apparently stable family relationships. Carlen's (1983) study of Scottish Sheriffs underlined the more punitive responses to those women defined as 'failed mothers'. On the theme of leniency, feminists who have researched the area of domestic violence have argued that violent male partners have traditionally enjoyed a high degree of leniency by the courts (e.g. Dobash and Dobash, 1979, 1992).

In a study of the women of Greenham Common peace camp, Young (1990) drew out two particularly relevant issues. First, that the police and the courts were here dealing with women who were not involved in run-of-the-mill 'ordinary' crime, and were themselves defined as 'unconventional' (with a media campaign of degradation). Second, that an analysis of sentencing decisions has to get behind mere surface appearances. The Greenham women who found themselves in court could potentially have been charged with a broad range of offences, and the choices made reflected the wide discretionary powers of the police (and later on the Crown Prosecution Service). As Young says, on the whole the women were charged with minor offences carrying light sentences. This 'chivalrous' response was seen as resulting from the desire of the courts to maintain a good public image, an image that would have been threatened if many prison sentences were handed out. According to Young, though, there were other considerations at work. One was that the courts were concerned that if Greenham women were imprisoned, they would continue their campaigning within the prison. Furthermore, in some cases the seriousness of the offence was such that defendants could have opted for a jury trial. This was seen as providing the women with dangerous publicity, and consequently the tendency was to charge them with lesser offences. However, Young (1990: 24) does acknowledge that in some cases very severe sentences were passed by the courts:

> Thus, the response of the criminal justice agencies has combined trivialisation with severe criminalisation. Despite the attempts of women to retain some control of the situation through disruption of court procedure and through the positive use of the

law as litigants, it would appear that the legal system has lent itself most profitably to the aims of the 'authorities'.

Finally, Matthews (1981) pointed out that if chivalry was a significant feature of British courtroom justice for women, then those women who were given custodial sentences must have been found guilty of particularly serious crimes. In fact, the majority of female prisoners were in prison for non-payment of fines or stealing.

Imprisonment

As many writers have observed, in a society such as ours, males are, in a sense, 'allowed' to behave in 'deviant' ways much more than females are: that is, certain activities, such as fighting, have traditionally been associated with masculine values. Thus female offenders are more likely to be viewed as doubly deviant, in that they have committed some offence *and* deviated from cultural expectations regarding 'feminine' behaviour. Especially important in this context are dominant understandings of female roles within the family. It is against this cultural backdrop that the imprisonment of women has to be understood. Dobash, Dobash and Gutteridge (1986), for example, expressed the view that the rehabilitative ideal figures much more prominently for women than it does for men, with rehabilitation strongly shaped by notions of domesticity. Zedner (1991) argued that as a result, women tend to experience prison regimes that are designed to foster dependency status and received understandings of 'femininity', with less emphasis placed on learning useful skills for use in the world outside. Studies such as those by Carlen (1983) and Dobash *et al.* (1986) continued to stress the relative lack of educational and recreational facilities for women prisoners. However, more recent studies of women in prison, especially in the United States, documented certain improvements with respect to family visits and styles of regime.

Studies of the effects of imprisonment on women (e.g., Carlen, 1985) suggested that it is more traumatising and generates more resentment than is the case with men. Partly because of this: 'A high proportion of women are charged with disciplinary offences, doses of tranquillizers prescribed are higher, and there is a significant incidence of self-mutilation' (Heidensohn, 1994: 1021). In Carlen's (1990) view, there should be an end to the imprisonment of women, except for a small number who commit the more serious offences.

Victimisation

Feminist research on women and children as victims of male violence had grown enormously since the beginning of the 1980s. This was paralleled by the growth of a broadly based 'victim movement' and the development of a field of research known as victimology. Studies of victims had been around in criminology for some time – the term 'victimology' was first introduced by an American psychiatrist, Wertham (1949), though the most important early work is credited to another American, Von Hentig (1948). (For good reviews of this field see Walklate, 1989, and Zedner, 1994.) Contemporary research on the theme of victimology, though, and especially feminist research, had been critical of the narrow social–psychological focus of the earlier work, and its emphasis on 'victim precipitation', which many have criticised for blaming the victim. Interest in crime victims during the 1980s and early 1990s, it should be noted, encompasses both academic research and campaigning or pressure group activities such as those associated with Victim Support.

Research by feminists on women as victims of crime, already building up in the 1970s, had a particularly strong influence on developments in the field. This, more than any other area perhaps, illustrated the impact of feminist perspectives in criminology. Left realists, for instance, acknowledged the debt that they owed to this work, as this comment indicates:

> Women bear the brunt of crime. For a long time it was supposed that they were irrational about crime, having, according to official statistics, a high fear of crime compared to men, but in reality a much lower chance of being victims . . . women are, in fact, more likely to be victims of crime than men.
>
> (Lea *et al.*, 1987: 15)

The dominant message from feminist research was that very large amounts of interpersonal violence, where the victims are women, had remained hidden from view. Thus official information had distorted actual patterns of victimisation, and criminology had failed to recognise that the fear of crime expressed by women was a reflection of their real experiences. Furthermore, when violence towards women did come to the attention of criminal justice agencies, and in particular the police, responses were less than satisfactory. One of the main complaints was that the police were reluctant to treat domestic violence in the same way that they treated other forms of assault, especially assaults by strangers (Dobash and Dobash, 1979; Stanko, 1985; Edwards, 1986). Up until the second half of the 1980s, when police attitudes and policies began to change, research pointed to a tendency for the police to categorise cases of domestic violence as 'family disputes'. In fact, Dobash and Dobash (1979) in their study of domestic violence in Scotland, found that only 2 per cent of women victims reported their assaults to the police; the rest went to friends or relatives for support. Of the women who pursued a prosecution, only a small minority – 6 per cent – subsequently dropped the complaint. This is important in that police officers very often argued against prosecution on the grounds that victims of domestic violence usually drop their complaint. In the case of victims of rape and sexual assault, there have been significant changes in police responses since the 1980s, partly as a result of bad publicity and partly as a result of a body of research highly critical of the police. As Brogden, Jefferson and Walklate (1988: 121) put it:

> These police attitudes reflect a victim precipitation view of such incidents, one which sees the victim's behaviour as being responsible for inviting a sexual response. This has been translated in the courts as 'contributory negligence'.

Because of its nature, it is not surprising that the interpersonal violence experienced by women has been largely unrecorded by official crime statistics. Although victim surveys were introduced to bring unrecorded crime to light, in the case of female victimisation they have not always been successful. The large-scale sweeps of the *British Crime Surveys*, for instance, have been notably unsuccessful. One reason is that because *British Crime Surveys* are householder-based, it is quite possible for victims of violence to be sitting next to their assailants when answering the questionnaire. Smaller, localised surveys appear to have overcome some of these difficulties, though feminists have preferred more intense ethnographic studies. As Zedner (1994: 1215) pointed out with reference to sexual assaults:

> The first two British Crime Surveys revealed only one (unreported) case of attempted rape and seventeen and eighteen cases of sexual assault respectively in the 1983 and 1985 reports . . . In stunning contrast, the first Islington Crime Survey estimated 1,200 cases of sexual assault in Islington during the period under review.

Stanko (1988) was critical of victim surveys such as these because they usually asked respondents to give details of their victimisation over the past twelve months. She argued that it is more satisfactory to follow the example set by the American research of Russell (1982), where women were not tied to a short time span, but were asked about their experiences over a lifetime. This, says Stanko, would allow surveys to be sensitive to the long-term effects of violence, and its impact on daily routines. In her sample of nearly 1,000 women, Russell found that 22 per cent had been raped at some time in their life, and a further 22 per cent had experienced an attempted rape.

British feminist studies had produced quite large variations in the number of women admitting to having been raped or sexually assaulted. Hall (1985) found that one-third of the women surveyed had in their lifetime been raped or sexually assaulted. Asking women about their experiences over the past twelve months, Hanmer and Saunders (1984) discovered that 59 per cent of respondents had been sexually assaulted, whilst in Radford's (1987) research the figure was 76 per cent. These variations will partly be explained by researcher's and respondent's definitions of these terms, and everyday understandings may not correspond with legal definitions. In fact, one of the important contributions made by feminist writers has been to show how legal categories will probably be incapable of capturing a woman's real experience of male intimidation and aggression; for example:

> Sexual harassment of women on the street is one form of intimidation. Ranging from leers to physical touching (and in some cases actual assault), sexual harassment reminds women that they are and can be targets for sexual assaults. It creates a climate of unsafety.
>
> (Stanko, 1988: 45)

Anderson *et al.*'s study of school-age children in Edinburgh, published in the early 1990s, shed some light on the extent to which children, and especially girls, experienced harassment by adults. Although often defined as frightening by the children, many of these incidents would not *per se* be categorised as criminal:

> For girls, the most common forms of adult harassment were being stared at (32%), being followed on foot (27%) and being 'asked things' (26%). For boys the most common were being asked things (17%) and being threatened (15%). Overall 52% [of] the girls had been harassed in some way during the previous nine months by an adult as had 36% of boys.
>
> (Anderson *et al.*, 1991: 155)

In addition to this, 17 per cent of the girls (compared with 4 per cent of the boys) had experienced men trying to 'touch them', and 12 per cent (4 per cent boys) had experienced indecent exposure by men.

Large-scale victim surveys tended not to pick up examples of domestic violence; however, small-scale local surveys were more successful. The first *Islington Crime Survey*, for instance, found that nearly one-quarter of all assaults took place within the home. From research into domestic violence it is clear that in the bulk of cases the victims are women. Out of the nearly 1,000 respondents in Dobash and Dobash's study, there were only ten cases where a wife had assaulted her husband; in three-quarters of the cases a husband had assaulted his wife. Worrall and Pease (1986) and Mawby (1987) have shown that in most cases of assaults on women their assailant is known to them, and this creates pressure not to inform the police. Stanko (1985) argued that further pressure from friends and neighbours to keep these events private, combined with the victim's apprehension about how the police will respond, helped to create a situation where violence in the home remained concealed.

GENDER AND CRIME

As we have seen, during the 1960s and 1970s, attempts to develop feminist perspectives within the discipline of criminology involved various critiques of existing criminology. Earlier criminology was criticised for the 'distortion' of women in analyses; later criminology for the 'neglect' of women. In an effort to remedy the situation, this was followed by research that focused specifically on female criminals and their experiences of the criminal justice system. A further development was to examine the issue of patriarchy and the social control of women, thus giving prominence to the question, 'why do women not break the law?' Research carried out in the 1980s and early 1990s, while acknowledging the important contribution made by those feminist writers who have helped redress the gender balance by addressing the theme of women, crime and criminal justice, had shifted the nature of the debate by stressing that the label 'gender and crime' should not be read, as it sometimes was, to mean women and crime. In other words, feminist work began to look at issues of criminality and social control from the point of view of men and women, in addition to continuing to challenge both the view that the criminal justice system is gender neutral and, on a broader level, the male assumptions underpinning discourses in the social sciences (for a detailed review see Walklate, 1995).

Brown (1986) pointed out that one of the dangers associated with equating gender and crime with women and crime is that a bifurcated, two-tier criminology was created, where (feminist) women are left to study women, and (non-feminist) men carry on studying men. In this situation, she argued, feminist research and ideas would become marginalised because men would continue to study the 'real' criminals, more or less immune from feminist critiques. This is likely to perpetuate the assumption made by mainstream criminology (sometimes referred to as 'malestream' – the penchant for puns among some feminist writers has been noted by Carlen, 1992) that although female offenders were neglected, analyses of male criminality were veracious. This was one of the reasons why feminist writing began to explore the concept of masculinity, or, more accurately, masculini*ties*.

Masculinities and crime

It is certainly the case that criminology has traditionally homed in on male rather than female offenders, and in the process often made reference to what are seen as essential masculine attributes: for example, toughness, daring and 'machismo'. Strong criticisms of this body of work have surfaced in feminist writing (as an aside, it should be noted that feminist writing does not necessarily come from the pens, or word processors, of women):

- Although based on research into male offenders, explanations of male criminal behaviour within mainstream criminology had, paradoxically, been put forward as explanations of criminal behaviour in general. Thus male criminality was equated with human criminality.

- Mainstream criminology had not problematised notions of femininity and masculinity. Analyses had tended to view femininity and masculinity as polar opposites, conceptualised around normative ideal types. Feminists argued that analyses should be sensitive to the different understandings and expressions of 'femininity' and 'masculinity' found within the same society. This is part of a critique of what is called essentialism, which is seeing the world in terms of two fundamentally different genders, each the product of universal and irreducible biological and/or socio-cultural factors.
- Mainstream criminology had failed to explore gender relationships in terms of structured relationships based upon both difference and power.
- There was insufficient appreciation of the multiplicity of socio-cultural contexts in which men and women construct their understandings of what it means to be a 'man' and a 'woman'. This requires a consideration of those factors (for example, poverty, a lack of respect, the mass media) that impact on men and women in gender-specific ways, as well as other situations where variables such as class, 'race' and age may be equally, or more, relevant.
- Little attention had been given to the actual ways in which groups and individuals via their interactions and interpretations of the social world come to understand themselves as men and women. Although acknowledging that men and women are caught up in wider structures and ideological forces pertaining to notions of 'proper' male and female behaviour, feminist writers rejected deterministic theories in favour of those that allow individuals some freedom to make choices. As far as crime was concerned, this, as Jefferson (1993) argues, allows the idea of pleasure (derived from, for instance, the risk involved, the approval of the group, or the behaviour in itself) as well as mere opportunity, to be introduced into the reckoning.

What should be obvious from even the above brief discussion is that feminist work on the theme of gender had stimulated highly complex theoretical debates that are central not just to sociological criminology, but to sociology in general. Unlike a large amount of criminological research which had, during the first half of the 1990s, concentrated on narrower questions linked to social policy, feminism had opened up a space within which deeper theoretical questions were addressed. Thus although the impact on policy and the criminological project may have been limited, resources were available for the development of a feminist theoretical discourse.

The causes of crime

Much criminology then (and now) was implicitly or explicitly, concerned with attempting to fathom the causes of crime. However, any attempt to uncover the salient causal factors associated with criminal behaviour will, to understate the case rather, have to grapple with a complex web of variables. At the same time certain variables may appear to operate at the level of causation, when they in fact can only be understood as correlations. Lombroso, for example, found that male criminals very often had tattoos; clearly, tattoos do not cause crime, no more than, on a different level, being unemployed or male causes crime.

For feminism a central issue had been the extent to which gender can be prioritised as a variable when explaining criminal behaviour, and reactions to that behaviour on the part of the criminal justice system. Put another way, what is the relative importance of gender compared to other variables such as class, 'race' and age? Before we examine this in a little more detail it should also be noted that criminology, of course, still has to cope with the ever-present difficulty that 'crime' is not an absolute behavioural category, and 'criminals'/'non-criminals' do not exist as two discrete types of human being. It may be reasonable for a criminologist to take an interest in, say, male violence in the street or in a domestic setting on the grounds that it causes human misery, or, if directed against women, on the grounds that it is an expression of patriarchy and is therefore of theoretical interest as well. However, male (and female) violence occurs at many levels and takes many forms, and sometimes is not actually criminal. This transports us back into the realms of ideology and the moral evaluation of harmfulness, and so forth, and reminds us that violence in the form of oppression or terror may be carried out on behalf of big business or the state.

As Walklate (1995: 161) pointed out:

> The literature on masculinity has increased markedly in recent years. However, whilst an increasing number of both academic and media commentators have endeavoured to draw attention to the relationship between maleness and crime, little work . . . has applied these developments systematically to either criminology or victimology.

As a result, discussions of masculinities and crime drew on a broader range of sources than those that are, strictly speaking, criminological in nature. One writer who specifically discussed the relationship between maleness and criminal behaviour was Grosz (1987), and she was not alone in putting forward the view that the problem of crime is fundamentally the problem of men. A similar position was taken by Campbell (1993: 319), who argued that: 'Crime and coercion are sustained by men'. Huge amounts of research in Britain and the United States, as well as the picture painted by official statistics, did little to contradict this kind of assertion, especially with respect to violent crime. Victim surveys underlined the fact that the fear of crime among women was largely the fear of male crime. In general, women did not expect to have their homes burgled by other women; or to have their cars stolen and raced around an estate by girls; or to be attacked in the home or on the street by other women. Importantly, and sometimes forgotten in this context, men too fear crime carried out by men. It is this fear that encourages individuals to join Neighbourhood Watch schemes, buy extra bolts for their doors and give considerable attention to how they manage their lives in terms of risk avoidance. As an example, residents in any town who wish to stay clear of trouble on a Saturday night usually know which pubs and other public spaces to avoid. Conversely, of course, there will be those who actively seek out such places, and because the police will also have this local knowledge, elements of a self-fulfilling prophesy may be present. Significantly, though, all parties will be aware that any trouble is likely to involve men, usually young men, and that drinking is heavily implicated. However, many men will avoid these places, and there will be pubs where, in spite of heavy drinking, trouble rarely occurs. Clearly, there is no simple causal connection between being male and, say, fighting. None the less, the much greater likelihood that it will be men rather than women who end up fighting has to be taken seriously.

Power

Feminism had stressed that gender relations are based on power rather than mere 'difference'. Thus, gender relations were not conceptualised simply in terms of socialisation processes through which men and women learn their respective masculine/feminine roles according to the particular culture. Not only did this 'role playing' model tend to stereotype and polarise gender divisions, it also ignored the existence of power, thereby sidestepping issues of inequality and oppression; men and women were characterised as different but equal.

A large amount of research had shown that 'women's crimes are the crimes of the powerless' (Carlen, 1992: 52; see also Messerschmidt, 1986; Worrall, 1990). In the case of men, much research, and especially that of a radical tradition, had suggested 'that the powerful (in both the gender and class spheres) do the most criminal damage to society' (Messerschmidt, 1986: 56). In his analyses of masculinity and crime, Messerschmidt argued that the power deriving from an integration of gender and class provided men with much greater opportunities than women to engage in corporate and white-collar crime. At the same time, the opportunity to commit different sorts of crime is distributed unequally among men: 'Just as the powerful have more legitimate opportunities, they also have more illegitimate opportunities' (ibid.: 56).

An important dimension to Messerschmidt's work was his discussion of the ways in which different men construct their own understandings of masculinity according to their 'access to power and resources' (ibid.: 119). These understandings are expressed in behavioural terms within three primary locations: the street, the place of work and the home. This type of approach, therefore, posited the existence of a range of masculinities, which find expression in various sorts of sometimes criminal behaviour, the nature of which will depend upon access to power and resources. Thus there is an attempt to pinpoint the continuities and discontinuities in masculine behaviour within a particular society. This is well summed up by Walklate (1995: 174):

> All of these accounts are offered as a means of demonstrating the ways in which men display their manliness to others and to themselves. So whilst the business executive might use his position and power to sexually harass his female secretary in perhaps more subtle ways than the pimp controls his women, the effects are both the same. In this particular example, the women concerned are subjugated and the men concerned are affirmed as normatively heterosexual men.

Walklate takes up a similar theme when she writes:

> Put simply, the following question should be asked: what makes the often rude and belligerent behaviour of the old boys' network of the House of Commons any different from the lads who shout, whistle and jostle hanging about on the street corner? The reply has to be very little. As expressions of masculine behaviour, the reply also has to be very little. What differs, of course, is their public and political acceptability.
>
> (Ibid.: 178)

This drew out the continuities in behavioural terms between the 'yob' on the street and the 'yob' in Parliament, yet also acknowledged the discontinuities because of differential access to power and resources. For Walklate these turned on public and political reactions. However, we have to recognise that the unwillingness to accept this behaviour when carried out on the street is often because of the fear that it might (as it sometimes does) escalate into violence; this is unlikely to occur in the House of Commons.

The discussion so far indicates that analyses of masculinity and crime need to consider the social contexts within which different men construct their understandings of masculinity, together with the opportunities available for law breaking. Furthermore, it is important to recognise that these social contexts will heighten the likelihood of *certain sorts* of offending and victimisation. For instance, young men living on tough housing estates, who have to use late-night public transport if they have a night out, are more likely to encounter and have to deal with threats of violence than those whose lives are more insulated (the victim studies carried out by Anderson *et al.*, 1991, and Hartless *et al.*, 1995, give an idea of the extent to which some young people have to cope with threats of violence).

In an influential study, the journalist Campbell (1993) addressed the theme of masculinity and crime among the least powerful men in our society. Focusing on a number of socially deprived housing estates that experienced outbreaks of rioting in 1991, Campbell examined the social contexts in which young men developed their understandings of masculinity. She noted that most analyses by the mass media and politicians concentrated on the familiar images of the 'underclass', lone female parents and undisciplined youngsters, but overlooked other important aspects. In particular, that the rioting involved young men, rather than women and, she argued, it was the young men on these estates who were responsible for the day-to-day crime and coercion. On the other hand, efforts to develop community-based projects, in the face of enormous difficulties (including a lack of support from central and local government and the police), mainly involved women. For Campbell, therefore, it was the women who made a positive effort to maintain a degree of stability and cohesion.

High levels of unemployment since the end of the 1970s had meant that a generation of young men had been denied the traditional working-class male anchor points of the workplace, the pub and the home. For an earlier generation of men, she argued, these provided the structures around which particular understandings of masculinity were developed. To a large extent traditional understandings of what it meant to be a 'proper man', based on the integrated roles of breadwinner, workmate and settled father, had been lost. These were replaced by new understandings shared by others who inhabited the same social space of the street. Rioting, burglary, car theft, and so on, had become ways of expressing this altered definition of manliness. From this perspective, their social situation offered few alternative sources of inspiration and strongly predisposed them to certain sorts of criminal behaviour. There were echoes here of Messerschmidt's argument, in that masculinity and crime are linked to the exercise of different types of power. Thus the possibilities regarding criminal activities will, for both men and women, be constrained by available opportunities. As Campbell pointed out, many of the young men living on Britain's run-down estates – 'dangerous places' as she calls them – can create fear. Some of them look and act tough, and intimidate so that witnesses are afraid to come forward, and yet, as the title of her book – *Goliath* – suggested, this power was severely circumscribed. Ultimately they met the power of the state, at which point other young men, in blue uniforms, will act out their own understandings of masculinity.

Campbell's work did not escape criticism, however. Some felt that it added fuel to a hard-line 'law and order' position which equated Britain's crime problem with the problem of a stereotypical 'yob culture' and 'underclass' (Coward, 1994; Walklate, 1995). Furthermore, a complete analysis of life in Britain's 'dangerous places' has to account for the existence of young men in a similar situation to those discussed above who do not riot, abandon their partners and children, carry out burglaries, or pick fights on a Saturday night. The emphasis on *constructing* masculinities implies some notion of choice and creativity and a corresponding rejection of determinism.

ADMINISTRATIVE CRIMINOLOGY

Administrative criminology was a product of research carried out by, or on behalf of, the Home Office, and in the 1980s superseded post-war liberal positivism and became 'the major paradigm in establishment approaches to crime' (Young, 1994: 91; for more detailed reviews see also Young, 1988; Downes and Rock, 1988; Roshier,

1989; Jefferson and Shapland, 1994). Clearly, as indicated in Chapter 12, this development has to be seen as part of more general social and political trends, and in particular within the context of the Conservative government's ideologies and policies.

Administrative criminology grew out of a critique of positivist-inclined attempts to discover the causes of criminality, whether pitched at the level of individual pathology, or at the level of socio-cultural factors. These approaches were not criticised for being 'wrong', so much as for failing to deliver the goods in terms of manageable explanations. Administrative criminology provided an alternative, and what is seen as a more realistic approach to crime, by focusing on its prevention rather than its causes. Thus even if causal connections (or correlations) were established between, say, deprivation and certain forms of criminality, the magnitude of the problem is so great that solutions would require sweeping social transformations, and the political will to carry them through. Administrative criminology argued that it is better to concentrate on more manageable crime control activities (for examples of this argument see Clarke and Mayhew, 1980; Clarke, 1980, 1984, 1992; Cornish and Clarke, 1986a, 1986b). Looked at from this perspective, administrative criminology clearly *was* 'realistic' – but it does raise the issue of what criminology as an academic discipline is for. This version was situated within a fairly narrow framework, where the primary concern is with the prevention of crime rather than the construction of broader criminological theory. Debates about, for instance, free will versus determinism were left off the agenda because they were made irrelevant. So too were fundamental theoretical questions pertaining to the nature of law and the role of the state in defining criminal behaviour and so on – certainly, whether or not Maradona did commit a foul was singularly irrelevant.

Administrative criminology modestly addressed issues of situational crime control, that is, those measures that can be taken at a local level; for example, surveillance cameras, better house and shop security, Neighbourhood Watch, and the like. To some extent there are links here with the classical school of criminology, in that the aim is to deter people from committing offences. There are also links with control theory given the central concern with factors that prevent law breaking. However, in each case there are important dissimilarities. For classicism, deterrence was seen as a function of the punishment handed out by the criminal justice system, whereas for administrative criminology deterrence was situationally based within the neighbourhood. In the case of Hirschi's control theory, the focus was on those controls that prevent individuals from being disposed to break the law, whilst administrative criminology focuses on those controls that prevent individuals breaking the law irrespective of their dispositions:

> This narrowing down of the focus of the original control theory seems to constitute a switch of attention from *offenders* to *situations*. Offenders are assumed to make rational choices . . . Consequently, the offenders are not important; what matters is that

opportunities must be reduced and risks increased and this requires that attention be given to the situations in which offences may occur.

(Roshier, 1989: 49)

Furthermore, as Young (1994) pointed out, although administrative criminology did draw on the notion of rational choice, as classical criminology did, there was a recognition that individuals were subject to various constraints that limited their rationality when making decisions. In fact, a major strand of administrative criminology as it developed came to be known as rational choice theory. Here the focus of attention is on the practical measures that can be taken to prevent a criminal event occurring, in other words, to make crime irrational by employing appropriate situational crime prevention strategies (for a useful overview of this field, see Crawford, 2007). Over the years rational choice theorists have refined and extended the list of strategies; most recently, Cornish and Clarke (2003) have identified the following (with each referenced against a potential offender's perception):

- Increasing the effort involved in committing crime (e.g. bars on windows, alarm systems).
- Increasing the risk of apprehension (e.g. CCTV, security personnel).
- Reducing the rewards of crime (e.g. systems for disabling electronic goods, policing distribution networks).
- Reducing the provocation to commit crime (e.g. polite staff in bars, cleaning up graffiti).
- Removing any possible excuses (e.g. publicising rules clearly, limiting alcohol consumption).

This work led to the introduction of a wide range of practical measures (including, notably, CCTV systems in the UK) aimed at the prevention, or at least reduction, of crime, which in turn stimulated a large number of 'does it work?' evaluative studies. One of the major themes to emerge from these studies concerned the issue of displacement (or deflection, see Pease, 2002). Hakim and Rengert (1981) suggest five different types of crime displacement:

- *Spatial displacement*, where the crime still occurs, but in an alternative location.
- *Temporal displacement*, where the crime occurs, but at a different time.
- *Tactical displacement*, where the crime occurs, but different methods are used.
- *Target displacement*, where the crime occurs in the same place, but with a different target.
- *Type of crime displacement*, where the crime occurs in the same place, but it involves a different type of crime to the one originally planned.

The underlying premise is that offenders make, or at least seek to make, rational choices when deciding whether or not to commit an offence. For critics, though, this is the 'fiction of economic man' (Rock, 2007: 16), that is, a crude understanding of behaviour that ignores an individual's social and psychological past and present, and views them as simply 'making decisions around the issues of risk, effort and reward' (ibid.: 16). Cultural criminologists (see the final chapter of this book) have been especially critical of this notion of coldly calculated decision-making, and argue that much offending behaviour is motivated by a desire to take risks, rather than avoid them. In these cases, the deterrence value of situational crime prevention measures becomes problematic. This raises a further important issue relating to the notion of rational choice. As rational choice theorists themselves acknowledge, the decision to engage in crime will be informed by the offender's subjective understanding of what is 'rational' and, therefore, the corollary of this is that some choices may be defined by an outside observer as utterly irrational. If this is the case, then it begs the question of how, when devising crime prevention measures based upon the idea of making crime irrational, is the rational choice theorist to know how potential offenders define what is rational?

Routine activity theory is another major strand of administrative criminology and the key figure here is the American Marcus Felson (Cohen and Felson, 1979; Felson, 1986, 1987, 2000). In a similar fashion to rational choice theory, routine activity theory does not concern itself with the original sources of criminal motivations, but focuses instead on practical crime prevention initiatives. It is also similar to rational choice theory in that there is an assumption that offenders make rational decisions in relation to risks, effort, rewards and opportunities. One important difference, however, is that unlike rational choice theory, which is oriented towards situational crime control, routine activity theory is interested in the relationship between criminal behaviour, seen as mundane and highly opportunistic, and the routines of everyday social life involving the family, shopping, work, leisure, etc. According to routine activity theory, these activities provide the context within which criminal opportunities arise. The theory is particularly associated with the argument that these opportunities result from the coming together of three crucial factors:

- A motivated offender
- A suitable target
- A lack of a capable guardian

Later on, Felson added a fourth factor to the list:

- An intimate handler (someone capable of restraining a motivated offender)

There are significant overlaps between this and Garofalo's (1987) work on the correlation between particular lifestyles and the chances of becoming a victim of crime. Proponents of routine activity theory see crime rises in the United States and elsewhere from the 1950s onwards as a function of increasing affluence combined with changes in the routine activities of everyday life. Thus they argue that such things as a growth in portable consumer goods and more unattended houses (due, for instance, to rises in the number of women working outside the home) led to an increase in criminal opportunities. As with rational choice theory and, indeed, administrative criminology in general, routine activity theory has been criticised for ignoring the causal factors leading to certain individuals being disposed, or motivated, to commit crime in the first place, except in the sense that there are more opportunities and fewer risks. These approaches have also been criticised for ignoring white-collar and corporate crime – though Alvesalo *et al.* (2006) suggest that the work of situational crime prevention theorists can be utilised in the control of corporate crime.

Administrative criminology is, *par excellence,* a representative of what Garland (1994) called the 'governmental project' within criminology. This is apparent in two important and interrelated respects:

1 It was entirely congruent with the Conservative government's commitment to what was described as efficiency and effectiveness and 'value for money' in the public sector, and also with the view of the public as 'consumers' of criminal justice services:

> Consumerism has also had a certain pay-off economically. If the costs of controlling a rising crime rate were apparently spiraling out of reach, demonstrating consumer satisfaction might just prove a more feasible (cheaper) alternative. Similarly, crime prevention initiatives which involved the community – the advent of which paralleled the new victim focus – were cheaper and maybe even more effective than increasing police establishments.
>
> (Jefferson and Shapland, 1994: 274)

2 It also provided a type of criminological theorising that could be used to counteract criticism of the government's 'law and order' record as measured by rises in amounts of recorded crime since 1980. In particular, the government had consistently resisted suggestions that rising crime was connected to economic recession and increasing gaps between rich and poor (for a review, see Box, 1987; and for a less accommodating example of Home Office research on this theme, see Field, 1990).

A key element of this symbiotic relationship between administrative criminology and government was the introduction of national victim-based studies through the Home Office *British Crime Surveys*. Gaining the approval of the government for the first survey at the beginning of the 1980s required some cogent arguments from the Home Office researchers, illustrating that all 'rational decision making' takes place within specific contexts. From the government's point of view the difficulty was that similar victim-based surveys carried out in the United States and other countries had, because of the 'dark figure' of crime, brought to light much more crime than was shown in official criminal statistics. The obvious worry was that this would both reflect badly on the government and lead to increased fears about crime. Although the research value of a national victim survey was to many self-evident because of the knowledge it would generate, its political utility had to be considered too. As it happened, Home Office researchers argued convincingly that although surveys in other countries had exposed large amounts of 'hidden' crime, all subsequent surveys, carried out at regular intervals and allowing trends to be plotted, had shown that crime was increasing at a *lower* rate than shown by official criminal statistics. This, indeed, was the case with the *British Crime Surveys* during the 1980s – however, the predictions were confounded for the period 1991–93 when, for the first time, acquisitive crime as measured by the *British Crime Survey* increased at a faster rate than indicated by official, police-generated figures (though the opposite was true for violent crime).

Concerns about the first *British Crime Survey* increasing the fear of crime among the public was reflected in the extraordinary statistical gymnastics used to allay any fear. Although (as predicted) things looked bad, we were told that they were not really *that* bad, and helpful comparisons were provided between the chances of being burgled or robbed and the chances (apparently much greater) of being certified as insane, or having one's house burn down. A further point about victim surveys is that they focus attention on the range of conventional crime, where householders are aware that they have been victimised, at the expense of corporate crime, and fail to pick up on sexual crime and domestic violence where women are the chief victims.

On a more complex level, administrative criminology had political utility because of its emphasis on the *crime* rather than the *criminal*. Rising levels of recorded crime were largely explained as being a function of police effectiveness and recording policies, coupled with the greater willingness of the public to report crime (due, for instance, to Neighbourhood Watch schemes). With the spotlight on situational crime control, crime was characterised as opportunistic, and the requirement, therefore, was to reduce opportunities for crime, through better locks, surveillance cameras, improved street lighting, and so forth. The assumption seemed to be that a more or less constant proportion of the population is always at the ready to commit 'conventional' crime, though why they should be motivated to break the law in the first place is irrelevant. For administrative criminology the trick is to close down opportunities available for law breaking. Along with other criminologies that became popular in the 1980s and 1990s, administrative criminology represented an impatient reaction to earlier social democratic approaches that saw their central task as one of illuminating the socio-cultural or psychological bases of criminality. It thus offered a theoretical framework that could seemingly deflect critical analyses of rising crime, to some extent blame the public for a lack of community vigilance, and obviate any need to consider the causes of criminal behaviour.

RIGHT-WING CLASSICISM

As with administrative criminology, right-wing classicism had a pedigree that went back to the classical school of criminology of the eighteenth century, and was associated with the growth of the New Right in Britain and the United States (although there are some differences in emphases: for an overview of New Right criminology, see Tame, 1991). There was, therefore, an insistence on free will and personal responsibility for one's actions. Attempts to explain criminal behaviour in terms of socio-cultural or psychological factors were rejected if they carried any suggestion that the individual was not to blame. Thus although the notion of an 'underclass' was important, with particular disapprobation being reserved for lone-parent families (Murray, 1990), such things as unemployment, poverty and deprivation were seen as products of the 'culture of poverty'. In other words, there is a repudiation of liberal democratic approaches linking certain forms of criminality to deprivation, and seeing those involved as victims of wider social and political structures. For right-wing classicists, these formulations had permeated social scientific thought and become part of the 'excuse making industry'. In this respect, social work was seen as being particularly culpable, and notions of rehabilitation were treated with some distaste (e.g., Morgan, 1978, 1981). Discussions of corporate, white-collar and state-level crime were left off the agenda. The chief source of criminal behaviour was seen to be the underclass, along with elements of a so-called 'yob culture', such as 'lager louts' who, like the underclass, had seemingly had their minds polluted with 'permissiveness' and 'moral relativism'. Under these circumstances, it was argued, crime control must proceed along two broad fronts. First, there was a need to instil self-discipline into those sections of society at fault, and this should involve a programme of moral education. Second, in view of the perceived failure of the rehabilitative model, the penal system should be used as a deterrent and as the basis for retribution; if individuals are responsible for their actions, then there should be no qualms about punishing them.

This view of crime and crime control harmonised well with common-sense understandings, and was incorporated into the popularist political ideology of Prime Minister Thatcher:

> The more orthodox conceptions of crime are broadly accepted and prioritized by the criminal justice agencies, mainstream politicians, the news media, Hollywood and other organs of popular culture. These social institutions legitimate each others' notions of what crime is, and which crimes are most worthy of attention, in mutually reinforcing and self-fulfilling circles.
>
> (Stenson, 1991: 9)

There were, however, 'libertarian' and 'conservative' versions of right-wing classicism. As Tame (1991) said, right-wing libertarianism covered a spectrum of thought from types of anarchy to that associated with nineteenth-century liberalism (when 'liberal' had a different meaning to the meaning that it has today). Unlike in the United States, right-wing libertarianism had lacked credibility within academic criminology in Britain (but see Davies, 1987, 1991). One of its hallmarks was a commitment to an unfettered, free-market economy, and a non-interventionist, though strong, central state. Not surprisingly, therefore, there was much enthusiasm for the privatisation of criminal justice agencies. There was also a belief in the idea of 'natural rights', and the freedom of the individual to pursue any actions providing that they do not harm others. This led to right-libertarian support for the decriminalisation of illicit drug use and pornography, and in the United States a vociferous defence of the citizen's right to own a firearm.

Conservative versions of right-wing classicism were less indulgent regarding these freedoms, and stressed the need for the state to intervene via the law in order to achieve social tranquillity, even at the expense of justice (see van den Haag, 1975, 1985). Efforts were made to mobilise the community around posited traditional moral values. In addition, and in a classical spirit, there was an emphasis on deterrence through punishment. This overlapped with the work of a number of right-wing economists, who had turned their attention to crime and crime control. Essentially, this has meant applying economic models based upon rational choice ('econometric' models) to crime. From this perspective, engaging in crime was the same as engaging in business-oriented behaviour and, following the classical school, the prevention of crime had to proceed on the basis of deterrence; that is, choosing crime had to be made irrational. In the United States, Posner's (1986) econometric approach to the analysis of law was particularly influential.

All of these right-wing classicists were united in the desire to deter criminal behaviour by having strong punishments available. In a critical discussion, Lilly *et al*. (1989: 200–1) make the point:

> For the most part, these commentators have focused on how increased punishment – scaring people straight – will reduce crime. It is instructive that these theorists have overlooked how increasing the rewards of conformity (e.g. more lucrative employment) can achieve similar gains in crime control.

NEO-POSITIVISM AND RIGHT REALISM

Broadly speaking, criminologies under this heading could be placed into two separate 'schools'. They each continued a positivist tradition, and also contained elements of control theory, but one was associated with the New Right, whilst the other contained a wide range of academic criminologists committed to what they saw as the scientific study of criminality.

New Right neo-positivism was particularly associated with James Wilson and Richard Herrnstein (1985) (see also Wilson, 1975). Their approach has also been labelled 'right realism', 'new realism' and 'neo-conservative' (Wilson was for a spell an adviser to the Reagan administration) and represented a rejection of the liberal democratic belief that welfare-oriented social reform will significantly reduce the crime rate. Needless to say, radical solutions based upon a total transformation of American society along socialist lines were also rejected. Interestingly, though, they agreed that major transformations would be required if crime rates were to be reduced to low levels, but rejected this scenario on the grounds that it would also bring with it a loss of freedoms, which they saw as worth preserving, even at the cost of more crime. As they saw it, the liberal policies introduced in the 1960s (poverty programmes, for instance) did not lead to lower crime rates; in fact, crime continued to rise, even though the United States was becoming more affluent. Crime for them did not result from social inequality. Rather, it was connected to the growth of 'permissiveness', and a 'dependency culture' among those existing on welfare benefits. Wilson and Herrnstein's 'realism' derived from a view that governments should seek to make modest, manageable, gains as far as crime control is concerned. 'Crime', for them, however, meant street crime (including burglary): they admitted that they were not concerned with other types of offences.

Wilson and Herrnstein's approach to criminality involved a complex interplay between social conditions and individualised constitutional factors. Thus they discussed the importance of children being properly socialised in the family so that they develop a conscience which leads them to reject criminal behaviour. This stress on social conditioning was combined with the argument that the deterrent effect of imprisonment will only operate if there is a strong certainty of being caught. However, they also introduced a biological dimension by arguing that some individuals are born with 'character defects', and this makes socialisation into law-abiding behaviour difficult: 'Crime cannot be understood without taking into account predispositions and their biological roots' (Wilson and Herrnstein, 1985: 103). They also drew on earlier criminological work linking criminality to body shape.

> It is also worth noting that a decade later, Herrnstein and Murray (1994) argued in their book *The Bell Curve* that black people and Latinos were, when compared with white people, handicapped by having lower, genetically-determined IQs, hence, according to the authors, their over-representation within the so called underclass and their greater propensity to engage in criminal behaviour. Clearly, these arguments proved, to put it mildly, to be controversial. Needless to say, the authors are neither black nor Latino. (Tierney, 2009)

Although Wilson's bio-social theory of the causes of criminality can be placed within a positivist tradition, he also produced work, with Kelling, which reflected the concerns of classicism, in that it was specifically oriented towards the issue of crime prevention and, in fact, was to have a significant influence on the subsequent development of administrative criminology. In combination, these two aspects of his work came to be known as right realism. What, from the point of view of its supporters, made this bundle of work 'realistic' was that as well as explaining why some individuals commit crime, it also put forward practicable policies aimed at controlling crime. Wilson and Kelling (1982, see also 1989) focused their attention on those economically and socially deprived neighbourhoods caught up in a seemingly inexorable downward spiral into serious problems of crime and disorder. In such neighbourhoods, a variety of interrelated factors conspire to create a gradual descent into chaos. A lack of close family and community bonds weakens informal processes of social control; respectable residents increasingly keep themselves to themselves, or, where possible, leave the neighbourhood; anti-social behaviour and low-level crime increases; an increasing number of 'disreputable' people – the homeless, alcoholics, drug users and, eventually, serious criminals – move into the area; and alongside all of this, the signs of physical deterioration become more and more pronounced. According to Wilson and Kelling, unless action is taken to halt this downward spiral, such neighbourhoods will inevitably become high crime areas. At the core of their argument was, famously, the notion of 'broken windows', a metaphor used to encapsulate the gradual, and highly visible, physical deterioration associated with the processes described above: boarded up doors, graffiti, litter, abandoned vehicles, run-down green areas and, of course, broken windows. Action should be taken, they said, before a neighbourhood reached the point of no return, and should be directed at 'mending broken windows', in other words, eradicating the outward signs of crime, disorder and neglect. The police were seen as having a particularly important role to play. Wilson and Kelling argued for a shift away from crime fighting to order maintenance based upon zero-tolerance policing (of marginalised 'disreputable' people), which they believed would ultimately strengthen community ties and encourage residents to once again become actively involved in maintaining a well-kept physical environment.

Three main criticisms of Wilson and Kelling's work can be noted. First, they avoid an analysis of the structural contexts and processes explaining the existence of homeless people, drug users, alcoholics and predatory criminals. Second, there is no discussion of what will happen to such people in areas where windows have been mended and an area reclaimed by 'respectable' people. Third, there are important issues regarding how to respond to those neighbourhoods that have apparently deteriorated beyond the point of no return. From the perspective of right realism, there is only one course of action: hard law enforcement and punitive sentencing.

In a debate between Wilson and the liberal American criminologist Elliott Currie (reproduced in Stenson and Cowell, 1991) a number of important critical points were made by Currie that could be applied to a range of New Right criminology. In essence, Currie said that although Wilson's views, and the views of others on the right, may appeal to common sense, and be widely agreed with among the general population (especially as these views are often carried by the popular media), this did not mean that they were correct. Two elements of this critique will be briefly outlined.

Leniency and permissiveness

In common with other representatives of the New Right, Wilson saw individuals as weighing up the costs and benefits of crime. A frequent complaint was that in the United States during the post-war period the courts had become too lenient, and society in general had become too permissive. Currie accepted the view that as far as serious offenders were concerned, the police were not particularly efficient, and therefore the certainty of punishment was lacking. However, he argued that the accusation of leniency when offenders are brought to trial did not square with the fact that the United States had much higher rates of imprisonment than most other industrialised nations, and in most cases these other nations had lower crime rates. Furthermore, as the rate of imprisonment rose in the 1980s, so too did the crime rate. As far as general permissiveness was concerned, Currie (1991: 55) made the point that:

> in recent years . . . we were, again by comparison with many other advanced industrial countries, extraordinarily punitive in many of our cultural values and institutional practices – as evidenced by such things as our continued support for the death penalty – and for corporal punishment of the young.

Human nature

Currie also made the point that by seeing criminality as being connected to some immutable 'human nature', so that a certain proportion of the population will be resistant to 'proper' socialisation, Wilson ignored the links between criminality and general social conditions. Thus Wilson was unable to account for the different crime rates in different cities in the United States (where there will be varying levels of unemployment, deprivation, racism, and so on). At an international level, there were industrialised countries with relatively low levels of crime, for instance Denmark, Switzerland and Japan.

Neo-positivism and free will

After a period of anti-positivism resulting from a barrage of criticism from interactionism and conflict theory, since the 1980s there was a renewal of interest in positivist criminology in the United States. Some examples of positivism attempted to trace criminal behaviour to in-born 'biological predispositions' (e.g., Wilson and Herrnstein, 1985), and they sustained a tradition that goes back to nineteenth-century Lombrosian criminology. These individualised explanations of criminality proved attractive to many on the right because they offered an alternative to other approaches that focused on such things as social inequality, class conflict and racism (see Lilly *et al.*, 1989 for a discussion of the political context of these developments). Other examples of neo-positivism, although they celebrated the eclectic approach, were largely based on the disciplines of sociology and social psychology. The resurgence of this type of criminological positivism was well represented by *Positive Criminology*, edited by Gottfredson and Hirschi (1987). The book consisted of a collection of readings that attempted to map out the defining features of a reconstructed positivist criminology, which Gottfredson and Hirschi confidently described as the 'dominant paradigm within criminology'.

One of the main arguments was that standard depictions of classical and positivist criminology, in which the differences between the two are polarised around 'free will' and 'determinism', were no longer valid. Indeed, positivism's incorporation of Hirschi's control theory indicated a degree of compatibility between the two traditions. However, Gottfredson and Hirschi also argued that, for the following reasons, the free will–determinism debate is now defunct:

- In the classical model, punishment should work to deter individuals from breaking the law. It was, though, acknowledged that not everyone would be deterred, and so the punishment that was there as a deterrent would sometimes actually be inflicted on an individual. There must, therefore, be certain variables determining the decision to offend, and a concern with those variables takes us into positivism.
- Control theory's contribution to positivism focused attention on social deterrents (for example, losing the respect of others), whilst classical criminology concentrated on legal penalties as deterrents. Neo-positivism acknowledged that in either case individuals may exercise 'free will': they can choose to ignore the feelings of others, and they can ignore the legal penalties. However, there are always deterministic factors shaping the choices made. Thus, said neo-positivists, whatever their relative importance, free will and determinism apply equally to the two schools of thought.

Even if this reasoning is accepted, it is still, of course, essentially about perceived overlaps between classicism and positivism, and does not provide a solution to the free will versus determinism debate. Neo-positivism was strongly committed to so-called scientific research: to the gathering of 'hard facts' and plotting correlates. Roshier (1989: 68) was sceptical about its success:

> It has failed to establish clear-cut causal variables that differentiate offenders from non-offenders . . . The best it has been able to achieve is loose, probabilistic associations which sometimes, in all but the terminology used, have treated individual offenders as at least partially free, rational and choice-making (and in so doing has to some extent converged with classical criminology).

RADICAL CRIMINOLOGY

In spite of the rise of the New Right, the growing influence of administrative criminology at the level of policy, and much soul searching regarding Marxist social theory, radical criminology continued to have a prime influence on academic criminology in Britain during this period under review. Although it encompassed a range of perspectives, taking in Marxism, anarchism and versions of feminism, for the purposes of this discussion radical criminology will refer to criminological work that was part of a left/socialist tradition. As such, it drew on interactionism and neo-Marxism, together with elements of other strands in criminology; for example, anomie and subcultural theory.

Although there existed various schisms, on a general level the main features of radical criminology were as follows:

- The nature and extent of crime were analysed within the context of a specifically capitalist society.
- Such a society was seen as characterised by inherent class conflict, and other conflictual divisions based upon, notably, patriarchy and racism.
- Crime, law and social control were to be understood by locating them within material and ideological contexts.
- The ultimate goal was the transformation of society along 'socialist' lines.
- Individualised, positivist explanations of criminality were rejected.

Identifying broadly based common features, however, provides only a vague indication of the nature of radical criminology. The question is: what did these things *mean*? To some extent this question has already been addressed in the discussion of radical criminology during the 1970s, but in this section, taking us up to the mid-1990s, subsequent developments need to be looked at. In order to do this, the discussion will be structured around a consideration of two important and competing paradigms that emerged in the 1980s, and provided the basis for intense theoretical debate among radical criminologists. These were left realism (or radical realism as it was sometimes called) and critical criminology (or left idealism, as it was called by left realists). Some of the principal writers associated with left realism in Britain were Richard Kinsey, John Lea, Roger Matthews, Geoff Pearson and Jock Young. Critical criminology was represented by, for example, Kathryn Chadwick, Paul Gilroy, Paul Gordon, Tony Jefferson, Phil Scraton, Joe Sim and Colin Sumner. The picture was complicated, however, because there were other criminologists on the left who, whilst being sympathetic to the left realist position, were nevertheless critical of some or much of the work (and some of those listed above may complain about this labelling exercise). The debate between these two paradigms did raise a number of important issues relating to the response of radical criminology (in terms of theory and practice) to the growth of the New Right and the dismantling of state socialism in the former Soviet

Union and eastern Europe. It also reintroduced questions of general interest to criminology, such as: what is criminology *for*?

What were left realists saying?

According to left realists, socialist criminology should 'take crime seriously'. This meant that it should mount a 'realistic', practical challenge to those on the right who have traditionally colonised the 'law and order' terrain. In order to accomplish this, left realism sought to:

- Build up an accurate picture of crime and its impact on victims.
- Develop causal explanations of criminality.
- Trace the relationship between offenders, victims and formal and informal controls.
- Develop 'progressive', yet realistic policies aimed at the reduction of victimisation rates, especially among more vulnerable poorer groups.

Crime and its impact

Although left realists had argued that the project of 'taking crime seriously' should include both 'conventional' crime such as burglary and robbery, and white-collar and corporate crime, in practice they concentrated on the former (see Pearce and Tombs, 1992). This was perhaps inevitable given the reliance on localised victim surveys for generating data on amounts and distribution of crime.

According to left realism, the fear of crime among working-class people was based upon their real experiences, and was therefore rational. It was not the result of false consciousness created by media-induced moral panics, as, said the realists, critical criminologists seemed to believe. Poorer people, in particular, had to contend with double victimisation: as victims of crime and as victims of poverty. Furthermore, in answer to the criticism of taking a ready-made conceptual category – 'crime' – left realists argued that across a range of criminal activities there existed a large consensus regarding its harmfulness. They also acknowledged, though, that the nature of crime was to some extent 'mystified' by, for example, mass media accounts; one of the tasks of criminology, then, was to demystify these stereotypes.

Explanations

Criminology was seen as a discipline that should concern itself with the development of explanations of crime. However: 'The trouble with criminology is that it cannot explain crime' (Young, 1987: 237). And, as far as left-wing versions are concerned: 'on crime, more than on most matters, the left seems bereft of ideas' (Gross, 1982: 51). Young (1994) in particular argued that within criminology there had been an 'aetiological crisis', that is, the discipline had been perplexed by the curious fact that crime rises correlated with both affluence and recession. Critical criminology and administrative criminology were both censured for a lack of interest in a causal explanation of crime. The former was seen as focusing on criminalisation (that is, the construction and application of the law), whilst the latter focused simply on crime control. Left realists supported the view that the post-war period had seen real increases in amounts of crime, coupled with greater sensitivity on the part of victims to its effects. This was the worst of all worlds: official statistics showed an increase in the crime rate, the fear of crime had increased, and there were real increases in the crime rate.

Critical criminologists were accused of refusing to recognise the harmfulness of predatory crime carried out by working-class males, because they concentrated mainly on the crimes of the powerful. When they did discuss working-class crime, said the left realists, they either approached it in a spirit of misplaced sympathy for the offender as victim, or romanticised it as proto-revolutionary action. The left realist position was that conventional crime is, in the main, carried out by poorer working-class males, and that the bulk of this is intra-class rather than inter-class. However, there was a rejection of the positivist view that unemployment or poverty *causes* crime. Jock Young, who had been the most prominent proponent of left realism, drew on Merton's concept of anomie, defined as a lack of opportunity to achieve cultural expectations, and it was poorer working-class people who experienced a lack of opportunity most acutely. Thus social class position was important in that it created a situation where, because of relative deprivation – that is, a subjective feeling that what one has achieved is less than what one deserves – there are greater pressures to commit property crime. He also pointed to the importance of working-class male subcultures as carriers of macho, patriarchal values. Focusing on the offender, though, was seen as offering only a partial explanation of crime. Left realists stressed the need for analyses to recognise that offenders are only one element of a set of relationships out of which is created the 'crime problem'. Young (1994), for instance, spoke of the 'square of crime': offenders, victims, formal controls and informal controls. Richard Kinsey and his colleagues favoured a pentagon: offender, victim/witness, public, the city, police (Anderson *et al.*, 1991).

Policies

In an effort to seize the 'law and order' debate from the right, left realists attempted to develop concrete, practical policies involving, for example, local authorities and police, and aimed at reducing crime levels and the unequal victimisation of the working class. This engagement with policy was not seen as mere 'reform', traditionally associated with liberal thought, but as progressive 'reformism', with the ultimate prize being the creation of a socialist society. Ian Taylor (1982) used the phrase 'transitional socialist criminology'; others spoke of 'pre-figurative socialism'. There were echoes here of what other socialists had argued for some time: E. P. Thompson, for example, took the view that historically the rule of law had to some extent protected the working class from the excesses of the ruling class, and Alan Hunt (1980) had argued that law will always be necessary, even in a socialist society. Such sentiments had not always gone down well with others on the left (see the earlier discussion of the 1970s).

A common theme among left realists was the notion of 'community' and a stress on responses to crime at the local level (see, for example, Gross, 1982; Matthews, 1992; McMullan, 1986; Taylor, 1981, 1982). This appeal to localism was seen as forging links with the historical struggle of the working class to improve their lot, and pitched progressive reform at a more manageable level. Gross (1982) argued for the establishment of self-help groups and 'citizen defence squads'; similarly, Einstadter (1984) proposed crime prevention programmes based upon 'supportive neighbourhood networks'; Michalowski (1983) argued for the democratisation of policing and 'authentic' forms of popular justice; Taylor (1981) pointed to the need for the participation of working-class people and 'marginalised groups' in such things as community homes and magistrates' courts. Broader-based 'progressive' state intervention was also suggested: for example, victim–offender mediation schemes, target-hardening, better youth facilities, and victim and family support schemes (see Matthews, 1992).

CRITICAL CRIMINOLOGY AND LEFT REALISM

The left realist criticism of 'left idealism'

Criticism of critical criminology, or 'left idealism' centred on the following themes:

- They had failed to recognise the real harm caused by conventional crime, and to this extent had failed to 'take crime seriously'. Concentrating on *criminalisation* and moral panics, rather than on actual offenders (the exception being the criminality of the powerful), and highlighting what they saw as other, more harmful problems faced by the working class, critical criminologists had ignored causal explanations of crime and at the same time allowed the right to dictate the terms of the 'law and order' debate.
- They had taken a stance based upon utopianism – that is, an all or nothing commitment to a crime-free socialist future – instead of engaging with practical problems of crime control in the present. This entailed a rejection of 'reformism', and any attempts to work constructively with agencies such as the police.

- They had tended to romanticise working-class crime, seeing it as proto-revolutionary action. Furthermore, there was a strong element of moral ambivalence regarding certain forms of expressive deviance; for example drug use.
- Some critical writers had opted for a naive 'abolitionist' stance; for example, arguing for the dismantling of the prison system, or for a declaration of peace, rather than war, on crime (see Pepinsky and Quinney, 1991).
- There was a rejection of the idea that real increases in crime had occurred. Amounts of recorded crime were seen as a function of reporting and recording processes, rather than as a register of increases in the crime rate.

Criticisms of left realism by critical criminology

Some of the main criticisms of left realism will be used to provide a framework within which to explore some of the wider criminological issues raised by this intra-left debate.

The concept of crime

> One of the strongest attacks on left realism has been that it is essentialist . . . that it attributes to the commonsense phenomenon 'crime' – a phenomenon that consists of many different types of lawbreaking and many different modes of criminalization – a unitary existence known to all people of good will and common sense.
>
> (Carlen, 1992: 59)

Clearly, this is an issue that raises major epistemological questions concerning the nature of criminology (for discussions within the context of left realism, see Brown and Hogg, 1992; Carlen, 1992; Hogg, 1988). According to critical criminologists, being 'realistic' meant surrendering to popular stereotypical conceptions of crime. Thus, left realism was seen as merely paying lip service to the requirement to consider white-collar and corporate crime, and concentrated on certain conventional forms of working-class crime, thereby helping to perpetuate dominant ideological understandings of the 'crime problem': 'I am not convinced that this emphasis of left realism is deserved. In my opinion, *inter-class* crime is an equally serious and real problem that exploits and victimizes working class people' (McMullan, 1986: 190).

Defending left realism, Young (1987) argued that popular fears and understandings have a 'rational kernel', and Rafter (1986: 12) wrote: 'It is time to face the fact that a core of consensus does lie at the heart of the criminal law and to consider the aetiology of serious offending in this light'. This, said critical criminologists, may be correct, but references to 'kernels' and 'cores' of rationality did not explicate those understandings that were 'irrational', and avoided a confrontation with the role of ideology. However, debates over the concept of crime involved more than the issue of focusing on only some forms of offending. While left realists acknowledged the contribution made by labelling theory, they contended that critical criminologists had exaggerated the importance of the 'reaction' in the creation and shaping of criminal behaviour. Left realists, therefore, underlined what they saw as a real, objective crime problem with it own genesis. For critical writers, though, this was to return to an earlier, uncritical and common-sensical view of 'crime', where both criminals and their behaviour are special:

> People who are involved in 'criminal' events do not appear in themselves to form a special category of people. Those who are officially recorded as 'criminal' constitute only a small part of those involved in events that legally are considered to require criminalisation. Among them young men from the most disadvantaged sections of the population are heavily over-represented.
>
> (Hulsman, 1986: 65)

Hulsman then made the point that the working class, towards whom left realists orient their work, experienced a whole range of non-criminal events in their lives that are harmful or distressing; for example, matrimonial difficulties, difficulties between parents and children, and housing problems. However, for those involved there is 'nothing which distinguishes those "criminal" events intrinsically from other difficult or unpleasant situations' (ibid.: 65). The task for criminology is, he said, to 'debunk' the conceptual category of 'crime' as it exists within the context of the criminal justice system, and to focus instead on 'problematic situations'.

In a similar vein, Steinert (1985: 329) wrote:

> To 'take crime seriously' in this situation means that we take troubles seriously, but not as 'crimes.' That people are mugged in the streets, that women are raped and beaten . . . that environments are poisoned by irresponsible production, that people who live together are alienated from each other – all this is undesirable irrespective of whether it is 'crime' or not.

On this basis, Steinert discussed 'socialist' policy interventions that are not tied inherently to a criminal justice frame of reference, for example into the area of public transport. As Brown and Hogg (1992: 144) have said:

> The most fundamental problem in the realist theory, programme and methodology lies in the diminution of concern with the concept of 'crime' itself. This is not a theoretical luxury, but a strategic relaxation with important political effects.

Critical criminologists, then, stressed the political and ideological bases of crime and crime control. The essential argument was that left realism had simply drifted back towards a traditional liberal position, though it was now graced with a progressive gloss, and in the process ditched many of the theoretical advances made by radical criminology:

> By their overall commitment to 'order through law' . . . [left realists] have retreated far from the theoretical gains of twenty years ago. Their regresssion into the assumptions of the standard criminal law model of social control – criminalization and punishment – is premature.
>
> (Cohen, 1986: 131)

This comment by Stan Cohen, and other criticisms of left realism, was addressed by John Lea (1987). In the course of his discussion he referred to the 'abolitionism' of Hulsman mentioned above and in the process touched on some important points regarding the nature of the criminological project. In Lea's view, to speak of 'problematic situations' begs the question of how do we identify them, especially as they will be so wide ranging. Thus he argued the case for taking 'crime' as the central concept on the basis of there being a large consensus of agreement regarding its harmfulness. Critics of this view, however, would say that not only does it fail to question the ideological sources of popular understandings, on which basis draconian criminal justice policies may be introduced (for example, the 1994 Criminal Justice and Public Order Act and its impact on travelling people), it also leads to what we might call a 'particularistic' criminology: a criminology empirically tied to a specific society at a specific moment. The result is that the criminologist is able to study *only* those activities that have been criminalised, with the assumption that they are 'bad'. This contrasts with the, at least potentially, 'universalistic' approach of critical and other criminologies. *In extremis,* the distinction between the two approaches can be illustrated if we imagine the criminological project within the context of Nazi society in Germany. 'Crime' here could not be equated with 'problematic situations' or 'badness' as these are understood by Lea, though from the point of view of the Nazi state they were. To say that Britain in the 1990s was not the same as Germany in the 1930s misses the point, and does not eradicate the intellectual problem for criminology. Even if we all agreed that, at a given moment, defined criminal events really are 'bad', it still leaves criminology as an academic discipline tied to definitions of crime that happen to coincide with its moment in history. Interestingly, in a study of offending and victimisation among school-age children in Edinburgh carried out by a leading proponent of left realism, Richard Kinsey, and colleagues, the researchers did in fact stray from a focus on 'crime' as such, and dealt with 'problematic situations'. Although the text was littered with references to 'the impact of crime', 'caused by crime', and 'contact with crime', many of the events referred to were not actually crimes (Anderson *et al.,* 1991). Focusing simply on current definitions of 'crime' is to ignore the point that in Britain today, in Britain's past and in other societies, there are examples of 'crime' that many of us, including the left realists, would not wish to conceive of as 'bad' and in need of eradication. As Carlen (1992: 58) said: 'Whereas the realism of Durkheim and Popper was aimed at subverting common sense, left realists appear to call for a theory of crime that will fit the facts of crime as popularly conceived of in common sense'.

Victims

Critical criminologists, along with others, frequently based their critiques of left realism on the theme of the uses and abuses of local victim surveys. Some argued that concentrating on the victims of crime in certain working-class neighbourhoods gave criminology too narrow a focus, and in effect surrendered to conceptualisations of the social world provided by survey respondents: 'Arguably, the advocacy of inner city victims, and an ill-concealed contempt shown for "suburban souls", constitutes a narrow platform for a socialist strategy dealing with crime' (Mugford and O'Malley, 1991; but see Young and Matthews, 1992, for a defence).

As has been indicated earlier, one of the biggest difficulties with victim surveys is that they fail to register instances of victimisation by big business and white-collar criminals. This raises the general point that the validity of a victim survey rests on the respondent's knowledge. Clearly, in some cases – for example, illegal currency dealing on the money markets – respondents will be far removed from the status of victim. However, in other cases – for example, the illegal use of antibiotics by a beef farmer – they may be direct victims, though they will not be aware of it. Furthermore, some left realists, such as Young, suggested that some people have a low tolerance of crime, and are therefore more victimised than are those with a high tolerance. It is an important point, but it raised huge theoretical problems that are yet to be resolved. On a methodological level, Walklate (1989) discussed a number of difficulties with local victim surveys; for example, that they do not always support the idea that working-class people are more likely to be victims of property crime than the middle class.

One of the primary tasks of victim surveys for left realism was to show that crime really is a problem for many working-class people, and that to a significant degree they worry about it (more than, for instance, housing or public transport). While this was valuable in terms of exposing the damage done by crime, it did reintroduce the notion of 'problematic situations' into the debate. What, we might ask, would be the relative importance of other problems not on the list in the lives of respondents? And, their significance is likely to change over time anyway.

Ruggiero (1992: 135) argued that left realists proceeded as if there was a convenient split between victims (that is, 'respectable' people) and offenders within the working class – or any social class:

> They imply a notion of working class centred on values such as ethical integrity, productivity, social merit and fairness. One is induced to think that what they describe as a neat divide between offenders and victims corresponds to a similar divide between legality and illegality.

In a study of the East End of London, Hobbs (1988) stressed the need to recognise that criminal activities cannot inevitably be equated with universal 'harm':

> By concentrating almost exclusively on intra-class crime, left realism is in danger of going the same way as its predecessors. For it is essential to stress the variety of criminal opportunities that are available to the working class and how, on occasions, these opportunities can enhance rather than encumber inner city life.
>
> (Quoted in Ruggiero, 1992: 136)

Crime control policies

Left realists were accused of 'idealism' in their characterisations of working-class 'community', and an overabundance of faith in the willingness of existing organisations to radically alter their structures and policies. Some of the main arguments were as follows:

- Closer attention needed to be paid to the nature of so-called 'communities', and to the allocation of resources that would underpin local action.
- Hulsman (1986) raised the issue of what the agency of reform will be. In other words, which individuals or groups will actually be willing and able to implement reformist policies? Extending this further, Stan Cohen (1988: 229) noted the wider social and political context: 'the essence of state power is not just the particular way it deploys its forces of criminalization and punishment but its initial normalizing power, that is, its radical monopoly to define what is right'.
- Jefferson (1986) suggested that left realists had failed to appreciate the limitations to police effectiveness, and that a closer involvement with the community on the part of the police will have implications for civil liberties.
- The call to mobilise the community around the idea of 'popular justice' was seen as highly problematic. If this occurred, then 'justice' might become more punitive and draconian than it was at present. When discussing popular justice, left realists did acknowledge the danger that those involved may resort to exemplary punishment or violent direct action against 'offenders' on the basis of moral panics and misinformation. Thus they logically argued that popular justice presupposes an appropriate information system is in place, that the education system should adjust accordingly, and that the mass media should be reformed to suit. Interestingly, this line of reasoning pushed left realism towards critical criminology, in that it fairly soon arrived at what appeared to be a socialist transformation of society. This returns us to one of the central issues: the extent to which justice can be achieved within an unjust society.

As is frequently the case with competing criminological paradigms, as time passed the debate between left realism and critical criminology became increasingly polarised.

One outcome of this might be an implication that radical criminologists had to make a choice and accept one of the paradigms whole cloth. However, this ignores areas of disagreement within each paradigm, as well as areas of agreement between them. It also ignores areas of agreement between them and other criminological paradigms.

Critical criminology's agenda emphasised the political, economic and ideological structures within which processes of criminalisation and deviantisation, especially of vulnerable and marginalised groups, occurred (see Scraton and Chadwick, 1991; Sumner, 1994). Out of this arose studies of apparatuses of state control and regulation seen within the context of class conflict, patriarchy and racism. This, though, did not mean that critical criminologists were disinterested in the victimisation of working-class people. There are, however, different sorts of victims, and different sorts of victimisation resulting not just from certain criminal offences, but from a range of experiences and events. Left realism's agenda emphasised the social reality of crime in terms of the criminal victimisation of, in particular, working-class people. Thus causal explanations of 'conventional' crime and an engagement with reformist policies became paramount. This, though, did not mean that left realists were disinterested in processes of criminalisation and the role played by ideology in constructing the 'crime problem'. The debate between the two flowed naturally from rather different primary agendas.

FINAL REMARKS ON THIS PERIOD

If we look at the general direction taken by criminological research in Britain during the 1980s and into the mid-1990s, the overall impression is that there was a trend towards more narrowly focused, policy-oriented approaches, though these were not *per se* to be criticised. However, such research had tended to take precedence over the 'big' theoretical debates, although, as we have seen, these debates still continued. This trend, and a degree of theoretical stasis, was partly accounted for by the institutional pressures surrounding criminology and the demands made on researchers by funding agencies.

Where, in the light of these developments, was criminology heading? A pessimistic (for some) prediction would conjure up the scenario of a post-theoretical version of criminology. More optimistic crystal gazing would note the enduring commitment to a theoretical discourse among many criminologists in this country, and the continuing importance of criminological theory for those teaching the discipline (and noted by Rock, 1994, in his survey of the social organisation of criminology). In the concluding chapters we shall see what happened.

Conventional crime

Over the years, for many criminologists the criminological project has coalesced around the types of offences and offenders that we are familiar with from the criminal statistics. We might say that the mainstay of criminological research has been 'conventional' crime, crime which, the evidence suggests, is disproportionately committed by lower-working-class males. Furthermore, and being 'realistic', it has to be acknowledged that these are the crimes that the public, understandably, worries about most. Not surprisingly, because of the lack of immediate personal impact, they are less worried about expense account fiddles, illegal arms deals, and so forth – the crimes of the powerful.

When a criminologist is invited into a television studio to participate in a programme on, for instance, 'crime today', or 'vandalism in the city', there is the same focus, and the criminologist is usually expected to explain why they, the criminals involved, do it. Certainly, he or she will not be expected to entertain the viewers with an exposition on the conceptual conundrums surrounding definitions of crime and deviance. Significantly, the same criminologists are not usually in the studio when issues such as pollution, nuclear testing in the South Pacific, bullying by employers, or the collapse of an international bank due to fraudulent practices is being discussed. Typically, criminologists get sucked into a milieu structured around common-sense understandings of the 'crime problem', and inevitably this means a preoccupation with the crimes of the powerless.

That the media concentrates on certain sorts of conventional crime is one thing, but to make it the *raison d'être* of academic criminology is something else. Obviously, when we consider that the criminal statistics are dominated by conventional crime, that victim surveys show that this is what people fear, and that such things as stealing cars, breaking into homes and engaging in random violence causes real misery and suffering, criminology's interest in conventional crime is understandable and important. The social distribution of different types of offending is partly accounted for by the different opportunities available. Those working in professional or managerial occupations are more likely to have access to less risky (and often more socially acceptable) criminal acts than are unskilled manual workers or the unemployed. Those owners of small businesses inclined to 'skim off' a few tax-free pounds from the day's takings, or the builders who for cash in hand will ignore VAT, or employees who add an extra mile or two to a mileage claim, have no need to take the risk of breaking into a house, or robbing someone on the street in order to top up their income. And the opportunities available at a corporate level take us into another league of criminality. Is behaviour such as this 'abnormal' or a function of 'disorganisation' as some versions of positivism suggest? The main point to make, though, is that a crude reading of the criminal statistics can give a rather misleading picture of the social distribution of crime and criminal motivations. Although no criminologist would argue that non-conventional crime should be ignored, in some quarters of criminology this is precisely what has happened, with the result that the 'underclass', or 'socially excluded' (or some functional equivalent) becomes *de facto* the source of Britain's crime problem.

During the 1980s and the first half of the 1990s, as we have seen, it was not positivism but administrative criminology that had most influence in government circles.

The attention was still on conventional crime, but the search for causes had been displaced by the search for ways of preventing offences taking place. The motivation to commit crime was taken as given; its aetiology, although interesting, was not under consideration.

WINNING THE FIGHT AGAINST CRIME?

In September 1995, as part of what was called a 'good news on crime' tour, the then Home Secretary, Michael Howard, was interviewed on a local radio station in Birmingham. He reported that government crime prevention policies were now beating crime, and he gave particular prominence to the value of security video cameras. Howard's 'good news' message made the front page in a number of national news papers. Although this is not strictly relevant, it is impossible to resist the temptation to mention that as the Home Secretary was being escorted by police and security staff from the studios through a back entrance, two youths came in by the front door and stole a large number of pictures of DJs off the wall. Ironically, they were filmed doing this by security cameras in the studio.

Although Howard based his argument on official statistics (with all the problems that that involves), supposing we took what was said at face value – that the number of offences committed had, because of various crime prevention initiatives, been significantly reduced – what did this really tell us? To learn that fewer houses were being burgled, cars stolen, or individuals beaten up on a Saturday night, *was*, in itself, obviously 'good news'. However, presenting the issue in this restricted format was misleading. The Home Secretary's fight against crime was based upon administrative criminology's search for ways of controlling criminally motivated individuals. Thus *control* was the key concept. People were still wanting to commit crime, but the project became one of somehow preventing them from doing it. Attractive as this project at first glance might seem, no one would argue that crime control at any cost is a good thing. Therefore, a 'real' reduction in crime, if that could be established, does not of itself mean that the quality of life (which, arguably, should involve such things as freedom, justice and rights) has necessarily improved. At a hypothetical level, one could imagine a situation where crime really did plummet to very low levels, but where, because of controls on behaviour, everyday life had become intolerable. The political, and in some quarters criminological, commitment to situational crime control involves a range of preventive measures: physical security (steering locks on cars, bars on windows, security cameras, etc.); personal and community-based strategies (risk avoidance, Neighbourhood Watch, etc.); different modes of policing. If, after consulting with security companies (and some companies have no qualms about using telephone marketing to inform householders that they are threatened by a crime wave), homes become virtual fortresses, if 'risk avoidance' means that the elderly imprison themselves in their houses and many people do not go into city centres in the evening, levels of crime may go down, but social life has clearly suffered. So although a reduction in crime may appear to be something that we should applaud, the overall circumstances in which it occurs need to be considered.

It is not, though, just a matter of how effective or draconian situational crime control measures are. The entire project pushes to one side the issue of criminal motivations and their socio-cultural contexts, whether relating to the crimes of the powerful or the crimes of the powerless. The existence of individuals who want to commit crime is simply taken as given: the trick is to prevent them doing it. Variations in levels of crime between one society and another are accounted for, therefore, simply in terms of the effectiveness, or otherwise, of the sorts of controls mentioned above. However, in itself 'successful' crime control tells us nothing about the nature, extent and sources of criminal motivations. Simply taking crime levels as an index of, for instance, the 'quality of life' in different societies is thus highly misleading. Equating a reduction in crime, however measured, with 'good news', and therefore implying that there has been a qualitative improvement in social life, is one-sided in the extreme. If the phenomenon of crime is used as an indicator of the quality of life within a society, then the nature and extent of criminal motivations cannot be ignored. This means examining the whole nature of that society in order to piece together and understand the structural roots of criminality. Indeed, rather than 'good news' from the front regarding the 'fight against crime', we would have been better served if we had had good news from the front regarding the fight against inequality, injustice, oppression and greed.

Selected further reading

An up-to-date report and analysis based upon the Cambridge Study of Delinquent Development is **Piquero, A. R., Farrington, D. P. and Blumstein, A. (2007)** *Key Issues in Criminal Career Research: New analyses of the Cambridge Study of Delinquent Development*, **Cambridge: Cambridge University Press**. A comprehensive, accessible and recent discussion of criminal career research is **Soothill, K., Fitzpatrick, C. and Francis, B. (2009)** *Understanding Criminal Careers*, **Cullompton: Willan**.

A good review of feminist research over the period covered in this chapter is **Heidensohon, F. (1994)** 'Gender and crime', in M. Maguire, R. Morgan and R. Reiner (eds) *The Oxford Handbook of Criminology*, 1st edn, Oxford: Clarendon Press.

For a discussion of violence towards women, see **Stanko, E. (1988)** 'Hidden violence against women', in M. Maguire and J. Pointing (eds) *Victims of Crime: A new deal?* Milton Keynes: Open University Press, a collection which addresses crime victimisation in general.

Walklate, S. (1995) *Gender and Crime,* Hemel Hempstead: Harvester Wheatsheaf, offers an accessible discussion of gender issues.

An influential study of masculinities is **Messerschmidt, J. (1993)** *Masculinities and Crime*, Lanham, MD: Rowman & Littlefield.

For an overview of the concerns of administrative criminology, see **Heal, D. and Laycock, G. (eds) (1986)** *Situational Crime Prevention: From theory into practice*.

A highly influential paper written from a conservative, 'right realist' perspective is **Wilson, J. Q. and Kelling, G. (1982)** 'Broken windows: the police neighborhood safety', *Atlantic Monthly*, March.

The collection of chapters in **Stenson, K. and Cowell, D. (eds) (1991)** *The Politics of Crime Control*, London: Sage provide a good overview of this period.

Discussions of left realism can be found in **Matthews, R. and Young, J. (eds) (1992)** *Issues in Realist Criminology*, London: Sage; and **Young, J. and Matthews, R. (eds) (1992)** *Rethinking Criminology: The realist debate*, London: Sage.

An example of an alternative 'critical' criminology is **Scraton, P. (ed) (1987)** *Law, Order and the Authoritarian State*, Milton Keynes: Open University Press.

For discussions of abolitionism see **Bianchi, H. and van Swaaningen, R. (eds) (1986)** *Abolitionism: Towards a non-repressive approach to crime*, Amsterdam: Free University Press.

Postscript

MIGHT

They are tough now

And so sure of themselves

That we even begin to accept it

Because they don't try to hide

And they don't care who sees.

They are confident

And that's what makes us weak

But when the change comes

(and it will)

The truth will shift

Because they are wrong

It just happens that

For a time

They have the power.

Nigel Mellor (1989), *For the Inquiry*,
London: Dab Hand Press.

PART VI

THE MID-1990S INTO THE NEW MILLENNIUM

THE DISCIPLINE OF CRIMINOLOGY
AND ITS CONTEXT – 5

Key themes

- New Labour, old problems
- Restorative justice
- Imprisonment
- Social policy and New Labour
- Crime prevention, crime reduction and community safety
- Crime and criminal justice: the wider context
- Criminology in the new millennium

INTRODUCTION

This final 'contextual' chapter takes us from the mid-1990s to the present day, a period that saw the replacement of a Conservative government by a (New) Labour government, which, at the time of writing, is in its third term of office. The chapter gives particular attention to New Labour's criminal justice policies, tracing both the continuities and discontinuities between them and the previous Conservative administration. The stress on a 'tough on crime' agenda is discussed, noting, for instance, the large increases in prison populations during the period under review. However, social policy and elements of welfarism are also referred to, and it is within this context that notions of community safety and restorative justice are discussed. The chapter concludes with an analysis of globalisation, social change and the late modern condition.

We now reach the final phase (in this review) in the historical development of sociological criminology. This coincides with a period that begins with the election of a Labour government in 1997 and takes us to the end of the first decade of the new millennium. At the time of writing, Labour is experiencing an unprecedented third term in office, and the UK, along with the rest of the world, is experiencing an economic recession of unprecedented – at least during the post-war period – proportions. The chapter here provides an overview of the social, economic and political contexts within which sociological criminology has continued to develop over this same period. In order to do this, the chapter works, as it were, from the inside outwards, and is thus organised into three sections addressing in turn:

- Criminal justice and other policies linked to issues of law and order introduced by New Labour.
- Shifts in the nature of criminal justice processes that developed prior to the election of New Labour, but continue to play an important role.
- Broader, and continuing, social, political and economic changes, some operating on a global level, that provide a backdrop to the above.

This will allow a discussion of the specific characteristics of New Labour's policies, the continuities and discontinuities between the past and the present, and the wider context within which these policies have been implemented, together with their broader implications. Of course, these different dimensions are not mutually exclusive; in various ways and to varying degrees they interact with each other.

As an aside, it can be noted here that in 2007 the Home Office was split into two organisations: a new Ministry of Justice (responsible for prisons, probation, criminal justice and sentencing), and a re-fashioned Home Office (responsible for terrorism, security, policing, drugs, immigration, ID cards and anti-social behaviour).

NEW LABOUR, OLD PROBLEMS

A political transformation

The project of creating *New* Labour, and thereby distancing the party from the 'old', was well under way prior to the general election of 1997. Officially, the logic guiding this transformation arose from a need to respond to a changing world by developing a more 'relevant' political agenda and a more appropriate set of policies. In other words, to become 'realistic' – a concept that, as we have seen, began to gain currency in various quarters during the 1980s. Allied to this was the conviction that the ideology and policies associated with Old Labour would make winning an election difficult, if not impossible. The central problem faced by New Labour, though, was (and is) devising a strong and coherent political platform, and attendant policies, that would distinguish the party from the two other major political parties and yet, at the same time, link it to the 'core' values associated with a perceived historical role for the Labour Party – though this role had to be responsive to a changing world. This project required the evolution of a particular type of discourse and the careful control of information and statements supplied to the media (distrust of the media, and in particular newspapers, among Labour politicians has – and not without some justification – had a long history). Gradually, the 'old' language of Labour – socialism, capitalism, working class, poverty, the poor, redistribution, equality, etc. – was replaced by a language seen as more appropriate to the condition of late modernity (and less contentious and abrasive among non-traditional Labour Party supporters, described in shorthand form as 'middle England'). Increasingly, references were made to the Third Way, market society, the socially excluded, and opportunities and choice for all. Clause 4 disappeared from the Labour Party constitution. Paralleling this, as the influence of Marxist social theory began to wane, the discourses of radical criminology were modified, as they too incorporated a new, and often similar, conceptual language. For New Labour, the goal was to achieve a national consensus on the basis of a non-ideological politics, one that broke with older notions of left and right (Becket and Hencke, 2004); in effect to rise above ideology by establishing a consensual 'Third Way' and leave behind notions of left and right associated with Old Labour (see, for example, Giddens, 1994).

Getting tough

Of particular importance was challenging the traditional perception among the electorate of the Conservatives as the party of law and order and, in the process, denying any suggestion that Labour was 'soft on crime'. While disillusionment with the Conservative government among large sections of the electorate in 1997 gave New Labour a powerful advantage at the polls, an election victory was no foregone conclusion. The electorate needed to be convinced of New Labour's managerial competence across a range of policy issues. Within the context of law and order, 'competence' equated with being tough on criminals. During the 1980s, there were major differences between the Conservatives in office and Labour in opposition over issues of law and order; however, these became much less significant during the 1990s. By 1997, Labour's election manifesto claimed that it was 'the party of law and order in Britain today'. One phrase in particular summed up New Labour's approach: 'tough on crime, tough on the causes of crime'. Among a cacophony of sound bites gracing the election process in 1997, this one grabbed the headlines. In fact, it first appeared in an article written for the *New Statesman* by Tony Blair in 1993, when he was shadow Home Secretary and, as Young and Matthews (2003: 5) say: 'the article . . . contains all the seeds of the subsequent crime policy of New Labour, both in terms of analysis and policy implications'. The phrase 'tough on crime, tough on the causes of crime', was highly effective because the *mélange* of possibilities regarding what it *could* mean made its appeal virtually universal, especially as few people had read the original article (for a left/social democratic audience, for instance, 'tough on the causes of crime' was equated with addressing the structural roots of criminality, seen in terms of inequality and social injustice). A pithy statement unencumbered by detail, making it difficult to argue against, often has the greatest impact.

During the 1997 election, it was the overall impression of toughness, rather than detailed disquisitions on planned criminal justice policies, that was crucial. The manifesto stated, for example, that 'we believe in personal responsibility and in punishing crime'. The core message, therefore, was seductively simple: New Labour is tough, not soft, on crime. Unsurprisingly, this intrusion into the rhetorical domain they saw as their own presented the Conservative Party with serious difficulties, and senior Tories reacted predictably by putting forward even 'tougher' policy suggestions. In 2004, for instance, as another election loomed, Michael Howard, then leader of the Conservatives, said that if elected, his government would end the current police practice of recording all stops and searches. This practice (which was recommended in 1999 by the Macpherson Report) was, for Howard, a reflection of 'sociological mumbo-jumbo and political correctness' (quoted by Garland, 2005: 63–4). This has to be seen against the backdrop of very large proportionate increase in the number of Asians subject to a stop and search, following the 2000 Terrorism Act. Once in power, New Labour's first Home Secretary, Jack Straw, was swift to underline the government's tough credentials. 'Squeegee merchants' and street beggars were vilified; the benefits of 'zero tolerance' policing were applauded; and, following a tabloid 'sting' involving his son and cannabis, he took parental responsibility by presenting his son to the police. The *Daily Mirror* christened him 'Dirty Jack' (a reference to Clint Eastwood's movie character, *Dirty Harry*) after he 'admonished' a youth in his constituency for spitting from a bridge (whether or not he said 'Are you feeling lucky punk' is unrecorded). In spite of this, and illustrating how difficult it is to please everyone, a leader in the *Daily Telegraph* made the remarkable assertion that 'At the Home Office, it is the soft-on-crime, liberal consensus that is back in charge'.

Since coming into office in 1997, this tough stance has been reflected in various pieces of legislation. As Downes and Morgan (2002: 297) put it:

> A string of largely punitive measures, announced in discussion papers in Opposition and mostly enacted in office, in the Crime and Disorder Act 1998 and other statutes, were designed to meet the 'tough on crime' agenda . . . all measures that would hardly have been countenanced by Labour before 1992.

The reluctance of New Labour to revert to more liberal pre-1992 approaches to law and order, coupled with a belief that its policies 'worked', resulted in further 'tough' legislation following their 2001 election victory.

For Downes and Morgan, New Labour have failed to capitalise on their 'political hegemony' in matters of law and order, and shift the emphasis towards a more liberal approach. Young (2003a) points to New Labour's failure to draw on the 'crime drop dividend' and the evidence from academic criminological research, choosing instead to continue with a populist approach. From this perspective, policy was driven by public opinion strongly influenced by 'a mass media which has consistently taken the most pessimistic view of the crime problem' (ibid.: 36). However, and regardless of its obsession with public opinion, the government was unlikely to alter its tough-on-crime stance (for example, by seeking a significant reduction in custodial sentences) because, first, there was political capital to be gained from linking existing policies to a continuing fall in the crime rate (though simultaneously not denying that crime risks continued) and, second, to do so would leave it open to accusations of vacillation. This was especially important if we note that according to the *British Crime Surveys*, and in spite of statistical evidence to the contrary, most people felt that crime was rising, and that courts were too lenient on offenders. Whilst a shift in policy informed by the evidence from research may bring dividends in the long term, short-term electoral considerations have always played a major role in governmental decision making. From a more cynical perspective, and alluded to above, there is some political capital to be gained by allowing public concerns about increasing risks to foment.

One inference that might be drawn from the above discussion, and especially the arguments put forward by Downes and Morgan and Young, is that New Labour's policies are simply a populist response to perceived public opinion and, if the truth be known, contradict what the government would actually want to do. However, whilst some of the law and order rhetoric may be characterised in this way, it seems perfectly reasonable to see these policies as being entirely consistent with the ideology of New Labour as manifested in so-called Third Way politics. There is no evidence that sufficient political hegemony or reductions in the crime rate would somehow trigger a covert, latent predilection to introduce more liberal policies. Tonry (2004) has added to this debate by suggesting that the more judicious of New Labour's criminal justice policies were introduced because they address non-controversial issues.

Having said that, it would be misleading to characterise New Labour's criminal justice policies, together with other policies intended to have an impact on problems of crime and disorder, as uniformly illiberal and simply a sop to tabloid-generated public opinion. Indeed, developing a coherent, simplified and easily digested overview of these policies is, because of the inconsistencies, difficult. As Morgan and Allen (2004: 3) put it: 'Contemporary criminal justice is difficult to characterise, with contrasts and contradictions at seemingly every turn'. Thus we can note, for instance, the Human Rights Act; minimum wage legislation; the Macpherson Inquiry into the racially motivated murder of Stephen Lawrence; Youth Justice partnerships and programmes aimed at the rehabilitation and reintegration of offenders; efforts directed at the regeneration of communities and tackling social exclusion; and a recognition that problems of crime and disorder are connected to the corrosive effects of deeper economic and social factors, such as long-term unemployment – a connection that the Conservative Party, when in government, refused to acknowledge. The link between social exclusion/unemployment and criminality is double edged though. Clearly, the evidence from official statistics on those convicted of 'volume crime' such as burglary and theft indicates the salience of forms of deprivation. However, as has been stated earlier, there is a danger that the problem of crime continues to be the problem of the so-called 'underclass', in the process recycling nineteenth-century images of the 'dangerous classes', and ignoring the huge amounts of crime committed by better-off, and, ostensibly, 'respectable', members of society. Karstedt and Farrell (2004), in their recent research, illustrate that 'inclusion' is no guarantee of law-abiding behaviour – 64 per cent of those classified as middle-class 'professionals' admitted that they committed at least one dishonest offence during the last year, compared with 43 per cent of those on lower incomes. The total cost of 'respectable' crime – fraud and forgery – is estimated at £14 billion per year. And, as recent revelations in the wake of the collapse of major global financial institutions have shown, there is also a danger of ignoring the harmfulness of *legal* ploys to avoid paying taxes:

> Royal Bank of Scotland tied up at least £25bn in complex international tax-avoidance schemes during its boom years, costing the British and US treasuries more than £500m in lost revenue . . . It is the first time that a major bank has admitted the existence of such deals on this scale. The new management at RBS, mindful of the fact that it is now 70% owned by the taxpayer, has disbanded the department responsible.
>
> (Lawrence and Leigh, 2009: 1)

A conceptual framework

The government's criminal justice legislation, including its flagship legislation, the 1998 Crime and Disorder Act, represents an attempt by New Labour to manage a fundamental tension present in all post-World War Two criminal justice policies aimed at dealing with offenders (and discussed previously): the tension between justice and welfare. Justice (which signals 'toughness' and has continued to play the dominant role) emphasises personal culpability and punishment as retribution and deterrence, whilst welfare emphasises the social causes of crime and the rehabilitation/treatment/reintegration of offenders (and, in some quarters at least, signals 'excuse making' and being soft on crime). Put another way, it reflects the tension between, on the one hand, classicism/neo-liberalism and individuals worthy of blame and, on the other, positivism and 'damaged' individuals. New Labour has sought to resolve the tension by incorporating what are seen as the strengths of each approach into a strategy based upon partnerships and managerialist principles. Young and Matthews (2003) argue that New Labour's attempt to manage these different approaches offers an alternative to Old Labour's positivism and neo-liberalism's classicism. Whether or not this has resulted in 'Third Way' law and order policies, in the sense of creating something new, rather than a continuation, or recycling, of already existing policies (and finding some middle ground somewhere between Attlee – see below – and Thatcher), is, however, debatable.

Young (1999) and Matthews and Young (2003), however, do provide useful analyses of the principles informing New Labour's policies relevant to crime and its reduction, and in the process indicate how these policies are intended to interact with one another. Unlike previous Conservative administrations, New Labour acknowledges that the causes of crime are ultimately located in the damaging effects of global economic and social factors over which individual offenders, and the families in which they are brought up, have no control. Particular attention is given to social exclusion and disintegrating communities deficient in social capital (for critical discussions of the concept of social exclusion, see Gans, 1995; Mooney and Danson, 1997; Young, 1999, 2007). The problems confronted by those living in such communities are multifarious, and therefore require 'joined-up' multi-agency interventions. Crime itself is specifically linked to poor socialisation within the family and the school, coupled with weak community-based social controls, leading to problems such as drug and alcohol abuse. Social policy interventions are oriented towards the creation of a flexible, skilled workforce and the regeneration of communities and, ultimately, the eradication of poverty and social exclusion and the establishment of strong social networks. Inherent in these control strategies is the idea of building up 'social capital' (Putnam, 2000) in 'problem' neighbourhoods:

> Social capital is conceived of as the 'social glue' that is derived from residents' active participation in local social networks that benefit the whole community in terms of making it a better place to live.
>
> (Innes, 2003: 152)

The broad thrust of social policy can, therefore, be seen to represent the second part of the tough on crime, tough on the causes of crime couplet. Ostensibly, this is very similar to the positivist-style policies of the two decades following World War Two, in that it acknowledges the links between offending and social and economic deprivation. There are, however, major differences, which become apparent when the 'tough on crime' half of the couplet, as reflected in New Labour's criminal justice policies, is taken into consideration. During the earlier post-war period, and beginning with Attlee's 1945 Labour government, there was a view that social reform would lead to a gradual reduction in crime, and criminal justice interventions were directed at what were seen as residual crime problems (see the discussion in Chapter 4). By the late 1960s, though, rising crime rates acted to challenge this optimism, and encouraged the political parties to develop alternative strategies, in terms of both general social policy and criminal justice policy.

In essence, three periods of post-war history can be identified, each exhibiting different understandings of, and approaches to, crime and criminality. In the first, immediate post-war period, offenders were seen as 'damaged', their criminality resulting from social and economic factors. From this deterministic perspective, offenders were not to blame and, therefore, criminal justice interventions should focus on their treatment/rehabilitation (especially children and young people). This reflected a positivist conceptual framework and prioritised structure over agency.

During the second, post-1979 period, the Conservative government worked within the framework of neo-liberal classicism, and stressed voluntarism; agency was prioritised over structure. Thus offenders were blameworthy and should be dealt with accordingly. In the third, New Labour period, understandings of, and approaches to, crime and criminality are more complicated. Criminal justice policies are a complex mixture of both neo-liberal classicism (linked to discourses of risk) and positivism. Although social policies aimed at regenerating communities and eradicating social exclusion appear to prioritise structure over agency, it is clear that criminal justice policies reflect a 'tough on crime' (which equates with tough on criminals) agenda, and this requires prioritising agency over structure. Ultimately, offenders are responsible for their behaviour. What is particularly interesting is the way in which both individual responsibility and potentially deterministic structural factors have been incorporated into New Labour's conceptual framework. In effect, it is an attempt to accommodate simultaneously a demand for welfare and a demand for justice, and at core relies on a variation of Hobbes's social contract theory. From the perspective of New Labour, between 1979 and 1997 Conservative governments did little to ameliorate the damaging consequences of post-industrialism and, indeed, exacerbated the consequences. Under those circumstances, it was relatively easy to be sympathetic in a liberal sense to the view that criminality was the result of social and economic factors. However, the introduction by New Labour of a range of measures aimed at improving the lot of the socially excluded has created a different situation, one where, from the government's perspective, excusing the behaviour of offenders is inappropriate. Offenders and the families that produced them are now blameworthy, for they have failed to grasp the opportunities that have been put in place. They may not have control over global social and economic forces, but they are now in a position to make rational decisions regarding personal behaviour. It is this stress on agency and voluntarism that provides the logic and justification for a 'tough on criminals' approach to criminal justice, and happens to tap into wider societal feelings of anger and resentment towards offenders (Pratt, 2000).

RESTORATIVE JUSTICE

However, as stated earlier, this does not mean that welfarist principles no longer feature in New Labour's criminal justice policies. The 1999 Youth Justice and Criminal Evidence Act, for instance, introduced the mandatory sentence of a referral order for some, but not all, young offenders. It is only applicable to first-time offenders aged 10 to 17, who plead guilty, or are convicted of, a non-custodial offence. The order requires the young person to attend a youth offender panel, which can consist of a wide range of people, for example members of the youth offending team, parents of the young offender, volunteers from the local community, and the victim. There are two key outcomes that the panel will seek to achieve: that the offender makes some reparation for his or her behaviour, and that a programme to prevent further offending is drawn up (Newburn *et al.*, 2001; Miers *et al.*, 2001). This approach to youth justice, which has occurred in many other countries, reflects the growing influence of restorative justice. Restorative justice is particularly associated with modes of dispute resolution found in small-scale societies – New Zealand Maori society is the archetypal example. It represents an alternative approach to one based upon retribution and/or deterrence, which is seen as alienating the offender from the community and likely to increase anger, conflict and further harm. With restorative justice, the offender is expected to repair the harm done to the victim and the community by some sort of reparation, whilst at the same time acknowledging the wrongfulness of their behaviour.

The theoretical underpinning for restorative justice is the work of Braithwaite (1989, 1998). His seminal *Crime, Shame and Reintegration* (1989) was an attack on the retributive tradition that dominated justice systems around the world. Drawing on ideas from labelling theory, he argued for a much more informal approach directed at the reintegration of offenders into the community, as opposed to their stigmatisation and marginalisation. This is accomplished by the 'reintegrative shaming' of the offender. Over the years the theoretical analysis has, on the basis of empirical research and academic debate, been refined and modified. In a recent discussion and review by Braithwaite and his colleagues (Ahmed *et al.*, 2001), an 'ethical identity' conception of shame and a theory of 'shame management' are developed. Briefly, ethical identity involves an offender feeling that their actions are bad, and that whilst *they* are not irretrievably bad, there is an aspect of self that has to change. Shame management refers to a process where an offender is enabled to develop a 'self-regulating conscience', thereby reducing the chances of further offending.

Evidence for the success of restorative justice programmes is at the moment inconclusive (Latimer *et al.*, 2001; Johnstone, 2003). As far as this country is concerned, Newburn *et al.* (2001) have highlighted the low levels of victim involvement in youth offender panels. Crawford and Newburn (2002) have pointed to the contradiction between the principle of restorative justice and the punitive tone of youth justice policy, as well as the punitive reality of custodial sentences for a large number of young offenders (restorative justice is reserved for those who commit relatively minor offences). In addition, they note the tension between the nature of the restorative justice process and a managerialist requirement for speedy and economic outcomes. There have been criticisms of restorative justice and reintegrative shaming arising from concerns regarding the nature of the communitarian ethos inherent in such concepts. Lacey (1998), for example, focuses on notions of inclusion and exclusion and the assumption of a neat 'good' and 'bad' division between offenders and non-offenders, seen respectively as 'them' and 'us'. In a similar vein, Scheingold (2000) argues that restorative justice may lead to a greater intolerance of difference, coupled with an attempt to create conformity by means of coercion.

Given their preoccupation with preserving a 'tough on crime' image, there has always been a degree of ambivalence towards community-based initiatives, such as restorative justice, on the part of the government. A recent example illustrates the Ministry of Justice's desire to manage that image by emphasising that such initiatives do not represent a 'soft' approach. At the end of 2008 a new community service programme was launched, which involves convicted offenders carrying out unpaid work in the community, whilst wearing bright orange bibs with the words 'community payback' on the back. According to the justice secretary, Jack Straw (2008: 6):

> The more we can get across to the public that community punishments are effective and tough, the fewer people the courts will find it essential to send to prison.

IMPRISONMENT

Wills (2007) has analysed the Labour government's track record in relation to juvenile justice, since coming to power in 1997. Summarising this record, she makes two important observations:

- Public debate about juvenile justice is characterised by two contradictory myths: that the past was a golden age of law and order, and that the treatment of juvenile criminals is more enlightened today.
- However, they have been used by the government to justify a punitive stance towards juvenile criminals which in many ways is more severe than at any point since the 1850s.

One indication of how punitive a society is when responding to criminal behaviour is its rate of imprisonment in comparison to other societies. In spite of the introduction of initiatives based upon notions of restorative justice (and other community-based, non-custodial sentences), there has been an extraordinary growth in the prison population – for children, young persons and adults – in this country since Labour came to power. Currently (as shown by the detailed statistics in Chapter 2), England and Wales has the highest rate of imprisonment among its European neighbours, apart from (and only just) Luxembourg and Spain. The number of adult prisoners has increased by 38 per cent since 1997. The growth in the prison population has, not surprisingly, stimulated a significant amount of critical research and comment within criminology in recent years (see, for instance, Cavadino and Dignan, 2002; O'Malley, 2004; Jewkes, 2007). Some of the factors that have led to this situation can be summarised as follows:

- The Labour government has introduced around 3,000 new criminal offences.
- Increased use of indeterminate sentences. There are now more people serving indeterminate sentences than there are serving sentences of less than 12 months.
- Increased number of mandatory minimum sentences.

- The use of the 'two strikes and you're out' principle.
- Longer sentences imposed by the courts. The average crown court sentence length has increased by 25 per cent over the last decade.
- More people have ended up being jailed because of the use of suspended sentence orders. Introduced in 2003, about 3,000 per month are now given out by the courts. They carry an implicit threat of a custodial sentence if an offender re-offends. Because they are subject to strict conditions, many end up breaching them (though the offence may be a relatively minor one) and, as a result, many are then given a prison sentence. Most orders are issued by magistrates' courts, almost half of them for summary offences such as driving while disqualified and common assault.
- While the 2003 Criminal Justice Act was intended to lead to heavier custodial sentences for violent and sexual offences, and a concomitant shift towards non-custodial, community-based sentences for less serious offences, courts have tended to embrace the former rather than the latter in their sentencing practices.
- Net widening. An Anti-Social Behaviour Order begins life as a civil instrument, as do official interventions into family life when children play truant from school. However, and regardless of what ministers had in mind when framing the respective legislation, in each case a failure to comply with what has been ordered may eventually transform a civil action into a criminal one, and with it the possibility of imprisonment. For instance, over the last six years, around 130 parents have been sent to prison because their children have truanted. This raises a further issue regarding blame for juvenile offending. The huge increase in parenting orders for parents of youngsters who offend suggests that it is the parents who are to blame; and yet, lowering the age of criminal responsibility to 10 in the 1998 Crime and Disorder Act, suggests that the offender is to blame. In practice, it seems that, somehow, both are to blame.

The government now plans to build two new 'titan' prisons, which between them will hold 5,000 prisoners, and the Ministry of Justice estimates that England and Wales will have a prison population of 96,000 by 2014. These will be private prisons (the privatisation of the prison estate during Labour's terms of office has also attracted a large amount of critical attention from criminologists).

SOCIAL POLICY AND NEW LABOUR

Social policy under New Labour is oriented primarily towards the achievement of equality of opportunity, rather then a redistribution of income and wealth and a reduction in material inequality *per se*, which raises an obvious question: how can equality of opportunity be achieved in a society that is fundamentally unequal? Blanden *et al.* (2004) have carried out research comparing the income of people born in 1958 with the income of those born in 1970 in order to assess amounts of social mobility during these respective periods. Those growing up in the earlier period, when material inequality was decreasing, moved further ahead of their parents' income than did those growing up in the latter period, a period when material inequality was increasing. Research by Paxton and Dixon (2004) showed that there had been a reduction in the number of people living in poverty in this country ('poverty' is defined as 60 per cent of median earnings after taking housing costs into account) since New Labour came to power. Furthermore, whilst the child poverty rate in Britain in 1998 was the highest among the then fifteen European member states, by 2001 it was in eleventh position. In 2004 the government achieved its target of reducing child poverty by 1 million, and has a target of halving child poverty by 2010 (it is highly unlikely that they will meet this target, especially given the current economic recession). However, inequalities in income and in wealth have continued to widen since 1997, continuing a twenty five-year trend beginning in the late 1970s. Of particular importance within the context of this discussion is that the living standards of the poorest 1 per cent have fallen. After falling each year since 1996/97, in 2005/06, then again in 2006/07, the proportion of people living in poverty in the UK rose; in 1996/97 the figure was 25 per cent and in 2006/2007, 22 per cent. Currently, 30 per cent of children live in poverty (for detailed, up-to-date information, see Palmer *et al.*, 2008; for a review of poverty and inequality since Labour came to power in 1997, see Hills *et al.*, 2009).

CRIME PREVENTION, CRIME REDUCTION AND COMMUNITY SAFETY

As we saw in Chapter 12, politicians and policy makers in both Britain and the United States had, by the 1980s, become disenchanted with the notion of rehabilitation and approaches to criminal justice based upon welfarist principles. In a 'nothing works' (Martinson, 1974) atmosphere, and encouraged by right-wing political agendas, there was a shift in policy towards informal, as well as formal, modes of social control, and crime prevention policies based upon the idea of situational crime control. This shift was influenced by the work of administrative and conservative criminologists, and in turn stimulated further academic work of this sort (for a brief review, see James and Raine, 1998).

Although 'Definitions of crime prevention . . . remain the subject of intense debate' (Crawford, 1998: 27), it became a key organising concept for criminal justice policy makers from the early 1980s onwards (see, for example: Tuck, 1988; Graham and Bennett, 1995; Ekblom, 2000; Pease, 2002), though it was largely used in relation to situational crime control. Throughout the 1980s and 1990s various governmental and non-governmental bodies were set up and charged with developing 'best practice' in areas of crime prevention, and a variety of reports on this theme were published. One such report published by the Standing Conference on Crime Prevention in 1991 – the Morgan Report – was destined to be particularly influential. The authors suggested that crime prevention should be a statutory responsibility of local authorities, though they preferred the term 'community safety' to that of crime prevention. The incumbent government may not have been overly impressed by the report, especially because of the Conservatives unwillingness to devolve crime prevention responsibilities to the local authorities (the government responded by replacing the Standing Conference with another body – a National Board for Crime Prevention), but the report's sentiments were in accord with those of nascent New Labour.

As the discussion that follows indicates, New Labour's approach to law and order exhibits both continuities and discontinuities with that of the previous administration, in addition to being contingent upon wider, global social and economic changes. Key examples of continuity are:

- a continuing core investment in strategies of situational crime control (linked, initially, to community safety, then to crime reduction);
- a commitment to the notion of partnerships and inter-agency cooperation;
- a commitment to market-style reforms, privatisation and the management of problems of crime and disorder through a process of devolution of responsibility to criminal justice managers and the local community;
- an emphasis on the management of risk and the reduction of victimisation, rather than on traditional criminal justice concerns such as the apprehension and conviction of offenders;
- presiding over a large, expanding prison population as part of an avowed mission to be 'tough on crime'.

In spite of the Conservative government's rejection of many of its recommendations, the ideas presented in the Morgan Report found fertile ground within many local authorities prior to the 1997 election. Although some local authorities had introduced strategies based upon the notion of community safety in the 1980s (when it was virtually synonymous with crime prevention), during the 1990s local authority discourses on crime and disorder were increasingly structured around the term, and by the mid-1990s a majority had policy statements on community safety in place. This process was encouraged by the availability of central government funding (in the shape of the Challenge Fund and partnership grants). Social policy was, it appeared, being criminalised. Community safety continued to have a powerful resonance among local authorities following the election of New Labour, and there was a proliferation of community safety coordinators/officers, and community safety strategies. However, there was (and is) no consensus regarding the precise definition of 'community safety'.

There is some agreement on a general level regarding its meaning, though. It is seen as encompassing a broader range of risk-related, quality of life issues than the concept of crime prevention, for example anti-social behaviour, the so-called fear of crime, road safety and environmental pollution. The obvious question to ask, though, is where is the line to be drawn? Writing prior to the election of a Labour administration, Hughes (1998: 10) argued that its conceptual vagueness opens up at least the possibility of progressive policies at the local level:

> . . . the very emptiness of the concept of community safety . . . perhaps offers the opportunity for creative ideological appropriation by local, progressive alliances and networks which could challenge regressive local and centralist tendencies on law and order.

It is also generally agreed (in conformity with the Morgan Report) that community safety is concerned with both the situational and the social aspects of crime and disorder, in the sense that dealing with such problems requires the involvement of the local community in general – local residents, the local authority, business and various agencies – so that on the basis of partnerships and multi-agency cooperation, all are actively mobilised in the pursuit of a safer social environment. The emphasis on the victim has made crime prevention virtually synonymous with victimisation avoidance, thereby continuing an approach to criminal justice based increasingly on the management of risk (the concept of 'risk' is discussed below). Such an approach, directed at risky situations, risky populations and populations *at* risk, requires the development of mechanisms capable of auditing and assessing risk within a local context. As a consequence, under the custodianship of New Labour, we have seen the further intrusion of an audit culture into criminal justice processes and beyond. Insurance companies have honed their actuarial skills and produced assessments of the risks of household burglary according to particular postcodes. This information can then be used to determine the costs of insurance premiums, and whether or not conditions involving extra security measures should be attached to a policy; in some cases, the information results in a refusal to provide insurance (actuarialism and criminal justice policy is discussed below). This offers another glimpse of an evolving process of what came to be termed 'responsibilisation' in this country, whereby individual citizens are expected to become active partners in the prevention and reduction of crime (O'Malley, 1996; Haggerty, 2003).

Beginning in the 1980s, and continuing today, the realm of penology has embraced the techniques of management through electronic tagging and the extension and increasing privatisation of the prison estate. In the case of the latter, attempts at rehabilitation (especially in relation to younger prisoners) still continue, but the primary concern is with cost effectiveness, and the control of prisoners through incapacitation. The high recidivism rates, especially among young offenders, provide a sobering counter-argument to the view that 'prison works'. Although managerialist techniques of risk reduction that seek to identify those thought to pose the greatest threat are very often directed at the socially excluded, a significant development over the past few years is the application of these techniques to the population in general, or at least those who happen to be present in a particular location, for example one covered by CCTV cameras (though research has shown that, in practice, operatives in CCTV control rooms often use common-sense and/or discriminatory understandings of 'risky people' – see Norris and Armstrong, 1999).

From community safety to community crime reduction

New Labour's ideas on law and order that were developed prior to their election victory culminated in the 1998 Crime and Disorder Act, which made local authorities and the police the 'responsible authorities' working in partnership with other agencies as members of a Crime and Disorder Reduction Partnership (CDRP). The government also provided a significant amount of funding linked to a National Crime Reduction Strategy, as part of its comprehensive spending review. The strategy reflected the government's enthusiasm for evaluative criminological research aimed at establishing examples of 'what works', and the use of the term 'crime reduction' rather than 'community safety', itself indicated a narrowing of focus and the creation of a policy domain where success or failure are more amenable to quantitative assessment. A 'what works' database has been produced by the Crime Prevention College; Home Office 'toolkits' provided practical advice to local CDRPs; and the Social Exclusion Unit works in unison with the Crime Prevention Agency in order to coordinate various cross-departmental initiatives. In addition, NVQ education programmes in this field have been developed as a way of enhancing practitioner expertise. In sum, it is a complex, and still developing, edifice built around notions of risk, crime reduction, community, partnerships and audits. Particularly worth noting in this respect is the statutory duty placed on the responsible authorities in England and Wales to produce three-yearly crime and disorder 'strategic asssessments in their locality, and to use the information as the basis for setting a crime and disorder reduction strategy, and assessing the success or otherwise of previous strategies' (Tierney, 2001). A number of writers have pointed out that the success of initiatives derived from a 'what works' principle is dependent upon local political and organisational contexts. As Tilley (2001: 81) says, the principle becomes 'dangerous nonsense' when these contexts are not taken into account.

Crime reduction may have replaced community safety as the central focus, but 'community' plays a central role in crime reduction discourses, and incorporates notions of social disorganisation, subcultural strain theory and relative deprivation. There is also a tendency to characterise neighbourhoods in terms of 'the community' – victims or potential victims of crime – and, regardless of whether or not they actually live in the neighbourhood, 'outsiders' – that is, offenders. The community is expected to involve itself in crime reduction (Neighbourhood Watch, improved security, providing witnesses, and engaging in consultation processes with CDRPs).

Research on inter- or multi-agency partnerships, including my own research (Tierney, 2001), has indicated some of the problems that can arise due to sectional interests and power differentials (Crawford, 1997; Gilling, 1997). The police, for instance, may dominate the local policy process because of their role of 'information brokers' (Ericson, 1994). Garland (2000) argues that these developments have created a 'crime complex' – a 'distinctive culture' where public opinion and media and political discourses are obsessively concerned with the risks of crime. As a consequence, people are acutely conscious of the requirement to manage and organise their lives in order to avoid victimisation, which in turn has led to the growth of a vast, and highly lucrative, security industry. And as Stenson (2001: 22–3) says:

> The introduction, *inter alia*, of CCTV, new insurance technologies, new means to assess and manage 'dangerousness' and other risks of crime . . . are among the host of ways in which new powers have, to use Michel Foucault's term, created a new 'governmentality'. This refers to the new means to render populations thinkable and measurable, through categorisation, differentiation, and sorting into hierarchies.

CRIME AND CRIMINAL JUSTICE: THE WIDER CONTEXT

Globalisation, social change and late modernity

By the last part of the twentieth century a variety of global social, economic and political changes were already having a profound impact on social life – locally and at the level of the nation state. As we have seen, criminology as an academic discipline was a product of the Enlightenment, and for most of its history has allied itself to what has been described as a modernist project. Criminology, along with other disciplines, has had to confront the challenges posed by these changes to the nature of social life, as well as the intellectual challenges emerging from the development of what purport to be more appropriate modes of theoretical analysis. The society that we now inhabit has been variously, and sometimes bewilderingly, labelled as late-modernity, high-modernity, liquid modernity, hypermodernity, postmodernity, post-fordist, post-industrial, New Times and risk society. If the social world can no longer be described as 'modernist', then, it is argued, modernist methodologies, intellectual assumptions and conceptual frameworks harnessed in an effort to explain and understand crime and deviance are singularly unsuited to the task at hand (South, 1997). The most strident expressions of such a view are associated with postmodernist social thought, and this and its influence on sociological criminology are examined in Chapter 15. However, although there is widespread agreement among sociologists that, since the mid-twentieth century, there have been major changes to social life, there are intense debates regarding the precise nature of these changes, as indicated by the various labels used to describe present conditions. For some, there has been a qualitative transformation of such magnitude that sociology's theories and concepts have ceased to be viable (Baudrillard, 1988), whilst others view the modernist project as unfinished (Habermas, 1987).

There is not the space here to delve into the complex nuances of these debates, but we can summarise the main social, economic and political changes that have been identified (needless to say, the impact of these varies from society to society, as well as in particular societies):

- globalisation;
- post-industrialism and post-fordism;
- the dominance of neo-liberal *laissez-faire* capitalism, accompanied by a stress on individualism and an intense consumerist culture, where consumption functions as the vehicle for exploring and developing identities;
- a restructuring of labour markets and social class relations, involving a flexible and rapidly changing workforce;
- the expansion of information technology and mass communications, impacting on the circulation of knowledge, which, together with greater amounts of geographical mobility, have led to what Garland and Sparks (2000) describe as 'the stretching of time and space';
- a restructuring of family and community life;
- enhanced opportunities to construct personal identities freed from the cultural constraints associated with class, ethnicity, gender and sexuality, leading to diverse and contradictory social processes;
- a heightened sense of uncertainty and ambiguity regarding social life and increasing concerns with risk and security;
- the (paradoxical) growth of both individually located moral relativism and fundamentalist appeals to moral absolutism.

Some time ago, Hood (1991) used the term New Public Management to describe the ways in which organisational techniques previously associated with the private sector were now being applied to public sector organisations, including those concerned with criminal justice. Driven by the principles of efficiency, effectiveness and economy, this approach continued with the election of New Labour in 1997. In consequence, the world of criminal justice is now steeped in managerialist concepts of targets, auditable performance, best value and consumer sovereignty, and strongly committed to market-based competition as well as, where thought appropriate, privatisation. It has also incorporated a process of decentralisation, whereby responsibility and accountability for implementing criminal justice policies are devolved by central government to smaller, localised organisational units. This is particularly evident in the case of local Crime and Disorder Reduction Partnerships. Thus overall policies derive from central government, which also controls the funding available, but these policies are put into practice at a local level, on the basis of inter-agency partnerships. Political theorists have described these developments as, for example: 'Hollowing out of the national state' (Jessop, 1993); 'Governing without government' (Rhodes, 1997); 'Death of the social' (Rose, 1996). As Leishman *et al.* (1996) have argued, though, processes of governance based upon elements of centralisation, decentralisation and fragmentation, carry the potential for conflict among the constituent parts.

This raises an important, general issue. In these analyses, such developments are situated within the context of an increasingly globalised world; however, the social, economic and political features of globalisation find expression in regional and local contexts. In other words, globalisation does not mean the end of the local. As Hobbs (1998: 416) puts it in a discussion of organised crime:

> The dialectics between the local and global . . . epitomises and underlines markets in both the legitimate and illegitimate spheres where complex affinities between global and local spaces are negotiated, creating an enacted environment consisting of indigenous renditions of global markets.

Risk and security

In recent years, a significant amount of academic work has focused on the notion of risk, including, notably, Beck (1992) and his concept of a 'risk society' (see also, Furedi, 1997; Leonard, 1997; Franklin, 1998; Giddens, 1998). In such a society, there is a heightened sensitivity to, and awareness of, threats to personal security. The risks involved permeate all areas of social life, taking in such things as crime, pollution, disease, contaminated foodstuffs and nuclear accidents. Whilst it is acknowledged that risks have been a feature of social life throughout history, in contemporary societies risks are seen as an unpredictable consequence of global technological and economic developments:

> The modern view of risk was as artefact, measurable, knowable, calculable, and predictable. Risks in late or postmodernity as it has been dubbed, are characterized by uncertainty, indeterminancy, contingency and their global impact. Contemporary risks also require personal choice and navigation, resulting in increased uncertainty, anxiety and reflexivity.
>
> (Kemshall, 2003: 8)

Kemshall (2003: 8), though, also points out that: 'risk is actually a highly politicized and contentious concept, and has changed both in terms of meaning and usage throughout history'.

The contentious nature of the concept of risk is indicated by a number of critical responses to, for example, Beck's characterisation of the 'risk society' (see, for instance,

Adams, 1995; Turner, 2001). Within the context of law and order, the politicised nature of discourses of risk has two important implications. First, an emphasis upon the risks of criminal victimisation can generate political capital if the public believes that a party in power, or a party seeking power, offers the best hope of minimising the chances of such victimisation. And, second, the public's preoccupation with the risk of victimisation can prepare the ground for the acceptance of new, more intrusive, legislative powers introduced as necessary if the public is to be protected. Current concerns with international terrorism following the attacks on the New York World Trade Center in 2001, London in 2005, and elsewhere around the world, have led to a wide range of global responses, involving both internal and external security. The British government's anti-terrorist legislation, for example, allows suspects to be detained for lengthy periods without charge or access to legal advice, a similar situation to that at Guantanamo Bay in Cuba, where hundreds of suspected terrorists are presently being held in detention (though US President Obama plans to have the facility closed down in the near future).

Surveillance

Allied to discussions of security and risk is the issue of surveillance. Developments in various forms of surveillance in the UK since 1997 have stimulated much research and debate among politicians, journalists and civil liberties organisations, as well as academic criminologists.

It is estimated that there are between 4 and 5 million CCTV cameras currently in use in the UK, a greater number than in any other country in the world. Cameras are increasingly incorporating automatic number plate recognition (ANPR), and in the near future this will allow all road vehicle journeys to be tracked and recorded. Information will be stored for up to five years. In addition, many CCTV cameras include facial recognition technology. Transport for London 'Oyster' cards record details of journeys made, and this information can be requested by authorised agencies.

If implemented through legislation, the government's 2008 communication data bill will create a central database able to track all telephone calls that an individual makes, every website visited, and every text and email they send. It is intended that this information will be routinely stored and analysed. The bill proposes that telecoms companies and internet service providers will be legally required to give this information to the Home Office in order to protect national security and aid in the detection of crime. Records based on mobile networks can now locate a caller to within 100 metres, wherever they are. The new database will be operated by the private sector. Since October 2008, telecoms companies have been required to store records of phone calls and text messages for twelve months. At the present time, under the Regulation of Investigatory Powers Act, approximately 700 bodies are licensed to make a certified request to telecoms or internet companies for information on the use of their services by individuals. During the last 12 months, around half a million requests were made. The Act allows local authorities to, in effect, spy on residents in order, for example, to satisfy themselves that a particular family actually lives within the catchment area of a school to which they have applied to send their child.

ID cards containing biometric information are gradually being introduced in the UK. The process began in 2008 with foreign residents and is scheduled to take four years to complete. Information from ID cards will be stored on the National Identity Register, a database capable of recording all instances where an individual discloses their identity in order to access a service, for example when hiring a car or booking a flight. This information will stay on the database until the cardholder dies.

Piloted in 2004, the National e-Borders Scheme uitilises advance passenger information from airlines etc. in order to establish personal profiles of anyone entering or leaving the UK. Where necessary, travel histories can be built up using biometric data, such as iris patterns and face recognition. The system is expected to become fully operational in 2009, and the information is primarily for use by the Home Office, though other government security agencies will, when necessary, have access to it. It is also worth noting that since the attacks on the World Trade Center in New York in 2001, major agreements relating to issues of security have been established between the European Union and the United States. As Bunyan (2008: 1) points out, there are six agreements covering justice and home affairs:

1   Europol (exchange of data)
2   Mutual assistance (yet to come into effect)
3   PNR (passenger name record)
4   SWIFT (all financial transactions, commercial and personal)
5   Extradition (yet to come into effect)
6   Container Security Initiative (CSI)

The first four involve the exchange of personal information on individuals. All have been controversial with the one on PNR going to the European Court of Justice with the result that its legal basis had to be changed.

In proportion to its population, the UK has the largest DNA database in the world. According to the Home Office, genetic samples from 7 per cent of the population are stored on the database. Virtually everyone arrested by the police for a recordable offence is required to provide a DNA sample, regardless of whether or not criminal proceedings follow, and the information is retained until the individual reaches their 100th birthday. Genetic information on just over 1 million children and juveniles aged under 18 years is now stored on this database. Home Office figures indicate that of these, 88 per cent were either charged, convicted or received a warning; however, the percentage of these who were charged but subsequently found not guilty has not been made public. Townsend and Asthana (2008: 1) report that:

> The director of forensic science at Scotland Yard and DNA spokesman for the Association of Chief Police Officers, said a debate was needed on how far Britain should go in identifying potential offenders, given that some experts believe it is possible to identify future offending traits in children as young as five.

The retention of the DNA of those not found guilty of a criminal offence has been of particular concern to many people. In fact, in 2008 the European Court of Human Rights ruled that the UK government was in breach of the European Convention by retaining the genetic material of innocent people.

Developments in surveillance technologies and techniques in the UK and other countries are a response to previous and possible future acts of terrorism, as well as increasingly sophisticated and globalised forms of (non-political) crime, notably illegal drug markets. Critical debate regarding these developments has focused on necessity and efficacy (do we need all of these measures and do they work?), and issues of privacy and civil liberties (has the reach and power of surveillance gone too far?). The answers to these questions are, of course, not at all self-evident, but depend upon both knowledge and subjective judgements. Few members of the public possess any significant relevant knowledge relating to, for instance, the amount and nature of terrorist actions that have been thwarted, or the number of criminal convictions resulting from the use of different sorts of surveillance. Thus, in general, judgements will be informed by beliefs and impressions regarding successful outcomes, combined with subjective perceptions regarding civil liberties, privacy and human rights.

Many writers have gathered together the issues raised above and discussed them within the context of human rights. Raab (2009), for example, provides a critical overview of the increase in the state's legal powers since Labour came to power in 1997, pointing out that since then, the Home Office has introduced more legislation than all previous governments combined.

Actuarial justice

The origins of actuarialism lie in the insurance business. It refers to the process of using statistical data in order to calculate the chances of a particular type of event, such as an injury or a burglary, occurring. This assessment of risk is based upon the production of aggregated data, for example all houses within a given postcode area, or all people of a certain age. Insurance premiums reflect the degree of risk: the greater the risk, the greater the premium. According to Feeley and Simon (1994) actuarialist principles have gradually permeated the criminal justice process. Referred to as actuarial justice, it involves identifying, classifying and, ultimately, managing populations that are considered to pose a threat to others. Borrowing from the world of insurance, the focus is on these populations as aggregates, rather than as individuals and, unlike traditional approaches to justice, where individuals are judged *after* they have offended, here judgements are anticipatory:

> Actuarial reasoning about risk gives rise to distinctive techniques for managing risk. Risk-management is forward-looking, predictive, oriented to aggregate entities and concerned with the minimization of harms and costs, rather than with the attribution of blame or the dispensation of individual justice.
>
> (Garland, 1997: 182)

Strategies of actuarial justice, then, depend upon the collation of information in order to build up profiles of high risk populations. The police (especially police Intelligence Units) are a key repository for this information, which can come from a wide range of sources: criminal records, beat officers, informers, Neighbourhood Watch members, targeted surveillance, CCTV operatives, etc. However, whilst actuarial discourses present an image of rational-scientific risk assessment and decision making, research shows that the authorities often use moral judgements, guesswork and hunches based upon stereotypical understandings of particular groups, and actuarial justice is to a significant extent mobilised to target the socially and economically deprived sections of society (Stillman-Ashby, 2004). Using the example of the regulation of student alcohol use in Canada, Moore (2000) shows how the authorities utilise common sense, as well as 'scientific' actuarial knowledge, as a basis for decision making. A further dimension to this, as Hudson (1995: 12) has argued, is that the use of actuarial, 'risk factor' assessment as the basis of sentencing can discriminate against black people: 'Criteria such as stable home or employment record obviously disadvantage black people who have higher rates of unemployment and face more discrimination in housing, than do their white counterparts'.

CRIMINOLOGY IN THE NEW MILLENNIUM

We can begin this section with some good news. Since the first edition of this book appeared in 1996, criminology's fortunes as an academic discipline have improved significantly. This includes sociological criminology, though the whole issue of once relatively discrete academic subject areas has become more contentious and problematic. However, the last few years have seen a large growth in the number of undergraduate and postgraduate degree programmes in criminology, and associated areas (helped partly by the government's commitment to expanding the number of people studying for a degree and, good or bad, by the popularity of the television series

Cracker and *CSI*), and NVQ courses in community safety have been introduced in the further education sector. There are also now 'benchmark statements' for criminology from the Quality Assurance Agency (these function to provide academic guidelines for undergraduate degree programmes in England and Wales). At the same time, individual modules in the sociology of crime and deviance, offered as components of a broader sociology undergraduate degree, continue to be popular. As Garland (2002: 45) says in a historical review of criminology: 'its continued expansion is perhaps a measure of the social and institutional forces that continue to underwrite the existence of British criminology'.

This expansion within higher education has had a multiplier effect in terms of the number of academics teaching and researching in the area of criminology and, obviously, work is more likely to be published if there exists a thriving market. This is good news for those working within the discipline, especially if they are the authors of criminology texts such as this. A further consideration here is the sword of Damocles hanging over the heads (and furrowed brows) of academics these days – the periodic Research Assessment Exercise (RAE). Under this system, examples of published research are submitted to a national body for assessment. The subsequent ratings contribute to the reputation of a university and its subject areas in terms of research activity and quality, as well as the amount of research funding that can be attracted. This too has contributed to the blossoming of research and publications among all academic disciplines, including criminology. However, debates about the overall quality of such publications, rather than the quantity, have trundled on since the inception of the RAE process, but these will be sidestepped here. We can also note that an expansion of student numbers in universities has led to increasing financial pressures on this sector, with the result that managers have increasingly encouraged academic staff to seek out research grants. For criminologists, evaluative research has provided one of these sources of income. The growth of what Marginson and Considine (2000) have called the 'enterprise university' has, however, had important ramifications in terms of advances in the development of criminological theory. Lacking 'practical' relevance and, if written from a critical perspective, antagonistic towards the machinery of social control within neo-liberal economies, funding directed at theoretical scholarship is likely to be in relatively short supply.

The development of an approach to criminal justice based on decentralisation and infused with notions of risk, performance indicators, audits and 'what works' has created a growing demand for various types of national and locally based research. Although much national research of this sort has been carried out by Home Office researchers, it has also been contracted out to academic criminologists. At a local level, as mentioned earlier, Crime and Disorder Reduction Partnerships (CDRP) are obliged to carry out yearly audits of crime and disorder (including community consultation and 'fear of crime' surveys), and develop crime and disorder reduction strategies – since 2006 these have been referred to as 'strategic assessments'. Along with this, they are expected to conduct evaluations of crime and disorder reduction initiatives introduced locally. As a consequence, and especially during the first few years following the 1998 Crime and Disorder Act (which introduced a three-yearly version) when 'in-house' expertise tended to be in short supply, criminologists found themselves in demand (though local authorities and their CDRPs also used private research organisations). Evaluative, policy-oriented research is, of course, not the same as research oriented towards the development of theory, and for this reason often has little status among those who have grander ambitions for criminology. Additionally, Bottoms (1995) argues that policy-oriented research of this kind often pushes the researchers into a world more familiar to accountants than criminologists. On a more optimistic note, though, local research of this type *could* provide opportunities to venture beyond 'evaluation' as narrowly conceived. There is the potential for academic researchers to influence the local policy process by utilising a critical perspective and drawing on the conceptual language of academic criminology. Furthermore, the findings from evaluation research can provide the raw materials for the development of theoretical ideas. As the American critical criminologist Currie (2007: 183) puts it: 'the bottom line question is . . . if we don't do this work, who will?'

Nonetheless, and as Walters (2001: 215) reminds us:

> Criminology throughout its development has largely been a state-directed enterprise and there is a growing trend by government to shape the type and production of criminological knowledge, that is, a pragmatic knowledge tied to the immediate needs of the state apparatus.

Thus the type of criminological research that is in demand, and listened to by policy makers, is circumscribed by particular political agendas and convictions. The research referred to above is directed at already existing criminal justice policies; the influence of criminological research on the actual creation of policy is much less apparent. This is an issue explored by Haggerty (2003) (see also, Becket, 1997; Caplow and Simon, 1999; and Walters, 2007). Although he discusses it within the context of the United States, it does have relevance to experiences in Britain. His basic argument is that since the 1970s, academic criminology's influence on the development of government policy has diminished significantly, due to (i) the growth of neo-liberalism (ii) the 'ascendancy of a highly symbolic public discourse about crime' (Haggerty, 2003: 217), making it a key factor in elections, and (iii) the introduction of new technologies of control. Under these conditions, the legitimisation and endorsement of criminal justice policies by experts from criminology becomes increasingly irrelevant, their places taken by political advisers and focus groups. Although criminological research still has an important role to play, its value is judged in terms of its pragmatic contribution to particular strategies of crime control: 'criminologists becoming experts in the operation of distinctive forms of panoptic power' (Haggerty, 2004: 217). This is not to say that criminologists have had no influence on policy formation over the last twenty-five years or so, rather, that when they have been influential it is because their expert contributions are congruent with that government's broad political agenda. This agenda has increasingly taken consumer preferences, located in perceptions of 'public opinion', into account. It is for this reason that administrative criminology (discussed in Chapter 13), with its emphasis on crime reduction through situational crime control, has continued to have an influential role in terms of policy. At the same time, mainstream criminology's empirical work on the correlation between various social and economic factors and the propensity to offend has found a ready audience among local CDRPs (see the discussion of criminal career research in Chapter 13). This has arisen from the requirement to identify such things as crime and disorder hot-spots and young people 'at risk', and in the process consider what are seen as relevant causal factors (though local strategies are dominated by situational crime control and 'community safety'). The criminal career research associated with mainstream criminology is nowadays subsumed under the title of developmental criminology, and is concerned with:

> . . . the development of offending and anti-social behaviour; risk factors at different ages; and the effects of life events on the course of development . . . efforts are made to investigate the prevalence of offending at different ages, the frequency of offending by offenders, the ages of onset and desistance, and specialization and escalation of offending over time.
>
> (Farrington, 2002: 658, in a useful overview)

The pressure on academic criminologists and contract researchers to attract outside research funding nowadays, and the implications of this from the point of view of the constraints it imposes on the nature of the research carried out, is for many a major source of concern. For example, in a fairly bleak assessment, Barton *et al.* (2007: 200) comment:

> Academic researchers, if they fail to break out of the state and policy-funded trap, are expected to spend their entire careers working to research specifications and answering research questions designed by bureaucrats. The disciplinary aspects of this process are obvious, as are the less remarked-upon effects of alienation experienced by this growing army of contract researchers in universities.

However, we should not ignore the progressive gains in relation to criminal justice policy that have been nudged along by important contributions from more critical researchers and theorists. Good examples are in areas of domestic violence, racially motivated violence, and rape.

Questions regarding the role and relevance of criminology have surfaced recently within the context of debates around the notion of public criminologies. These debates have been influenced by Burawoy's (2004, 2005) arguments in favour of developing a public sociology, with criminologists shifting the focus from one academic discipline to another. Following Burawoy, advocates of public criminologies (see, for example, Chancer and McLaughlin, 2007; Currie, 2007) take the argument beyond the need to simply engage in policy-oriented research. Whilst there are disputes as to its precise meaning, on a general level 'public' criminology looks beyond academia, and seeks to inform broader public and political debate and media representations, in order to have a significant (and progressive) influence on public policy relating to crime and criminal justice. Thus, for example, instead of writing books that will only be read by a handful of academics, criminologists are encouraged to put their energies into informative criminological books that are aimed at a much wider audience – in the United States such books are referred to (sometimes disparagingly) as 'trade' books (Currie, 2007). When governments place great emphasis on attempting to match their policies to 'public opinion' – as assessed by, for instance, so-called focus groups – then influencing public opinion could play a part in, in turn, influencing public policy.

This is an interesting and important issue, and raises the fundamental question of what is criminology for? There is a long-standing complaint within the discipline that academic criminology has made little impact on actual criminal justice policy and practice. The extent of this influence has, though, ebbed and flowed over the years. In the immediate post-war period, when the government was striving to construct a welfare state, British criminologists worked closely with politicians and policy makers (Garland and Sparks, 2000). In the United States the early 1960s saw strong influence on policy coming from strain theorists such as Cloward and Ohlin (1960). However, as mentioned above, the influence of criminological ideas and knowledge on public policy will always be contingent upon the degree to which they are in tune with the broader political ideas, or ideologies, of those in power. Since the 1950s and 1960s the world has, of course, changed enormously. As Chance and McLaughlin (2007: 157) put it:

> The categorizations that a generation of post-war criminologists took for granted have been sidelined by (a) the politicization of crime fears (b) victim-oriented criminal justice policy shifts and (c) the extension of private sector involvement in crime control and the delivery of criminal justice services.

At the same time (as this book illustrates), there has been an exponential growth in the sheer volume of criminological research and theory, bringing with it a huge number of competing, and often contradictory voices from within the discipline. Policy makers have to decide which of these voices to listen to. For Currie (2007: 179), part of the problem lies within the (largely university-based) discipline itself:

> . . . we are not well set up institutionally to do this job. There are few structural incentives for it, and indeed there are very powerful *dis*incentives to doing the kind of work

we need to do if we want to affect the public mind. The hard fact is that you get few points in the academic discipline of criminology . . . for doing this work, and indeed you may get hurt if you do too much of it, especially in the institutions that wield the most 'clout' and credibility in the wider world – the research universities.

The nature and role of radical or critical criminology under these circumstances has been the subject of some debate since the mid-1990s, and is obviously of particular interest for those whose work has grown out of a left-wing, socialist tradition (Walton and Young, 1998; Carrington and Hogg, 2002). The fall from grace of Marxism – which provided radical criminology's theoretical foundations – and the dismantling of state socialism in the former Soviet Union, etc., and with it the seemingly inexorable growth of neo-liberal market societies, have clearly had a major impact. The response among writers belonging to this tradition has been to theorise the nature of law-and-order policies within the context of these social, economic and political changes (see, for example, Taylor, 1999; Garland, 2000; Pitts, 2001; Stenson and Sullivan, 2001; Lea, 2002; Matthews and Young, 2003), whilst exploring the possibilities in terms of developing a distinctive, coherent and convincing radical/critical criminology in a post-Marxist period (this is examined in detail in the next chapter). There are significant challenges attached to this task:

> Very few would have predicted the rapid demise of radical criminology, a brand of theorizing that once seemed so strong that it would sweep all before it, at least in large parts of Europe, Canada, and Australasia.
>
> (Rock, 2002: 75)

One prominent writer, Jock Young, who continues to address these challenges, makes an important, positive point regarding critical criminology at the present time:

> My argument so far is that critical criminology in this age of the gulag and the punitive turn is massively needed – it is the counter-voice to neoliberalism and conservatism. And what is more, critical criminology is flourishing.
>
> (Young, 2002: 259)

Young then goes on to substantiate his claim, listing a large number of texts in this genre, including this book. Personally, I am happy to endorse this view, whilst at the same time acknowledging that there is no simple answer to the question of precisely what is meant by the appellation 'critical' in this context. Notwithstanding this, inevitably, undergraduate students of criminology will be introduced to the ideas contained in these texts, and these students will provide the next generation of theorists and researchers (including those who will conduct evaluative research similar to that discussed above).

Selected further reading

A good introduction to the area of crime prevention and community safety is **Hughes, G. (1998)** *Understanding Crime Prevention*, Buckingham: Open University Press; and to the theme of social control in contemporary society, **Innes, M. (2003)** *Understanding Social Control: Deviance, crime and social order*, Maidenhead: Open University Press.

For more detailed analyses of crime prevention and community safety see **Crawford, A. (1998)** *Crime Prevention and Community Safety: Politics, policies and practice*, London: Longman; and Matthews, R. and Pitts, J. (eds) (2001) *Crime, Disorder and Community Safety*, London: Routledge. Gilling, D. (2007) *Crime Reduction and Community Safety: Labour and the politics of local crime control*, Cullompton: Willan analyses New Labour's policies and their impact at a local level. See also, **Hughes, G. (2007)** *The Politics of Crime and Community*, Basingstoke: Palgrave.

Critical discussions of a range of issues pertaining to contemporary crime control are provided by: Stenson, K. and Sullivan, R. R. (eds) (2001) *Crime, Risk and Justice*, Cullompton: Willan; Matthews, R. and Young, J. (eds) (2003) *The New Politics of Crime and Punishment*, Cullompton: Willan; and Blomberg, T. G. and Cohen, S. (eds) (2003) *Punishment and Social Control*, 2nd edn, New York: Aldine de Gruyter. A critical analysis of government responses to so called anti-social behaviour is provided by **Burney, E. (2005)** *Making People Behave: Anti-social behaviour, politics and policy*, Cullompton: Willan.

The use of imprisonment within the context of market society is examined by **Stern, V. (2006)** *Creating Criminals: Prisons and people in market society*, London: Zed Books. A very comprehensive overview of imprisonment will be found in **Jewkes, Y. (ed) (2007)** *The Prisons Handbook*, Cullompton: Willan.

For an authoritative guide to current key anti-terrorist legislation in this country, see **Walker, C. (2009)** *Blackstone's Guide to the Anti-Terrorism Legislation*, 2nd edn, Oxford: Oxford University Press. The 'extraordinary rendition' programme of the United States, which involved the secret transfer of terrorist, or terrorism-connected, suspects to prisons in various parts of the world, is examined by **Grey, S. (2006)** *Ghost Plane: The true story of the CIA torture program*, New York: C. Hurst and Co.

The classic text on 'risk society' is **Beck, U. (1992)** *Risk Society: Towards a new modernity*, London: Sage, and Kemshall, H. (2003) *Understanding Risk in Criminal Justice*, Maidenhead: Open University Press, offers an accessible introduction to notions of risk, risk assessment and actuarialism within the context of criminal justice.

For a critical discussion of the Labour government's legislative programme and its impact on civil liberties, see **Raab, D. (2009)** *The Assault on Liberty*, London: HarperCollins. A good introduction to surveillance and CCTV is **Coleman, R. (2004)**, *Reclaiming the Streets: Surveillance, social control and the city*, Cullompton: Willan. Also on the theme of surveillance: **Lyon, D. (2007)** *Surveillance Studies: An overview*, Oxford: Polity and Mathiesen, T. (2004) 'The rise of the surveillant state in times of globalization', in C. Sumner (ed) *The Blackwell Companion to Criminology*, Oxford: Blackwell.

The concept of actuarial justice was originally put forward in **Feeley, M. and Simon, J. (1994)** 'Actuarial justice: The emerging new criminal law', in D. Nelken (ed), *The Futures of Criminology*, London: Sage.

Restorative justice has a theoretical basis in the work of John Braithwaite: **Braithwaite, J. (1989)** *Crime, Shame and Reintegration*, Cambridge: Cambridge University Press; for a more recent discussion, see **Ahmed, E., Harris, N., Braithwaite, J. and Braithwaite, V. (2001)** *Shame Management Through Reintegration*, Cambridge: Cambridge University Press. A discussion of restorative justice from a practitioner's perspective is provided by **Liebmann, M. (2007)** *Restorative Justice: How it works*, London: Jessica Kingsley. See **Walgrave, L. (2008)** *Restorative Justice, Self-interest and Responsible Citizenship*, Cullompton: Willan for a sophisticated discussion of the concept. A comprehensive overview of the theory and practice of restorative justice is provided by **Johnstone, G. and Van Ness, D. W. (eds) (2006)** *Handbook of Restorative Justice*, Cullompton: Willan. The journal *Theoretical Criminology*, **10(1), February 2006** is a special issue on the theme of gender, race and restorative justice.

For an interesting discussion of crime and crime control in historical context and contemporary manifestations, see **Lea, J. (2002)** *Crime and Modernity*, London: Sage.

An American study of the crime control industry, which seeks to steer a course between traditional liberal and conservative outlooks, is **Ruth, H. and Reitz, K. R. (2003)** *The Challenge of Crime: Rethinking our response*, Cambridge, MA: Harvard University Press.

The notion of 'public criminology' is explored in detail in **Loader, I. and Sparks, R. (2008)** *Public Criminology? Studying crime and society in the twenty-first century*, Abingdon: Routledge.

CHAPTER 15

THEORETICAL PERSPECTIVES: RECENT DEVELOPMENTS

Key themes

Postmodernist perspectives

Feminist perspectives

Perspectives on masculinities

Control perspectives

Cultural perspectives

Critical perspectives

INTRODUCTION

In this final chapter, the discussion of theoretical developments in criminology is structured around the notion of 'perspectives' rather than, for example, 'schools of thought'. This is to emphasise the continuing fragmentation and diversity characterising contemporary criminological theory in Britain, the United States and elsewhere in the world. The continuing influence of postmodernist thought, along with various critiques, is examined. The chapter gives due weight to more recent feminist perspectives on crime, criminality, social control and social justice, as well as ongoing debates surrounding the concept of masculinity. A resurgence of interest in control theory among academic criminologists and the directions taken by more recent theorists are discussed in detail. So too are highly influential and significant theoretical developments associated with cultural criminology. The chapter concludes with an analysis of critical perspectives and their theories, agendas and relevance as we reach the end of the first decade of the twenty-first century.

This chapter examines developments in criminological theory from the mid-1990s to the present day. The discussion in the previous chapter covered the same period, and provided a general social, political and economic context within which these developments may be situated. This, of course, does not reflect a neat rupture between developments up to the mid-1990s and developments since then.

In order to underline the fact that contemporary criminological theory is characterised by fragmentation and the cross-fertilisation of ideas, the discussion that follows is based upon 'perspectives' rather than 'schools'. Referring to schools gives the wrong impression regarding how criminological theory has evolved in recent years, suggesting as it does, self-contained theoretical clusters. Tracing the recent trajectories of these major perspectives will draw out continuities and discontinuities, complexity and uncertainty and, it is hoped, the vibrancy that still animates this field of study. At the same time, however, the use of the term perspective does allow for the retention of a sense of history in terms of particular theoretical traditions. Whilst not an exhaustive list, in combination, these perspectives are major components of the contemporary criminological project.

This book has introduced the reader to a very wide range of perspectives found within sociological criminology and the sociology of deviance. Many of the ideas constituting this history – sometimes from the relatively distant past – continue to have a presence within contemporary criminology, often reworked in an effort to make them more relevant to a world that has experienced irrevocable global changes over the last quarter of a century. On the other hand, for some criminologists influenced by postmodernist social theory, these ideas are largely associated with a (failed) modernist project and are, therefore, nowadays singularly irrelevant (though none of this is peculiar to criminology). The result is that the recent past has witnessed an intensification of debates regarding what criminology *is*. Ostensibly, this is sobering news for students grappling with the theoretical concerns of criminology, and yet, more positively, such debates are important in that they signal a willingness among at least some criminologists to respond critically to profound social, political and economic change, and in the process address important and interesting theoretical challenges.

At the present time and, indeed, throughout its history, these debates have sprung from the diverse ways in which criminologists have endeavoured to answer certain fundamental questions:

- *What to study*? For example, offending behaviour, social control reactions and criminalisation processes, the nature of the criminal justice system, the meaning of 'crime' and 'deviance', activities that produce social harms, etc.
- *Whom to study*? For example, the usual suspects associated with conventional crime, corporate criminals, professional criminals, the poor, the rich, the state, etc.
- *How to study*? For example, library-based theoretical work, 'hands on' ethnography, from a feminist standpoint, 'number-crunching' using computer software.
- *Why study*? For example, to find the causes of crime, to help in the fight against crime, to transform society, to create gender equality, to fight racism, to attract departmental funds, to enhance one's Research Assessment Exercise rating.

The different ways in which these are answered will shape the theories and research methodologies constituting the discipline – or, as Lea (1998) describes it, 'field' – of criminology. Clearly, the range of possibilities is enormous, and this is reflected in the many different understandings of what is meant by the 'criminological project', and one principal aim of this book is to make problematic the issue of what criminology *is*. The fact that no universal agreement exists, so that we have to speak of criminolog*ies*, is no bad thing; the time to worry is if academic freedom were to be so constrained that intellectual disputes no longer exist. The process of developing and refining criminological theories is unfinishable, rather than unfinished business. From a more negative position (though not one they take themselves), and referring specifically to the sociology of deviance, Downes and Rock (2003: 352) point out that: 'One significant development over the past decade or so has projected the view that it is exhausted, unable to cope with new trends in crime and society or with new perspectives in social theory'.

These views being associated with, respectively, Sumner (1994); Morrison (1995); and Nelken (1994). Sumner's 'obituary' for the sociology of deviance has already been referred to, though this, together with the contributions from the other two sources, is returned to below. Again, it has to be stressed that whilst the various theoretical perspectives addressed in this chapter do not represent an exhaustive list of possibilities, they are, in combination, intended to indicate the main currents within contemporary sociological criminology.

POSTMODERNIST PERSPECTIVES

Postmodernism is discussed here in terms of some of the key themes and ideas with which it is associated, rather than as a 'school' of criminology. Emerging during the second half of the twentieth century, theories described as postmodernist had their origins not in the social sciences, but in fields such as literary criticism and architecture. Postmodernist thought has, though, increasingly influenced the work of sociologists and other social scientists, including those interested in areas of crime and deviance. However, this influence is complex and varied. In some cases, criminological discourses have, wittingly or unwittingly, incorporated a variety of themes and ideas associated with postmodernism, in other cases, discourses are informed by what we might more loosely describe as a postmodern sensibility. The criminologists involved, though, do not necessarily label themselves as 'postmodernists'. Very often, they prefer the term 'late' or 'high' modernity to postmodernity when discussing contemporary society, reflecting a view that we are 'witnessing an acceleration or radicalisation of modernity itself' (Valier, 2002: 171). Furthermore, as Cohen (1998: 101) argues, some of these ideas could be found within criminological theory 'well before Foucault made these subjects intellectually respectable' (see, also, Young, 1998). On the theme of 'deconstruction' – a key postmodernist concept – Cohen traces the deconstruction of the concepts of crime and deviance in new deviancy theory, the new criminology and abolitionism. In their discussion of postmodern criminology, Lilly *et al.* (2007) designate a whole range of criminological work as 'postmodern'; for example, feminist perspectives, the new criminology, abolitionism, peacemaking criminology and constitutive theory. They do this, not simply because the work concerned was produced during a period supposedly following modernity, but because the work represents a critique of the modernist project, and especially positivism. It is, therefore, important to reiterate the point made elsewhere in this book: that although in broad terms particular traditions can be identified, contemporary criminology is characterised by a significant degree of fragmentation. This is not a conspiracy to make life difficult for students of criminology; it reflects the fact that there are no neat divisions between one perspective and another. As a consequence, aspects of postmodernist thought, as outlined below, reappear throughout this chapter.

A further complication is that postmodernism puts forward a philosophical position that is antagonistic towards the idea of grand narratives, including, by definition, a postmodernist grand narrative. Thus as Lea (1998: 165) points out:

> Postmodernism is a bit like criminology in that it too is best described as an area, a loose collection of themes, rather than as in itself a coherent philosophy. To attempt a description of postmodernism in the latter sense would be to fall precisely into the trap of attempting to articulate it as a grand narrative, or global world view, when one of its main thrusts is precisely the denial of the possibility of such standpoints.

However, and acknowledging the above points (and some writers argue that it does represent a grand narrative), we can outline some of the main themes and ideas associated with postmodernism by focusing on three key dimensions.

- First, postmodernist thought developed as a critique of modernism: the philosophical principles that emerged during the Enlightenment period in the eighteenth and nineteenth centuries. Modernism is associated with an optimistic belief in progress, based upon an assumption that the social and physical world can be understood and controlled through the application of scientific rationality. Therefore, as knowledge increased, so would society's ability to solve problems such as crime. As we have seen, and particularly following its absorption of positivist ideas, for much of its history criminological work was dominated by this modernist view of the world (a break with this tradition began with the advent of new deviancy theory): 'Modernity was underpinned by a faith in certain grand narratives . . . particularly those of progress, self-advancement and emancipation' (Morrison, 1995: 453). From a postmodernist perspective this faith was naïve in the extreme. The application of science and technology has in many ways improved the lot of humankind, say postmodernists, but it has also brought with it major problems, such as the destruction of the environment and the power to wage war on a massive scale; it has also provided the basis for enhanced systems of surveillance and control. Furthermore, the so called rationality of modernism orchestrated such things as imperialism, slavery, and class, 'race' and gender inequalities.

- Second, postmodernists argue that during the second half of the twentieth century there was a qualitative transformation in the nature of the social world: a previously modern social world became postmodern. The postmodern social world, or condition, is associated with such things as globalisation, post-industrialism, hyper-consumerism, reflexivity, the dissolution of traditional (left–right) political ideologies, pluralism, diversity and difference.
- Third, postmodernists believe that new – postmodernist – ways of understanding the social world are required.

At the core of modernism is the belief that the application of scientific rationality will gradually reveal the true nature of social reality. Thus from a modernist perspective the social world is, as it were, waiting to be made into an ordered whole on the basis of appropriate concepts (such as capitalism, class structure, masculinity and femininity) and appropriate methodologies (based upon science). For postmodernists, this entire project is fatally flawed and, historically, has created illusions, rather than a truthful model, of social reality. One of the major influences on postmodernist thought came from the post-structuralist theory associated with various French writers, notably Foucault (1977) – who had the greatest influence on a specifically postmodern criminology – Lyotard (1984), Baudrillard (1984) and Derrida (1976). Post-structuralists theorists rejected the view that social processes, relations and behaviours should be analysed and understood by seeing them as products of interrelated and relatively stable, economic, political, kinship etc. institutions constituting the deeper structural basis of social life. Instead, they prioritised human agency and subjectivities, and argued that the 'reality' of social life arises from language and texts; that is, it is embedded in, and constituted by, discourse. From this perspective, there is no other, more 'truthful' (let alone structural) reality.

For post-structuralists, the illusions of modernist thought derive from the nature of language. As mentioned above, a key concept in postmodernism is deconstruction, an intellectual device associated with Derrida (1976). Deconstructionists argue that the words used to give meaning to the social world do not create a 'real' understanding of that world. Rather, they create bodies of knowledge that in effect exclude other, alternative, though ultimately equally valid, bodies of knowledge. At first glance this may seem similar to Marx's notion of ideology. However, for Marx, an ideology is a false representation of reality, and science would unmask ideology in order to provide a true picture of reality. Postmodernists, on the other hand, argue that there is no essential, deeper reality in the social world that can be brought to light; all that we have are texts and signs representing versions of reality and, therefore, the possibilities are limitless. The process of constructing a meaningful social world is, therefore, an expression of power and domination. This is because, say postmodernists, the words used to give meaning to the world require dualities; they are always referenced against an opposite: crime and non-crime, good and bad, feminine and masculine, terrorist and non-terrorist, for instance, as if there existed an essential difference between each of them. Official discourses may create an ordered social world, but by definition it is one based upon seemingly 'fixed' hierarchical social divisions. From the point of view of postmodernists, then, the task should be one of deconstructing language in order to expose the processes whereby knowledge is created.

We can develop this further by examining briefly some aspects of the postmodern condition as seen by postmodernist writers. Of particular importance is the argument that social life has become increasingly pluralistic:

> The basic theme is the 'loss of the social' in the old sense that societies consisted of stable structures, classes and institutions, into which individuals were integrated and from which they took their outlook and social roles . . . Class is being replaced by identity, and stable social and political institutions by a fluid, pluralistic and contingent informalism.
>
> (Lea, 1998: 166)

For postmodernists, therefore, the human subject is free to explore and experiment with a plethora of identities and lifestyles. Unencumbered by the past, or by class, etc., or even by moral foundations (Gardiner, 1996), individual identities are fluid and contingent, and do not constitute a unified whole; indeed, the postmodern condition is seen as requiring this fluidity (Schrag, 1997). This does not mean that there is an absence of morality; rather that the previous, stable, sources of morality have dissolved. The result is a social world characterised by fragmentation and diversity, and a multiplicity of models of order of such complexity as to be unamenable to so called scientific inquiry. As Williams (2000: 71–2) says:

> One strategy – of the sceptical version of postmodernism – invokes the contemporary presence and growth of new kinds of individuals without singular identities, or indeed any of the conventional attributes of stable subjectivities. Such individuals are portrayed as the product of their own autonomous actions chosen without regard to consistency, alignment with collectivities or attachment to moral values.

'Sceptical' postmodernism referred to in the above quote, has been distinguished from 'affirmative' postmodernism. The latter draws back from an utterly relativistic view of competing claims to knowledge, and exhibits an inclination to engage positively with political programmes (see Rosenau, 1992, for a detailed discussion).

This discussion raises an important, fundamental issue regarding postmodernist analyses: an often implicit assumption that analyses of the 'postmodern condition' can only be accomplished by using postmodernist theory and method. This suggests that all other theories and methods are, as far as contemporary society is concerned, irrelevant. It is, though, an assumption that has been rightly challenged by some, for example Carlen (2008: 528) in a discussion of Young's (2007) book *The Vertigo of Late Modernity*:

> Too often sociological and criminological texts have a chronicity of reference that suggests that late or postmodern conditions can only be analysed by reference to postmodern texts; so it was a relief to read a text which demonstrates that sociology can be scientific in the sense of creating new knowledge and new ways of knowing from bits and pieces of classical sociology.

As indicated above, the postmodernist perspective presents a number of key challenges to sociological studies of crime and deviance. Crucially, crime and deviance cannot be distinguished from behaviour in general in terms of some essential meaning; so-called criminal or deviant behaviour is literally everywhere, and contingent upon a plurality of models of order. Furthermore, traditional attempts to identify causal factors (or correlations) become highly problematic because these 'factors' (for instance, class, ethnicity, gender) and the institutional arrangements that supported them no longer have salience.

Constitutive criminology provides an example of affirmative postmodernist theorising oriented explicitly towards the issue of crime. Unsurprisingly, given its intellectual roots, its approach is strikingly different to the approaches associated with the bulk of criminological theorising, and its influence on the discipline of criminology has, at least up to now, been limited. Frankly, and leaving aside the validity of its analyses and ideas, the reason for this probably lies in its theoretical complexity and, reflecting this, the mode of exposition associated with its proponents. As one sociological criminologist puts it: 'Henry and Milovanovic's (1999) almost incomprehensible (to me, at least) constitutive criminology . . .' (Snider, 2004: 245). From the perspective of constitutive criminology, 'crime' is the product of unequal relations of power between one person (the victim) and another (the offender). More specifically: 'the power to deny others their ability to make a difference' (Henry and Milovanovic, 1996: 116). Crime exists when individuals are treated in disrespectful ways so that they are unable to freely express their humanity, thus they are prevented from becoming 'fully social beings'. Crime, therefore, equates with the harm arising from the disrespect shown to victims by offenders. Instead of explaining crime in terms of causal factors as normally understood, constitutive criminologists view it as 'co-produced' by society as a totality. Using what is referred to as a 'holistic' approach, victims and offenders are seen as social identities discursively co-produced, or constructed, by all participants through discourse. Looked at like this, crime, criminality and related phenomena are discursively constituted through social and cultural processes – from policing to film-making.

Postmodernism, sceptical or otherwise, has been subject to a variety of criticisms. Callinicos (1989) sees it as an intellectual fad, which some academics have latched on to as a substitute for Marxism. In his view, so-called postmodernist ideas have been around for many years and can be found in the work of classical sociological theorists such as Marx, Weber and Durkheim. He also says that postmodernism is itself a grand narrative. From the field of literary theory, Eagleton (1996) takes postmodernism to task for its extreme relativism, whereby all tastes and beliefs are seen as being of equal validity. A common criticism is that postmodernism is unable to develop progressive ideas and policies that can change the social world for the better. This, however, is not only associated with postmodernist thought. As Cohen (1998) points out, within the radical tradition in criminology, there are tensions between the merits of deconstructionism and a sceptical outlook, and the merits of engaging with the 'real' world and its problems and harms. He traces these tensions back to the 1960s and new deviancy theory: 'the urge on the one hand to be "relevant", and on the other to detach ourselves from what others define as relevant' (Cohen, 1998: 120). Whilst recognising the practical difficulties that it presents, Cohen (1998: 122) argues the case for a 'triple loyalty' on the part of the criminologist:

> first, an overriding obligation to honest intellectual enquiry itself (however sceptical, provisional, irrelevant and unrealistic); second, a political commitment to social justice, and third (and potentially conflicting with both), the pressing and immediate demands for short-term humanitarian help. We have to appease these three voracious gods.

For critical criminologists in particular, this is problematised around a desire to stay in without 'selling out', that is, attempting to develop a criminological project that is capable of satisfying simultaneously academic, political and human rights agendas. Critical criminology is discussed later.

FEMINIST PERSPECTIVES

Criminology and feminisms

> It might be supposed that today there are few silences left to articulate and the 'classic masculine discourse' of criminology . . . has been well and truly (if paradoxically) 'penetrated' by feminism. This is not the case. Doubts are still expressed . . .
> (Gelsthorpe, 2002: 112)

In spite of the theoretical, institutional and political gains over recent years, from the point of view of feminist writers there is still some way to go before Naffine's (1997) charges that criminology is male-dominated, and that men still tend not to recognise their own maleness (as opposed to women's femaleness), can be dropped. Gelsthorpe (2002: 131) adds a further note of pessimism by suggesting that: 'over the past decade

. . . a popular backlash against feminism . . . has impinged upon the academic world of criminology'. Carrington (2002: 114) argues that post-structuralist ideas and a commitment to anti-essentialism have led to feminism becoming: 'a vital and vibrant part of critical criminology, not some add-on or afterthought', though she also argues that in some quarters of critical criminology there is: 'a continuing and deeply problematic denial of the legitimacy of victimisation still prevalent' (2002: 115). Howe (2004: 269), on the other hand, lambastes new/critical criminology for failing to 'meet feminist challenges on the man question', adding:

> The new criminologies might purport to make an epistemological and political break with positivist paradigms. Yet when faced with the issue of pervasive men's violence, they soon retreat into victim-blaming etiologies and antediluvian conceptualisations of 'gender' reminiscent of the old-order criminology they claim to have supplanted.

Once again, we are reminded of the diversity and divergences characterising contemporary criminology. The above comments also indicate that debates regarding the relationship between feminism and criminology, whether or not a feminist criminology is possible and, guided specifically by postmodernist ideas, whether or not feminism should free itself from criminology and develop an alternative epistemology (as discussed in Chapter 13), continue to thrive. These debates reflect the different approaches and agendas existing within feminism itself (which is why feminisms is preferred to feminism). Walklate (2003) provides a useful summary of the major strands within feminism and their implications in terms of 'doing' criminology. The relationship between liberal feminism and traditional, mainstream criminology is relatively unproblematic, given that each strives to apply social scientific methodologies in an effort to improve knowledge relating to offending behaviour and criminal justice processes. On this basis, liberal feminists concern themselves with the issue of gender discrimination. Radical feminism focuses on men and the problems they create for women, thus the nature of the relationship with criminology is: 'largely dependent upon whether or not "men" as men are considered the central concern of the criminological agenda' (Walklate, 2003: 80). Research carried out from the perspective of socialist feminism situates the experiences of men and women within the social, political and economic structures of market society, with a view to ultimately replacing that society with a socialist one. Clearly, the degree of compatibility between this and criminological agendas depends upon the degree of convergence in relation to understandings of the wider market society, the gendered nature of that society, and the desire for a socialist transformation. Postmodernist feminism 'poses the most fundamental challenge for criminology' (Walklate, 2003: 81). This is because of the postmodernist rejection of the idea that 'correct' knowledge regarding the nature of social reality can be assembled by social scientists, making the link between postmodernist feminism and a criminology oriented towards issues of social policy highly problematic (see the discussion of postmodernism in the previous section of this chapter). As is the case with critical criminologists, a central issue for feminists is that of staying in without selling out. We can add another perspective to the above, that of black feminism. This developed out of the complaint that the various types of feminism had failed to acknowledge the significance of minority ethnic status when analysing women's experiences (for instance, because of racism).

In a recent overview, Heidensohn and Gelsthorpe (2007) suggest that since its beginnings in the 1970s, feminist criminology has, broadly speaking, passed through three main phases. 'Empiricism', where the aim was to increase the visibility of women in criminology; 'standpointism', where the aim was to provide accounts of the social world from the perspective of women; and 'deconstructionism', which drew on postmodernist thought in order to confront and challenge conventional discourses. Clearly, because of the ways in which they represent the 'reality' of gender, crime and social control, and thus understandings of (gendered) social identity and the 'other' (viewed as, for example, abnormal or perverted), language and texts are of particular interest to criminologists. A key dimension to this is the rejection of essentialist representations of women and men, in favour of an approach that sees no necessary (or, by definition, 'normal') coincidence of sex, gender and sexuality in each individual. Having said that, some feminist writers sympathetic to a postmodernist approach, have sought to analyse social life in terms of both discourse and social relations (for example, Smart, 1995; Daly, 2006).

While there are diverse perspectives among feminists, gender remains the core concept (with equal weight being given to understandings of both femininity and masculinity). However, feminist work has increasingly moved away from an earlier tendency (in the 1970s and 1980s) to essentialise gender/sex. An anti-essentialist stance is one that rejects the idea that gender can function as a single, totalising, explanatory concept, as if all women (and men) are the same in terms of experiences and identities: 'Most feminist scholars today are concerned with linking sex/gender to other social relations and with making particular (not generic) claims about women or men' (Daly, 1997: 41).

A tendency to essentialise, especially with reference to the concept of crime, is, as we have seen, associated with much criminological theorising over the years. Early versions of radical/critical criminology, for instance, did this in relation to 'the working class' and 'capitalists'. Both critical criminology and feminist-influenced criminology have, however, moved on:

> A founding claim of feminism was that women have common interests arising from a common experience, of which they should be aware ... over the last two decades ... this has been challenged by the recognition of important differences among women.
>
> (Valier, 2002: 148)

Thus, increasingly, feminist analyses of female (and male) criminal behaviour, victimisation, or experiences of the courtroom or prison, have pointed to the interplay between such things as gender, class and ethnicity. From this perspective experiences and identities are highly fluid and contingent upon particular circumstances (see, for example, Carrington, 2002). The complexity of these processes makes it difficult (some would say impossible), though, to discern the precise role and relative salience of the various factors.

Offending and punishment

In the discussion of feminism and criminology in Chapter 13, reference was made to the argument found in some circles that the influence of feminism and the growth of the women's movement had, in effect, liberated women, triggering an upsurge in female criminality. Whether linked explicitly to the women's movement or not, stories about apparent increases in female transgressive behaviour (which is always likely to be judged as 'doubly deviant', because it steps outside of notions of accepted *female* behaviour) have routinely appeared in the mass media over the last few years. Chesney-Lind and Irwin (2007) argue that recent attempts to deviantise young women represent an attempt to punish those viewed as transgressing stereotypical understandings of female propriety. What is particularly interesting about these debates is that they concentrate on the issue of women becoming more like men. However, as Heidensohn (2002: 497) says: 'Questions which have scarcely ever been considered, yet could be equally valid, are why males are not more like females, and how the sex/crime ratio could be altered from their perspective'.

The most recent, and highly detailed, statistical report on women and the criminal system in England and Wales is by Hunter *et al.* (2009). The report uses data from the Ministry of Justice relating to, for instance, victimisation, offending – recorded and self-reported – and sentencing. In 2006–07, 17 per cent of those arrested for a notifiable offence were women and 83 per cent men. The number of people arrested has increased since 2002–03, though at a slightly greater rate for women. Of those issued with a caution, warning or reprimand in 2006–07, 28 per cent were women and 72 per cent men; 14 per cent of those proceeded against (that is, taken to court) were women and 86 per cent men; 8 per cent of women and 92 per cent of men were given a custodial sentence. Figures based upon known offenders give a ratio of around 5 to 1 for men and women, a ratio that has remained virtually the same over the past twenty years. As the report notes, there has been some convergence since 2002–03; however, this involves less serious, rather than more serious, offending. Self-report studies, though, continue to put this ratio – in relation to serious and less serious offending – at around 2.5 to 1. An increase in alcohol consumption among young women is one of the latest areas of concern (linked by the media to the growth of a so-called 'ladette' culture). A self-report study for the Office for National Statistics (2003) found that between 1992 and 2002 alcohol consumption among young women aged 16 to 24 had doubled; over the same period alcohol consumption among men had decreased. However, the study also found that in 2002 males were still heavier drinkers than females. As far as underage drinking is concerned, a recent study of 15–16-year-old teenage girls found that there had been a sharp rise in alcohol consumption over the past eight years among this group, to the extent that in 2003 they had overtaken their male counterparts in units of alcohol consumed within the previous month (Centre for Research in Public Health and Primary Care Development, 2004). Reviewing the literature on changes in female offending, Williams concludes (2004: 474):

> These studies point to the absence of any strong direct causative link between the women's movement and women's criminality . . . They suggest that even if the women's movement has made a difference in the power or control of women . . . this would not necessarily lead to a large difference in female crime rates because other traditional socialising aspects may remain, or because women may be less likely to choose such behaviour.

Females represent a small, though rising, proportion of the prison population in England and Wales. Of the total prison population in 1992, 3.4 per cent were females, rising to 4.4 per cent and 6 per cent in 1997 and 2004 respectively. In 2007 it had fallen to a figure of 5 per cent, a downwards trend following a steep rise in the proportion of female offenders given a custodial sentence in the 1990s. This decrease, though, is largely due to a significant reduction in the number of women remanded in custody prior to a court appearance. The number of women receiving a custodial sentence doubled between the beginning and the end of the 1990s, although the length of sentence decreased, and was significantly less than that for men. Around 30 per cent of female and 20 per cent of male prisoners are from minority ethnic groups, and 20 per cent are foreign nationals compared to 11 per cent for males. The earlier increase in female imprisonment, during a period when the number of women found guilty of, or cautioned for, an indictable offence was declining, is seen by Carlen (2000) as reflecting a significantly more punitive response on the part of the courts to female offending, especially for the economically disadvantaged. She also links this to judgements about a woman's culpability in terms of both her offending behaviour and her sexual behaviour and perceived track record as a mother and 'good wife'/partner. Gelsthorpe and Morris (2002), on the other hand, point to a shift towards an increasingly punitive sentencing policy guided by risk assessment, that is, the likelihood of further offending. Deakin and Spencer (2003: 133) sum up these developments as follows:

> Our argument is quite simply that there is little evidence to justify the significant increase in the use of custody for women. There has been a failure on the part of policy makers and practitioners to take account of women's needs within the 'what works' strategy . . . The over-use of custody for women is a serious issue with far-reaching consequences on those women sentenced to periods of imprisonment.

One far-reaching consequence concerns those female prisoners who have children – 55 per cent of women in prison have children under the age of 16, and one-third of these have a child under the age of 5. Another concerns the psychological impact of imprisonment on women; each year 25 per cent are involved in some kind of self-harm incident (for a useful introductory discussion of women's imprisonment, see Carlen and Worrall, 2004). Although a small number of dedicated women's prisons have been built recently, the earlier feminist argument that the criminal justice system has problems dealing with female offenders, because it is basically designed for men, still has relevance (see Worrall, 2003, for a discussion of women offenders and the use of community sentences). On a different level, Alison Young (1998) draws on feminist and post-structuralist methodologies in her analysis of the experiences of victims of rape during cross-examination. Using the technique of deconstruction, she argues that legal discourses act as a masculinist coercive instrument, an established and one-sided exercise in power, which effectively silences the victim's account. Feminist research has continued to emphasise the point that the criminal justice system does not respond to crime victims (and offenders) in a gender-neutral way. In the case of female victims of violent crime especially:

> A range of rich gendered symbols and signifiers, such as dress, manner, conduct, appearance, associates, place and time are called upon in a variety of insinuation strategies to imbue the female victim with contempt and suspicion . . . Men . . . are rarely scripted into such narrow victim-blaming typologies, unless of course they happen to be gay or transsexual, that is outside of hegemonic forms of masculinity.
>
> (Carrington, 2002: 117)

Offenders

As the above discussion indicates, when compared to men, women are still much less likely to engage in criminal behaviour, especially serious criminal behaviour. Clearly, this raises important issues relating to gender and criminality, though from the point of view of both femininity and masculinity (see below). In recent years, feminist research into female criminality has continued, most of it sceptical of mainstream criminology's ability, or willingness, to incorporate gender into analyses. On a general level, it is recognised that understandings and experiences of gender have a significant influence on the propensity to commit crime. In this way, gender-based social structures and processes, together with attendant learned behaviour, create particular controls on women's behaviour (Heidensohn, 2000). It is important to recognise, though, that gender roles within a particular society only provide a general context, and analyses need to take into consideration (i) specific understandings of femininity and masculinity, (ii) the relevance of other contingent factors such as class and ethnicity, (iii) the specific contexts and circumstances in which female and male criminal behaviour occurs, and (iv) the ways in which all three interact with each other. Specific contexts will include, for example, the experience of victimisation, the desire for retaliation or resistance, and the mobilisation of defensive and control strategies.

A number of recent studies of female criminality have stressed the importance of 'agency' and social context, and the variety of dynamic and creative processes at work. In their Glasgow-based study, Burman *et al.* (2000) found that the minority (10 per cent) of teenage girls in their sample who admitted to being involved in violent behaviour did so for instrumental reasons based on gaining respect and status; thus, the authors argue, the behaviour could not be written off as 'irrational'. Placing the behaviour within a broader context, when compared with the rest of the sample, those involved in violence were much more likely to have personal experience of being physically assaulted. They also had relatively low socio-economic status and tended to engage in other, non-violent criminal behaviour. In a study of females who engaged in street robbery, Miller (1998) found that although the women concerned faced various constraints deriving from their gender, they managed to open up their own spaces on the street, within which to negotiate and explore their identities. In her study of female drug dealers in the United States, Maher (1997) too shows how the women concerned were able to challenge traditional, gender-based expectations. The women had similar motivations to their male counterparts, but the ways in which they organised their dealing had to be tailored to suit the opportunities available to women in a male-dominated market constructed around traditional understandings of gender. The constraints imposed by male understandings of gender roles was noted in an earlier study of delinquent girls by Campbell (1981). Although the girls concerned were prepared to join delinquent gangs, they entered a milieu where they were expected to conform to notions of female roles based upon subordination and support.

The importance of context and circumstances in relation to female offending is well illustrated in Jamieson's (1999) paper on genocide in Bosnia-Herzegovina and Rwanda in the 1990s. Taking the example of extreme violence, she challenges essentialist readings of gender that cast women in the role of victims, and shows how violent behaviour should be understood in terms of its relationship to socially constructed identities, which include gender. In the case of Rwanda, nearly all the Hutu – women, children and men – were involved in the genocide directed at the Tutsi and, she says, this involvement of women 'has been largely ignored by feminist theorists' (ibid., 1999: 138). Thus, although throughout the world violence is overwhelmingly associated with men, the potential for violence among women should not be overlooked. The capacity for violence cannot be fully understood 'if we insist on endowing it only in the masculine or the "ethnic" rather than in the feminine, the "human", or the "social"' (Jamieson, 1999: 142). In Rwanda, as one example:

> Women along with children acted as 'finishers off'. Their task was to locate those who were still living and kill them, using whatever – usually 'low tech' – weapons were available to them (knives, machetes, 'masus' (nail-studded clubs) or sharpened sticks.
>
> (Ibid.: 142)

This is not to downgrade the importance of masculinities and violence. Looking back through history, we will find situations where a large proportion of the female population in a particular country participated in acts of violence. However, it would be surprising if a large proportion of men in that country were not themselves also involved in that violence. It is worth making one further point regarding Jamieson's work. Sadly, and I have to say ludicrously, there may be those of a certain twist of mind who would wish to racialise her discussion. For this reason, it has to be stressed that being, say, a white European or North American woman is no guarantee of non-violence (Nazi extermination camps is one example that comes to mind).

PERSPECTIVES ON MASCULINITIES

The last few years have seen a sharp increase in theoretical studies of masculinities, many focusing on the core issue that men are more likely to involve themselves in crime, and especially violent crime, than women are. For some, the significance of criminal behaviour in the construction of male identities has been given particular attention. Other work, though, has broadened the debate considerably, by examining notions of masculinity within the context of, for instance, victimisation (Newburn and Stanko, 1994); probation (Holland and Scourfield, 2000); the deviantisation of homosexuality (Groombridge, 1999); and sport (Jefferson, 1998). In addition, some studies have explored the relationship between the male body, gender characteristics and behaviour. Hobbs *et al.* (2003), for example, in their detailed study of bouncers, indicate how the physiques of the men involved (as well as evidence of earlier battles) provides a crucial resource, in terms of both preventing and responding to violence. Here the body is commodified; its image, strength and potential for violence is for sale:

> The authority of the vast majority of bouncers is embodied in their physicality . . . for the majority who ply their trade in the night-time economy, authority is derived from local reputation and the potential physicality of their bodies. This potential can be suggested by bulk, in the case of body builders, evidence of engagement in combat, for instance a battered or scarred visage, or the presence of highly specialized skills and capabilities.
>
> (Hobbs *et al.*, 2003: 144)

However, whilst a consideration of the male body is obviously important, some analyses of masculinity tend to conflate gender and sex, drawing a neat division between men and women:

> In the popular accounts . . . masculinity runs through men like writing through rock. But this is a collapse of gender (masculinity) into sex (men). For example, all the

contributors to that recent *British Journal of Criminology* special issue (1996) speak, always, about men and masculinities . . . there are no masculine women or feminine men on these pages.

(Hood-Williams, 2001: 39)

This is an important point to make, though, since the special issue referred to, a number of writers have noted that masculine behaviour and identity can be found among those with female, as well as male, bodies (Connell, 2000, for example). However, this in turn raises an equally important issue, and one that indicates the complexities involved in these debates. If men/male bodies are much more likely to engage in crime than women/female bodies are, and masculine attributes are overwhelmingly associated with men rather than women, does this mean that criminal women are more masculine than non-criminal women? Does it also mean that criminal men are more masculine than non-criminal men? Presenting the issue in such stark terms, though, raises a whole range of additional questions, such as, how is 'masculinity' to be defined in the first place? And what *kinds* of criminal behaviour are being referred to?

Many writers have conceptualised the issue of masculinity in late modernity in terms of transformation and crisis. Collier (2004: 289) puts it like this:

> From this perspective, the debate about masculinities and crime is itself, in effect, seen as emblematic of wider concerns and anxieties around the meaning of social, economic, cultural and political changes since the 1980s, not least those between men and women . . . the idea that *something* is happening to men and their shifting 'masculinities' and that this relates to crime. (Emphasis in original)

Messerschmidt's (1993) 'structured action theory' approach to masculinities and crime was discussed briefly in Chapter 13 (for a further development, see Messerschmidt, 1997). His theory drew on Connell's (1995) notions of 'hegemonic' and 'subordinated' masculinities, ideal types of, respectively, 'accredited' and 'discredited' models of manliness. 'Hegemonic' masculinity provides the dominant, culturally approved, yardstick against which men create and define themselves as men and, in contradistinction to (sociologically speaking) ideal-type notions of subordinated masculinity (or notions of femininity), emphasises attributes commensurate with criminal, and especially violent, behaviour: 'practices toward authority, control, competitive individualism, independence, aggressiveness, and capacity for violence' (Messerschmidt, 1993: 82). Looked at like this, crime represents one way in which men 'do' or accomplish gender – it is a way of providing evidence of manliness and resisting accusations of weakness. Furthermore, for Messerschmidt, the different types of crime associated with different men arise from their structural location in society: factors of class and 'race' will influence both the amount of pressure to be 'manly' in this sense, and the nature of the response to this pressure.

Messerschmidt's analysis of masculinities has now assumed an important place within criminological theory; it has, though, stimulated a number of criticisms. First, it has been noted that much crime, because of its nature, does not require the attributes associated with hegemonic masculinity. Second, it has been said that the central argument is tautological. As Collier (2004: 293) puts it (see also, Walklate, 1995; Hood-Williams, 2001):

> Masculinity is depicted as both primary and underlying *cause* (or source) of a social effect (crime); and, simultaneously, as something which itself *results from* (after all, it is accomplished through) recourse *to* crime. (Emphases in original)

Third, as Hood-Williams (2001) points out, Messerschmidt's formulation is unable to clarify why it is that only *some* men use crime to accomplish masculinity and, as Jefferson (1996) says, only a minority within class or ethnic groupings. Fourth, it is noticeable that the attributes apparently associated with masculinity are negative ones; there is little room for the kind or sensitive man.

Jefferson (1997; see also Hollway and Jefferson, 2000) has addressed these theoretical debates by placing particular emphasis upon individual male subjectivities and how these are contingent upon not social structure, but (using the lens of post-structuralism) discourses of masculinity. This psycho-social approach rejects what is seen as the determinism found in structured action theory. On the basis of, for instance, a case study of the boxer 'iron' Mike Tyson, Jefferson (1998) seeks to illustrate the complexity of 'masculinity' as subjectively understood – the deeper psychological dimensions involving anxiety, uncertainty and contradiction. This approach to understanding male criminality has also been explored by Gadd (2000, 2002) within the context of violence towards women. Unlike Messerschmidt (1993), who equates domestic violence with men 'doing masculinity', as part of a process of reaffirming their (dominant) masculinity, Gadd emphasises the complex tensions and ambiguities surrounding the actions of violent men, their accounts of these actions, and their 'real' feelings about what has happened. In the case of domestic violence perpetrators, Gadd (2002) argues that they often experience intense feelings of shame, rather than guilt-free satisfaction that honour has been restored. He also argues that many men have a contradictory, and hence volatile, relationship with their female partner, deriving from a perception of women that oscillates between two extremes: idealisation and denigration. Psycho-social approaches have generated a fair amount of criticism. One of the chief ones is that the conscious and unconscious processes, referred to as the 'psyche', cannot be categorised as 'masculine' or 'feminine' (Hood-Williams, 2001).

The complexity of the issues – especially the contradictions and ambiguities – raised by notions of masculinity, and in particular the relationship between masculinity and violence, is indicated in a recent review, by ex-lifer Erwin Jones (2009), of a newly released film called *Bronson*. The film is based on the life of Michael Peterson who, when he was younger and fighting as an unlicensed boxer, changed his name to Charles Bronson. Apart from a few months outside, Bronson has spent the last thirty-five years in prison. He has a reputation for extreme violence, and over the years was frequently described by the media as 'Britain's most dangerous prisoner'. Currently:

> he is being held in a specially constructed cage deep in the bowels of Wakefield high-security prison. He lives in total isolation, is fed through a hatch and spends his time exercising, writing and drawing ... his cartoon art sells well ... and much of the money he makes from his art he gives to children's charities.
>
> (Ibid.: 3)

Jones goes on:

> We have had some correspondence recently. His first letter made me want to cry. 'It has been nine years since I caused anyone any harm,' he wrote. 'Surely it must be time now to give me chance?' I was touched by his vulnerability. Having been a prisoner with little hope once, I wanted to reach out and reassure him.
>
> (Ibid.: 3)

A further dimension to this is that returning Bronson to the prison wings could be risky for him, in that a younger prisoner might see this as an opportunity to enhance their (masculine) reputation through violence. The year 2009 also sees the release of *Tyson*, a documentary film about the boxer Mike Tyson, who provides a commentary throughout the film. At one point, as the audience see archival footage of him entering the ring for a major fight, Tyson says: 'I come and I have supreme confidence, but I'm scared to death.'

In their more recent work, Connell and Messerschmidt (2005) have acknowledged the dynamic nature of masculinity, as identity and guide to action, and, in the process, emphasised the ways in which it can alter during the course of a lifetime. They have also spent more time analysing masculinities and femininities as interrelational phenomena; in other words, that one cannot exist without the other.

Male sexuality is a further area of contention within contemporary criminology. Writing from the perspective of what has been called 'queer theory', Groombridge (1999), for example, makes the point that throughout its history criminology has resisted engaging with male sexuality, except in the sense of absorbing implicitly the view that heterosexuality equates with 'normal' sexuality (see also Bernstein, 2004).

CONTROL PERSPECTIVES

In Chapter 13 there was a discussion of Hirschi's (1969) control theory, an explanation of criminality that seeks to answer the question: why do people *not* break the law? Since then, a variety of control perspectives has emerged, especially within

American criminology. In addition, Hirschi and Gottfredson (1993, 2000) have explored further the concept of control, as part of a general theory of crime. In this work, the core argument is that criminal behaviour (as well as more broadly defined deviant and risk-taking behaviour) is a result of low levels of self-control. The degree of self-control that an individual exercises is dependent upon the ways in which an individual has been socialised, especially within the family, during the first few years of their life. In fact, for Gottfredson and Hirschi, to a large extent the die has been cast round about 8 years of age. They also suggest that the effectiveness of early socialisation processes will be influenced by genetic differences between one child and another. Low self-control is associated with various attributes, such as impulsiveness and a commitment to immediate gratification, a propensity for risk-taking, and a lack of concern for victims. In combination, it is argued, such attributes significantly increase the likelihood of someone engaging in criminal behaviour when the opportunity presents itself. It should be noted, though, that this version of control theory is quite different to Hirschi's original version. In the first version, criminality was dependent upon the quality of the social bonds tying an individual to the wider society, whereas in the new version, low self-control is given priority. As Lilly *et al.* (2007: 112) say:

> Hirschi changed his mind over the years. He once thought that social bonds were the main determinant of crime. Later, however, he (and Gottfredson) came to believe that social bonds were merely a manifestation of a person's level of self-control and thus had no independent causal relationship to criminal involvement.

Control theory, including Gottfredson and Hirschi's formulation, has had a continuing influence on criminological theorising and, whilst it is difficult to test, some empirical research does support the theory (for instance, Pratt and Cullen, 2000). As mentioned earlier, some writers explain the lower rates of female offending by drawing on control theory (see, for example, Hagan and Kay, 1990 and, more recently, Hayslett-McCall and Bernard, 2002). On the other hand, criticisms of control theory have also continued to appear. Schinkel (2002), for instance, criticises Hirschi's original version of control theory on two counts. First, for being tautological:

> the idea that the criminal has a weakened bond to conventional society tells us nothing new, since the criminal is part of the non-conventional, rather than the conventional, and a criminal, someone who commits non-conventional acts, is thus by definition someone who commits less conventional acts (since these constitute the 'bond' to conventional society).
>
> (Ibid.: 141)

And, second, for conceptually placing the criminal outside society (in a realm of the 'non-conventional'), rather than seeing 'the criminal' as part of society. Gottfredson and Hirschi's more recently formulated self-control theory has also been criticised for being tautological. The basis for this criticism is that, in effect, the theory is simply stating that people with low self-control engage in behaviours that reflect low self-control, and this still leaves the problem of explaining the source of this low self-control – socialisation within the family is only one among many possibilities (Akers, 1991; Geis, 2000; and for responses to this charge, see Hirschi and Gottfredson, 1993, 2000). A final point we can note is that, whilst Hirschi and Gottfredson suggest that deviant behaviour does correlate with class position, it is clear that for the authors, low self-control is primarily associated with those of low socio-economic status – the lack of material and social success reflecting low self-control. This is in contradistinction to Hirschi's (1969) original formulation, where he argued that his empirical research did not indicate that lower class youths were disproportionately involved in offending.

A further variant of the control perspective is control balance theory, introduced by Tittle (1995), and subsequently refined by him (Tittle, 1997, 2000, 2004). Control balance theory attempts to provide an explanation of a wide range of activities that result in social harms, including criminal ones (research oriented towards harms, rather than crime *per se,* is called zemiology). The concept of 'balance' in this theory refers to the balance between, on the one hand, those controls acting *on* an individual and, on the other, those controls exercised *by* an individual. Too much of the former produces a 'deficit' of control; too much of the latter produces a 'surplus' of control. Deviant, or socially harmful behaviour, results from the pressure created by an imbalance in the 'control ratio', due to either a deficit or a surplus of control. If there is a deficit, says Tittle, deviant behaviour may be used in an attempt to redress the balance, and if there is a surplus, it may be used in order to enhance an individual's existing power to control others. In the second case, this power reduces the chances of attracting a social or legal censure, making deviant behaviour a more viable option. Control balance theory, therefore, offers a theoretical model that is relevant to the deviant behaviour of the powerful as well as the powerless. It also applies to individuals *and* other 'social entities', such as organisations (it could, therefore, be used to explain the illegal invasion of one country by another, more powerful, country – referred to as 'autonomous' deviance, see below).

This discussion, however, does not exhaust the theoretical ingredients of this explanation of deviant behaviour. As a theory, it is made more complex because Tittle incorporates a number of factors, other than relative amounts of power, into his analysis in an effort to provide a general theory of crime and deviance (for this reason, it is extremely difficult to test the theory). Specifically, he identifies four key factors that will influence the decision to deviate:

- According to Tittle, we are all predisposed to resist the controls placed upon us by others. All human beings carry the potential to develop deviant motivations because of an inherent desire for personal autonomy. Individuals who experience

an imbalance in the control ratio are more likely to deviate in situations where this is combined with a lack of opportunities to acquire desired goals in life.
- The motivation to deviate arises out of a situation where an individual, having become 'acutely aware of an imbalance in the control ratio, and experienced belittlement by others, feels that deviant behaviour can be used to strengthen their autonomy' (Tittle, 2000: 320).
- Social circumstances must provide an opportunity to engage in deviant behaviour.
- The individual has to be free from various constraints, such as the social bonds tying them to significant others, the risk of being caught or suffering in some way, the extent to which they can exercise self-control, and their moral feelings regarding the deviant behaviour involved.

Of particular interest in this version of control theory is the view that deviance can arise because an individual experiences either too much *or* too little control. It thus acts as an antidote to the view among some policy makers that the solution to crime and deviance lies in more control. One problem with the theory, however, is that control balance is put forward as the central causal concept, but deviant behaviour only occurs when a whole range of other factors are present. It is thus difficult to assess the relative salience of all of these variables and, indeed, whether other variables are, at least sometimes, more relevant. As Lilly *et al.* (2007: 116) argue:

> His emphasis on autonomy as the wellspring of human motivation seems unnecessarily limited. Why not consider, for example, the desire for self-gratifications, a drive that many other control theories claim is universal and central to the motivation to deviate?

In a recent paper, Tittle (2004) has further refined control balance theory and, in the process, acknowledged a 'logical flaw' and 'conceptual inconsistencies' in the earlier formulation. There is not the space to delve into this in detail here, though one example can be noted. Originally, Tittle had differentiated between 'repressive' and 'autonomous' forms of deviance, and argued that the first of these is mainly linked to those experiencing control deficits. Repressive deviance is where the perpetrator is directly involved in the deviance or confronts the victim (for example, burglary); autonomous deviance is where this is not required, and 'typically makes use of third parties, organisations or structural arrangements' (2004: 399). However, Tittle accepts that in practice it is difficult to distinguish between these two forms of deviance, and that 'there is no necessary reason within the logic of the theory why a person with a control surplus would choose mainly from among "autonomous" deviant acts' (ibid.: 400).

Colvin's (2000) differential coercion theory – put forward as an 'integrated theory' – also focuses on the exercise of power and its implications for criminality. According to Colvin, as individuals go through life they experience different degrees of coercion, stretching from non-coercion to coercion (for example, in the family). The coercion is used in order to get individuals to comply with notions of approved and appropriate behaviour. The manner in which this coercion is applied, says Colvin, can be 'consistent' or 'erratic', and it is erratic coercion that is more likely to lead to criminal behaviour. The degree of coercion experienced varies according to an individual's structural position in society. Thus, says the theory, criminality is more likely to be found among those who are subject to the coercion arising from such things as poverty, racism and a lack of educational opportunities. Whatever its merits, a familiar difficulty here is that not all of, say, the poor turn to crime, meaning that the precise origins, nature and impact of coercion require explication.

In recent years there has been a resurgence of interest in varieties of control theory, especially in the United States, where the 'life-course' theory of Laub and Sampson (2003) has been particularly influential (and see Laub *et al.*, 2006, for a review). One of the attractions of this work is that it puts forward a non-determinstic theoretical understanding of criminality based upon an integration of social structure, life events, and subjective interpretations on the part of the individuals concerned. Life events, such as the nature of family relationships during childhood, employment opportunities, marriage, and so on, are important in that the theory is sensitive to the changing possibilities associated with these experiences as an individual goes through life. From this perspective, nothing is fixed or inevitable. Laub and Sampson reserve particular criticism for the impact of formal involvement with the criminal justice system, especially imprisonment, which they see as a major factor influencing subsequent offending.

CULTURAL PERSPECTIVES

Cultural criminology is characterised by a fairly eclectic mix of themes and ideas linked to a variety of criminological traditions, notably phenomenology, the naturalistic perspective associated with David Matza, interactionism, critical criminology and subcultural theory, together with significant influences from postmodernist thought. As the name suggests, the writers concerned have a common interest in the study of crime, deviance, modes of social control and related phenomena within the context of culture. Work of this genre has focused on the nature and role of the mass media in late modernity (or postmodernity, depending on one's preference), together with transgressive behaviour and processes of social control, conceptualised as products and representations of culture.

For cultural criminologists, a key feature of the late modern world is that it is 'media-saturated' (Ferrell and Sanders, 1995). Global electronic communications systems have made time and space much less relevant than previously, and created a world awash with constantly changing information, images and signs. One dimension to this are the cultural meanings attached to such things as crime, criminals, deviants, heroes and monsters. These meanings are produced, reproduced, circulated, reshaped, absorbed or rejected in a multiplicity of complex and continuous processes of interaction and interpretation. Individuals enjoy their fifteen minutes of fame, or infamy; a small boy becomes a feral, uncontrollable 'rat-boy'; violent criminals are transformed into romanticised lovable celebrities; whole communities are stigmatised as the barbarians at the gate; exploited migrant labour is recast as a threat to the 'British way of life'. In this frenzy of images and signs, where the media act as mediators of reality, the distinction between fact and fiction dissolves. Hollywood and South Central, Los Angeles, are in, one sense, worlds apart, and yet converge as 'the street scripts the screen and the screen scripts the street' (Hayward and Young, 2004: 259). Instead of seeking to determine the causes of crime – seen as a futile task – many cultural criminologists have turned their attention to the ways in which representations of crimes and criminals are socially constructed by the mass media and reproduced in the form of textual images (A. Young, 1997; Ferrell *et al.*, 2004). These images permeate the cultural realm and, in effect, become reality, but it is a fragmented reality. They become part of the 'maps of meaning' (Clarke *et al.*, 1976: 9) among the public in general, those defined as criminals and deviants, and the agents of social control whose job it is to respond to their transgressions (Tzanelli, *et al.*, 2005).

Importantly, though, cultural criminology emphasises that cultural meanings arise from interactional processes, in which individuals play an active and creative role. Cultural criminologists, therefore, eschew the deterministic methodologies and models of positivism, in favour of ethnographic research oriented towards interpretative understandings of the cultural meaning of crime, deviance and transgression among those involved. This connects these criminologists to a long lineage of qualitative criminological work, work that aims to give an insight into the ways in which people see, experience and shape their social worlds as active participants. Thus studies have analysed criminal and deviant behaviour in terms of emotion, thrill and visceral excitement: a 'sociology of the skin', as Ferrell and Sanders (1995) describe it (see, for example, Winlow, 2001; Presdee, 2000; Hayward, 2004). Katz's (1988) now classic study, the *Seductions of Crime*, offers a rich enthnography of the sensual attractions of risky behaviour. Fenwick and Hayward (2000) situate their analysis of youthful transgression within the context of a postmodern culture characterised by intense consumerism. Transgression in the form of illegal drug use or football hooliganism, for example, is seen as one more leisure option, satisfying the consumer's desire for novelty and immediate gratification. The notion of risky, challenging behaviour is important in this context, for as O'Malley and Mugford (1994) point out, although Katz focuses on crime, the core theoretical arguments apply to other, non-criminal behaviours, which open up sensual spaces in an otherwise mundane, controlled social world, where consumers experience leisure and thrill as commodities. Other writers have explored these possibilities by analysing forms of behaviour that are exciting, or dangerous or provocative (or all three), though they do not necessarily involve rule-breaking and are difficult to situate on a spectrum of public approval–disapproval; for example, rock climbers scaling not rock faces, but dizzyingly tall city centre skyscrapers. Lyng (1990, 1998) describes such activities as 'edgework'.

Cultural criminologists are also highly critical of administrative criminology's characterisation of offenders as instrumentally motivated rational decision makers, who, employing a form of cost–benefit analysis, weigh up the risks associated with a criminal act. For cultural criminologists, this approach to crime control ignores the emotional dimension to the motivation to offend. In other words, that offenders are often seeking a thrill, or adrenaline rush. One implication of this is that, rather than acting as a disincentive, the increased risk arising from crime control measures may provide an extra incentive (for example, because of the 'thrill of the chase') to go ahead with the criminal act.

Although this kind of criminology will, of course, provoke the usual criticisms from proponents of a positivist perspective (as well as criticisms from administrative criminology), some versions of cultural criminology have also been criticised by some writers sympathetic to its methods and ideas. Young (2003b) is critical of Katz (1988) for over-emphasising culture at the expense of social structure, and therefore detaching individuals from background factors such as poverty and education. These factors are important because of the bearing they have on the ways in which individuals experience, understand and interpret social life. Additionally, analyses need to be sensitive to the wider structural context within which cultural experiences are situated and shaped in late modern society. A good example is the night-time economy in this country – those city and town centre nocturnal leisure zones oriented primarily towards young people and the consumption of alcohol. Although the cultural dimension to this is clearly important, analyses should, as Hobbs *et al.* (2003) argue, also appreciate that the nature, shape and evolution of this economy are closely linked to an intensely competitive market dominated by a handful of very large companies, who, as part of a process of urban regeneration, have worked with local authorities on the basis of private–public entrepreneurial partnerships. Likewise, whilst it is correct to stress people's creative engagement with culture, it should also be noted that the mass media are dominated by a small number of global multinational corporations whose messages have a major influence on understandings of, for instance, the good life, good taste, good food, good sex and good war. As Sumner (2004: 25) says: 'Cultural studies have taken over so much of sociology and we even now have "cultural criminology" . . . which proclaims the culturalness of much to do with crime. But what of economics and politics, and the "social"?'

O'Brien (2005) has also criticised cultural criminology for giving insufficient attention to economic, political, psychological etc. factors. In addition, he is critical of the way in which 'culture' and 'subculture' are conceived of, and dichotomised, in the work of some cultural criminologists (see also, Garland, 2006). Subcultures, such as the one associated with the urban graffiti artists in Ferrell's (2006) study, tend to be presented as 'edgy', exciting, risk-taking, politicised and praiseworthy, whilst culture equates with 'mainstream' society, which is characterised as dull, mundane, bored and boring, and is hence much less praiseworthy. However, not everyone makes a public display of their transgression; lots of transgressive behaviour goes on, as it were, behind the closed doors of ordinary life.

Finally, some cultural criminologists have been criticised for avoiding issues of harm and morality, and painting a one-sided, romanticised picture of criminal behaviour. There is a reminder here of earlier criticisms of new deviancy theorists for concentrating on deviance without victims (or where victimisation was obscured). Referring to Katz's *Seductions of Crime*, Howe (2004: 279), for instance, puts it like this:

> Getting caught up in the 'wonderful attractions within the lived experience of criminality', losing yourself to the 'seductive appeal' of violence, and grasping the 'magic in the criminal's sensuality' can so deplete your resources that you overlook the dead bodies of the victims . . . Tellingly, sex killings and sexual assaults are omitted from Katz's list of 'transcendent' criminal projects.

CRITICAL PERSPECTIVES

By the mid-1990s, and as discussed in Chapter 14, it was possible to broadly characterise 'radical' criminology in terms of two strands: a still avowedly Marxist critical criminology (or 'left idealism') and a democratic socialist left realism. Now, nearing the end of the first decade of the twenty-first century, and the nature of what was called radical criminology has become much less clear-cut, though not necessarily any less interesting and relevant. There are still recognisable differences between the left realists and others situated on what used to be more commonly described as the left of the political spectrum. However, the term 'radical' has largely been discarded, and in general nowadays the preferred collective term is critical criminology. One enduring quality of critical criminology since its emergence as the 'new' criminology in the early 1970s (Taylor *et al.*, 1973) has been a penchant for being iconoclastic. Young (2002: 254–5) illustrates this delight in upsetting taken for granted understandings of crime and social control by outlining a series of 'ironies' which 'served to turn establishment criminology on its head':

- *Self-fulfilment* – that illusions and stereotypes of crime can be real in their consequences and self-fulfilling in reality.
- *Seriousness* – that crime occurred throughout the social structure and that the crimes of the powerful were more serious in their consequences than the crimes of the poor.
- *Ontology* – that crime has no ontological reality and that the 'same' behaviour can be constructed totally differently. Thus, for example, a serial killer could be either a psychopathic monster or a hero if dropping bombs daily in the Afghan War.

- *Decentring* – that the criminal justice system is not the front-line defence against crime but a minor part of the system of social control, itself crucially dependent on informal norms of civil society.
- *Selectivity* – that criminal law, although phrased in a language of formal equality, is targeted in a way that is selective and substantially unequal.
- *Counter-productivity* – that the prison and the criminal justice system produce criminals rather than defuse criminality.
- *Socialisation* – that the core values of competitiveness, acquisitiveness, individualism and hedonism are close to the motivations for crime, so that the well-socialised person is more likely to offend than the undersocialised.
- *Contradiction* – that the ideals which legitimate and hold the system together are the very ones which society thwarts and the frustrations generated seem to break the system apart.
- *Function* – that 'the criminal', 'the outsider', 'the other', far from destroying the fabric of society, produces stereotypes which hold the fabric together.
- *Secondary harm* – that the primary harm of a social problem is frequently of a lesser order than the secondary harm accruing from the intervention to control it. The prime example of this being the regulation of drug use.

In defence of the continuing influence and relevance of critical criminology, Young argues that these ironies still have a contemporary resonance, adding: 'critical criminology is flourishing . . . the majority of centres that teach criminology are within the rubric of critical criminology' (2002: 259). In the same vein, Scraton (2002: 35) states:

> Critical research, publication and teaching within criminology has a significant role in resisting the political and ideological imperatives of official discourse, state-sponsored evaluations of official policy initiatives and the correspondence of vocational training to the requirements of the crime control industry.

Not all of those who would label themselves 'critical theorists' are as positive when assessing the current state of critical criminology. Hill and Robertson (2003: 111), for example, argue for 'a different approach to both theory construction and activism'. They suggest an approach that shifts the emphasis away from crime and penalty towards the notion of 'social harms', guided by a central commitment to human rights. This echoes the views of Hulsman (1986), discussed in Chapter 13, and raises major epistemological issues revolving around the use of 'crime' as a key referent (and will be returned to). From a somewhat different perspective, one expressing a post-modernist sensibility, Pavlich (1999) chastises critical criminology for failing to respond appropriately to the conditions of late/post modernity. The failure is seen as being manifested in either what he sees as a highly constraining engagement with aspects of crime and the control of crime, or a misplaced faith in the possibility of achieving a 'better' world. This too raises major issues which will be returned to;

suffice at this stage to say that Pavlich's alternative lies in the concept of 'paralogic' – a concept introduced by Lyotard (1984) – a form of reasoning which seeks to generate innovative ideas by breaking free from the intellectual constraints imposed by the suppositions inherent in already existing versions of reason. Thus, as Pavlich (1999: 43) puts it: 'Paralogy legitimates knowledge claims on the grounds of a *relentless iconoclasm* through which new vistas of language and practices are sought' (emphasis in original).

A changing context

As we have seen in earlier chapters, critical criminology had its intellectual roots in neo-Marxism (though it did draw on what was then more recent work on crime and deviance, notably interactionism and labelling theory), and its political roots in socialism. Based upon a fundamental critique of capitalism, seen as an inherently criminogenic and unjust system, its ultimate goal was the creation of a socialist/communist society. Over the last few years, though, and in tandem with a rejection of grand narratives, Marxist social theory has ceased to be an intellectual force; state socialist societies, such as the former Soviet Union, have abandoned their versions of socialism and embraced neo-liberal market economies; and across Europe there has been the rise of what some call a liberal democratic consensus – as personified by New Labour – which is purported to represent the 'end of ideology'. Certainly, the definition of 'socialism' and the viability and desirability of a future socialist society are, to put it mildly, highly problematic issues – issues that, put in those terms, only rarely now find their way into the writings of critical criminologists. Marxism, though, is concerned with both interpreting the world and changing it. Thus neo-Marxism provided the conceptual tools for critical criminologists to analyse the workings of capitalism, and to situate crime, deviance, social control, etc. within their analyses. At the same time, and although capitalism was seen to contain 'the seeds of its own destruction' in the shape of various contradictions, neo-Marxist critical criminologists were also committed to playing a part in its destruction. As far as the first of these is concerned, there are some contemporary writers who suggest that in the context of a rampant, global neo-liberal capitalism, we may see a resurgence in neo-Marxist social theory in the new millennium, for example:

> Far from being over, the argument with Marxism is only just about to begin all over again, this time in the context of a capitalism careering out of control and without the counterpoint of communism exerting a counter-pressure for egalitarian policies in welfare, income and wealth distribution, and the equivalent in international terms of the controls exercised by nation states over business and finance before the 'big bang' of global capitalism in the 1980s . . . a host of highly criminogenic trends have been set in motion.
>
> (Downes and Rock, 2007: 323)

This may be so, but it is significant that the focus of critique in recent critical criminology has tended to be on 'out of control' neo-liberal markets, rather than on capitalism *per se,* and illustrates the distance travelled since the early 1970s when, drawing on neo-Marxist theory, the ultimate goal was the replacement of capitalism ('out of control' or otherwise) with socialism. However, at the time of writing, global capitalism is experiencing its most serious financial crisis since the Depression of the inter-war years, and, in retrospect, Downes and Rock's words are remarkably prescient.

In this section the focus is on those writers whose work can, at least loosely, be seen as a product of the neo-Marxist-influenced tradition discussed earlier on in this book. It is acknowledged that, in common with criminology as a whole, present manifestations of this critical criminological tradition are characterised by degrees of diversity and fragmentation, partly resulting from the dissolution of its explicit links with Marxist social theory. Furthermore, the past decade or so has seen the emergence of a range of work that could also, reasonably, be described as 'critical' (for example, cultural criminology, discussed above). Indeed, potentially, *any* criminologist could describe their work as 'critical'. None the less, in terms of the structure of this book, which is guided by a sensitivity to historical context, this section conforms to the definition of critical criminology outlined above.

The agendas of critical criminology

We can indicate on a very general level the sort of work produced by contemporary critical criminologists by using the framework provided by the four key questions posed at the beginning of this chapter. Some examples of this work are discussed below.

What to study? Crime, criminality and control within the context of neo-liberal market societies; penality; private–public systems of social control and governmentality in late modern society; injustice, corruption and human rights violations; ethnicity, gender and masculinities; green issues.

Who to study? The 'powerful', for example, in the shape of corporate and state crime; perpetrators of 'conventional' crime, linking their criminality to neo-liberal market societies, inequality and globalisation.

How to study? 'Radical' ethnography; through the perspective of cultural criminology; on the basis of anti-positivism, anti-essentialism and deconstructionism; theoretical work on social censures and socially constructed representations of crime and the crime problem; as a critique of the conceptual language and claims of administrative and conservative criminologies.

Why study? For neo-Marxist critical criminologists the ultimate goal was the achievement of socialism (or communism), though what was meant by a socialist (or communist) society was by no means agreed upon. Although 'socialism' is still referred to among critical criminologists (and even, though very occasionally, among New Labour cabinet ministers), its ideological power has, over the last quarter of a century, been hugely diminished. Furthermore, large-scale, radical social movements in, for example, Europe and North America now mobilise around issues of globalisation and environmentalism, rather than socialism – understandable given the collapse of (state) socialism around the world, and its track record of oppression and environmental degradation. Whilst the *raison d'être* of critical criminology continues to be a commitment to *critique* oriented explicitly towards the realisation of a more equal and just society, there is now 'the problem of the narrative which guides such a transformation' (Young, 2002: 269; see also Cohen, 1996, who sees 'universal human rights' as the last remaining meta-narrative). Jock Young addresses this problem by drawing on Bauman's argument that rather than being a project that can be completed, socialism represents a sort of utopian beacon:

> a horizon constantly on the move, perpetually receding, but guiding the travel . . . keeping humans forever on the move . . . calling them to fight over new injustices and to take the side of the successive echelons of the left behind, injured, humiliated.
>
> (Bauman and Tester, 2001, quoted by Young, 2002: 269)

Some years earlier, George Orwell put it like this:

> The real objective of socialism is not happiness . . . Men use up their lives in heart-breaking political struggles, or get themselves killed in civil wars, or tortured in the secret prisons of the Gestapo, not in order to establish some central-heated, air-conditioned, strip-lighted Paradise, but because they want a world in which human beings love one another instead of swindling and murdering one another. And they want that world as a first step. Where they go from there is not so certain, and the attempt to foresee it in detail merely confuses the issue.
>
> (Orwell, 1943: 5)

Critical perspectives on concepts of crime and deviance

Since its genesis at the beginning of the 1970s, a key feature of critical (and postmodern-influenced) criminological theory has been 'anti-essentialism': a refusal to take 'crime' (and 'deviance') for granted, as if there was some essential, inherent difference between those activities designated as criminal and those designated as non-criminal. From this perspective, the difference between them derives from the existence or absence of a rule, or, more specifically, a legal censure. The adoption of an anti-essentialist perspective challenges the ontological status of 'crime' – criminology's central referent. Thus activities officially defined as criminal cannot be distinguished objectively from other activities in terms of, say, essential moral qualities or notions of harmfulness. Having said that, it would, however, be surprising to find anyone describing themselves as a criminologist who argued that crime was inherently different to non-crime, though there are those who, in spite of this, have attempted to identify a characteristic or quality shared by those who engage in criminal behaviour, for example an aggressive personality or a lack of self-control. Notwithstanding this, the rejection of essentialism – at least at an ideational level – became routine following the influence of new deviancy theory in the 1960s. Relativism in this sense, though, was not born with new deviancy theory. As Reiner (1988: 138) says (and referred to earlier in this book), that deviance is not a quality of the act 'may have been news to criminology, but it was platitudinous to criminal lawyers'.

The notion of anti-essentialism is important because of its implications for debates regarding what critical criminologists believe they should study. Although they recognise that crime has no essential meaning, many criminologists working outside the critical tradition show little interest in these debates. This is particularly so when carrying out policy-oriented research – a police force spending large amounts of money on mapping crime 'hot spots', for instance, would hardly be thrilled by the revelation that 'there is no "ontological reality" of crime' (Hulsman, 1986: 65). An anti-essentialist stance makes the issue of what to study particularly problematic for critical criminologists because the legal rules defining crime are seen as ideological constructs created by the powerful (though left realism sees a significant degree of congruence between these and public opinion). Therefore, as discussed earlier, and put simply, the study of crime as traditionally understood necessarily requires accepting and working within the categorical constraints imposed by the 'rule makers'.

Internal debates regarding what should properly be the object of inquiry for critical criminology have been in evidence since the early 1970s, and continue today. Indeed, these and other debates relating to the theoretical concerns of critical criminology have been on the increase since the mid-1990s (partly because of the platform provided by the publication in 1997 of a new journal, *Theoretical Criminology*). As a result, within contemporary critical criminology there exist a number of approaches purporting to offer ways of studying crime that are congruent with a fundamental commitment to anti-essentialism. In spite of their differences, they all see 'crime' as the product of socially constructed criminalisation processes; the different conceptions of crime derive from the fact that each is focusing on, and giving priority to, different social processes. In other words, depending upon the nature of the particular discourse, the signifier 'crime' is referring to a variety of phenomena. None of them is 'wrong'; they are all 'right' within the context of their specific discourses. These approaches are discussed in turn.

Social censures

As stated in Chapter 13, Sumner (1990, 1994) is particularly associated with the notion of deviance or crime as a social censure (an adverse judgement). With this model there is no implication that practices designated as criminal are inherently bad, or necessarily harmful, but various publics may judge them as such, depending upon the circumstances in which ideological moral discourses are created and evolve. What is not always appreciated, though, is that social censures may be analysed on two levels. First, at a general abstracted level, where no reference is made to specific, substantive examples. Thus, for instance, the social censure (or crime) of murder can be discussed without reference to actual practices defined as murder; such practices need not exist in order for the censure to exist. On a second level, substantive, actual examples of practices subject to a social censure may be selected and the censuring processes analysed, for example acts of violence (Sumner, 1997). Alison Young (1997) has taken up a similar, though more broadly based, theme in her analysis of cultural imagery and the 'crimino-legal complex'. Here Young is concerned with representations of criminality/deviance, rather than with putting forward an explanation or understanding of the practices represented. Although, for example, in her section on the James Bulger case (the toddler James Bulger was killed by two young boys), she discusses various attempts within the wider society to make sense of what happened, these are used to illustrate further processes of cultural representation; they are not evaluated as viable or otherwise explanations *per se*. In these examples we see how crime is studied in terms of criminalisation and representational processes and, because of this, analyses are seen as congruent with an anti-essentialist position.

Victims and criminalisation: left realism

Left realist criminologists have continued to defend their position as anti-essentialist in spite of the criticisms to the contrary discussed in Chapter 13. Jock Young's (1997) 'holistic' approach is an attempt to encompass both the signifier, 'crime', and the signified, 'the criminal'. Again, a specific type of discourse, seen as anti-essentialist, is constructed, in this case on the basis of a left realist understanding of the criminalisation process. Fundamentally, this process is derived from victims' accounts of crime. Through their interpretation of certain events as crimes, victims are assigned a primary role in the criminalisation process. Public understandings in the shape of tolerance, disapproval and perceived harmfulness (and seen as largely reflecting a rational consensus) are the basis of this process and, in effect, create the 'crime problem'. Whereas other critical theorists focus on criminalisation by the state and its agencies of social control, left realists focus on crime as a product of the will of the people, and it is this notion of crime that provides the criminologist's object of inquiry. The left realists' approach is discussed further below.

Dispensing with legalism

Some have argued that the concept of 'criminal' behaviour should be retained, though severed from its link to criminal law. An early version of this has been discussed already: Schwendinger and Schwendinger's (1975) argument that 'crime' should be redefined in terms of universal codes of conduct based upon human rights. This new, liberating, understanding of crime is, they said, what criminologists should study. More recently, and from a similar standpoint (though as part of a much more sophisticated analysis), Henry and Milovanovic (1996) seek to redefine crime as resulting from unequal relations of power. 'Crime', they say, is 'the harm resulting from any attempt to reduce or suppress another's position or potential standing through the use of power that limits the other's ability to make a difference' (ibid.: 13).

As with the Schwendingers, this approach severs the links between crime and criminal law, thereby dissolving official boundaries separating crime from non-crime and allowing a range of non-criminalised, or legally censured, behaviours to come under scrutiny. However, freeing analyses from official definitions of crime also means that the power of the state to criminalise certain behaviours is removed from the frame, except in the negative sense of *not* criminalising, which puts it at variance with the social censure model of crime. A further issue is one of selection: how is it to be decided which practices transgress what the authors refer to as 'universal codes of conduct', or create harm, and on that basis are treated as 'crimes'? If these are construed as identifiable, objective categories, then it would seem to subvert an anti-essentialist model.

Dispensing with crime

As we saw in an earlier period of critical criminology's development, Steinert (1985) and Hulsman (1986) wished to dispense with the concept of crime altogether, preferring to speak of 'troubles' or 'problematic situations' (we can add De Haan, 1991, and Hill and Robertson, 2003, to this list). As with the Schwendingers and Henry and Milovanovic, from this perspective the activities selected for attention should not be dependent upon their pre-categorisation on the basis of criminal law. However, whilst the challenge to common sense, ideologically informed understandings of crime is to be recommended, there is, again, still the problem of deciding which activities to select for attention; whose voices are to be listened to? A lack of decent olive oil in the neighbourhood might be a problem for some people, but it hardly amounts to a 'problematic situation' as envisaged by Hulsman; but how, or where, is the line to be drawn? Furthermore, we might ask why it is that (critical) criminologists should be restricted to studying only those activities deemed to be troublesome or problematic.

Dispensing with criminology

With Smart's postmodernist 'deconstruction' of crime, criminology as an academic discipline would disappear as its subject matter is dispersed among a variety of alternative 'domains':

> The thing that criminology cannot do is deconstruct 'crime'. It cannot locate rape or child sexual abuse in the domain of sexuality, nor theft in the domain of economic activity, nor drug use in the domain of health. To do so would be to abandon criminology to sociology; but more importantly it would involve abandoning the idea of a unified problem which requires a unified response – at least at the theoretical level.
>
> (Smart, 1990: 7)

However, whilst this signals a rejection of essentialism, it does not constitute an argument for dispensing with 'crime' as a concept – references to rape and theft, etc. are references to legal categories. According to Smart's 'anti-criminology' perspective, though, analyses of these phenomena should be freed from the constraints imposed by criminological discourses. Thus crime would be studied, but not by criminologists *as* criminologists.

There are echoes of this approach in Van Hoorebeeck (1997), though there is no suggestion here that criminology should be abandoned. For Van Hoorebeeck, the criminologist can avoid falling into an 'essentialist trap' by recognising that activities defined as criminal cannot be distinguished from other, non-criminal activities in terms of causal factors. Put another way, there are no special (for example, psychopathological) factors specifically linked to criminality, but not to non-criminality.

Left realism and the 'crime problem'

Criminologists associated with left realism have, since the mid-1990s, continued to develop their version of critical criminology (see, for example, J. Young, 1998; Taylor, 1999; Lea, 2002). One dimension to this has been further theoretical work on the role of victims of crime in left realist understandings of the criminalisation process. Fundamentally, through their interpretation of certain events as crime, victims are assigned a prime role in this process.

Jock Young (1998) argues that crime is a product of a dyadic relationship between 'action' by an offender and 'reaction' as manifested in victims' accounts, though he acknowledges that measuring 'real' amounts of crime is a chimera. Nevertheless, drawing on evidence from victim surveys, he is led to conclude that since the 1960s amounts of crime – meaning conventional crime – have increased in Britain. Developing the point that public sensitivity to crime will vary over time, as well as from group to group, he introduces the idea of a continuum stretching from 'tolerated' to 'criminalised'. According to Young, public sensitivity has increased since the 1960s, leading to more behaviour being situated at the 'criminalisation' end of the contin-uum, as registered in victim surveys. Therefore, from this perspective, we have expe-rienced the worst of both worlds in Britain: on the one hand, rising levels of relative deprivation coupled with an increasing emphasis on individualism have, since the 1960s, led to an increase in crime incidents (see the discussion of left realism in Chapter 13) and, on the other hand, the public is less tolerant of crime, leading to a greater propensity for crime victims to register their victimisation in surveys. One difficulty with this is that there is no way of assessing the extent to which relative dep-rivation and individualism were relevant to explanations of criminality prior to the 1960s. Whilst these two factors might explain crime *rises* since then, they are not explanations of criminality in general; that is, if other causal factors are believed to have been at work up to the 1960s, what were they, and what role do they continue to play? And, as far as the measurement of crime is concerned, how can comparisons be made between the pre-1960s and more recent times, when no comparable data from victim surveys in the earlier period exist?

A further difficulty emerges if we examine more closely the 'action–reaction' relationship. What is put forward as 'realistic' evidence for increases in crime is pro-vided by victims' accounts, and these increases are explained in terms of relative dep-rivation and individualism – factors associated with an increasingly aggressive neo-liberal market economy. At the same time, public sensitivity is said to have heightened since the 1960s and, as a consequence, more events have been crimi-nalised in the sense of being defined as crimes by victims. However, when examining amounts of crime registered in victim surveys, there is no objective way of quantify-ing the relative importance of the 'external' factors (relative deprivation and individu-alism) and the factors associated with public perceptions and tolerance when explaining crime rises. Thus we cannot know how much of the crime registered by victims is 'new' and how much is the result of increased sensitivity. According to the logic of the tolerance–criminalisation model proposed by Young, less tolerance is highly likely to lead to more criminalisation in the above sense. In fact, in theory, less tolerance could account for the entire crime rises referred to by Young. One is reminded of Durkheim's society of saints, discussed earlier, where crime as normally understood may have decreased dramatically, and yet 'crime' as understood within that context may have increased equally dramatically. Data from the *British Crime Survey* (a victim survey) indicate that crime has been falling since the mid-1990s in Britain: is this because there has been a 'real' decrease due to less relative depriva-tion/individualism, or because the public has become *more* tolerant?

Although a lack of tolerance is not coterminous with moral panic, it is allied to it in that each involves a notion of heightened sensitivities. In its original formulation (see Cohen, 1980), a moral panic may simply create an illusion that crime has increased, or it may set in motion an amplification spiral, leading eventually to actual increases in crime. For left realists, 'real' amounts of crime *have* risen (at least up until the mid-1990s) since the 1960s, due to more relative deprivation and individualism, thus a suggestion of any illusion on the part of victims is rejected. Indeed, one of the main criticisms aimed at so called left idealists by left realists was that the former see increases in crime as an illusion. What is left unexplored in Young's analysis is the extent to which an amplification spiral is implicated in these 'real' increases in crime. The issue becomes even more complex if his 'square of crime' – comprising offenders, victims, formal controls and informal controls – is brought into the frame. The argument that public (or police, or media, etc.) intolerance is a rational response to real increases in crime suggests that the public, as victims, are simply responding to events that have their origins elsewhere. In fact, looked at in this way, we could equally argue that an increase in crime in a particular neighbourhood might eventually *reduce* people's sensitivity, making them more tolerant, and according to the 'tolerance–criminalisation' model, this should lead to less criminalisation, that is, less crime. A final point to make, one commented on earlier, is that respondents' views in victim surveys are mediated by a set of pre-given legal categories; therefore, non-criminal harmful activities are excluded, and so too are those crimes such as white-collar crime, untouched by victim surveys.

Morality, tolerance and the 'crime problem'

Clearly, public sensitivities regarding crime and victimisation are central to debates about the nature of the 'crime problem'. For this reason, it is worth returning to the postmodernist argument that in contemporary society individuals are relatively detached from moral foundations, and can draw on a plurality of moral universes. If the social world is more fractured and fragmented in this sense, then it will have major implications for deviantisation and criminalisation processes. According to the logic of Young's tolerance–criminalisation model discussed above, a reduction in the influence of previously widely accepted moral strictures, and the emergence of a society characterised by cultural pluralism, as suggested by postmodernists, should lead to a shift in public attitudes towards 'tolerance'. Yet Young argues that public sensitivities regarding crime have become more heightened since the 1960s, leading to a shift towards 'criminalisation', that is, less tolerance. As they stand, neither of these perspectives allows for the possibility that, since the 1960s, both processes have been at work: that a more 'liberal', open-minded moral outlook can coexist with less tolerant attitudes towards crime and criminals. There is, though, an alternative way of approaching this issue, one that is capable of accommodating the coexistence of both processes. In order to illustrate this, it is necessary to go back to the work of the new deviancy theorists in the 1960s. Although there was a celebration of cultural pluralism, and a rejection of the notion of consensus, the types of behaviour chosen for study tended to be based upon a perception of widespread societal disapproval of that behaviour, rather than small-scale, sectional disapproval (for example smoking marijuana rather than drinking real ale). Looking back, and applying contemporary sensibilities, many of the choices now appear *passé*, in the sense that the behaviours chosen would be unlikely to be defined, on that basis, as deviant today. Some examples are: naturists, gays, lesbians, green-haired punks, shaven-headed skin-heads, topless barmaids and marijuana users. There does seem to have been a weak-ening of moral disapprobation on a general level, suggesting a shift towards a more tolerant attitude. We can, though, be more specific: the shift has been towards a more tolerant attitude regarding what have been referred to as 'crimes/deviance without victims'. In short, a whole range of behaviours are now much less likely to attract a social censure of deviance. Indeed, going back further into the twentieth century, we can include such things as unmarried mothers, divorcees and couples 'living in sin'. At the same time, though, a more sensitised, less tolerant attitude towards crimes *with* victims appears to have developed, partly reflecting the increasing emphasis placed upon victims and rights. Young does not make this distinction when dis-cussing his tolerance–criminalisation continuum, and neither does he incorporate notions of approval and disapproval. This is returned to below within the context of a discussion of more recent work from Young.

Critical criminology, globalisation and neo-liberal markets

In recent years, various critical criminologists have focused on the criminogenic fea-tures of globalised neo-liberal markets. Some examples will indicate the key arguments.

Critical criminologists have continued to explore the area of white-collar and cor-porate crime (as crimes of the powerful), though now within the context of unfet-tered, footloose, neo-liberal global markets (see, for example, Bonanno *et al.*, 1997; Slapper and Tombs, 1999; Snider, 2000; Cottino, 2004). To digress slightly, an impor-tant point to make here is that labelling different types of crime as white-collar, cor-porate, professional, organised, state and conventional is not to suggest that these are in practice discrete categories. On the contrary, there is a significant degree of overlap among all of them. Pearce and Tombs (2004) provide a good, recent overview of multinational corporations (MNCs), paying special attention to the international oil industry, and crime. They begin by questioning the current orthodoxy, suggesting that globalisation has led to nation states becoming less powerful when compared to MNCs. Whilst true in some respects, the reality, they say, is rather more complex: 'in creating the condition within which MNCs can operate more freely and on an increasingly international scale, advanced capitalist states have been crucial actors' (ibid.: 361).

The authors point out that MNCs share three basic features:

- the control of economic activities in a number of countries;
- they are able to take advantage of geographical differences among countries;
- they are in a position to move resources and functions around the world.

In combination, these lead to four important consequences.

- First, MNCs have significant opportunities to bypass the legal system of a country in which they operate, and there are few bodies of law that are international in scope. This allows 'regime shopping', that is, searching out those parts of the world where there are fewer regulations; usually these are in the developing world. It also allows MNCs to 'export hazard', to use methods of production or sell products that in their home country would be against the law.
- Second, MNCs can threaten to locate elsewhere if controls on their activities are not reduced.
- Third, MNCs ensure that the companies they establish in other countries are, from a legal point of view, of independent status. This complicates any situation where illegal behaviour is suspected, and limits the liability of the MNC as whole (the Bhopal disaster in India involving a Union Carbide plant is a good example of this occurring – see Pearce and Tombs, 1998).
- Fourth, because the criminal law is largely based upon the individual and the concept of *mens rea* – the criminal intent of an act – it does not easily apply to a 'fictional individual' in the shape of a 'corporate person'.

Currie's (1997: 147) central thesis is that market societies (seen as societies where market principles pervade the whole social fabric) 'are especially likely to breed high levels of violent crime'. As he says, many commentators in the United States (and elsewhere) pointed to the increases in crime, including violent crime, in Russia and China when free market economies replaced state socialism, a transformation previously applauded as a move towards democracy and freedom. Whilst in these accounts the lawlessness was linked to the advent of a free market, the same commentators saw no reason to make a corresponding link between the market and high levels of violent crime in the United States. For Currie, this link is crucial, though his analysis also takes into consideration the significant differences in amounts of violent crime between one society and another:

> Are there some common features which help explain why homicide is so startlingly high in *one* advanced Western industrial society – the US – and also in some (but not all) developing countries and (only recently) in some parts of the former Soviet bloc? And relatedly, are there some common factors that help explain why most of the *rest* of the post-industrial family of nations, including even its poorer cousins, suffer so much less of it?
>
> (Currie, 1997: 149–50, emphases in original)

From Currie's (left realist) perspective, then, some market societies are worse than others, in that they are more competitive, more unequal, and provide less welfare for the poor and marginalised and, because of this, they are particularly prone to high rates of violent crime. Alternative forms of capitalism – 'compassionate' and 'keiretsu' – lead to social structures and relationships that are less harsh. Compassionate capitalism is seen to stress 'social solidarity, equity and community values . . . as in Scandinavia' (Currie, 1997: 153), whilst keiretsu capitalism 'is paternalistic . . . Japan being the classic example' (ibid.: 153) (for a detailed study of crime and Japanese society, see Leonardsen, 2004). The United States, on the other hand, argues Currie, provides a distinct example of a capitalist society where protection from the worst excesses of the market is extremely limited. He identifies a number of highly criminogenic and interrelated mechanisms that have come together in a concentrated form in the United States, and these provide the basis for an explanation of the comparatively high rates of violent crime in that society:

- the progressive destruction of livelihood;
- the growth of extremes of economic inequality and material deprivation;
- the withdrawal of public services and supports, especially for families and children;
- the erosion of informal and community networks of mutual support, supervision and care;
- the spread of a materialistic, neglectful and 'hard' culture;
- the unregulated marketing of the technology of violence;
- and, not least, the weakening of social and political alternatives.

By the end of the 1990s a more 'Europeanised' critical criminology was emerging in Britain. This was linked to such things as the political and economic changes occurring within the context of neo-liberal market capitalism; the notion of the 'European dream' arising from the European Community; cross-border crime; and the growth in European-wide treaties relating to, for example, increasing cooperation among law enforcement agencies, including the exchange of intelligence. Ian Taylor (1999), for example, discusses what he calls the 'five defining features of market-liberal discourses on crime in Europe'.

There is, first, 'crime and social anxiety'. Market-liberalism, says Taylor, encourages anxiety and a sense of risk among citizens. As a result, people work harder because of job insecurities; buy more, because of insecurities over consumer goods; and take financial risks, such as buying on credit cards and speculating on shares. There are further anxieties concerning economic stability because of the intrusion of free market criminal enterprises into the legitimate market. He also notes the increases in corporate fraud that followed the deregulation of the market in the 1980s. Overall, he argues, contemporary societies are characterised by a culture of anxiety and a psychological sense of risk, as reflected in 'fear of crime' surveys (seen as a device by which generalised anxieties are articulated). With this as a backdrop, criminal justice policy is based upon the management of risk.

Second, Taylor points to 'the nation and the state'. Persistent poverty and long-term unemployment have led to the institutionalisation of inner-city, or outer-edge, ghettoes in older, now post-industrial European cities. The poor are seen as the marginalised casualties of market-liberalism, creating problems that the nation state finds increasingly difficult to solve, leading, again, to a response based upon the management of problems.

Third, he refers to crime and 'the other'. The argument here is that aggressive markets create a situation where sections of the population are increasingly subject to a process of demonisation. Media-generated moral panics target more and more folk devils, who are judged not to be full members of society (for example, asylum seekers, Yardies and paedophiles). This too heightens the sense of risk and danger.

Taylor's fourth feature is 'crime, dislocation and social care'. Here he points to the reductions in welfare and social care provided by the state, as governments across Europe have cut taxes and social spending. Unfortunately, this has taken place within the context of deindustrialisation and the restructuring of European economies. Various social problems, including crime, have resulted from this intensification of social inequality.

Finally, Taylor discusses what he calls 'market liberalism, hyperbole and critical evaluation'. By this he means that market societies invest huge amounts of energy in the 'almost messianic' project of convincing citizens that such societies provide unlimited opportunities for success and happiness. An extreme emphasis on the consumption of material goods, says Taylor, intensifies a striving for success, bringing with it the inevitable losers as well as winners, and an increase in (Mertonian) relative deprivation.

Vertiginous late modernity

While contemporary critical criminology contains a number of unifying themes (such as a commitment to critique and anti-essentialism, and a concern to challenge inequality, injustice and punitive responses to crime), there is also fragmentation, diversity and fluidity in terms of its ideas, concerns and methodologies. One criminologist who has figured prominently in the development of critical criminology in Britain and, indeed, around the world during the last forty years or so is Jock Young. Although he has not, of course, made the journey alone, he has had a significant presence in the twists and turns associated with the history of critical criminology: a late 1960s study of illegal drug users guided by new deviancy theory; the 'new criminology' that emerged in the early 1970s; the growing influence of left realism in the 1980s; and, in the new millennium, the incorporation of cultural criminology into a left realism sensitive to the profound social, economic and political transformations characterising late (and, as it is sometimes called, 'liquid') modernity. Young's (2007)

The Vertigo of Late Modernity, is an invigorating, wide-ranging, erudite and polemical statement of where he now stands:

> Vertigo is the malaise of late modernity: a sense of insecurity of insubstantiality, and of uncertainty, a whiff of chaos and a fear of falling. The signs of giddiness, of unsteadiness, are everywhere . . . The obsession with rules, an insistence on clear uncompromising lines of demarcation between correct and incorrect behaviour, a narrowing of borders, the decreased tolerance of deviance, a disproportionate response to rule-breaking, and easy resort to punitiveness and a point at which simple punishment begins to verge on the vindictive.
>
> (Ibid.: 12)

In this book, Young revisits and develops his earlier work on the theme of social exclusion (Young, 1999), in the process seeking to dissolve the binary distinction between exclusion and inclusion. For one commentator, *Vertigo* could signal a shift away from left realism back towards left idealism: 'Famous for his previous repudiation of Left Idealism in favour of Left Realism (a transformation that may by slowly reversing again)' (Maruna, 2008: 534). Certainly, Young's claim that 'moral panics abound' (Young, 2007: 13) does seem to depart from left realism's view that public concerns about crime and disorder should not be written off as exaggerated, or disproportionate, and makes a reliance on the views of victims, or the 'community', problematic. Furthermore, the cultural criminology he has aligned himself with is infused with themes, ideas and intellectual influences that emerged in the heady days of the late 1960s under the rubric of new deviancy theory, for example (along with moral panic) an 'appreciation', even celebration, of forms of deviance, a recognition of cultural pluralism, and a concern with politicising deviant behaviour. At the same, though, notions of relative deprivation and equality of opportunity, derived originally from Merton and subsequently embraced by left realists, still have an important presence in Young's analysis of the late modern condition.

In *Vertigo,* Young compares and contrasts late modernity, that is the present, with an earlier 'modern' period of the 1950s and the 1960s, noting the massive changes that have occurred in terms of employment, family and community:

> Late modern society involves insecurities of economic position and of identity. A turbo-charged capitalism shifts manufacturing industries abroad, out-sources, downsizes, deskills and automates; it undermines the social embeddedness of job, community and very often family, creating a high level of instability and a pervasive sense of unfairness. Such a sense of disembeddedness is further exacerbated by the shock of the plural, an unprecedented pluralism of values, engendered by mass migration and global media.
>
> (Young, 2008: 524)

These transformations, argues Young, have resulted in strong feelings of resentment among members of a lower or underclass and members of an 'insecure' middle class ('middle class' is here defined as a broad tranche of the population occupying a class position between an 'underclass' and a rich upper class, and is distinguished from a fourth strata, a 'secure' middle class). It is the insecure middle class who are seen as experiencing a sense of 'vertigo': a fear of falling due to an intensification of anxieties about jobs, social status and a lack of ontological security. According to Young, this has led to what he calls 'othering': demonising the poor as culturally inferior, and the source of the crime problem. Along with this, he says, has been a trend towards 'defining deviancy up', that is, a diminution in the tolerance of other people's behaviour, together with a more punitive stance. The end result is an increase in rules and prohibitions, as the (insecure) middle class attempt to recapture a world of security and stability.

Drawing on Merton's model, Young argues that for those in the lower reaches of the class structure, problems arise because of a disjunction between cultural *inclusion* and structural *exclusion*. Thus the least well off are socialised into the same value system as the wider society – one stressing material success and equal opportunities – and yet face the structural barriers deriving from low wages and a lack of opportunities for upward mobility. The ensuing relative deprivation intensifies the 'transgressive anger', and this is often directed at others in the same position:

> For the poor predate the poor, the stigma of being a 'loser' is countered by a hardening, an essentialist self-othering, often of machismo, race, religion, even locality and postal code; internecine splits of spurious identity striating an obscured class structure.
>
> (Ibid.: 526)

There is in Young's *The Vertigo of Late Modernity* an echo of an argument discussed above within the context of left realist criminology: that public sensitivity towards crime/deviance can be located on a continuum stretching from 'tolerated' to 'criminalised'. In *Vertigo,* the argument is that 'othering' on the part of an insecure middle class has led to less tolerance of difference and, therefore, a 'defining up' of deviancy. This, it is argued, has resulted in an increase in rules and prohibitions (something that the current recession is likely to accentuate even further). As we have seen in the previous chapter, criminal justice (and other) policies introduced by the Labour government do support the idea of less tolerance, and a more vindictive, punitive stance in relation to difference, together with an expansion of the means of surveillance. However, this does raise questions regarding the source of these censures, as well as the linkages between the public, the media and government. In other words, how and why does greater intolerance among the insecure middle class get translated into actual policy, and what role do the media play? If, as Young argues, late modern society is, from the point of view of cultural affiliations, much more pluralistic than it was in, say the 1950s, then it would suggest a trend towards greater, rather than less, tolerance among the public. The problem is that the issue is so complicated that it is impossible to draw up a simple balance sheet of gains and losses in degrees of tolerance (not the least because an individual's values are necessarily inherent in any assessment). Furthermore, while the criminalisation of certain behaviours may reflect greater intolerance, it could be reasonably argued that sometimes such criminalisation – for example, in relation to domestic violence and marital rape – is something to welcome. In addition, and referred to in the earlier discussion of left realism, during the last fifty years or so the public have become more tolerant towards certain behaviours previously viewed as deviant. In some cases, for example, in relation to gambling and alcohol consumption, a more liberal attitude has been reflected in the state decriminalising such behaviour.

Hall *et al.* (2008) also discuss offending within the context of the intense individualism and consumerism characterising late modern society. This is an ethnographic study concentrating on criminal identities among those ostensibly at the bottom end of the class structure. Here, aspirations were oriented towards the status, respect and sense of achievement delivered by an ostentatious display of material consumption, and criminality – especially dealing in drugs – was seen as providing *the* mechanism for satisfying these aspirations. None of those interviewed, though, saw themselves as part of a socially excluded underclass. In fact, it was crucially important they were able to distance themselves from the 'losers' (for example 'Aldi bashers', a label given to those who had sunk so low that they had to shop in discount stores). Allied to this, none of them displayed any allegiance to traditional notions of working class community or conventional values. They were committed to an ethos of individualism and consumerism, rather than collectivism and class-based struggle.

Green perspectives

Here the concerns of criminology are extended to include activities that harm the environment and animals (in terms of activism, there are links with the environmental movement and the animal rights movement). At the moment, it is premature to suggest that a 'green' criminological theory exists, rather it is, as South (1998: 212) puts it, 'a sensitising *perspective*', and encompasses such things as risk, human and animal rights, and a critique of the activities of multinational corporations (Vol. 2, No. 2, 1998, special issue of *Theoretical Criminology* is devoted to the theme 'for a green criminology'). More recently, Lynch and Stretsky (2003) develop further a theoretical understanding of green perspectives. As they say, this has been a neglected area within criminology and 'Has allowed little room for critical examination of individuals or entities who/which kills, injures and assaults other life forms (human, animal or plant) by poisoning the earth' (ibid.: 231).

They outline three 'guiding principles' for a green perspective. First, the harms done to the environment result from the priority given to economic interests over environmental interests, and this will determine whether or not these harms are defined as crimes. Second, those harms that impact upon the least powerful in society, for example poorer people or minorities, are the ones least likely to be criminalised or subject to law enforcement. Third, they argue that a green perspective should seek to integrate social structural considerations with subjective understandings on the part of those who suffer from harms and/or involve themselves in ecological movements.

The future of critical criminology

The above discussion has given some indication, albeit a brief one, of more recent developments and debates located in what is now a broad church of critical criminology. In spite of intellectual challenges from postmodernists and others, and a changed world where talk of socialist utopias is seen as naïve and totally unrealistic, the work of critical criminologists continues to have a significant presence in criminological discourses. Founded on a fundamental commitment to critique, it is not unreasonable to suggest that in the present social, political and economic context, critical criminology is even more relevant than it was when it was on the crest of a wave in the 1970s. It will obviously continue to evolve, and the nature of its evolution will, of course, be contingent upon a multitude of wider changes, internal and external to criminology as an academic field. One obvious source of fluidity is the people involved. With the passage of time, new *galacticos* with different biographies and new challenges to those discussed on the pages of this book will emerge. However, there are a number of key agendas that, one hopes, will continue to excite the minds of the critical criminologist, notably:

- theoretical debates about the nature of criminology and its conceptual language;
- critical analyses of the social, political and economic contexts, global and local, within which social harms, criminalised or otherwise, are situated;
- a theoretical and practical engagement with issues of social and criminal justice policy and a commitment to the eradication of injustice;
- an interest in not only criminalisation processes, but also issues of aetiology, culture and identity among those subjected to these processes.

One also hopes that for those involved, this is accompanied by, as Currie (2002: vii) puts it; 'a willingness to apply a critical lens not only to the work of their more conventional counterparts in the discipline but their own as well'.

FINAL REMARKS

This book has been about criminology as an academic discipline and the various ways in which the criminological project has been conceived and socially organised; it has also been about criminological theory and the different ways in which issues of crime, deviance and control have been studied. A very broad array of criminological theories have been discussed in this text and, whatever their particular merits, each did at least for a period capture the imagination of some academic criminologists; occasionally they even influenced criminal justice policy. And then something else came along. Out of the discipline's internal and external history have come many different types of criminology, and now, well into the new millennium, intense, complex and sometimes vitriolic debates continue. Thank goodness. Whatever their personal preferences, it is hoped that readers of this book will find these debates both important and interesting. In the future, it is from their ranks that books such as this will draw their inspiration.

Selected further reading

Postmodernism and criminology are discussed by **Morrison, W. (1995)** *Theoretical Criminology: From modernity to post-modernism*, London: Cavendish Publishing, and South, N. (1997) 'Late-modern criminology: "late" as in "dead" or "modern" as in "new"', in Owen, D. (ed) *Sociology After Postmodernism*, London: Sage. A key text written from the perspective of constitutive criminology is **Henry, S. and Milovanovic, D. (1996)** *Constitutive Criminology: Beyond post-modernism*, London: Sage.

For reviews of feminist perspectives, gender and crime, see **Heidensohn, F. and Gelsthorpe, L. (2007)** 'Gender and crime', in M. Maguire, R. Morgan and R. Reiner (eds) *The Oxford Handbook of Criminology*, 4th edn, Oxford: Clarendon Press. Silvestri, M. and Crowther-Dowey (2008) *Gender and Crime*, London: Sage, provide an accessible introduction.

More detailed analyses will be found in **Naffine, N. (1997)** *Feminism and Criminology*, Cambridge: Polity, and **Heidensohn, F. (2000)** *Sexual Politics and Social Control*, Buckingham: Open University Press. On the relationship between gender and justice, see Heidensohn, F. (ed) (2006) *Gender and Justice: New concepts and approaches*, Cullompton: Willan. Renzetti, C. (2008) *Feminist Criminology*, Abingdon: Routledge, examines the intersection of gender, race and class within the context of crime and justice.

An accessible and up-to-date discussion of masculinities and crime is **Collier, R. (2004)** 'Masculinities and crime: Rethinking the "man question"', in C. Sumner (ed) *The Blackwell Companion to Criminology*, Oxford: Blackwell Publishing.

For a 'structured action' approach, see **Messerschmidt, J. W. (1997)** *Crime as Structured Action: Gender, race, class and crime*, Thousand Oaks, CA: Sage, and for an iconoclastic analysis of this area, **Hood-Williams, J. (2002)** 'Gender, masculinities and crime: From structures to psyches', *Theoretical Criminology*, 5(1). Connell, R. (2002) *Gender*, Cambridge: Polity Press examines gender theory, paying particular attention to masculinities.

An excellent introduction to psycho-social criminology (with or without the hyphen) is provided by **Gadd, D. and Jefferson, T. (2007)** *Psychosocial Criminology: An Introduction*, London: Sage.

Control theory is represented by **Gottfredson, M. R. and Hirschi, T. (1990)** *A General Theory of Crime*, Stanford, CA: Stanford University Press; and 'control balance' theory by **Tittle, C. R. (2000)** 'Control balance', in R. Paternoster and R. Bachman (eds) *Explaining Criminals and Crime: Essays in contemporary theory*, Los Angeles, CA: Roxbury, with a 'refinement' in **Tittle, C. R. (2004)** 'Refining control balance theory', *Theoretical Criminology*, **8(4)**. A useful review of Laub and Sampson's influential 'life course' theory is provided by **Laub, J. H., Sampson, R. J. and Sweeten, G. (2006)** 'Assessing Sampson and Laub's life-course theory of crime', in F. T. Cullen, J. P. Wright and K. R. Blevins (eds) *Taking Stock: The status of criminological theory* (*Advances in Criminological Theory*, Vol. 15, pp. 313–33), New Brunswick, NJ: Transaction Publishing.

A good, introductory, starting place for exploring cultural criminology is **Ferrell, J., Hayward, K. and Young, J. (2008)** *Cultural Criminology: An invitation*, London: Sage.

A now classic text from twenty years ago is **Katz, J. (1988)** *Seductions of Crime*, New York: Basic Books. For discussions of more recent developments, see **Ferrell, J. and Sanders, C. (eds) (1995)** *Cultural Criminology*, Boston, MA: Northeastern University Press; Ferrell, J., Hayward, K., Morrison, W. and Presdee, M. (2004) *Cultural Criminology Unleashed*, London: Glasshouse; and **Hayward, K. (2004)** *City Limits: Crime, consumer culture and the urban experience*, London: Glasshouse.

A synthesis of structural and cultural approaches is **Young, J. (2003)** 'Merton with energy, Katz with structure', *Theoretical Criminology*, **7(3)**. Following the recent popularity of cultural criminology, **Jefferson, T. and Hall, S. (eds) (2006)** *Resistance Through Rituals: Youth subcultures in post-war Britain*, 2nd edn, Abingdon: Routledge (and as a measure of its continuing influence) has been re-issued as a 2nd edition, 30 years after it was first published (published originally as Hall, S. and Jefferson, T. (eds) (1976)).

A number of recent edited collections written from a critical perspective are available, notably: **Sumner, C. (ed) (2004)** *The Blackwell Companion to Criminology*, Oxford: Blackwell Publishing; Carrington, K. and Hogg, R. (eds) (2002) *Critical Criminology: Issues, debates, challenges*, Cullompton: Willan; and, making links with the earlier *New Criminology*, **Walton, P. and Young, J. (eds) (1998)** *The New Criminology Revisited*, Basingstoke: Macmillan.

Barton, A., Corteen, K., Scott, D. and Whyte, D. (eds) (2007) *Expanding the Criminological Imagination: Critical readings in criminology*, Cullompton: Willan, is a useful introduction. **Scraton, P. (2007)** *Power, Conflict and Criminalisation*, Abingdon: Routledge draws on various 'case studies', such as the Dunblane shootings and the 'war on terror', in order to analyse the processes involved in the marginalisation and criminalisation of specific groups. From critical criminologists in Australia and New Zealand: **Anthony, T. and Cunneen, C. (eds) (2008)** *The Critical Criminology Companion*, Cullompton: Willan.

Young, J. (2007) *The Vertigo of Late Modernity*, London: Sage is an erudite, polemical analysis of transgression and control in contemporary, late modern societies, and incorporates ideas from R. K. Merton, left realist critical criminology and cultural criminology.

For critical work on corporate and white-collar crime, see **Pearce, F. and Tombs, S. (1998)** *Toxic Capitalism: Corporate crime and the chemical industry*, Aldershot: Ashgate; and **Green, S. P. (2007)** *Lying, Cheating and Stealing: A moral theory of white-collar crime*, Buckingham: Open University Press.

For an interesting discussion on the theme of state crime, see **White, R. (2008b)** 'Depleted uranium, state crime and the politics of knowing', *Theoretical Criminology*, 12(1), pp. 31–54.

Critical arguments in favour of orienting criminology towards 'harm' rather than 'crime' are gathered together in **Hillyard, P., Tombs, S., Pantazis, C. and Gordon, D. (eds) (2004)** *Beyond Criminology: Taking harm seriously*, London: Pluto.

For critical work on surveillance and issues surrounding security, see **Lyon, D. (2007)** *Surveillance Studies: An overview*, Oxford: Polity; Goold, B. (2008) *Surveillance*, Abingdon: Routledge; Wood, J. and Shearing, C. (2006) *Imagining Security*, Cullompton: Willan; and Zedner, L. (2007) *Security*, Abingdon: Routledge.

A 'Europeanised' criminology is well represented by **Taylor, I. (1999)** *Crime in Context*, Cambridge: Polity Press; and van Swaaningen, R. (1997) *Critical Criminology: Visions from Europe*, London: Sage.

A useful book on social theory and criminology is **Garland, D. and Sparks, R. (eds) (2000)** *Criminology and Social Theory*, Oxford: Oxford University Press.

For an introduction to 'green' criminology, see **Lynch, M. J. and Stretsky, P. B. (2003)** 'The meaning of green: contrasting criminological perspectives', *Theoretical Criminology*, 7(2); and for further theoretical elaboration: **Beirne, P. and South, N. (eds) (2007)** *Issues in Green Criminology: Confronting harms against environments, humanity and other animals*, Cullompton: Willan. A useful discussion of environmental criminology is provided by **White, R. (2008a)** *Crimes Against Nature: Environmental criminology and ecological justice*, Cullompton: Willan.

A well-written, up-to-date American overview of criminological theories of delinquency is **Shoemaker, D. J. (2005)** *Theories of delinquency: An examination of explanations of delinquent behavior*, 5th edn, Oxford: Oxford University Press.

Tierney, J. (2009) *Key Perspectives in Criminology*, Milton Keynes: Open University Press provides an up-to-date, detailed discussion of the major theoretical perspectives in criminology.

Postscript to the 2nd Edition

In the paradise of plenty all the palaces of fun

Are standing cold and empty as you shiver in the sun

In the shadows of ambition where you learned to buy and sell

The ghosts of all your wishing are now lying where they fell

While the felons of the language and the psycho-racketeers

Eat their bare faced sandwiches and never taste the tears

As disciples of the message and the refugees of thought

Go fleeing from the wreckage of the dream that they once bought

Are you waiting for some saviour to come tripping from the train

With points for good behaviour and some pills to ease the pain

Do you know what you are doing is your conscience clean and clear

As you stand amongst the ruin of all you once held dear.

'Crazy Days', written by, and reproduced
by kind permission of Willy Russell,
© Willy Russell Music 2003.
From the CD *Hoovering the Moon*.

Postscript to the 3rd Edition

Me and Javi

Shouted slogans in Spanish

Like it was our world to win

Then they moved the plant

Down to Ojeda

Time to bite your tongue again

I've seen the fabled city

And its streets are paved with gold

But an iron fence runs round it

And its iron gate is closed

What ain't right ain't right

He told me
But something else passed behind his eyes
Now he's downtown on his knees
Washing floors for somebody
And quietly biding his time

I've seen the fabled city . . .

At the gas station
On Sunset and Crescent
I met an angel sad and old
She lived in the alley
Behind the market
In the shadows maybe hidden from the Lord
And for a dollar
She sang a song
That sounded more like a prayer
A wish that her dead mother and father
Couldn't look down and see her there

I've seen the fabled city . . .

On the wire outside my window
There sit 100 swallows
And I suspect that if one flew
Then 99 would follow

Tom Morello: The Nightwatchman
'The Fabled City' Taken from the album
The Fabled City © 2008 The Nightwatchman
Music (BMI).Myspace.com/the nightwatchman

REFERENCES

Adams, J. (1995) *Risk*, London: UCL Press.

Adamson, M., Briskin, L. and McPhail, M. (1988) *Feminist Organising for Change: A contemporary women's movement in Canada*, Toronto: Oxford University Press.

Adler, F. (1975) *Sisters in Crime*, New York: McGraw-Hill.

Agnew, R. (1987) 'On testing structural strain theories', *Journal of Research in Crime and Delinquency*, **24**(4), pp. 281–6.

Agnew, R. (1991) 'The interactive effects of peer variables on delinquency', *Criminology*, **29**, pp. 47–72.

Ahmed, E., Harris, N., Braithwaite, J. and Braithwaite, V. (2001) *Shame Management Through Reintegration*, Cambridge: Cambridge University Press.

Akers, R. L. (1967) 'Problems in the sociology of deviance: social definitions and behavior', *Social Forces*, **46**(4), pp. 455–65.

Akers, R. L. (1991) 'Self-control as a general theory of crime', *Journal of Quantitative Criminology*, **7**(2), pp. 201–11.

Allen, H. (1987) *Justice Unbalanced! Gender, Psychiatry and Judicial Decisions*, Milton Keynes: Open University Press.

Althusser, L. (1971) *Lenin and Philosophy and Other Essays*, London: New Left Books.

Amir, M. (1971) *Patterns of Forcible Rape*, Chicago, IL: University of Chicago Press.

Anderson, E. (1976) 'The "chivalrous" treatment of the female offender in the arms of the law: a review of the literature', *Social Problems*, **23**(3), pp. 49–57.

Anderson, N. (1975; first pub. 1923) *The Hobo: The story of Chicago's prohibition era*, London: Hutchinson.

Anderson, P. (1968) 'Components of the national culture', *New Left Review*, **50**.

Anderson, S., Kinsey, R., Loader, I. and Smith, C. (1990) *The Edinburgh Crime Survey*, Edinburgh: Scottish Office.

Anderson, S., Kinsey, R., Loader, I. and Smith, C. (1991) *'Cautionary Tales': A study of young people in Edinburgh*, Edinburgh: Centre for Criminology, University of Edinburgh.

Anthony, T. and Cunneen, C. (eds) (2008) *The Critical Criminology Companion*, Cullompton: Willan.

Atkinson, J. M. (1971) 'Societal reactions to suicide: the role of coroners' definitions', in S. Cohen (ed), *Images of Deviance*, Harmondsworth: Penguin.

Atkinson, J. M. (1979) *Discovering Suicide*, London: Macmillan.

Austin, A. L. (1977) 'Commitment, neutralization and delinquency', in T. N. Ferdinand (ed), *Juvenile Delinquency*, London: Sage.

Bagot, J. H. (1941) *Juvenile Delinquency: A comparative study of the position in Liverpool and England and Wales*, London: Cape.

Baldwin, J. and Bottoms, A. (1976) *The Urban Criminal*, London: Tavistock.

Bankowski, Z. and Mungham, G. (1975) *Images of Law*, London: Routledge & Kegan Paul.

Barnardo's (2008) *Locking Up Or Giving Up: Is custody for children always the right answer?*, Ilford: Barnardo's.

Barton, A., Corteen, K., Scott, D. and Whyte, D. (eds) (2007) *Expanding the Criminological Imagination: Critical readings in criminology*, Cullompton: Willan.

Bates, J. E., Bayles, K., Bennett, D. S., Ridge, B. and Brown, M. N. (1991) 'Origins of externalizing behaviour problems at 8 years of age', in D. J. Pepler and K. H. Rubin (eds), *The Development and Treatment of Childhood Aggression*, Hillsdale, NJ: Erlbaum.

Baudrillard, J. (1988) *Selected Writings*, Cambridge: Polity Press.

Bauman, Z. and Tester, K. (2001) *Conversations with Zymunt Bauman*, Cambridge: Cambridge University Press.

Baumer, E. P. (2007) 'Untangling research puzzles in Merton's multilevel anomie theory', *Theoretical Criminology*, **11**(1), pp. 63–93.

Beccaria, C. (1963) *On Crime and Punishments* (H. Paolucci, trans.) Indianapolis, IN: Bobbs-Merrill (first published in 1764 as *Dei Delitti e Delle Pene*).

Beck, U. (1992) *Risk Society: Towards a new modernity*, London: Sage.

Becker, H. S. (1963) *Outsiders: Studies in the sociology of deviance*, London: Macmillan.

Becker, H. S. (1967) 'Whose side are we on?' *Social Problems*, **14**(3), pp. 239–47.

Becker, H. S. (1974) 'Labelling theory reconsidered', in P. Rock and M. McIntosh (eds), *Deviance and Social Control*, London: Tavistock.

Becket, F. and Hencke, D. (2004) *The Blairs and Their Court*, London: Aurum Press.

Becket, K. (1997) *Making Crime Pay: Law and Order in Contemporary American Politics*, New York: Oxford University Press.

Beirne, P. (1979) 'Empiricism and the critique of Marxism on law and crime', *Social Problems*, **26**(4), pp. 373–84.

Beirne, P. (1993) *Inventing Criminology: Essays on the rise of 'homo criminalis'*, Albany, NY: State University of New York Press.

Beirne, P. (2005) *The Chicago School of Criminology, 1914–1945*, Abingdon: Routledge.

Beirne, P. and South, N. (eds) (2007) *Issues in Green Criminology: Confronting harms against environments, humanity, and other animals*, Cullompton: Willan.

Bellamy, R. (ed) *Beccaria: On crimes and punishments and other writings*, Cambridge: Cambridge University Press.

Belson, W. (1975) *Juvenile Theft: The casual factors*, London: Harper & Row.

Bernard, T. J. (1987) 'Testing structural strain theories', *Journal of Research in Crime and Delinquency*, **24**(4), pp. 262–80.

Bernstein, M. (2004) '"Abominable and detestable": understanding homophobia and the criminalization of sodomy', in C. Sumner (ed), *The Blackwell Companion to Criminology*, Oxford: Blackwell Publishing.

Bianchi, H. and van Swaaningen, R. (eds) (1986) *Abolitionism: Towards a non-repressive approach to crime*, Amsterdam: Free University Press.

Biderman, A. D. and Reiss, A. J. (1967) 'On exploring the "dark figure" of crime', *Annals of the American Academy of Political and Social Science*, **374**, pp. 1–15.

Bilton, T., Bonnett, K., Jones, P., Stanworth, M., Sheard, K. and Webster, A. (1981) *Introductory Sociology*, Basingstoke: Macmillan.

Bittner, E. (1967) 'The police on skid row: a study of peacekeeping', *American Sociological Review*, **32**(5), pp. 699–715.

Black, E. (2003) *War Against the Weak: Eugenics and America's campaign to create a master race*, New York: Four Walls Eight Windows.

Blanden, J., Goodman, A., Gregg, P. and Machin, S. (2004) 'Changes in intergenerational mobility in Britain', in M. Corak (ed), *Generational Income Mobility in North America and Europe*, Cambridge: Cambridge University Press.

Block, A. (1991) *Perspectives on Organised Crime*, Boston, MA and London: Kluwer.

Bolling, K., Clemens, S., Grant, C. and Smith, P. (2003) *2002–2003 British Crime Survey (England and Wales): Technical report*, Vol. 1, prepared for the Measuring and Analysing Crime Programme, Research, Development and Statistics Directorate, Home Office, London: Home Office.

Bonanno, A., Constance, D. H. and Lyman, K. L. (1997) 'Corporate crime in the global era', *Critical Sociology*, **2**, pp. 63–88.

Bordua, D. (1970) 'Recent trends: deviant behavior and social control', in C. Bersani (ed) *Crime and Delinquency*, London: Collier Macmillan.

Bottomley, A. K. and Pease, K. (1986) *Crime and Punishment: Interpreting the data*, Milton Keynes: Open University Press.

Bottoms, A. (1995) 'The philosophy and politics of punishment and sentencing', in C. Clarkson and R. Morgan (eds), *The Politics of Sentencing Reform*, Oxford: Oxford University Press.

Bottoms, A., Mawby, R. I. and Walker, M. A. (1987) 'Localised crime survey in contrasting areas of a city', *British Journal of Criminology*, **27**, pp. 125–34.

Box, S. (1981) *Deviance, Reality and Society*, 2nd edn, Eastbourne: Holt, Rinehart & Winston.

Box, S. (1983) *Power, Crime and Mystification*, London: Tavistock.

Box, S. (1987) *Recession, Crime and Punishment*, Basingstoke: Macmillan.

Box, S. and Hale, C. (1983) 'Liberation and female criminality in England and Wales', *British Journal of Criminology*, **23**(1), pp. 35–49.

Braithwaite, J. (1989) *Crime, Shame and Reintegration*, Cambridge: Cambridge University Press.

Braithwaite, J. (1998) 'Restorative justice', in M. Tonry (ed), *The Handbook of Crime and Punishment*, Oxford: Oxford University Press.

Brewer, C. and Lait, J. (1980) *Can Social Work Survive?* London: Temple Smith.

Brewer, C., Morris, T., Morgan, P. and North, M. (1981) *Criminal Welfare on Trial*, London: Social Affairs Unit.

Broadhead, R. R. (1974) 'A theoretical critique of the societal reaction approach to deviance', *Pacific Sociological Review*, **17**, pp. 287–312.

Brogden, M. (1982) *The Police: Autonomy and consent*, London: Academic Press.

Brogden, M., Jefferson, T. and Walklate, S. (1988) *Introducing Policework*, London: Unwin Hyman.

Brown, B. (1986) 'Women and crime: the dark figures of criminology', *Economy and Society*, **15**, pp. 355–402.

Brown, D. and Hogg, R. (1992) 'Law and order politics – Left realism and radical criminology: a view from down under', in R. Matthews and J. Young (eds), *Issues in Realist Criminology*, London: Sage.

Browne, A. (1987) *When Battered Women Kill*, London: Collier Macmillan.

Browne, S. (1994) *Whose Challenge? Youth Crime and Everyday Life in Middlesbrough*, Middlesbrough: Middlesbrough City Challenge Partnership.

Brownmiller, S. (1975) *Against Our Will*, Harmondsworth: Penguin.

Bullock, S. and Mulchandani, R. (2009) *Police Service Strength in England and Wales*, Home Office Statistical Bulletin, 03/09, London: Home Office.

Bunyan, T. (2008) 'EU agrees US demands to re-write data protection agreement', *Statewatch*, **18**(4), October–December, pp. 1–2.

Burawoy, M. (2004) 'Public sociology: contradictions, dilemmas and possibilities', *Social Forces*, **82**(4), pp. 1603–18.

Burawoy, M. (2005) 'For public sociology', *American Sociological Review*, **70**(1), pp. 4–28.

Burgess, E. (1925) 'The growth of the city', in R. E. Park and E. Burgess, *The City*, Chicago, IL: University of Chicago Press.

Burman, M., Brown, J., Batchelor, S. and Tisdall, K. (2000) *A View from the Girls: Exploring violence and violent behaviour*, Glasgow: University of Glasgow.

Burt, C. (1925) *The Young Delinquent*, London: University of London Press.

Cain, M. (1973) *Society and the Policeman's Role*, London: Routledge & Kegan Paul.

Cain, M. (1989) *Growing Up Good*, London: Sage.

Cain, M. (1990) 'Towards transgression: new directions in feminist criminology', *International Journal of the Sociology of Law*, **19**, pp. 1–18.

Cain, M. and Hunt, A. (eds) (1979) *Marx and Engels On Law*, London: Academic Press.

Callinicos, A. (1989) *Against Postmodernism: A Marxist Critique*, Cambridge: Polity Press.

Campbell, A. (1981) *Girl Delinquents*, Oxford: Blackwell.

Campbell, A. (1984) *The Girls in the Gang*, Oxford: Blackwell.

Campbell. A. (1986) 'Self-report of fighting by females', *British Journal of Criminology*, **26** (1), pp. 28–46.

Campbell, B. (1993) *Goliath: Britain's dangerous places*, London: Virago.

Campbell, K. (ed) (1992) *Critical Feminism: Argument in the discipline*, Buckingham: Open University Press.

Caplow, T. and Simon, J. (1999) 'Understanding prison policy and population trends', in M. Tonry and J. Petersilia (eds), *Prisons*, Chicago, IL: University of Chicago Press.

Carlen, P. (1976) *Magistrates' Justice*, Oxford: Martin Robertson.

Carlen, P. (1980) 'Radical criminology, penal politics and the rule of law', in P. Carlen and M. Collison (eds), *Radical Issues in Criminology*, Oxford: Martin Robertson.

Carlen, P. (1983) *Women's Imprisonment*, London: Routledge & Kegan Paul.

Carlen, P. (1985) *Criminal Women*, Oxford: Polity Press.

Carlen, P. (1988) *Women, Crime and Poverty*, Milton Keynes: Open University Press.

Carlen, P. (1990) *Alternatives to Women's Imprisonment*, Buckingham: Open University Press.

Carlen, P. (1992) 'Criminal women and criminal justice', in R. Matthews and J. Young (eds), *Issues in Realist Criminology*, London: Sage.

Carlen, P. (2000) 'Women's imprisonment at the millennium', *Criminal Justice Matters*, **38**, pp. 20–1.

Carlen, P. (2008) 'Vertigo', *Theoretical Criminology*, **12**(4), pp. 528–31.

Carlen, P. and Collison, M. (eds) (1980) *Radical Issues in Criminology*, Oxford: Martin Robertson.

Carlen, P. and Worrall, A. (2004) *Analysing Women's Imprisonment*, Cullompton: Willan.

Carr-Saunders, A. M., Mannheim, H. and Rhodes, E. G. (1942) *Young Offenders*, Cambridge: Cambridge University Press.

Carrington, K. (2002) 'Feminism and critical criminology: confronting genealogies', in K. Carrington and R. Hogg (eds), *Critical Criminology: Issues, debates and challenges*, Cullompton: Willan.

Carrington, K. and Hogg, R. (eds) (2002) *Critical Criminology: Issues, debates and challenges*, Cullompton: Willan.

Carson, W. G. (1970) 'White collar crime and the enforcement of factory legislation', *Bristish Journal of Criminology*, **10**, pp. 383–98.

Carson, W. G. (1982) *The Other Price of Britain's Oil*, Oxford: Martin Robertson.

Carson, W. G. and Wiles, P. (eds) (1971) *The Sociology of Crime and Delinquency in Britain*, Vol. 1, *The British Tradition*, Oxford: Martin Robertson.

Carter, M. P. and Jephcott, P. (1954) 'The social background of delinquency', unpublished, University of Nottingham.

Cashburn, M. (1979) *Girls Will Be Girls*, London: Women's Research and Resources Centre.

Caudill, H. M. (1977) 'Dead leaves and dead men', *Nation*, **226**, pp. 492–7.

Cavadino, M. and Dignan, J. (2002) *The Penal System: An introduction*, 3rd edn, London: Sage.

Centre for Research in Public Health and Primary Care Development (2004) *The 2003 European School Survey Project on Alcohol and Other Drugs*, Bristol: University of the West of England.

Cernkovich, S. A. (1978) 'Value orientation and delinquency involvement', *Criminology*, **15**, pp. 443–57.

Chambliss, W. J. (1964) 'A sociological analysis of the law of vagrancy', *Social Problems*, **12**(1), pp. 67–77, repr. in W. G. Carson and P. Wiles (eds) (1971) *The Sociology of Crime and Delinquency in Britain*, Vol. 1, *The British Tradition*, Oxford: Martin Robertson.

Chambliss, W. J. (1969) *Crime and the Legal Process*, New York: McGraw-Hill.

Chambliss, W. J. (1975) 'Towards a political economy of crime', *Theory and Society*, **2**, pp. 152–3.

Chambliss, W. J. (1976) 'The state and criminal law', in W. J. Chambliss and M. Mankoff (eds), *Whose Law, What Order?*, New York: Wiley.

Chambliss, W. J. (1978) *On the Take: From petty crooks to presidents*, Bloomington, IN: Indiana University Press.

Chancer, L. and McLaughlin, E. (2007) 'Public criminologies: diverse perspectives on academia and policy', *Theoretical Criminology*, **11**(2), pp. 155–73.

Chapman, J. (1980) *Economic Realities and the Female Offender*, Lexington, MA: Lexington Books.

Chesney-Lind, M. (1973) 'Judicial enforcement of the female sex role: the family court and the family delinquent', *Issues in Criminology*, **8**, pp. 51–69.

Chesney-Lind, M. (1978) *Chivalry Re-Examined: Women and the criminal justice system*, Lexington, MA: Lexington Books.

Chesney-Lind, M. (1986) 'Women and crime: the female offender', *Signs*, **12**(1), pp. 78–96.

Chesney-lind, M. and Irwin, K. (2007) *Beyond Bad Girls: Gender, violence and hype*, Abingdon: Routledge.

Christie, N. (2004) *A Suitable Amount of Crime*, Abingdon: Routledge.

Cicourel, A. V. (1968) *The Social Organization of Juvenile Justice*, New York: Wiley.

Clarke, J. (1976) 'The skinheads and the magical recovery of community', in S. Hall and T. Jefferson (eds), *Resistance through Rituals*, London: Hutchinson.

Clarke, J. and Jefferson, T. (1973a) 'Politics of popular culture: cultures and subcultures', Occasional Paper No. 14, Centre for Contemporary Cultural Studies, University of Birmingham.

Clarke, J. and Jefferson, T. (1973b) 'Down these mean streets: the meaning of mugging', Occasional Paper No. 17, Centre for Contemporary Cultural Studies, University of Birmingham.

Clark, J. and Jefferson, T. (1976) 'Working-class youth cultures', in G. Mungham and G. Pearson (eds), *Working-Class Youth Culture*, London: Routledge & Kegan Paul.

Clarke, E. J. (2008) *Deviant Behavior*, 7th edn, Basingstoke: Palgrave Macmillan.

Clarke, J., Hall, S., Jefferson, T. and Roberts, B. (1976) 'Subcultures, cultures and class: a theoretical overview', in S. Hall and T. Jefferson (eds), *Resistance through Rituals: Youth subcultures in post-war Britain*, London: Hutchinson.

Clarke, M. (1990) *Business Crime: Its nature and control*, Cambridge: Polity Press.

Clarke, R. (1980) 'Situational crime prevention: theory and practice', *British Journal of Criminology*, **20**(2), pp. 136–47.

Clarke, R. (1984) 'Opportunity-based crime rates', *British Journal of Criminology*, **23**(1), pp. 74–83.

Clarke, R. (1992) *Situational Crime Prevention: Successful case studies*, New York: Harvard & Heston.

Clarke, R. and Mayhew, P. (eds) (1980) *Designing Out Crime*, London: HMSO.

Clinard, M. B. and Yeager, P. C. (1981) *Corporate Crime*, New York: Free Press.

Cloward, R. and Ohlin, L. (1960) *Delinquency and Opportunity*, London: Collier Macmillan.

Cohen, A. K. (1955) *Delinquent Boys*, London: Free Press.

Cohen, A. K. and Short, J. F. (1958) 'Research in delinquent subcultures', *Journal of Social Issues*, **14**(3).

Cohen, L. E. and Felson, M. (1979) 'Social change and crime rate trends: a routine activities approach', *American Sociological Review*, **44**, pp. 588–608.

Cohen, P. (1972) 'Subcultural conflict in working-class community', Working Papers in Cultural Studies, No. 2, Centre for Contemporary Cultural Studies, University of Birmingham.

Cohen, S. (1969) 'Ideological and criminal violence', *Phalanx*, **2**, University of Durham.

Cohen, S. (ed) (1971) *Images of Deviance*, Harmondsworth: Penguin.

Cohen, S. (1973) 'Protest, unrest and delinquency: convergences in labels and behaviours', *International Journal of Criminology and Penology*, **1**, pp. 117–28; repr. in P. N. P. Wiles (ed) (1976) *The Sociology of Crime and Delinquency in Britain*, Vol. 2, *The New Criminologies*, Oxford: Martin Robertson.

Cohen, S. (1974) 'Criminology and the sociology of deviance in Britain', in P. Rock and M. McIntosh (eds), *Deviance and Social Control*, London: Tavistock.

Cohen, S. (1980) *Folk Devils and Moral Panics*, 2nd edn, Oxford: Martin Robertson.

Cohen, S. (1981) 'Footprints in the sand: a further report on criminology and the sociology of deviance in Britain', in M. Fitzgerald, G. McLennan and J. Pawson (eds), *Crime and Society: Readings in history and theory*, London: Routledge & Kegan Paul/Open University Press; repr. in S. Cohen (1988) *Against Criminology*, New Brunswick, NJ: Transaction Books.

Cohen, S. (1985) *Visions of Social Control*, Cambridge: Polity Press.

Cohen, S. (1986) 'Community control: to demystify or to reaffirm?' in H. Bianchi and R. van Swaaningen (eds), *Abolitionism: Towards a non-repressive approach to crime*, Amsterdam: Free University Press.

Cohen, S. (1988) *Against Criminology*, New Brunswick, NJ: Transaction Books.

Cohen, S. (1993) 'Human rights and crimes of the state: the culture of denial', *Australian and New Zealand Journal of Criminology*, **26**(1), pp. 87–115.

Cohen, S. (1996) 'Crime and politics: spot the difference', *British Journal of Sociology*, **47**(1), pp. 1–21.

Cohen, S. (1998) 'Intellectual scepticism and political commitment: The case for radical criminology', in P. Walton and J. Young (eds), *The New Criminology Revisited*, Basingstoke: Macmillan.

Cohen, S. and Taylor, L. (1972) *Psychological Survival: The experience of long-term imprisonment*, Harmondsworth: Penguin.

Cohn-Bendit, D. and Cohn-Bendit, G. (1968) *Obsolete Communism: The Left-wing alternative*, London: Deutsch.

Coleman, A. (1988) *Altered Estates*, London: Adam Smith Institute.

Coleman, R. (2004) *Reclaiming the Streets: Surveillance, social control and the city*, Cullompton: Willan.

Collier, R. (2004) 'Masculinities and crime: rethinking the "man question"', in C. Sumner, (ed), *The Blackwell Companion to Criminology*, Oxford: Blackwell Publishing.

Colvin, M. (2000) *Crime and Coercion: An integrated theory of chronic criminality*, New York: St Martin's.

Conklin, J. E. (1977) *Illegal but not Criminal: Business crime in America*, Englewood Cliffs, NJ: Prentice-Hall.

Connell, R. W. (1995) *Masculinities*, Berkeley, CA: University of California Press.

Connell, R. W. (2000) *The Men and the Boys*, Sydney: Allen & Unwin.

Connell, R. W. and Messerschmidt, J. W. (2005) 'Hegemonic masculinity: rethinking the concept', *Gender and Society*, **19**(6), pp. 829–59.

Cooley, C.H. (1902) *Human Nature and the Social Order,* New York: Scribner's.

Cornish, D. and Clarke, R. (eds) (1986a) *The Reasoning Criminal,* New York: Springer-Verlag.

Cornish, D. B. and Clarke, R. V. (1986b) 'Situational prevention, displacement of crime and rational choice theory', in D. Heal and G. Laycock (eds), *Situational Crime Prevention: From theory into practice,* London: HMSO.

Cornish, D. B. and Clarke, R. V. (2003) 'Opportunities, precipitators and criminal decision', *Crime Prevention Studies,* **16**, pp. 41–96.

Corrigan, P. and Frith, S. (1976) 'The politics of youth culture', in S. Hall and T. Jefferson (eds) *Resistance through Rituals,* London: Hutchinson.

Cottino, A. (2004) 'White collar crime', in C. Sumner (ed), *The Blackwell Companion to Criminology,* Oxford: Blackwell Publishing.

Coulter, J. (1973) *Approaches to Insanity: A philosophical and sociological study,* London: Martin Robertson.

Cousins, M. (1980) 'Mens rea: a note on sexual difference, criminology and the law', in P. Carlen and M. Collison (eds), *Radical Issues in Criminology,* Oxford: Martin Robertson.

Coward, R. (1994) 'Whipping boys', *Guardian Weekend,* 3 September.

Cowie, J., Cowie, V. and Slater, E. (1968) *Delinquent Girls in London,* London: Heinemann.

Crawford, A. (1997) *The Local Governance of Crime,* Oxford: Clarendon Press.

Crawford, A. (1998) *Crime Prevention and Community Safety: Politics, policies and practice,* London: Longman.

Crawford, A. (2007) 'Crime prevention and community safety', in M. Maguire, R. Morgan and R. Reiner (eds), *The Oxford Handbook of Criminology,* 4th edn, Oxford: Oxford University Press.

Crawford, A. and Newburn, T. (2002) 'Recent developments in restorative justice for young people in England and Wales: community participation and restoration', *British Journal of Criminology,* **42**(2), pp. 476–95.

Crawford, A., Jones, T., Woodhouse, T. and Young, J. (1990) *Second Islington Crime Survey,* London: Middlesex Polytechnic.

Croal, H. (1992) *White Collar Crime,* Milton Keynes: Open University Press.

Cuff, E. C. and Payne, G. C. F. (eds) (1979) *Perspectives in Sociology,* London: Allen & Unwin.

Cullen, F. T. and Messner, S. F. (2007) 'The making of criminology revisited: an oral history of Merton's anomie paradigm', *Theoretical Criminology,* **11**(1), pp. 5–37.

Cullen, F. T. and Wozniak, J. (1982) 'Fighting the appeal of repression', *Crime and Social Justice,* **18**, pp. 23–33.

Currie, E. (1991) 'The politics of crime: the American experience', in K. Stenson and D. Cowell (eds), *The Politics of Crime Control,* London: Sage.

Currie, E. (1997) 'Market, crime and community: toward a mid-range theory of post-industrial violence', *Theoretical Criminology,* **1**(2), pp. 147–72.

Currie, E. (2002) 'Preface', in K. Carrington and R. Hogg (eds), *Critical Criminology: Issues, debates, challenges,* Cullompton: Willan.

Currie, E. (2007) 'Against marginality: arguments for a public criminology', *Theoretical Criminology,* **11**(2), pp. 175–90.

Dahrendorf, R. (1959) *Class and Class Conflict in an Industrial Society,* London: Routledge & Kegan Paul.

Dahrendorf, R. (1968) 'Towards a theory of social conflict', *Journal of Resolution of Conflict,* **2**, pp. 170–83.

Dahrendorf, R. (1985) *Law and Order,* London: Stevens.

Daly, K. (1989) 'Rethinking judicial paternalism: gender, work, family relations and sentencing', *Gender and Society,* **3**(1), pp. 9–36.

Daly, K. (1997) 'Different ways of conceptualizing sex/gender in feminist theory and their implications for criminology', *Theoretical Criminology,* **1**(1), pp. 25–51.

Daly, K. (2006) 'Feminist criminologies', in E. McLaughlin and J. Muncie (eds), *The Sage Dictionary of Criminology,* 2nd edn, London: Sage.

Davies, P. M., Francis, P. and Greer, C. (eds) (2007) *Victims, Crime and Society,* London: Sage.

Davis, F. (1967) 'Why all of us may be hippies someday', *Transaction,* **15**(2), pp. 10–18.

Davis, S. (1987) 'Towards the remoralization of society', in M. Loney (ed), *The State of the Market: Politics and welfare in contemporary Britain,* London: Sage.

Davies, S. (1991) *The Historical Origins of Health Fascism,* London: FOREST.

De Haan, W. (1991) 'Abolitionism and crime control: a contradiction in terms?' in K. Stenson and D. Cowell (eds), *The Politics of Crime Control,* London: Sage.

Deakin, J. and Spencer, J. (2003) 'Women behind bars: Explanations and implications', *Howard Journal,* **42**(2), pp. 123–36.

Dell, S. (1971) *Silence in Court,* London: Bello.

Dennis, N. (1993) *Rising Crime and the Dismembered Family,* London: IEA, Health and Welfare Unit.

Derrida, J. (1976) *Of Grammatology,* trans. G. C. Spivak, London and Baltimore, MD: Johns Hopkins University Press.

Ditton, J. (1977) *Part-Time Crime,* London: Macmillan.

Ditton, J. (1979) *Controlology: Beyond the new criminology,* London: Macmillan.

Dobash, R. E. and Dobash, R. P. (1979) *Violence Against Wives,* New York: Free Press.

Dobash, R. E. and Dobash, R. P. (1992) *Women, Violence and Social Change,* London: Routledge.

Dobash, R. E., Dobash, R. P. and Gutteridge, S. (1986) *The Imprisonment of Women,* Oxford: Blackwell.

Dodd, T., Nicholas, S., Povey, D. and Walker, A. (eds) (2004) *Crime in England and Wales 2003/2004,* Home Office Statistical Bulletin 10/04, London: Home Office.

Domhoff, G. W. (1970) *The Higher Circles: The governing class in America,* New York: Random House.

Dominelli, L. (1992) 'More than a method: feminist social work', in K. Campbell (ed), *Critical Feminism: Argument in the discipline,* Buckingham: Open University Press.

Dorn, N. and South, N. (eds) (1987) *A Land Fit for Heroin? Drug Policies, Prevention and Practice,* London: Macmillan.

Dorn, N., Murji, K. and South, N. (1992) *Traffickers: Drug markets and law enforcement,* London: Routledge.

Douglas, J. D. (1967) *The Social Meaning of Suicide*, Princeton, NJ: Princeton University Press.

Douglas, J. D. (ed.) (1971a) *Understanding Everyday Life*, London: Routledge & Kegan Paul.

Douglas, J. D. (1971b) *American Social Order: Social rules in a pluralistic society*, New York: Free Press.

Douglas, J. W. B. (1964) *The Home and the School*, London: MacGibbon & Kee.

Dowie, M. (1988) 'Pinto madness', in S. Hill (ed.), *Corporate Violence: Injury and death for profit*, Totowa, NJ: Rowman & Littlefield.

Downes, D. (1966) *The Delinquent Solution*, London: Routledge & Kegan Paul.

Downes, D. (1978) 'Promise and performance in British criminology', *British Journal of Sociology*, **29**(4), pp. 91–101.

Downes, D. (1988) 'The sociology of crime and social control in Britain, 1960–1987', in P. Rock (ed.), *The History of British Criminology*, Oxford: Oxford University Press.

Downes, D. and Morgan, R. (2002) 'The politics of law and order', in M. Maguire, R. Morgan and R. Reiner (eds), *The Oxford Handbook of Criminology*, 3rd edn, Oxford: Oxford University Press.

Downes, D. and Rock, P. (2003) *Understanding Deviance*, 4th edn, Oxford: Oxford University Press.

Downes, D. and Rock, P. (2007) *Understanding Deviance*, 5th edn, Oxford: Oxford University Press.

Drapkin, I. (1983) 'Criminology: intellectual history', in S. Kadish (ed), *Encyclopedia of Crime and Justice*, Vol. 2, New York: Free Press, pp. 546–56.

Dunhill, C. (ed.) (1989) *The Boys in Blue: Women's challenge to the police*, London: Virago.

Durkheim, E. (1970) *Suicide: A study in sociology*, London: Routledge & Kegan Paul.

Durkheim, E. (1982) *Durkheim: The rules of sociological method*, ed. S. Lukes, London: Macmillan.

Duster, T. (2003) *Backdoor to Eugenics*, 2nd edn, London: Routledge.

Eagleton, T. (1996) *The Illusions of Postmodernism*, Oxford: Blackwell.

Eaton, M. (1983) 'Mitigating circumstances: familiar rhetoric', *International Journal of the Sociology of Law*, **11**, pp. 385–400.

Eaton, M. (1985) 'Documenting the defendant', in J. Brophy and C. Smart (eds), *Women in Law*, London: Routledge & Kegan Paul.

Eaton, M. (1986) *Justice for Women?*, Milton Keynes: Open University Press.

Edwards, S. S. M. (1984) *Women on Trial*, Manchester: Manchester University Press.

Edwards, S. S. M. (1986) *The Police Response to Domestic Violence in London*, London: Polytechnic of Central London.

Edwards, S. S. M. (1989) *Policing 'Domestic' Violence*, London: Sage.

Ehrlich, I. (1975) 'The deterrent effect of capital punishment: a question of life or death', *American Economic Review*, **65**, pp. 397–417.

Einstadter, W. J. (1984) 'Citizen patrols: prevention or control?' *Crime and Social Justice*, **21–22**, pp. 199–212.

Ekblom, P. (2000) 'The conjunction of criminal opportunity – a tool for clear, joined-up thinking about community safety and crime reduction', in S. Ballantyne, K. Pease and

V. Maclaren (eds), *Secure Foundations: Key issues in crime prevention, crime reduction and community safety,* London: Institute for Public Policy Research.

Elliot, N. (1990) *Making Prison Work,* London: Adam Smith Institute.

Engels, F. (1969) *The Condition of the Working Class in England,* London: Panther.

Ericson, R. V. (1994) 'The division of expert knowledge in policing and society', *British Journal of Criminology,* **45**(2), pp. 149–76.

Erikson, K. T. (1962) 'Notes on the sociology of deviance', *Social Problems,* **9**, reprinted in H. S. Becker (ed) (1964), *The Other Side: Perspectives on deviance,* New York: Free Press.

Erikson, K. T. (1966) *Wayward Puritans,* New York: Wiley.

Eron, L. D. and Huesmann, L. R. (1990) 'The stability of aggressive behaviour – even unto the third generation', in M. Lewis and S. M. Miller (eds), *Handbook of Developmental Psychopathology,* New York: Plenum.

Erwin, J. (2009) 'Ultra-ultra-violence', *The Guardian, Film and Music,* 27.02.09.

Faragher, T. (1981) 'The police response to violence against women in the home', in J. Pahl (ed), *Private Violence and Public Policy,* London: Routledge & Kegan Paul.

Farrington, D. P. (1986) 'Age and crime', in M. Tonry and N. Morris (eds), *Crime and Justice,* Vol. 7, Chicago, IL: University of Chicago Press.

Farrington, D. P. (1989) 'Self-reported and official offending from adolescence to adulthood', in M. W. Klein (ed), *Cross-National Research in Self-Reported Crime and Delinquency,* Dordrecht: Kluwer.

Farrington, D. P. (1992a) 'Explaining the beginning, progress and ending of antisocial behaviour from birth to adulthood', in J. McCord (ed), *Advances in Criminology Theory,* Vol. 3, *Facts, Frameworks and Forecasts,* New Brunswick, NJ: Transaction Books.

Farrington, D. P. (1992b) 'Juvenile delinquency', in J. C. Coleman (ed), *The School Years,* 2nd edn, London: Routledge & Kegan Paul.

Farrington, D. P. (1993) 'Childhood, adolescent and adult features of violent males', in L. R. Huesmann (ed), *Aggressive Behavior: Current perspectives,* New York: Plenum.

Farrington, D. P. (1994) 'Human development and criminal careers', in M. Maguire, R. Morgan and R. Reiner (eds), *The Oxford Handbook of Criminology,* Oxford: Clarendon Press.

Farrington, D. P. (1995) 'The development of offending and antisocial behaviour from childhood: Key findings from the Cambridge study in delinquent development', *Journal of Child Psychology and Psychiatry,* **36**, pp. 929–64.

Farrington, D. P. (2002) 'Development criminology and risk-focused prevention', in M. Maguire, R. Morgan and R. Reiner (eds), *The Oxford Handbook of Criminology,* 3rd edn, Oxford: Oxford University Press.

Farrington, D. P. and Morris, A. M. (1983) 'Sex, sentencing and reconviction', *British Journal of Criminology,* **23**(3), pp. 229–48.

Farrington, D. P. and West, D. J. (1990) 'The Cambridge study in delinquent development: a long-term follow-up of 411 London mates', in H. J. Kerner and G. Kaiser (eds), *Criminality: Personality, behaviour and life history,* Berlin: Springer-Verlag.

Farrington, D. P., Snyder, H. N. and Finnegan, T. A. (1988) 'Specialization in juvenile court careers', *Criminology,* **26**, pp. 461–87.

Feeley, M. and Simon, J. (1994) 'Actuarial justice: the emerging new criminal law', in D. Nelken (ed), *The Futures of Criminology*, London: Sage.

Felson, M. (1986) 'Routine activities, social controls, rational decisions and criminal outcomes', in D. B. Cornish and R. V. Clarke (eds), *The Reasoning Criminal*, New York: Springer-Verlag.

Felson, M. (1987) 'Routine activities and crime prevention in the developing metropolis', *Criminology*, **25**, pp. 911–31.

Felson. M. (2000) 'The routine activity approach as a general social theory', in S. S. Simpson (ed), *Of Crime and Criminality: The use of theory in everyday life*, Thousand Oaks, CA: Pine Forge Press.

Fenton, S. (ed) (1984) *Durkheim and Modern Sociology*, Cambridge: Cambridge University Press.

Fenwick, M. and Hayward, K. (2000) 'Youth crime, excitement and consumer culture: the reconstruction of aetiology in contemporary theoretical criminology', in J. Pickford (ed), *Youth Justice: Theory and practice*, London: Cavendish Publishing.

Ferguson, T. (1952) *The Young Delinquent in his Social Setting: A Glasgow study*, Oxford: Oxford University Press.

Ferguson, T. and Cunnison, J. (1951) *The Young Wage-Earner: A study of Glasgow boys*, London: Oxford University Press.

Ferguson, T. and Cunnison, J. (1956) *In Their Early Twenties: A study of Glasgow youth*, London: Oxford University Press.

Fergusson, D. M., Horwood, L. T. and Lynskey, M. T. (1992) 'Family change, parental discord and early offending', *Journal of Child Psychology and Psychiatry*, **33**, pp. 1059–75.

Ferrell, J., Hayward, K., Morrison, W. and Presdee, M. (2004) *Cultural Criminology Unleashed*, London: Glasshouse.

Ferrell, J., Haywood, K. and Young, J. (2008) *Cultural Criminology: An invitation*, London: Sage.

Ferrell, J. and Sanders, C. (eds) (1995) *Cultural Criminology*, Boston, MA: Northeastern University Press.

Ferri, E. (1895) *Criminal Sociology*, London: Unwin.

Field, S. (1990) *Trends in Crime and their Interpretation: A study of recorded crime in post-war England and Wales*, Home Office Research Study No. 119, London: HMSO.

Fine, B. (ed) (1979) *Capitalism and the Rule of Law: From deviancy theory to Marxism*, London: Hutchinson.

Fine, B. and Millar, R. (eds) (1985) *Policing the Miners' Strike*, London: Lawrence & Wishart.

Finkelhor, D. (1979) *Sexually Victimized Children*, New York: Sage.

Foucault, M. (1977) *Discipline and Punish: the birth of the prison*, London: Allen Lane.

Foucault, M. (1979) *The History of Sexuality: An introduction*, London: Allen Lane.

Franklin, J. (ed) (1998) *The Politics of Risk Society*, Cambridge: Polity Press.

Furedi, F. (1997) *Culture of Fear: Risk-taking and the morality of low expectation*, London: Cassell.

Fyvel, T. R. (1961) *The Insecure Offenders*, London: Chatto & Windus.

Gadd, D. (2000) 'Masculinities, violence and defended social subjects', *Theoretical Criminology*, **4**(4), pp. 429–49.

Gadd, D. (2002) 'Masculinities and violence against female partners', *Social and Legal Studies*, **11**(1), pp. 61–80.

Gadd, D. and Jefferson, T. (2007) *Psychosocial Criminology*, London: Sage.

Galliher, J. F. (1978) 'The life and death of liberal criminology', *Contemporary Crises*, **12**(3), pp. 245–63.

Gans, H. (1995) *The War Against the Poor*, New York: Basic Books.

Gardiner, M. (1996) 'Alterity and ethics', *Theory, Culture and Society*, **13**, pp. 120–43.

Garfinkel, H. (1967) *Studies in Ethnomethodology*, Engelwood Cliffs, NJ: Prentice-Hall.

Garland, D. (1985a) 'Politics and policy in criminological discourse: a study of tendentious reasoning and rhetoric', *International Journal of Sociology of Law*, **13**, pp. 1–33.

Garland, D. (1985b) *Punishment and Welfare*, Aldershot: Gower.

Garland, D. (1990) *Punishment and Modern Society: A study in social theory*, Oxford: Oxford University Press.

Garland, D. (1992) 'Criminological knowledge and its relation to power', *British Journal of Criminology*, **32**(4), pp. 403–22.

Garland, D. (1994) 'Of crimes and criminals: the development of criminology in Britain', in M. Maguire, R. Morgan and R. Reiner (eds), *The Oxford Handbook of Criminology*, 1st edn, Oxford: Clarendon Press.

Garland, D. (1997) '"Governmentality" and the problem of crime', *Theoretical Criminology*, **1**(2), pp. 173–214.

Garland, D. (2000) 'Ideas, institutions and situational crime prevention', in A. von Hirsch, D. Garland and A. Wakefield (eds), *Ethical and Social Perspectives on Situational Crime Prevention*, Oxford: Hart Publishing.

Garland, D. (2002) 'The development of British criminology', in M. Maguire, R. Morgan and R. Reiner (eds), *The Oxford Handbook of Criminology*, 3rd edn, Oxford: Clarendon Press.

Garland, D. (2006) 'Concepts of culture in the sociology of punishment', *Theoretical Criminology*, **10**(4), pp. 419–47.

Garland, D. and Sparks, R. (eds) (2000) *Criminology and Social Theory*, Oxford: Oxford University Press.

Garland, D. and Sparks, R. (2000) 'Criminology, social theory and the challenge of our times', *British Journal of Criminology*, **40**(2), pp. 189–204.

Garland, J. (2005) 'Surfing the crime net: issues and challenges in police community relations', *Crime Prevention and Community Safety: An International Journal*, **7**(1), pp. 63–8.

Garofalo, J. (1987) 'Reassessing the lifestyle model of criminal victimization', in M. R. Gottfredson and T. Hirschi (eds), *Positive Criminology*, Newbury Park, CA: Sage.

Garofalo, R. (1968; first pub. 1914) *Criminology*, Boston, MA: Little, Brown; Patterson-Smith.

Geis, G. (2000) 'On the absence of self-control as the basis for a general theory of crime: a critique', *Theoretical Criminology*, **4**(1), pp. 35–53.

Gelsthorpe, L. (2002) 'Feminism and Criminology', in M. Maguire, R. Morgan and R. Reiner (eds) *The Oxford Handbook of Criminology*, 3rd edn, Oxford: Oxford University Press.

Gelsthorpe, L. and Morris, A. (1988) 'Feminism and criminology in Britain', *British Journal of Criminology*, **28**(2), pp. 93–109.

Gelsthorpe, L. and Morris, A. (eds) (1990) *Feminist Perspectives in Criminology*, London: Routledge & Kegan Paul.

Gelsthorpe, L. and Morris, A. (2002) 'Women's imprisonment in England and Wales in the 1990s: a penal paradox', *Criminal Justice*, **2**(3), pp. 277–301.

Gelsthorpe, L. and Padfield, N. (eds) (2003) *Exercising Discretion: Decision-making in the criminal justice system and beyond*, Cullompton: Willan.

Giallombardo, R. (1966) *Society of Women: A study of a woman's prison*, New York: Wiley.

Gibbs, J. P. (1966) 'Conception of deviant behaviour: the old and the new', *Pacific Sociological Review*, **14**(1), pp. 20–37.

Gibbs, J. P. (1975) *Crime, Punishment and Deterrence*, New York: Elsevier.

Giddens, A. (1978) *Durkheim*, Glasgow: Fontana.

Giddens, A. (1993) *Sociology*, 2nd edn, Cambridge: Polity Press.

Giddens, A. (1994) *Beyond Left and Right: The future of radical politics*, Cambridge: Polity Press.

Giddens, A. (1998) *The Third Way: The renewal of social democracy*, Cambridge: Polity Press.

Gill, O. (1977) *Luke Street*, London: Macmillan.

Gilligan, C. (1982) *In a Different Voice*, Cambridge, MA: Harvard University Press.

Gilling, D. (1997) *Crime Prevention: Theory, policy and politics*, London: UCL Press.

Gilling, D. (2007), *Crime Reduction and Community Safety: Labour and the politics of local crime control*, Cullompton: Willan.

Goldman, N. (1959) 'A socio-psychological study of school vandalism', Final Report on Office of Education Contract No. SAE 181 (8453), Syracuse, NY: University Research Institute.

Goold, B. (2008) *Surveillance*, Abingdon: Routledge.

Gordon, D. M. (1971) 'Class and the economics of crime', *Review of Radical Political Economy*, **3**, pp. 51–75.

Goring, C. (1919) *The English Convict*, London: Methuen.

Gottfredson, M. R. and Hirschi, T. (eds) (1987) *Positive Criminology*, London: Sage.

Gottfredson, M. R. and Hirschi, T. (1990) *A General Theory of Crime*, Stanford, CA: Stanford University Press.

Gouldner, A. W. (1968) 'The sociologist as partisan: sociology and the welfare state', *American Sociologist*, **3**, pp. 103–16.

Gouldner, A. W. (1971) *The Coming Crisis of Western Sociology*, London: Heinemann.

Gove, W. (ed) (1975) *The Labelling of Deviance*, London: Wiley.

Graham, J. M. (1976) 'Amphetamine politics on Capitol Hill', in W. J. Chambliss and M. Mankoff (eds), *Whose Law? What Order?*, New York: Wiley.

Graham, J. and Bennett, T. (1995) *Crime Prevention Strategies in Europe and North America*, Helsinki Institute for Crime Prevention and Control Finland, HEUNI, No. 28, Finland: United Nations.

Grant, C., Harvey, A., Bolling, K. and Clemens, S. (2006) *2004–2005 British Crime Survey Technical Report*, London: Home Office.

Green, S. P. (2007) *Lying, Cheating and Stealing: A moral theory of white collar crime*, Buckingham: Open University Press.

Greenberg, D. (1976) 'On one-dimensional Marxist criminology', *Theory and Society*, **3**, pp. 610–21.

Greenwood, V. (1981) 'The myths of female crime', in A. M. Morris with L. R. Gelsthorpe (eds), *Women and Crime*, Cropwood Conference Series, No. 13, Cambridge: Cambridge Institute of Criminology.

Greenwood, V. (1983) 'The role and future of female imprisonment', mimeo, Middlesex Polytechnic.

Gregory, J. (1986) 'Sex, class and crime: towards a non-sexist criminology', in R. Matthews and J. Young (eds), *Confronting Crime*, London: Sage.

Groombridge, N. (1999) 'Perverse criminologies: the closet of Doctor Lombroso', *Social and Legal Studies*, **8**(4), pp. 529–48.

Gross, B. (1982) 'Some anti-crime proposals for progressives', *Crime and Social Justice*, **17**, pp. 51–4.

Grosz, E. A. (1987) 'Feminist theory and the challenge to knowledge', *Women's Studies International Forum*, **10**(5), pp. 208–17.

Haag, E. van den (1975) *Punishing Criminals: Concerning a very old and painful question*, New York: Basic Books.

Haag, E. van den (1985) *Deterring Potential Criminals*, London: Social Affairs Unit.

Habermas, J. (1987) *The Philosophical Discourse on Modernity*, Cambridge MA: MIT Press.

Hagan, J. (1977) *The Disreputable Pleasures*, Toronto: McGraw-Hill Ryerson.

Hagan, J. and Kay, F. (1990) 'Gender and delinquency in white-collar families: a power-control perspective', *Crime and Delinquency*, **36**, pp. 391–407.

Hagan, J., Simpson, J. H. and Gillis, A. R. (1979) 'The sexual stratification of social control: a gender-based perspective on crime and delinquency', *British Journal of Criminology*, **30**(1), pp. 25–38.

Hagel, A. and Newburn, T. (1994) *Persistent Young Offenders*, London: Policy Studies Institute.

Haggerty, K. D. (2003) 'From risk to precaution: the rationalities of personal crime prevention', in R. V. Ericson and A. Doyle (eds), *Risk and Morality*, Toronto: University of Toronto Press.

Hall, R. (1985) *Ask Any Woman*, London: Falling Wall Press.

Hall, S. (1974) 'Deviance, politics and the media', in P. Rock and M. McIntosh (eds), *Deviance and Social Control*, London: Tavistock.

Hall, S. (1980) 'Popular-democratic vs authoritarian-populism: two ways of "taking democracy seriously" ', in A. Hunt, *Marxism and Democracy*, London: Lawrence & Wishart.

Hall, S. (1988) 'The hard road to renewal', *British Journal of Criminology*, **34**(3), pp. 14–28.

Hall, S. and Jefferson, T. (eds) (1976) *Resistance through Rituals: Youth subcultures in postwar Britain*, London: Hutchinson.

Hall, S., Critcher, C., Jefferson, T., Clarke, J. and Roberts, B. (1978) *Policing the Crisis: Mugging, the state and law and order*, London: Macmillan.

Hall, S., Winlow, S. and Ancrum, C. (2008) *Criminal Identities and Consumer Culture: Crime, exclusion and the new culture of narcissism,* Cullompton: Willan.

Hanmer, J. (1978) 'Male violence and the social control of women', in G. Littlejohn, B. Smart, J. Wakefield and N. Yuval-Davies (eds), *Power and the State,* London: Croom Helm.

Hanmer, J. and Saunders, S. (1984) *Well Founded Fears: A community study of violence to women,* London: Hutchinson.

Han-Pile, B. (2008) *Foucault,* Abingdon: Routledge.

Harding, S. (1991) *Whose Science? Whose Knowledge?,* Buckingham: Open University Press.

Hargreaves, D. H. (1967) *Social Relations in a Secondary School,* London: Routledge & Kegan Paul.

Hargreaves, D. H., Hester, S. and Mellor, F. (1976) *Deviance in Classrooms,* London: Routledge & Kegan Paul.

Harris, R. (1992) *Crime, Criminal justice and the Probation Service,* London: Routledge.

Harris, R. and Webb, D. (1987) *Welfare, Power and Juvenile Justice,* London: Tavistock.

Hartless, J. M., Ditton, J., Nair, G. and Phillips, S. (1995) 'More sinned against than sinning: a study of young teenagers' experience of crime', *British Journal of Criminology,* 35(1), pp. 114–33.

Hay, W., Sparks, R. and Bottoms, A. E. (1994) *Prisons and the Problem of Order,* Oxford: Oxford University Press.

Hayslett-McCall, K. L. and Bernard, T. J. (2002) 'Attachment, masculinity and self-control: a theory of male crime rates', *Theoretical Criminology,* 6(1), pp. 5–33.

Hayward, K. J. (2004) *City Limits: Crime, consumer culture and the urban experience,* London: Glasshouse.

Hayward, K. L. and Young, J. (2004) 'Cultural criminology: some notes on the script', *Theoretical Criminology,* 8(3), pp. 259–73.

Heal, L. and Laycock, G. (eds) (1986) *Situational Crime Prevention: From theory into practice,* London: HMSO.

Hebdige, D. (1979) *Subculture: The meaning of style,* London: Methuen.

Heidensohn, F. (1968) 'The deviance of women: a critique and an enquiry', *British Journal of Criminology,* 19(2), pp. 160–75.

Heidensohn, F. (1969) 'Prison for women', *The Criminologist,* 4(12), pp. 113–22.

Heidensohn, F. (1985) *Women and Crime,* London: Macmillan.

Heidensohn, F. (1986) 'Models of justice: Portia or Persephone? Some thoughts on equality, fairness and gender in the field of criminal justice', *International Journal of the Sociology of Law,* 14, pp. 287–98.

Heidensohn, F. (1989) *Crime and Society,* Basingstoke: Macmillan.

Heidensohn, F. (1994) 'Gender and crime', in M. Maguire, R. Morgan and R. Reiner (eds), *The Oxford Handbook of Criminology,* 1st edn, Oxford: Clarendon Press.

Heidensohn, F. (2000) *Sexual Politics and Social Control,* Buckingham: Open University Press.

Heidensohn, F. (2002) 'Gender and crime', in M. Maguire, R. Morgan and R. Reiner (eds), *The Oxford Handbook of Criminology,* 3rd edn, Oxford: Oxford University Press.

Heidensohn, F. and Gelsthorpe, L. (2007) 'Gender and Crime', in M. Maguire, R. Morgan and R. Reiner (eds), *The Oxford Handbook of Criminology*, 4th edn, Oxford: Oxford University Press.

Henry, S. (1978) *The Hidden Economy*, Oxford: Martin Robertson.

Henry, S. and Lanier, M. M. (1998) 'The prism of crime: arguments for an integrated definition of crime', *Justice Quarterly*, **15**(4), pp. 609–27.

Henry, S. and Milovanovic, D. (1996) *Constitutive Criminology: Beyond postmodernism*, London: Sage.

Henry, S. and Milovanovic, D. (eds) (1999) *Constitutive Criminology at Work: Applications to crime and punishment*, New York: State University of New York Press.

Hepburn, J. R. (1977) 'Social control and the legal order: legitimated repression in a capitalist state', *Contemporary Crises*, **1**, pp. 77–90.

Hester, S. and Eglin, P. (1992) *A Sociology of Crime*, London: Routledge.

Hill, R. and Robertson, R. (2003) 'What sort of future for critical criminology?', *Crime, Law and Social Change*, **39**, pp. 91–115.

Hills, J., Sefton, T. and Stewart, K. (2009) *Poverty, Inequality and Policy Since 1997*, London: Policy Press.

Hillyard, P., Tombs, S., Pantazis, C. and Gordon, D. (eds) (2004) *Beyond Criminology: Taking harm seriously*, London: Pluto.

Hinch, R. (1983) 'Marxist criminology in the 1970s: clarifying the clutter', *Crime and Social Justice*, **19**, pp. 65–73.

Hindelang, M. J. (1974) 'Decisions of shoplifting victims to invoke the criminal justice process', *Social Problems*, **21**, pp. 580–91.

Hindelang, M. J., Hirschi, T. and Weis, J. G. (1981) *Measuring Delinquency*, Beverly Hills, CA: Sage.

Hirsch, A. von (1993) *Censure and Sanctions*, Oxford: Oxford University Press.

Hirschi, T. (1969) *Causes of Delinquency*, Berkeley, CA: University of California Press.

Hirschi, T. and Gottfredson, M. R. (1993) 'Commentary: testing the general theory of crime', *Journal of Research in Crime and Delinquency*, **30**(1), pp. 52–3.

Hirschi, T. and Gottfredson, M. R. (2000) 'In defence of self-control', *Theoretical Criminology*, **4**(1), pp. 55–69.

Hirst, P. Q. (1975a) 'Marx and Engels on law, crime and morality', in I. Taylor, P. Walton and J. Young (eds), *Critical Criminology*, London: Routledge & Kegan Paul.

Hirst, P. Q. (1975b) 'Radical deviancy theory and Marxism: a reply to Taylor, Walton and Young', in I. Taylor, P. Walton and J. Young (eds), *Critical Criminology*, London: Routledge & Kegan Paul.

Hirst, P. Q. (1980) 'Law, socialism and rights', in P. Carlen and M. Collison (eds), *Radical Issues in Criminology*, Oxford: Martin Robertson.

HM Treasury (2008) *Public Expenditure Statistical Analyses*, London: HM Treasury.

Hobbs, D. (1988) *Doing the Business: Entrepreneurship, the working class, and detectives in East London*, Oxford: Clarendon Press.

Hobbs, D. (1998) 'Going down the glocal: the local context of organized crime', *Howard Journal*, **37**(4), pp. 407–22.

Hobbs, D., Hadfield, P., Lister, S. and Winlow, S. (2003) *Bouncers: Violence and governance in the night-time economy,* Oxford: Oxford University Press.

Hobsbawn, E. J. (1959) *Primitive Rebels,* Manchester: Manchester University Press.

Hogg, R. (1988) 'Taking crime seriously: Left realism and Australian criminology', in M. Findlay and R. Hogg (eds), *Understanding Crime and Criminal Justice,* Sydney: Law Book.

Holdaway, S. (ed) (1979) *The British Police,* London: Edward Arnold.

Home Affairs Committee (1993) *Juvenile Offenders,* 6th Report, London: HMSO.

Holland, S. and Scourfield, J. B. (2000) 'Managing marginalized masculinities: men and probation', *Journal of Gender Studies,* **9**(2), pp. 199–211.

Hollway, W. and Jefferson, T. (2000) *Doing Qualitative Research Differently: Free association, narrative and the interview method,* London: Sage.

Home Office (1985) *Criminal Careers of Those Born in 1953, 1958, 1963,* Statistical Bulletin No. 5/89, London: Home Office Statistical Department.

Home Office (1987) *Criminal Careers of Those Born in 1953: Persistent offenders and desistance,* Statistical Bulletin No. 35/89, London: Home Office Statistical Department.

Home Office (2009) *Crime in England and Wales: Quarterly update to September 2008,* Home Office Statistical Bulletin 01/09, London: Home Office.

Hood, C. (1991) 'A public management for all seasons?' *Public Administration,* **69**(1), pp. 3–19.

Hood, R. (1987) 'Some reflections on the role of criminology in public policy', Address to the British Society of Criminology, 28 January.

Hood-Williams, J. (2001) 'Gender, masculinities and crime: from structures to psyches', *Theoretical Criminology,* **5**(1), pp. 37–60.

Hooper, J. and Stratton, A. (2009) 'Mills gets jail term in Berlusconi bribe case', *The Guardian,* 18th February.

Hope, T. (2006) Review of Smith, M. J. and Tilley, N. (eds), *Crime Science: New approaches to preventing and detecting crime,* Cullompton: Willan, in *Theoretical Criminology,* **10**(2), pp. 245–50.

Horowitz, I. L. and Leibowitz, M. (1969) 'Social deviance and political marginality: towards a redefinition of the relation between sociology and politics', *Social Problems,* **15**(3), pp. 280–96.

Hough, J. M. and Mayhew, P. (1985) *Taking Account of Crime: Key findings from the second British crime survey,* Home Office Research Study No. 85, London: HMSO.

Howe, A. (2004) 'Managing "men's violence" in the criminological arena', in C. Sumner (ed), *The Blackwell Companion to Criminology,* Oxford: Blackwell Publishing.

Hoyle, C. and Zedner, L. (2007) 'Victims, victimization, and criminal justice', in M. Maguire, R. Morgan and R. Reiner (eds), *The Oxford Handbook of Criminology,* 4th edn, Oxford: Oxford University Press.

Hudson, B. (1987) *Justice Through Punishment,* Basingstoke: Macmillan.

Hudson, B. (1993) 'Racism and criminology: concepts and controversies', in D. Cook and B. Hudson (eds), *Racism and Criminology,* London: Sage.

Hudson, B. (1995) 'Racial justice in the risk society', paper presented at the American Society of Criminology conference, Boston, Massachusetts, 15–18 November.

Hughes, G. (1998) *Understanding Crime Prevention,* Buckingham: Open University Press.

Hughes, G. (2007) *The Politics of Crime and Community,* Basingstoke: Palgrave.

Hugill, B. (1995) *The Observer,* 23 July.

Hulsman, L. (1986) 'Critical criminology and the concept of crime', *Contemporary Crises,* **10**, pp. 63–80.

Hunt, A. (1980) 'The radical critique of law: an assessment', *International Journal of the Sociology of Law,* **8**, pp. 33–46.

Hunter, G., Hearnden, I. and Gyateng, T. (2009) *Statistics on Women in the Criminal Justice System,* ICPR King's College London, London: Criminal Justice Reform.

Innes, M. (2003) *Understanding Social Control: Deviance, crime and social order,* Maidenhead: Open University Press.

James, A. and Raine, J. (1998) *The New Politics of Criminal Justice,* Harlow: Longman.

Jamieson, R. (1999) 'Genocide and the social production of immorality', *Theoretical Criminology,* **3**(2), pp. 131–46.

Jay, P. and Rose, B. (1977) *Children and Young Persons in Custody,* Working Party Report, London: NACRO.

Jefferson, T. (1973) 'The Teds: a political resurrection', stencilled occasional papers, No. 22, Centre for Contemporary Cultural Studies, University of Birmingham.

Jefferson, T. (1986) 'Unpopular perceptions: a reply to Richard Kinsey', *Marxism Today,* July, p. 39.

Jefferson, T. (1993) 'Theorising masculine subjectivity', plenary address, Masculinities and Crime Conference, University of Brunel, September.

Jefferson, T. (1996) 'From "little fairy boy" to the "compleat destroyer": subjectivity and transformation in the biography of Mike Tyson', in M. Mac an Ghaill (ed), *Understanding Masculinities,* Buckingham: Open University Press.

Jefferson, T. (1997) 'Masculinities and crime', in M. Maguire, R. Morgan and R. Reiner (eds), *The Oxford Handbook of Criminology,* 2nd edn, Oxford: Oxford University Press.

Jefferson, T. (1998) ' "Muscle", "hard men" and "iron" Mike Tyson: reflections on desire, anxiety and the embodiment of masculinity', *Body and Society,* **4**(1), pp. 103–18.

Jefferson, T. and Hall. S. (eds) (2006) *Resistance Through Rituals: Youth subcultures in postwar Britain,* 2nd edn, Abingdon: Routledge.

Jefferson, T. and Shapland, J. (1994) 'Criminal justice and the production of order and control', *British Journal of Criminology,* **34**(3), pp. 265–90.

Jeffery, C. (1960) 'The historical development of criminology', in H. Mannheim (ed), *Pioneers in Criminology,* London: Stevens.

Jessop, B. (1993) 'Toward a Schumpeterian workforce state? Preliminary remarks on post-fordist political economy', *Studies in Political Economy,* **40**, pp. 7–39.

Jewkes, Y. (ed) (2007) *The Prisons Handbook,* Cullompton: Willan.

Johnson, R. E. (1979) *Juvenile Delinquency and Its Origins,* Cambridge: Cambridge University Press.

Johnstone, G. (ed) (2003) *A Restorative Justice Reader: Texts, sources, context,* Cullompton: Willan Publishing.

Jones, H. (1958) 'Approaches to an ecological study', *British Journal of Delinquency,* **18**(4), pp. 277–93.

Jones, P. (1993) *Studying Society: Sociological theories and research practices,* London: Collins.

Jones, S. (1987) 'Women's experience of crime and policing', mimeo, Centre for the Study of Community and Race Relations, Brunel University.

Jones, T., Maclean, B. and Young, J. (1986) *The Islington Crime Survey,* Aldershot: Gower.

Jupp, V. R. (1989) *Methods of Criminology Research,* London: Unwin Hyman.

Karstedt, S. and Farrell, S. (2004) 'The moral maze of the middle class: the predatory society and its emerging regulatory order', in H-J. Albrecht, T. Serassis and H. Kania (eds), *Images of Crime II,* Freiburg: Edition Iuscrim (Max Planck Institute).

Katz, J. (1988) *Seductions of Crime,* New York: Basic Books.

Kemshall, H. (2003) *Understanding Risk in Criminal Justice,* Maidenhead: Open University Press.

Kershaw, C., Budd, T., Kinshott, G., Mattinson, J., Mayhew, P. and Myhill, A. (2000) *The 2000 British Crime Survey: England and Wales,* Home Office Statistical Bulletin 18/00, London: Home Office.

Kershaw, C., Chivite-Matthews, N., Thomas, C. and Aust, R. (2001) *The 2002 British Crime Survey: First results, England and Wales,* Home Office Statistical Bulletin 18/01, London: Home Office.

Kershaw, C., Nicholas, S. and Walker, A. (eds) (2008) *Crime in England and Wales 2007–2008: Findings from the British Crime Survey and police recorded crime,* Home Office Statistical Bulletin 7/08, London: Home Office.

Kinsey, R. (1984) *The Merseyside Crime Survey: First report,* Liverpool: Merseyside County Council.

Kitsuse, J. I. (1962) 'Societal reaction to deviant behavior: problems of theory and method', *Social Problems,* **9,** pp. 247–56, reprinted in E. Rubington and M. S. Weinberg (eds) (1968), *Deviance: The interactionist perspective,* Basingstoke: Macmillan.

Kitsuse, J. I. and Dietrick, D. (1959) 'Delinquent boys', *American Sociological Review,* 24, pp. 208–15.

Klein, D. (1973) 'The etiology of female crime', *Issues in Criminology,* **8**(2), pp. 3–30.

Kornhauser, R. (1978) *Social Sources of Delinquency,* Chicago, IL: University of Chicago Press.

Kolko, G. (1976) *Railroads and Regulations,* Princeton, NJ: Princeton University Press.

Krinsky, C. (ed) (2008) *Moral Panics Over Contemporary Children and Youth,* Abingdon: Ashgate.

Kroeber, A. L. (1952) *The Nature of Culture,* Chicago, IL: University of Chicago Press.

Lacey, N. (1988) *State Punishment,* London: Routledge.

Lacey, N. (1998) *Unspeakable Subjects: Feminist essays in legal and social theory,* Oxford: Hart.

Laing, R. D. (1967) *The Politics of Experience and the Bird of Paradise,* Harmondsworth: Penguin.

Laing, R. D. (1968) 'The obvious', in D. Cooper (ed), *The Dialectics of Liberation,* Harmondsworth: Penguin.

Landesco, J. (1968) *Organized Crime in Chicago,* Chicago, IL: University of Chicago Press.

Latimer, J., Dowden, C. and Muise, D. (2001) *Effectiveness of Restorative Justice Practices: A Meta-Analysis*, Ottawa: Department of Justice Research and Statistics Division.

Laub, J. H. and Sampson, R. J. (2003) *Shared Beginnings: Divergent Lives: Delinquent boys to age 70*, Cambridge, MA: Harvard University Press.

Laub, J. H., Sampson, R. J. and Sweeten, G. (2006) 'Assessing Sampson and Laub's life-course theory of crime', in F. T. Cullen, J. P. Wright and K. R. Blevins (eds), *Taking Stock: The status of criminological theory* (*Advances in Criminological Theory*, Vol. 15, pp. 313–33), New Brunswick, NJ: Transaction Publishing.

Lawrence, F. and Leigh, D. (2009) 'RBS avoided £500m of tax in global deals', *The Guardian*, 13th March.

Lea, J. (1987) 'Left realism: a defence', *Contemporary Crises*, **11**, pp. 357–70.

Lea, J. (1998) 'Criminology and postmodernity', in P. Walton and J. Young (eds), *The New Criminology Revisited*, Basingstoke: Macmillan.

Lea, J. (2002) *Crime and Modernity*, London: Sage.

Lea, J., Matthews, R. and Young, J. (1987) *Law and Order Five Years On*, London: Middlesex Polytechnic, Centre for Criminology.

Leishman, F., Loveday, B. and Savage, S. P. (1996) *Core Issues in Policing*, London: Longman.

Lemert, E. M. (1951) *Social Pathology*, New York: McGraw-Hill.

Lemert, E. M. (1967) *Human Deviance, Social Problems and Social Control*, Englewood Cliffs, NJ: Prentice-Hall.

Leonard, E. B. (1982) *A Critique of Criminological Theory: Women, crime and society*, New York: Longman.

Leonard, P. (1997) *Postmodern Welfare*, London: Sage.

Leonardsen, D. (2004) *Japan as a Low-Crime Nation*, Basingstoke: Palgrave Macmillan.

Levi, M. (1987) *Regulating Fraud*, London: Tavistock.

Levi, M. (1994) 'White-collar crime', in M. Maguire, R. Morgan and R. Reiner (eds), *The Oxford Handbook of Criminology*, Oxford: Clarendon Press.

Liazos, A. (1972) 'The poverty of the sociology of deviance: nuts, sluts and preverts', *Social Problems*, **20**, pp. 103–20.

Liebmann, M. (2007) *Restorative Justice: How it works*, London: Jessica Kingsley.

Lilly, J. R., Cullen, F. T. and Ball, R. A. (1989) *Criminological Theory: Context and consequences*, London: Sage.

Lilly, J. R., Cullen, F. T. and Ball, R. A. (2007) *Criminological Theory: Context and consequences*, 4th edn, London: Sage.

Little, W. R. and Ntsekhe, V. R. (1959) 'Social class background of young offenders from London', *British Journal of Delinquency*, **16**(2), pp. 130–5.

Loader, I. and Sparks, R. (2008) *Public Criminology? Studying crime and society in the twenty-first century*, Abingdon: Routledge.

Loeber, R. and Stouthamer-Loeber, M. (1986) 'Family factors as correlates and predictors of juvenile conduct problems and delinquency', in M. Tonry and N. Morris (eds), *Crime and Justice*, Vol. 7, Chicago, IL: University of Chicago Press, pp. 29–49.

Lombroso, C. (1876) *L'Uomo Delinquente*, 5th edn, Turin: Bocca; first pub. Milan: Hoepli.

Loomis, C. P. (1957) *Community and Society,* Michigan, Il: Michigan State University Press. Translation and edited version of Tonnies, F. (1887), *Gemeinschaft und Gesellschaft.*

Lowson, D. (1960) 'Delinquency in industrial areas', *British Journal of Criminology,* **1**(1), pp. 50–5.

Lukes, S. (1973) *Emile Durkheim, His Life and Work: Historical and critical study,* Harmondsworth: Penguin.

Lynch, M. J. and Stretsky, P. B. (2003) 'The meaning of green: contrasting criminological perspectives', *Theoretical Criminology,* **7**(2), pp. 217–38.

Lyng, S. (1990) 'Edgework: a social psychological analysis of voluntary risk-taking', *American Journal of Sociology,* **95**(4), pp. 876–921.

Lyng, S. (1998) 'Dangerous methods: risk-taking and the research process', in J. Ferrell and M. Hamm (eds), *Ethnography at the Edge,* Boston, MA: Northeastern University Press.

Lyon, D. (2007) *Surveillance Studies: An overview,* Oxford: Polity.

Lyotard, J. F. (1984) *The Postmodern Condition: A report on knowledge,* Minneapolis, MN: University of Minnesota Press.

MacDonald, E. (1991) *Shoot the Women First,* London: Fourth Estate.

MacGregor, S. (ed) (1989) *Drugs and British Society: Responses to a social problem in the 1980s,* London: Routledge.

McCord, J. (1979) 'Some child rearing antecedents of criminal behaviour in adult men', *Journal of Personality and Social Psychology,* **37**, pp. 1477–86.

McCord, J. (1982) 'A longitudinal view of the relationship between paternal absence and crime', in J. Gunn and D. P. Farrington (eds), *Abnormal Offenders, Delinquency and the Criminal Justice System,* Chichester: Wiley.

McLeod, E. (1982) *Women Working: Prostitution Now,* London: Croom Helm.

McMullan, J. L. (1986) 'The "law and order" problem in socialist criminology', *Studies in Political Economy,* **21**, pp. 175–92.

McRobbie, A. and Garber, J. (1976) 'Girls and Subcultures', in S. Hall and T. Jefferson (eds), *Resistance through Rituals,* London: Hutchinson.

Maguire, M. (1994) 'Crime statistics, patterns and trends: changing perceptions and their implications', in M. Maguire and R. Reiner (eds), *The Oxford Handbook of Criminology,* 1st edn, Oxford: Clarendon Press.

Maguire, M. (2002) 'Crime statistics: the "data explosion" and its implications', in M. Maguire, R. Morgan and R. Reiner (eds), *The Oxford Handbook of Criminology,* 3rd edn, Oxford: Oxford University Press.

Maguire, M. (2007) 'Crime data and statistics', in M. Maguire, R. Morgan and R. Reiner (eds), *The Oxford Handbook of Criminology,* 4th edn, Oxford: Oxford University Press.

Maguire, M., Morgan, R. and Reiner, R. (eds) (1994) *The Oxford Handbook of Criminology,* 1st edn, Oxford: Clarendon Press.

Maguire, M., Morgan, R. and Reiner, R. (eds) (1997) *The Oxford Handbook of Criminology,* 2nd edn, Oxford: Oxford University Press.

Maguire, M., Morgan, R. and Reiner, R. (eds) (2002) *The Oxford Handbook of Criminology,* 3rd edn, Oxford: Oxford University Press.

Maher, L. (1997) *Sexed Work: Gender, race and resistance in Brooklyn Drug Market*, Oxford: Oxford University Press.

Mankoff, M. (1971) 'Societal reaction and deviant career: a critical analysis', *Sociological Quarterly*, **12**, pp. 204–18.

Mannheim, H. (1940) *Social Aspects of Crime in England Between the Wars*, London: Allen & Unwin.

Mannheim, H. (1965) *Comparative Criminology*, London: Routledge & Kegan Paul.

Manning, P. (1977) *Police Work: The organisation of policing*, Cambridge, MA: MIT Press.

Marginson, S. and Considine, M. (2000) *The Enterprise University: Power, Governance and reinvention in Australia*, Melbourne: Cambridge University Press.

Martinson, R. (1974) 'What works? Questions and answers about prison reform', *Public Interest*, **35**, pp. 22–54.

Maruna, S. (2008) 'Merton with energy, Katz with structure, Jock Young with data', *Theoretical Criminology*, **12**(4), pp. 534–9.

Marx, K. (1969) *Theories of Surplus Value*, Vol. 1, London: Lawrence & Wishart.

Marx, K. and Engels, F. (1965) *The German Ideology*, London: Lawrence & Wishart.

Marx, K. and Engels, F. (1970a) *Selected Works*, London: Lawrence & Wishart.

Marx, K. and Engels, F. (1970b) 'Manifesto of the Communist Party', in K. Marx and F. Engels (1970a), *Selected Works*, London: Lawrence & Wishart.

Mathiesen, T. (2004) 'The rise of the surveillant state in times of globalization', in C. Sumner (ed), *The Blackwell Companion to Criminology*, Oxford: Blackwell.

Matthews, J. (1981) *Women in the Penal System*, London: NACRO.

Matthews, R. (1992) 'Replacing "broken windows": crime, incivilities and urban change', in R. Matthews and J. Young (eds), *Issues in Realist Criminology*, London: Sage.

Matthews, R. and Young, J. (eds) (2003) *The New Politics of Crime and Punishment*, Cullompton: Willan Publishing.

Matza, D. (1964) *Delinquency and Drift*, New York: Wiley.

Matza, D. (1969) *Becoming Deviant*, Englewood Cliffs, NJ: Prentice-Hall.

Matza, D. and Sykes, G. M. (1961) 'Juvenile delinquency and subterranean values', *American Sociological Review*, **26**, pp. 712–19.

Mawby, R. I. (1987) 'From victimization rates to the crime experience', mimeo, Plymouth Polytechnic.

Mayhew, P. (2000) 'Researching the state of crime: local, national and international victim surveys', in R. D. King and E. Wincup (eds), *Doing Research on Crime and Justice*, Oxford: Oxford University Press.

Mayhew, P., Elliot, D. and Dowds, L. (1989) *The 1988 British Crime Survey*, London: HMSO.

Mayhew, P. and Hough, M. (1983) 'Note: the British crime survey', *British Journal of Criminology*, **23**, pp. 394–5.

Mayhew, P. and Maung, N. A. (1993) *The 1992 British Crime Survey*, London: HMSO.

Mays, J. B. (1954) *Growing Up in the City: A study of juvenile delinquency in an urban neighbourhood*, Liverpool: Liverpool University Press.

Mays, J. B. (1959) *On the Threshold of Delinquency*, Liverpool: Liverpool University Press.

Mays, J. B. (1975) *Crime and its Treatment*, 2nd edn, London: Longman.

Mead, G. H. (1934) *Mind, Self and Society*, Chicago, IL: University of Chicago Press.

Menard, S. (1995) 'A developmental test of Mertonian anomie theory', *Journal of Research in Crime and Delinquency*, **31**, pp. 136–74.

Merton, R. K. (1957) 'Priorities in scientific discoveries: A chapter in the sociology of science', *American Sociological Review*, **22**(6), pp. 635–9.

Merton, R. K. (1993; first pub. 1938) 'Social structure and anomie', in C. Lemert (ed), *Social Theory: The multicultural readings*, Boulder, CO: Westview Press.

Messerschmidt, J. W. (1986) *Capitalism, Patriarchy and Crime: Towards a Socialist–Feminist Criminology*, Totowa, NJ: Rowman & Littlefield.

Messerschmidt, J. W. (1993) *Masculinities and Crime*, Lanham, MD: Rowman & Littlefield.

Messerschmidt, J. W. (1997) *Crime as Structured Action: Gender, race, class and crime*, Thousand Oaks, CA: Sage.

Messner, S. F. and Rosenfeld, R. (2001) *Crime and the American Dream*, 3rd edn., Belmont, CA: Wadsworth.

Michalowski, R. J. (1983) 'Crime control in the 1980s: a progressive agenda', *Crime and Social Justice*, **20**.

Michalowski, R. J. and Bohlander, E. W. (1976) 'Repression and criminal justice in capitalist America', *Sociological Inquiry*, **46**(2), pp. 95–106.

Miers, D., Maguire, M., Goldie, S., Sharpe, K., Hale, C., Uglow, S., Doolin, K., Hallam, A., Enterkin, J. and Newburn, T. (2001) *An Exploratory Evaluation of Restorative Justice Schemes*, Crime Reduction Series Paper 9, London: Home Office.

Miles, I. and Irvine, J. (1981) 'The critique of official statistics', in J. Irvine, I. Miles and J. Evans (eds), *Demystifying Social Statistics*, 2nd imp., London: Pluto Press.

Miliband, R. (1969) *The State in Capitalist Society*, London: Weidenfeld & Nicolson.

Miller, E. (1986) *Street Women*, Philadelphia, PA: Temple University Press.

Miller, J. (1998) 'Up it up: gender and the accomplishment of street robbery', *Criminology*, **36**(1), pp. 37–65.

Miller, W. B. (1958) 'Lower class culture as a generating milieu of gang delinquency', *Journal of Social Issues*, **14**(3), pp. 5–19.

Mirrlees-Black, C., Mayhew, P. and Percy, A. (1996) *The 1996 British Crime Survey: England and Wales*, Home Office Statistical Bulletin 19/96, London: Home Office.

Mirrlees-Black, C., Budd, T., Partridge, S. and Mayhew, P. (1998) *The 1998 British Crime Survey: England and Wales*, Home Office Statistical Bulletin 21/98, London: Home Office.

Mooney, G. and Danson, M. (1997) 'Beyond culture city: Glasgow as a dual city', in N. Jewson and S. MacGregor (eds), *Transforming Cities*, London: Routledge.

Moore, D. (2000) 'Risking Saturday night: regulating student alcohol use through "common sense"', *Theoretical Criminology*, **4**(4), pp. 411–28.

Moore, S. (1995) 'Barking up the family tree', *The Guardian*, 9 March.

Morgan, P. (1978) *Delinquent Fantasies*, London: Maurice Temple Smith.

Morgan, P. (1981) 'The Children's Act: sacrificing justice to social worker's needs?', C. Brewer, T. Morris, P. Morgan and M. North, *Criminal Welfare on Trial*, London: Social Affairs Unit.

Morgan, R. (1994) 'Imprisonment', in M. Maguire, R. Morgan and R. Reiner (eds), *Criminal Welfare on Trial,* London: Social Affairs Unit.

Morgan, R. and Allen, R. (2004) 'Editorial: whose justice?' *Criminal Justice Matters,* 57.

Morris, A. (1987) *Women, Crime and Criminal Justice,* Oxford: Blackwell.

Morris, T. P. (1957) *The Criminal Area: A study in social ecology,* London: Routledge & Kegan Paul.

Morrison, W. (1995) *Theoretical Criminology: From modernity to postmodernism,* London: Cavendish Publishing.

Moulds, E. (1980) 'Chivalry and paternalism: disparities of treatment in the criminal justice system', in S. Datesman and F. Scarpitti (eds), *Women, Crime and Justice,* New York: Oxford University Press.

Mugford, S. and O'Malley, P. (1991) 'Heroin policy and deficit models: the Limits of Left realism', *Crime, Law and Social Change,* **15,** pp. 19–36.

Mullins, C. (1945) *Why Crime? Some causes and remedies from the psychological standpoint,* London: Methuen.

Muncie, J. (1984) *The Trouble With Kids Today,* London: Hutchinson.

Muncie, J. (2009) *Youth and Crime,* 3rd edn, London: Sage.

Muncie, J. and Sparks, R. (eds) (1991) *Imprisonment: European perspectives,* London: Harvester Wheatsheaf.

Murphy, D. S. and Robinson, M. B. (2008) 'The Maximizer: clarifying Merton's theories of anomie and strain', *Theoretical Criminology,* **12**(4), pp. 501–21.

Murray, C. (1990) *The Emerging British Underclass,* London: Institute of Economic Affairs, Health and Welfare Unit.

Naffine, N. (1987) *Female Crime,* Sydney: Allen & Unwin.

Naffine, N. (1997) *Feminism and Criminology,* Sydney: Allen and Unwin.

Nagin, D. S. and Farrington, D. P. (1992) 'The onset and persistence of offending', *Criminology,* **30,** pp. 501–23.

Nelken, D. (1994) *The Futures of Criminology,* London: Sage.

Nelken, D. (2007) 'White-collar and corporate crime', in M. Maguire, R. Morgan and R. Reiner (eds), *Oxford Handbook of Criminology,* 4th edn, Oxford: Oxford University Press.

Nettler, G. (1978) *Explaining Crime,* New York: McGraw-Hill.

Newburn, T. (1992) *Permission and Regulation: Law and morals in post-war Britain,* London: Routledge.

Newburn, T. and Stanko, A. E. (1994) 'When men are victims: the failure of victimology', in T. Newburn and A. E. Stanko (eds), *Just Boys Doing Business? Men, masculinities and crime,* London: Routledge.

Newburn, T., Crawford, A., Earle, R., Goldie, S., Hale, C., Masters, G., Netten, A., Saunders, R., Sharpe, K. and Uglow, S. (2001) *The Introduction of Referral Orders into the Youth Justice System,* RDS Occasional Paper No. 70, London: Home Office.

Nicholas, S., Kershaw, C. and Walker, A. (2007) *Crime in England and Wales 2006–2007,* Home Office Statistical Bulletin 11/07, London: Home Office.

Nicholas, S., Povey, D., Walker, A. and Kershaw, C. (2005) *Crime in England and Wales 2004–2005,* Home Office Statistical Bulletin 11/05, London: Home Office.

Norrie, S. and Adelman, S. (1989) '"Consensual authoritarianism" and criminal justice in Thatcher's Britain', *Journal of Law and Society*, **16**(1).

Norris, C. and Armstrong, G. (1999) *The Maximum Surveillance Society: The rise of CCTV*, Oxford: Berg.

Nuttall, J. (1970) *Bomb Culture*, St Albans: Paladin.

Obama, B. (2008) 'America Can Change', *The Guardian*, 6th November.

O'Brien, M. (2005) 'What is *cultural* about cultural criminology?', *British Journal of Criminology*, **45**(5), pp. 599–612.

Office for National Statistics (2003) *General Household Survey*, www.statistics.gov.uk.

O'Malley, P. (1996) 'Risk and responsibility', in A. Barry, T. Osborne and N. Rose (eds), *Foucault and Political Reason: Liberalism, neo-liberalism and rationalities of government*, Chicago, IL: University of Chicago Press.

O'Malley, P. (2004) 'Penal policies and contemporary politics', in C. Sumner (ed), *The Blackwell Companion to Criminology*, Oxford: Blackwell.

O'Malley, P. and Mugford, S. (1994) 'Crime excitement and modernity', in G. Barak (ed), *Varieties of Criminology*, Westport, CT: Praeger.

Orwell, G. (1943) 'Can Socialists be happy?', http://www.readprint.com/work-1257/George-Orwell.

Palmer, G., MacInnes, T. and Kenway, P. (2008) *Monitoring Poverty and Social Exclusion*, London: Joseph Rowntree Foundation.

Parker, H. (1974) *View From the Boys*, Newton Abbot: David & Charles.

Parker, H. (1976) 'Boys will be men: brief adolescence in a down-town neighbourhood', in G. Mungham and G. Pearson (eds), *Working Class Youth Culture*, London: Routledge & Kegan Paul.

Parnaby, P. F. and Sacco, V. F. (2004) 'Fame and strain: the contributions of Mertonian deviance theory to an understanding of the relationship between celebrity and deviant behavior', *Deviant Behavior*, **25**, pp. 1–26.

Parton, N. (1992) *Governing the Family*, Basingstoke: Macmillan.

Passas, N. and Agnew, R. (eds) (1997) *The Future of Anomie Theory*, Boston, MA: Northeastern University Press.

Pavlich, G. (1999) 'Criticism and criminology: in search of legitimacy', *Theoretical Criminology*, **3**(1), pp. 29–51.

Paxton, W. and Dixon, M. (2004) *The State of the Nation: An audit of injustice in the UK*, London: Institute for Public Policy Research.

Pearce, F. (1976) *Crimes of the Powerful*, London: Pluto Press.

Pearce, F. and Tombs, S. (1992) 'Realism and corporate crime', in R. Matthews and J. Young (eds), *Issues in Realist Criminology*, London: Sage.

Pearce, F. and Tombs, S. (1998) *Toxic Capitalism: Corporate crime and the chemical industry*, Aldershot: Ashgate.

Pearce, F. and Tombs, S. (2004) '"Dance your anger and your joys": multinational corporations, power, "crime"', in C. Sumner (ed), *The Blackwell Companion to Criminology*, Oxford: Blackwell Publishing.

Pearson, G. (1975) *The Deviant Imagination*, London: Macmillan.

Pearson, G. (1976) 'Cotton town: a case study and its history', in G. Mungham and G. Pearson (eds), *Working Class Youth Culture*, London: Routledge & Kegan Paul.

Pearson, G. (1978) 'Social work and law and order', *Social Work Today*, **9**(30).

Pearson, G. (1983) *Hooligan: A history of respectable fears*, London: Macmillan.

Pearson, G. (1987) *The New Heroin Users*, Oxford: Blackwell.

Pearson, G. (1994) 'Youth, crime and society', in M. Maguire, R. Morgan and R. Reiner (eds), *The Oxford Handbook of Criminology*, Oxford: Clarendon Press.

Pearson, R. (1976) 'Women defendants in magistrates' courts', *British Journal of Law and Society*, **3**, pp. 265–73.

Pease, K. (2002) 'Crime reduction', in M. Maguire, R. Morgan and R. Reiner (eds) *The Oxford Handbook of Criminology*, 3rd edn, Oxford: Oxford University Press.

Pepinsky, H. E. and Quinney, R. (eds) (1991) *Criminology As Peacemaking*, Bloomington, IN: Indiana University Press.

Phillipson, M. (1971) *Sociological Aspects of Crime and Delinquency*, London: Routledge & Kegan Paul.

Piquero, A. R., Farrington, D. P. and Blumstein, A. (2007) *Key Issues in Criminal Career Research: New analyses of the Cambridge Study in Delinquent Development*, Cambridge: Cambridge University Press.

Pitts, J. (1988) *The Politics of Juvenile Crime*, London: Sage.

Pitts, J. (2001) *The New Politics of Youth Justice*, London: Palgrave.

Pizzey, E. (1973) *Scream Quietly or the Neighbours Will Hear*, Harmondsworth: Penquin.

Player, E. (1989) 'Women and crime in the city', in D. Downes (ed), *Crime in the City*, London: Macmillan.

Plummer, K. (1975) *Sexual Stigma*, London: Routledge & Kegan Paul.

Plummer, K. (1979) 'Misunderstanding labelling perspectives', in D. Downes and P. Rock (eds), *Deviant Interpretations*, Oxford: Martin Robertson.

Pollak, O. (1950) *The Criminality of Women*, New York: Barnes/Perpetuo.

Pollner, M. (1974) 'Mundane reasoning', *Philosophy of Social Sciences*, **4**(1), pp. 35–54.

Poole, E. D. and Regoli, R. M. (1979) 'Parental support, delinquent friends and delinquency', *Journal of Criminal Law and Criminology*, **70**, pp. 188–93.

Posner, R. A. (1986) *Economic Analysis of Law*, Boston, MA: Little, Brown.

Poulantzas, N. (1973) 'The problem of the capitalist state', in J. Urry and J. Wakeford (eds), *Power in Britain*, London: Heinemann.

Pratt, J. (2000) 'Emotive and ostentatious punishment: its decline and resurgence in modern society', *Punishment and Society*, **2**(4), pp. 417–39.

Pratt, T. C. and Cullen, F. T. (2000) 'The empirical status of Gottfredson and Hirschi's general theory of crime', *Criminology*, **38**, pp. 931–64.

Presdee, M. (2000) *Cultural Criminology and the Carnival of Crime*, London: Routledge.

Putnam, R. (2000) *Bowling Alone: The collapse and revival of American community*, New York: Simon & Schuster.

Quinney, R. (1969) *Criminal Justice in American Society*, Boston, MA: Little, Brown.

Quinney, R. (1970a) *The Social Reality of Crime*, Boston, MA: Little, Brown.

Quinney, R. (1970b) *The Problem of Crime*, New York: Dodd, Mead.

Quinney, R. (1974) *Critique of the Legal Order: Crime control in capitalist society*, Boston: Little, Brown.

Quinney, R. (1975) *Criminology: Analysis and critique of crime in America*, Boston, MA: Little, Brown.

Quinney, R. (1977) *Class, State and Crime: On the theory and practice of criminal justice*, New York: McKay.

Raab, D. (2009) *The Assault on Liberty*, London: HarperCollins.

Radford, J. (1987) 'Policing male violence', in J. Hanmer and M. Maynard (eds), *Women, Violence and Social Control*, London: Macmillan.

Radzinowicz, L. (1961) *In Search of Criminology*, London: Heinemann.

Rafter, N. H. (1986) 'Left out by the Left: crime and crime control', *Socialist Review*, **16**, pp. 7–23.

Reiner, R. (1988) 'British criminology and the state', *British Journal of Criminology*, **29**(1), pp. 138–58.

Reiner, R. (1992) *The Politics of the police*, 2nd edn, Hemel Hempstead: Wheatsheaf.

Reiner, R. (1994) 'Policing and the police', in M. Maguire, M. Morgan and R. Reiner (eds), *The Oxford Handbook of Criminology*, Oxford: Clarendon Press.

Reiner, R. and Cross, M. (eds) (1991) *Beyond Law and Order*, London: Macmillan.

Renzetti, C. (2008) *Feminist Criminology*, Abingdon: Routledge.

Rex, J. and Moore, R. (1967) *Race, Community and Conflict*, London: Institute of Race Relations/Oxford University Press.

Rhodes, R. A. W. (1997) *Understanding Governance: Policy networks, governance, reflexivity and accountability*, Buckingham: Open University Press.

Riley, D. (1986) 'Sex differences in teenage crime: the role of lifestyle', Research Bulletin No. 2, Home Office Research and Planning Unit, HMSO, London, pp. 34–80.

Riley, D. and Shaw, M. (1985) *Parental Supervision and Juvenile Delinquency*, Home Office Research Study No. 83, London: HMSO.

Robins, L. N. and Rutter, M. (eds) (1990) *Straight and Devious Pathways From Childhood To Adulthood*, Cambridge: Cambridge University Press.

Rock, P. (1973) *Deviant Behaviour*, London: Hutchinson.

Rock, P. (1988) 'The present state of criminology in Britain', *British Journal of Criminology*, **28**(2), pp. 188–99.

Rock, P. (1994) 'The social organization of British criminology', in M. Maguire, R. Morgan and R. Reiner (eds), *The Oxford Handbook of Criminology*, 1st edn, Oxford: Clarendon Press.

Rock, P. (2002) 'Sociological theories of crime', in M. Maguire, R. Morgan and R. Reiner (eds), *The Oxford Handbook of Criminology*, 3rd edn, Oxford: Oxford University Press.

Rock, P. (2007) 'Sociological Theories of Crime', in M. Maguire, R. Morgan and R. Reiner (eds), *The Oxford Handbook of Criminology*, 4th edn, Oxford: Oxford University Press.

Rodger, J. (1995) 'Family policy or moral regulation?', *Critical Social Policy*, **43**.

Roe, S. and Ashe, J. (2008) *Young People and Crime: Findings from the 2006 offending. Crime and justice survey*, Home Office Statistical Bulletin 09/08, London: Home Office.

Rose, N. (1996) 'The death of the social? Refiguring the territory of government', *Economy and Society*, **25**(3), pp. 327–56.

Rosenau, P. (1992) *Post-Modernism and the Social Sciences*, Princeton, NJ: Princeton University Press.

Roshier, B. (1977) 'The function of crime myth', *Sociological Review*, May.

Roshier, B. (1989) *Controlling Crime*, Milton Keynes: Open University Press.

Ruggiero, V. (1992) 'Realist criminology: a critique', in J. Young and R. Matthews (eds), *Rethinking Criminology: The realist debate*, London: Sage.

Russell, D. E. H. (1982) *Rape in Marriage*, New York: Macmillan.

Rutter, M. and Giller, H. (1983) *Juvenile Delinquency*, Harmondsworth: Penguin.

Sacco, V. F. (2005) *When Crime Waves*, London: Sage.

Sainsbury, P. (1955) *Suicide in London*, London: Institute of Psychiatry.

Scheingold, S. A. (2000) 'Constructing the new political criminology: power, authority, and the post-liberal state', *Law and Social Inquiry*, **23**(4), pp. 857–95.

Schervish, P. G. (1973) 'The labelling perspective', *American Sociologist*, **8**, pp. 47–56.

Schinkel, W. (2002) 'The modernist myth in criminology', *Theoretical Criminology*, **6**(2), pp. 123–44.

Schlossman, S., Zellman, G. and Shavelson, R., with Sedlak, M. and Cobb, J. (1984) *Delinquency Prevention in South Chicago: A fifty-year assessment of the Chicago area project*, Santa Monica, CA: Rand.

Schrag, C. O. (1997) *The Self after Postmodernity*, London: Yale University Press.

Schur, E. M. (1971) *Labelling Deviant Behaviour*, New York: Harper & Row.

Schutz, A. (1972) *The Phenomenology of the Social World*, London: Heinemann.

Schwendinger, H. and Schwendinger, J. (1975) 'Defenders of order or guardians of human rights?', in I. Taylor, P. Walton and J. Young (eds), *Critical Criminology*, London: Routledge & Kegan Paul.

Scott, P. (1956) 'Gangs and delinquent groups in London', *British Journal of Delinquency*, **7**, pp. 8–21.

Scraton, P. (1985) *The State of the Police*, London: Pluto Press.

Scraton, P. (ed) (1987) *Law, Order and the Authoritarian State*, Milton Keynes: Open University Press.

Scraton, P. (2002) 'Defining "power" and challenging "knowledge": Critical analysis as resistance in the UK', in K. Carrington and R. Hogg (eds), *Critical Criminology: Issues, debates, challenges*, Cullompton: Willan Publishing.

Scraton, P. (2007) *Power, Conflict and Criminalisation*, Abingdon: Routledge.

Scraton, P. and Chadwick, K. (1991) 'The theoretical and political priorities of critical criminology', in K. Stenson and D. Cowell (eds), *The Politics of Crime Control*, London: Sage.

Sellin, T. (1938) *Culture, Conflict and Crime*, New York Social Science Research Council.

Shacklady Smith, L. (1978) 'Sexist assumptions and female delinquency: an empirical investigation', in C. Smart and B. Smart (eds), *Women, Sexuality and Social Control*, London: Routledge & Kegan Paul.

Shaw, C. R. (1930) *The Jack-Roller: A delinquent boy's own story*, Chicago, IL: Chicago University Press.

Shaw, C. R. and McKay, H. D. (1942) *Juvenile Delinquency and Urban Areas*, Chicago, IL: Chicago University Press.

Shaw, C. R. and Moore, M. E. (1931) *The Natural History of a Delinquent Career,* Chicago, IL: Chicago University Press.

Shaw, C. R., McKay, H. D. and MacDonald, J. F. (1938) *Brothers in Crime,* Chicago, IL: Chicago University Press.

Shearing, C. and Stenning, P. (1987) 'Say cheese! From the panopticon to Disney World', in C. Shearing and P. Stenning (eds), *Private Policing,* Beverly Hills, CA: Sage.

Short, J. F. and Strodtbeck, F. (1965) *Group Process and Delinquency,* Chicago, IL: University of Chicago Press.

Shover, N. (1985) *Aging Criminals,* Beverly Hills, CA: Sage.

Silvestri, M and Crowther-Dowey, C. (2008) *Gender and Crime,* London: Sage.

Sim, J. (1990) *Medical Power in Prisons: The Prison Medical Service in England 1774–1989,* Milton Keynes: Open University Press.

Simmel, G. (1903) *The Metropolis and Mental Life,* Dresden: Peterman.

Simmons, J. and Dodd, T. (eds) (2003) *Crime in England and Wales 2002/2003,* Home Office Statistical Bulletin 07/03, London: Home Office.

Simmons, J. *et al.,* (2002) *Crime in England and Wales 2001/2002,* London: Home Office.

Simon, R. J. (1975) *Women and Crime,* Toronto: Lexington Books.

Slapper, G. and Tombs, S. (1999) *Corporate Crime,* London: Addison Wesley Longman.

Smart, C. (1976) *Women, Crime and Criminology: A feminist critique,* London: Routledge & Kegan Paul.

Smart, C. (1979) 'The new female criminal: reality or myth?', *British Journal of Criminology,* **19**(1), pp. 50–9.

Smart, C. (1981) 'Response to Greenwood', in A. M. Morris and L. R. Gelsthorpe (eds), *Women and Crime,* Cropwood Conference Series, No. 13, Cambridge: Institute of Criminology.

Smart, C. (1989) *Feminism and the Power of Law,* London: Routledge.

Smart, C. (1990) 'Feminist approaches to criminology, or postmodern woman meets atavistic man', in L. R. Gelsthorpe and A. M. Morris (eds), *Feminist Perspectives in Criminology,* London: Routledge & Kegan Paul.

Smart, C. (1995) *Law, Crime and Sexuality: Essays in feminism,* London: Sage.

Smith, C. (1970) *Adolescence,* 2nd edn, London: Longman.

Smith, D. J. and Grey, J. (1985) *Police and People in London: The PSI Report,* Aldershot: Gower.

Smith, L. J. F. (1988) 'Image of women: decision-making in courts', in A. M. Morris and C. Wilkinson (eds), *Women and the Penal System,* Cropwood Conference Series, No. 10, Cambridge: Institute of Criminology.

Snider, L. (2000) 'The sociology of corporate crime: an obituary (or whose knowledge claims have legs?)', *Theoretical Criminology,* **4**(2), pp. 169–206.

Snider, L. (2004) 'Female punishment: from patriarch to backlash?' in C. Sumner (ed), *The Blackwell Companion to Criminology,* Oxford: Blackwell Publishing.

Soothill, K., Fitzpatrick, C. and Francis, B. (2009) *Understanding Criminal Careers,* Cullompton: Willan.

South, N. (1994) 'Drugs: control, crime and criminological studies', in M. Maguire, R. Morgan and R. Reiner (eds), *The Oxford Handbook of Criminology,* 1st edn, Oxford: Clarendon Press.

South, N. (1997) 'Late-modern criminology: "late" as in "dead" or "modern" as in "new"', in D. Owen (ed), *Sociology after Postmodernism*, London: Sage.

South, N. (1998) 'A green field for criminology? A proposal for a green perspective', *Theoretical Criminology*, **2**(2), pp. 211–33.

Sparks, R., Genn, H. G. and Dodd, D. J. (1977) *Surveying Victims*, Chichester: Wiley.

Spencer, J. L. *et al.* (1961) 'Preliminary report of the British social project', unpublished.

Spivack, G., Marcus, J. and Swift, M. (1986) 'Early classroom behaviour up to age 30', *British Journal of Criminology*, **29**, pp. 124–31.

Standing Conference on Crime Prevention (The Morgan Report) (1991) *Safer Communities: The local delivery of crime prevention through the partnership approach*, London: Home Office.

Stanko, E. (1985) *Intimate Intrusions*, London: Routledge & Kegan Paul.

Stanko, E. (1988) 'Hidden violence against women', in M. Maguire and J. Pointing (eds), *Victims of Crime: A new deal?*, Milton Keynes: Open University Press.

Stanko, E. (1993) *Men and Crime*, Milton Keynes: Open University Press.

Stanley, L. and Wise, S. (1983) *Breaking Out*, London: Routledge & Kegan Paul.

Stattin, H., Magnusson, D. and Reichel, H. (1989) 'Criminal activity at different ages: a study based on a Swedish longitudinal research population', *British Journal of Criminology*, **29**, pp. 368–85.

Stedman-Jones, G. (1971) *Outcast in London*, Oxford: Oxford University Press.

Steinert, H. (1985) 'The amazing New Left law and order campaign', *Contemporary Crises*, **9**, pp. 327–33.

Stenson, K. (1991) 'Making sense of crime control', in K. Stenson and D. Cowell (eds), *The Politics of Crime Control*, London: Sage.

Stenson, K. (2001) 'The new politics of crime control', in K. Stenson and R. R. Sullivan (eds), *Crime, Risk and Justice: The politics of crime control in liberal democracies*, Cullompton: Willan Publishing.

Stenson, K. and Cowell, D. (1991) *The Politics of Crime Control*, London: Sage.

Stenson, K. and Sullivan, R. R. (eds) (2001) *Crime, Risk and Justice: The politics of crime control in liberal democracies*, Cullompton: Willan Publishing.

Stern, V. (2006) *Creating Criminals: Prisons and people in a market society*, London: Zed Books.

Stillman-Ashby, A. B. (2004) *The Actuarial Community: A study investigating actuarial justice and its adoption into strategies of crime control*, unpublished PhD thesis, School of Applied Social Sciences, University of Durham.

Strang, J. and Gossop, M. (eds) (1993) *Responding to Drug Misuse: Treatment and control in Britain*, London: Tavistock.

Straw, J. (2008) quoted by P. Lewis, *The Guardian*, 2nd December.

Sudnow, D. (1965) 'Normal crimes: sociological features of the penal code in a public defender office', *Social Problems*, **12**.

Sumner, C. S. (1976) 'Marxism and deviancy theory', in P. Wiles (ed), *The Sociology of Crime and Delinquency in Britain*, vol. 2, *The New Criminologies*, Oxford: Martin Robertson.

Sumner, C. S. (1981) 'Race, crime and hegemony', *Contemporary Crises*, **5**(3), pp. 277–91.

Sumner, C. S. (ed) (1990) *Censure, Politics and Criminal Justice,* Buckingham: Open University Press.

Sumner, C. S. (1994) *The Sociology of Deviance: An obituary,* Buckingham: Open University Press.

Sumner, C. S. (ed) (1997) *Violence, Culture and Censure,* London: Taylor & Francis.

Sumner, C. S. (ed) (2004) *The Blackwell Companion to Criminology,* Oxford: Blackwell Publishing.

Sutherland, E. H. (1937) *The Professional Thief: By a professional thief,* Chicago, IL: University of Chicago Press.

Sutherland, E. H. (1939) *Principles of Criminology,* Philadelphia, PA: J.B. Lippincott.

Sutherland, E. H. (1940) 'White-collar criminality', *American Sociological Review,* **5,** pp. 1–12.

Sutherland, E. H. (1983; first pub. 1949) *White-Collar Crime,* New York: Holt, Rinehart & Winston.

Sykes, G. M. and Matza, D. (1957) 'Techniques of neutralization: a theory of delinquency', *American Sociological Review,* **22,** pp. 664–70.

Szasz, T. S. (1973) *The Manufacture of Madness,* St Albans: Paladin.

Takagi, P. (1974) 'A garrison state in a "democratic" society', *Crime and Social Justice,* **1,** pp. 27–30.

Tame, C. R. (1991) 'Freedom, responsibility and justice: the criminology of the "New Right"', in K. Stenson and D. Cowell (eds), *The Politics of Crime Control,* London: Sage.

Tannenbaum, F. (1938) *Crime and the Community,* New York: Columbia University Press.

Taylor, I. (1971) 'Soccer consciousness and soccer hooliganism', S. Cohen (ed.), *Images of Deviance,* Harmondsworth: Penguin.

Taylor, I. (1981) *Law and Order: Arguments for socialism,* London: Macmillan.

Taylor, I. (1982) 'Against crime and for socialism', *Crime and Social Justice,* Winter, pp. 14–15.

Taylor, I. (1999) *Crime in Context,* Cambridge: Polity Press.

Taylor, I. and Walton, P. (1971) 'Hey, mister, this is what we really do; some observations of vandalism in play', *Social Work Today,* **2**(12), pp. 25–7.

Taylor, I., Walton, P. and Young, J. (1973) *The New Criminology: For a social theory of deviance,* London: Routledge & Kegan Paul.

Taylor, I., Walton, P. and Young, J. (eds) (1975) *Critical Criminology,* London: Routledge & Kegan Paul.

Taylor, L. (1971) *Deviance and Society,* London: Michael Joseph.

Taylor, L. (1980) 'Bringing power to particular account: Peter Rajah and the Hull Board of Visitors', in P. Carlen and M. Collison (eds), *Radical Issues in Criminology,* Oxford: Martin Robertson.

Taylor, L. (1984) *In the Underworld,* Oxford: Blackwell.

Taylor, L., Lacey, R. and Bracken, D. (1980) *In Whose Best Interests?,* London: Cobden Trust/Mind.

Thio, A. (1973) 'Class bias in the sociology of deviance', *American Sociologist,* **8,** pp. 1–12.

Thomas, C. W., Kreps, G. A. and Cage, R. J. (1977) 'An application of compliance theory to the study of juvenile delinquency', *Sociology and Social Research,* **61,** pp. 156–75.

Thomas, T. (2007) *Criminal Records: A database for the criminal justice system and beyond*, Basingstoke: Palgrave Macmillan.

Thompson, E. P. (1975) *Whigs and Hunters: The origins of the Black Act*, London: Allen Lane.

Thrasher, F. M. (1963; first pub. 1927) *The Gang*, Chicago, IL: Phoenix Press.

Tierney, J. (1980) 'Political deviance: a critical commentary on a case study', *Sociological Review*, **28**(4), pp. 829–50.

Tierney, J. (1987) 'Police discretion: raising the age of consent', *The Police Journal*, **60**(4), pp. 283–6.

Tierney, J. (1988) 'Viewpoint: romantic fictions: the re-emergence of the crime as politics debate', *Sociological Review*, **36**(1), February, pp. 133–45.

Tierney, J. (1989) 'Graduating in Criminal Justice', *Policing*, **5**, pp. 208–23.

Tierney, J. (2001) 'Audits of crime and disorder: some lessons from research', *Crime Prevention and Community Safety: An International Journal*, **3**(2), pp. 7–17.

Tierney, J. (2009) *Key Perspectives in Criminology*, Milton Keynes: Open University Press.

Tierney, J. and Hobbs, D. (2003) *Alcohol-Related Crime and Disorder: Guidance for Local Partnerships*, Home Office On-Line Report 08/3, London: Home Office.

Tifft, L. L. (1995) 'Social harm definitions of crime', *The Critical Criminologist*, **7**, pp. 9–13.

Tilley, N. (2001) 'Evaluation and evidence led crime reduction policy and practice', in R. Matthews and J. Pitts (eds), *Crime, Disorder and Community Safety*, London: Routledge.

Tittle, C. R. (1995) *Control Balance: Toward a general theory of deviance*, Boulder, CO: Westview.

Tittle, C. R. (1997) 'Thoughts stimulated by Briathwaite's analysis of control balance theory', *Theoretical Criminology*, **1**(1), pp. 99–110.

Tittle, C. R. (2000) 'Control balance', in R. Paternoster and R. Bachman (eds), *Explaining Criminals and Crime: Essays in contemporary theory*, Los Angeles, CA: Roxbury.

Tittle, C. R. (2004) 'Refining control balance theory', *Theoretical Criminology*, **8**(4), pp. 395–428.

Tonry, M. (2004) *Punishment and Politics*, Cullompton: Willan Publishing.

Townsend, M. and Asthana, A. (2008) 'Put young children on DNA list, urge police', *The Observer*, 15th March.

Travis, A. (2008) 'Row over police statistics', *The Guardian*, 24th October, p. 10.

Tuck, M. (1988) *Crime Prevention: A shift in concept*, Home Office Research and Planning Unit, Research Bulletin No. 24, London: Home Office.

Turk, A. T. (1969) *Criminality and the Legal Order*, Chicago, IL: Rand McNally.

Turner, B. S. (2001) 'Risks, rights and regulation: an overview', *Health, Risk and Society*, **3**(1), pp. 9–18.

Tzanelli, R., Yar, M. and O'Brien, M. (2005) '"Con me if you can": exploring crime in the American cinematic imagination', *Theoretical Criminology*, **9**(1), pp. 97–117.

Vagg, J. (1994) *Prison Systems: A comparative study of accountability in England, France, Germany and the Netherlands*, Oxford: Oxford University Press.

Valier, C. (2002) *Theories of Crime and Punishment*, Harlow: Pearson Education.

Van Hoorebeeck, B. (1997) 'Prospects for reconstructing aetiology', *Theoretical Criminology*, **1**(4), pp. 501–18.

Veljanovski, C. (1990) *The Economics of Law: An introductory text*, London: Institute of Economic Affairs.

Vilar, P. (1985) 'Constructing Marxist history', in J. le Goff and P. Nora (eds), *Constructing the Past: Essays in historical methodology*, Cambridge: Cambridge University Press.

Vold, G. (1958) *Theoretical Criminology*, New York: Oxford University Press.

Von Hentig, H. (1948) *The Criminal and His Victim*, New Haven, CT: Yale University Press.

Wadsworth, M. (1979) *The Roots of Delinquency*, Oxford: Martin Robertson.

Walgrave, L. (2008) *Restorative Justice, Self-interest and Responsible Citizenship*, Cullompton: Willan.

Walker, A., Kershaw, C. and Nicholas, S. (2006) *Crime in England and Wales 2005–2006*, Home Office Statistical Bulletin 12/06, London: Home Office.

Walker, C. (2009) *Blackstone's Guide to the Anti-Terrorism Legislation*, 2nd edn, Oxford: Oxford University Press.

Walker, N. (1965) *Crime and Punishment*, Edinburgh: Edinburgh University Press.

Walker, N. D. (1991) *Why Punish?*, Oxford: Oxford University Press.

Walklate, S. (1989) *Victimology: The victim and the criminal justice process*, London: Unwin & Hyman.

Walklate, S. (1995) *Gender and Crime*, Hemel Hempstead: Harvester Wheatsheaf.

Walklate, S. (2003) *Understanding Criminology: Current theoretical debates*, Buckingham: Open University Press.

Walklate, S. (2007) *Handbook of Victims and Victimology*, Cullompton: Willan.

Walsh, D. and Poole, A. (eds) (1983) *A Dictionary of Criminology*, London: Routledge & Kegan Paul.

Walters, R. (2001) 'Social defence and international reconstruction: illustrating the governance of post-war criminological discourses', *Theoretical Criminology*, **5**(2), pp. 203–21.

Walters, R. (2007) 'Critical criminology and the intensification of the authoritarian state', in A. Barton, K. Corteen, D. Scott and D. Whyte (eds), *Expanding the Criminological Imagination: Critical readings in criminology*, Cullompton: Willan.

Walton, P. and Young, J. (eds) (1998) *The New Criminology Revisited*, Basingstoke: Macmillan.

Ward, D. A. and Kassebaum, G. G. (1966) *Women's Prison*, London: Weidenfeld & Nicolson.

Werkentin, F., Hofferbert, M. and Baurmann, M. (1974) 'Criminology as police science or "How old is the new criminology?"', *Crime and Social Justice*, **2**, pp. 24–41.

Wertham, F. (1949) *The Show of Violence*, Garden City, NY: Doubleday.

West, D. J. (1982) *Delinquency: Its roots, careers and prospects*, London: Heinemann.

West, D. J. and Farrington, D. P. (1973) *Who Becomes Delinquent?*, London: Heinemann.

West, D. J. and Farrington, D. P. (1977) *The Delinquent Way of Life*, London: Heinemann.

White, R. (2008a) *Crimes Against Nature: Environmental criminology and ecological justice*, Cullompton: Willan.

White, R. (2008b) 'Depleted uranium, state crime and the politics of knowing', *Theoretical Criminology*, **12**(1), pp. 31–54.

Whyte, W. F. (1955; first pub. 1943) *Street Corner Society*, 2nd edn, Chicago, IL: University of Chicago Press.

Wiles, P. N. P. (1976a) 'Criminal statistics and sociological explanations', in P. N. P. Wiles (ed.), *The Sociology of Crime and Delinquency in Britain*, Vol. 2, *The New Criminology*, Oxford: Martin Robertson.

Wiles, P. N. P. (ed) (1976b) *The Sociology of Crime and Delinquency in Britain*, Vol. 2, *The New Criminologies*, Oxford: Martin Robertson.

Wilkins, L. (1964) *Social Deviance: Social policy, action and research*, London: Tavistock.

Willcock, H. O. (1949) *Mass Observation Report on Juvenile Delinquency*, London: Falcon Press.

Williams, K. S. (2004) *Textbook on Criminology*, 5th edn, Oxford: Oxford University Press.

Williams, R. (2000) *Making Identity Matter: Identity, society and social interaction*, Durham: Sociology press.

Willis, P. (1978) *Profane Culture*, London: Routledge & Kegan Paul.

Willmott, P. (1966) *Adolescent Boys of East London*, London: Routledge & Kegan Paul.

Wills, A. (2007) 'Historical myth-making in juvenile justice policy', *History and Policy*, www.historyandpolicy.org/papers/policy-paper-60.html#concl.

Wilson, H. (1980) 'Parental supervision: a neglected aspect of delinquency', *British Journal of Criminology*, **20**, pp. 203–35.

Wilson, H. and Herbert, G. (1978) *Parents and Children in the Inner City*, London: Routledge & Kegan Paul.

Wilson, J. Q. (1975) *Thinking About Crime*, New York: Vintage.

Wilson, J. Q. and Herrnstein, R. (1985) *Crime and Human Nature*, New York: Simon & Schuster.

Wilson, J. Q. and Kelling, G. L. (1985) 'Making Neighborhoods Safe', *Atlantic Monthly*, March, p. 29.

Winlow, S. (2002) *Badfellas: Crime, tradition and new masculinities*, Oxford: Berg.

Wolfe, A. (1971) 'Political repression and the liberal state', *Monthly Review*, **23**, 20 December.

Wolfgang, M. E. (1958) *Patterns in Criminal Homicide*, Philadelphia, PA: University of Pennsylvania Press.

Wolfgang, M. E., Thornberry, T. P. and Figlio, R. M. (1987) *From Boy to Man, from Delinquency to Crime*, Chicago, IL: University of Chicago Press.

Wood, J. and Shearing, C. (2006) *Imagining Security*, Cullompton: Willan.

Worrall, A. (1981) 'Out of place: female offenders in court', *Probation Journal*, **28**, pp. 90–3.

Worrall, A. (1990) *Offending Women*, London: Routledge.

Worrall, A. (2003) '"What works" and community sentences for women offenders', *Criminal Justice Matters*, **53**, p. 40.

Worrall, A. and Pease, K. (1986) 'The prison population in 1985', *British Journal of Criminology*, **26**(2), pp. 184–7.

Yeager, P. C. (1991) *The Limits of Law: The public regulation of private pollution*, Cambridge: Cambridge University Press.

Young, A. (1990) *Femininity in Dissent*, London: Routledge.

Young, A. (1997) *Imagining Crime*, London: Sage.

Young, A. (1998) 'The waste land of law, the wordless song of the rape victim', *Melbourne University Law Review*, **22**(2), pp. 442–65.

Young, J. (1971) *The Drugtakers: The social meaning of drug use*, London: MacGibbon & Kee/Paladin.

Young, J. (1975) 'Working class criminology', in I. Taylor, P. Walton and J. Young (eds), *Critical Criminology*, London: Routledge & Kegan Paul.

Young, J. (1986) 'The failure of criminology: the need for a radical realism', in R. Matthews and J. Young (eds), *Confronting Crime*, London: Sage.

Young, J. (1987) 'The tasks facing a realist criminology', *Contemporary Crises*, **11**, pp. 337–56.

Young, J. (1988) 'Radical criminology in Britain: the emergence of a competing paradigm', in P. Rock (ed), *A History of British Criminology*, Oxford: Oxford University Press.

Young, J. (1994) 'Incessant chatter: recent paradigms in criminology', in M. Maguire, R. Morgan and R. Reiner (eds), *The Oxford Handbook of Criminology*, 1st edn, Oxford: Clarendon Press.

Young, J. (1997) 'Left realist criminology: radical in its analysis, realist in its policy', in M. Maguire, R. Morgan and R. Reiner (eds), *The Oxford Handbook of Criminology*, 2nd edn, Oxford: Oxford University Press.

Young, J. (1998) 'Writing on the cusp of change: a new criminology for an age of late modernity', in P. Walton and J. Young (eds), *The New Criminology Revisted*, Basingstoke: Macmillan.

Young, J. (1999) *The Exclusive Society*, London: Sage.

Young, J. (2002) 'Critical criminology in the twenty-first century: critique, irony and the always unfinished', in K. Carrington and R. Hogg (eds), *Critical Criminology: Issues, debates, challenges*, Cullompton: Willan Publishing.

Young, J. (2003a) 'Winning the fight against crime? New Labour, populism and lost opportunities', in R. Matthews and J. Young (eds), *The New Politics of Crime and Punishment*, Cullompton: Willan Publishing.

Young, J. (2003b) 'Merton with energy, Katz with structure', *Theoretical Criminology*, **7**(3), pp. 389–414.

Young, J. (2007) *The Vertigo of Late Modernity*, London: Sage.

Young, J. (2008) 'Vertigo and the global Merton', *Theoretical Criminology*, **12**(4), pp. 523–7.

Young, J. and Matthews, R. (eds) (1992) *Rethinking Criminology: The realist debate*, London: Sage.

Young, J. and Matthews, R. (2003) 'New Labour, crime control and social exclusion', in R. Matthews and J. Young (eds), *The New Politics of Crime and Punishment*, Cullompton: Willan Publishing.

Young, M. (1993) *In the Sticks: An anthropologist in a shire force*, Oxford: Oxford University Press.

Zedner, L. (1991) *Women, Crime and Custody in Victorian England*, Oxford: Blackwell.

Zedner, L. (1994) 'Victims', in M. Maguire, R. Morgan and R. Reiner (eds), *The Oxford Handbook of Criminology*, 1st edn, Oxford: Clarendon Press.

Zedner, L. (2002) 'Victims', in M. Maguire, R. Morgan and R. Reiner (eds), *The Oxford Handbook of Criminology*, 3rd edn, Oxford: Oxford University Press.

Zedner, L. (2007) *Security*, Abingdon: Routledge.

NAME INDEX

Adamson, M. 258
Adelman, S. 225
Agnew, R. 106
Akers, R.L. 157–8, 174
Allen, H. 267
Allen, R. 309
Althusser, L. 199
Amir, M. 37
Anderson, E. 219
Anderson, N. 73, 98
Anderson, S. 39, 46, 271
Aristotle 211
Asthana, A. 325
Atkin, Lord 14, 15
Atkinson, J.M. 175

Ball, R.A. 257
Barton, A. 329
Bates, J.E. 250
Baudrillard, J. 338
Bauman, Z. 362
Baumer, E.P. 102
Beck, U. 322
Becker, H. 7–8, 14–15, 138, 139, 148, 149–50, 151, 154, 155, 156, 157, 185, 211, 226
Bell, M. 252–3
Berlusconi, S. 31
Bernard, T.J. 102
Biderman, A.D. 35
Black, E. 64
Blair, T. 307
Blanden, J. 315–16
Block, A. 42
Booth, C. 95
Bottomley, A.K. 28, 38, 39, 44
Bottoms, A. 80, 328
Box, S. 35–6, 41–2, 92, 111, 174, 208–9, 213, 214–15, 217, 235, 261
Bradbury, M. 179–80

Braithwaite, J. 313
Brewer, C. 226
Brogden, M. 270
Brown, B. 258, 272
Brown, D. 294
Browne, S. 253, 262
Bulgar, J. 252, 364
Bunyan, T. 324
Burawoy, M. 329–30
Burgess, E. 97–8
Burman, M. 347
Burt, C. 61, 76

Cain, M. 259
Callinicos, A. 340–1
Campbell, A. 217, 262, 263, 347
Campbell, B. 274, 276–7
Capone, A. 100
Carlen, P. 8, 169, 259, 260, 262, 263, 267, 268, 272, 293, 295–6, 340, 345
Carrington, K. 342, 346
Carter, M.P. 79, 120–1
Caudill, H.M. 208
Cavadino, M. 314
Chadwick, K. 289
Chambliss, W.J. 42, 169, 172, 186, 187–8
Chancer, L. 330
Chapman, J. 263–4
Chesney-Lind, M. 319, 344
Churchill, W. 71
Cicourel, A.V. 34, 175
Clarke, J. 199, 200
Clarke, K. 253
Clarke, R.V. 279
Clinard, M.B. 208
Cloward, R. 84, 86, 112–15, 116, 117, 119, 127, 330
Cohen, A.K. 84, 109–12, 116, 117, 118, 119, 120, 123, 124, 126, 127

Cohen, P. 199
Cohen, S. 12, 21, 72–5, 76, 77, 78, 80, 82, 137, 153, 166, 174, 177, 190, 202, 236, 295, 297, 336, 341, 362
Cohn-Bendit, D. 143, 144
Collier, R. 349, 350
Colvin, M. 354–5
Comte, A. 55, 89
Conklin, J.E. 159
Connell, R.W. 349, 351
Considine, M. 327
Cooley, C.H. 152
Cornish, D.B. 279
Corrigan, P. 200
Coulter, J. 175
Cousins, M. 259
Cowie, J. and V. 218
Crawford, A. 40, 313
Cuff, E.C. 57
Cullen, F.T. 257
Currie, E. 286, 287, 328, 330–1, 370–1

Dahrendorf, R. 186, 235
Daly, K. 267
Davis, F. 141
Deakin, J. 345
Dell, S. 219
Derrida, J. 338
Dignan, J. 314
Ditton, J. 20, 42, 174
Dixon, M. 316
Dobash, R.E. 268, 269, 271
Dobash, R.P. 268, 269, 271
Douglas, J. 210
Douglas, J.W.B. 28, 79
Dowie, M. 208
Downes, D. 75, 78–9, 81, 124–6, 130–1, 135, 144, 199, 210, 211, 215, 231, 232, 237, 260, 262–3, 277, 308, 309, 336, 360–1
Drapkin, I. 54
Durkheim, E. 52, 87–95, 96, 102, 113, 154, 210, 341
Duster, T. 64

Eagleton, T. 341
Edwards, S.S.M. 266–7
Einstadter, W.J. 292
Elgin, P. 176, 210–11
Engels, F. 184, 193–5, 194, 204

Erikson, R.V. 94, 139, 156
Eron, L.D. 250
Eysenck, H. 75

Farrell, S. 310
Farrington, D.P. 177, 247, 248, 249–50, 267, 329
Feeley, M. 325–6
Felson, M. 280–1
Fenwick, M. 356
Ferrell, J. 357
Ferri, E. 55
Fine, B. 15, 170, 205
Finkelhor, D. 30
Finstone, H. 101
Foucault, M. 170, 205, 238, 320, 338
Frith, S. 200

Gadd, D. 350
Galliher, J.F. 202
Galton, Francis 62
Garland, D. 51, 53–4, 55, 57, 60, 70, 71, 74, 77, 144, 231, 226–7, 281, 320, 326
Garofalo, J. 55, 280
Gelsthorpe, L. 258, 265, 341–2, 343, 345
Gibbs, J.P. 155
Giddens, A. 21
Gilligan, C. 263
Gilroy, P. 289
Glueck, E. and S. 212
Goldman, N. 166, 197
Gordon, D. 187–8
Gordon, P. 289
Goring, C. 60–1
Gottfriedson, M.R. 176, 288, 352–3
Gouldner, A. 156, 157, 160, 168, 174, 189, 192
Graham, J.M. 169–70
Gramsci, A. 167, 205
Greenwood, V. 258
Gregory, J. 258, 265
Groombridge, N. 351
Gross, B. 292
Grosz, E.A. 274
Gutteridge, S. 268

Habermas, J. 143, 197
Hagan, J. 264
Hagel, A. 252, 254, 255, 256
Haggerty, K.D. 328

Hale, C. 261
Hall, R. 40, 270
Hall, S. 166, 167, 171, 190, 202, 207, 235, 375
Hanmer, J. 270
Hargreaves, D. 126–7, 137
Harris, R. 265
Hartless, J.M. 40
Hayward, K. 356
Heidensohn, F. 12, 24, 100, 104, 128, 129,
    216–17, 259, 263, 343, 344
Henry, S. 42, 340, 365
Herrnstein, R. 284–5
Hester, S. 176, 210–11
Hill, R. 359
Hinch, R. 196
Hirschi, T. 71, 176, 211–13, 214, 278, 288, 351,
    352–3
Hirst, P.Q. 23, 53, 168–9, 192, 194, 196, 206
Hobbs, D. 42, 297, 322, 348, 357
Hobbs, T. 312
Hobsbawm, E. 166, 197
Hogg, R. 294
Hood, C. 321
Hood-Williams, J. 349, 350
Hooper, J. 31
Horowitz, I.L. 157, 166, 189–90, 202
Howard, M. 300, 308
Howe, A. 342
Hudson, B. 246, 326
Huesmann, L.R. 250
Hughes, G. 318
Hulsman, L. 294, 359, 365
Hunt, A. 292
Hunter, G. 344

Innes, M. 311
Irvine, J. 43
Irwin, K. 344

Jamieson, R. 347, 348
Jefferson, T. 200, 225, 233, 234–5, 236,
    238, 242, 270, 273, 278, 281, 289,
    297, 350
Jeffery, C. 57–8
Jephcott, P. 79, 120–1
Jessop, B. 322
Jones, E. 350–1
Jones, T. 40
Jowell, T. 31

Karstedt, S. 310
Katz, J. 356, 358
Kelling, G.L. 285–6
Kelly 43
Kemshall, H. 322
Kinsey, R. 40, 289, 291, 295
Kitsuse, J.I. 139, 151, 156
Kolko, G. 160
Kroeber, A. 8

Lacey, N. 313
Laing, R.D. 166
Lait, J. 226
Lakotos, I. 226
Landesco, J. 100
Laub, J.H. 355
Lawrence, F. 310
Lea, J. 269, 289, 295, 335, 337, 339
Leibowitz, M. 157, 166, 189–90, 202
Leigh, D. 310
Leishman, F. 322
Lemert, E. 22, 149, 150, 151–2, 155, 160, 185
Leonard, E.B. 216, 262
Levi, M. 42, 232
Liazos, A. 138, 158, 159, 168, 186
Lilly, J.R. 86, 257, 284, 336, 352, 354
Lombroso, C. 55, 59, 95, 218, 274
Lyng, S. 357
Lyotard, J.F. 338, 360

McCord, J. 251
MacDonald, E. 262
McKay, H.D. 83–4, 98, 100
McLaughlin, E. 330
McLeod, E. 262
Maguire, M. 18, 32–3, 39, 252
Maher, L. 347
Mankoff, M. 160
Mannheim, H. 72, 75, 79, 80
Manning, P. 34
Marcus, J. 250
Marcuse, H. 140, 142, 143
Marginson, S. 327
Marx, K. 51–3, 184, 192, 193–5, 204, 239, 338
Matthews, J. 268
Matthews, R. 289, 307, 310–11
Matza, D. 57–8, 98, 100, 116, 126, 128, 129–30,
    148, 150, 180, 214–15, 355
Mawby, R.I. 271

Mayhew, H. 79, 95, 96
Mays, J.B. 79, 80, 82, 119, 120, 121
Mead, G.H. 148, 174
Merton, R.K. 82, 87, 88, 102–7, 109, 111,
    149, 291
Messerschmidt, J.W. 275, 277, 349–50, 351
Messner, S.F. 102, 106–7
Michalowski, R.J. 292
Miles, I. 43
Millar, R. 15
Miller, E. 263
Miller, J. 347
Miller, W. 123
Mills, D. 31
Milovanovic, D. 340, 365
Moore, D. 118, 326
Moore, M.E. 98
Morgan, R. 308, 309
Morris, A. 258, 265, 267, 345
Morris, T.P. 80, 82, 121–2
Moulds, E. 259
Mugford, S. 356
Mullins, C. 62–4, 243
Murphy, D.S. 106

Naffine, N. 263, 341
Nelken, D. 42, 171, 336
Newburn, T. 252, 254, 255, 256, 313
Nicolaus, M. 146
Nixon, R. M. 159
Norrie, S. 225
Nuttall, Jeff 141

Obama, B. 85, 323
O'Brien, M. 357
Ohlin, L. 84, 86, 112–15, 116, 117, 119, 127, 330
O'Malley, P. 356
Orwell, G. 362

Pailthorpe, G. 60
Park, R. 96–7
Parker, H. 174
Parsons, G. 137
Parsons, T. 57
Parton, N. 262
Pashukanis, E. 205–6
Pavlich, G. 359–60
Paxton, W. 316
Payne, G.C.F. 57

Pearce, F. 42, 208, 369–70
Pearson, G. 62, 66, 143, 167, 197, 226, 289
Pearson, K. 61
Pease, K. 28, 38, 39, 271
Peterson, M. 350–1
Phillipson, M. 175
Pitts, J. 225, 226
Player, E. 262, 265
Plummer, K. 157, 174
Pollak, O. 218
Pollner, M. 155–6, 211
Poole, A. 11
Posner, R.A. 284
Poulantzas, N. 205

Quinney, R. 186, 188–9, 205

Raab, D. 325
Radford, J. 270
Radzinowicz, L. 70, 73
Rafter, N.H. 293
Reiner, R. 14–15, 33, 154
Reiss, A.J. 35
Rhodes, R.A.W. 322
Riley, D. 251, 264
Robertson, R. 359
Robinson, M.B. 106
Rock, P. 167, 202, 210, 211, 215, 228–9234,
    237, 262–3, 277, 280 331, 336, 360–1
Rodger, J. 251
Rosenfeld, R. 102, 106
Roshier, B. 54, 61, 93, 94–5, 175, 212, 249, 277,
    278–9, 288
Ruggiero, V. 296, 297
Russell, D.E.H. 270

Sainsbury, P. 79, 121
Sampson, R.J. 355
Saunders, S. 270
Scheingold, S.A. 313
Schlossman, S. 84
Schultz, A. 209
Schur, E.M. 160
Schwendinger, H. and J. 16, 170–1, 365
Scraton, P. 34, 235, 289, 359
Seeger, P. 140
Sellin, T. 16
Shapland, J. 225, 233, 234–5, 236, 238, 242,
    278, 281

Shaw, C.R. 83–4, 98, 100, 101
Shaw, M. 251
Short, J.F. 122
Sim, J. 289
Simmel, G. 89
Simon, J. 325–6
Slater, E. 218
Smart, C. 172, 216, 217–18, 258, 259,
    261–2, 366
Smith, C. 198
Smith, H. 60
Smith, L.J.F. 266
Socrates 94
South, N. 232, 375
Sparks, R. 29, 37, 321
Spencer, H. 89
Spender, J. 345
Spivak, G. 250
Stanko, E. 270, 271
Stanley, L. 260
Stedman-Jones, G. 169
Steinert, H. 294, 365
Stenson, K. 283, 320
Stratton, A. 31
Straw, Jack 308, 314
Strodtbeck, F. 122
Sumner, C.S. 10, 13–14, 23, 24–5, 91, 93,
    159–60, 167–9, 193, 206–7, 224, 235,
    242, 289, 336, 357
Sutherland, E.H. 42, 84, 98–9, 100, 110, 115,
    121, 171, 207
Swift, M. 250
Sykes, G.M. 116, 126, 129–30, 214
Szasz, T.S. 158

Tame, C.R. 283
Tannenbaum, F. 149
Taylor, I. 23, 53, 54, 151, 155, 156, 157, 166–7,
    292, 371–2
Taylor, L. 42, 104, 206
Tester, K. 362
Thatcher, M. 179, 225, 283
Thio, A. 159
Thompson, E.P. 169, 292

Thrasher, F.M. 98, 122
Tierney, J. 197, 285, 319, 320
Tittle, C.R. 353–4
Tombs, S. 369–70
Tonnies, F. 89
Tonry, M. 309
Townsend, M. 325
Tracy, J. 72
Turk, A. 186–7, 188

Valier, C. 343
Vilar, P. 239
Vold, G. 55, 74, 257
Von Hentig, H. 269

Walker, N. 75
Walklake, S. 43, 270, 272, 274, 276, 296, 342
Walt, D. 11
Wallets, R. 328
Walton, P. 23, 166–7, 190–1
Weber, M. 156, 186, 341, 62, 63, 71, 305, 312
Wertham, F. 269
West, D.J. 23, 177, 249
Whyte, W.F. 98, 110, 123
Wiles, P.N.P. 79, 137
Wilkins, L.T. 152–3, 174
Williams, R. 339, 345
Willis, P. 199
Willmott, P. 80, 123–4
Wilson, J.Q. 284–7
Wise, S. 260
Wolfe, A. 204–5
Wolfgang, M.E. 36
Worrall, A. 271

Yeager, P.C. 42, 208
Young, A. 267–8, 346, 364
Young, J. 19, 23, 57, 139, 144, 166–7, 168, 174,
    177–8, 190–3, 206, 277, 279, 289, 291,
    293, 296, 307, 308, 309, 310–11, 331,
    340, 358–9, 362, 364, 366–7, 368–9,
    372–5

Zedner, L. 41, 268, 270

SUBJECT INDEX

abolitionism, and critical criminology 240–1, 293, 295
academic disciplines 12, 69–70, 234
ACPO (Association of Chief Police Officers) 254
action-reaction relationship 367
Acts of Parliament 25
see also legislation
actuarial justice 325–6
adaptive function of crime 93, 94
the adjustment problem 126–8
administrative criminology 74, 144, 245, 257, 277–82, 299–300
and crime control 277–82, 300–1
and government 281–2
and left realism 291
and neo-positivism 285–6
and New Labour 316
and policy 329
and rational choice theory 279–80
and routine activity theory 280–1
adult offenders, defining 25
affiliation theory 122
affirmative postmodernism 339, 340
age
and academic criminologists 228–9
and conflict theory 187
of criminal responsibility 25, 315
and criminality 247–8
and self-report studies 18
victims of crime 40, 233
alcohol consumption 344–5, 375
altruistic suicide 92
American criminology
conflict theory 119, 172, 185, 186–9, 191, 203, 223–4
influences on British criminology 116–17, 136
neo-positivism 284–5

and ring-wing classicism 283, 284
sociological criminology 79–80, 81, 82–6
victim-based surveys 281–2
see also United States
anomie
Durkheim's concept of 87, 88, 91, 92, 93
and female offenders 216
and left realism 258, 291
and radical criminology 289
and strain theory 102, 103, 104–5, 106–7
and subcultural theory 129
ANPR (automatic number plate recognition) 323
anthropology 69
anti-criminology perspective 366
anti-essentialism 342, 362–3, 364
anti-social behaviour 249–50, 318
Anti-Social Behaviour Orders 315
arrestable offences 25
attachment, and control theory 213, 215
audits 19, 40
authoritarian populism 179
authority, and conflict theory 186–7
aversion therapy 75

BCS see British Crime Surveys (BCS)
belief, and control theory 213
bias, and policy-oriented research 230
biology 69
biometric data 324
Birmingham Centre for Contemporary Cultural Studies 128, 167, 171, 198–9, 200, 207
black feminism 343
black people
and actuarial justice 326
imprisonment rates 45
and 'muggings' and black youth 171, 207
and victim surveys 40, 41
boundary maintenance function of crime 93–5

British Crime Surveys (BCS) 17, 23, 37–8, 39, 40,
  41, 47, 48, 49, 270, 367
  and administrative criminology 281, 282
  and 'tough on crime' policies 309
British criminology
  early twentieth century 59–62
  late twentieth century 239–43
  post-war period 70–6
  see also sociological criminology
British Journal of Criminology 72, 75, 349
British Journal of Delinquency 72
British Society of Criminology 72, 75
Bronson (film) 350–1
burglaries
  age and criminality 248
  and left realism 290
  public reporting of 30
  recorded offences 28–9, 49, 246
  victim surveys of 38–9, 40

Cambridge Institute of Criminology 74
Cambridge Study in Delinquent Development
  247, 249–50
Cambridge University, Department of Criminal
  Science 72
capitalism
  and American conflict theory 189
  and critical criminology 360–1
  globalisation and neo-liberal markets
    369–72
  Marx and Engels on crime and 193–5
  and the New Left 142
  and the politicisation of deviance 196–7
  and radical criminology 139, 170
CCTV cameras 279, 319, 323
CDRPs *see* Crime and Disorder Reduction
  Partnerships (CDRP)
Chernobyl disaster 208
Chicago School 60, 82–4, 87, 88, 95–107
  assessment of 99–101
  and British sociological criminology 119–22
  criticisms of 101
  and cultural transmission 98, 101, 117
  ecological models of the city 96–7, 98, 101,
    116–17
  and new deviancy theory 147
  and policy-oriented research 233
  and social disorganisation theory 99
  and subcultural strain theory 112, 116–19

and symbolic interactionism 98, 100
and the Zone of Transition 97–8, 99, 115
children
  adult harassment of 271
  child abuse/offenders 25, 30
  child poverty in Britain 240, 316
  in custody 46
  and doli incapax 25
  of female prisoners 346
  as victims of crime 253
civil liberties 234, 325
class
  and American conflict theory 188
  class conflict approach to statistics 43–4
  and crime as political 167
  and criminality 248–9
  and critical criminology 190, 192
    the ruling class and the law 203–4
  and cultural diversity theory 122–6
  and delinquency 116–19, 120–2
  and feminist criminology 263, 264, 344
  and late modernity 374
  and left idealism 293
  and left realism 291, 293, 294
  Marx and Engels on crime and 193–4
  and non-delinquent values 118–19, 119–20
  and police characterisations of the public 34
  and the politicisation of deviance 196–7
  radical criticism and the middle classes
    179–80
  and research on victims of crime 233
  and right-wing classicism 283
  schools and the adjustment problem 126–8
  and subcultural strain theory 109–12,
    113–14, 117–19
  and subterranean values 129, 130–1
  the underclass 118, 283, 309–10
  and victims of crime 296–7
  and youth subcultures 198–200
classical criminology 51, 54–5, 55–6, 58,
  241, 257
  and administrative criminology 279
  right-wing classicism 283–4, 310
collective conscience 90, 91, 92, 93
commitment, and control theory 213, 215
common law 25
common sense 7–8
  and left realism 295–6
  and New Right criminology 226, 228, 241

communities
    crime reduction 319–20
    and left realism 97, 292
    and restorative justice 312–14
community safety 305, 317–20, 327
community service orders/programmes 266, 314
computer data
    DNA databases 324–5
    measuring crime using 18–19
conduct norms 16, 19, 21
conflict subcultures 115
conflict theory 119, 172, 185, 186–9, 191,
        203, 223–4
Conservative Party/governments
    and administrative criminology 281
    and New Labour 307, 308, 312, 317
    and New Right ideology 224–6, 239–40
constitutive criminology 10, 153, 154, 155–6,
        340
consumerism 140–2, 356, 375
contagion view of delinquency 122
control balance theory 353–4
control perspectives 351–5
control theory 92, 100, 145, 174, 184,
        211–15, 334
    and administrative criminology 278
    criticisms of 352–3
    and feminist criminology 263, 264
    and positivism 288
conventional crime 298–300
corporate crime
    and administrative criminology 281
    and critical criminology 369
    and labelling theory 159
    and left realism 290
    and policy-oriented research 231
    powerful law breakers 207–9
    and radical criminology 171–2
    and self-report studies 249
    and strain theory 106
    unrecorded 217
    and victim surveys 41–2
    see also white-collar crime
correctionalism 75
Council for National Academic Awards 232
counter-culture 167
    and new deviancy theory 140–2, 144
    and the New Left 142–3
    and the politicising of deviance 189–90

crime
    defining 13–16, 25
    and deviance 14–15
    varieties of 19–21
crime control
    and administrative criminology 277–82,
        300–1
    and left idealism 292
    left realism and crime control policies 297–8
    New Labour policies 316–20
    and the production of knowledge 53
    research on 233, 234–5
    see also situational crime control
Crime and Disorder Reduction Partnerships
        (CDRPs) 19, 40, 319, 321, 327–8, 329
crime mapping 19
crime prevention see crime control
Crimewatch UK 38
criminal careers, longitudinal research on 246–56
criminal damage (vandalism) 246, 248, 261
    statistics 30–1
    and strain theory 106, 111
    and victim surveys 42
criminal justice
    and actuarial justice 325–6
    and left realism 297
    New Labour policies 308–9, 310
        and restorative justice 312–14
    and positivism 58
    privatisation of 236, 284
    research 234, 236
    and women 272, 345–6
        feminist criminology 218–19, 264–5
criminal statistics 10, 298–9
    and administrative criminology 281–2
    and changes in the law 30–1, 34–5
    and the police 18, 19, 31–4, 39
    recent trends 47–9
    usefulness of 43–7
    see also official statistics
criminal subcultures 115
criminology
    competing agendas in 12–13
    defining 11, 53–4
    emergence of 70–6
    focus of 12
critical criminology 70, 75, 160, 168–9, 170,
        184, 185, 190–3, 258, 331, 355, 358–76
    and abolitionism 240–1, 293, 295

agendas of 361–2
anti-criminology perspective 366
changing context of 360–1
concepts of crime and deviance 362–3
and conflict theory 188–9, 191, 203
deviance, crime and power 202–9
dispensing with crime 365
divisions within 183
and feminism 342, 343
future of 376
globalisation and neo-liberal markets 369–72
green perspective 375–6
'ironies' of 358–9
and late modernity 372–5
and left realism 206, 289, 291, 292–8, 358,
    363, 373
and policy-oriented research 238–9
and postmodernism 341
and radical criminology 298
and social censures 364
and victims 296–7
see also left realism; Marxist criminology
cultural criminology 280, 334, 355–8
cultural diversity theory 122–6
cultural pluralism 99, 100
cultural symbolisation 200–1
cultural transmission 98, 101, 117, 122
culture of poverty 241, 283
cynical rule breakers 171–2

'dark figure' of crime 10, 17, 19, 29
    and victim surveys 35, 37, 282
deconstruction 336, 338
deconstructionism 343
delegated legislation 25
delinquency
    and cultural diversity theory 122–6
    defining 25
    and sociological criminology 81–2
    and subcultures 109–15, 116–19, 120–2
    see also Chicago School; youth crime
determinism 58, 59, 60, 75, 311
    and critical criminology 192
    and feminism 273
    masculinities and crime 277
    and subcultural theory 128, 130
deterrence 284
deviance 12, 14–15, 21–5
    defining 21

and labelling theory 22–3
politicisation of 189–90, 196–7
and positivism 59
and power 185–6, 202–9
and radical criminology 22–5
sociology of 336
see also new deviancy theory
deviancy amplification 152–3, 173–4
differential association 99, 110, 115, 117,
    121, 122
    and female offenders 216
differential coercion theory 354–5
differentiation 58
discrimination, and actuarial justice 326
displacement 279
DNA databases 324–5
doli incapax 25
domestic violence 30, 217, 219, 267, 269
    victim surveys of 271
drug use 42, 145
    female drug-dealers 347
    and gender 261
    and labelling theory 149–50, 174
    and left idealism 293
    and persistent offenders 255
    and policy-oriented research 232
    and strain theory 104, 115
    and surveillance 325

economic marginalisation, and feminist
    criminology 263–4
economic recession, and corporate crime 208–9
Economic and Social Research Council 229, 236
economics 69
edgework 357
egoistic suicide 92
empiricism 73
England and Wales
    crime statistics 16–17, 18, 28–9
    imprisonment in 45, 46
environmental factors in criminality 59, 60,
    61, 62
environmentalism 362, 375–6
equality of opportunity
    and New Labour social policy 315–16
    and strain theory 85, 103, 105, 107, 112, 113
ethical identity 313
ethnographic research
    and the Chicago School 97, 100

ethnographic research (*continued*)
  and labelling theory 174
  and new deviancy theory 146
  and phenomenology 175
  and policy-oriented research 231
ethnomethology 175–6, 184, 210–11
eugenics 62–4
Europe
  imprisonment rates in European countries 45
  market-liberalism in 371–2
  security issues and the European Union 324
European Community 25, 371
European Court of Human Rights 325
experimental method 57
'exposé' criminology 207–8
external history of criminology 226–8

facial recognition technology 323
family context, and criminality 250–1, 255
fear of crime
  and administrative criminology 282
  data relating to 19
  and gender 274–5
  and left realism 291
  and local crime surveys 46–7
  and New Labour 318
  and radical criticism 181–2
feminist perspectives 2, 24, 37, 172–3,
      184, 216–19, 242, 258–71, 334,
      341–8
  and the causes of crime 274
  core elements of 258–9
  and criminal justice 218–19, 264–5
  distortion 217–18, 262–4
  feminisms 258, 341–4
  on imprisonment 268
  invisibility 216–17, 260–2
  and masculinities 272–3
  on offending and punishment 344–6
  and the police 265–6
  and power 275–7
  and research 233, 261
  on sentencing 266–8
  standpointism 260, 343
  and victimisation 173, 219, 268–71
  see also gender
Ford Motor Company 208
forensic science 74
Frankfurt School 142–3, 188

free will, and neo-positivism 287–8
functionalism 22, 52, 56–7, 88

gangs 98, 122
Gay Liberation Movement 166, 190
gender 271–7
  and academic criminologists 228, 229
  and alcohol consumption 344–5
  and the causes of crime 273–5
  and conflict theory 187
  and crime rates 261
  and feminist criminology 263
  masculinities and crime 272–3, 274, 275–6,
      348–51
  offenders 173
    persistent 255
  and power 275–7
  and research on victims of crime 233
  and subcultural theory 128
  and victim surveys 40, 261
  see also feminist perspectives; men; women
General Household Surveys 38–9
globalisation 320–2, 338, 362, 369–72
governmental project 70
green perspectives 375–6
Greenham Common peace camp women 267–8

hegemonic masculinity 349, 350
hereditary factors in criminality 59, 60–1, 62
  and eugenics 62–4
higher education, courses in criminology
      326–7
Home Office
  classification of offences 30–1
  criminal statistics 16–17
  Offending, Crime and Justice Survey 18
  and orthodox criminology 176
  and the police 31, 32
  re-fashioned 306
  and recent crime trends 47–8
  Research and Planning Unit 72, 74, 229,
      236, 254
  research projects 233
  and sociological criminology 78
  see also British Crime Surveys (BCS)
homeless people 42
human nature and criminality 287
human rights 16, 170–1, 259, 325, 341,
      362, 365

iceberg analogy 19–20, 29
ID cards 324
ideological violence 145
illegitimate children 63–4
imperialism 16
individual delinquents 76, 77
individuation 90–1
industrial sabotage 145
innovation, and strain theory 103–4
Institute of Criminology 72
Institute for the Scientific Treatment of
    Delinquency (ISTD) 72, 74
institutional roots of criminology 72
institutional-anomie theory 107
institutionist view of crime 10
insurance fraud 42
interactionism 136, 145, 147–8, 173–5, 257, 355
    and the constitutive model of deviance 153
    and control theory 215
    and critical criminology 190, 258, 360
    criticisms of 185
    and labelling theory 148–9
    and New Right criminology 242
    and radical criminology 289
    see also labelling theory; new deviancy
      theory
interdisciplinary conception 74–5
international terrorism 323
interpretive sociology 97
Islington Victim Survey 40–1, 46, 47, 271
ISTD (Institute for the Scientific Treatment of
    Delinquency) 72, 74
Italian school of criminology 55

just deserts 58, 182
juveniles see delinquency; youth crime; youth
    justice
labelling theory 22–3, 119, 136, 146, 147, 148–9
    and conflict theory 186, 223–4
    and control theory 213
    and critical criminology 168, 170, 191, 360
    criticisms of 185
    deviance and power 185–6
    and deviancy amplification 153–4
    and deviant acts 154–6
    divisions within 183
    and Durkheim 88
    and ethnographic research 174
    and ethnomethodology 211

    and female offenders 216
    'nuts, sluts and preverts' 138, 156,
      158–60, 168
    and policy-oriented research 230
    and the politicisation of deviance 189
    and politics 165–7
    and primary and secondary deviation
      151–2
    and radical criminology 170, 171
    and the reality and fear of crime 181–2
    and society 173
    underdog critique 156–8, 165, 168
    see also new deviancy theory
Labour Party/government
    and juvenile justice 225
    and left realism 227, 228
    and policy-oriented research 238
    post-war 71–2, 311
    and radical criminology 178, 179
    see also New Labour government
late modernity 372–5
law 25
    changes in 30–1, 34–5
    and consensus on deviant behaviour 23
    and crime 9, 14–16, 19
    and criminal behaviour 365
    and criminology 12
    and critical criminology 203–6
    ethnomethology and law making 176
    powerful law breakers 207–9
    sociology of 167–72
law and order
    and administrative criminology 281
    and left realism 290, 291–2
    and New Right ideology 224–5
    and risk 323
left idealism 183, 206, 223, 289, 358, 373
    left realist criticism of 292–8, 368
left realism 78, 183, 223, 227, 228, 258
    and crime control policies 297–8
    and the 'crime problem' 366–8
    and critical criminology 206, 289, 291,
      292–8, 358, 363, 373
    and deviance 23–4
    and late modernity 372–5
    and local crime surveys 46–7
    and neo-liberal markets 370–1
    and policies 291–2
    and policy-oriented research 237–8, 239

left realism (*continued*)
    and radical criminology 289–92, 294–5
    and victims of crime 38, 41, 233, 296–7,
        364, 366–8
legislation
    Children and Young Persons Act (1969)
        182, 225
    communication data bill 323–4
    Crime and Disorder Act (1998) 19, 40, 310,
        315, 319, 328
    Criminal Justice Act (1948) 72
    Criminal Justice Act (1991) 232
    Criminal Justice Act (2003) 315
    Criminal Justice and Public Order Act 240,
        253, 256, 295
    Education Act (1944) 61
    Police and Criminal Evidence Act (1984) 232
    Police and Justice Act (2006) 19
    Regulation of Investigatory Powers Act 323–4
    Terrorism Act (2000) 308
    Youth Justice and Criminal Evidence Act
        (1999) 312
leisure and delinquency 125–6
liberal criminology 241, 242
liberal feminism 342
libertarianism, right-wing 283–4
Liberty 234
'life history' approach 84
life-course theory 355
local crime surveys 39–41, 46–7
Lombrosian project 70, 78
London School of Economics 72, 75
lone-parent families 250–1
longitudinal research
    and criminal careers 246–56
    and orthodox criminology 177
    and self-report studies 18
'looking glass self' 152

magistrates' courts 15, 17
mainstream criminology 245–6
    and gender 272, 273
man fighting-back image of deviancy
    189, 192
managerialism 321–2
Marxist criminology 22, 23, 166–7, 168–9, 170,
    172, 174, 331
    Dan postmodernism 341
    and conflict theory 185, 187, 188–9

    and critical criminology 24, 168–9, 190–3,
        203–7, 358, 360–1
    neo-Marxism 257, 258, 289, 360–1, 362
    and new deviancy theory 145, 165, 166
    and policy-oriented research 238
    structuralism Marxism 204–6, 207
    see also critical criminology; left idealism
masculinities and crime 348–51
Maudsley Hospital 75
measuring crime 16–19, 27–49
    changes in the law 30–1
    computer-based data 18–19
    the `dark figure' of crime 10, 17, 19, 29, 35
    iceberg analogy 19–20, 29
    official statistics 16–17, 27–9
    and the police 18, 31–3
    public reporting 29–30
    self-report studies 17–18
    victim surveys 17, 29, 30, 35–43, 46–7
    see also criminal statistics
mechanical solidarity 89–92
media
    and cultural criminology 355–6
    and the Frankfurt School 188
    and gender 273
    and labelling theory 173
    moral panics 153, 171, 251–4
    and non-delinquent values 118–19
medicine and criminology 74
men
    and female criminals 262
    male offenders 173
    male sexuality 351
    masculinities and crime 272–3, 274–5
        and power 275–7
    and victim surveys 40
    as victims of crime 276
    violence against women 270–1
MFY (Mobilization for Youth) programme 86
miners' strike (1984-85) 15
misfit sociology 137, 166
mitigation, neoclassical principle of 58
MNCs (multinational corporations) 369–70
Mobilization for Youth (MFY) programme 86
modernity
    globalisation and social change 320–2
    late modernity 372–5
    and postmodernity 337, 338
moral absolutism/relativism 321

moral panics 153, 171, 292, 367–8, 372, 373
    and criminality 251–4
moral standards, and criminal law 15–16, 19
Morgan Report (Standing Conference on Crime
        Prevention) 316–17, 318
motoring offences 17
multinational corporations (MNCs) 369–70

NACRO (National Association for the Care and
        Resettlement of Offenders) 234
NAPO (National Association of Probation
        Officers) 254
National Crime Reduction Strategy 319
National Deviancy Conference (NDC) 144–5,
        167, 170, 174, 190
National e-Borders Scheme 324
National Identity Register 324
Nazi Germany 295
NDC (National Deviancy Conference) 144–5,
        167, 170, 174, 190
neighbourhood decay, and right realism 286
Neighbourhood Watch schemes 30, 274, 282,
        300, 319, 326
neo-liberal markets 369–72
neo-liberalism 231, 285, 328
neo-Marxism 257, 258, 289, 360–1, 362
neo-positivism 257, 284–8
neoclassical principle of mitigation 58
neutralisation techniques 129, 130
new criminology see critical criminology
new deviancy theory 21–2, 23, 79, 81, 135,
        136–42, 147–60, 223
    and anti-essentialism 363
    conceptualising deviance 153–4
    and the counter-culture 140–2
    criticisms of 154–60
    and cultural criminology 358
    deviancy amplification 152–3
    divisions and disputes within 145–6
    and left-wing criminologists 139–40
    and orthodox criminology 136–8, 147, 177
    and policy-oriented research 231
    and positivism 59, 136–7, 138
    primary and secondary deviation
        149, 151–2
    and radical criminology 144–6
    see also labelling
New Labour government 305, 306–20
    and changes in the law 30

creation of New Labour 306–7
crime control policies 316–20
    and expenditure on policing 33
    and imprisonment 314–15
    and managerialism 321–2
    and restorative justice 312–14
    social policy 315–16
    'tough on crime' policies 307–10
New Left 135, 138, 140, 142–3, 167
    and new deviancy theory 139
    and the politicising of deviance 189–90
New Public Management 321
new realism 285
New Right 178–9, 223, 224–6, 228,
        239–40, 243
    classicism 257
    neo-positivism 257, 284–8
    positivism 246
    and radical criminology 289
    and radical criticism 179–81, 182
    right realism 257
    and ring-wing classicism 283–4
non-arrestable offences 25
non-delinquent values, and subcultures 118–19,
        119–20, 129–30
normative criminology 191–2
norms of conduct 16, 19, 21
Northern Ireland 233
    official crime statistics 16
Norwood Report (1943) 61
notifiable offences 16–17, 19, 47–8
'nuts, sluts and preverts' label 138, 156,
        158–60, 168

official statistics 16–17, 27–9, 41, 246
    and youth crime 252
ontology 358, 363
organic solidarity 89–92
organised crime
    and American conflict theory 188
    and the Chicago School 100–1
    and globalisation 322
    and powerful law breakers 208
    and victim surveys 41–2
orthodox criminology
    in the 1970s 176–8
    and critical criminology 193
    and new deviancy 136–8, 147, 177
othering 374

paralogy 360
parental influences on criminality 250–1
parenting orders 315
participant observation, and the Chicago
    School 100
pathology and positivism 58
patriarchy 263
    and the criminal justice system 264–5
permissiveness, and right realism 287
persistent offenders 254–6
phenomenology 175, 184, 209–10, 355
    and American conflict theory 188
    and critical criminology 192
    and new deviancy theory 137, 145, 148
Piper Alpha oil rig 208
police
    and actuarial justice 326
    characterisations of the public 33–4
    and crime reduction policies 320
    and domestic violence 269
    expenditure on policing 33
    and female offenders 265–6
    gatekeeping role 31–3
    number of police officers 33
    and rape/sexual assault 269–70
    recorded crime figures 18, 19, 39, 48
    research on policing 232, 234
    zero-tolerance policing 286
policy-oriented research 230–3, 242, 328–9, 330
    and critical criminology 363
    and radical criminology 237–9
political orientations of criminology 13
political revolutionaries, and strain theory 104
politicisation of deviance 189–90, 196–7
politics 184
    and labelling theory 165–7
    and youth subcultures 198–202
positivism 51, 54, 55, 56–60, 79, 223, 257, 299
    and administrative criminology 277, 278
    and the Chicago School 95, 96, 97, 100
    and the concept of crime 58–9
    and critical criminology 192
    and cultural criminology 356
    and Durkheim 87
    and free will 287–8
    and interactionism 174
    and mainstream criminology 246
    neo-positivism 257, 284–8
    and new deviancy theory 59, 136–7, 138

and New Labour 310, 311, 312
New Right 246
and orthodox criminology 176–7, 178
the positivist trap 75
and postmodernism 337
and radical criticism 182
and sociological criminology 79, 82
post-new deviance theory 24
post-structuralism 338, 342, 350
postmodern feminism 342–3
postmodernism 243, 320, 334, 335, 336–41,
    342, 355, 356, 376
poverty 16
    and American conflict theory 189
    child poverty in Britain 240, 316
    culture of 241, 283
    and delinquency 121
    and feminist criminology 264
    and gender 273
    and liberal markets 372
    and New Labour policies 311, 316
poverty programmes, and strain theory 11,
    85–6, 105, 112, 113
power
    and conflict theory 186–7
    and crime control 301
    crime and power relations 365
    and deviance 185–6, 202–9
    and gender 275–7
pragmatism, in post-war British criminology
    73–4, 77–8, 79
prediction of criminality 76
prescriptive policies 182
primary deviation 149, 151–2, 155
Prison Department, and orthodox
    criminology 176
prisons
    and abolitionism 241
    criminal statistics on imprisonment 45–6
    imprisonment rates and crime rates 287
    New Labour and imprisonment 314–15, 318
    prison populations
        in Britain 240, 305, 314, 315
        and gender 173, 266, 345–6
    privatisation 315
    sentencing policies and gender 267–8
privatisation 180
    criminal justice system 236, 284
    prisons 315

proactive policing 31–2
probation orders 266
productivity, Marx on crime and 51–3
progressive movement 83
property crime
  and criminal subcultures 115
  and criminality 250
  and gender 262, 263–4
  persistent offenders 255
  and strain theory 104
prostitutes, and police officers 266
PSI (Policy Studies Institute), report on the
      Metropolitan Police 34
psychiatry 12, 60, 74
  anti-psychiatry movement 166
psychoanalytical criminology 72, 74–5
psychogenic factors in delinquency 110
psychology 12, 60, 69, 72, 74
  and scientific criminology 55, 59
public criminologies 329–30
public opinion 22, 329, 330
public reporting of crime 29–30

Quality Assurance Agency 76
queer theory 351

race/ethnicity
  and conflict theory 187
  and crime as political 167
  and feminist criminology 264, 265, 343,
      344
  and imprisonment rates 45
  in late twentieth-century Britain 240
  Paki-bashing studies 197, 202
  policy-oriented research on 232, 2333
  racially motivated violence 38
  racism 16, 64
  and strain theory 85
  and victim surveys 40, 41
  see also black people
radical criminology 169–72, 174, 223, 243, 258,
      289–92, 331
  and American conflict theory 186, 188
  and critical criminology 298, 358
  cynical rule breakers 171–2
  and deviance 22–5, 167, 202
  divisions within 183
  features of 289
  and left realism 289–92, 294–5

  and new deviancy theory 144–6, 165
  and New Labour 307
  and orthodox criminology 177–8
  and policy-oriented research 237–9
  the politicisation of deviance 189–90
  self-interested rule makers 169–71, 238
  see also left realism
radical criticism 179–83
radical feminism 342
rape
  and feminist criminology 269–71, 346
  and strain theory 106
  and victim surveys 40
  and victimisation 37, 219
rational choice
  and administrative criminology 279–80
  and right-wing classicism 284
reaction formation 111–12, 120
reactive policing 31
realism
  and criminal statistics 10
      victim surveys 35–6
rebellion, and strain theory 103, 104
recidivism, and scientific criminology 75
recorded crime see criminal statistics; official
      statistics
rehabilitation 182, 316, 318
reintegrative shaming 313
relative deprivation 85
relativism 59, 363
Research Assessment Exercise (RAE) 327
restorative justice 305, 312–14
retreatism 103, 104, 115
retribution 58, 257, 313
right realism 257, 284–8
right-wing classicism 283–4, 310
  see also New Right
risk assessment, actuarial justice 325–6
risk avoidance 275, 300–1
risk society 322–3
risky behaviour 356–7
ritualism, and strain theory 103, 104
routine activity theory 280–1
rule-breaking behaviour 155
Rwanda 347

sceptical postmodernism 339, 340
schools, and the adjustment problem 126–8
scientific criminology 55, 56–9, 75

Scientific Group for the Discussion of
        Delinquency Problems 72
Scotland, official crime statistics 16
secondary deviation 151–2
selectivity, and subcultural theory 128
self-control theory 352, 353
self-fulfilling prophecy, labelling theory as 149
self-interested rule makers 169–71, 238
self-report studies
    and control theory 212–13, 215
    of criminality
        and age 247–8
        and gender 261
        persistent offenders 254
        and socio-economic status 248–9
    of female offenders 344
    and feminist criminology 217
sentencing
    and children in custody 46
    disparities in 45
    female offenders 266–8
    New Labour and imprisonment 314–15
    see also restorative justice
sex offenders 248, 253
sexism 16, 265–6
sexual assaults 269–71
    and victim surveys 40, 42, 43
sexual offences, reporting 30
sexuality, male 351
shame management 313
situational crime control 233, 234–5, 300–1
    and administrative criminology 280, 281,
        282, 329
    and New Labour 316
social capital 311
social censures 364
social change 320–2
social class see class
social constructionism 10, 11, 48, 356
social Darwinism 96
social democracy 72
social exclusion 311, 318, 373
Social Exclusion Unit 319
social harms 335, 359
social marginalisation, and feminist
        criminology 264
social order, Durkheim on 89–92
social reaction theory 136
social security fraud 42

social welfare programmes 71–2, 80–1
socialisation 285, 352, 359
socialism 191–2, 360, 361, 362
    and left realism 291–2
socialist feminism 342
socio-economic status see class
sociological criminology 13, 74, 75, 77–86, 224
    in Britain 77, 78–82, 119–31, 326
        American influences on 116, 119–22, 136
        development of 135–6
        and New Labour 305–12
    and orthodox criminology 177
    teaching and research in 234
    in the United States 79–80, 81, 82–6
sociology
    and criminology 12, 60, 69, 72, 74
    and Durkheim 88–9
Soviet Union (former) 190, 289–90, 331, 360
Spens Report (1938) 61
Standing Conference on Crime Prevention
        (Morgan Report) 316–17, 318
statistics see criminal statistics; official statistics
sterilisation policies 63, 64
strain theory 82, 84–6, 87, 102–7, 330
    and anomie 102, 103, 104–5
    criticisms of 105–7
    and modes of individual adaptation 103–4,
        105, 106
    subcultural 109–15
        and the Chicago School 112, 116–19
structuralist Marxism 204–6, 207
structured action theory 349, 350
style, and youth subcultures 200–1
subcultural strain theory 109–15
    and the Chicago School 112, 116–19
    and sociological criminology in Britain
        118–20
subcultural theory 128–31, 258, 355
    and feminist criminology 263
    and radical criminology 289
subcultures
    and cultural criminology 357–8
    and cultural diversity theory 122–6
    and left realism 291
    and policy-oriented research 231
    schools and the adjustment problem 126–8
    youth subcultures
        and policy-oriented research 231
        and politics 198–202

radical theory of 167
subordinated masculinity 349
subterranean values 129, 130–1
suicide 121, 145
    Durkheim's study of 88–9, 91–2, 102, 210
    and phenomenology 210
summary offences 17
surveillance 323–5, 374
suspended sentences 315
symbolic interactionism 98, 100, 174

targeted offences 32
Tavistock Institute 75
tax fraud 42
techniques of neutralisation 129, 130
terrorism 323, 325
Thatcherism 178–9, 225–6, 227, 228, 237
theft 42, 246
    recorded offences 28–9
Theoretical Criminology (journal) 363, 375
tolerance–criminalisation model 367, 368–9
'tough on crime' policies 307–10
transactionalism 136
treatment programmes, individually
        tailored 76
treatment/punishment regimes, common sense
        8–9
Tree of Knowledge 53–4
Tree of Sin 53, 239
Tyson (film) 351

underclass
    in modern Britain 118, 309–10
    and ring-wing classicism 283
underdog critique of deviance 156–8, 160,
        165, 168
unemployment 277, 291, 309
    and liberal markets 372
United States
    eugenics movement 64
    Kennedy administration 85, 113
    Mobilization for Youth (MFY)
        programme 86
    and neo-liberal markets 371
    progressive movement 83
    Reagan administration 178, 285
    security issues 324
    Vietnam War 159, 186
    see also American criminology; strain theory

vagrancy laws 187
vandalism *see* criminal damage (vandalism)
Victim Support 269
victim surveys 17, 29, 30, 35–43
    and administrative criminology 281–2
    and critical criminology 296–7
    and feminist criminology 270, 271
    findings 38–9
    and gender 40, 261, 274
    limitations and problems of 41–3
    local 39–41, 46–7
    see also British Crime Surveys (BCS)
victimisation
    and gender 173, 219, 268–71, 276, 348
    and New Labour policies 318
    and risk 323
victimology 17, 36–7, 224, 269
victims of crime
    children as 253
    and left realism 38, 41, 296–7, 364, 366–8
    research on 232–3
    women as 266, 268–71, 346
victims, crimes without 42
Vietnam War 159, 186
violence
    and conflict subcultures 115
    ideological 145
    and masculinity 350–1
violent crime
    and criminality 248, 250
    female offenders 347–8
    female victims of 346
    and masculinity 173
    'muggings' 171, 207
    notifiable assaults 47–8
    persistent offenders 255
    policy-oriented research on 232
    recorded offences 29

white-collar crime
    and administrative criminology 281
    and the Chicago School 100–1
    and critical criminology 369
    and left realism 290
    and policy-oriented research 231
    powerful law breakers 207–9
    and radical criminology 171–2
    and self-report studies 249
    and strain theory 105, 106

white-collar crime (*continued*)
  studies of 145
  and victims of 296
  see also corporate crime
women
  and crime 271–2
    and power 275
  and the criminal justice system 218–19,
    264–5, 272
  female criminality 172–3, 216–19, 260–8,
    272, 344–8
  female prisoners 345–6
  and victim surveys 40
  as victims of crime 266, 268–71, 346
Women, Crime and Criminology (Smart)
    172, 216
work record and criminality 249
World War II 61–2, 71, 77

youth crime
  age and criminality 247–8
  and the Chicago School 98
  defining 25
  and imprisonment 314, 315
  and moral panics 251–4
  and policy-oriented research 231, 232
  and post-war British criminology 76
  and sociological criminology 81
  and welfarism 62
  see also delinquency; subcultures
youth justice
  and moral panics 251–4
  and New Labour 314
  and New Right idcology 225
  and restorative justice 312–14

Zone of Transition 97–8, 99, 115